Dictionary of Asian American History

EDITED BY
HYUNG-CHAN KIM

GREENWOOD PRESS
NEW YORK • WESTPORT, CONNECTICUT • LONDON

Library of Congress Cataloging-in-Publication Data
Main entry under title:

Dictionary of Asian American history.

Bibliography: p.
Includes index.
1. Asian Americans—History—Dictionaries. 2. Asian
Americans—History—Addresses, essays, lectures.
I. Kim, Hyung-chan.
E184.06D53 1986 973′.0495 85–30188
ISBN 0–313–23760–3 (lib. bdg. : alk. paper)

Library of Congress Catalog Card Number: 85–30188
ISBN: 0–313–23760–3

First published in 1986

Greenwood Press, Inc.
88 Post Road West, Westport, Connecticut 06881

Printed in the United States of America

∞

The paper used in this book complies with the
Permanent Paper Standard issued by the National
Information Standards Organization (Z39.48–1984).

10 9 8 7 6 5 4 3 2 1

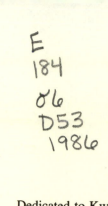
Dedicated to Kwang-oak, my wife,
and my sons, Jerome and Justin

Contents

Contributors

HUNGDAH CHIU, School of Law, University of Maryland, Baltimore, Maryland

JESSE HIRAOKA, Department of Foreign Languages, Western Washington University, Bellingham, Washington

GAIL P. KELLY, Department of Educational Organization, Faculty of Educational Studies, State University of New York, Buffalo, New York

ELAINE KIM, Asian American Studies, University of California, Berkeley, California

ILLSOO KIM, Department of Sociology, Drew University, Madison, New Jersey

TRICIA KNOLL, Portland, Oregon

LYDIA KOTCHEK, School of Nursing, University of Washington, Seattle, Washington

H. BRETT MELENDY, San Jose State University, San Jose, California

S. FRANK MIYAMOTO, Department of Sociology, University of Washington, Seattle, Washington

DON T. NAKANISHI, Graduate School of Education, University of California, Los Angeles, California

PARMATMA SARAN, Department of Sociology and Anthropology, Baruch College, New York, New York

BOB H. SUZUKI, Vice President for Academic Affairs, California State University, Northridge, California

SHIH-SHAN HENRY TSAI, Department of History, University of Arkansas, Fayetteville, Arkansas

Consultants

ALBERT ACENA, College of San Mateo, San Mateo, California

RUBEN R. ALCANTARA, American Studies Department, University of Hawaii, Honolulu, Hawaii

GUNTHER BARTH, Department of History, University of California, Berkeley, California

DANILO BEGONIA, School of Ethnic Studies, San Francisco State University, San Francisco, California

BONG-YOUN CHOY, Berkeley, California

ROGER DANIELS, Department of History, University of Cincinnati, Cincinnati, Ohio

MAXINE P. FISHER, Department of Sociology, Queens College, CUNY, New York, New York

WON MOO HURH, Department of Sociology and Anthropology, Western Illinois University, Macomb, Illinois

JOAN M. JENSEN, Department of History, New Mexico State University, Las Cruces, New Mexico

GEORGE KAGIWADA, Asian American Studies, Department of Applied Behavioral Sciences, University of California, Davis, California

TETSUDEN KASHIMA, Department of American Ethnic Studies, University of Washington, Seattle, Washington

EUGENE KIM, School of Education, California State University, Sacramento, California

HARRY H. L. KITANO, School of Social Welfare, University of California, Los Angeles, California

HUM MARK LAI, Chinese Historical Society, San Francisco, California

STANFORD M. LYMAN, Department of Sociology, Graduate School of the New School for Social Research, New York, New York

DARREL MONTERO, School of Social Work, Arizona State University, Tempe, Arizona

FRANKLIN ODO, Department of Ethnic Studies, University of Hawaii, Honolulu, Hawaii

WAYNE PATTERSON, St. Norberg College, Greenbay, Wisconsin

STANLEY SUE, Department of Psychology, University of California, Los Angeles, California

Preface

When I was offered the opportunity to take on the enormous task of writing a dictionary of Asian American history in August 1981, I accepted the challenge in trepidation, for I felt, as I feel now, that it was beyond one man's ability to survey a wide spectrum of the collective memory of the countless Asian immigrants and their descendants in the United States. As the end of research and writing on the dictionary draws near, I can only hope that I have done justice to the topic. In trepidation I shall await the judgment of the critics.

The *Dictionary* is divided into two major sections: (1) essays and (2) entries. In addition, an extensive bibliography on literature about Asian and Pacific Americans, an up-to-date historical chronology of Asians in America, a census report on people of Asian descent living in the United States, and a general subject index are appended to the end of the dictionary for the reader's convenience.

The first seven essays of the essay section treat the historical development of different ethnic groups of people from Asian countries and the Pacific Islands who are now called Asian and Pacific Americans; the last eight essays are treatises on the place of Asian and Pacific Americans in the American social order. The authors of these essays have been teaching in the field of Asian and Pacific American Studies for many years, and they have written extensively on the general topic of Asians in America.

All entries in the second section were written by the editor. They are arranged alphabetically and include major events, persons, places, and concepts that have left indelible marks on the collective experience of Asian and Pacific Americans. There are approximately 800 entries, and the majority of them center on the historical experiences of persons of Chinese, Japanese, Korean, Asian Indian, and Filipino ancestry—although some attention is also paid to contemporary events in the lives of refugees from Vietnam, Kampuchea, and Laos.

Only a minimal number of entries on the experience of the Pacific Islanders are included in the *Dictionary*. One of the reasons is the lack of available literature on the history of Pacific Islanders in the United States. It should also be pointed out that the Hawaiian historical experience receives coverage only when it is directly related to the Asian American experience in those islands. I do believe, as others do, that the collective experience of the native people of Hawaii occurred under circumstances similar to those of Native Americans in the United States mainland. Therefore, the title of the *Dictionary* does justice to the coverage.

Within the entries themselves, in presenting the names of Asians from China, Japan, and Korea, the following rules have been observed: (1) the surname is listed first if the given name is not Anglicized, but if the given name is Anglicized, then the given name is listed first; (2) this principle is applied to all Asians born in the United States of Chinese, Japanese, and Korean ancestry; (3) the names of Asian Indians and Filipinos are given in the same way as those of people whose first names are Anglicized; (4) when individuals use their names consistently in a particular way, that is, Syngman Rhee, then no change is made to those names; and (5) all personal names in the entry headings, regardless of whether or not they are Asian, are given with surnames first, followed by their given names.

Asterisks used in the text indicate names or terms that appear as entry headings in the *Dictionary*.

No book is envisioned, conceptualized, written, and produced in isolation from a community of concerned scholars interested in developing, promoting, and criticizing socially produced knowledge. The present volume is no exception. In the course of research and writing for this book, I have been indebted to many people who have generously given their time and effort beyond the call of duty. There are too many to mention all their names in such limited space. I hope they will forgive me if I fail to acknowledge my indebtedness to them all individually.

I would like to express my deep gratitude to the scholars who have enriched the *Dictionary* with their individual essays. I would also like to extend my special thanks to the scholars who served as consultants (see the separate list of consultants) during the research and writing of the *Dictionary*. Particular thanks go to Professor Gunther Barth of the University of California at Berkeley, and to Professor Hum Mark Lai of the Chinese Historical Society in San Francisco.

Special thanks go to the following individuals without whose support I would have been less sanguine about the probability of completing the manuscript: Professor Ray McInnis of the Wilson Library, Western Washington University, for his willingness to obtain the necessary material and to listen to my emotional ups and downs during the course of research and writing; Professor Philip B. Vander Velde, Department of Educational Administration and Foundations, Western Washington University, for his flexibility to arrange and oftentimes to rearrange my class schedule to my convenience; Professor Marvin Klein, former Dean, School of Education, Western Washington University, for providing me with extra office space for research and writing; Professor Choy Bong-youn, Contra Costa College, for his words of encouragement and faith in the value of the present volume; Professor Frank Miyamoto, University of Washington, for his kindness in answering my questions at any time of the day; Professor Elaine Kim, the University of California at Berkeley, for her eagerness to spend time with me in discussing how best to organize the *Dictionary*; Professor Don Nakanishi, the University of California at Los Angeles, for his sound advice on editorial matters; Professor T. Kashimura, University of Washington, for the time we spent together in identifying scholars to work as consultants and contributors, and Mr. Art Ruffier, Assistant Law Librarian, Washington State Law Library, for his assistance and for providing me with information and documents to research state and federal court cases.

I would also like to express my deep gratitude to Mrs. Jane Clark for her patience and perseverance. She spent countless hours typing the manuscript. Misses Paige Payne and Laura Jessup should be thanked and commended for their wonderful editorial assistance. Mrs. Cynthia Harris, Greenwood Press, deserves a special thanks from me for her time and effort in transforming an unpolished manuscript into a readable book.

DICTIONARY
OF ASIAN
AMERICAN
HISTORY

ESSAYS

Chinese in the United States

SHIH-SHAN HENRY TSAI

The history of the Chinese in America has been marked by cultural conflicts, political alienation, and a stream of economic and social injustices. In the midst of this, American images of the Chinese have changed from highly unfavorable in the nineteenth century, to more realistic in the 1930s and 1940s, to highly favorable in recent years. The unfavorable American perception of the Chinese was for the most part the product of the experience of the latter part of the nineteenth century when China was weak and poor, and the Chinese who came to America were largely uneducated, cheap laborers. Pressed by poverty at home and induced by job opportunities in America, hundreds of thousands of Chinese from the southern province of Kwangtung flocked to the United States. They tunneled through mountains, cleared forests, built railroads, worked in the mines, reclaimed swamps, fished along the California coast, gathered wheat and cash crops, and helped to open up the great American West for settlement.

It is generally believed that the Chinese population in the United States reached a peak in the early 1880s, although its actual number will probably never be known. The 1880 Census counted 105,465 Chinese on the mainland and some 10,000 living in Hawaii, and immigration records indicated that in the first two years of that decade 57,271 arrived and 26,788 departed, leaving a net gain of 30,483. The depression of the 1870s and mass unemployment caused growing tension between laborers and capitalists and accelerated the growth of organized labor in the United States. The Chinese, then appearing as a new ethnic group on the American scene, quickly became the target of racial hatred and victims of labor-management disputes. Anti-Chinese propaganda initiated by organized labor and the sand-lot orations of wily politicians resulted in a series of exclusion laws to bar the entry of Chinese laborers. Consequently, the Chinese population in America fell from 152,000 (including Hawaii) in 1882, when Congress passed the first exclusion law, to 122,789 in 1890. A drastic decline took place in the 1890s and continued until World War II when the new immigrants and students and the birth of a second generation caused the number of Chinese in America to climb slowly upward again.

In America the Chinese lived in an abnormal society full of young males—wandering sojourners whose dream was to put in a few years of hard labor and to return home wealthy and respected "Gold Mountain Guests." Hence, Chinese immigrants did not establish a miniature replica of traditional Chinese society in the United States. The Chinese population was almost totally transient, and there was a great scarcity of females. This social phenomenon combined with the anti-Chinese outrages gave rise to the Chinese quarters or Chinatowns in American cities. In the small and often crowded quarters of San Francisco, Sacramento, Honolulu, and other urban communities, the Chinese built temples and public halls, established stores and businesses, and opened restaurants and wash-houses. They retained their native customs and formed a nation within a nation, a tendency characteristic of all immigrant groups in America. They formed clan associations, regional associations, and secret societies for the control, protection, and general welfare of their kinsmen. But the fact that they retained Chinese traditions instead of the Judeo-Christian culture set them off from the American mainstream. In the final analysis, their lofty effort to maintain the Chinese heritage, language, and religion in America retarded the acculturation of the first and second generations of Chinese in the New World.

Until the Japanese attacked Pearl Harbor and the United States and China became wartime allies, those Chinese who remained in the United States were driven into Chinatown ghettos, uncomplaining, withdrawing, being apolitical and passive. They were mostly limited to non-competitive jobs and were largely left to benign neglect. World War II changed the American perception of China and the Chinese, and resulted in the repeal of all anti-Chinese exclusion laws in 1943. The more tolerant social environment along with better political conditions opened new educational and career opportunities to Chinese Americans, greatly improving their economic position. The 1950s saw a significant portion of Chinese easing into previously restricted areas of employment, and growing numbers were hired as technicians and engineers. The income gap between whites and Chinese, though still considerable, contracted somewhat during the war years.

Nowhere was the new Chinese American role better exemplified than in the armed services. As soon as the United States entered the conflict, Chinese community leaders urged young Chinese to enlist in the armed forces of the United States as a demonstration of their loyalty to the American cause. The New York Chinatown cheered itself hoarse when the first draft numbers included Chinese Americans. Of the only eleven Chinese of draft age in Butte, Montana, all enlisted before being drafted. In the battlefields of Europe and Asia, Chinese soldiers fought side by side with white comrades whose grandfathers had tried to expel their ancestors. Of the 59,803 Chinese adult males in the United States, including citizens, residents, and students, over 20 percent were drafted or enlisted in the U. S. Army. In addition, a smaller number served in the navy and the air force. Two hundred fourteen Chinese died in World War II combat.

That number, though small when compared to the national average, nevertheless showed the patriotism of a people long discriminated against in the United States. Many young Chinese veterans used the G. I. Bill to go to college and began a pursuit of the American dream. The inroads the Chinese had made into the American labor force were never to be reversed.

Equally important gains were made on political, legal, and social fronts. With the repeal of the exclusion laws and naturalization prohibition, more and more Chinese could and did build normal lives in America. The old sojourner's bachelor society was being replaced by a better structured social order and family system that was to become a mainstay of Chinese stability and distinctiveness. Their educational achievements and occupational skills, together with their low delinquency and crime rate and rare recourse to social welfare, convinced many whites that the Chinese were, and could be, valuable members of American society. In the 1940s and 1950s, the pace of acculturation increased markedly. Moreover, in the period 1890–1940, the number of foreign-born Chinese dropped from 100,000 to 40,000. By World War II the former laboring sojourners had become mostly older people.

The rise of an acculturated generation ultimately entailed the development of art and literature in a Chinese American context. Beyond the world of chop suey and laundry, Chinese Americans were becoming better educated and more English speaking, were reading more books, and were seeking ethnic self-definition in art and literature. American-born Chinese writers began to adopt themes from American life, attacking the discrimination of the immigration laws and the evils of racism, and speaking in terms of alienation and anguish in contemporary American life. Creative work became a vehicle by which Chinese Americans could characterize their sensibilities as members of a minority group and could develop their ethnic consciousness. Over and over, they expressed the pain of cultural estrangement and *alexia*, or the deprivation of a natural language of identity. C. Y. Lee's *Flower Drum Song* (1957), Frank Chin's *Aiiieeeee! An Anthology of Asian American Writers* (1974), and Maxine Hong Kingston's *The Woman Warrior* (1977) were but a few examples that reflected the American-born Chinese quest for identity.

Collateral to the acute identity crisis was the phenomenal increase of the Chinese population after 1965. Thanks to the liberal Immigration Act of 1965, the 1980 U. S. Census showed that there were 806,027 Chinese in the fifty states of the Union and that the Chinese had overtaken the Japanese to become America's largest Asian population. This figure represented an increase of 239 percent since the 1960 Census, which had recorded 237,292, but over half of all Chinese still lived in the Pacific states. However, an increasing number had settled in the East, notably New York, New Jersey, and Massachusetts, and in such Midwestern states as Illinois, Michigan, and Ohio. The greatest percentage increase since 1970 was in the South, especially in Texas and Florida. Eleven percent of the Chinese population resided in the South in 1980 as compared with only 8 percent in 1970. Consequently, there were slight decreases in the percentages of Chinese living in Hawaii and California, in spite of the fact that California remained the state with the largest Chinese population, 322,340, and Hawaii led all states with the highest Chinese population percentage at 5.8 percent.

The Chinese population was overwhelmingly urban in the 1980 Census. The largest concentrations were in the New York-New Jersey metropolitan area and in the San Francisco Bay area, each of which listed more than 100,000 Chinese residents. Other urban and suburban counties also showed high rates of population gain for the Chinese. In Los Angeles, the Chinese population grew 129 percent between 1970 and 1980 whereas the county's growth was only 6 percent. San Diego showed a 139 percent gain for the Chinese as compared with an overall population gain of 37 percent. About 97 percent of the Chinese lived in urban areas; other cities showing marked gains included Houston, Chicago, Boston, Dallas, Seattle, San Jose, Detroit, Philadelphia, Phoenix, Washington, D. C., Honolulu, and Sacramento. Cities that had concentrations of over 4,000 Chinese included Stockton, Anaheim-Santa Ana-Garden Grove, and Fresno in California, Portland in Oregon, Minneapolis-St. Paul, and Miami-Fort Lauderdale.

The Chinese in America are still treated, at least in government ethnic reckonings, as a singular minority group, even though they are as diversified and, to a certain extent, as individualistic as the Americans of European origin. Like other Americans, the Chinese community includes those who have been established in America for several generations along with newly arrived immigrants, economically disadvantaged and non-English speaking workers as well as wealthy businessmen, high school dropouts, and Ivy League-trained Ph.D.s. Unlike the early "faceless and nameless" Chinese immigrants of the nineteenth century, contemporary Chinese Americans include such nationally recognized personalities as Senator Hiram Fong of Hawaii, Republican activist Anne Chennault, world renowned architect Ieoh Ming Pei, NBC anchorwoman Connie Chung, prominent California politician March Fong Eu, computer wizard Dr. An Wang, ice skate champion Tiffany Chin, and astronaut Taylor Wang. Unlike the early Cantonese-speaking peasants from rural villages, many of the recent arrivals are well educated and speak the standard Mandarin plus the distinct Taiwan or Shanghai dialects. Not only do these recent arrivals speak different Chinese dialects and organize associations completely independent of the Six Companies (q.v.), they also prefer different cuisines and support mutually hostile political groups. In short, sharp ethnic and class distinctions and a politically fragmented population are characteristics of the post–1965 Chinese American community.

Japanese in the United States

S. FRANK MIYAMOTO

The main Japanese immigration to the continental United States began around 1890. (Due to space limitations, little is said here about the Japanese minority in Hawaii.) The U. S. Census reported 2,039 persons of Japanese background in 1890, 24,326 in 1900, 126,947 in 1940, and 461,226 in 1980. Of the 1940 and 1980 totals, 63 and 80 percent, respectively, were American-born.

The earliest immigrants were predominantly young males, most of whom came as sojourners intent on gaining wealth quickly and returning to Japan as persons of status. They came on the whole from farming and small trades backgrounds, especially from the southwestern prefectures such as Hiroshima, Kumamoto, Yamaguchi, and Fukuoka. In America, the owning classes of the Pacific Coast welcomed this new source of cheap labor, for the Chinese Exclusion Act of 1882 had shut off their previous source. With the help of Japanese labor contractors, hundreds of workers were recruited into railroading, lumbering, fishing, mining, and farming. On the other hand, a strong impulse toward individual entrepreneurship was prevalent among these workers. After accumulating small savings, substantial numbers started individually operated farms or city trades such as market stands, gardening, groceries, hotels, barbershops, restaurants, cleaners, and laundries.

Farmers and tradesmen soon felt the need for wives who could help with the enterprises, and the importation of wives became a major concern. Japan's traditional arranged marriage, including a variant called the "picture-bride marriage," facilitated quick marriages. The resulting rapid increase of families had multiple effects, such as the diminishing of the earlier sojourner's concern to return to Japan.

Another effect was an intensification of the anti-Japanese movement. This movement was an extension of the earlier anti-Chinese agitation and as in the Chinese case was led by San Francisco labor leaders. Publishers of powerful California newspapers joined the attack, and politicians quickly discovered that a campaign for Japanese exclusion was an unfailing method of winning public support. In 1905 labor organizations met in San Francisco to form the Asiatic Exclusion League, the prime aim of which was to halt Japanese immigration. It fostered boycotts of Japanese enterprises, its members attacked Japanese on the streets, and in 1906 it brought pressure on the San Francisco Board of Education to segregate all Japanese children and youths in an Oriental school. When the Japanese government protested the school segregation to President Theodore Roosevelt, the President persuaded the city to retract the segregation rule. However, knowing that the underlying concern of Californians was to stop Japanese immigration, he negotiated the so-called Gentlemen's Agreement by which Japan agreed, beginning in 1908, to restrict the issuance of passports to the United States only to non-laborers and to parents, wives, and children of those who had already immigrated.

The signing of the Gentlemen's Agreement did little to curb the anti-Japanese agitation. Proposals to restrict the land holdings of Japanese farmers now appeared before the state legislature. In 1913 the Alien Land Act of California was enacted which prohibited land ownership by any alien ineligible for citizenship, a bill clearly directed against the immigrant Japanese. Similar land laws were later passed in Washington and Oregon in 1921 and 1923. As immigration continued and the number of families increased, exclusionists set up the cry that the Japanese were "breeding like rabbits" and would soon overrun the Pacific Coast. Others foresaw "the Yellow Peril," the likelihood of a Japanese military invasion of the Pacific Coast. Pressure groups, politicians, and newspapers, especially in California, redoubled their efforts for Japanese exclusion. The effort culminated in the passage by Congress of the Immigration Act of 1924 which specifically excluded from immigration any alien ineligible for citizenship. In 1922 the U. S. Supreme Court had rejected the claim of Ozawa Takao, an immigrant Japanese with considerable American education, for the right of citizenship.

The majority group's hostility contributed substantially to the tendency of the immigrant Japanese to remain socially isolated. Within their segregated communities which dotted the Pacific Coast states, the minority developed an unusually active and highly organized community life. Entrepreneurs evolved a self-sufficient ethnic economy that served virtually all needs, although many also competed for a place in the larger economy and thus promoted assimilation. Churches, both Christian and Buddhist, flourished. Recreational clubs and sports organizations mushroomed. The basis of these organizations was a network of bonds that existed within families, among kinfolk, and among *kenjin* (fellow prefectural members). The *kenjin* often organized themselves into a *kenjinkai* (prefectural association). In the larger communities, all these various organizations were often loosely coordinated under an umbrella organization, the Japanese Association.

As long as the Issei (first generation) dominated, adaptations of Old World customs prevailed in the communities, but as the Nisei (second generation) increased in number and maturity, the Americanization of the communities progressed rapidly. The interests and activities of the Nisei were not markedly different from those of American youths elsewhere, except that Nisei activities were more highly organized. They were also set apart by segregation barriers. The organization of the Japanese American Citizens League in 1930 symbolized the two dominant concerns of the Nisei in those years: to overcome the discrimination that barred them from jobs and social opportunities in the larger society, and to become assimilated.

Japan's bombing of Pearl Harbor on December 7, 1941, incited, after a brief period of restraint, an intense campaign for the removal of the Japanese minority from Pacific Coast areas. The campaign climaxed on February 19, 1942, with President Franklin D. Roosevelt's signing of Executive Order 9066 which authorized military commanders to designate military areas from which any and all persons might be excluded. General John L. DeWitt, commanding general of the Western Defense Command, then issued orders designating broad zones of the Pacific Coast from which persons of Japanese ancestry were excluded, and quickly effected the evacuation from these areas of about 110,000 Japanese minority residents.

The evacuees were removed first to temporary centers, called assembly centers, and then to more permanent relocation centers. Ten of the relocation centers, administered by a new federal agency called the War Relocation Authority (WRA), were established in isolated semi-desert areas. The relocation centers, with capacities ranging from 8,000 to 20,000 residents, consisted of rows of army barracks surrounded by barbed-wire fences and guard towers. Within each center the WRA attempted to create a semblance of normal community life, but in less than a year the administration concluded that detention was mentally and morally unhealthy for the evacuees. The WRA thereupon attempted to institute a program of loyalty registration and resettlement of the evacuees to non-restricted areas. A minority of the evacuees for a variety of reasons refused to sign the loyalty oath; these people, totaling 18,000, were isolated in the Tule Lake Segregation Center and were labeled "the Disloyal."

Many evacuees, especially the Nisei, took the opportunity to seek employment or education outside the centers, and new communities of the Japanese minority emerged in Chicago, New York City, Denver, and many scattered places throughout the country. But others, especially the Issei, refused to leave the centers and remained until the end of the war.

At the end of the war when the exclusion orders on the Pacific Coast were lifted, many who had moved to regions outside the Pacific Coast states chose to stay in their new locations, but the majority returned to their former communities on the Pacific Coast, to communities that had been dramatically altered by the evacuation. Most Issei were now too old and lacked the financial means to reestablish their farms and businesses or regain their former employment, and only a shadow of the old ethnic economy was revived. It was now the Nisei's turn to dominate, and their activities gave the primary imprint to the revived communities. Fortunately for the Nisei, majority group prejudice and discrimination was now substantially less than before the war. Job opportunities in the larger economy, especially for professionals, semi-professionals, and skilled workers, opened up as they never had before. Residential segregation and social discrimination which were flagrant before likewise gradually declined. These improved conditions were in part due to the general decline of white prejudice toward racial minorities in the post-war decades, but they were also very much due to the brilliant military performance recorded during World War II by the all-Nisei 442nd Regimental Combat Team as well as the Nisei in the Pacific War.

As post-war American society became steadily more hospitable, the Nisei flourished. Studies in the 1960s showed that they had achieved exceptionally high median educational levels, twice as many proportionately in the professions than among white Americans, and equally high median family income as among white Americans. A number of Nisei have now gained national prominence: for example, sculptor Noguchi Isamu, architect Yamasaki Minoru, furniture designer George Nakashima, and Senators Daniel Inouye, Spark Matsunaga, and S. I. Hayakawa. The Nisei are perhaps most widely known in art and politics, but many in various other professions are well recognized within their own fields. Although the Sansei (third generation) are only now reaching maturity, evidence indicates that they are establishing themselves much more securely in the larger society than did the Nisei.

The assimilative process among Japanese Americans, however, is following a bifurcated course. The job discrimination and residential segregation which were flagrant before the war have greatly diminished, and many Nisei now associate predominantly with non-Japanese. The intermarriage rate of the Sansei, overwhelmingly with Caucasians, is now over 50 percent. Because of such evidence, some writers forecast a rapid decline of the Japanese American identity. On the other hand, the Japanese American Citizens League, the only national organization of Japanese Americans, shows a surprising persistence, not only on the Pacific Coast but in every region of the country as well. The organization persists because it is able to mobilize a nationwide concern among Nisei and Sansei around such issues as "redress for the injustices of the evacuation" inflicted on the Japanese minority. Japanese American churches, both Christian and Buddhist, also endure in surprising numbers. That is, substantial numbers of Nisei and even of Sansei appear to prefer associating with Japanese Americans to non-Japanese, or at least have an interest in not cutting their ties with other Nisei and Sansei. The overall evidence indicates that the Japanese American identity will persist for some time to come.

Today, over forty years after the evacuation, two issues which arose from that event are finally approaching resolution. One concerns the constitutionality of the forced evacuation and related restrictions that were imposed by the federal government on citizens of Japanese ancestry. In 1942, even as the evacuation and detention programs were proceeding under orders issued by General John

L. DeWitt, four Nisei separately initiated court tests of those orders. Gordon K. Hirabayashi and Yasui Minoru deliberately violated a curfew restriction issued on March 24, 1942, that restricted all persons of Japanese ancestry residing in Military Area No. 1, and were apprehended, tried, and convicted of a criminal offense. Later, Fred T. Korematsu failed to comply with General DeWitt's exclusion order, was arrested, and was also found guilty of a criminal violation. In its review of these three cases in 1943 and 1944, the Supreme Court of the United States handed down decisions concluding that the evidence of military necessity justified General DeWitt's imposition of the curfew and evacuation orders on citizens of Japanese ancestry, and upheld the convictions. On the other hand, in the case of Endo Mitsuye, a Nisei woman who challenged the right of the government to hold her in detention at a War Relocation Authority center, the Supreme Court unanimously declared that detention was invalid and ordered her unconditional release by the War Relocation Authority.

In 1981, Peter Irons, a Harvard Law School graduate who had joined the political science faculty of the University of California at San Diego, uncovered documents in the Federal Archives which clearly indicated that high-level federal officials had suppressed evidence, known at the time of the evacuation decision, which raised serious doubts about the army's claim of military necessity for the evacuation. Informed of this new evidence, Korematsu, Hirabayashi, and Yasui initiated petitions for a writ of error *coram nobis*, which requires evidence that the original conviction was tainted by government misconduct, in an effort to have their earlier convictions overturned.

At a hearing before the federal court in San Francisco on November 10, 1983, Korematsu's previous conviction was vacated and the case was dismissed. A similar finding was handed down for Yasui in January 1984. In the Hirabayashi case heard in a Seattle federal district court on May 18, 1984, however, Judge Donald Voorhees overrode the plea of the U. S. Department of Justice to have the case dismissed if the conviction was vacated. Instead he ordered an evidentiary hearing on Hirabayashi's *coram nobis* petition. At this hearing, the date for which has not yet been set at this writing, evidence on the claim of government misconduct, including cross-examination of those who were directly involved in the evacuation decision and are still alive, will be presented.

The second unresolved issue concerns the question of redress, compensation to the evacuees for damages and losses suffered because of evacuation. In 1948 an Evacuation Claims Act was passed by which persons of Japanese ancestry could file claims against the U.S. government for real or personal property losses incurred demonstrably as a result of the evacuation. The act had several limitations, however, particularly in its requirements of elaborate proof of loss and its unwieldy mechanism for processing claims. Ultimately, a total of $38 million was paid to the evacuees under the act, less than 10 percent of a conservatively estimated total property loss suffered by the evacuees. And the act did not allow claims for lost income or for pain and suffering.

In the 1970s when ethnic consciousness rose among all minorities, Japanese

Americans became increasingly vocal in their demand for redress of the evacuation injustices. Congress responded in 1980 by establishing a Commission on
Wartime Relocation and Internment of Civilians, composed of an eminent group
of Americans, to investigate the circumstances and effects of the evacuation and
detention, and to recommend appropriate remedies. After more than two years
of hearings and investigations, the commission submitted findings which concluded that the evacuation had inflicted a grave injustice on the Japanese minority.
It recommended various forms of restitution, including a one-time per capita
compensatory payment of $20,000 to each of the approximately 60,000 surviving
persons who were subjected to the evacuation. In 1983 a redress bill was introduced in Congress, and at this writing hearings are proceeding within a House
Judiciary subcommittee.

Thus, four decades after the nadir of Japanese minority experiences in the
United States, the fortunes of the group are tending in a positive direction.

Koreans in the United States

HYUNG-CHAN KIM

The first group of 101 Korean immigrants arrived in Hawaii on January 13, 1903, to work on Hawaiian sugar plantations. Since that time, during the last eighty-three years, many different historical and sociological factors have pushed Koreans out of their homeland and pulled them to the United States. Some of these push-and-pull factors resulted from events taking place in Korea, and other factors were international in origin and scope. In order to better understand the nature of the influencing forces, it seems appropriate to divide the history of Korean immigration to the United States into four distinctive periods: (1) 1902–1905; (2) 1906–1945; (3) 1946–1964; and (4) 1965–present.

A combination of historical, socioeconomic, and political forces worked together to push approximately 8,000 Koreans out of their native land between 1902 and 1905. At the turn of the century, following Japan's victory over China in 1895, a general political uncertainty hovered over the Korean peninsula as Japan began to aggressively pursue commercial and economic interests in Korea. Because the war was fought on their own soil, large numbers of Korean peasants were uprooted from their ancestral land and began to move into population centers in search of work. Unemployment became a very serious problem in these population centers. In addition, a severe famine struck a number of northern provinces of Korea in 1902, driving more peasants from their farmlands in search of food. General economic and political conditions in Korea were then conducive to immigration. At this time, the Hawaiian Sugar Planters' Association made arrangements with Horace N. Allen, American Minister to Korea, to have Koreans recruited by David Deshler for work on Hawaii's plantations.

A careful examination of the socioeconomic and cultural characteristics of Koreans who were recruited to work in Hawaii suggests that Korean immigrants to Hawaii were quite different from Chinese and Japanese immigrants already in Hawaii working for the Hawaiian Sugar Planters' Association. First, unlike Chinese and Japanese immigrants, Koreans came from various parts of Korea.

No one district or province could be singled out as the predominant geographic area of origin of Korean immigrants. Whereas Chinese and Japanese immigrants came to Hawaii primarily from Kwangtung Province and Hiroshima Prefecture, respectively, the geographic distribution of Korean immigrants to Hawaii in terms of their place of residence before immigration was distributed over the entire Korean peninsula. Second, half of the Korean immigrants were city-dwellers in the Seoul-Inchon-Suwon area, and the other half came from other population centers. Wayne Patterson in his unpublished essay, ''Koreans in Hawaii: The Linkage Between Immigration and Adjustment,'' suggests that these Koreans were urbanized people,[1] but his claim is highly questionable.

There were no genuine major urban centers in Korea at the turn of the century. These city-dwellers had moved away from their farms into population centers in search of work during, or immediately after, the end of the Sino-Japanese War in 1895. Before the war they probably had been engaged in farming, but they were no longer farmers and were not inclined to do farming after their arrival in population centers. Their children, particularly, were not accustomed to farming. These city-dwellers were not urbanized people in the genuine sense of the word ''urbanization.'' It would be more appropriate to characterize them as people who were in transition from rural to urban life.

A third difference between these immigrants and the Chinese and Japanese, according to the author of *A Fifty-Year History of Koreans in America*, was their literacy rate of 40 percent. If this estimate by Kim Won-yong is correct,[2] then the literacy rate of Korean immigrants was extremely high, particularly when compared with literacy rates among Chinese and Japanese immigrants. Fourth, although a majority of Korean immigrants were single young men, the ratio between men and women among them was much higher than that among Chinese and Japanese immigrants. This more balanced ratio suggests that many Korean immigrants had a different motive from that of their Chinese and Japanese counterparts: whereas Chinese and Japanese immigrants came to work to make money with which to return to their native country, many Korean immigrants came with the purpose of staying in Hawaii and making it their home. This challenges the notion that early Korean immigrants were sojourners who were interested only in making money with which to return to Korea to live out their lives in wealth and comfort. Unlike the Chinese and Japanese who had their mother country to return to, Korean immigrants did not think they could return to their unstable country and feel safe and secure. Fifth, many Korean immigrants, unlike the Chinese and Japanese, were already Christians before they decided to come to Hawaii.

These five major characteristics set the Koreans apart not only from the Chinese and Japanese immigrants to Hawaii, but also from Eastern Europeans who immigrated to the mainland United States. According to some sociologists, including Ilsoo Kim, author of *New Urban Immigrants: The Korean Community in New York*, Korean immigrants who have come to the United States since 1965

are different from those who immigr̲ ̲ ̲ ̲ ̲ica before the passage of the
1965 Immigration Act. They are espe̲ ̲ ̲ ̲ ̲tern European
immigrants who arrived in the Unit̲
sociologists argue that a different so̲
ing the post–1965 immigrants in th̲
urban backgrounds. The paradigm̲
priate to studying the post–1965̲
orientation used in studying the̲
new paradigm would help us to̲
methods with regard to the post̲
too simplistic to think that the̲
be captured in two separate soc̲
development and expansion of̲
differentiated theoretical pers̲

As suggested above, the K̲
were in transition from rura̲
from this transition stage̲
rural in their economic and cu̲
left the plantations faster than any other ethni̲
of the plantations even before their contract expired. They su̲
into Hawaii's urban centers and recorded one of the highest rates of urbaniza̲ ̲.
Therefore, strict application of the folk-to-urban paradigm to studying the pre–
1965 immigrants in the United States and of the urban-to-urban paradigm to
researching the post–1965 immigrants is too simplistic, for it fails to take into
consideration other complex factors involved in international migration. Not all
immigrants to the United States before the passage of the 1965 Immigration Act
moved from rural areas of their native country to urban centers of the United
States. The Chinese and Japanese, for instance, came from rural areas of their
respective countries to sugar plantations in Hawaii. These plantations were anything but urban. On the other hand, Korean immigrants were in transition from
rural to urban in both places.

The social backgrounds of Korean immigrants contributed to the development
of different social organizations and institutions. Although the Chinese and Japanese established community organizations based on the regional, geographic,
and kinship affiliations of their respective homeland, Korean immigrants, lacking
such ties, created entirely different institutions: namely, churches and village
councils. Korean immigrants established churches as soon as they arrived in
Hawaii. Village councils were later created on plantations after the Koreans were
dispersed into small groups to be sent to their work places. A village council
was organized on every plantation that had more than ten Korean families, and
it functioned as an agency of law enforcement. The Korean immigrants also
organized secret societies to offer extra protection to their members. Although
the institution of rotating credit associations known as Kye was brought to Hawaii

[handwritten annotation on note:]
1. various part. (5 major)
2. city-dwellers → not accustomed to farming
   urbanization.
3. literacy. population.
4. different motive
   sojourners
5. Christians.

and was therefore available, it was not extensively used by the Koreans. It was especially not used to capitalize small businesses among Korean immigrants in Hawaii.

The first wave of Korean immigration to Hawaii was abruptly halted by Japanese officials. First, the government in Tokyo was under pressure from Japanese immigrants in Hawaii to stop Korean immigration, inasmuch as Japanese employers frequently used Koreans as strike-breakers. Japanese workers would go on strike demanding better working conditions and higher wages, but the Hawaiian Sugar Planters' Association would bring in Koreans to replace the striking workers. Second, the Japanese government did not want to see the American government adopt a policy of exclusion against the Japanese as it had adopted against the Chinese. The Tokyo government considered it rather demeaning for Japan to undergo the same treatment accorded the Chinese by the government in Washington. Because of the anti-Japanese agitation on the United States' West Coast, the Tokyo government was willing to discourage its subjects from moving to the West Coast from Hawaii and to put an end to the Korean immigration in exchange for Washington's continued support for Japanese immigration to Hawaii. When the government of Korea complained that Korean immigrants in Hawaii had been mistreated, Japanese authorities in Korea seized the opportunity to halt Korean immigration under the pretext that strict measures were to be taken for the protection of Korean emigrants going abroad.

During the second period of immigration, extending from 1906 to 1945, only a limited number of Koreans came to the United States. Among them were picture-brides, students, and political refugees. After the conclusion of the Gentlemen's Agreement between the United States and Japan in 1908, Koreans in Hawaii were granted permission to bring their wives and family. The first picture-bride arrived in Hawaii on November 28, 1910: Sara Choe, who became Mrs. Yi Nae-su. Subsequently, more than 800 picture-brides came to join their husbands between 1910 and 1924, the latter being the year of the Asian Exclusion Act. In addition, a limited number of Korean students, sponsored either through private means or by the Japanese colonial government in Korea, came to the United States for study. Some of them decided to stay in America after completing their studies in order to pursue a professional career or to work toward Korean independence. There were also a number of political refugees who escaped to the United States from Korea, which was then under Japanese rule. Among those political refugees was Syngman Rhee, who later worked to consolidate Koreans in Hawaii for the Korean independence movement.

Because of the diverse socioeconomic, cultural, and political backgrounds of Koreans who came to the United States between 1906 and 1945, it would be almost impossible to apply one sociological paradigm to the research and study of these people. Picture-brides, who came to Honolulu to live, came from rural backgrounds; students who were born and raised in urban areas in Korea chose to go to small colleges and universities in rural areas of America; others from rural areas of Korea went to colleges and universities in American cities; and still other Koreans, who had lived in urban areas, felt more comfortable with America's urban life.

During the second period one major driving force among Korean immigrants both in Hawaii and in mainland United States became a rallying point for their organizations. After Korea became a protectorate of the Japanese Empire in 1905, Koreans in America were politically mobilized for the cause of Korea's political independence. Nationalism among Koreans in America was high, as Korea was forced to give up more autonomy under Japanese pressure between 1905 and 1910. During this period of national shame, more than twenty organizations were created among Koreans in America. Among them were the United Korean Society in Hawaii and the Mutual Assistance Society in mainland United States. The two organizations merged into one and became the Korean National Association on February 1, 1909, a year before Japan decided to make Korea its official colony.

The Korean National Association had noble objectives: to promote educational and business development in the Korean community, to protect freedom and equality among Koreans, and to work toward restoration of Korean independence. Although its objectives were noble, high-minded leaders who were willing to work together at the expense of their personal interests were rare among Koreans in America. The struggle to restore Korea's independence was unfortunately a long and protracted one, spanning over forty years. It was hard for Korean community leaders not to disagree on the philosophy and methods of gaining Korean independence. Ultimately, differences in opinion developed over philosophy and methods among leaders, and a widening gap between them became solidified and unbridgeable until factionalism destroyed any sense of unity among Koreans in America. Leaders such as Syngman Rhee, Ahn Chang-ho, and Pak Yong-man were as obstinate about their determination to work toward Korea's independence as they were about their philosophy and strategy for achieving their goal. Ultimately, leaders and their followers were to be blamed for the factionalism that continued to plague the Korean community in America even after Korea's liberation in 1945. During this period, even churches were divided to support particular political philosophies and the individual interests of their leaders. In spite of the factionalism among churches, they continued to play a major role by providing Korean immigrants and their descendants with opportunities to gather to exchange information, to share the Korean heritage, to speak their native tongue, to strengthen their sense of identity, and to satisfy their spiritual needs.

The third period of Korean emigration, stretching from 1946 to 1964, was caused and influenced as much by internal factors as by those external to the Korean peninsula. Because of these multiplex factors, which determined the sociocultural, economic, and political characteristics of Koreans emigrating to the United States, it would again be extremely difficult to use one sociological paradigm to study these people. Among the factors pushing Koreans out of their country were the establishment of the American occupational administration in

South Korea, which was followed by the propping of the fledgling South Korean government by American military support during the Korean War (1950–1953), and the subsequent deployment of more than 40,000 American soldiers on the Korean peninsula for more than three decades. American influence in Korea resulted in increasing sociocultural, economic, and political ties between South Korea and the United States; a strong desire among young Koreans to study in the United States; and the exodus of large numbers of Korean women married to American soldiers.

The United States emerged from World War II as the world's strongest nation, both economically and militarily. This American supremacy was supported by the American industrial power, which was in need of trained manpower that was not readily available in the United States. This situation ultimately led to the relaxing of restrictions previously imposed on the immigration of non-white people to the United States. During this period, Congress approved a number of specific pieces of legislation, which allowed dependents of American citizens as well as highly trained professionals to immigrate to America. Among the laws were the War Brides Act of 1945, the Luce-Celler Act of 1946, the McCarran-Walter Immigration and Naturalization Act of 1952, and the Refugee Relief Act of 1953.

Three major groups of Koreans came to the United States during the third period of Korean emigration. The first group consisted of large numbers of Korean students selected by the government to study at American colleges and universities. More than 10,000 Korean students came to America after the end of the Korean War, but only a minority of them returned to their country, as 7,542 adjusted their legal status in the United States from student to permanent resident during the ten-year period between 1966 and 1975. This meant that most of these people who had their immigration status adjusted had come to America before the passage of the 1965 Immigration Act. They had completed their study and found employment before they were able to file petition for status adjustment. According to an official report released by the South Korean government in 1968, only about 6 percent of Korean students who had completed their advanced studies in the United States returned to Korea over the previous fourteen-year period. This continued to be true even after 1965, as evidenced by the fact that only 64 out of 325 Korean students who received doctoral degrees in 1968 in the United States returned to Korea.

The second group of immigrants consisted of large numbers of Korean women who followed their American husbands to America after marrying American servicemen stationed in Korea. Many women saw marriage to American soldiers as their ticket out of poverty in Korea into relative wealth in America. Upon arrival in America, however, they confronted problems associated with interracial marriage, language difficulty, employment, differences in dietary and other cultural habits, and finally readjustment in case of divorce from their American husbands. The third group, composed of thousands of Korean children, who were either orphaned during the war or born of Korean women and American soldiers and later deserted by their parents, were brought to the United States to be adopted by American families.

Because of the nature of Korean immigrants in the United States during this period, the social organizations established among them were not drastically different from those of the previous periods. In fact, most of the political organizations established before 1945 became dormant when they lost organizational appeal among Korean immigrants. A few of these organizations redirected their attention in support of, or against, the regime in South Korea. Regardless of whether they were for or against the government in South Korea, organizations were highly conservative in their political orientation with the exception of one organization. This left-wing organization was called the Korean National Revolutionary Party. Organized in 1942 in Los Angeles by Korean intellectuals with a more progressive political consciousness, the party supported the political and military actions of the Korean National Revolutionary Party in China against the Japanese Army. After Korea's liberation in 1945, the organization was radically politicized to denounce the policies of the American military government in South Korea. Several members of this organization openly criticized the American-backed government in South Korea and expressed their sympathy with Communists in North Korea. As a result of their support of the Communists and their policies, members were harassed by American immigration authorities and were subsequently investigated by government security personnel. A few Koreans finally decided to leave America and cast their lot with Communists in North Korea. One of these people, Diamond Kimm, decided to challenge his deportation order in the U. S. Supreme Court, which ruled against him in the famous case of Diamond Kimm v. Rosenberg on June 13, 1960. Before the Court delivered its opinion, however, Diamond Kimm had already gone to North Korea, later to be purged by North Korean authorities.

The current wave of Korean immigration to America began with the passage of the 1965 Immigration Act, signed into law by President Lyndon B. Johnson on October 3, 1965. The law brought about fundamental changes in American immigration policies, thus affecting not only the nature of Korean immigrants coming to America, but also their ability to adapt to and assimilate in American society. The law did away with the nationality origin's quota system which had been the basis of the American immigration policy since 1924. In its place, the law created new national policy by setting a world quota allowing 270,000 immigrants to enter the United States every year. The law made provisions for the spouses, children, and parents of American citizens to come as non-quota immigrants without numerical limitations. This law has been largely responsible for the tremendous increase in the number of Koreans coming to the United States since 1965. For instance, there were only 70,598 Koreans in America according to the 1970 Census, but this population reached 354,529 in 1980, no less than a 402-percent increase over the ten-year period. This phenomenal increase, however, tells only part of the story behind the push-and-pull factors inseparably interwoven into the warf and woof of the sociological and political fiber of Korean society.

Among the push factors identified by many researchers were Korea's population explosion after the end of the Korean War, rapid urbanization which inevitably exposed Koreans to American culture represented in Korea by American soldiers, a frenzied industrialization geared to supporting an export-oriented economy, the Korean government's labor policy of exporting Korean workers abroad, the Korean educational system's willingness to train people for immigration, and the political and military uncertainty hovering over the Korean peninsula since 1945. These push factors working more in cooperation with rather than independently of pull factors have continued to bring more than 20,000 Korean immigrants to the United States every year since 1973.

One of the major pull factors created by the United States was the passage of the 1965 Immigration Act, which, working in close cooperation with labor policy of the American government, set in motion a selective process through which highly skilled and professional manpower has been drained out of Korea into the United States. The immigration of Korean medical professionals is a good case in point. It is estimated that 13,401 doctors have been licensed to practice medicine in Korea since 1948, but only 8,700 were to be found in Korea in 1973. It is now estimated that between 45 and 60 percent of the graduates of the eleven medical schools in South Korea have found employment outside Korea, and more than 3,000 of them are now in the United States. Certainly, these people were both highly educated and urbanized, and were part of a special class of people who were allowed entry into the United States as a result of the 1965 Immigration Act. But another class of Koreans who were allowed entry to America by the same law were large numbers of relatives of Korean women married to American soldiers. After the women had acquired American citizenship, they made arrangements to bring their relatives to the United States. Many of these people were neither highly educated nor urbanized. In fact, most of these people came from the rural areas of Korea. The average number of years of schooling these Korean women completed was 7.2, which is far below 12.7, the average number of years of schooling completed by all other Korean immigrants. This factor alone suggests that the relatives of these Korean women were probably not as highly educated as other Koreans. Given this difference between two major classes of Korean immigrants, it is again difficult to claim that the post–1965 Korean immigrants in America are to be studied only within the context of the urban-to-urban paradigm.

The organizational activities that lay dormant among Koreans in America before 1965 came alive as new Korean immigrants began to settle in America's urban centers where jobs were easier to find, public transportation was more readily available, housing was cheaper, and loneliness could be mitigated by the presence of other Koreans. Because of the diversity of Korean immigrants and their differing interests, various organizations again began to develop in Korean

Figure 1

Country of Emigration	Urban	Transition	Rural
Country of Immigration			
Urban	1	4	7
Transition	2	5	8
Rural	3	6	9

communities across America. Most of them were social, religious, educational, and political organizations providing a variety of social services for Koreans. In this respect, they were not too different from those that existed during the previous three periods of Korean emigration. Organizations unique to the post–1965 Korean immigrants emerged to meet the special interests of professionals in various fields: of businessmen in small business enterprises, of people with a common recreational pursuit, and of people who established alumni associations. Some of these organizations are still in initiative or formative stages in terms of the social network of their members, whereas others have gone through these two stages to reach the stage of institutionalization. With institutionalization comes a more intense social network among members who participate in organizational affairs more actively. Still others have reached the stage of segmentation during which time their members become further solidified around very specialized collective interests. As more Koreans immigrate to the United States, other organizations will be created to meet special interests, and organizations will continue to go through the same process of development. It is also possible that with the increasing assimilation of Korean immigrants into American culture and society, these organizations may decline and disappear.

In conclusion, the discussion above demonstrates the inadequacy of the folk-to-urban and urban-to-urban paradigms and suggests a more differentiated paradigm building. If we are to accept the notion that immigrants to America could be more adequately studied in terms of their sociological orientation on the rural-urban continuum, then it is quite clear that the paradigmatic schema shown in Figure 1 will be more valuable to researchers in view of the facts presented above.

The schema in Figure 1 suggests nine different paradigms on the rural-urban continuum: (1) urban-to-urban, (2) urban-to-transition, (3) urban-to-rural, (4) transition-to-urban, (5) transition-to-transition, (6) transition-to-rural, (7) rural-to-urban, (8) rural-to-transition, and (9) rural-to-rural. Many of the post–1965 Korean immigrants belong to Paradigm One, whereas Vietnamese refugees fit into Paradigm Two. *Ganen-Mono*, the so-called first-year Japanese immigrants recruited by Eugene Van Reed to come to Honolulu in 1868 for work on Hawaii's sugar plantations, fit into Paradigm Three. Paradigms Four, Five, and Six are applicable to the study of certain segments of Korean immigrants in the United States as they were in the stage of transition in Korea before their departure, regardless of whether they came to the United States before or after 1965. These Korean immigrants settled in urban or rural areas in their newly adopted country, or underwent a brief period of transition before they finally settled in an urban or a rural area. Early Japanese and Chinese immigrants to mainland United States, as well as Eastern European immigrants, belong to Paradigm Seven, and some Vietnamese refugees fit into Paradigm Eight. The last paradigm, rural-to-rural, may well be used in explaining the vast majority of Chinese and Japanese immigrants to Hawaii before the turn of the century.

NOTES

1. Wayne Patterson, "Koreans in Hawaii: The Linkage between Immigration and Adjustment," paper presented at the Asian Studies on the Pacific Coast conference, June 17–19, 1977.

2. Kim Won-yong, *Chae-Mi Hanin Osimnyon-sa* (A Fifty-Year History of Koreans in America) (Los Angeles: Charles Ho-Kim, 1959).

3. Kim Ilsoo, *New Urban Immigrants: The Korean Community in New York* (Princeton: Princeton University Press, 1981).

Asian Indians in the United States

PARMATMA SARAN

BRIEF HISTORY OF INDIAN MIGRATION

American history is the history of ethnic groups. This sentiment has increasingly been expressed in recent times with regard to American society. Since 1607, when the English first settled in America, millions of people from every corner of the earth have immigrated to the United States. An incredible diversity of people, languages, cultures, and values have found new homes in America. For many years observers assumed that immigrants came to America simply to find sanctuary from the oppressiveness of European society: Catholics, Jews, and some Protestants migrated, for example, to avoid religious persecution, whereas others sought to escape war, political repression, and the poverty of their home-lands. It also seems, however, that many immigrants chose America as much because it was seen as a land of opportunity as because it offered a refuge.

As a result of changes in the immigration laws of 1965, many immigrants have come to the United States from Asia. A significant amount of Asian im-migration has taken place from India. According to the 1980 Census, close to 400,000 Asian Indians have immigrated to the United States.

The phenomenon of Indian migration is not new. Indians have migrated to different parts of the world to settle, and they continue to do so wherever opportunities exist. However, the Indians who have migrated to the United States in recent times represent a population that is highly educated and professional.

With the exception of the Sikh farmers from the Punjab who came here some eighty years ago and settled on the West Coast with heavy concentration in the Fresno Valley area, there has not been a permanent Indian community in the United States. However, the United States has always had a small population of Indians. This population included graduate students at various universities and people working for Indian as well as international agencies such as the Indian embassy, the Indian consulate, Air India, and the United Nations, among others.

Nevertheless, this population was transitory. Starting in 1969–1970, because of changes in the immigration laws (passage of Public Law 89–236, 1965), scores of Indians came with their families to live and to earn a living in this country. Now, for the first time, we find the emergence of permanent Indian communities, at least in large urban centers like New York, Chicago, Los Angeles, and San Francisco. According to our estimate, nearly 1 million Indians are living in the United States at the present time. Approximately one-fourth of them have taken out American citizenship, and the rest are permanent residents.

MAJOR HISTORICAL EVENTS

In the short history of the settlement of Indian immigrants in the United States, only a few historical events are seen as important. One of the most important was the election of Dalip Singh Saund from California to the House of Representatives in 1956. Saund is the only American of Asian Indian origin to have achieved this distinction. In more recent times others have sought political office but without any success.

Another important event was the inclusion of a separate category, "Asian Indians," in the 1980 Census. The Indian community considered this a major victory and as recognition of the Indian community by federal agencies. This category also resulted in the recognition of Asian Indians as a minority group and enabled them to receive federal assistance in business loans and other benefits. This became possible because in the last ten years Asian Indians won a number of lawsuits establishing that they had been discriminated against in employment, promotions, and other areas.

Events of the recent past—the proclamation of Emergency in India in 1975, military intervention to clear the Golden Temple in Amritsar, India's war with Pakistan in 1971, resulting in the emergence of Bangladesh—all have had important bearings on the Asian Indian population in the United States.

NOTABLE INDIANS

For the past several years, a number of Pan-Indian organizations have honored Indians for their achievements and contributions to American society. Because the list of these award recipients is so long, only a few are mentioned here. Some of these outstanding and distinguished Indians are Zubin Mehta, Ravi Shankar, Har Gobind Khorana, and Subrahmanyan Chandrashekhar.

Zubin Mehta, conductor and director of the New York Philharmonic Orchestra, is undoubtedly the best known Indian in the United States. After he made his Metropolitan Opera debut on December 29, 1965, with a highly acclaimed performance of *Aida*, Alan Rich of the *New York Herald Tribune* wrote: "Mehta . . . brought to the conducting of the score a kind of bedazzlement that has no peer in recent times." The government of India awarded Mehta one of its highest honors, Padme Bhushan, in 1976 for his contribution to the world of music and for doing more to build bridges of understanding between East and West than almost any of his generation in India.

Ravi Shankar, the renowned Indian sitarist, was named Artist of the Year by the music industry's *Billboard* Magazine in 1968. He enjoys the unusual distinction of being admired by both lovers of classical Indian music and lovers of classical Western music. In 1966 he was invited by Yehudi Menuhin to play at England's Bath Festival, and for the first time, Western critics began to notice him. George Harrison, one of the Beatles, was captivated by the sound of the sitar and became Shankar's disciple. This gave Shankar worldwide publicity. Music critic Alan Rich has ranked Shankar as "among the greatest musicians of any sort of music in the world today."[1]

Dr. Har Gobind Khorana's long efforts at the University of Wisconsin to define the structure of the gene—the basic unity of heredity—won him a Nobel Prize in physiology and medicine for 1968, which he shared with two others. It has been said that through his work he has quite possibly ushered in an era when humans can hope to gain control of their heredity, with awesome implications for both good and evil. But even while conceding that in all human knowledge there is "this duality of nature to do good and evil," Khorana says: "I do have a basic faith that survival of our civilization is soon not going to be possible without the proper use of science."[2] His discovery remains a major breakthrough in our quest to understand creation.

Dr. S. Chandrashekhar is regarded as a superstar in the world of astrophysics. *Fortune* Magazine called him "the outstanding pure theorist of modern astronomy." The recipient of a number of awards, including the Royal Astronomical Society's Gold Medal in 1953 and the Draper Award of the United States National Academy of Sciences in 1968, Chandrashekhar was also awarded the Padma Vibushan, the second highest award India can give. The citation read: "Dr. Chandrashekhar has not only played a leading role in modern India's contribution to scientific research, but is also a link between India and the West." Dr. Chandrashekhar, too, received the Nobel Prize in 1983.

EMERGENCE OF SOCIAL AND CULTURAL ORGANIZATIONS

One of the most important developments that has taken place as a result of the establishment of a permanent Indian community in the United States is the emergence of a large number of social and cultural organizations, some with political overtones, and, more recently, the formation of political action committees.

Basically, we can classify these organizations into three categories: (1) those that are Pan-Indian in character and believe they must leave their Indian linguistic and regional differences behind and work together to maintain their Indian heritage and at the same time adapt to the new society; (2) those that are organized on an Indian linguistic and regional basis, and feel it is an important part of their identity and are more concerned with its maintenance than with adapting to the new society; and (3) those that are organized with the realization that unless Indians organize themselves politically they will be at a disadvantage and lack any political pressure.

At least one dozen organizations throughout the country fall into the first category. Leadership of these organizations is in the hands of older groups of Indian immigrants, who did not necessarily arrive after 1965, have done quite well in their respective professions, use English as a medium of conversation, in some cases are married to Americans or non-Indians, and became American citizens. Although they show an interest in India and the maintenance of an Indian identity, they are rather keen to assimilate to the degree possible. The leadership of these organizations is competent and intelligent, but their membership is limited and they have not been able to reach out to the Indian population at large.

The number of Indian organizations that fall in the second category has increased by leaps and bounds. It is estimated that there are at least several hundred such organizations in the United States. In the New York City area alone there are nearly fifty such organizations, which are quite well established and have a large membership. The leadership of these organizations is in the hands of those who for the most part came after 1965, are professionals, and have done well but not as well as those involved in the Pan-Indian organizations. They use both English and their native language for conversation, have Indian spouses, are less likely to take out American citizenship, and, although they show some commitment to America, are more keen to maintain their Indian ties and identity.

The third category, a recent phenomenon, consists of organizations that are essentially political in nature. Leadership of such groups is a mixed bag, including those who came before as well as after 1965. In terms of the profile of its leadership as well as membership, which is limited, we would find representatives from the two groups we have described earlier. They are involved in raising funds for political candidates, endorsing them and trying to establish liaison with both the Republican and Democratic parties, although the majority of the members show a preference for the Democrats.

In addition, some religious organizations are involved in building temples and organizing other kinds of religious activities. Although only a small core of the larger population is involved in this effort, they seem to be well organized and effective in raising funds for their activities and projects.

Unlike other ethnic groups, so far there is a complete absence of service-oriented Indian organizations. Because until recently the majority of Indian immigrants who came had a high level of education and professional backgrounds, the need to form service-oriented organizations to provide assistance to these immigrants was not felt. More recently, the composition of the Indian population has been changing as many new immigrants have come on the basis of their relationship to those already here. These newcomers are not as well educated as the earlier immigrants and lack professional skills. In view of such demographic changes, growing tension and conflict are being experienced in the community, and the formation of service-based organizations in employment, mental health, and other areas is ever increasing.

NOTES

1. M. V. Kamaph, ed., *The U. S. and India, 1776–1976* (Washington, D. C.: Embassy of India, 1976).

2. Ibid.

Filipinos in the United States

H. BRETT MELENDY

Filipino immigration to the United States is a twentieth-century phenomenon. The first large wave of immigration occurred between 1907 and 1934 while the Philippines was an insular possession of the United States, a fact that proved dichotomous for the archipelago inhabitants who desired independence but thrived on the economic benefits of dependency. Filipinos migrating eastward across the Pacific came as American nationals with free access to the United States and the "fundamental rights" of life, liberty and property as defined by the Supreme Court in the Insular Cases in 1901. No Filipino, unless he had served in World War I, could obtain American citizenship. This limitation exposed the immigrants to overt discrimination by several states. Many states also prohibited the marriage of Filipinos with Caucasians.

The Tydings-McDuffie Independence Act of 1934, which provided for the eventual independence of the Philippines, restricted the entry of Filipinos to only fifty a year. In 1946 President Harry Truman by proclamation set the annual quota at 100 and made it possible for those Filipinos to apply for American citizenship. The 1952 McCarran-Walter Act removed any remaining ambiguities about citizenship and permitted the immediate relatives of citizens and non-resident aliens to enter the United States. The 1965 immigration law has provided the opportunity of access for large numbers of highly trained Filipinos.

Filipino immigration commenced in 1907 as Hawaiian Sugar Planters' Association (HSPA) agents sent Filipinos to Honolulu. The HSPA, always searching for cheap labor, at first felt that these new arrivals would not do, but a Japanese-led sugar strike in 1909 changed planters' minds. That year HSPA agents forwarded 803 Tagalogs from Manila and Visayans from Cebu and other Visayas islands. In 1910 there were 2,361 Filipinos in Hawaii and only 406 on the mainland. After 1915, HSPA recruiters focused on northern Luzon's Ilocanos barrios. Fifteen years later, the Ilocanos formed the largest ethnic group working in Hawaiian fields.

The HSPA guaranteed work at set wages, housing, and medical care. After 1915, free transportation back to the Philippines was established, but only after the worker had paid for his Hawaiian passage. Most of these single young men anticipated that their Hawaiian stay would be brief and that they would soon return home. Whether in Hawaii or on the American West Coast, these men were viewed as social outcasts. Those who returned to Luzon's barrios with some measure of financial affluence and able to posture as men of means gained the appellation *Hawaiianos*.

Following the pineapple industry's collapse in 1931, the HSPA refused to accept any new workers and induced many to return to the Philippines. From 1909 through 1931, about 113,000 Filipinos arrived in Hawaii; over 55,000 remained, 39,000 returned home, and 18,600 moved to the West Coast or to Alaska's salmon canneries.

When two major strikes against Hawaii's plantations failed in 1920 and 1924, many Filipinos left for California. In 1910 only five Filipinos resided in that state; ten years later that number reached 2,674, and by 1930 there were 30,470 in the Golden State—86 percent of the total lived either in California or Hawaii.

Others came directly to California from Manila. Some sought a college education, but only a few graduated. Most became migrant farm workers, following the crops from the Imperial Valley northward to Washington's Yakima Valley and Idaho. These "birds of passage" barely endured, captive to an economic system over which they had no control. During the winter months, they moved into "Little Manilas" in Los Angeles, Salinas, San Francisco, Stockton, and other cities where they lived in cramped quarters while seeking employment in hotels and restaurants or as house servants.

West Coast agriculturalists, like their Hawaiian counterparts, wanted cheap labor, and after 1920 the Filipinos, along with the Mexicans, formed the backbone of field labor. These workers encountered prejudice and intolerance in Hawaii and on the West Coast. In the islands, the dominant white socioeconomic group, the territory's small area, and strictly drawn ethnic lines forced them to turn inward. West Coast Filipinos also remained in a closed society, but their great mobility made their numbers appear larger than they were, leading to hostile and violent acts against them.

Many Americans believed that Filipinos were headhunting savages with cannibalistic tendencies, and others feared that they presented a health hazard. But the cause of greatest excitement was the attention they lavished on white women, which presumably would lead to sex crimes. With a sex ratio of fourteen males to one female in 1930, Filipinos, of course, sought companionship with white women. This led to explosive incidents at Yakima in 1928 and at Exeter and Watsonville, California, in 1929 and 1930, respectively. In the 1930 riot, one Filipino was killed and several others wounded. Prominent Californians, including the University of California president, congressmen, and several judges, verbally attacked Filipinos and persons who engaged in prostitution or operated taxi-dance halls. The State of California conducted a prejudicial study of Filipinos in 1930 which viewed with alarm the increasing importance of these immigrants in agriculture.

Filipinos also worked as unskilled laborers in salmon canneries and the merchant marine. Some worked in restaurants, civil service jobs, and at naval shore stations in Chicago, Detroit, Philadelphia, and New York. The navy recruited Filipino mess stewards, and about 4,000 men served in that billet prior to 1942.

Second-generation Filipinos and those coming to the United States from 1946 to 1967 as the second immigrant wave were restricted to unskilled or semi-skilled jobs, partly because of inadequate education and partly because of union discrimination against them. Integrated unions in Hawaii made it easier for them to become skilled laborers there.

In 1959 Larry Itilong organized the Agricultural Workers Organizing Committee and then led California's Filipino agricultural workers on a strike against Delano grape growers. This union merged with Cesar Chavez's National Farm Workers Organization to form the United Farm Workers Organizing Committee (UFWOC), which has significantly improved working conditions and wages.

Since 1968, with the sole exception of 1978, the Philippines has sent more immigrants to the United States than any other country except Mexico. The third immigration wave, consisting of 312,700 Filipinos, arrived between 1971 and 1979. The Philippines replaced all European countries as the leading foreign provider of engineers, physicians, and technical workers. These new arrivals, better educated than earlier ones, came as family units, intending to make their homes in the United States where economic opportunity appeared better and the political atmosphere was freer. But many newly arrived dentists, doctors, lawyers, and pharmacists encountered state regulating agencies that forced them into other short-term occupations until they could qualify through citizenship or education at an American university.

In 1980 a total of 774,652 Filipinos lived in the United States—almost half were recent arrivals—and 92 percent of these lived in urban areas. About two-thirds of the total population resided in California and Hawaii, and more than 50 percent of all Filipinos were women. Other states with more than 10,000 Filipinos in rank order were New York, New Jersey, Washington, Texas, Florida, Maryland, and Virginia.

Given their educational and employment levels, most older Filipinos have remained anonymous contributors to the American scene. By 1980 several had ventured into politics, gaining election to various offices, including the California and Hawaii legislatures. Eduardo E. Malapit of Kauai became the first Filipino to be elected mayor of an American city. Alfred Laureta, the first to hold a state cabinet position, director of Hawaii's Department of Labor and Industrial Relations from 1962 through 1967, received appointment as Hawaii's Fifth Circuit judge in 1969. In Los Angeles, Maria L. Obrea served as a municipal judge, and G. Monty Manibog and Leonard Velasco were elected mayors of Monterey Park and Delano, respectively.

Filipinos show prominence in the field of labor. Carl Damsco served as president of the Hawaii branch of the International Longshoremen's and Warehouse-men's Union; Filipinos constituted 50 percent of that union's membership and 40 percent of Hawaii's Hotel and Restaurant Workers' Union. In California, the important leaders of the farm workers movement were Larry D. Itilong, Philip Vera Cruz, Pete Velasco, and Andrew Imutan.

The several linguistic groups, religious affiliations, and economic levels among Filipinos have made it difficult to bring them into one or even a few major organizations. In California, for example, there were in 1980 more than 400 cultural and social organizations representative of the many Philippine provinces. Recognizing the need for voter solidarity, Filipinos have formed several political organizations, but these have not endured. Two such California organizations were the Filipino-American Political Association and the Filipino-American Co-ordinating Committee. Typical of local organizations was the Filipino-American Council of San Francisco. In Hawaii, the United Filipino Council sought to provide some centralized direction.

Union organizations and the church, particularly the Catholic Church, have provided a unifying network for Filipinos. There are also historical fraternal and social organizations with roots in the Philippines: Caballeros de Dimas-Alang, Legionarios del Trabajo, the Filipino Federation of America, and the Philippine Commonwealth Club.

The first of these, in cooperation with federal and city agencies, has erected the Dimas-Alang House in San Francisco to care for the elderly and low-income families. UFWOC has established the Paulo Agbanyani Retirement Village near Delano, named after a man who died on the picket line fighting for better conditions. Many have worried about the aging Filipino population, and in 1972 Pilipino Bayanihan, the largest federally funded community organization, was started in Stockton. With branches in Tulare County, Coachella, Brawley, and Ventura, it has tried to meet the needs of unemployed, underemployed, and senior citizens.

Pacific Islanders in the United States

LYDIA KOTCHEK

INTRODUCTION

Migration eastward to the West Coast of the continental United States has come primarily from the countries of the Asian mainland and the large offshore islands. These countries have added noticeable millions to the population of the United States. Scattered throughout the Pacific Ocean between Asia and the Americas are much smaller lands, the many Pacific Islands. From these have come migrants to the United States also, but this migration has been one of thousands rather than millions and has been—in part because of numbers, but also because of political history—a relatively invisible one. Yet the migration from the Pacific Islands is a significant one, which illustrates the effects of colonialism, militarism, and culture on both migration and the subsequent adaptation of the migrant to the host country.

The Pacific Islands are divided here into three groups on the basis of physical and cultural identities. The first group, the Melanesian Islands, are in the Southwest Pacific, clustered northeast of Australia, and include New Guinea, Fiji, and the Solomon Islands. These islands were initially colonized by European countries and now are independent nations or part of Indonesia. The 3.5 million Melanesians are foreigners, according to the United States. So few have migrated to the United States that no known study of this group has been made; this essay does not refer to this culture area again.

The islands of Micronesia, located in the middle western portion of the Pacific, are very small dots scattered over more than 3 million square miles. The largest island is Guam, with a population of 105,000 and a mass of 206 square miles. The United States acquired possession of Guam from Spain in 1898, and its residents became citizens of the United States in 1952. Most of the other Micronesian islands, some ninety-three with a total land area of 708 square miles and a population of some 125,000—who are also foreigners according to the

United States—are the Trust Territory formed by the United Nations after World War II. The trustee of this territory is the United States whose main interest in the lands has been their strategic military positions.

The third group, the larger Polynesian islands, in the central and eastern Pacific, have been colonized by Great Britain (New Zealand, Tonga), by France (Marquesa, Tahiti), and by the United States (Samoa, Hawaii). In 1980 the total Polynesian population of these islands was 440,000.

PACIFIC ISLAND MIGRATION IN GENERAL

Migration to the United States from these various Pacific Islands reflects the political history of the region. Before 1941 immigration was minimal. However, the intense military and political activities during and after World War II profoundly changed the area and emigration from it. The self-sufficient horticultural economies of the pre-war era have now become almost exclusively dependent on a wage economy that does not have enough jobs for those seeking them. With increasing survival rates after birth, the Pacific Islands have the world's most rapidly increasing populations. Most residents have acquired the taste and expectations of Western technology. But most islands have few resources to support this technology. Islands such as New Zealand and Hawaii, which have sufficient resources to do so, have already been settled by colonists, and the indigenous Polynesian populations have been widely displaced from their homelands. Thus, with the push of population and economics and with the pull of expectations for life in a developed country, Pacific Island migration has increased exponentially.

Access to the United States is limited primarily by citizenship. The Immigration Act of 1965 removed national origin quotas from migration to the United States but replaced them with occupational and kinship preference categories. Most Pacific Islanders who are not citizens of the United States do not qualify for the preferred occupations and thus can migrate primarily by kinship networks. Relatively few foreigners from these islands migrate to the United States. An estimated 3,000 Tongans live on the West Coast. Some 4,000 Micronesians from the Trust Territory are scattered throughout the United States; most of these are college students supported by federal scholarships. The presence of Tahitians or of Marqueseans is undocumented. Hawaiians will not be discussed as migrants for they are residents within the fifty states. Although census count is taken of them in each state, Hawaiians are more like surrounded Native Americans than they are like migrants moving to a new country.

SPECIFIC MIGRATION: SAMOANS

Samoan migration to the United States typifies much of Pacific migration: the problems of citizenship, the effects of culture contact, movement of a technologically unskilled population from rural areas to urban areas. The original

Samoan Islands were culturally homogeneous. The islanders were first contacted by European and American traders; next, by missionaries who were so successful in their work of conversion that by 1850 Samoa had become—and still is—the most Christian country in the world. More than 99 percent of the islanders were, and are, nominally members of a Christian church. During the late 1800s the United States and Germany vied for control of these islands and their important harbors. These two nations exchanged hostile diplomatic notes, shot at each other by arming rival Samoan groups, and came close to war over the islands. In 1899, at a conference table without Samoan representatives, the islands were partitioned. Germany assumed control of the larger islands, now known as Western Samoa; New Zealand continued this control after World War I. In 1962 Western Samoa became an independent nation; as such, its residents are foreigners in the United States, although many Western Samoans have family ties with residents of American Samoa.

American Samoa was governed by the U. S. Navy until 1952. Since then, this territory has been the charge of the Department of the Interior. The navy firmly controlled American Samoa, with its 76 square miles and its 5,000 residents. Samoan leaders who protested were imprisoned or deported. Indigenous medical treatment was banned. Gradually the economy became dependent on jobs created by the navy. During World War II, American Samoa became an important transfer station; nearly every adult male in the islands was employed in some way by the military. But after the war the navy considered its Samoan base to be obsolete and moved out. With the closing of the naval base, the economic depression in American Samoa was profound—and the population was growing.

Although the navy was in charge, emigration of American Samoans was discouraged. Nonetheless, some few did move to Hawaii and to California. When the navy closed its Samoan base, it offered to transfer all of its Samoan personnel and their dependents to Pearl Harbor, Hawaii. Nearly 1,000 Samoans, or 5 percent of the then 20,000 residents moved within the year to Hawaii. Since that move and during the past thirty years, migration to Hawaii and to the West Coast of the United States has increased markedly. It has been estimated that nearly 50,000 Samoans now live in the fifty United States, in comparison to the 1980 resident population of 30,000 in American Samoa.

As migrants from Europe came initially to the eastern United States, so immigrants from the Pacific now live primarily in the West, although the 1980 Census noted some Samoans living in every state. Samoan migration occurs primarily through a network of kin. The original migrants, who often moved to the states through a military assignment, became the first link of a long interconnected chain. Kin came to visit them and stayed to become in turn another link. Family units moved into an area to join a brother, an older son, a married daughter who had previously come on a visit and who had remained. A family with young children might send back to Samoa for a sister, a cousin, or an aunt to come and help them. When one household becomes too large, by Samoan measures, some of the adults and their dependents will move out and form another kin-connected residence.

CHANGES WITH MIGRATION

In common with immigrants from other Pacific Islands, Samoans must adapt to an urban environment that is markedly different from the rural or semi-rural village at home. Although quantitatively the difference in potential living space is vast (there are 3 million square miles in the continental United States), qualitatively Samoan migrants to the mainland have both a decrease and an increase in living space. Back home, one can move from one kin household to another; the children can be sent out of the home to play, for someone will always be watching them. If the homelife grows too uncomfortable in one village, a kind aunt or uncle will provide lodging in another. The beach is close, the hills are near, and the climate is tropical. The surrounding houses contain relatives or friends who are ethnically similar. In the mainland, the distances between Samoan households are greater; the available kin are scattered in cities from Hawaii to California and Washington State. The surrounding populations are strangers and are ethnically different, and speak another language. Crime is reported to be in the streets, and the climate is harsher. Samoans often stay within their homes or visit another Samoan household—an indoor existence. On the other hand, in Samoa an individual who wants to escape the watching eyes of friends and kin has difficulty doing so. On the mainland, crowds are larger; Samoans are a numerical minority. Those who wish to live apart from and to avoid other Samoans can do so.

In addition to being dark skinned in a dominant culture that disvalues increased melanin, and to having difficulties with the dominant language of English, Samoans also must deal with other problems. In American Samoa, medical care is subsidized by the government, and, covertly, indigenous cures and curers are available. In the United States, such care is not free; moreover, Samoans are suspicious of medical personnel and comment, "They will put you in jail if you don't do what they want." This reflects a memory that has persisted for more than thirty years of the coercion practiced by the navy in American Samoa. Students in American Samoan schools are surrounded by other Samoans, all of whom value behaviors that demonstrate consensus, non-competitiveness, and respect for elders. Samoans in American schools are a small minority of those students for whom English is a second language; they are greatly outnumbered by more recent Asian immigrants and may receive less community attention. Dropout rates among Samoan high school students are high because Samoans often have trouble learning necessary study skills. Samoan students are often discomfited by the atmosphere of competition and aggressiveness in public schools.

Housing is difficult to find. Landlords are reluctant to rent to Samoans with such large families—on the average 5.2 persons in a household (the average in the total United States is 3.3). Most professional jobs in American Samoa are filled by non-Samoans. Therefore, migrants come with few job skills, and they compete with many other such workers for jobs in a tight labor market. In addition, workers on the mainland are expected not to let family matters interrupt their work. However, Samoan family ties are extensive and can often so intrude. Moreover, this is a young population with high birthrates and the lowest median age (19.5) of any reported group in the United States (the median age for the whole population is 30). Thus, the adult Samoan workers support several dependents.

The 1980 Census, which was the first to include Samoans as a labeled category, reported that Samoans in the fifty states were the poorest of all ethnic groups, with the lowest reported household median income (an income that supports more people than in most American homes) and the lowest per capita income. Samoans report that their greatest needs are for more job training and help in improving their proficiency in English.

ADAPTIVE STRATEGIES

Samoans continue to migrate in anticipation of achieving what they wish. Many, when queried, speak of returning home and some do. More, however, stay, survive, and are raising American-born Samoans. Some young adults are attending college; some older adults have reached a degree of relative affluence. The Samoan's extended family is the primary adaptive mechanism for coping within the new environment. One such family may have several households living in Hawaii, in southern California, or in Washington. One unit of this family will assist with an individual's initial migration. The several households throughout the West provide a network for members to move through until the proper combination of education, employment, and family constellation is negotiated. The family is also a means for pooling resources. With any crisis such as illness or with a transition event such as a marriage, family members are expected to contribute goods, services, and money toward helping those in immediate need. In their turn, contributors will receive reciprocal assistance. Information about jobs and housing opportunities is passed along family lines. Membership in churches, the main Samoan community organization, is primarily a matter of family alliance. Although individual Samoans may have few resources, the collectivity of the family can redistribute what is available and needed.

Survival through such a family has its costs. With such redistribution, all are helped, but a single individual has difficulty accumulating a sufficient amount for such individual achievements as attending college. Moreover, the ambient culture tends to denigrate extensive family ties. Employers of Samoans do not understand or appreciate the many kinship ties and obligations that may call a Samoan worker away from his or her job. Political organization which will speak collectively to the dominant culture in requesting assistance is one strategy of migrant groups. However, Samoan intrafamilial ties are so strong that interfam-

ilial alliances are brittle. Samoans have difficulty maintaining larger, more com-
munity-based organizations. Traditional Samoan politics were based on changing
alliances between family units. These shifting liaisons continue to be formed,
but they continue to splinter the community rather than to consolidate what is
already a small fragment of the larger population.

In addition, another division, one based on citizenship, exists among Samoans.
Those born in American Samoa are nationals; they are neither foreigners nor
citizens. However, nationals can migrate to the United States without a passport,
and with six months' residence can apply for citizenship. Western Samoans are
aliens, from a foreign country even though they may be closely tied to American
Samoans by kinship. Western Samoans in the United States may be reluctant to
work with American Samoans for community assistance that may only benefit
the American Samoans.

Although in the color-coded United States, Samoans and other Pacific Islanders
are physically visible, in comparison with other migrant populations Samoans
are relatively invisible. They are a very small minority. Few mainlanders are
aware of the islands' history. There are no painful memories of political problems
with the donor countries as there are, for example, with Vietnam which makes
these Southeast Asian migrants quite visible. There is an advantage of invisibility:
the host environment will impose few, if any, unfavorable stereotypes on Samoans. But Samoans will also be ignored, as they have been for the past ninety
years during which the United States has been associated with Samoa. Some
federal and public recognition of Samoans has recently occurred. The 1980
Census counted Samoans as a separate group. In 1984 the Department of Labor,
Employment Training Division, contracted for a study of unemployment, poverty, and training needs of American Samoans. More federal recognition and
possible funds will have consequences. More job and language training may
become available. But the Samoans most active in organizing the use of these
funds are the younger college-educated adults. Therefore, more power and authority may become invested in younger Samoans, a reverse of tradition. Reciprocity based on family ties may become less acceptable; kinship ties may be
less helpful. Yet, Samoans have persisted as a relatively cohesive culture in their
islands in spite of centuries of change and political control, in spite of more than
eighty years of being partitioned. The Samoan migration to the Western states
is a recent one, beginning after World War II and becoming a more voluminous
one in the past two decades. Previous migrant groups have followed a sequence:
the first generation in the new land clings as much as possible to their home
ways; their children reject the "old"; but their grandchildren rediscover their
ethnicity. The first-generation Samoan migrants are busy trying to survive in a
somewhat hostile new environment; Samoan traditions, especially close and
extended family ties, aid in the survival. Younger Samoans, teenagers who
remember little of "home," are showing signs of disaffection with their ethnicity;
they chafe under the discipline of their elders, and they often wish to become
more isolated from the Samoan community. How subsequent generations will
cope is a story for future study.

Southeast Asians in the United States

GAIL P. KELLY

In April 1975 the U. S.-backed government of Vietnam collapsed, setting in motion one of the largest refugee movements in the past twenty years. In 1975 alone approximately 130,000 of these refugees entered the United States from Vietnam, Kampuchea (formerly Cambodia), and Laos. In subsequent years additional refugees followed. By March 1980, 235,000 Vietnamese (some of whom were ethnic Chinese), 35,000 Laotians, 30,000 Hmongs, and 20,000 Kampucheans had resettled in the United States. By late 1981 the refugee population in the United States had reached 560,333.[1] The U. S. government called the refugees "Indochinese," a term that refers to French Indochina, rather than to the nation-states that pre- and post-date colonial domination. In the pages that follow, the refugees are referred to by their nationalities rather than the term "Indochinese." Although the term "Indochinese" permeates government documents and the research literature, it masks the very real differences among the peoples who came to the United States from Vietnam, Laos, and Kampuchea.

The refugees from Vietnam, Laos, and Kampuchea arrived in the United States in three waves.[2] Those who came in 1975 were part of a U. S. evacuation and came from their home country directly to refugee camps on the U. S. mainland. This first wave was predominantly Vietnamese. Between 1975 and 1977, approximately 1,800 additional refugees arrived per month. This second wave consisted of "boat" people and overland refugees who spent considerable and often harrowing time in refugee camps in Thailand, Malaysia, Singapore, Hong Kong, and other parts of Southeast Asia. They were not part of a U. S. evacuation; rather, they left, in the case of the Vietnamese, out of opposition to the new government's economic and rural resettlement programs. The refugees from Laos and Kampuchea were fleeing from famine, civil war, and political repression of ethnic groups that had worked with the U. S. Central Intelligence Agency (CIA) in the years of the Vietnam War. The third wave of refugees, which began in 1978, was marked by the expulsion of ethnic Chinese from Vietnam. Between

1975 and 1980, Kampucheans, Laotians, Hmongs, Mien, and Tai Dem came to the United States as the Pol Pot regime fell and the new Laotian government sought to consolidate its control over ethnic minorities.[3] The United States admitted only a fraction of the millions of people fleeing from wars and famines in Laos and Kampuchea. Nearly 1 million refugees in 1982 remained in camps in Southeast Asia.

This chapter will survey U. S. policy toward the refugees from Vietnam, Laos, and Kampuchea. It will describe the social background characteristics of the refugee population, where they resettled, and their adjustment to living in the United States.

U. S. REFUGEE POLICY

Since World War II there has been no single policy toward refugees; rather, policy toward their admission and resettlement has been formulated on an *ad hoc* basis. For example, little regularity can be found in the policies and practices established with regard to the Hungarian refugees of 1954, the Cubans of the 1960s, or the Vietnamese, Kampucheans, Laotians, and Hmongs of the 1970s and 1980s. Consistent American policy has yet to be formed and uniformly applied to the Vietnamese, Laotians, Kampucheans, and Hmongs.[4]

The refugees who arrived in the United States before 1980 were admitted as parolees; between 1975 and 1979 ten separate authorizations with differing criteria for entry were made at the discretion of the Attorney General. In the month preceding the fall of Saigon, the U. S. government raised, lowered, and re-raised the number of Vietnamese who would be allowed access to the United States. The eligible, in order of priority, were dependents and relatives of American citizens or resident aliens of the United States; employees of the U. S. government and private corporations; and individuals who had good reason to believe they would be in mortal danger should a Communist government come to power.[5] The criteria for entry into the United States shifted after 1975. Through 1976 and 1977 refugees allowed into the United States were only those who were blood relatives of Americans, resident aliens, and refugees who had entered the United States in 1975. In subsequent years, the government changed criteria for special populations: parolee status was offered to Hmongs, Laotians, and Kampucheans, who had been employees of the U. S. government; in the case of "boat people" the criteria shifted to those persecuted by Communist governments in power.[6] The 1980 Refugee Act gave future refugees resident alien rather than parolee status, which meant they were automatically eligible for U. S. citizenship, unlike their compatriots who had entered before that date. The 1980 act also changed the definition of "refugee" who was eligible to enter the United States; it broadened the term to include those suffering economic hardship as a result of changed political circumstance.[7]

REFUGEES: BACKGROUND CHARACTERISTICS

The refugee population that entered the United States between 1975 and 1980 from Laos, Kampuchea, and Vietnam did not represent a cross-section of the populations of their home countries. The Vietnamese who entered the United States in the first wave were well educated, not only by Vietnamese standards, but by American standards as well. Close to 20 percent had university education or better; another 38 percent had secondary education. The Vietnamese refugees were predominantly Catholic (over 50 percent were Catholic, coming from a country where at best 10 percent of the population profess that faith); most were urban professionals, technicians, and managers (including military officers); but 4.9 percent were rural farmers or fishermen.[8] The first-wave Vietnamese refugees may have been relatively well educated, representative of the urban Catholics, and more likely to have direct ties to Americans either as employees or relatives than their fellow countrymen at home, but they were scarcely fluent in English. As of March 1976, almost a year after their arrival in the United States, 64.7 percent of all first-wave Vietnamese spoke no English at all; 21 percent could make themselves understood in the language; and only 13.9 percent were able to communicate effectively in English.[9]

Second- and third-wave refugees were not as urbanized, well educated, or acquainted with Americans as the 130,000 Vietnamese who entered in 1975. Although most second- and third-wave Vietnamese were related to 1975 entrants, Laotians, Hmongs, and Kampucheans admitted after 1975 were not as well prepared to live in the United States. For example, the 20,000 Hmong refugees in the United States contrast sharply with first-wave Vietnamese. Hmong society was outside the mainstream of twentieth-century Laos; the language is not a written one, and few Hmong refugees could read or write any language. Although Vietnamese refugees tended to be urban dwellers employed in wage sectors of the modern economy in their homeland, for most Hmong their first urban experience was in the United States. In Laos, before the CIA armed them to fight the Pathet Lao, they had practiced slash and burn subsistence agriculture. Even though they were organized as an army, that organization still followed clan lines and traditional hierarchical patterns. The Hmong refugees also had few ties across traditional ethnic and social lines to other refugees from Laos who fled to the United States. Few were Catholic or Buddhist like the Vietnamese, Kampucheans, and Laotians; they were animists whose religious practices were vested in clan shamans.[10]

Although the refugees from Vietnam, Laos, and Kampuchea exhibit clear differences as to education, religion, occupation, and urban experience, these refugees share several characteristics. In all cases, they represent young populations who came to the United States in extended family groupings. Among first-wave Vietnamese, 45.9 percent were under age eighteen; another 35.6 percent were between eighteen and thirty-four years of age. The Hmong population was even younger than the Vietnamese: 51.6 percent were under age eighteen. Although there were unaccompanied minors and single people among the refugees, most brought their families with them. This was the case even with first-wave Vietnamese who fled while Saigon was under rocket attack in late April 1975. The average household size was 5.1 persons. Only 16,819 of first-wave Vietnamese came without family; 62 percent came in households of over five persons. Among the Hmong refugees of the late 1970s, the average household size was 7.6; among Laotians, 6.9.[11]

RESETTLEMENT: DIASPORA AND SECONDARY MIGRATION

Until 1980 the United States had no single set of enforceable policies and practices relating to refugee resettlement. Resettlement, in fact, was not government-run, but rather the province of private voluntary agencies such as the United States Catholic Conference, the International Rescue Committee, the Lutheran Immigration and Refugee Service, and the Tolstoi Foundation. The State Department contracted each of the voluntary agencies to find sponsors—individuals who would be responsible for the refugee's welfare until he or she could become self-supporting. Sponsors were to feed, clothe, and shelter the refugee, find the head of household a job, help enroll the children in school, and generally help the refugee and his or her family to adjust to American society. The government's obligation was to supply a resettlement grant of $500 per refugee to the voluntary agency to spend as it saw fit.[12]

Although resettlement was delegated to voluntary agencies, the U. S. government urged these agencies to disperse refugees throughout the United States and prevent the development of large ethnic communities which might create political tensions between state, local, and national governments or put undue strain on local communities. Voluntary agencies in 1975 tried to follow government guidelines, with moderate success. As early as December 1975, 27,199 of the 129,792 refugees resettled thus far were concentrated in California, 9,130 in Texas, and 7,159 in Pennsylvania. Despite these beginnings, the refugees were scattered throughout the country, placed wherever voluntary agencies could locate a church, community organization, corporation, or individual who would act as sponsor.[13]

The resettlement of first-wave refugees was arranged while refugees were housed in camps in the United States at Fort Chaffee in Arkansas, Fort Indiantown Gap in Pennsylvania, Camp Pendleton in California, and, for a very brief period, Eglin Air Force Base in Florida. Refugees, for the most part, had little negotiating power; they were sent where the agencies could find American sponsors. Within six months after they were resettled by the voluntary agencies, these first-wave refugees tended to relocate. They abandoned their sponsors and regrouped so as to develop the ethnic community the U. S. government had tried to discourage. For the most part, their movement was from rural to urban areas, from Northeastern states to Southern and Western states. By 1978 one-third of all refugees were residing in California; another 10 percent were in Texas. By 1983, 90 percent of the refugees were located in ten states.[14]

No constraints were placed on the refugees' secondary migration, despite the government's dim view of refugees who did so. Most sponsors were unable to provide for the refugees until they became self-supporting simply because most refugees had great difficulty entering the American labor market in a time of economic recession and in gaining adequate compensation for work once they found a job. Sponsors ended up channeling refugees to welfare offices. Ties that might have held refugees to a community—jobs and dependency on a local sponsor—did not form. There was little the government or the voluntary agencies could do to prevent migration, given the complete absence of coordination of refugee resettlement assistance services.

The development of refugee population concentrations was further exacerbated in the second- and third-wave migrations. Although many willing American organizations and churches and, to a lesser extent, individuals could be located to sponsor refugees while sympathy for Vietnamese fleeing from a Communist takeover could be drummed up, such sympathy, coupled with a deepening U. S. recession, made Americans less likely to step forward to sponsor refugees. Those who had served as sponsors in 1975 were reluctant to assume additional responsibility. By 1980 it became clear that the major groups sponsoring incoming refugees were refugees who had arrived in the United States in 1975. In 1983 it was estimated that over 50 percent of all new refugees were being sponsored by relatives and families without any American sponsors involved. This practice meant that preexisting refugee concentrations grew larger. In the period January through November 1978 alone, the 41,514 refugees in California welcomed 5,121 newly admitted refugees to their midst. The 13,717 refugees in Texas were joined by 2,177 second- and third-wave arrivals. The way the U. S. government delegated responsibility for resettlement, or more precisely diffused that responsibility, contradicted professed public policy. In 1979 urban areas in four states accounted for 75 percent of all refugees resettled in the country. The greatest concentration was in three zip code zones in the Los Angeles area; the second largest concentration was in New Orleans, Louisiana.[15]

Although the initial resettlement and secondary migration patterns for refugees have meant the development of large ethnic communities in California, Louisiana, and, to a lesser extent, Texas, this pattern represents the Vietnamese, the numerically largest of the refugees the U. S. government labeled "Indochinese." The resettlement patterns of Hmongs, Laotians, and Kampucheans were not the same, although these groups have also tended to form their own ethnic communities. The Hmongs in the United States, while initially scattered, like the Vietnamese of 1975, have engaged in spontaneous concentration through secondary migration. As of 1981 one-third of the Hmongs were in Santa Ana, California, and another third had moved to St. Paul, Minnesota. Significant communities had formed in Missoula, Montana; Denver, Colorado; and Providence, Rhode Island. In short, the Hmongs have formed communities where there are no Vietnamese, Kampucheans, or Laotians. Of the more than 1,000 refugees in Montana, in 1981 all but 68 were Hmongs. In St. Paul, when the Hmongs moved in, two-thirds of the Vietnamese located in the city moved out.

The Hmongs are not the only refugees who have formed their distinctive ethnic communities in areas where there are few other refugees from Vietnam, Kampuchea, and Laos. The Mien, another highland people from Laos, 3,000 to 4,000 of whom moved to the United States, have established a community of over 1,500 in Portland, Oregon; 1,000 or more Laotians are clustered in Des Moines, Iowa, where the number of Vietnamese is low.[16]

In sum, despite U. S. policy, refugee communities have developed in the United States through secondary migration. These concentrations are not ''Indochinese,'' but rather are based on nationality, with concentrations of Vietnamese in geographic spaces often distinct from those of Hmongs, Kampucheans, or Laotians. The regrouping represents the reestablishment of community and cannot be explained by simplistic notions of economic opportunity or variations in the provision of social services by individual states.[17]

LIVING IN THE UNITED STATES

Refugees from Vietnam, Laos, and Kampuchea may have successfully formed their own communities, but this does not mean they have become self-sufficient. Far from it. For a majority of refugees, coming to the United States has meant downward occupational and social mobility and marginal integration into low-paying blue collar and service employment. For many refugees it has meant unemployment, underemployment, and dependency on the American welfare system.[18]

Refugees have entered the work force at rates comparable to, if not higher than, the American population as a whole. In 1975 the employment rate of Vietnamese refugees was 68.2 percent among men and 50.9 percent among women. Within three years 94.9 percent of all first-wave Vietnamese refugees over the age of sixteen were employed (versus 94.5 percent of all Americans). Of those employed 82 percent had full-time work. Despite this high rate of employment, which characterizes only those refugees who have been in the United States at least three years (for those in the country less than three years, the employment rate is closer to 68 percent), family income remains below the poverty level for a family of four. As of 1978, only 33.9 percent of first-wave Vietnamese refugees earned more than $200 per month. Mean household income, with two or more wage earners, stood at $800 per month, or $9,600 per year. As of 1981, 67 percent of all refugees received some form of welfare assistance.[19]

Although refugees have been able to find work, for the vast majority the jobs they have taken in the United States do not correspond to those they held in their country of origin. This is particularly the case for Vietnamese refugees who had been managers, professionals, and technicians. A survey taken in late 1978 indicated that only 31.7 percent of Vietnamese professionals and 11.2

percent of managers and technicians were able to find similar jobs in the United States. Most took on clerical and sales or unskilled blue collar work. The small proportion of refugees who had been unskilled and semi-skilled laborers were employed similarly in the United States. Although they hold low-status, low-paying jobs in the United States, they were in similar positions before coming to the United States.[20]

The dependent economic position of refugees from Vietnam, Laos, and Kampuchea is due to several factors. Most refugees' English language skills upon entry into the United States were negligible. The ability to obtain and hold work in other than unskilled, poorly paid jobs depends on communication skills in English. For the first-wave Vietnamese, who were relatively highly educated and literate, developing English language skills, given the availability of special programs liberally funded by the U. S. government through 1980, has been a difficult but not insurmountable task. For second- and third-wave refugees from Laos and Kampuchea, English language skills have been more difficult to master. Unlike many first-wave Vietnamese, they were not employed by U. S. corporations and the government in clerical and technical positions. These refugees had less exposure to English and to Americans before their arrival in the country. The refugees from Kampuchea and Laos tended to be less well educated than first-wave Vietnamese; many were illiterate, and the Hmongs and Mien spoke languages that lacked writing systems. English language programs that have successfully taught the Vietnamese have been noticeably ineffective with these groups, and their work force participation rates, which are considerably lower than those of the Vietnamese (67 percent), reflect in large part their inability to speak English and obtain a job.[21]

English language skills are not the only factor that affect the economic status of the refugees. Just as important is the state of the American economy at the time of the refugees' arrival. These refugees came at a time of high unemployment. Thus, although the lack of English language skills and job skills handicapped them, equally important was the inability of the American economy to provide employment for both Americans and for refugees who desired work. In addition, according to a 1983 Government Accounting Office report, the concentration of refugees may have hampered their ability to gain well-paying jobs, for large refugee communities have formed in some areas like Portland, Oregon, Washington State, and Pennsylvania where high unemployment is endemic among Americans as well as among refugees.

Although in the short term the refugees from Vietnam, Kampuchea, and Laos are in a precarious economic position, whether such a situation will persist in the future is not clear. The refugees have been in the United States scarcely ten years and most have been here less than five years. In that short period it is remarkable that they have managed to achieve the degree of economic self-sufficiency that they have, given the American economy and the refugees' general lack of preparedness to enter the U. S. job market. Over time it is likely that refugee income will go up as more become fluent in English and enter the many job retraining programs the U. S. government has made available to them. Although refugee income levels today are dismally low compared to 1975 levels, family income has risen appreciably and labor force participation rates have risen rather than declined in the economic recession of the early 1980s.

The refugee adjustment to the United States has not been easy, for most have had to cope not only with moving from one culture to another but, in the case of the Hmongs and Mien, with moving from a rural to a modern industrial urban society. Most have experienced considerable downward social mobility. Almost all have been aware of the hostility of many Americans toward them.[22] American involvement in Vietnam, in particular, was strongly contested in the United States, and the opposition to the war spilled over into suspicion, distrust, and downright hostility to refugees from Vietnam as well as from Kampuchea and Laos. The refugees were not always perceived as victims of political persecution, but rather as those who did the persecuting. At the time of the fall of Saigon in 1975 most Americans did not support the government's offer of asylum to first-wave refugees. Refugees who had undergone the trauma of flight, in some cases where family members had died in transit, found themselves in a country where they were hardly welcome. In addition, many Americans perceived these refugees, coming as they did in a time of high unemployment and deepening economic recession, as individuals who would undermine Americans' opportunities to find a job.[23] As Vietnamese, Laotians, and Kampucheans moved into communities around the country, they came into conflict with American minorities who feared that the U. S. government was providing more services and benefits to refugees than to themselves. In New Orleans, for example, American blacks charged local governments with discriminating in favor of Vietnamese in job placement services and in allocating public housing. Similar incidents occurred in Albuquerque, where Mexican-American resentment against the Vietnamese ran high. Ugly incidents concerning fishing rights have erupted into violence in Texas and Louisiana.[24] The extent of conflict between the refugees and Americans is hard to gauge. Its existence has not helped the refugees' adjustment to the United States.

Despite the difficulties the refugees have faced in adjusting to a new social milieu, they have begun to set the terms of their integration into American society. Vietnamese, Laotians, Kampucheans, Mien, and Hmongs have formed associations designed to promote their interests, to assist them in becoming self-sufficient, and to maintain their cultural and religious heritages. In 1977 alone, 143 self-help organizations were formed, 119 of which were Vietnamese, 16 Kampuchean, and 8 Laotian.[25] The goals of these groups are varied: some, such as the Vietnamese Alliance of Boulder, Colorado, provide Vietnamese language books, celebrate holidays like Tet, and tutor children so that they can succeed well in school. Other associations have provided job placement services and counseling; still others perform religious functions. The diversity of such organizations and their number indicate that these new refugees are relying less on the American government and more on themselves to define their place in U. S. society.

NOTES

The author would like to thank Brian Anderson and Cherif Sadki for their assistance in gathering data for this essay.

1. For statistics on the refugees, see Gail P. Kelly, *From Vietnam to America: A Chronicle of the Vietnamese Immigration to the United States* (Boulder, Colo.: Westview Press, 1977), ch. 2; Wever Gim and Tybel Litwin, *Indochinese Refugees in America: Profiles in Five Communities: A Case Study*, 22d Session, Executive Seminar in National and International Affairs (Washington, D. C.: Department of State, 1980), p. 3; Report by the U. S. General Accounting Office, *Greater Emphasis on Early Employment and Better Monitoring Needed in Indochinese Refugee Resettlement Program* (Washington, D. C.: General Accounting Office, March 1, 1983), p. 1.

2. For a description of the three waves, see Scott C. S. Stone and John E. McGowan, *Wrapped in the Wind's Shawl: Refugees of Southeast Asia and the Western World* (San Rafael, Calif.: Presidio Press, 1980).

3. Ibid.; see also Tricia Knoll, *Becoming Americans: Asian Sojourners, Immigrants and Refugees in the Western United States* (Portland, Oreg.: Coast to Coast Books, 1982).

4. For an excellent overview of U. S. immigration policy, see Charlotte J. Moore, *Review of U. S. Refugee Resettlement Programs and Policies: A Report Prepared at the Request of Senator Edward M. Kennedy, Chair, Committee on the Judiciary United States Senate by the Congressional Research Service, Library of Congress*, 96th Cong., 2d sess. (Washington, D. C.: U. S. Government Printing Office, 1980), especially Appendix II.

5. See Senate Subcommittee to Investigate Problems Connected with Refugees and Escapees, *Indochina Evacuation and Refugee Problems, Part II. The Evacuation*, 94th Cong., 1st Sess., April 15, 25, and 30, 1975, p. 71; *Part IV. Staff Reports Prepared for the Use of the Subcommittee*, 94th Cong., 1st Sess., June 9 and July 8, 1972, p. 2.

6. See Michael J. deSherbinin and Carol Weeg, eds., *1980 World Refugee Survey* (New York: U. S. Committee for Refugees, 1980), especially pp. 12–18; Moore, *Review*; Gim and Litwin, *Indochinese Refugees*; Astri Suhrke, "Indochinese Refugees and American Policy," *World Today* 37, No. 2 (February 1981): 54–62.

7. Gim and Litwin, *Indochinese Refugees*; Moore, *Review*.

8. See Kelly, *From Vietnam to America*, ch. 2; William Liu, Maryanne Lamanna, and Alice Murata, *Transition to Nowhere: Vietnamese Refugees in America* (Nashville, Tenn.: Charter House Publishers, 1979), pp. 43–63; P. D. Starr and A. E. Roberts, "Community Structure and Vietnamese Refugee Adaptation: The Significance of Context," *International Migration Review* 16, No. 3 (1982): 595–618.

9. HEW Refugee Task Force, *Report to the Congress* (Lithograph), March 15, 1976, p. 28.

10. See Knoll, *Becoming Americans*, chs. 7–9; Gertrude Roth Li, "The State of Hmong Resettlement and Possible Approaches to Solve Some of Its Problems" (Nyack: N. Y.: World Relief, 1981), 27 pp. (ED 219 471); Robert Deaton, "What to Do When the Smoke Clears: Stage I and Stage II Planning with Asian Refugees," Paper presented at National Institute on Social Work in Rural Areas, Columbia, South Carolina, July 26–

29, 1981 (ED 230 630); Marshall Hurlech, "Preliminary Nutritional and Demographic Assessment of Hmong Refugees in the Area of Puget Sound, Washington," in William H. Meredith and Bette J. Twenton, eds., *Compiled Proceedings: Helping Indochinese Families in Transition* (Lincoln: University of Nebraska, College of Home Economics, May 11–12, 1981) (ED 206 768); William H. Meredith and Sharon Cramer, "Nebraska Indochinese Refugee Needs Assessment," in Meredith and Twenton, eds., *Compiled Proceedings*; Jean S. Baldwin, "Community Outreach and Health Education Classes Among Hmong and Mien in N. E. Portland," in Meredith and Twenton, *Compiled Proceedings*; see also Gim and Litwin, *Indochinese Refugees*.

11. Most U. S. government documents do not provide any breakdown on refugees by nationality. The figures presented here are based on extrapolations from regional studies. Although there are some regional studies of Vietnamese, Mien, and Hmongs, I could not locate any on Kampucheans in the United States. For information on Vietnamese, see Kelly, *From Vietnam to America*; other figures on Hmongs and Laotians are based on: Kathleen B. McInnis, "Secondary Migration Among the Indochinese: The Wisconsin Study" (Milwaukee, Wis.: Marquette University, unpublished paper, 1981) (ED 205 636); Young Y. Kim, "Dynamics of Intrapersonal and Interpersonal Communication: A Study of Indochinese Refugees in the Initial Phase of Acculturation," paper presented at the Annual Meeting of the Speech Communication Association, San Antonio, Texas, November 10–13, 1979 (ED 181 511); Meredith and Cramer, "Nebraska Indochinese"; and Gim and Litwin, *Indochinese Refugees*.

12. For a survey of the roles of voluntary agencies, see Kelly, *From Vietnam to America*, chs. 5 and 6; U. S. Department of State and Department of Health, Education and Welfare, *Report to the Congress by the Comptroller General of the United States, Domestic Resettlement of Indochinese Refugees—Struggle for Self-Reliance* (Washington, D. C., May 10, 1977); Robert G. Wright, "Voluntary Agencies and the Resettlement of Refugees," *International Migration Review* 15, No. 1 (Spring-Summer 1981): 157–74; Elizabeth Winkler, "Voluntary Agencies and Government Policy," *International Migration Review* 15, No. 1 (Spring-Summer 1981): 95–98.

13. HEW Refugee Task Force, *Report to the Congress*, p. 29.

14. See especially Report by the U. S. General Accounting Office, *Greater Emphasis on Early Employment*, p. 51.

15. Ibid.; see also Julia Vadala Taft, David S. North, and David Ford, *Refugee Resettlement in the United States: Time for a New Focus: A Report* (Washington, D. C.: New Transcentury Foundation, 1979), p. 186.

16. Li, *State of Hmong Resettlement*; Knoll, *Becoming Americans*, ch. 7; Gim and Litwin, *Indochinese Refugees*.

17. This conclusion is not mine, but rather was stated by the GAO in its 1983 report. See U. S. General Accounting Office, *Greater Emphasis on Early Employment*.

18. Employment is perhaps the most studied aspect of adaptation. See, for example, Robert L. Bach, "Employment Characteristics of Indochinese Refugees," *Migration Today* 8, No. 3 (January 1979): 10–14; Darrel Montero, *Vietnamese Americans: Patterns of Resettlement and Socioeconomic Adaptation in the United States* (Boulder, Colo.: Westview Press, 1979); Starr and Roberts, "Community Structure"; Christine Robinson Finnan, "Occupational Assimilation of Refugees," *International Migration Review* 15, No. 1 (Spring-Summer 1981): 292–309; Liem T. Nguyen and Alan B. Henkin, "Vietnamese Refugees in the United States: Adaptation and Transitional Status," *Journal of Ethnic Studies* 9, No. 4, (Winter 1982): 101–16; Barry N. Stein, "Occupational Ad-

justment of Refugees: The Vietnamese in the United States," *International Migration Review* 13, No. 1 (1979): 25–45; Opportunity Systems, Inc., *Sixth Wave Report: Indochinese Resettlement Operational Feedback*, Vietnamese Refugee Group (Washington, D. C. August 1979).

19. Indochinese Refugee Assistance Program, *Report to the Congress*, December 31, 1978, pp. 241–45; see Report by the U. S. General Accounting Office, *Greater Emphasis on Early Employment*, tables 3–1 and 3–2 and p. 17.

20. See Opportunity Systems, Inc., *Sixth Wave Report*.

21. Gim and Litwin, *Indochinese Refugees*, especially the chapter on Minneapolis-St. Paul, Minnesota; U. S. General Accounting Office, *Greater Emphasis on Early Employment*, tables 3–1 and 3–2 and p. 17.

22. See, for example, Ken-Ming Lin, Laurie Tazuma, and Minoru Masuda, "Adaptational Problems of Vietnamese Refugees. I. Health and Mental Health Status," *Archives of General Psychiatry* 36 (August 1979): 955–81; Liang Tien Redick and Beverly Wood, "Cross Cultural Problems for Southeast Asian Refugee Minors," *Child Welfare* 61, No. 6 (June 1982): 365–73; David Haines, Dorothy Rutherford, and Patrick Thomas, "Family and Community Among Vietnamese Refugees," *International Migration Review* 15, No. 1 (Spring-Summer 1981): 310–19; Barry N. Stein, "The Refugee Experience: Defining the Parameters of a Field Study," *International Migration Review* 15, No. 1 (Spring-Summer 1981): 320–30; C. Michael Lanphier, "Refugee Resettlement: Models in Action," *International Migration Review* 17, No. 1 (Spring 1983): 4–33; Tran Tuong Nhu, "The Trauma of Exile: Viet-Nam Refugees," *Civil Rights Digest* (Fall 1976): 59–62; J. Donald Cohon, Jr., "Psychological Adaptation and Dysfunction Among Refugees," *International Migration Review* 15, No. 1 (Spring-Summer 1981): 255–75.

23. The initial hostility to the Vietnamese has been well documented. See, for example, Richard T. Schaefer and Sandra L. Schaefer, "Reluctant Welcome: U. S. Response to the South Vietnamese Refugees," *New Community* 4, No. 3 (Autumn 1975): 366–70; James P. Sterba, "Captain Midnight Becomes Civilian Ky," *New York Times Magazine*, January 11, 1976, pp. 34–40; "Refugees: A Cool and Wary Reception," *Time Magazine*, May 12, 1975, pp. 24, 26.

24. Paul D. Starr, "Troubled Waters: Vietnamese Fisher-folk on America's Gulf Coast," *International Migration Review* 15, No. 1 (Spring-Summer 1981): 226–38; Knoll, *Becoming Americans*; Vuong G. Thuy, "The Needs and Expectations of Indochinese in America," paper delivered at the National Conference on Indochinese Education and Social Services, Arlington, Virginia, March 28, 1980 (ED 191 966); Rawlein Soberano, "The Vietnamese of New Orleans: Problems of America's Newest Immigrants," 1978 (ED 173 525); Gim and Litwin, *Indochinese Refugees*.

25. Indochinese Refugee Assistance Program, *Report to the Congress*, p. 240.

Asian Americans and American Immigration Law

TRICIA KNOLL

Successive immigrations of Asians to the United States have historically been referred to as "waves." Nineteenth-century labor leaders screamed "Yellow Peril" as if a rising tide of Asian arrivals on Western shores threatened every American institution. In fact, after Chinese laborers thronged California's mining camps, for more than a hundred years state and national immigration laws conspired to hold those waves to spurts and trickles.

Before the Civil War, no uniform national policy governing immigration existed in the United States. Although Congress regulated both the deportation of dangerous aliens and the condition of passenger ships accommodating immigrants, states freely recruited laborers and oversaw their entry into the United States. Ironically, the legal foundation used to restrain Asian immigration until 1952 was an early federal law that ostensibly had little to do with immigration policy: the Naturalization Act of 1790 which limited citizenship by naturalization to free, white aliens. Although an 1870 revision made people of African birth or descent eligible for citizenship by naturalization, court cases and treaties such as the 1868 Burlingame Treaty (in which China and the United States outlined a reciprocal immigration, consular, and trade agreement) specifically denied the privilege to Chinese.

After the Civil War, pressure mounted for a national immigration policy. The Gold Rush had fizzled. Railroads were well on the way to completion. A labor glut halted state recruitment of foreign-born laborers. Although Western states taxed the Chinese to discourage immigration, labor leaders called for broader congressional action to overthrow the Burlingame Treaty. Then, in 1874, the U. S. Supreme Court ruled that state immigration laws usurped the federal government's constitutional power to regulate foreign commerce. Congress responded with narrow bills that banned the admission of persons for lewd purposes, required the consent of Chinese and Japanese laborers on labor contracts, and ordered the inspection of passenger vessels on entry to U. S. ports.

The 1882 Immigration Act sought to end the conflict of state regulations. It banned the admission of lunatics, idiots, convicts, and persons likely to become public charges. A companion act, the Chinese Exclusion Act, violated the spirit of the Burlingame Treaty by barring anyone not eligible for citizenship under the 1790 Naturalization Act from immigrating to the United States—specifically the Chinese. This first immigration act to discriminate against citizens of one nation effectively halted the arrival of Chinese laborers. A few skilled workers and merchants were allowed in as exceptions.

From 1882 to 1917 Congress further extended federal control of immigration. It established holding camps for immigrants, created quarantine procedures, and banned the admission of epileptics, beggars, and anarchists. In 1907 President Theodore Roosevelt, fearing the diplomatic repercussions of a Japanese exclusion act which labor leaders demanded as passionately as they had Chinese exclusion, negotiated a Gentlemen's Agreement with Japan which limited the immigration of Japanese and Korean laborers to fill vacancies created by the Chinese cutoff. Disappointed exclusionists looked to state alien land laws which forbade aliens not eligible for citizenship to own land and anti-miscegenation laws to discourage the arrivals of Japanese, Korean, and Filipino laborers.

With the 1882 Chinese Exclusion Act as a precedent, however, by 1917 exclusionist lobbies pressured Congress to pass an immigration act that severely reduced the immigration of laborers from an "Asiatic Barred Zone" including India, Indochina, Burma, Siam, the Malay States, and the Polynesian and East Indian Islands—all Asians who were not banned by earlier legislation or executive agreement. It also established a literacy requirement.

Through the 1920s shifts in immigration policy continued to suppress Asian immigration. In 1921 Congress passed the first national quota law which created preferences for family reunification and those eligible for citizenship. Legislation passed in 1924 established the "national origins" principle for setting quotas, a primary criterion in U. S. immigration until 1965. Quotas favored Western and Northern Europeans while banning Japanese and Koreans. Filipino laborers entered during this decade because, as U.S. nationals, they could not be excluded. Although eligible for citizenship if they served in the U.S. military, alien land laws and other discriminatory state laws applied to Filipinos as they did to all other Asians.

With the onset of the depression in 1929, during the next decade more persons of all nationalities left the United States than arrived. The Repatriation Act of 1935 encouraged Filipinos to return to the Philippines by offering to pay their transportation fees.

In theory, the period from 1940 to 1952 reversed the trend of earlier Asian exclusions. Embarrassed to exclude military allies during wartime, Congress repealed the Chinese Exclusion Act in 1943 and granted citizenship by naturalization to foreign-born Chinese. Then in 1946, when the Philippines gained independence, Filipinos in the United States were offered citizenship by naturalization as were Asian Indian immigrants. At the same time, however, these Asian groups were subject to small, token immigration quotas. During the 1940s, 105 Chinese were allowed to enter annually: half the slots went to professionals, and half to wives or children of immigrants already here.

Foreign policy concerns challenged this rigid quota system well into the 1950s. Special legislative responses allowed numerous admissions of non-quota individuals: the Displaced Persons Act of 1948 admitted refugees displaced by Communist takeovers and orphans from World War II and later the Korean conflict; and the War Brides Act allowed spouses of American military men to immigrate. Legislative arguments erupted over whether to charge these admissions against future quotas, a ludicrous proposal in the face of rapidly swelling refugee populations in both Asia and Europe and the small, token quotas set for Asian nations not entirely banned by the 1917 and 1924 legislation.

The McCarran-Walter Act of 1952 addressed these confusions. It codified all previous law but retained the bias of the national origins quota system toward Northern and Western Europeans. Then it artificially delineated the Asia-Pacific Triangle, an area embracing half the world's population in twenty-three Asian nations including China, Japan, Korea, the Philippines, India, Burma, Indonesia, Thailand, Vietnam, Laos, and Kampuchea. Each nation in the Triangle was allowed 100 immigrants per year, the total for the Triangle not to exceed 2,000 in one calendar year. Italy's quota was over 5,000, but Germany's more than 25,000.

Despite this discrimination against the Eastern Hemisphere, detractors grudgingly applauded two other aspects of the McCarran-Walter Act. First, it guaranteed all immigrants the right to citizenship—finally repealing earlier legislation that hung on the Naturalization Act of 1790. Japanese and Koreans residing in the United States—some for more than four decades—could become citizens. Second, the act defined the concept of parole for refugees and the procedure for a change of status to permanent resident which was expanded and renewed in subsequent Refugee Relief Acts in 1953, 1957, 1958, and 1959. The provisions of these acts outlined emergency procedures and permitted President John F. Kennedy to authorize 15,000 Chinese who had fled China to Hong Kong to enter the United States from 1962 to 1967.

These refugee acts eroded the intent of the restrictive quotas of the McCarran-Walter Act. The quotas themselves also became an embarrassment in U. S. international relations. By 1965 Congress was ready to pass a comprehensive immigration act that radically altered the restrictionist philosophy of the last century. The act eliminated national origins quotas in favor of hemispheric ceilings which were further revised in 1978 to create a non-discriminatory immigration preference system based on family reunifications and educational background. By establishing high preferences for professional and technical workers, the 1965 act allowed hundreds of thousands of Korean, Filipino, and Asian Indian professionals to enter the United States. In demographic terms, the impact of the 1965 Immigration Act was enormous: Asian Indian populations here jumped from 6,000 in 1960 to 312,000 in 1980; Korean from 11,000 to 354,000; and Filipino from 180,000 to 775,000.

If the 1965 legislation encouraged the skilled Asian professional to immigrate to the United States, it also prepared a refugee admissions policy to handle the homeless and displaced in Southeast Asia after Communist takeovers there in 1975. Although it continued to tie refugee admissions specifically to Communist persecution, a narrower definition than United Nations conventions, it included refugees as the seventh, or last, preference. From 1975 through the present, the United States has extended parole—or refugee—status to hundreds of thousands of Southeast Asian refugees from Vietnam, Laos, and Kampuchea. The Refugee Act of 1980 tried to regularize procedures which this large-scale exodus challenged by creating a more equitable basis for cash and medical assistance, increasing refugee ceilings, outlining the President's authority to admit emergency groups outside the normal flow, and redefining refugee flight to conform with the U. N. definition by eliminating references to communism.

The refugee problem in Southeast Asia—as well as other areas of the globe—is currently receiving substantial legislative attention. Because public opinion appears to favor decreasing immigration numbers generally, the executive branch is responding to congressional concerns by reducing the refugee admissions ceilings. Commissions are studying the impact of refugee resettlement on both assistance programs and sponsorship organizations. Whether refugees applying for resettlement are actually economic migrants or genuinely subject to persecution if they return to their homeland is coming under closer scrutiny. Unlike recent highly skilled Asian immigrants and their families, the newest refugees include unaccompanied minors, the aged and handicapped, and the unskilled who test the American commitment to easing the plight of refugees. These concerns will continue to challenge American immigration policy for the decade to come.

Asian Americans and American Justice

HUNGDAH CHIU

The experience of Asian Americans with American law lies primarily in the areas of immigration, naturalization, and discrimination. Until the post-World War II period, most Asian Americans were Chinese, Japanese, and Filipinos. The Filipinos, because of U. S. administration, enjoyed a special status. Therefore, the related laws and judicial decisions discussed below are related principally to Chinese or Japanese.

IMMIGRATION

Under traditional Chinese law, the Chinese were not allowed to leave China without special permission. However, a few Chinese did come to the United States between 1820 and 1840. In 1848 gold was discovered in California, and entrepreneurs sought cheap labor from China. In 1850 there were 4,000 Chinese working in California, and the first anti-Chinese legislation was enacted there—a special tax on Chinese laborers. In 1855 California enacted another law to impose an entry tax of $55 per person on Chinese and subsequently even enacted laws to exclude the entry of Chinese, but the exclusionary legislation was declared unconstitutional by the Supreme Court.

After the end of the Civil War in 1865, there was a great demand for Chinese laborers to lay railways and work in other construction in the West. Thus, in 1868 the United States urged China to agree in Article 5 of the Additional Articles to the Sino-American Treaty of June 18, 1858 (generally known as the Reed Treaty) to the principle of free emigration so that Chinese would come legally to the United States. However, after the major construction work was finished, native workers sensed keen competition from the Chinese workers, who were more efficient and demanded less pay. The resulting friction manifested itself in several anti-Chinese riots in the West. Not surprisingly, the federal and local authorities took no effective actions to protect the Chinese during riots.

Their omissions were in disregard of legal obligations under international law and various Sino-U. S. treaties. In 1882 Congress adopted the first anti-Chinese legislation. Later, on October 1, 1888, Congress enacted the so-called Chinese Exclusion Act, 25 Stat. L. 504, in violation of several Sino-U. S. treaties. This act effectively excluded Chinese immigration to the United States. In 1892 another act was enacted by Congress, 27 Stat. L. 25, to require Chinese laborers already in this country to acquire certification of residence within a stated period. All Chinese laborers without such certificates would be deemed unlawfully within the United States and would be deported. The act imposed strict requirements to acquire the certificate, and many Chinese could not meet such requirements. They were thus subject to deportation. In Fong Yue Ting v. United States, 149 U. S. 698 (1893), the Supreme Court held the act constitutional. At least fifteen anti-Chinese laws were enacted by the U. S. Congress between 1882 and 1913.

During the World War II period, the Republic of China (Nationalist) became an ally of the United States. Hence, on December 17, 1943, Congress enacted Public Law 78–199, 57 Stat. 600, which repealed all Chinese exclusion legislation and granted a quota for Chinese immigration based on the national origin system computed in accordance with the acts of 1921 and 1924. As a result, an immigration quota of 105 persons was allocated to Chinese annually.

In accordance with the 1894 and 1907 U. S.-Japanese treaties, citizens or subjects of each country should "have liberty to enter, travel and reside in the territories of the other . . . ''; and they should "enjoy in this respect the same rights and privileges" which might "be granted to native citizens or subjects." The Immigration Act of 1924, however, contained in Section 13 (c) a provision excluding the immigration of aliens "ineligible to citizenship" to the United States. Because not all Asians were eligible for citizenship, this provision in fact excluded all Asians, except the Filipinos, to immigrate to the United States, including the Japanese, whose right to emigrate was provided in the treaties.

The Philippine Islands were ceded by Spain to the United States in 1898 and thus came under U. S. administration, so the Filipinos were eligible to enter the United States. After the adoption of the Philippine Independence Act in 1934, 48 Stat. 456—although the entry of the Filipinos into the United States had to comply with the U.S. Immigration Act of 1924—the discriminatory Section 13(c) stated above was not applicable to them.

The 1952 Immigration and Nationality Act, 66 Stat. 235, abolished the exclusion of non-white immigration to the United States, but the allocation of quotas based on the national origin system remained strongly unfavorable to non-whites, especially Asians. The national origin system as defined under the 1924 and 1952 acts intended to preserve the racial composition of the United States as of 1920, and the quota for immigrants from any one nation was calculated in terms of one-sixth of 1 percent of persons of that origin then in the United States. There was an absolute ceiling of 2,000 on immigrants originating from the so-called Asia-Pacific Triangle, embracing most Far Eastern countries. The total number of immigrants a year was limited to 150,000. The allocation of the number of immigrants based on national origin resulted in 65,000 for Great Britain and minimum quotas of 100 immigrants for most non-white countries. The larger quotas allocated to European countries in fact remained unused to a substantial extent, whereas applicants from countries with minimal quotas remained on long waiting lists.

In the 1965 amendment to the Immigration and Nationality Act, Public Law 89–236, 79 Stat. 911, the immigrant quotas based on national origin were abolished. The new system allows the admission of up to 170,000 immigrants per fiscal year, with preferences allocated under Section 203 of the amended act on the basis of a series of priorities such as family ties and occupational skills. There is a limitation of 20,000 per fiscal year on immigrants from any one country. This amendment removed the racial prejudices against the non-whites, including Asians. Since then the number of Asian immigrants to the United States has increased significantly.

NATURALIZATION

By the act of 1790 only "free white persons" and "aliens of African nativity and persons of African descent" were capable of naturalization; thus, Asians were not eligible for naturalization. In late 1943, when Congress abolished all Chinese exclusion acts, it also made the Chinese eligible for naturalization. The Immigration and Nationality Act of 1952 abolished all racial prejudice in naturalization.

DISCRIMINATION

Although the Fourteenth Amendment of the Constitution provides that "all persons born . . . in the United States . . . are citizens of the United States," the question was once raised whether persons born of Chinese parents, who were not eligible for naturalization, would acquire U. S. citizenship through birth. In 1895 a person of Chinese origin, Wong Kim Ark, was denied entry into the United States after his short visit to China, despite the fact that he was born in California in 1873. He brought action against the United States before a U. S. federal district court. In the habeas corpus proceedings, the question was raised whether Wong was a citizen. The case finally reached the Supreme Court which found in Wong's favor (United States v. Wong Kim Ark, 169 U. S. 649 (1898)). The Court stated that "the fourteenth amendment . . . , in clear words and in manifest intent, includes the children born within the territory of the United States of all other persons, of whatever race or color, domiciled within the United States"; therefore, Wong acquired his U. S. citizenship by birth and was entitled to enter the United States. The Court further stated that "no act of omission of Congress, as to providing for the naturalization of parents or children of a particular race, can affect citizenship acquired as a birthright, by virtue of the Constitution itself without any aid of legislation."

This case is of great significance to Asians and other non-white groups in the United States, because it assured their descendants born in the United States of acquiring U. S. citizenship and banned Congress from using legislation to deprive them of this right. Under such circumstances, the number of Americans of Asian origin was able to grow.

During the World War II period, while the United States was at war with Japan, the military command of the Western Defense Command, pursuant to Presidential Executive Order No. 9066 issued on February 19, 1942, promulgated an order requiring, *inter alia*, that all persons of Japanese ancestry within a designated military area ''be within their place of residence between the hours of 8 p. m. and 6 a. m.'' In the case of Hirabayashi v. United States, 320 U. S. 81 (1943), the Supreme Court decided that such a measure was not unconstitutionally discriminatory against citizens of Japanese ancestry. The Court stated: ''We cannot close our eyes to the fact, demonstrated by experience, that in time of war, residents having ethnic affiliations with an invading enemy may be a greater source of danger than those of a different ancestry.'' This reasoning is highly questionable, because the United States was at war with Germany and Italy too, and none of the Americans of German or Italian ancestry in the East Coast states was subject to a similar restriction. Moreover, after the defeat of the Japanese Navy in the 1942 Midway Island engagement, there existed no immediate threat of invasion to Hawaii and the West Coast. Thus, at the time of the Court's decision in 1943, even the existence of such a military necessity to justify such a measure was questionable.

Pursuant to Presidential Executive Order No. 9066 and Act of Congress of March 21, 1942, 56 Stat. 173, the commanding general of the Western Defense Command directed that after May 9, 1942, all persons of Japanese ancestry should be excluded from the area. The implementation of this measure resulted in the removal of 110,000 Japanese, two-thirds of them citizens of the United States by birth, from their homes and properties, and in their temporary segregation in ''assembly centers'' and later in ''relocation centers.'' Fred T. Korematsu, an American citizen of Japanese ancestry, refused to follow the order and was therefore convicted under the act of March 21, 1942. In Korematsu v. United States, 323 U. S. 214 (1944), the Supreme Court upheld the constitutionality of the criminal conviction of Korematsu. However, it refused to rule on the basic constitutional issues of relocation, confinement, and segregation of Japanese Americans. The order was lifted by President Harry S. Truman on December 31, 1946, more than a year after the Japanese surrender and the cessation of active hostilities. Hindsight makes it clear that there was no necessity for the Japanese segregation measures, as not one single Japanese, citizen or otherwise, in the United States was found guilty of one single effort at sabotage or espionage. Subsequently, congressional legislation provided for compensation for certain categories of losses caused by the relocation (62 Stat. 1231 [1948]).

Since the enactment of the Civil Rights Acts of 1957, 1960, 1964, and 1968 and the Voting Rights Acts of 1965 and 1970, all discrimination against Americans of different racial groups has been banned. Asian Americans certainly benefited from these laws. Recently, in 1982, a twenty-seven-year-old Chinese, Vincent Chin, was beaten to death by two whites in Detroit, but the court there merely sentenced the killers to three years' probation and a fine of $3780 each. This unjust sentence caused great indignation among Asian Americans; later, the Justice Department decided to investigate the case to see whether Chin's civil rights had been violated. The case indicates that whether the administration of justice, even under the recent anti-discrimination legislation, is in practice fair to Asian Americans is an open question.

Asian Americans and American Politics

DON T. NAKANISHI

The participation of Asian Americans in American politics represents one of the most glaring gaps in our historical knowledge of Asian Americans. Most works on the topic such as Roger Daniels' *Politics of Prejudice*[1] emphasize how American political institutions, especially political parties and state governments, had a decisive impact on creating and maintaining a system of exclusion and discrimination against Asian Americans. Until recently less academic attention was given to the flip-side of that structural condition, namely, how Asian Americans responded to such treatment and, more generally, how they engaged in a variety of political activities, electoral and non-electoral, domestic and international, to confront political situations that threatened their group survival, and to advance their group interests.[2]

In understanding the involvement of Asian Americans in American politics, several key distinguishing features of their historical experiences must be highlighted. First, early Asian immigrants were politically disenfranchised and could not become naturalized citizens, register to vote, or be fully involved in other aspects of American society because of a plethora of discriminatory laws and policies, one of the most crucial being Ozawa v. United States (1922), which forbade Asian immigrants from becoming American citizens. This legal barrier prevented early Asian immigrants from being involved in electoral politics of any form—be it the type of ward politics practiced by European immigrants in the East or Midwest or simply voting for their preferences in a presidential election—and restricted the development of electoral participation by Asian Americans to the second and subsequent generations. Although groups like the Japanese American Citizens League launched limited voter registration drives during the 1930s, the most sustained and visible involvement of Asian Americans in electoral politics did not occur until the 1950s in Hawaii and the 1970s in mainland United States. At present, Asian Americans hold a variety of elected and appointed positions in over twenty states, especially in Hawaii, California, and Washington, and are courted by both major political parties for their financial contributions and to a lesser extent for their voting potential. Some of the more prominent Asian American politicians include U. S. Senators Daniel Inouye and Spark Matsunaga from Hawaii; U. S. Congressmen Norman Mineta and Robert Matsui from California and Daniel Akaka from Hawaii; Governor George Ariyoshi of Hawaii; Secretary of State March Fong Eu of California; and Lieutenant Governor S. B. Woo of Delaware.[3]

Electoral politics has become a significant focus of attention for Asian American communities in recent years, but it represents only one form of political participation by Asian Americans. Another key distinguishing feature of their history is that Asian Americans have been concerned about and affected by events, issues, and relationships involving their Asian ancestral homelands. They have been active transnational participants in major revolutionary, nationalistic, and independence movements that have emerged in their respective homelands during the past century, and have sought to contribute to subsequent national development efforts in those countries.[4] They have also been victimized to a greater extent than other American immigrant groups by the dramatic shifts in bilateral relations between the United States and their homelands as the World War II internment of Japanese Americans demonstrates. At present, concern among Asian Americans in Asian affairs ranges from restoring democratic rule to both right-wing and Communist political systems in Asian countries to playing a greater role in U. S.–Pacific Rim relationships in trade, cultural exchanges, and economic development activities. In general, Asian Americans have not been as successful as other American immigrant groups in becoming an influential lobbying force in American foreign policy decision-making, but this should not minimize the significance which Asian-oriented political involvement has had in Asian American history or, more specifically, in competing with domestic political issues in mobilizing Asian American communities.

Asian Americans, like other American racial minorities which have been historically disenfranchised from the American electoral system, have engaged in a variety of non-electoral political activities to advance their group interests. As recent research has documented, they have been active participants in labor-organizing efforts in the Far West, Hawaii, New York, and the Rocky Mountain states, and indeed were at the forefront of creating labor unions for agricultural workers in California and Hawaii.[5] They have also sought justice and equal treatment by continuously engaging in legal challenges against discriminatory laws and practices in education, employment, housing, land ownership, immigration, and other policy issues, and many of their legal cases, be it Korematsu v. United States (1943) or Lau v. Nichols (1974), have become landmark civil rights decisions. Although electoral participation is increasing among Asian Americans, it is clear that non-electoral forms of political participation are still vigorously being pursued by the Asian American community. In recent years, for example, Asian Americans have formed a number of their own parallel organizations in conjunction with broader social movements in American society

dealing with the Vietnam War, civil rights, women's issues, and nuclear proliferation, and have established an assortment of leftist organizations, which
perpetuate a long-standing Marxist-oriented sector in Asian American communities. They have also launched major nationwide protest campaigns seeking
justice for individuals such as Lee Chol Soo and Iva Ikuko Toguri D'Aquino,
commonly known as Tokyo Rose, who were viewed as victims of discriminatory
legal treatment; challenged the initial lenient sentences given to two Detroit
unemployed auto workers who murdered Vincent Chin, a Chinese American
who was mistaken for a Japanese American and was therefore viewed as being
responsible for the declining American automobile industry; and registered their
anger over the Soviet downing of Korean Airlines Flight 007, and the assassination of Philippine opposition leader Benigno Aquino. They have also protested
against the perpetuation of negative Asian stereotypes in the media, lobbied
against discriminatory legislation like the Simpson-Mazzoli immigration bill,
and have sought to gain redress and reparations for the World War II internment
of Japanese Americans.[6]

Although there has been a dramatic increase in political involvement by Asian
Americans in all forms of political activity in recent years, it would be incorrect
to conclude that they have become a powerful and unified political entity, or
that they are now capable of competing equally with other actors, be they other
minority groups or special interests, in realizing their specific political goals.
Asian Americans still have not fully developed and used the wide array of real
and symbolic resources that are needed to compete on an equal basis with other
groups, and their internal diversity (of ethnic origins, generations, social classes,
political perspectives, organizational aims, and other features) has often prevented them from being a unified political force. In some mainland cities such
as San Francisco, Gardena, Monterey Park, and to a lesser extent Seattle and
Los Angeles, Asian Americans have become increasingly viable and recognized
political participants, but in most areas aside from Hawaii and at higher levels
of state and federal decision-making they remain largely ignored and underrepresented. Indeed, as a result of both structural and group-specific constraints,
they have not been able to sufficiently cultivate a national political presence, or
an explicit set of national priorities, which is at least recognized when minor
policy issues dealing with the poor, elderly, or U. S. relations with Asia are
legislated and implemented. At best, their contemporary impact on American
politics has been regional and sporadic rather than national and continuous, and
their reputed success as a model minority disguises their lack of influence and
representation in the most significant political and social arenas and institutions
of American society.

The future of Asian American political involvement cannot be fully forecast
because of the profound political transitions that appear to be occurring in Asian
American communities, Asian countries, and American politics in the mid–
1980s. Many Asian American elected officials, for example, optimistically believe that Asian Americans will play an increasingly significant role in American

electoral politics in coming years as the large number of recent Asian immigrants and refugees—who bolstered the Asian Pacific American population by 153 percent from 1970 to 1980—become naturalized citizens and augment the present Asian American electorate. However, there is no guarantee that these new citizens will actually register to vote, believe that their participation will enhance the political influence of Asian Americans, or will develop an efficacious orientation toward the American political system without special organized activities in Asian American communities like voter registration drives or political education forums. At the same time, the passage of Proposition 0 in San Francisco in 1983 and Proposition 38 in California's 1984 general election, both of which called for the elimination of bilingual ballots and other election materials, may not only have sent a signal to new immigrants that the electoral system is less than fully accessible, but may also have provided added impetus to a national conservative movement that seeks to eliminate all equal rights and equal opportunity provisions in voting and other policy areas. Similarly, in relation to Asian nations, it is difficult to predict how and in what ways their internal political conflicts, as well as their potentially explosive external relations with neighboring countries, will be resolved, and, more importantly, what stake Asian Americans, especially new immigrants and refugees, will have in those future developments. One cannot forecast, for example, whether these international issues will dominate the political agendas of Asian American communities and overwhelm efforts to steer Asian Americans toward greater involvement in the American political system. At the same time, the volatile political economies of most Asian nations will probably play havoc with the present goals of many Asian American leaders in assuming a greater instrumental role in Pacific Rim activities. And finally, it is perhaps too early to predict the future course of the Democratic Party, which has been the most receptive to the involvement of Asian Americans as an organized interest group within its party structure. If the party, based on its embarrassing national presidential defeats in recent elections, abandons its interest group strategy or significantly alters its ideological premises, there may be major shifts in campaign fund-raising and voting patterns among Asian Americans, which are decisively oriented toward the Democratic Party at this time.

Although future trends in Asian American politics cannot be accurately predicted, it is perhaps reasonable to conclude that Asian Americans will continue to engage in a diverse array of political activities, be they electoral or nonelectoral, domestic or international. By doing so, they will hardly be doing something new. Their political legacy is as old as their experiences in this country.

NOTES

1. Roger Daniels, *The Politics of Prejudice* (New York: Atheneum Press, 1968).
2. Yuji Ichioka, "The Early Japanese Quest for Citizenship: The Background of the 1922 Ozawa Case," *Amerasia Journal*, Vol. 4 (1977): 1–22; Him Mark Lai, "A Historical

Survey of the Chinese Left in America,'' in Emma Gee, ed. *Counterpoint* (Los Angeles: Asian American Studies Center, 1976), pp. 63–80; Victor Low, *The Unimpressible Race: A Century of Educational Struggles by the Chinese in San Francisco* (San Francisco: East West Publishing Co., 1982); and Kingsley Lyu, ''Korean Nationalistic Activities in Hawaii and the Continental United States, 1900–1945,'' Parts I and II, *Amerasia Journal*, Vol. 4 Nos. 1 and 2, (1977): pp. 23–90; pp. 53–100.

3. Don T. Nakanishi and Bernie LaForteza, *The National Asian Pacific American Roster, 1984*. Los Angeles: Asian American Studies Center, 1984.

4. Shih-Shan Henry Tsai, ''The Emergence of Early Chinese Nationalist Organizations in America,'' *Amerasia Journal*, Vol. 8, 1981, pp. 121–144; Lyu, *op. cit.*; Mark Juergensmeyer, ''The Ghadar Syndrome: Nationalism in an Immigrant Community,'' *Center for South and Southeast Asian Studies Review*, Vol. 1, 1978, pp. 9–13; Lucie Cheng, et al. ''Chinese Emigration, the Sunning Railroad, and the Development of Toisan,'' *Amerasia Journal*, Vol. 9, 1982, pp. 59–74.

5. Peter Kwong, *Chinatown, New York: Labor and Politics, 1930–1950*. New York: Monthly Review Press, 1981; Cletus Daniel, *Bitter Harvest: A History of California Farmworkers, 1870–1941*. Ithaca, NY: Cornell University Press, 1981; Howard DeWitt, *Violence in the Fields: California Filipino Farm Labor Organizing During the Great Depression*. Saratoga, CA: Century Twenty One Publishing, 1980; Karl Yoneda, *Ganbatte*. Los Angeles: Asian American Studies Center, 1983.

6. Rocky Chin, et al. ''The Long Road—Japanese Americans Move on Redress,'' *Bridge*, Vol. 7, 1981–82, pp. 11–29; Amy Uyematsu, ''The Emergence of Yellow Power in America,'' in Amy Tachiki, et al. (eds.) *Roots: An Asian American Reader*. Los Angeles: Asian American Studies Center, 1971, pp. 9–13.

Asian Americans and the American Economic Order

ILLSOO KIM

The early Asian immigrants entered the United States over the period of time extending from the discovery of gold in California in 1848 to the passage of the national Origins Act in 1924. This period of American history was marked by economic transformation caused by industrial and commercial expansion. It was an era of the advance of Western civilization across the American continent. It was also the period of great transatlantic migration involving the arrival of millions of European "huddled masses" of peasants and unskilled workers on the East Coast of the American continent.

In contrast with the transatlantic migration, Asian immigrants with cultural and racial characteristics quite different from those of the Europeans crossed the Pacific toward either the Hawaiian Islands or the West Coast—the last frontiers of America. The exploration of these areas demanded an abundant supply of cheap labor. This is the historical setting against which the basic economic adjustment patterns of early Asian immigrants evolved.

THE CHINESE AS AN ASIAN ECONOMIC FORERUNNER

Largely owing to the ever-expanding economic opportunities on the West Coast, the Chinese immigrants, who began to arrive as early as the 1840s, broadened the range of their occupational structure. Stereotypical Chinese occupations such as hand laundry and restaurant businesses had not yet distinctively emerged. From 1850 to 1882, when the Chinese Exclusion Act went into effect, some 322,000 Chinese, including returnees, arrived on the West Coast and Hawaiian Islands. The overwhelming majority of them were peasants and unskilled laborers from the rural areas of Kwangtung and Fukien; they penetrated into almost all occupations and industries on the West Coast.[1] Chinese workers were notably employed in the construction of the Central Pacific portion of the transcontinental railroad as well as the western section of the Southern Pacific and Northern Pacific railroads.

The Chinese entry into major industries contributed to the anti-Chinese movement led largely by white immigrants on the East Coast. The agitation was spurred on by the whites' fear of "Yellow Peril"—the idea being that Asians, pushed by the "population explosion" in their homelands, would inundate white American society. The proponents of the anti-Chinese movement, which was led by the labor unions and supported by small businessmen and small farmers, alleged that Chinese immigrants being servile, docile, and undemocratic were unassimilable. The Chinese depressed wages and undercut the American standard of living. These Asian immigrants were frequently subjected to physical violence. Nineteen Chinese were murdered in a riot in Los Angeles in 1871; in 1885 a white mob killed twenty-eight Chinese in a racial riot at Rock Springs, Wyoming. As a result, an involuntary occupational segregation began to take place among the Chinese.[2]

The organizers and supporters of the anti-Chinese movement held conventions in California. In 1877 the California Legislature appealed to the U. S. Congress to limit Chinese immigration. The federal government was initially hesitant in assisting California because it was deeply involved in working out its international relations with China, with the aim of advancing and expanding the imperial interests of the United States in China. As a political result of the complex interplay between America's relations with, and imperial interests in, China and America's domestic "labor problem" associated with Chinese immigrants, Congress passed the Chinese Exclusion Act in 1882.

Other Asian immigrant groups, who began to enter the United States later than the Chinese, shared the economic adjustment patterns that the Chinese had established in a broader context of national and international events. Three patterns emerged affecting other Asians—Japanese, Koreans, and Filipinos. The first pattern relates to the success of the labor union-led Chinese exclusion movement at the turn of the century. Asians were excluded from labor unions and thereby blue collar occupations. The historic Chinese exclusion movement began to shape the Asian underrepresentation in labor unions, which continues to the present. The second pattern is that in the face of white racism, Asians—especially the Chinese and Japanese—turned to small businesses. They relied on ethnic resources—ethnic organizations and values—for the economic "success" in small businesses. The third pattern can be found in the consistent roles the federal government played in determining the "fate" among Asians. The basic pattern of Asian immigration to the United States has been governed by international relations between the United States and Asian nations.

THE JAPANESE EXPERIENCE

By the time 22,000 Japanese came to the West Coast between 1890 and 1900, local and national legislation had succeeded in excluding the Chinese from the mainstream of American life. The Japanese had undergone economic adjustment patterns quite similar to those of the Chinese. As in the case of the Chinese, they were employed as laborers on the railroads, in the canneries, in logging, and in mining, meatpacking, and salt industries.[3] Like the Chinese, too, the Japanese were industrious and willing to work for low wages. However, they could not enter higher paying occupations such as shoe, cigar, and clothing industries largely because of the effect of earlier white labor agitation against the Chinese. The Japanese also found it difficult to find jobs in cities. These external conditions channeled a high proportion of them into agriculture.

By 1909 some 39,000 Japanese were engaged in farming and allied agricultural work, particularly menial labor. The figure accounted for more than half of all the Japanese in the United States. Many of them made efforts to advance themselves as independent farmers and pioneers. The Japanese economic ventures evoked the organized white hostility in the same manner of the anti-Chinese agitation. Roger Daniels calls the anti-Japanese movement "a tail to the anti-Chinese kite." The white lobby of California placed a legal barrier on the Japanese economic expansion. In 1913 the California Legislature passed the Alien Land (Webb-Heney) Act. According to the law, those aliens who were "ineligible for citizenship" could not own agricultural property. The law was intended for Asian immigrants who were legally designated as "aliens ineligible for citizenship."

The anti-Japanese movement in California, as in the case of the anti-Chinese movement, contributed to the evolution of the Japanese service jobs which did not compete with whites. Most Japanese were employed in domestic service in towns and cities "or ran small curio shops, cafes, laundries, dry cleaners, rooming houses, grocery stores and barber shops."[4] As Roger Daniels notes, Issei workers were seldom hired by white firms for factory or office work because of unionization and anti-Asian movements.[5]

THE KOREAN AND THE FILIPINO EXPERIENCE

Between 1903 and 1905 some 8,000 Korean immigrants came to the Hawaiian Islands to succeed Japanese immigrants in the supply of labor to Hawaiian sugar plantations. The annexation of Hawaii to the United States led thousands of Japanese contract laborers to move to the mainland, necessitating the importation of other groups of cheap but industrious laborers—Koreans and Filipinos. Upon being freed from their labor contracts, Koreans followed the Japanese suit: from 1905 to 1910 some 2,000 Koreans, previously living on the islands, largely enticed by better economic opportunities, moved to the West Coast. Like the Japanese and the Chinese, the Koreans faced economic adjustment and exposure to the anti-Oriental movement on the West Coast. The Koreans engaged in rice and vegetable farming, railroad construction, and the restaurant and hotel business. Their economic ventures were greatly limited by the anti-Oriental movement. Koreans were lumped together with the Chinese and Japanese as

"Mongolians," and all were subjected to the same discrimination. The Japanese and Korean Exclusion League, which was formed by foreign-born white laborers in 1905 in San Francisco, included as one of its aims the extension of the Chinese exclusion laws to all classes of Japanese and Koreans.[6] This kind of hostility against all Asians led some Koreans to turn to small businesses. However, as we will see, the Koreans were far less active in small businesses than the Chinese and the Japanese.

Filipinos immigrated as American nationals after the Philippine Islands were placed under American colonial rule as a result of the Spanish-American War in 1898. Filipinos had been granted the right to enter the United States freely under a legal arrangement with the United States until 1934 when the Tydings-McDuffie Independence Act conferred commonwealth status on the islands. The Filipinos arrived in Hawaii and on the West Coast, enticed by the agricultural industries which continued to seek cheap labor in the face of the growing difficulty of recruiting Chinese, Japanese, and Korean immigrants. The National Origins Act of 1924 effectively barred immigration from Asian nations other than the Philippine Islands. Thus, the decade of the 1920s saw a dramatic increase of Filipino immigrants; some 45,000 Filipinos arrived on the West Coast.

Filipinos were employed mostly as migratory farm workers whose lives were characterized by both a high geographical mobility and a lack of social stability.[7] They also encountered white hostility and agitation—especially during the Great Depression. In the 1950s and the early 1960s the Filipinos and the Mexicans were the major source of labor supply to California's agricultural industry.

Unlike the Chinese and the Japanese, they did not turn to small businesses as an alternative to being exploited and discriminated against in the general economy. This difference in the Filipinos' economic adjustment patterns is partly attributed to the fact that the Filipinos, consisting of divergent linguistic and racial groups, lacked cultural, religious, and racial homogeneity, a prerequisite to the formation of ethnic solidarity necessary for economic advancement in a hostile social environment.

ETHNIC RESOURCES

The Chinese and Japanese immigrants, as well as their second generations, were heavily concentrated in small business or service occupations. By 1920 more than 50 percent of the Chinese in the United States were employed or self-employed in restaurants or laundries. By 1919 the Japanese owned 47 percent of the hotels and 25 percent of the grocery stores in Seattle. By 1929 some 9,000, or 30 percent, of the Japanese in Los Angeles were engaged in small businesses ranging from groceries and fruit stands to hotels, cafés, restaurants, and barbershops. Given the structural factor or situational factor of the anti-Asian movement or racial discrimination, ethnic values and organizations contributed to the Japanese and Chinese overrepresentation in self-employment.

The Chinese, Japanese, and Koreans share a common value system largely derived from Confucianism. Asians cherish such Confucian values as a concern for propriety, the control of impulses and emotions, respect for age, devotion to the family, deference to authority, and diligence and industriousness. As William Caudill and George De Vos indicate, the Confucian values in a Japanese context are compatible with, but not identical to, white middle-class Protestant values such as emphasis on hard work, politeness, family authority, diligence, cleanliness, and neatness.[8]

Many social scientists and journalists have attributed the "Asian success" to the compatability of Asian cultural values with Protestant values. According to this cultural explanation of the "Asian success," Asians have achieved tremendous economic mobility by overcoming all kinds of adversity through their cultural strength.[9] They are dubbed a "model minority." This cultural thesis, although a useful theoretical framework for partial explanation of the "Asian success," should be subject to refinement and delimitation. First, it should be distinguished from Max Weber's thesis of individualistic, achievement-oriented Protestant ethics as a spiritual foundation of modern, rational capitalism, for it emphasizes a pre-modern, collective solidarity and achievement as expressed in Confucian familism. Second, the cultural thesis ignores the "class" resources or factors associated with the differential mobility patterns of Asian groups.

Given the whites' agitation and hostility against all Asian groups and the commonality of cultural values of the Chinese, Japanese, and Koreans, the degree of occupational expansion and adjustment was nonetheless significantly different from one group to another. The Japanese were more successful and mobile than other Asian groups. The Japanese immigrants and their children, the Nisei, entered and prospered in major small businesses and the agricultural industry on the West Coast. Compared with the Japanese and the Chinese, Korean ventures into business enterprises were quite insignificant. Before the end of World War II, according to Choy Bong-youn, fewer than 5 percent were engaged in business, individually or on a partnership or corporate basis.[10] The answer to this different pattern of economic adjustment among Asian groups can be found in the pre-emigration socioeconomic characteristics of immigrants.

The Japanese immigrants had been exposed to Japanese modernization prior to their entry into the United States. They experienced the process of a great transformation from a feudal to an urban industrial society, which was set in motion by the Meiji Restoration in 1867. The majority of Issei had the equivalent of an eighth-grade education. They were young, ambitious, and ready to seize their economic opportunities. They came with modernized "class" resources to be utilized for their economic ventures.[11]

In contrast, the Chinese and Korean immigrants were largely drawn from uneducated, unskilled, "pre-modern" peasants and laborers.[12] Most of the Korean immigrants, too, were common laborers from Korean port cities and towns. These differences in socioeconomic characteristics among Asian groups had a great effect on the different patterns of economic adjustments.

ETHNIC ORGANIZATIONS

Ethnic organizations formed another resource which was central to Asian solidarity in business enterprise in America. The Chinese and the Japanese formed ethnic organizations to develop the resources of entrepreneurship as well as to control intraethnic competition and conflict. Again, the communal or ethnic solidarity was derived from the cultural baggage which immigrants brought with them.

Chinese immigrants organized Hui, an association in which each member was obliged to contribute a stipulated sum of money to a common pool. A member in need of a lump sum of money would receive it through either a bidding system or a lottery system. A member could receive the lump sum only once, rotating the turn until the outstanding member automatically received the total. Memberships were usually restricted to persons from the same village or district in China. This financial cooperative system was an ancient institution prevalent in variant forms in China, Korea, and Japan. The Japanese and Koreans called it, respectively, Ko and Kye. The Japanese Ko association, like the Hui association, had its membership restricted to immigrants from the same prefecture or village. Ko meetings were combined with social and recreational activities. This financial cooperative system or rotating credit association, as Ivan Light has indicated, was decisive to the capitalization of both Chinese and Japanese business enterprises when both groups were discriminated against in securing loans from white-owned banks.[13] According to Kim Hyung-chan, Korean immigrants did not organize Kye associations with the same characteristics of the Hui or the Ko.[14] The answer as to why Korean immigrants did not transplant their traditional economic organization in America may be found in a demographic factor. The total number of Koreans—some 10,000—was so small and so scattered over the West Coast and the Hawaiian Islands that they could not form territorial communities. This demographic factor might have prevented them from organizing informal organizations whose memberships were derived from the same regions or clans in Korea.

The Chinese and Japanese rotating credit associations were a derivative of regional or clan associations, for they were operated within the context of regional or clan ties. The Japanese founded regional associations, or the *kenjinkai*, whose memberships were based on the provincial origin of immigrants. The formal functions of the *kenjinkai* were social and benevolent: *kenjinkai* gave social welfare assistance to destitute or needy members. The *kenjinkai* also acted as an employment agency for members and organizations of rotating credit associations, and supported the organization and operation of Japanese trade guilds such as boardinghouses and hotels, shoemakers, restaurants, and grocery stores. By both controlling the location of shops and protecting the interests of its members in various ways, the Japanese trade guild played a key role in the Japanese concentration in small businesses. The *kenjinkai* also supplied Japanese agricultural labor to California farmers through the Japanese "boss" system.

The Japanese "boss" was an ethnic labor broker with the multiple roles of recruiting, supervising, and representing Japanese workers. He was dependent on the *kenjinkai* for the supply of his agricultural crew.

Because virtually all Chinese immigrants came from several districts of Kwangtung in southern China, predominantly from Toishan District, it was quite natural for them to form district associations or *hui kuan*. The confederation of district associations is now officially known as the Chinese Consolidated Benevolent Association, an informal government in Chinatown. The *kenjinkai* and the *hui kuan* had the same functional characteristics. But the scope of organizational characteristics of the *hui kuan* was much more inclusive than that of the *kenjinkai*. Being involuntarily segregated from the larger society and being less urbanized and modernized than the Japanese, the Chinese in Chinatown were dependent on the *hui kuan* for almost all life activities.[15]

Reflecting Confucian familism, the Chinese also organized clan or family associations on the basis of surnames. The memberships of the *hui kuan* and clan association overlapped, for the memberships of the clan association included everyone bearing the same name, regardless of lineage. There was some overlapping of activities between the *hui kuan* and clan association. But the clan association tended to focus on benevolent and fraternal activities, whereas the *hui kuan* accentuated business and political matters.

THE NEW ECONOMIC STRUCTURE AFTER WORLD WAR II

World War II effected a great deal of change in the economy of Asian Americans. The U. S. government played a key role in determining the opportunities of both Asian Americans and the prospective immigrants from Asian nations. The United States repealed the Chinese exclusion acts to show good will to Nationalist China, an ally of the United States against the Japanese aggression. A token immigration quota was given to China. Chinese women were admitted as non-quota immigrants under the provisions of the War Brides and G. I. Fiancees Act. The provisions greatly facilitated the influx of women from other Asian nations—the Philippines, Japan, and Korea. The defeat of Chiang Kai-shek's forces on mainland China effected the political exodus of Chinese intellectuals, students, government officials, and businessmen to the United States. The U. S. occupation of South Korea after World War II and its military involvement in the Korean War (1950–1953) were pre-emigration factors critical to Korean immigration after World War II. Korean refugees, war brides, orphans, and students began to enter the United States. All these post-World War II immigrants promoted a source of change in the Asian economic structure.

Japanese Americans, however, had experienced great economic and psychological loss during World War II owing to the U. S. government's prejudice toward them. The Japanese attack on Pearl Harbor on December 7, 1941, set in motion a final solution to the "Japanese problem" in California. A complex interplay of wartime hysteria, patriotism, and white farmers' economic interests led President Franklin D. Roosevelt to sign Executive Order 9066 on February 19, 1942, which empowered military commanders to remove "dangerous persons" from designated areas. As a result, more than 110,000 Japanese, the majority of whom were native-born American citizens, were removed to concentration camps. The evacuation meant the loss of homes, neighbors, farmland, and businesses. On June 16, 1983, the Commission on Wartime Relocation and Internment of Civilians, established in 1980 by Congress, recommended that the U. S. government pay $20,000 to each of the 60,000 surviving Japanese Americans who had been held in the concentration camps. The evacuation, which had shattered the close-knit Japanese community, generated an unintended consequence: it greatly contributed to the Japanese economic and cultural assimilation to the larger society.

The wartime manpower shortage and the rapid economic development after World War II opened up economic opportunities to Asians. They began to enter technical, administrative, professional, white collar occupations. The second- or third-generation Chinese and Japanese were no longer confined to small businesses based on ethnic resources. In addition, all kinds of federal anti-discrimination policies and legislation, most of which were formulated and enacted in the 1960s, facilitated a tremendous economic mobility of the second or third generation of Asians. Asians began to tap and utilize "class" resources such as proficiency in English, marketable skills, and professional licenses for their upward social mobility. A bipolarity of Asian occupational structure was shaped: Asians overrepresented labor-intensive, service, small business and professional, technical, white collar professions. Asian professionals or new middle classes were well integrated into the corporate capitalism in the United States. Many Asian business enterprises, free of ethnic resources, emerged and constituted an integral part of the general economy. This new economic pattern of Asian Americans has been increasing with the influx of new Asian immigrants after the passage of the Immigration Act of 1965.

During the 1965–1981 period, a total of 2.1 million Asian immigrants entered the United States. They came largely from the Philippines, South Korea, the two Chinas including Hong Kong, India, and Vietnam. In 1981 Asia overtook North/Central America, including the Caribbean Islands, as the largest source of immigrants to the United States. Unlike the earlier Asian immigrants, the overwhelming majority of the new Asian immigrants were drawn from large cities in their home countries. They had undergone urbanization or modernization prior to their entry into the United States. A high proportion of them were well-educated, middle-class, professionals, students, and businessmen. Some 70,000 Asian medical professionals—physicians, nurses, and pharmacists—came from the Philippines, South Korea, and India. A majority of Asians, with the exception of South Asian refugees, brought with them "class" resources such as education, dollars, and professional skills, a key factor in their rapid upward economic mobility in the "post-industrial" American society.

According to the 1980 U. S. Census, 37 percent of Asian immigrants—Chinese, Koreans, Asian Indians, and Filipinos—received four or more years of college education, in sharp contrast with 16 percent of the native-born Americans. Asians, including native-born Americans of Asian ancestry, had higher median family income than whites: $22,075 for Asians against $20,980 for whites. According to the Census, 42 percent of the Asians were suburbanized or settled in suburbs surrounding large central cities, whereas 36 percent of the whites were. This upward mobility pattern is partly attributed to the fact that Asians have more family members working than other ethnic groups. According to the Census, 63 percent of Asian families, but only 55 percent of white families, had two or more workers. However, Asians had a higher poverty rate than whites: 13 percent of Asians were below poverty level compared with 9 percent of whites. Given the average family income figures, this indicates a widening income gap or class division among Asians.

The 1980 Census confirmed the bipolarity of the Asian occupational structure: 56 percent of the employed Asian immigrants—Chinese, Korean, Asian Indians, Filipinos, and Vietnamese—engaged in managerial, professional, technical, and administrative occupations; another 33 percent were found both in menial labor-intensive service occupations and in unskilled or semi-skilled jobs. The representation of Asian immigrants in both farming and fishing industries and in higher paid skilled blue collar occupations was insignificant. Two factors are responsible for the bipolarity. The first factor is the emergence of highly mobile, white collar, professional Asian "yuppies" among both native-born and foreign-born Asians. Their upward mobility has been facilitated by affirmative action programs and "spirit," as well as other federal policies and programs for racial minorities. The other factor is the Asian—especially Korean, Chinese, and Asian Indian—concentration in small businesses. In 1976, for instance, 34 percent of Korean male householders in the New York metropolitan areas were running commercial businesses, compared with 16 percent for native-born whites across the nation. Asian immigrant businesses such as Korean fruit and vegetable stores, Asian Indian newsstands, Chinese restaurants, and garment industries recruit workers from among their own immigrant group, thus creating the concentration of Asian immigrant labor in service or unskilled jobs.

Asian immigrant businessmen also take advantage of the development of international trade between the United States and Asian nations—especially South Korea, Hong Kong, and Taiwan. The total volume of U. S. trade with Asia has exceeded that with Europe. Asian immigrants have emerged as agents facilitating trade. In Los Angeles, for instance, some 7,000 Korean business enterprises were identified in 1983, of which some 300 were trading companies dealing with South Korean products. In 1983 California's total trade volume was over $71 billion; over two-thirds of this trade was with nations along the Pacific Rim. In this context, Asian Americans will increasingly play a key role in further developing international trade with the Pacific.

NOTES

1. Stanford M. Lyman, *Chinese Americans* (New York: Random House, 1974), p. 73.

2. H. Brett Melendy, *The Oriental Americans* (New York: Hippocrene Books, 1972), p. 53.

3. Harry H. L. Kitano, *Japanese Americans: The Evolution of a Subculture* (Englewood Cliffs, N. J.: Prentice-Hall, 1969), p. 15.

4. Stephen Thernstrom, ed., *Harvard Encyclopedia of American Ethnic Groups* (Cambridge: Belknap Press of Harvard University Press, 1980), p. 563.

5. Roger Daniels, *The Politics of Prejudice* (Gloucester, Mass.: Peter Smith, 1966), pp. 11–12.

6. Raymond Leslie Buell, "Anti-Japanese Agitation in the United States," *Political Science Quarterly* 37 (1922):614–23.

7. Grayson Kirk, "The Filipinos," *Annals of the American Academy of Political and Social Science* 367 (1966):44–52.

8. William Caudill and George De Vos, "Achievement, Culture and Personality: The Case of the Japanese Americans," *American Anthropologist* 58 (1956):1103–26.

9. See William Petersen, "Success Story, Japanese American Style," *New York Times*, January 9, 1966.

10. Bong-youn Choy, *Koreans in America* (Chicago: Nelson-Hall, 1979), p. 128.

11. John Higham, ed., *Ethnic Leadership in America* (Baltimore: Johns Hopkins University Press, 1978), p. 63.

12. Elmer Clarence Sandmeyer, *The Anti-Chinese Movement in California* (Urbana: University of Illinois Press, 1978), p. 13.

13. Ivan H. Light, *Ethnic Enterprise in America* (Berkeley: University of California Press, 1972), pp. 19–61.

14. Hyung-chan Kim, "Ethnic Enterprises Among Korean Immigrants in America," in Hyung-chan Kim, ed., *The Korean Diaspora* (Santa Barbara: ABC-Clio Press, 1977), p. 104.

15. Illsoo Kim, *New Urban Immigrants: The Korean Community in New York* (Princeton, N. J.: Princeton University Press, 1981), p. 102.

Asian Americans and American Education

BOB H. SUZUKI

This essay provides a brief overview of the education of Asian Americans in the United States. The first section summarizes the historical background of the education of Asian Americans, beginning with their immigration in the 1840s. The second section describes the educational attainment and socioeconomic status of Asian Americans and the relationship between these two social indices. Finally, the third section discusses some of the present and future problems and issues in education facing Asian Americans.

The term "Asian American" as used here refers primarily to the three largest Asian American ethnic groups: the Chinese, the Filipinos, and the Japanese. Information on other groups, such as the Koreans and the Indochinese, is still quite limited because of their smaller numbers and relatively recent history in the United States.

HISTORICAL BACKGROUND

The first of the Asian immigrants, the Chinese, began to arrive in the United States in the late 1840s. The vast majority of these early Chinese immigrants were poor and largely uneducated peasants, nearly all single males who were unmarried or had left their wives at home. In 1882, as a result of a virulent anti-Chinese movement, Chinese immigration was brought to a halt by an exclusion act passed by the U. S. Congress.[1]

The major proportion of the Japanese immigrants arrived in Hawaii and on the U. S. mainland between 1890 and 1920. They were brought in to work as cheap laborers in many of the same areas in which the earlier Chinese immigrants had worked. Unlike the Chinese immigrants, many of them were able to bring their wives with them or to get married through "picture-bride" marriages arranged through photographs. In 1924 another exclusion act was passed by the U. S. Congress prohibiting further immigration from Japan.[2]

The last of the Asian immigrants to arrive were the Filipinos. Most of them began to immigrate in the early 1900s and continued to arrive until the mid–1930s, when yet another congressional exclusionary act brought their immigration to a halt. The first few Filipino immigrants were mostly students. However, the much larger numbers of immigrants who came later were mostly young males who, like the Chinese and Japanese, were recruited as cheap laborers.[3]

The discrimination encountered by the early Asian immigrants was pervasive, and it also affected the education of their children. A segregated Oriental School in San Francisco's Chinatown was created by the city's Board of Education in 1885. The school segregation of Chinese children in California lasted until at least 1946.[4]

In 1906, because of intense anti-Asian hostility, the San Francisco Board of Education attempted to segregate Japanese children in the segregated Oriental School. However, as a result of vociferous protests from Japan, the matter became an international incident, and the board was ultimately forced to rescind its action. However, in other areas of California, such as the Sacramento River Delta, Japanese children were forced to attend segregated schools with other minority children up until World War II.[5]

In Hawaii, through the 1920s and 1930s, so-called English Standard elementary and secondary schools were established. Only students who passed an English Standard examination could attend these schools; others had to attend the regular public schools. The vast majority of the students who passed the examination were white, whereas the vast majority who failed were Asian. Thus, the English Standard schools served, in effect, to partially segregate the public schools until after World War II.[6]

With the outbreak of World War II, anti-Asian hostility lessened toward the Chinese, Filipinos, and Koreans. It intensified against the Japanese, however, resulting in the incarceration of over 110,000 Japanese Americans on the West Coast in detention camps.[7] With the end of World War II, discrimination against Asian Americans gradually began to subside. Several blatantly discriminatory laws against Asians, such as the alien land laws, were repealed, and naturalization rights were finally extended to resident Asian aliens. Job opportunities for Asian Americans also began to increase in the 1950s with the rapid post-war expansion of the American economy.

Perhaps the most significant change was the passage in 1965 of a more equitable immigration law, which finally lifted the discriminatory restrictions against Asians imposed by previous legislation. Partially as a result of this law, immigration from Asia, particularly from Hong Kong, Taiwan, Korea, and the Philippines, increased enormously. Much of the several-fold increase in the Chinese, Filipino, and Korean populations in the United States since 1965 has been the result of this recent immigration. There has also been an influx of over 500,000 Indochinese into this country since the end of the Vietnam War in 1975.

EDUCATIONAL ATTAINMENT AND SOCIOECONOMIC STATUS

The 1980 U. S. Census counted approximately 3.7 million Asians and Pacific Islanders living in the United States, amounting to about 1.6 percent of the total U. S. population. The three largest Asian ethnic groups were the Chinese, Filipinos and Japanese, with populations of 812,000, 782,000, and 716,000, respectively. There were also some 387,000 Asian Indians, 357,000 Koreans, and 245,000 Vietnamese.[8]

According to a 1978 survey of the U. S. Office of Civil Rights, 593,597, or 1.4 percent, of the 41,836,257 students enrolled in public elementary and secondary schools (K–12) in the fall of 1978 were Asian/Pacific Americans (APAs).[9] Over 86,000, or 14.5 percent, of these APA students were limited- or non-English speaking. Only 54 percent of these limited- or non-English speaking APA students were receiving English-as-a-second language (ESL) or bilingual education services. These figures may be compared with the 1980 U. S. Census data which showed that 809,475 of the 47,245,559 students enrolled in grades K–12 were APAs.

Data collected by the National Center for Education Statistics in the fall of 1978 showed that 238,382 APA students were enrolled in colleges and that they constituted 2.1 percent of the total student enrollment in institutions of higher education. Approximately 180,000 of these students were undergraduates, and the remainder were graduate students, in professional schools, or unclassified.[10] Again, these figures may be compared with the 1980 U. S. Census data which showed that 378,199 APA students were enrolled in college and that 278,234 of them were undergraduates. These data indicate that APAs attend institutions of higher education in considerably higher proportions than their representation in the general population.

The Census data also show that Asian Americans are among the most highly educated ethnic groups in the country. In particular, the 1970 U. S. Census found that the median years of schooling completed was 12.5 for Chinese, 12.5 for Japanese, and 12.2 for Filipinos, compared to 12.2 for the U. S. population as a whole. Comparable figures for each of these three groups are not yet available from the 1980 U. S. Census. However, for APAs as a group, the 1980 U.S. Census found that the median years of schooling completed was 13.0, compared to 12.6 for the U. S. population as a whole.

Income figures for the three groups are equally impressive. In 1969 the median annual family income was $10,600 for Chinese, $12,500 for Japanese, and $9,300 for Filipinos compared to $9,600 for U. S. families as a whole. Again, comparable figures for each of these groups are not yet available from the 1980 U. S. Census but, for APAs as a group, the median annual family income in 1979 was $22,713, compared with $19,917 for U. S. families as a whole.

These glowing social indices on Asian Americans have led a number of writers to hail them as the "model minority" who have overcome the adversities of racial discrimination through hard work, patience, and perseverance to achieve unparalleled success in American society. Indeed, an article in *Newsweek* magazine proclaimed that Japanese Americans were "outwhiting the whites," implying that they were even more successful than whites.[11]

Although the statistics cited appear to lend support to this "model minority" image of Asian Americans, a number of Asian American social scientists who have analyzed the data more closely and critically have taken strong exception to this characterization and have found it to be inaccurate, misleading, and a gross overgeneralization.[12] Athough many Asian Americans have, indeed, achieved middle-class status, the U. S. Census, including the 1980 Census, has consistently shown that there is a far larger proportion of people with incomes below the poverty level among Asian Americans than among whites. Many of these poorer Asian Americans live in inner-city ghettos, such as the Chinatowns and Manilatowns, which are often among the most impoverished areas of the cities in which they are located.

Even for the more educated, middle-class Asian Americans, the "model minority" stereotype remains quite problematic. Although the median incomes of Asian American families are higher than those of white families, the median incomes of individuals are found to be lower for Asian Americans than for whites. This apparent paradox is due to the following factors: (1) there is a larger proportion of Asian American families in which both spouses work than among white families, (2) Asian American children remain with the family longer and thereby contribute longer to family income, and (3) Asian-American families are larger on the average and, therefore, have more earners contributing to family income.

Furthermore, when income figures for Asian Americans are adjusted for such demographic variables as education, age, geographic location, and hours per week worked, it is found that they are earning considerably less than their white counterparts. On the basis of such an analysis, it can be said that Asian Americans are typically underemployed in lower level positions that are not commensurate with their levels of education, age, and experience. Although Asian Americans have invested heavily in education, it obviously does not gain nearly as much earning power for Asian Americans as it does for whites. This disparity has been largely attributed to the persistence of racial discrimination.

PRESENT AND FUTURE PROBLEMS AND ISSUES IN EDUCATION

In view of the educational attainments of Asian Americans, it may seem absurd even to suggest that serious educational problems exist for Asian Americans. Indeed, educators almost universally see Asian American students as industrious, conscientious, and well-behaved high achievers. Such a view is superficial at best, and its perpetuation will worsen the widespread misconceptions that have impeded efforts to identify and meet the educational needs of Asian American students.

In this section, some of the present and future problems and issues facing Asian Americans in education are discussed. These problems and issues may be categorized into the following general areas: (1) bilingual education, (2) multicultural education, (3) adult education, (4) higher education, and (5) parental and community involvement in education.

Bilingual Education

The 1980 U. S. Census data indicate that over 50 percent of the current Asian American population are recent immigrants who are limited- or non-English speaking. Consequently, many of them face formidable language and cultural barriers that affect their lives in major ways. This lack of English competency is particularly debilitating for teenagers who often experience severely dysfunctional family/school discontinuities, become alienated from school, and drop out. A number of them end up joining youth gangs which are gaining notoriety for their involvement in criminal activities, including a number of gang-related slayings that have been sensationalized by the press.[13]

Under these circumstances, bilingual education is clearly one of the pressing needs of a substantial proportion of the Asian American student population. Because of the projected major influx of Asian immigrants over the foreseeable future, this need is likely to grow. Although a survey in 1980 identified over 450 Asian bilingual education programs throughout the nation, they appear to be underfinanced and are often fragmented and uncoordinated. Moreover, as a result of a shortage of qualified bilingual teachers and the unavailability of adequate curriculum materials, there are still numbers of limited- and non-English speaking Asian American students whose needs are not being met.[14]

Multicultural Education

American-born Asian students who are quite competent in English are not without their problems in the schools either. They face many subtle forms of discrimination in their education because of the ''Anglo-centric'' orientation of most schools. For example, the curriculum usually projects negative stereotypes of Asian Americans, or omits their experiences and contributions altogether. Such distortions and omissions subtly convey the message that Asian Americans have little significance, a message that can have detrimental effects on the self-concepts of Asian American students.[15]

Another common problem is that teachers often stereotype Asian American students as industrious, conscientious high achievers, especially in math and science. Students who do not fulfill this stereotype may have unrealistic expectations imposed on them. Those who do are often counseled in disproportionate numbers into the technical/scientific fields. Asian American students are also frequently stereotyped as quiet, docile, and exceptionally well behaved. Students who do not conform to this stereotype, but are boisterous, assertive, and aggressive, may be considered unusual by teachers, even though similar behavior by non-Asian students would be accepted as normal. Such treatment by teachers may partially explain why Asian American students frequently do not develop the ability to express and assert themselves verbally, become overly conforming, and have their academic and social development narrowly circumscribed.[16]

These problems in cross-cultural conflict could be ameliorated to a considerable degree if schools would adopt a multicultural approach to education. Such an approach requires major changes in school curricula and teaching practices. Multiple learning environments would have to be provided that match the academic and social needs of students from a variety of cultural backgrounds. However, as is often the case, if multicultural education is implemented in superficial ways, such as by simply incorporating ethnic content into the curriculum, it will have little or no impact on improving the school environment for Asian American and other minority students.[17]

Adult Education

The enormous influx of Asian immigrants since 1965 has created a major need for adult education programs. Many of these immigrants must seek gainful employment immediately upon arrival in order to subsist. Yet, because most of them are limited- or non-English speaking, they are in urgent need of gaining competency in English. Many of them would also like to learn a new vocation to enable them to obtain jobs with opportunities for advancement and decent pay. However, as a result of the lack of appropriate adult education programs, a large proportion of them find themselves trapped in low-paying, dead-end, and menial jobs.[18]

These problems are exacerbated for Asian immigrants who are in their late teens and early twenties. As indicated earlier, these young adults often drop out of school, and many of them join youth gangs. Because they speak little or no English and have no high school diploma, their chances of finding a decent job are practically nil.

To meet the different needs of these groups, a variety of well-conceived, innovative programs in adult education are needed. These programs should offer both English language instruction and vocational training. They should also include culturally sensitive approaches to job placement and family counseling. Although a few such programs exist, they are hardly sufficient to meet existing needs, much less future needs.

Higher Education

As shown earlier, Asian Americans are enrolled in colleges and universities in higher proportion to their representation in the general population. Despite this high college-going rate, Asian Americans face a number of serious problems in higher education.

Studies have indicated that a disproportionate number of Asian Americans pursue degrees in the technical/scientific disciplines, such as engineering, accounting, and computer science. On the other hand, there is an underrepresentation of Asian Americans in such fields as the humanities, arts, and social sciences. This state of affairs has been attributed to cultural orientation, the influences of schooling, and racial discrimination.[19]

In recent years, increasing numbers of Asian American students from low-income and/or recent-immigrant families have gone on to college, even though many of them are ill prepared to do so. Because such students often lack financial aid, have inadequate competency in English, and do not receive adequate tutorial and remedial assistance once they are on campus, many of them drop out after one or two terms.

Although the enrollment of Asian American students in institutions of higher education has increased markedly, Asian American Studies programs appear to be on the decline as a result of budgetary cutbacks, declining interest, and changing priorities. Yet, these programs have demonstrated that they meet important academic and social needs of Asian American students, as well as contribute significantly to the body of knowledge of Asian Americans.

Asian Americans appear to be well represented on the faculties of institutions of higher education. However, American-born Asians are still underrepresented on higher education faculties and are outnumbered 10 to 1 by foreign-born Asians. It should also be noted that very few Asian American faculty have been appointed to positions as senior-level academic administrators.[20]

The problems described above will require a variety of approaches to solve. Pre-college and in-college counseling programs are needed to assist Asian American students to explore a wider range of career options. Programs in Asian American Studies, for remedial instruction in basic skills, for bilingual tutoring, and in cross-cultural psychological counseling need to be instituted and/or expanded to meet the social, psychological, and academic needs of Asian American students. Finally, institutions of higher education must become more sensitive to the problems faced by Asian American faculty and pursue affirmative action more vigorously on their behalf.

Parental and Community Involvement in Education

Asian American parents are usually both very concerned and involved with their children's education. However, because of the respect they have traditionally accorded teachers, they are often reluctant to complain when they are dissatisfied with the education their children are receiving. Their reluctance is compounded by the insensitivity of many teachers to the special problems and needs of Asian American students.

Because an unusually high proportion of Asian American families have two working parents, they often find it difficult to attend conferences with teachers or PTA meetings. Furthermore, many of them distrust and are intimidated by the large, impersonal bureaucracies of most urban school systems. Because of these barriers, Asian Americans in some communities have organized themselves so that they can act collectively in getting school systems to address the problems and needs of Asian American students.

To overcome these problems, teachers and administrators must become more knowledgeable of and sensitive to the special problems and needs of Asian American students. They must also become more familiar with the nature and functioning of Asian American families. For their part, Asian American community organizations need to become more involved in the educational arena by supporting candidates for school board elections and by speaking for the interests of Asian American students before school boards and other governmental bodies that influence education. School administrators need to devise ways of reducing the structural barriers between the schools and parents.

NOTES

1. Mary R. Coolidge, *Chinese Immigration* (New York: Arno Press Reprint, 1969); Betty Sung, *The Story of the Chinese in America* (New York: Collier Books, 1967).

2. Yamato Ichihashi, *Japanese in the United States* (New York: Arno Press Reprint, 1969); Bill Hosokawa, *Nisei: The Quiet Americans* (New York: William Morrow and Co., 1969).

3. H. Brett Melendy, *The Oriental Americans* (Boston: Twayne Publishers, 1972); Bruno Lasker, *Filipino Immigration to the Continental United States and Hawaii* (Chicago: Chicago University Press, 1939).

4. Jack Chen, *The Chinese of America: From Beginning to the Present* (San Francisco: Harper and Row, 1981); Stanford Lyman, *Chinese Americans* (New York: Random House, 1974).

5. Roger Daniels, *The Politics of Prejudice* (Berkeley: University of California Press, 1962); Ken Suyama, "The Asian American Experience in the Sacramento River Delta," in A. Tachiki et al., eds., *Roots: An Asian American Reader* (Los Angeles: University of California Press, 1971).

6. Lawrence Fuchs, *Hawaii Pono: A Social History* (New York: Harcourt, Brace and World, 1961).

7. Michi Weglyn, *Years of Infamy: The Untold Story of America's Concentration Camps* (New York: William Morrow and Co., 1976); Audrie Girdner and Anne Loftis, *The Great Betrayal: The Evacuation of the Japanese Americans During World War II* (London: Macmillan, 1969).

8. U.S. Bureau of the Census, *Asian and Pacific Islander Population by State: 1980*, PC80-S1-12 (Washington, D. C.: U. S. Government Printing Office, 1983).

9. U. S. Office of Civil Rights, *State, Regional and National Summaries of Data from the 1978 Civil Rights Survey of Elementary and Secondary Schools* (Alexandria, Va.: Killalea Associates, 1980). It should also be noted here that Pacific Americans comprised only 7 percent of the total APA population counted in the 1980 U. S. Census.

They included 172,346 Hawaiians, 39,520 Samoans, 30,695 Guamanians, and 17,005 "Other Pacific Islander" persons.

10. National Center for Education Statistics, *Fall Enrollment in Higher Education, 1978* (Washington, D. C.: U. S. Department of Education, 1980).

11. William Petersen, "Chinese and Japanese Americans," in Thomas Sowell, ed., *Essays and Data on American Ethnic Groups* (Washington, D. C.: Urban Institute, 1978); "Success Story of One Minority Group in U. S.," *U. S. News and World Report,* December 26, 1966, pp. 73–76; "Success Story: Outwhiting the Whites," *Newsweek,* June 21, 1971, pp. 24–25.

12. Ki-Taek Chun, "The Myth of Asian American Success and Its Educational Ramifications," *IRCD Bulletin* 15, nos. 1 & 2, (1980): 1–12; Bob H. Suzuki, "Education and the Socialization of Asian Americans: A Revisionist Analysis of the 'Model Minority' Thesis," *Amerasia Journal* 4, no. 2 (1977):23–52; Amado Y. Cabezas, "A View of Poor Linkages Between Education, Occupation and Earnings for Asian Americans," Paper presented at the Third National Forum on Education and Work, San Francisco, 1977.

13. Betty L. Sung, *Gangs in New York's Chinatown* (New York: Department of Asian Studies, City University of New York, 1977); Robin Wu, "Front Page Chinatown: What the *** Is Going on?" *Bridge* 5 (Fall 1977): 4–7.

14. Asian American Bilingual Center et al., *Directory of Asian and Pacific American Bilingual Programs in the United States* (Berkeley, Calif.: Asian American Bilingual Center, 1980).

15. Albert H. Yee, "Myopic Perceptions and Textbooks: Chinese Americans Search for Identity," *Journal of Social Issues* 15, no. 2 (1973): 99–113; "Asian Americans in Children's Books," *Interracial Books for Children Bulletin* 7, nos. 2 & 3 (1976): 1–34.

16. Colin Watanabe, "Self-Expression and the Asian American Experience," *Personnel and Guidance Journal* 51 (February 1973): 390–96.

17. Robert H. Suzuki, "Curriculum Transformation for Multicultural Education," *Education and Urban Society* 16, no. 3 (1984): 294–322; Nicholas Appleton, *Cultural Pluralism in Education: Theoretical Foundations* (New York: Longman, 1983).

18. Betty L. Sung, *A Survey of Chinese-American Manpower and Employment* (New York: Praeger, 1976).

19. Watanabe, "Self-Expression and the Asian American Experience"; Derald W. Sue and Austin C. Frank, "A Typological Approach to the Psychological Study of Chinese and Japanese American College Males," *Journal of Social Issues* 29, no. 2 (1973): 129–48.

20. Dorothy M. Gilford and Joan Snyder, *Women and Minority Ph. D.'s in the 1970s: A Data Book* (Washington, D. C.: National Academy of Sciences, 1977); Thomas Sowell, *Affirmative Action Reconsidered* (Washington, D. C.: American Enterprise Institute, 1975).

Asian Americans and Mental Health

HYUNG-CHAN KIM AND MARK PETERSEN

The United States has often been called a nation of immigrants. For three and a half centuries people from many nations have come to the "melting pot" to seek fortunes, start new lives, or escape political or religious persecution. Americans of Asian ancestry share this background with Americans of other origins. Asian Americans include ethnically diverse people of Japan, China, Korea, Southeast Asia, the Philippines, and the Pacific Islands of Hawaii, Samoa, and Guam. They are one of the nation's fastest growing populations: according to the 1980 census, the number of Americans of Asian ancestry and of Pacific Island origin has ballooned by 120 percent over the past decade to 3.5 million and this population is expected to reach 10 million by 2000 A.D.

In order to understand the psychological orientation of the Asian Americans one must have some idea of their cultural background and the roles that assimilation and acculturation play in the lives of immigrants and of their descendants. When we speak of a group's culture, we are referring to certain shared experiences that result in ways of perceiving, interpreting, and behaving. Whether it be the Chinese Americans with a longer history in the United States than the Korean Americans, or the now emerging Vietnamese Americans, each group has its own history and culture. A culture is a functional whole and the disruption of a single aspect of a particular culture may upset its balance. The assimilation and acculturation process has been shown to play a key role in the development of the Asian American personality as it develops in the host country.

The results of a study by Fong[1] indicate that as the Chinese Americans become increasingly exposed to the values and standards of the larger host culture, there is a progressive inculcation of those norms. It further shows that those Chinese families which had been in the United States for two or more generations have largely assimilated. In several other studies the number of generations in the United States has been singled out as a measure of assimilation. In comparing first, second and third generations of Japanese Americans with Caucasian Americans, Conner[2] found that the number of the generation was directly related to the strength of self-reported "American" identity. Although Japanese Americans had higher scores than Caucasian Americans on a questionnaire dealing with family cohesiveness, Sansei (third-generation Japanese Americans) were closer to the Caucasian Americans than were earlier generations of Japanese Americans. This whole process of acculturation and assimilation adds much stress and anxiety to the entire development of the Asian American family. The degree of tension will depend on the stage of acculturation that a family has reached.

Racism, individual and institutional, is another force that affects Asian Americans. Individual racism involves a person's attitudes and behaviors towards Asian Americans; this can also be a positive prejudice. Institutional racism refers to systematic discrimination in various institutions, i. e., laws, education, government, and industry. According to Sue and Morishima,[3] Asian Americans encounter an oppressed image which casts them as the victims of racism. Statistics on their well-being tend to be misleading and often ignore the major problems that they encounter as a result of prejudice and discrimination. It is important to understand those patterns that have evolved around values, interactions, stereotypes, and practices between Asian Americans and the American society.

A third major force which is important in the development of the Asian Americans is the family. In American society the individual moves away from the family to go on his own. However, in Asian American culture, the trend is to place great emphasis on the family as the central unit. Most family theories and research focus on Japanese and Chinese Americans. Two main theorists, Hsu and De Vos, believe that the main characteristics of the Asian American family are achievement orientation, closeness, conformity, and the importance of the family; within the family, role structures and filial piety are emphasized. Hsu believes that the Chinese American family is better able to satisfy a basic need for interpersonal intimacy and to provide social support. De Vos contends that the integrity of Japanese American family roles and structures defends against the impact of stress.

There is much pressure placed upon the individual by the family to gain a good education, to be obedient to parents, and to give the family a good name. Exhibiting anti-social behavior or low achievement brings shame to the entire family. Guilt is used as a controlling technique by the parents to maintain individual obligation to the family. Research investigations have shown that there are changing attitudes on family practices and child rearing due to the assimilation process. Conner[4] found that the later generations of American-born Japanese had a weaker tendency to identify with, and to respect, the family name.

An Asian American personality paradigm, developed by Sue and Sue[5] viewed the Asian American on a spectrum of development. The Sues not only considered Asian and American culture but also racism as factors that influence personality. They developed a typological scheme to describe what they saw as the "types." The first type, the "traditionalist," strongly adheres to and internalizes Asian values. They identify with their particular culture and conform to parental wishes; they also tend to socialize with members of their own ethnic group. The second type, the "marginal" individual, adapts to Western values, rejects ethnic values, and often exhibits racial self-hatred. Marginal individuals tend to associate with Caucasian Americans and are at the opposite end of the acculturation-assimilation dimension from the traditionalists. The third type, the "Asian American," attempts to formulate a new identity by integrating ethnic values, Western influences, and minority group experiences. They tend to make alliances with Asian Americans and other oppressed minority groups. The main issue for the Asian Americans is not of assimilation versus separatism, but of personal respect versus disrespect by others. Aspects of cultural conflict and racism place the Asian American under a great deal of emotional stress. When these sources of stress become too great, mental health problems frequently result.

Are there specific kinds of mental health problems encountered by Asian Americans? According to Dohrenward and Dohrenward,[6] different cultural groups do have different distributions with respect to types of psychopathology, and cultural groups may manifest different symptoms of a disorder. In a study of behavioral patterns of Japanese and Filipino Americans, patients diagnosed as paranoid schizophrenic[7] results showed that the Japanese American group expressed more depression, withdrawal, and disturbances in inhibition and thinking, while the Filipino Americans exhibited greater delusions of persecution and overt signs of disturbed behavior. Finney's study[8] showed that different kinds of defense mechanisms were manifested by various ethnic groups. Asian Americans appear to believe that mental disturbance is associated with organic or somatic factors. It has been noted that Asian Americans, more frequently than Caucasian Americans, tend to express psychological distress through somatic complaints of pain or discomfort.[9] It is speculated that Asian American groups tend to somaticize due to their view of unity between physical and psychological status. Secondly, Asian groups tend to control self-disclosure; thus, physical complaints are an allowable form of expression of personal and interpersonal problems. The third speculation is that mental disturbance is highly stigmatized and reflects poorly on the family. Presently, there is a low visibility of mental illness among the Asian American people; this is largely due to fear of social stigma and the handling of problems within the family. The under-utilization of mental health services by Asian Americans was evidenced in a study by Sue and Sue.[10] The study indicates that the under-utilization of psychiatric clinics by Asians may be due to cultural factors rather than a paucity of mental problems.

What type of mental disorders are displayed by Asian Americans? In looking at mental disorders among the various groups of Asian Americans it is difficult to ascertain the reliability of the classification system used for the diagnosis of mental disorders. *The Diagnostic and Statistical Manual of the American Psychiatric Association* is the main tool used to diagnose mental disorders. A main question of the tool is: how valid is it to diagnose disorders between different groups. According to Sue,[11] Asian American clients do not seem to exhibit large differences from Caucasian American clients in diagnosis. However, among users of mental health services, Asian Americans are more likely to receive a psychotic diagnosis than Caucasian Americans. Also, the diagnosis of neurosis is greater among Asian Americans, especially anxiety neurosis. Occasionally, depressive neurosis is seen when an Asian American has been unable to fulfill the obligations of filial piety before his parents died. These findings may be attributable to various reasons: (1) The less severely disturbed Asian Americans avoid using mental health hospitals, thus the small number that do use them are more highly disturbed; (2) the diagnostic categories which were developed in a Western culture conceal striking and significant symptomatic differences between Western and non-Western groups. At this time few studies have been done to single out specific Asian American groups and their mental disorders. Methodological problems of doing research also play a key role in specifying the disorders of Asian Americans.

A key factor that plays a role in the development and continual growth of the Asian Americans is language. The common stereotype is that of the verbally inhibited Asian American. According to Kloph and Cambra,[12] Asian Americans appear to be less verbal because of personality of situational variables, i. e., conformity to authority, speech anxiety, and reserve. Cambra, Kloph, and Oka observed that anxiety or communication apprehension may have devastating consequences on well-being. According to Allard,[13] the language handicap has compelled many immigrants to seek employment in garment sweat shops. A major reason for continued language problems is the educational system which has failed to provide Asian American children with special programs to help them acquire language proficiency. Thus, language barriers not only hinder Asian Americans from succeeding in education, but also prevent them from integrating into the larger society. Narrow social networks remain among Asian Americans, and this process can not be widened into the host society.

A major factor in the language barrier is the communication between cultures, especially in the mental health field. The American society tends to promote directness and openess as its ideals. Within the Asian American community many variables play a significant role, i. e., status, concepts of obligation, shame and loss of face, among others. In order for the mental health worker to be accurate in his assessment of Asian Americans he must have knowledge of these important variables; otherwise, he may impose his own cultural views and values onto the Asian American mental health needs. It is important to note that Asian Americans do not communicate in direct verbal communication; thus, many messages may be communicated nonverbally. One new tool that is being utilized in the mental health field is ethnotherapy. In ethnotherapy, participants who share a common ethnic background are encouraged to air their feelings, positive and negative, about their heritage and talk about the conflicts. Ethnotherapy is a great tool in that it helps those participants who have internalized society's negative views of their ethnic group. At this time the issue of the language barrier is just beginning to be broken down.

In looking at Asian American crime and delinquency, little is actually known due to lack of information. Most studies in the past have focused on the Chinese and Japanese Americans. Studies by Abbot and Abbot[14] and Kitano[15] acknowledged that there is a low rate of crime and juvenile delinquency. According to Abbot and Abbot,[16] the relationship between family members and their psychosocial development represents a critical factor in juvenile delinquency in the Chinese American community. Kitano[17] summarized that Japanese delinquents do not identify with their ethnic community, are not a part of their families or neighborhoods, experience considerable family conflict, and evidence disturbed personalities. Sollenberger stated four reasons why the deliquency rate may be low for Chinese Americans: (1) An abundance of nurturance and protection during childhood; (2) physical aggression is discouraged from an early age; (3) the child comes from a tightly integrated family where mutual respect prevails; and (4) the child generally has wide exposure to positive models of behavior within the family and community.[18] Sue and Morishima briefly focussed on youth gangs in Chinatowns; they pointed to a study that linked the increased number of youth gangs with an increase in the number of youths, particularly immigrants, frustrations of racism and powerlessness, inability to succeed in school due to English language problems and cultural conflict, and the financial gains obtained through gang activities.[19] It is apparent that as the stressors continue to be increased upon the individual Asian American, the resultant stress will be manifested in their community.

Other areas of major concern are: (1) Programs should be developed to meet the needs of the elderly; (2) treatment centers should be located in the Asian American community and staffed with bilingual-bicultural professionals; (3) research methodologies should be developed to ascertain information concerning individual Asian American groups, thus attaining more accurate information; and (4) a more accurate diagnostic tool should be developed for assessing mental health needs among Asian Americans. These are a few of the main areas of concern which require continued research in order to assist Asian Americans in becoming better adjusted in their host culture. Acculturation cannot be achieved without exacting a price in terms of psychic conflict and emotional turmoil. Asian Americans need help in the process of acculturation to minimize these stresses.

NOTES

1. S. L. M. Fong, "Assimilation of Chinese in America: Changes in Orientation and Social Perception," *American Journal of Sociology*, Vol. 71, (1965), pp. 265–73.

2. J. W. Conner, "Acculturation and Changing Need Patterns in Japanese American and Caucasian American College Students," *Journal of Social Psychology*, Vol. 93, (1974), pp. 293–94.

3. S. Sue and K. Morishima, *The Mental Health of Asian Americans*. San Francisco: Jossey-Bass Publishers, 1982.

4. Conner, *op. cit.*

5. S. Sue and D. W. Sue, "Chinese American Personality and Mental Health," *American Journal*, Vol. 1, (1971), pp. 36–44.

6. B. P. Dohrenward and B. S. Dohrenward, "Social and Cultural Influences on Psychopathology, *Annual Review of Psychology*, Vol. 25, (1974), pp. 417–52.

7. J. B. Enright and W. R. Jaeckle, "Psychiatric Symptoms and Diagnosis in Two Subcultures," *International Journal of Social Psychology*, Vol. 9, (1963), pp. 12–17.

8. J. C. Finney, "Psychiatry and Multiculturality in Hawaii," *International Journal of Social Psychology*, Vol. 9, (1963), pp. 5–11.

9. S. Sue and D. W. Sue, "MMPI Comparisons between Asian American and Non-Asian Students Utilizing a Student Health Psychiatric Clinic," *Journal of Counseling Psychology*, Vol. 21, (1974), pp. 423–27.

10. *Ibid.*

11. S. Sue, "Psychological Theory and Implications for Asian Americans," *Personnel and Guidance Journal*, Vol. 55, (1977), pp. 381–89.

12. D. W. Kloph and R. E. Cambra, "Communicating Apprehension among College Students in America, Australia, Japan, and Korea," *Journal of Psychology*," Vol. 102, (1979), pp. 27–31.

13. W. A. Allard, "Chinatown, the Gilded Ghetto," *National Geographic*, Vol. 148, (1975), pp. 626–43.

14. K. A. Abbott and E. L. Abbott, "Juvenile Delinquency in San Francisco's Chinese American Community: 1961–1966," *Journal of Sociology*, Vol. 4, (1968), pp. 45–56.

15. H. H. L. Kitano. *Japanese Americans: The Evolution of a Subculture*. Englewood Cliffs, New Jersey: Prentice-Hall, 1969.

16. Abbott, *op. cit.*

17. H. H. L. Kitano, "Japanese American Crime and Delinquency," *Journal of Psychology*, Vol. 66, (1967), pp. 253–63.

18. R. T. Sollenberger, "Chinese American Child-rearing Practices and Juvenile Delinquency," *Journal of Social Psychology*, Vol. 74, (1968), pp. 13–23.

19. Sue and Morishima, *op. cit.*

Asian American Literature

JESSE HIRAOKA

Asian American writing emerged as a body of literature in the 1960s when the civil rights movement provided a politically unifying base for works describing and explaining the experiences of Asians in the United States. The movement also lent impetus to the emergence of a collective identity which was different from any previous group consciousness in that it focused principally on the experiences shared by the various Asian peoples in their encounters with the established American social system. In addition to explaining specific group experiences, such as those of the Chinese, the Japanese, the Filipinos, the Koreans, the Pacific Islanders, and others, writers turned their attention to those experiences shared in common, which enlarged the context of Asian American writing and led to use of the term "Asian American literature."

Informative articles, poetry, and fiction were obviously written by and about Asians in the United States before the term "Asian American literature" came into usage. The experiences of the first generation of Asian immigrants to the United States, particularly up to 1924, were expressed in private chronicles not written in English or were commented on by outsiders. In the first case, the immediate concerns of survival and the language barrier would limit the emergence of a significant amount of writing. In the latter case, the relentless emphasis on Americanization, particularly during the early decades of the 1900s, and the two major contexts for discussion, American labor and immigration policies, would foster negative images and develop stereotypes about Asians in the United States.

Even with the emergence of a generation of English-speaking and English-educated Asians in the United States, there remained the obstacle of publishing writings on the experiences of Asians in the United States. Publications remained strongly European-oriented, and publishers saw little need to concern themselves with the existence of an Asian population, which was relatively small in number and concentrated primarily on the West Coast. Thus, the writings of this second group were relegated to small journals, to community newspapers, and only occasionally to scholarly journals. Two clear examples are the short stories of Toshio Mori and the sociological studies of the Chinese in the United States by Rose Hum Lee. Mori's stories were first met with stated concerns about his command of English, and Lee's writings did not initially find a readily available audience of scholars. Their writings would receive a new and more appreciative reception after the 1960s.

The extent to which any writings about Asians in the United States could become available to a wider and more appreciative audience required certain conditions, two of which are of special significance: (1) the development of an identifiable community of readers; (2) the development of a discursive arena where information in various terms by and about Asian Americans could be presented and discussed. With the arrival of the 1960s and the concomitant political and social unrest, the needed conditions developed and Asian American writing began to assume the nature of a published body of literature. The publication of poetry, fiction, and journalistic and scholarly writings by and about Asian Americans escalated.

As Ronald Tanaka has explained in his systems analysis of ethnic minority literature, there was not only the development of an increased readership of Asian Americans, but the majority community which influenced publication and information channels became interested in American ethnic minority writing, in major part, because the civil rights struggles and the identity issues raised by the ethnic minorities affected the survival and safety of the majority group. Given the degree of dissent and social disorder, the majority society needed information about the minorities in the United States for its own purposes. Therefore, the political and social unrest was given broad attention, if only to help stabilize the situation as quickly as possible. Thus, publishers could be assured of a wider readership of writings about Asian Americans as well as about other ethnic minorities. Foundation support for small presses increased, university presses enlarged their scope of what could be considered scholarly materials, and private publication efforts met with a more satisfactory response.[1]

The need for a discursive arena was fulfilled by the development of Ethnic Studies programs with an Asian American Studies component, which included courses on Asian American history, politics, and literature. The inclusion of academic programs in Ethnic Studies led to the subsequent emergence of professional and social organizations and conferences, all of which provided an arena for the presentation and discussion of writings by and about Asian Americans. Two works that exemplify the interest of a larger reading audience are *The Woman Warrior* (1977) by Maxine Hong Kingston and the anthology of Asian American writings *Aiiieeeee* (1974) edited by Frank Chin, Lawson Inada, Shawn Wong, and Jeffrey Chan. Both works received favorable critical acclaim from a readership that extended well beyond the Asian American community.

With the rapidly expanding interest, there developed an organizing criterion that controlled, to a certain extent, the selection and publication of materials on

Asian Americans. The overriding objective became that of establishing an Asian American heritage in terms of the arrival and stay of the Asians in the United States, and the changes that occurred as they consolidated their presence in American society. More importantly, because this period of publication received its impetus from the civil rights movement, a major concern of the writings was racism in America, a concern that easily preempted the establishing of other criteria for the publication of a rapidly growing body of literature.

For purposes of organization and discussion, Asian American literature can be divided into three categories: (1) Anthologies that emphasize the roots or heritage of Asians in America. These collections of writings vary in terms of the period of time covered and the types of materials included. Two representative examples, their publication dates about a decade apart, are *Roots* (1971) and *Ayumi* (1980). (2) Social scientific writings, largely sociological in scope and intent, that analyze the experiences of Asians in the United States and present data on them. Studies on early labor history, the characteristics of the Issei and Nisei, demographic studies on Chinatowns, and larger works on each Asian group are prominent. The study of Japanese Americans by Harry Kitano and the articles appearing in *Amerasia*, the periodical specializing in Asian American Studies, are representative. (3) Poetry, fiction, short stories, and plays. This category of writing escalated in terms of publication beginning with the mid–1970s. Small presses, some with foundation support, university presses, and private publishing efforts lent considerable support to the publication of Asian American creative writing. The area had been largely ignored in the past, particularly since the scope of American literature had generally excluded ethnic minority literature. Evidence of this type of growth in Asian American writing is reflected not only in the reissuing of early works of the 1950s, such as John Okada's *No No Boy* (1957) and Monica Sone's *Nisei Daughter* (1953), but also in the significant number of published poets including Mei Berssenbrugge, Lawson Inada, Garret Hongo, Janice Mirikitani, Nellie Wong, Ronald Tanaka, Alan Lau, Stephen Liu, James Mitsui, and Alex Kuo.

Cutting across the categories are three organizational themes that drew the attention of Asian American writers: America as Gold Mountain, Chinatown, and the wartime relocation of the American Japanese. Each of these themes provides a focal point for discussing the process of Americanization and the degree of acceptance of Asians in the United States. The Gold Mountain metaphor provides a ready backdrop for writings on the life and experiences of the early period of Asian immigration. Although the quest for a new beginning and for wealth is not uncommon to American literature in general, the Gold Mountain metaphor is particularly suited to the early history of Asian immigration, especially because the period of the entry of Chinese laborers from 1850 to 1882 coincided with the development of the railroad. Within this setting there is reflected the early experiences and the history of Asian immigration. The physical labor required, the portrayal of Chinese labor as coolie or slave labor, the use of the epithets "heathen" and "sojourner," and the view of the Chinese as "strangers in the land" who would not readily assimilate—all set the pattern for the Asian immigration that followed and seeded the stereotypes of Asians which were to be used against each subsequent entry of immigrants from Asia. It is within this minimal landscape, especially delineated by the hard physical labor demanded, that Asian American writers of later generations sought ties to their own past history. Most strikingly, the Gold Mountain metaphor would lead Carlos Bulosan to reflect on the meaning of the American Dream in *America Is in the Heart* (1946).

Chinatown, by its very boundaries which permit the maintenance of a place with its food, spirit, style, and language, provides a spatial setting for the encounter of Eastern and Western cultures. While influenced by the American culture, Chinatown's very structure holds that American culture at bay. Within Chinatown, where the language and culture are sheltered by clear boundaries, the dynamic encounter between the world of Chinatown and that of the surrounding society can be presented, and at another level the personal and collective experiences related so as to reflect the effects of the Americanization process. Short stories and plays draw on Chinatown as the logical setting for the experiences of the Chinese in America. Just as the white farmer's field was a spatial setting for the experiences of Chicanos in the United States, with the Teatro Campesino clearly reflecting that setting as an available form of expression, so, too, Chinatown provided a theatrical setting, readily suited to presentation in dramatic form, as reflected in Frank Chin's *The Year of the Dragon* (1974) and *The Chicken-Coop Chinaman* (1972).

The wartime relocation and incarceration of the American Japanese in 1942 is the source of the most prolific writing on the Asian experience in the United States. The government's decision to remove over 110,000 American residents of Japanese ancestry, including those who were citizens, revealed the distinction that could be made between citizenship and nationality. It became a topic that would be treated in a continuing stream of words, from articles and books on the constitutionality of the imprisonment to autobiographical accounts of the impact of the event on personal lives and on families. The publication in the 1980s of Yoshiko Uchida's *Desert Exile* (1982) and *Obasan* (1981) by the Canadian writer and poet Joy Kogawa reflects the continuing interest in the subject of the relocation and imprisonment of the American Japanese. Even earlier publications, such as the sketches of life in the concentration camps by Mine Okubo, have been reissued. This single event has served as a focal point for the discussion of American society's acceptance not only of its Asian population, but also of its total identifiable minority populations, thus attracting the attention of a wider range of readers.

It would be difficult to impose a strict historical pattern on Asian American writing, and it would be inaccurate to suggest that the boundaries of Asian American literature are in any way limited to the stated categories and themes. The continuing efforts of Asian American writers will alter any existing boundaries. What is significant is that the specific conditions under which the body of

Asian American writing took shape and emerged provided readers, writers, and publishers with a collaborative frame of mind during a two-decade period, to the extent that even the earlier writings by Asian Americans could be reexamined and included in a more favorable context. The basis for a body of literature written by and about the Asian experience in the United States had been formulated.

NOTES

1. Ronald Tanaka, ''The Circle of Ethnicity,'' in *Journal of Ethnic Studies*, vol. 8, no. 3, Fall 1980, pp. 1–65.

Asian Americans and American Popular Culture

ELAINE KIM

Stereotypes of racial minority groups are found in many areas of American life: in radio and television programs and films, in advertising, and in children's literature and comic books as well as in pornographic materials. They appear on restaurant menus and as part of the half-time entertainment at college football games. Nor are these stereotypes confined to popular culture; they are supported by learned perspectives.[1] Powerful politicians are in no way exempt: shortly after his election in 1980, President Ronald Reagan's doodled drawing of a Fu Manchu figure during an official meeting was published in a weekly news magazine.

Racial stereotypes are so deeply ingrained in American attitudes and daily life that it is sometimes difficult to distinguish fact from fantasy or to see members of racial minority groups as individuals. Not only are individuals perceived as generalized representatives of their particular racial group; distinctions among the different racial groups are blurred: the shuffling servant, the menacing savage, and the plodding peasant could be black, brown, red, or yellow.[2] Moreover, although white Americans are also featured in the popular media as villains, sex sirens, sidekicks, or servants, they are not limited to one-dimensional caricatures that mask their complex and diverse humanity.

Because the Asian population in the United States was kept small by racially discriminatory immigration laws until quite recently, and because Asians in America were segregated from the mainstream of American life, most Americans were more likely to have encountered Fu Manchu, Charlie Chan, or Suzy Wong on the printed page or the silver screen than an ordinary Asian or Asian American in real life. Children can still read about the five Chinese brothers, hear the ditty about the "ching chong Chinaman" whose English is limited to "no tickee no washee," or laugh about Japanese houseboys who say "ah so." American-born Asians are still commonly viewed as exotic aliens, complimented when they speak fluent English and asked when they are "going back." Asian men are popularly expected to be mathematicians or laundry workers who speak English with grotesque accents and excel in the martial arts, and Asian women are expected to know, either by instinct or by training, how to please men. Even today, a television program featuring a multidimensional Asian protagonist would hardly be marketable. It is still difficult for an Asian American writer to publish a story except as autobiography, because publishers know that American readers might have trouble distinguishing stereotype from reality. Contemporary Chinese American playwright Frank Chin notes that New York critics of his play *Chickencoop Chinaman*, complained in the early 1970s that his characters did not speak, dress, or act "like Orientals." Maxine Hong Kingston says that her highly successful book, *The Woman Warrior* (1977), is actually a work of fiction and is autobiographical only in the way that life itself is a fusion of history, myth, dreams, and desire. Although American readers do not expect Erica Jong's or Norman Mailer's work to be autobiographical, Kingston's publishers advised her that her writing would sell better as nonfiction autobiography.[3]

There are two basic kinds of stereotypes of Asians in American popular culture: the "bad" Asians—sinister villains and brute hordes who cannot be controlled and must therefore be destroyed—and the "good" Asians—helpless heathens, loyal sidekicks, docile servants, and seductive female sex partners who pose no apparent threat.[4] What both the "bad" and the "good" Asian stereotypes have in common is that they define the Anglo as physically and morally superior. The villains and savages must succumb to courageous white heroes; the servants and sidekicks are foils to their strong and benevolent white masters; and the sensuous Asian woman reflects the virile Anglo man. Instead of describing Asians, the racial stereotypes describe Anglos as "not Asian": what is emphasized are the permanent and irreconcilable differences that make Anglos superior and Asians inferior.

The Western European image of "bad" Asians as faceless masses of barbaric savages probably originated with the spectre of Attila the Hun and the crusade against Islam centuries ago. The fear that Western civilization might be subsumed by Asiatic hordes still figures in U.S. foreign and domestic policies.

Long before the first Chinese laborer set foot on American soil, the image of the degraded Chinese coolie whose racial and cultural characteristics made him a threat to the American way of life was vivid in the popular imagination.[5] Although Asian cheap labor was desperately needed on Hawaii's sugar plantations and on farms and construction sites in the American West, Asians were not considered suitable as permanent settlers. Although European immigrants were described in school textbooks as individuals in search of political, religious, and economic freedom, Asian immigrants were usually depicted as "hordes" bent on milking this country of its riches and funnelling them back to Asia. During the latter half of the nineteenth century and the first decades of this century, pseudo-scientific assertions about Asian fertility, fecundity, and innate tolerance for pain and harsh life and work conditions served as a warning that unchecked Asian immigration would result in white civilization being outlasted, indeed overrun, in much the way that germs, cockroaches, and other low forms of life can survive human beings. A poem by Daniel O'Connell, anthologized in the 1970s, depicts this fear:

We will make a second China by your pleasant Western seas;
We will swarm like locusts that scourged the East of old;
. . . We can do your women's labor at half a woman's rate. . . .
We'll monopolize and master every craft upon your shore,
And we'll starve you out with fifty—aye, five hundred thousand more![6]

Journalists, politicians, and labor leaders, particularly in California and the Pacific Northwest, contributed to the fear of the "Yellow Peril," adding momentum to the movement to exclude Asians from the United States. The Chinese were the first to be excluded by law on the basis of nationality in 1882, and all Asians were prohibited from immigrating or becoming naturalized U. S. citizens after 1924.

The notion that Asian and other non-white immigrants threaten the American way of life, taking away "American" jobs and lowering the standard of living, persists on an unofficial level even today, as can be seen in the attempts to restrict Vietnamese immigrant fishermen in Texas, Louisiana, and California, as well as on an official level, as part of the rationale for contemporary congressional efforts to revise American immigration policies. The "Yellow Peril" was the theme of Atwell Whitney's 1878 novel, *Almond-Eyed*, which ends with a stream of Chinese immigrants "pouring in, filling the places which should be occupied by the Caucasian race, poisoning the atmosphere, tainting society, undermining the free institutions of this country, degrading labor.''[7] It was also the implication in the feature essay of a 1983 issue of *Time* Magazine, "The New Ellis Island," which warns that the English language and Anglo-American culture are endangered by the influx of Asian and other non-white immigrants into the city of Los Angeles.[8]

Stereotypes override specifically human detail. The generalization of Asians into an undifferentiated mass is reflected in U. S. foreign policy. The mistaken notion that Asian lives are cheap and dispensable and that Asians themselves do not value human life undoubtedly influenced the decision to use atomic bombs in Japan during World War II. News coverage of the Korean conflict three decades ago promoted the image of hordes of Chinese and Korean footsoldiers pitted against American forces striving to protect human freedom and Western civilization and helped make conceivable wars of attrition in Southeast Asia in recent years. Even today the image persists: after normalization of relations with mainland China, the U. S. news media continues to focus on crowds, regimentation, and unisex clothing in China. On the home front, the familiar belief that all Asians look and are alike concretely affects Asian Americans' lives: young Korean immigrant Lee Chol Soo, for example, was convicted without a shred of material evidence of a 1973 slaying he did not commit and spent ten years in prison because he was identified as looking somewhat like the Chinese American culprit.

According to popular belief, the most potent threat of the "Yellow Peril" to Western civilization is the possibility that mindlessly obedient Chinese might be harnessed under the leadership of the clever and mimetic Japanese, who have supposedly learned to utilize technology devised by "Caucasian minds" for their own purposes. Fear of the Japanese grew with Japan's defeat of the Russian Baltic fleet in 1905: for the first time in modern memory, a "white" nation had succumbed to a "colored" one. The spectre of Japanese military might profoundly alarmed popular American writer Jack London, who wrote that the Japanese might be clever enough to acquire the white man's material achievement, but that Anglo-Saxon "soul stuff" is "the product of an evolution which goes back to the raw beginnings of the race and not a coin to be pocketed by the first chance comer." The Anglo-Saxon, according to London, is imbued with "a certain integrity, sympathy and comradeship and warm human feel, which is ours, indubitably ours, and which we cannot teach to the Orientals as we would teach logarithms or the trajectory of projectiles."[9] Even today, Japan's political and economic ascendancy is viewed with alarm in the United States, where Japan is popularly blamed for American economic woes. The strength and tenacity of this view, coupled with the common inability to distinguish among Asian nationality groups, can be seen in the 1982 bludgeoning murder of Vincent Chin, a young Chinese American, by two unemployed white men in Detroit. The killers mistook Chin for a Japanese, whom they blamed for unemployment problems in the U. S. automobile industry. The American criminal justice system supported their views: the killers were given suspended sentences and fined $3,780 each for the murder. Only under severe public pressure did the justice system change its verdict.

The popular belief that Asian Americans are all foreigners has its origins in white supremacism. From the days of the Founding Fathers, European immigrants expected America to be a white man's country. Over a century ago, Asian immigrants were excluded from the United States because they were thought to be racially undesirable, a race that could never be successfully assimilated into the mainstream of American life. In a series of studies on "racial distance" conducted between 1926 and 1966, Anglo Americans were asked to rank a score of nationality groups, including both Asians and Asian Americans, by nationality, according to whether or not they could be accepted as co-workers, neighbors, or in-laws. Chinese, Chinese Americans, Filipinos, Japanese, Japanese Americans, and Koreans were consistently ranked near the bottom of the list.[10]

Ironically, the ethnic ghettos to which Asians were relegated were popularly viewed as concrete evidence of their unassimilability—foreign settlements where they could cling stubbornly to their native languages and cultures. It was argued that if immigration were allowed to continue, un-American habits and practices would take root in American soil, posing a grave threat to the "sweetness and purity of our national waters." Japanese Americans were criticized fiercely for establishing Japanese language schools for children in California and the Pacific Northwest, although no one seemed to see the connection between the schools and the limited opportunities for both immigrant and American-born Japanese in all arenas of American life. The situation was even worse for the Chinese: prevented by exclusion and anti-miscegenation policies from marrying and establishing normal family lives, immigrant men of Chinatown worked as waiters and laundrymen in bachelor communities, where recreation was largely limited to gambling and prostitution. The popular image of the Chinese American community as a den of vice peopled by opium addicts, *tong* assassins, and slave girls has a long history. According to Robert McClellan, the American people's "insatiable appetite" for lurid stories about Chinatown made almost every area of Chinese life a popular topic in American life and culture for generations.[11]

Stereotypes about Chinatown strengthened already widespread misconceptions about the Chinese in America, even among persons who had little contact with Chinese Americans. In one 1929 study of race attitudes, American children asked to describe the Chinese called them crafty, backward, and clannish, adding that they disliked the Chinese because they steal, do "underhand work," bring opium into America, stab people in the back with knives, and have "a sneaking, slimy air" and "slant eyes (that) give me a chill."[12] Interviews of adults in Chicago in 1935 revealed that many Americans feared the "criminal appearance" of Chinese laundrymen, whom they believed "did all kinds of sinister and mysterious things in their back rooms," ate rats, and kidnapped little boys in their laundry bags and hid them in rooms behind secret sliding panels.[13]

Even today, the supposed mysteries and vices of Chinatown life attract tourists to the Chinese communities of New York and San Francisco in search of bizarre sights and exotic quaintness. No other ethnic community has added so many tourist dollars to its city's coffers as San Francisco Chinatown. Long-lived interest in Chinatown crime was recently revived with the arrival of Chinese immigrant families after the immigration quotas were changed in 1965. Like the problems of black and white urban youth, Chinese youth crimes can be attributed to poverty and a variety of environmental factors, including poor schools and lack of recreational facilities and the alienation that sometimes arises among struggling immigrant families with multiple wage earners. Even though Hong Kong-born youth have no affiliation with old south China secret societies and evidence little interest in mainland Chinese politics, California Attorney General Evelle Younger issued a pamphlet in 1973 in which Chinatown youth crime was linked to both *tongs* and Chinese communism. What underlies this conjecture is the assumption that the problems of the Chinese in America must come from China: they cannot have developed here. In this way, the victims are blamed for their own failures and problems, and American society is completely absolved.

After the exclusion of all Asian immigrants, discriminatory policies and laws confined those Asians who had already settled in the United States to subordinate social and economic status. In general, the Chinese were limited to "Chinese" or "Chinatown" jobs—in laundries and ethnic restaurants and businesses. Japanese, Filipinos, and Koreans worked as farm laborers or domestic servants. Even American-born Asians were largely unable to find employment in other arenas: according to employers, priority was given to "Americans." Other forms of segregation separated Asians from other Americans: before the 1950s, it was almost impossible for them to find housing outside their ethnic communities, and Asians in California and the Pacific Northwest could not use public recreational facilities. They were barred from "white" hotels, restaurants, barbershops, and beauty parlors, and they sat, together with other non-whites, in the balconies of movie theatres. Attempts were also made to prevent Asian American children from attending "white" schools. Parents and community groups objected when Japanese American children were selected for parts in school plays about American history, and in one case, when a Japanese American child won a school debate, the ensuing uproar resulted in the runner-up representing the school at a nationwide contest.[14]

According to the popularly accepted mythology, no matter how "American" the Asian might seem, he was ultimately an unassimilable alien. In "Young Mr. Van," Wallace Irwin writes:

> Yu can take a Chink from 'is hop,
> 'is lanterns and gals and pigs and chop,
> Yu can dress 'im up in yer Christian clo'es,
> Put texts in 'is head and hymns in 'is nose,
> But yu'll find, when he's actin' a dead straight part
> He's a Chinaman in 'is yellow heart.[15]

The notion that attitudes, behavior, and political loyalties are racially inherited made logical the internment of more than 110,000 Japanese Americans, two-thirds of whom were American-born U.S. citizens, as enemy aliens during World War II. Even orphanage children of Japanese ancestry were not exempt. Institutional acceptance of the popular belief that nothing could change the racial unacceptability of Asians as American citizens is reflected in the 1922 Supreme Court decision to deny the possibility of naturalization to Ozawa Takao. In this case Ozawa argued that he should be eligible for citizenship because he had lived in Hawaii for most of his life, spoke English at home, was a practicing Christian, and had attended American public schools and the University of California at Berkeley.

One of the traditional explanations for racial inequality in America has been that racial minorities lack the intellectual aptitude and accomplishments of whites. In study after study, the figures for educational attainment have been correlated with occupational status and wage, suggesting that racial minorities might achieve equality if they would change their attitudes toward schools. Although historically educational attainment has been lower for blacks, Hispanics, and Native Americans than for whites, Asians in the United States have ranked higher than whites in median years of school completed for many decades, even though their socioeconomic status has been lower. Half a century ago, Korean Americans were ten times as likely as other Americans to have attended college. As long ago as 1927, a California study revealed that the IQ test scores and grades of Japanese American students equaled or surpassed those of white students, suggesting that race discrimination and not lack of schooling has been the barrier to social and economic equality.[16] Even today, Asian Americans continue to surpass all other Americans in years of school completed, but the correlation between educational attainment and socioeconomic status is not equal with whites. Asians continue to be clustered in low-profile, low-mobility occupations, requiring detail work and very little public contact. No matter what their credentials or level of formal education, Asians are underrepresented in all areas of administrative work. This may well result from the belief that no amount of formal education can result in racial equality. Half a century ago, American geneticists and biologists were still arguing that the brains of black, yellow, and white people suited them to manual labor, detail work, and administration, respectively.[17] Although American sociogeneticists continued the effort to attribute the subordinate social and economic status of black Americans to biological factors, they ignored the fact that Asian IQ's were higher than whites. In the case of Asians, it might be asserted, subordinate social status stems from other factors.

The notion that Asians make good computer technicians but lack social skills is directly related to popular stereotypes of Asians. Brilliant but arrogant and cruel, the archetypal sinister Asian villain appears frequently in films and popular literature. He is the power-crazed tyrant who wants to hoard the world's dinosaur fossils in Walt Disney's films for children. He is the sworn enemy of James Bond and the heroes of "Star Trek." Although he has been educated at the best universities in the West, and although he speaks fluent, if stilted, English, like the evil Asian genius in Jack London's imagination, he lacks the moral fibre and physical qualities of the white man, and no mental powers, no veneer of Westernization, can make him the white man's equal.

The epitome of this stereotype is the insidious Dr. Fu Manchu. Created in 1913 by British author Sax Rohmer (Arthur Sarsfield Ward), by 1964 Fu Manchu had appeared in thirteen novels, which were translated into more than a dozen languages, including Braille, as well as scores of films and radio programs in Great Britain and the United States. Fu Manchu brought Rohmer wealth and fame: he was even awarded an honorary doctorate at Harvard, and the FBI consulted him when the U. S. State Department received a threatening letter from the fictitious "Chinese" organization Rohmer had invented for his stories. Although he did not originate the fear of the "Yellow Peril," Sax Rohmer can no doubt be credited for having linked "Asian" with "evil" in Western imaginations for many generations.

Rohmer's Fu Manchu is a figure of towering intellect, but he has mastered Western knowledge and science without comprehending "Western ethics." He is endowed with "an intellect so cold and exact, that the man in whose body it was set could sacrifice his own flesh and blood to the interests of his giant impersonal projects.'' Fu Manchu himself says that the brain, not the heart, is the seat of power, and it is lust for power that drives him. He will use any means to achieve his goal, which is nothing less than the overthrow of the white race. He invents drugs that turn white men yellow and change dead men into zombies obedient to his will. With a pitiless smile, he can command rape and torture and the killing of both his enemies and his bungling followers. Fu Manchu is the dialectical opposite of the white hero: although his mind is more powerful, he is, in Rohmer's words, ''not a normal man. He is superman, Satan materialized and equipped with knowledge which few had ever achieved; a cold, dominating intellect, untrammelled by fleshly ties, a great mind unbound by the laws of man.'' Ultimately, of course, nothing can defeat the wholesome, warmly human white protagonists of the Fu Manchu stories—not superior intelligence, not ingenious weapons, not overwhelming numbers, not black magic—because the battle is between good and primordial, Satanic, Chinese evil.[18]

The profoud impact of the Fu Manchu stereotype can be seen in print and visual media portrayals of Asian political leaders like Mao Tse Tung, Kim Il Sung, and Ho Chi Minh. Training materials about these men produced by the U. S. Defense Department bear a striking resemblance to the Fu Manchu stories. The stereotype has had a role on the domestic scene as well: in 1969, Los Angeles County Coroner Thomas Noguchi almost lost his job when he was accused of ''smiling enigmatically'' over the bodies of slain white men like Robert Kennedy.

Because race stereotypes essentialize or ignore specifically human qualities, there are no ''favorable'' stereotypes. ''Good'' Asians are simply friendly to whites, and ''bad'' Asians are hostile. Both are grotesque parodies, portrayals in a vacuum, and both serve to emphasize the inherent superiority of the white race. Barbaric Asian hordes can be seen as masses of helpless heathens; all are faceless, lacking in individual identities, and both are defined by the white hero that subdues or saves them. The stock character of comical Asian servant, a ''good'' Asian stereotype, serves primarily to demonstrate the courage and virility of his white master. Hop Sing in the ''Bonanza'' television series hides trembling under a table while the brave white cowboys fight the marauding Indians, just as his predecessors did in the popular melodramas of the nineteenth century.[19] Cowardly, grotesquely dressed, speaking hilariously broken English, the Asian servant does possess the virtue of intense loyalty to his master. Likewise, the stereotype of the loyal Asian sidekick underscores the importance of the white protagonist. Even the ''positive'' portrayal of Asians in American popular culture today, the Japanese American laboratory technician in the television drama ''Quincy,'' is marginal and one-dimensional. He exists solely to show the viewers Quincy's cleverness and integrity, asking questions that help Quincy demonstrate his knowledge and intelligence. A clean-cut, helpful assistant in a white coat, he knows his pharmaceutical terms, but he is never permitted to engage in romance or adventures himself, which is only a problem because there are no multidimensional characterizations of Asian men in any print or visual media in America today.

It is occasionally argued that because he is clever and foils villains when he solves mysteries, Charlie Chan is a positive portrayal of Asians in American media. Certainly Earl Derr Biggers, creator of Charlie Chan, meant the character to be a positive one. "Sinister and wicked Chinese are old stuff," Biggers once said, "but an amiable Chinese on the side of law and order has never been used."[20] Between 1925 and 1932, Biggers wrote six Charlie Chan novels, all of them serialized in the *Saturday Evening Post* before being published in book form, and some of them translated into as many as ten foreign languages. Forty-seven Charlie Chan films were produced in four Hollywood studios, featuring six different non-Chinese actors in the title role. When Charlie Chan television programs and films were proposed in the 1970s and 1980s, many Chinese Americans objected strenuously, and merchants in San Francisco's Chinatown refused to allow cameramen to film near their shops. To them, the pudgy detective with the half-closed, beady eyes held up with scotch tape, wearing baggy pants and speaking fortune-cookie English, was a racial insult. Far from being a positive or realistic portrayal, they argued, Charlie Chan was simply another drearily familiar stereotype, another "good" Asian caricature—an amusingly non-threatening, asexual ally of the white people for whose sake he works so hard to solve murder mysteries.

According to Chinese American writers Frank Chin and Jeffrey Paul Chan, what is unique to stereotypes of Asian men, whether as villains, servants, or sidekicks, is their total lack of sexual dimension.

> Devil and angel, the Chinese is a sexual joke glorifying white power. . . . Fu Manchu, a man wearing a long dress, batting his eyelashes, surrounded by muscular black servants in loin cloths, and with his bad habit of caressingly touching white men on the leg . . . is not so much a threat as . . . a frivolous offense to white manhood. Charlie Chan's gestures are the same except he doesn't touch, and instead of being graceful . . . in flowing robes, he is awkward in a baggy suit and clumsy. His sexuality is the source of a joke running through all of the forty-seven Chan films. The large family of the bovine detective isn't the product of sex, but animal husbandry. . . .[21]

It is difficult to recall any characterization of Asian men with a sexual identity in American popular culture, even in recent years; certainly the Asian characters in television programs such as "Bonanza," "Cane," "Star Trek," and "Shogun" have none. Martial arts expert Bruce Lee starred in one Hollywood film before he died, and although the portrayal was supposed to be positive, the character was less a human being than a fighting machine. Lee had played many multidimensional roles in Hong Kong-made films, but Warner Brothers' *Enter the Dragon* features him as uniquely unlike his black and white cohorts. His single-minded focus on perfecting his fighting skills precludes all other interests, including an interest in women, friendship, or a social life. The other major

Asian character in the film is the adversary, an evil man with an iron claw and modeled after Fu Manchu. Narrow in a different way, he is driven by lust for power. He has no interest in human relationships. The beautiful Asian women around him are intensely attractive to the non-Asian men in the film, but to him they are only objects to be used in his quest for power.

Stereotypes of both "bad" and "good" Asian men as not being manly are a reflection of a white male perspective that defines the white man's virility. Because of this perspective, it is possible for the Asian man to be viewed as asexual and the Asian woman as only sexual. Although the Asian man is portrayed as a machine—whether he is a laundryman, an engineer, or a Kungfu fighter—the Asian woman is popularly thought to be warmly sensual, imbued with an innate understanding of how to please her man and how to serve him. The strength and resilience of this stereotype is no doubt responsible for the phenomenal success of Singapore Airlines, which bases its entire advertising effort on the image. It also helps explain the enormous demand for X-rated films featuring Asian women and the emphasis on bondage in pornographic materials about Asian women. Moreover, the popular image of alluring and exotic "dream girls of the mysterious East" has created a demand for "Oriental" bath house workers in American cities from Cincinnati and Indianapolis to Tacoma and Corpus Christi, as well as a booming business in mail order marriages and expensive introduction services for middle-aged and older American men seeking young Asian brides.[22]

We would be hard pressed to think of many portrayals in American popular culture of Asian men as lovers of white or Asian women, but almost every exotic Asian woman character is the devoted sexual slave of a virile white man. The image of the Asian woman as exotic sex object describes the sexual power and significance of the white man at the expense of the Asian man. According to the fantasy, whether as sex tourist in Asia or mail order marriage client in California, the white man is the key to the Asian woman's liberation from Asian men and Asian culture, the supposed sources of her own oppression and suffering. The mystique of the Asian woman is in fact only a reflection of the subordination of one group by another, as are all stereotypes of racial or sexual servility. Factors such as poverty and social disruption, which are at the root of prostitution, sex tourism, and the sex services industry in Asia, are ignored because they are neither erotic nor exotic. Acceptance of the stereotype impedes efforts to end exploitation and subordination and adversely affects white women's emancipation struggles as well.[23] The popular image of the Asian woman as obedient, eager to please, and simple to satisfy makes it all the more difficult for them to overcome race and sex discrimination. It is no coincidence that the majority of Asian women in America today, no matter what their level of formal education and work experience, are clustered in either sewing factory and food services work or in low-profile, low-wage, and low-mobility clerical jobs requiring hard work, attention to detail, and low autonomy—the qualities of good subordinates.[24]

The popular contemporary stereotype of Asian Americans as a "model minority'' is but a variation on old themes, casting Asians as well-behaved subordinates. The myth of the ''model minority'' functions mostly to encourage American racial minorities to persevere as ''good'' non-whites so that the status quo can be effectively maintained. As a ''model minority,'' Asian Americans today are supposed to be restrained, humble, well-mannered, hardworking believers in law and order and education. In the 1980s newspapers and news magazines have frequently carried feature stories about Asian American ''success.''[25] Most of the emphasis in these stories is on educational attainment—the high percentage of Asian American students enrolled at Harvard, MIT, and the University of California at Berkeley, the disproportionate number of Asian American high school and college valedictorians and academic prizewinners. Very little is said about the persistent barriers faced even by highly educated Asian Americans in hiring and promotion, which have little to do with grade point averages: at every level of education, from none to postgraduate, Chinese, Korean, and Filipino males, whether educated in the United States or in Asia, make less than their white counterparts, and Japanese American high school graduates make less than whites with the same level of education. Asian American males with more than a high school education make less than their white counterparts. When adjustments are made for education, both men and women of all Asian national origins make less than whites with similar qualifications.[26] Nor is it mentioned that the educational achievements of Asian Americans in the 1980s are simply a continuation of past patterns. The achievements have become more noticeable because the Asian American population has increased considerably since 1965 when the immigration quota laws were changed.

The image of Asian American success is important because it suggests that there is no fundamental difference between the history and conditions of the non-white poor of today and the ethnic poor of past generations: everyone, according to this line of argument, works his or her way up the ladder to the American Dream. The model minority myth reinforces the belief that if non-whites try hard enough, they can succeed in America, and that where inequality does persist, the problem is with the racial minority group itself and not with external factors, such as race discrimination.

Ironically, the ''success'' of today's Asian Americans is attributed to the same ancestral cultures that were formerly blamed for their unassimilability. Contemporary American sociologists and anthropologists have devised what they call the ''culture and personality theory'' to explain Asian American adaptation patterns.[27] Confucian mores and traditional Japanese values, which used to be considered incompatible with white American culture, are now called the key to Asian American acceptability: Confucian emphasis on respect for the law and the maintenance of social control through close-knit family units and the Tokugawa values of frugality, patience, obedience, and diligence are now deemed highly compatible with American middle-class values and the Protestant ethic in Western culture.

No doubt the degree of compatibility between the immigrant and the host

cultures is important in determining what the minority group's American experiences might be. However, the implications of the culture and personality
notion can be misleading: on the one hand, if Asians are more successful than
other racial minorities because of something inherent in their cultures and personalities, the relative failure of other groups of attain the Asian level of "success" must be the result of some deficiency in their cultures and personalities
or to their own lack of effort. The underlying assumption is that failure to attain
the Anglo American cultural norm must result in permanent subordinate status.

The contemporary function of the model minority stereotypes can be seen in
a *U. S. News & World Report* article published in the mid–1960s, when militant
demands for social equality were being voiced by American racial minorities,
led by American blacks. At the height of the civil rights movement, the Chinese
were held up as an example for blacks and other "troublesome" minority groups
to follow. Although their past hardships would "shock those now complaining
about the hardships endured by today's Negroes," the article contends, the
Chinese are succeeding "on their own" now:

> At a time when it is being proposed that hundreds of billions be spent to uplift
> Negroes and other minorities, the nation's 300,000 Chinese are moving ahead on
> their own ... with no help from anyone else. Still being taught in Chinatown is
> the old idea that people should depend on their own efforts ... not a welfare check
> ... in order to reach America's "promised land."[28]

The "promised land" referred to in the article is not self-determined well-
being; it is not even economic security. It is low incidence of reported crime.
New York Chinatown is hailed as a "haven of law and order," an "island of
peace and stability," the "safest place" in New York City. Although the essay
is purportedly about Chinese Americans, there are numerous references to blacks,
for an implicit comparison is being made between Chinatown and the black
communities, where racial unrest was manifested in uprisings that terrified the
nation's white population. The essay suggests that blacks and Hispanics ought
to follow the Chinese example of "overcoming their handicaps quietly" instead
of making demands and causing trouble.

The model minority notion is largely an attempt to rationalize the relationship
between black and white Americans at the expense of both blacks and Asians.
Whites emerge as superior to both, with Asian Americans occupying a "buffer
zone" position that protects the existing power relationships and pins the blame
for racial inequality on the victims themselves. Thus, American institutions and
white racism are vindicated.

The Asian model minority stereotype is used as evidence of a racial equality
that does not exist. Even the existence of a notion such as a model minority,
which is in reality a "mascot minority," grows from the popular view that
acceptance of white supremacy is the key to acceptability for non-white Americans. The shuffling "coon" is infinitely preferable to the rebellious "buck
nigger."

Generalizations about the characteristics of a particular culture or the people of a particular nation help define a national identity. Combined with political domination, they also involve generalizations about the people of the dominated culture or nation as inferior and so provide justification for the existing power relationship. Thus, Western European stereotypes about backwardness, degeneracy, inefficiency, and eccentricity in the cultures of Asia, Africa, Latin America, and the Arab world became particularly developed and refined during the nineteenth century, when European colonial dominion increased from 35 to 85 percent of the globe. These fantasies passed into the New World as part of America's European heritage and have helped rationalize America's international political, economic, and cultural preeminence. White supremacist stereotypes have also served to explain the domination of racial minority groups within the nation's borders. Racially discriminatory policies against blacks, Hispanics, Native Americans, and Asian Americans are related to the notion of whiteness as an essential aspect of the American national identity. Historically, both the people of the nations within the American political domain and America's racial minorities have been viewed as "problems" to be solved, confined, or vanquished. Just as the images of impoverished masses of culturally alien non-whites in other countries has helped to justify conquest and domination, the stereotype of Native Americans as either brutal or noble savages has helped rationalize extermination and relocation policies, and stereotypes of servile or menacing blacks have served as a justification for slavery and continued subjugation after emancipation.

Far from being an incidental collection of grotesque lies, then, racial stereotypes are both the products and tools of political and cultural domination. They systematically and continually reaffirm what Nigerian novelist Chinua Achebe has called the "positional superiority" of one group over another, emphasizing the supremacy of the one by disregarding or denying the essential humanity of the other.[29]

Because they are essentially fiction, not fact, the body of "knowledge" represented by racial stereotypes has not increased in size or accuracy with time. Instead, the old images have simply become more complex and refined, while the basic distortions persist. For this reason, it is fruitless to try to change the images without changing the institutional structures of inequality that give rise to and maintain them in the first place. At the same time, it is important to recognize the popular stereotypes and to understand their origins and implications. Challenging racial stereotypes could be one way of critiquing the ideologies and practices that impede fulfillment of the promise of American justice and democracy, which cannot be realized within the context of continued racial inequality. Indeed, continued popular acceptance of racist stereotypes inhibits the fullest possible development of American life and culture, diminishing the American imagination by reinforcing a limited and limiting point of view that inhibits the development of sound domestic and foreign policies and perpetuates self-deception among those who at first glance seem to benefit from them. For Asian Americans, the most constructive response to racial stereotyping is to continue to challenge both the stereotypes and the political and cultural hegemony that allows them to flourish, creating instead self-images based on the diversity and complexity of their real life experiences and aspirations.

NOTES

1. See Edward W. Said, *Orientalism* (New York: Vintage Books, 1978), and Elaine H. Kim, "Images of Asians in Anglo-American Literature," in *Asian American Literature: An Introduction to the Writings and Their Social Context* (Philadelphia: Temple University Press, 1982), pp. 3–22.

2. See Ronald Takaki, *Iron Cages: Race and Culture in 19th-Century America* (New York: Alfred A. Knopf, 1979).

3. Berkeley, California, interview, June 9, 1980.

4. Frank Chin and Jeffrey Paul Chan, "Racist Love," in Richard Kostelanetz, ed., *Seeing Through Shuck* (New York: Ballantine Books, 1972), pp. 65–79.

5. See Stuart Creighton Miller, *The Unwelcome Immigrant: The American Image of the Chinese, 1785–1882* (Los Angeles: University of California Press, 1969).

6. Daniel O'Connell, "Song of the Tartar Horde," quoted in William Purvience Fenn, *Ah Sin and His Brethren in American Literature* (Peking: College of Chinese Studies, 1933), pp. 18–19.

7. Atwell Whitney, *Almond-Eyed: The Great Agitator: A Story of the Day* (San Francisco: Bancroft, 1878), p. 168.

8. *Time*, June 13, 1983, pp. 18–25.

9. Jack London, "The Yellow Peril," *Revolution and Other Essays* (New York: Macmillan Co., 1910), pp. 284–85.

10. Emory S. Bogardus, "Social Distance: A Measuring Stick," *The Survey* 56, No. 3 (May 1, 1926): 169–70 and 206–10, and Emory S. Bogardus, "Comparing Racial Distance in Ethiopia, South Africa, and the United States," *Sociology and Social Research* 52 (1968):149–56.

11. Robert McClellan, *The Heathen Chinee* (Columbus: Ohio State University Press, 1971), p. 13.

12. Bruno Lasker, *Race Attitudes in Children* (New York: Henry Holt and Co., 1929), pp. 140–41.

13. Paul C. P. Siu, "The Chinese Laundryman: A Study of Social Isolation," Ph.D. diss., University of Chicago, 1953, pp. 11–14.

14. Eliot Grinnell Mears, *Resident Orientals on the American Pacific Coast* (New York: Institute of Pacific Relations, 1927), pp. 366–67.

15. Wallace Irwin, *Chinatown Ballads* (New York: Duffield and Co., 1906), p. 16.

16. Edward K. Strong, *The Second-Generation Japanese Problem* (London: Oxford University Press, 1934), pp. 191–94.

17. See, for example, Robert Bennett Bean, *The Races of Man* (New York: University Society, 1935).

18. Sax Rohmer (Arthur Sarsfield Ward), *The Trial of Fu Manchu* (London: Alan Wingate, 1978, originally published c. 1934), p. 49; Sax Rohmer (Arthur Sarsfield Ward), *The Island of Fu Manchu* (New York: Doubleday and Co., 1940).

19. The stock image of the comical Asian servant made its first appearance as "John Chinaman" in popular melodramas set in the American West and performed on both

coasts during the latter half of the nineteenth century: cowardly, grotesquely dressed, speaking hilariously broken English, he had the virtue of intense loyalty to his virile and courageous white employer.

20. Dorothy B. Jones, *The Portrayal of China and India on the American Screen, 1896–1955* (Cambridge: MIT Press, 1955), p. 38.

21. Chin and Chan, "Racist Love," p. 66.

22. See Elaine Kim, "Sex Tourism in Asia: A Reflection of Political and Economic Inequality," *Critical Perspectives* 2, No. 1 (Fall 1984): 225–29.

23. According to University of Texas sociologist Davor Jedlicka, who studies American mate selection patterns, many American men think that, in comparison to Asian women, American women are "too competitive" and not suitable as wives and mothers (Raymond A. Joseph, "American Men Find Asian Brides Fill the Unliberated Bill," *Wall Street Journal*, January 25, 1984).

24. The labor force participation of Asian American women has historically been high: in 1980, 57 percent were in the labor force, in contrast to 49.4 percent of white women. Like other American women, Asian women are clustered in low-wage, low-status occupations, but Asian American women are heavily represented in unskilled and semiskilled menial work. In 1970, 57 percent of all employed Chinese women in the United States were seamstresses and food service workers, whereas the rest were concentrated primarily in four low-profile clerical occupations as file clerks, typists, office machine operators, and bookkeepers. See Betty Lee Sung, *Chinese Manpower and Employment* (Springfield, Va.: NTIS, 1975), pp. 90–92 and 115–18. In the same year, two-thirds of all garment factory workers and one-third of private household domestics in the San Francisco Bay Area were Asian American women. Today, about one-third of private household domestics in the San Francisco Bay Area were Asian American women. Today, about one-third of the 6,000 employees in San Francisco's thirty-six major hotels are Asian American women, who work as room cleaners, linen menders, kitchen helpers, and laundry workers. Asian American women are underrepresented in all levels of management and administration as well as in the skilled trades ("Selected Statistics on the Status of Asian-American Women," *Amerasia Journal* 4, No. 1 (1977): 138–39). Although all women in America face problems of sex discrimination in employment, Asian American women fare worse than their white sisters: in 1981, women earned only 64.7 cents for every dollar earned by a man, a gap that is the same as it was thirty years ago. Income levels for Asian American women are even lower: in 1970 Filipino American women earned only 47.5 percent, Japanese American women 43.7 percent, Chinese American women 39.6 percent, and Korean American women 37.0 percent of white men's income. See Gloria Kumagai, "The Asian Women in America," *Explorations in Ethnic Studies* 1, No. 2 (July 1978): 72. According to the 1980 U. S. Census, the median annual income for Asian American women ($6,685) was about half that of white men ($12,881). College-educated white women earn less than white male high school graduates, but the disparity between education and income is greater for Asian American women, who have completed more years of school (12.7 years) than either white women (12.5 years) or white men (12.4 years). See Pauline Fong, "Economic Status of Asian Women," Paper presented to the National Advisory Council on Women's Educational Programs, San Francisco, 1976).

25. See, for example, "Asian Americans: A Model Minority," *Newsweek*, December 6, 1982; "Making It: The Saga of Min Chul Shin and His Family Fruit Store," *New York*, December 20, 1982; "New Version of Success Story: Asians in U. S. Make Rapid

Economic Rise," Los Angeles *Times*, October 5, 1982; "The Promise of America," *Parade*, June 2, 1985; and "Asians: To America with Skills," *Time*, July 8, 1985.

26. Amado Y. Cabezas, "Disadvantaged Employment Status of Asian and Pacific Americans," *Civil Rights Issues of Asian and Pacific Americans: Myths and Realities* (Washington, D. C.: Consultation Proceedings, U. S. Commission on Civil Rights, 1979), pp. 434–44. See also Amado Y. Cabezas et al., *Discriminatory Employment of Asian Americans: Private Industry in the San Francisco-Oakland SMSA*, Report to the U. S. Equal Opportunity Commission (San Francisco: Asian American Service Institute for Assistance to Neighborhoods, 1977); David N. Moulton, "The Socio-Economic Status of Asian American Families in Five Major SMSA's," San Francisco: Asian American Service Institute for Assistance to Neighborhoods, 1978.

Indeed, while much has been written and said about the strong representation of Asian Americans in institutions of higher learning, little attention has been paid to the correlation between level of education and occupational status and wage. Moreover, critics and observers argue that even Asian American "success" in schooling as compared with white Americans will not be tolerated indefinitely. In 1985 the Asian American Task Force of University Admissions in San Francisco charged that the University of California at Berkeley was making "deliberate policy changes" to curtail admission of Asian applicants, citing an unexpectedly sharp drop in enrollment in 1984 despite an increase in the number of eligible applicants. The Task Force cited a 1983 report to the Chancellor's Office expressing concern that there were "too many Asians on campus" (*East/West*, June 19, 1985). In the same year, Asian American community leaders asserted that Asian American students were subject to discrimination in admission to Ivy League colleges: statistics showed that lower percentages of Asian American applicants were accepted than whites, despite the Asians' higher academic qualifications and test scores. They referred to Princeton University's Professor Uwe Reinhardt's statement that when he was serving on a graduate school admissions committee in 1983, other members of the committee argued that "we have enough" Asian American students, indicating that an unofficial quota had already been reached (*Asian Week*, June 7, 1985).

27. See, for example, George De Vos, "A Quantitative Research Assessment of Maladjustment and Rigidity in Acculturating Japanese Americans," *Genetic Psychology Monograph* 52, No. 1 (August 1955):51–87; William Caudill, "Japanese Personality and Acculturation," *American Anthropologist* 58 (1956); William Caudill and George De Vos, "Achievement, Culture and Personality: The Case of the Japanese Americans," in Staten W. Webster, ed., *Knowing the Disadvantaged* (San Francisco: Chandler Publishing Co., 1966); William Petersen, *Japanese Americans: Oppression and Success* (New York: Random House, 1971); and Ivan Light, *Ethnic Enterprise in America* (Berkeley: University of California Press, 1972).

28. "Success Story of One Minority Group in U. S.," *U. S. News & World Report*, December 26, 1966, p. 49.

29. Chinua Achebe, *Morning Yet on Creation Day: Essays*, Garden City: Anchor Press/Doubleday, 1975, pp. 3–28.

DICTIONARY

A

ABE v. FISH AND GAME COMMISSION, a case argued in the California District Court of Appeals in 1935 which challenged the right of the California Fish and Game Commission to prohibit persons not having resided in the United States or the State of California for at least one year from bringing fish caught on the high seas into California for sale. This regulation, a 1933 amendment to Section 990 of the Fish and Game Code, was tested in this landmark case by T. Abe, the holder of a California commercial fishing license. Abe had hired a crew of Japanese aliens, none of whom had resided in the United States for the requisite year prior to coming into the San Diego harbor, to fish from his vessel off the coast of California and unload their catch. The Fish and Game Commission attempted to prevent them from unloading their cargo, and charged that they had violated Section 990. Presiding Justice Charles R. Barnard of the District Court of Appeals held in this decision that Section 990 was void because it discriminated unreasonably between residents and non-residents of the United States, and therefore was in violation of the equal protection clause of Section 1 of the Fourteenth Amendment of the Constitution.

This was not, however, the end of attempts to prohibit Japanese fishermen from operating in California. In 1943, while the Japanese were interned in concentration camps, the California Legislature again amended Section 990 to specifically prohibit "alien Japanese" from obtaining commercial fishing licenses. This amendment remained in force until after the release of loyal Japanese in 1945, at which time Section 990 was again amended to prohibit the granting of licenses to "any person other than a person eligible for citizenship," for the legislature realized that the 1943 amendment would be easily overturned on the basis of blatant discrimination. This provision was overturned in 1948 only after being taken to the Supreme Court of the United States by Takahashi Torao,* a Japanese alien released from Manzanar in 1945. Thus was this blatant attempt

to eliminate competition from the highly successful Japanese fishing operations finally laid to rest.
FURTHER READING: Frank F. Chuman, *The Bamboo People*, Del Mar, Calif.: Publisher's Inc., 1976.

ABIKO KYUTARO (1865–1936), a leader of the Japanese community of San Francisco, editor of the *Nichi Bei Times*,* and head of the Japanese American Business Promotion Company (Nichibei Kangyosha). Abiko is best known for his organization of the Central California Land Company, which bought up desert land near Livingston, California, and sold it on liberal terms financed by his own *Nichi Bei Bank* to young immigrants from Japan. One hundred Japanese were involved in the first phase of this pioneering project, settling and reclaiming 2,000 acres of land hitherto regarded as sheer wasteland. Their efforts were so successful that Abiko also bought parcels to the east of the original settlement around Cressy, known as the Yamato Colony, and additional tracts to the north of it, in the area of Cortez. Despite his foresight in this and other projects, Abiko lost both his bank (as a consequence of the depression of 1913) and his newspaper. (*See also Nichi Bei Times.*)
FURTHER READING: Bill Hosokawa and Robert A. Wilson, *East to America*, New York: William Morrow and Co., 1980; Bill Hosokawa, *Nisei*, New York: William Morrow and Co., 1969.

ACT NO. 2486—AN ACT FIXING A TAX UPON EVERY PERSON OR ENTITY ENGAGED IN RECRUITING OR CONTRACTING LABORERS IN THE PHILIPPINES, a law enacted by the government of the Philippines in 1915 to regulate and control both Filipino and non-Filipino labor contractors involved in the recruitment of Philippine nationals for work on the plantations of Hawaii. This law also provided taxation powers to each province in which recruitment was occurring. In addition, Act No. 2486 set forth certain stipulations regarding the workers' return to the Philippines once the specified term of the contract had expired. All persons or entities involved in the recruitment of workers would be licensed by the Philippine government, with their activities being supervised by the Bureau of Labor. The governor-general would appoint commissioners to oversee the activities of contractors outside of the Philippines, including the hearing of complaints by the contracted laborers in regard to their relationships with employers while under contract.
FURTHER READING: Bruno Lasker, *Filipino Immigration*, Chicago; University of Chicago Press, 1931.

ACT TO PROHIBIT THE COOLIE TRADE BY AMERICAN CITIZENS IN AMERICAN VESSELS, 1862, a bill ending the coolie trade* completely, passed on February 19, 1862. During the first session of the 37th Congress, the House asked President Abraham Lincoln for information on the coolie trade, but no legislative action was taken at that time. In the second session, two steamship bills were introduced in the Senate, one of which was the Coolie Bill.* This bill was passed and sent to the House. Thomas Eliot of Massachusetts introduced his own Coolie Trade Bill at the opening of the second session. It was reported back with amendments on January 15, 1862, and passed the House on the same day. Although the original bill by Eliot had a qualifying phrase, "against their will and without their consent," the Senate committee decided to delete it, thus prohibiting the coolie trade entirely. President Lincoln signed the bill on February 19, 1862. (*See also* Coolie Trade.)

FURTHER READING: E. P. Hutchinson, *Legislative History of American Immigration Policy, 1798–1965*, Philadelphia: University of Pennsylvania Press, 1981; Robert L. Irick, *Ch'ing Policy Toward the Coolie Trade, 1847–1878*, San Francisco: Chinese Materials Center, 1982.

ACT TO EXECUTE CERTAIN TREATY STIPULATIONS RELATING TO CHINESE, May 6, 1882. *See* Chinese Exclusion Act of 1882.

ACT TO AMEND AN ACT ENTITLED "AN ACT TO EXECUTE CERTAIN TREATY STIPULATIONS RELATING TO CHINESE," APPROVED MAY SIXTH, EIGHTEEN HUNDRED AND EIGHTY-TWO; July 5, 1884, an amendment of the Chinese Exclusion Act.* This act primarily specified the term "Chinese" as referring to both subjects of China and Chinese subjects of any other country. It also placed restrictions on the entry of Chinese merchants identified as "hucksters, peddlers or those engaged in taking, drying, or otherwise preserving shell or other fish for home consumption or exportation." The amendment also granted to "peace officers of the several States and Territories of the United States: the same authority to carry out the provisions of the Chinese Exclusion Act as marshals of the United States Government." (See also Chinese Exclusion Act.)

FURTHER READING: William L. Tung, *The Chinese in America*, Dobbs Ferry, N.Y.: Oceana Publications, 1974.

ACT TO PROHIBIT THE COMING OF CHINESE LABORERS TO THE UNITED STATES, September 13, 1888, a bill banning the immigration of working class Chinese for twenty years. The first session of the 50th Congress convened on December 5, 1887, and immediately began to work on nine bills introduced to prohibit Chinese immigration. Only two bills received attention, one originating in the House and one in the Senate. The Senate Committee on Foreign Relations introduced a bill to prohibit the coming of Chinese laborers, and the Senate passed the bill without debate and astonishingly without a recorded count of votes. The House had begun to work on an identical bill, but it decided to table it. It was then decided to transmit the Senate bill to the Committee on Foreign Relations, which reported an amended bill that was designed to repeal not only the 1884 act (an Act to Amend an Act entitled "An Act to Execute Certain Treaty Stipulations Relating to Chinese," Approved MAY SIXTH,

EIGHTEEN HUNDRED AND EIGHTY TWO; July 5, 1884*) but also the Chinese Exclusion Act of 1882.* The House passed the bill on August 20, and with Senate agreement, it was sent to the President for signature. The bill was signed on September 13, 1888. The act, in essence, imposed a twenty-year suspension on Chinese immigration, with the exception of officials, teachers, students, merchants, and travelers. When the Chinese government refused to ratify the treaty that was being negotiated at the time, the suspension provisions of the act were considered void.

FURTHER READING: E. P. Hutchinson, *Legislative History of the American Immigration Policy, 1798–1965*, Philadelphia: University of Pennsylvania Press, 1981; William L. Tung, *The Chinese in America*, Dobbs Ferry, N.Y.: Oceana Publications, 1974.

ACT TO SUPPLEMENT AN ACT ENTITLED "AN ACT TO EXECUTE CERTAIN TREATY STIPULATIONS RELATING TO CHINESE," APPROVED THE SIXTH DAY OF MAY, EIGHTEEN HUNDRED AND EIGHTY-TWO, October 1, 1888. *See* Scott Act of 1888.

ACT TO PROHIBIT THE COMING OF CHINESE PERSONS INTO THE UNITED STATES, May 5, 1892. *See* Geary Act of 1892.

ACT TO PROHIBIT THE COMING INTO AND TO REGULATE THE RESIDENCE WITHIN THE UNITED STATES, ITS TERRITORIES AND ALL TERRITORY UNDER ITS JURISDICTION, AND THE DISTRICT OF COLUMBIA, OF CHINESE AND PERSONS OF CHINESE DESCENT, April 29, 1902, a bill enacted twenty years after the Chinese Exclusion Act of 1882,* extending indefinitely the provisions of the earlier bill. In addition, it went beyond the scope of the Exclusion Act by setting down restrictions on the movement of laborers of Chinese origin from the new island territories of the United States to the mainland, as well as their movement from one area of U.S. control to another. Chinese residing in any U.S. island territory, with the exception of Hawaii, were given one year to obtain a certificate of residence in order to remain there legally. Special consideration was given to the Philippine Islands, where a Philippine Commission was given authority and responsibility to set up and implement a plan to register all Chinese and persons of Chinese origin.

Another section of the bill specifically allowed Chinese laborers to enter the United States as employees of foreign nations, hired to aid in the setting up or conducting of exhibits in any kind of legally authorized fair or exhibition. The Secretary of the Treasury was also authorized by a section of the bill to set up, change, or eliminate rules and regulations governing the entry and residence of Chinese in the United States under the auspices of the original exclusion act. (*See also* Chinese Exclusions Act of 1882.)

FURTHER READING: Jack Chen, *The Chinese of America*, New York: Harper and Row, 1980; William L. Tung, *The Chinese in America*, Dobbs Ferry, N.Y.: Oceana Publications, 1974, pp. 75–76.

ACT TO REPEAL THE CHINESE EXCLUSION ACTS, TO ESTABLISH QUOTAS, AND FOR OTHER PURPOSES, December 17, 1943, a bill that amended the Nationality Act of 1940. During World War II there was strong public opinion in favor of a more relaxed immigration policy toward China and the Chinese. Many Americans felt that the government policy to exclude the Chinese was an inappropriate policy with which to treat a wartime ally. In addition, an attitude favoring the repeal of Chinese exclusion laws was being formed in Congress after Generalissimo Chiang Kai-shek's wife, Soong Mei-ling, had addressed Congress in February 1943. Many civic organizations openly supported the idea of repeal. Among these organizations was the American Legion, which had been known for its support of anti-Chinese immigration legislation. In May 1942 a Citizens Committee to Repeal the Exclusions Acts was formed, and in the following year Representative Warren Magnuson of Washington introduced a bill entitled "An Act to Repeal the Chinese Exclusions Acts, to Establish Quotas, and for Other Purposes." The chief goal of this bill was to amend Section 303 of the Nationality Act of 1940—to add to the classes eligible for naturalization Chinese persons and persons of Chinese descent and to give them an annual quota of 105 immigrants. The House passed the bill on October 21, 1943, and the bill was reported without amendment by the Senate committee. Although a number of attempts were made to amend the bill, they were all rejected and the Senate passed the bill on November 26, 1943. This act ended more than sixty years of discriminatory policy by the American government toward Chinese immigration.

FURTHER READING: Jack Chen, *The Chinese of America*, New York: Harper and Row, 1980; E. P. Hutchinson, *Legislative History of American Immigration Policy, 1798–1965*, Philadelphia: University of Pennsylvania Press, 1981; S. W. Kung, *Chinese in American Life*, Seattle: University of Washington Press, 1962.

ACUTE REFUGEES, a refugee model proposed by E. F. Kunz. According to Kunz, two separate patterns in the movement of refugees can be recognized: flight-arrival and associative. Included in the flight-arrival patterns are two models: the acute refugees and the anticipatory refugees*. Kunz defines acute refugees as people who are compelled to move because of great political or other drastic changes. They move from one place to another in large numbers, their main purpose being to reach a place of safety where they will be allowed to stay. Soon after their arrival in a new place or country they begin to redefine their relationship to their native land, for they realize that they will probably not return to their homeland. This redefinition often serves as the first step toward changing their status from refugees to exiles. (*See also* Anticipatory Refugees.)

FURTHER READING: E. F. Kunz, "The Refugees in Flight: Kinetic Models and Forms of Displacement," *International Migration Review* 7 (Summer 1973), pp. 125–146; Darrel Montero, *Vietnamese Americans*, Boulder, Colo.: Westview Press, 1979.

ADUJA, PETER (1920–), the first Filipino to be elected to the legislature of the Hawaiian Territory prior to statehood. Elected to a seat in the lower house in 1955, Aduja served a single term and was subsequently defeated in a bid for reelection. Governor Samuel W. King appointed him Deputy Attorney General. After Hawaii attained statehood, he was elected, beginning in 1966, three times to the Hawaii House of Representatives from the district of Windward, Oahu. Born October 19, 1920, in the Province of Ilocos Sur in the Philippines, Aduja came to Hawaii at the age of eight, graduated from Hilo High School, and served in the First Filipino Infantry Regiment* in World War II. Following the war he attended the Boston University School of Law, and after becoming a lawyer he returned to Hilo to practice.

FURTHER READING: H. Brett Melendy, *Asians in America*, Boston: Twayne Publishers, 1977.

AGRICULTURAL WORKERS ORGANIZING COMMITTEE. *See* United Farm Workers Organizing Committee.

AGUINALDO, EMILIO (1869–1964), a leader of the Filipino independence movement during the last years of Spanish colonial rule, who at the age of twenty-seven emerged as a national leader after the death of Jose Rizal.* Aguinaldo was elected head of the Revolutionary Central Government in March 1897 and received much support from those who were formerly members of the Katipunan, a secret society established by Andres Bonafacio. When promised by the Spanish governor-general, Primo de Rivera, that the reform demands would receive due consideration and that he and his staff would be paid $400,000, he and his men went into exile in Hong Kong. There he came into contact with American officials who, according to Aguinaldo's claims, had promised an independent Philippines. Returning to his native land, Aguinaldo began to organize armed resistance against the American military government in the Philippines. He was finally captured in March 1901, and on April 19, he pledged allegiance to the United States and told his followers to do the same.

FURTHER READING: Edwin Wildman, *Aguinaldo*. Boston: Lothrop Publishing, 1901.

AHN, CHANG-HO (1878–1938), an educator, social reformer, and leader of the Korean national independence movement. Ahn was born on November 9, 1878, in Kangso County of Korea and came to America at the age of twenty-five. His purpose in immigrating to America in 1902 was to study and learn from Western civilization, but he decided to postpone his study after he saw various community problems facing Korean immigrants in the Bay Area. He worked very hard to improve the Koreans' living conditions by establishing an employment agency, community improvement projects, and social and political organizations. Ahn was responsible for the first Korean community organization known as the Friendship Society (Ch'inmok-hoe).* He also established the first Korean political organization, called the Mutual Assistance Society* (Kongnip Hyop-hoe), which later merged with the United Korean Society* (Han-nin Hapsong Hyop-hoe) on February 1, 1909, to become the Korean National Association* (Tae-Han Kungmin Hyop-hoe). In 1913 he also founded an educational and cultural organization known as the Corps for the Advancement of Individuals (Hungsa-dan)* which was established to help develop Korea's national leadership.

Ahn, though deeply committed to his family, left his wife and children (one of whom was Philip Ahn*) and returned to Korea in order to continue his struggle for Korea's independence from Japan. He died on March 10, 1938, in a prison under Japanese rule.

AHN, PHILIP (1911–1978), an actor and community activist, born on March 29, 1911, of Korean parentage. His father was Ahn Chang-ho,* an educator, reformist, and prominent leader of the Korean national independence movement while Korea was under Japanese rule. Philip Ahn entered films in the mid–1930s and usually played the role of an Oriental in numerous Hollywood productions. Although he appeared in more than 300 films in his lifetime, he is probably best known for his role in the television series, "Kung Fu." Among the films in which he appeared are *The Good Earth* in 1936 with Paul Muni, *Love Is a Many Splendored Thing*, with William Holden, and *Battle Hymn* with Rock Hudson.

In recognition of his contributions to Hollywood moviedom, the Hollywood Chamber of Commerce's Committee of the Walk of Fame decided to inscribe the name of the actor in the "Walk of Fame." He is the first Asian actor to receive such an honor. (*See also* Ahn, Chang-ho.)

AISO, JOHN (1909–), the first Nisei* to be appointed the the Municipal Court of Los Angeles by Governor Earl Warren* on the U.S. mainland. Born on December 14, 1909, he attended Le Conte Junior High School in Hollywood where he was elected president of the student body. Because of parental pressure and prejudice against Japanese, however, he was denied his position. Later, in 1926, he won an oratorial contest at Hollywood High School which entitled him to go for the national competition in Washington that year. Instead, his debating partner was sent to represent Hollywood High School. He attended Brown University and graduated cum laude, and he received a law degree from Harvard Law School. He was drafted into the U.S. Army in April 1941 and was assigned to a truck repair unit. He was later transferred to the Fourth Army Intelligence School as a Japanese language instructor. After the Pacific War, he served as commissioner in the Superior Court of California for a year before he was appointed to the Municipal Court of Los Angeles. He then served as a Superior Court judge for ten years before he was appointed a justice in the California Court of Appeals in 1968.

Commenting on his initial appointment by Governor Earl Warren, Aiso felt that he was appointed because of Warren's remorse for supporting the evacuation of persons of Japanese ancestry during World War II.

AKAKA, ABRAHAM KAHIKINA (1917–   ), a clergyman born in Honolulu on February 21, 1917. Akaka attended the University of Hawaii between 1934 and 1937 and received the Doctor of Divinity degree from the University of Chicago in 1958. He was ordained in 1944 as a minister of the United Church of Christ. Between 1958 and 1960 he served as chaplain of the Hawaiian Senate. Akaka was responsible for organizing Friends of Kamehameha Schools* in order to support these schools. He believed that Hawaiians were better suited to take advantage of growing opportunities because of their intermixture with other peoples. He worked with future state legislators in order to protect Hawaiian interests. He was very optimistic about Hawaii's statehood when his people were deeply disappointed over the decision by Congress to grant statehood to the islands. He challenged his people to view it as a new opportunity for all peoples of Hawaii. (*See also* Kamehameha Schools.)

AKAKA, DANIEL KAHIKINA (1924–   ), U.S. Representative. Akaka was born in Honolulu on September 11, 1924, and attended public schools there. He graduated from the University of Hawaii with a B.Ed. degree in 1952 and began to teach in the following year, retaining that position until 1960. He served as vice-principal of Ewa Beach Elementary School, Honolulu, from 1960 to 1964 when he moved to Pohakea Elementary School where he was appointed principal.

Akaka's political career began when he was made director of the state Office of Economic Opportunity in 1971. As a close ally of George Ariyoshi,* Akaka was picked by Ariyoshi as his running mate for lieutenant governor in the Democratic primary in 1974, but Akaka was defeated. Governor Ariyoshi chose him as his special assistant for human resources.

When Patsy Takemoto Mink* was defeated in her unsuccessful bid for the U.S Senate, she opposed Akaka for the 2nd District House seat in Hawaii in 1976. With the support of Ariyoshi and the state AFL-CIO, he defeated his formidable opponent and won the seat to become the only native Hawaiian ever to be elected to the U.S. House of Representatives.

ALA MOANA CASE, a case involving Mrs. Thalia Massie, the twenty-year-old wife of a submarine lieutenant stationed in Pearl Harbor, who was allegedly raped on the night of September 12, 1931, by a gang of five "dark-skinned youths" in Ala Moana Park. In the 1930s there had already been strong racial antagonism among whites against non-whites in the islands. Mrs. Massie's claim stirred up strong feelings against non-whites among the *haole** population who felt that their white womanhood had been violated. The five young men—two Hawaiians, two Japanese, and one Chinese—were not convicted, as the racially mixed jury in Honolulu was not able to reach a verdict.

While one of the two Hawaiian youths, Kahahawai, was awaiting trial, Lieutenant Thomas Hedges Massie, his mother-in-law, Mrs. Grace Hubbard Bell Fortescue, and two sailors kidnapped him and took him to Mrs. Fortescue's place and killed him. Lieutenant Massie and his accomplices were arrested and convicted of their crime, and they were sentenced to ten years in prison on May 4, 1932. But they did not spend even a single day in prison, as Governor Lawrence M. Judd, under severe pressure from the navy, altered their prison sentence from ten years to one hour, which was to be served in the custody of the high sheriff. FURTHER READING: Gavan Daws, *Shoal of Time*, Honolulu: University Press of Hawaii, 1968; Lawrence H. Fuchs, *Hawaii Pono: A Social History*, New York: Harcourt, Brace and World, 1961.

ALABAMA AND CHATTANOOGA RAILROAD, established shortly after the Civil War by John C. Stanton and his brother, Daniel L., who acquired bankrupt railroad lines, including the Wills Valley Railroad, the Northeast and Southwest Railroads, and combined them to form the Alabama and Chattanooga Railroad. The two brothers persuaded financiers in the East and legislators in Alabama to float bonds to provide the needed capital for their design to connect Chattanooga, Tennessee, with Meridian, Mississippi, a distance of some 295 miles, largely through Alabama. Cornelius Koopmanschap* promised John Stanton that 1,000 or 2,000 Chinese laborers could be delivered to him. Each of them was to cost him $60. Stanton was also to pay $16 per month and board. After the two reached an agreement, the Chinese workers were sent to Alabama from California by railroad. In early August 1870 about 960 Chinese arrived in Alabama, but W. A. Kissam, a Chinese labor contractor, lured some of them into leaving for plantation work in Louisiana.

In June 1871 the Alabama and Chattanooga Railroad received a bankruptcy judgment and all work had to stop, although the decision was later reversed. But because of increasing financial difficulty, Koopmanschap petitioned for bankruptcy in May 1872, as he was unable to liquidate $160,000 in railroad bonds and $100,000 in notes given by the Chinese. After the bankruptcy of the Alabama and Chattanooga Railroad, the largest group of Chinese ever to be gathered together in the South was dispersed. Many of them moved on to Louisiana to work on plantations. FURTHER READING: Gunther Barth, *Bitter Strength*, Cambridge, Mass.: Harvard University Press, 1964; Lucy M. Cohen, *Chinese in the Post-Civil War South: A People Without a History*, Baton Rouge: Louisiana State University Press, 1984; Robert Seto Quan, *Lotus Among the Magnolias: The Mississippi Chinese*, Jackson: University Press of Mississippi, 1982.

ALASKA CANNERY WORKERS, predominantly Asian immigrants, especially Filipinos. Cannery work in Alaska, particularly in salmon fish industries, attracted many cheap and unskilled laborers, most of whom were Asian immigrants. Among them were many Filipino workers who had come to America between 1907 and 1930. Asian laborers were concentrated in Alaskan fishing industries for a number of reasons. First, cannery work was highly seasonal, with most of it being done during three or four summer months. Second, the seasonal nature of the fishing industry did not appeal to white laborers, who did not like the work of cleaning, cutting, and trimming fish, a task in which the majority of Asian immigrants were engaged.

As early as 1921 as many as 957 Filipinos were working in canneries in Alaska. By 1928 their number had grown to 3,939. But only 16 of them were fishermen, 7 were transporters, and the rest were shoremen. Bruno Lasker,* commissioned to study Filipino immigration in 1929 by the Research Committee of the American Council of the Institute of Pacific Relations, found that there were approximately 36,303 Asians in Alaska, including nationals from China, Japan, Korea, and the Philippines. Although Filipino cannery workers in Alaska fared better than their countrymen in other industries, they also suffered during the 1930s. Wages in Alaskan cannery industries were the lowest in years, and many left Alaska in search of work in Washington, Idaho, and even Minnesota.

A number of attempts were made to organize Filipino cannery workers, but all efforts failed until 1957 when Local 37 of the International Longshoremen's and Warehousemen's Union* in Seattle settled their labor dispute over wages and became the sole bargaining agent for all employees hired from California, Washington, and Oregon. (*See also* Cannery Workers; International Longshoremen's and Warehousemen's Union.)

FURTHER READING: Hyung-chan Kim, *The Filipinos in America, 1898–1974*, Dobbs Ferry, N.Y.: Oceana Publications, 1976; Tricia Knoll, *Becoming Americans*, Portland, Oreg.: Coast to Coast Books, 1982; Bruno Lasker, *Filipino Immigration*, Chicago: University of Chicago Press, 1931; H. Brett Melendy, *Asians in America*, Boston: Twayne Publishers, 1977.

ALEXANDER AND BALDWIN. *See* Big Five.

ALIEN LAND ACT OF CALIFORNIA, 1913, a law that prohibited the Japanese from leasing land for agricultural purposes. A number of alien land bills were submitted for debate in the California legislative session of 1913. After long debate over the various bills, one called the Webb-Heney Bill finally passed both houses and went before the governor for signature. President Woodrow Wilson, concerned about the reaction of the Japanese government, sent Secretary of State William Jennings Bryan* to Sacramento to meet with members of the legislature and cooperate with them in framing a law that would satisfy the people of the state and still leave the treaty obligations of the United States intact. Bryan and the California Legislature could not come up with a bill in harmony with the views of the federal government. President Wilson then sent a letter of disapproval to California governor Hiram Johnson, urging him to veto the bill. The Japanese government issued an immediate response to President Wilson who then sent the letter on to the governor of California. In this letter the Japanese government stated that the bill was unfair and discriminatory, inconsistent with treaty provisions, and was opposed to the spirit and principles of amity and good understanding. The governor responded to the Japanese government's letter by saying that the act did not violate the treaty. He signed the bill on May 19, 1913. Section One of the act stated:

> All aliens eligible to citizenship under the laws of the United States may acquire, possess, enjoy, transmit and inherit real property, or any interest therein, in this State, in the same manner and to the same extent as citizens of the United States, except as otherwise provided by the laws of this State.

Section One excluded all Asians because they were ineligible for citizenship in the United States. Sections Two and Three prohibited all aliens other than those specified in Section One of the Act from holding a majority interest in land. It also limited the leasing of agricultural land to three years. The three-year limit was very damaging to the Japanese strawberry producers, who were producing 70 percent of California's strawberries, because it takes at least three years for the vines to produce berries. Section Four of the act related to the distribution of property in the event a Japanese owner died and willed his land to a U.S. citizen or a Japanese citizen, or a U.S. citizen willed his property to a Japanese citizen. In all of the cases the State of California would sell the land and give the proceeds to the appropriate heir.

For over a year the Japanese filed several formal protests expressing the Japanese government's belief that the act was not a violation of the treaty but a violation of the spirit of the treaty.

On June 9, 1914, the Japanese government issued a response that sought to end the dispute over this act and produce better relations between the two governments. The sentence that summarizes its response says that spokesmen of "the Imperial Government are confident that the action complained of stands without historical parallel, and they are happy to believe that the legislation in question forms no part of the general policy of the Federal Government but is the outcome of unfortunate local conditions."

The Alien Land Act of 1913 remained unchanged until numerous court cases showed its loopholes. Strong public reaction to these loopholes caused the passage of the 1920 initiative. The 1920 law omitted the leasing clause in the 1913 law prohibiting the leasing of land by Japanese for agricultural purposes. It also stated that aliens ineligible for citizenship could not acquire stock in any organization authorized to enjoy real property other than provided in the treaty.

After the Alien Land Act of 1920, cropping contracts were often used. A cropping contract was made with a valid land owner, giving him a percentage of the profit for permitting the Japanese farmer to use his land. The cropping contracts did not last long before they were prohibited by the 1923 amendment to the 1913 and 1920 Alien Land acts.

The 1923 amendment stated that Japanese who did not own land previously could not work it legally as hired laborers. This amendment to California's Land Act closed nearly all of the loopholes in the 1913 Alien Land Act. Between 1921 and 1923 many other states, including Washington, initiated such legislation.

FURTHER READING: Sidney L. Gulick, *The American Japanese Problem*, New York: Charles Scribner's Sons, 1914; Yamato Ichihashi, *Japanese in the United States*, Stanford, Calif.: Stanford University Press, 1932; T. Iyenaga and Kenoske Sato, *Japan and the California Problem*, New York: G. P. Putnam's Sons, 1921; Robert A. Wilson and Bill Hosokawa, *East to America*, New York: William Morrow and Co., 1980.

ALIEN LAND LAWS, laws preventing the Chinese and Japanese from owning real property, passed in response to the reaction of whites to the presence of Chinese and Japanese farmers on the West Coast. As early as 1889 the California Legislature attempted to prohibit aliens from owning real property. In 1909 Assembly Bill 78, introduced by Assemblyman A. M. Drew of Fresno, was considered by the California Legislature, and the Assembly Judiciary Committee reported on January 15, 1909, in favor of the bill known as the Alien Land Bill. The bill required that an alien acquiring title to land become a citizen within five years or dispose of his holdings. The bill was defeated, but this was only a prelude to what was to come in 1913. During that year the California Legislature was inundated with more than thirty anti-Japanese measures. Of these measures the bill that was drafted by Senator Francis J. Heney and Ulysses S. Webb, California Attorney General, passed the Senate and the Assembly within two days after it had been amended and was sent to the governor for his signature on May 3, but he did not sign the bill until May 19, 1913, in order to allow the federal government to state its position on the matter in order to placate the Japanese government. The Heney-Webb Alien Land Law has its loopholes which became a source of court battles. Californians passed an initiative in 1920 to close up these loopholes. In 1923 a further amendment to the original Heney-Webb Alien Land Law was made in order to close up any loopholes left in the law.

Many other states on the West Coast followed suit in the following years. In 1917 Arizona passed a law preventing ineligible citizens from holding title to any real property. In 1921 the State of Washington strengthened its alien land law, and again in 1923 other restrictive measures were added to plug any loopholes. During the same year Oregon and Idaho passed legislation basically patterned after the California Alien Land Law. Then came Texas, Kansas, Nebraska, Montana, Minnesota, New Mexico, Missouri, and Louisiana.

These alien land laws did not go unchallenged by those whose lives were severely affected by them. Some of the cases challenging the constitutionality of alien land laws went to the highest court of the land for decision. The Supreme Court ruled the California Alien Land Law constitutional in Porterfield v. Webb,* thereby dealing a severe blow to the agricultural interests of the Japanese on the West Coast.

These racist laws were fully enforced until 1948 when the U.S. Supreme Court handed down a major decision on Oyama v. California.* In a six to three decision the Supreme Court found the California Alien Land Law unconstitutional and in violation of the equal protection clause of Section I of the Fourteenth Amendment

of the federal Constitution. On November 6, 1956, Californians approved Proposition 13* repealing their state's Alien Land Law.
FURTHER READING: Frank F. Chuman, *The Bamboo People: The Law and Japanese-Americans*, Del Mar, Calif.: Publisher's Inc., 1976; Roger Daniels, *The Politics of Prejudice*, Berkeley: University of California Press, 1972; Yamato Ichihashi, *Japanese in the United States*, Stanford, Calif.: Stanford University Press, 1932; K. K. Kawakami, *The Real Japanese Question*, New York: Macmillan Co., 1921.

ALL-INDIA MUSLIM LEAGUE, an organization originally established in India by leaders of the Muslim religion to provide Muslim youths with opportunities to participate in politics, thereby preventing them from joining the Indian National Congress, which was a Hindu political organization. The organization was established on December 30, 1906, when Nawab Slimullah of Dacca called for a meeting of Muslim leaders, who were attending the Muhammadan Educational Conference in Dacca, and proposed a plan to found a Central Muhammadan Association. The All-India Muslim League was established to promote loyalty to the British government among the Musalmans of India, to protect and enhance the political rights of the Musalmans, and to promote feelings of friendship and harmony among those not opposed to the goals of the league.

Under the intellectual leadership of Muhammad Iqbal (1873–1938), the league became a catalyst for the creation of Pakistan, a name the league adopted in 1940 as its official aim. In 1947 it became a political reality as Pakistan was established with more than 70 million people.

In the United States the All-India Muslim League struggled for passage of a bill through Congress that would give Asian Indians an annual quota of 100 who would be allowed to immigrate to the United States. Their efforts finally resulted in passage of the Celler Bill which allowed the admission of persons of races indigenous to India and their naturalization in 1946. (*See also* Celler, Emanuel.)
FURTHER READING: H. H. Dodwell, *The Cambridge History of India*, Vol. 6, New York: Macmillan Co., 1932; R. C. Majumdar, ed., *Struggle for Freedom*, Bombay, India: Bharatiya Vidya Bhavan, 1969; Vincent A. Smith, *The Oxford History of India*, Oxford, England: Oxford University Press, 1958.

ALLEN, HORACE N. (1858–1932), missionary, physician, and diplomat. Born on April 23, 1858, in Delaware, Ohio, Allen graduated from Ohio Wesleyan University in 1881 and from Miami Medical School in 1883. Upon graduation he decided to enter the field of mission work and went to Korea in 1884. Although he was not able to get along with his missionary colleagues, he did become a close friend and advisor to Korea's penultimate king, King Kojong,* chiefly as a result of his tending to the king's nephew who was severely wounded during a palace coup d'etat. Because of his trust in Allen, Kojong appointed the doctor as Foreign Secretary of Legation in 1887 to guide Korean diplomats sent to the United States. In 1890 Allen finally left the mission field for a diplomatic career and became Secretary of American Legation in Korea with the assistance of his associate, David W. Deshler.* Deshler was a step-son of Governor George Nash of Ohio, a close friend of Senator John Sherman, who became Secretary of State under William McKinley. Nash, a Republican, belonged to the Sherman-Hanna-McKinley wing of the party. Deshler became the intermediary between Allen and Nash, who, upon his son's urging, recommended Allen to President-elect McKinley for the top position in the American legation in Korea.

Allen became concerned about Korea's future as its powerful neighbors—Japan, China, and Russia—began to vie for control over the Korean peninsula. He felt strongly that the American government should help Korea maintain its independence. In spite of his repeated appeals to Washington, however, no help was in sight, and Allen decided to take in his own hands the course of action which he felt would influence American diplomacy in Korea. As part of his scheme, he actively sought to place American business interests in Korea, for he believed that the American government would protect America's economic interests wherever they were found. When he was asked to explore the possibility of sending Korean laborers to Hawaii, he persuaded Kojong to establish a government office to process and facilitate the immigration of Koreans to Hawaii to work for the Hawaiian Sugar Planters' Association* (HSPA). He asked Deshler to become a recruiter for the HSPA, thus paying off the political debt he owed Deshler. As a result of his effort, approximately 8,000 Koreans came to Hawaii to work on sugar cane fields between 1903 and 1905. Allen deeply believed that where the American dollar went there also went the American flag, but he was proven wrong, as the Roosevelt administration decided in November 1905 to withdraw American interests, political or otherwise, from Korea altogether in compliance with the Taft-Katsura memorandum, which was concluded on July 29, 1905 in secrecy. Through this memorandum of understanding, America acknowledged Japan's exclusive right to have control over the Korean peninsula, and in return it received Japan's concession to America's exclusive interests in the Philippines.

Allen died on December 11, 1932.

FURTHER READING: Fred H. Harrington, *God, Mammon and the Japanese*, Madison: University of Wisconsin Press, 1944; Hyung-chan Kim, *The Korean Diaspora*, Santa Barbara, Calif.: ABC-Clio Press, 1977; Andrew Nahm, "The Impact of the Taft-Katsura Memorandum on Korea—A Reassessment," *Korea Journal* 25 (October 1985), pp. 4–17, 74; Wayne K. Patterson, "The Korean Frontier in America: Immigration to Hawaii, 1896–1910," Ph.D. diss., University of Pennsylvania, 1977.

AMAE, a concept used to describe the basic dependency needs of the Japanese, meaning specifically the individual's need to be loved and cherished by others. Although it is almost impossible to translate it into English, Takeo Doi characterizes it as "the need for a passive love," as this need for love resides in the deepest inner being of the Japanese, albeit not readily and outwardly expressed. *Amae* begins as a result of the infant's realization that his mother is a separate being, and he attempts to deny this fact of separation from his mother, who becomes the object of his *amaeru-ing*. *Amae* plays an important role in the mother-infant relationship; without *amae*, a healthy personality in the infant would not develop. When *amae* is frustrated or thwarted, the Japanese tend to turn inward and are likely to blame themselves. Gerald Meredith points out that this passive behavior might have something to do with the lack of leadership among Japanese males. Takeo Doi suggests that a Japanese feels victimized by the object of his *amae* because he cannot completely control the object. This sense of being victimized is similar to the sense of being interfered with or hindered, and Takeo Doi characterizes this as the *amae* mentality.

FURTHER READING: Takeo Doi, *The Anatomy of Dependence*, Tokyo: Kodansha International Ltd., 1973; Harry Kitano, *Japanese Americans: The Evolution of a Subculture*, Englewood Cliffs, N.J.: Prentice-Hall, 1969; Gerald Meredith, "Amae and Acculturation among Japanese-American College Students in Hawaii," *Journal of Social Psychology*, 70 (December 1966); Dennis M. Ogawa, *Kodomo no tame ni* [For the sake of the children], Honolulu: University Press of Hawaii, 1978.

AMERASIA JOURNAL, a quarterly publication started by the Asian American Students Association at Yale University in 1971. The journal began in March 1971 with the intention of publishing four issues annually. Beginning with Volume 2, which was published in the fall of 1973, the Asian American Studies Center of the University of California at Los Angeles agreed to co-sponsor the journal, at which time the journal became a semi-annual publication. In 1974 the journal became a publication of the University of California at Los Angeles Asian American Studies Center. Although the center intended to publish the journal in the spring and fall of every year, it continued to publish only one issue a year until 1976. Beginning with the first issue of Volume 4, which was published in early 1977, the center began to publish the journal twice a year.

Amerasia Journal has had several editors through the years. The first editor was Lowell Chun-Hoon who was followed by Megumi Dick Osumi in the fall of 1974. Osumi and Carolyn Yee became co-editors of the journal in 1976. The following year, with the publication of the first issue of Volume 4, Yee became sole editor of the journal. In 1977 she was succeeded by Russell C. Leong who remains the editor.

Although many scholarly journals are devoted to the publication of academic and professional studies on American ethnic groups, *Amerasia Journal* is the only publication devoted exclusively to Asian American history as well as to the contemporary issues and problems facing Asian Americans and their communities.

AMERICA IS IN THE HEART. *See* Bulosan, Carlos.

AMERICAN BOARD OF COMMISSIONERS FOR FOREIGN MISSIONS, a missionary organization founded on June 29, 1810, when the General Association of Massachusetts Proper, an organization of conservative Congregational ministers, approved a plan to establish a foreign missionary board. The plan had been submitted by a group of four young men from Andover Seminary as a result of their dedication to the association. The association accepted the plan and elected nine members to the board, and left them with the responsibility of working out the details of the organization. The original nine members on the board were John Treadwell, Timothy Dwight, Jedediah Huntington, Calvin Chapin, Joseph Lyman, Samuel Spring, William Bartlet, Samuel Worcester, and Samuel Walley. The first group of missionaries dispatched by the board consisted of Samuel and Harriet Newell, and Adoniram and Ann Judson. The group left Salem on February 19, 1812, on the *Harmony*, which brought them to Calcutta, India, on June 17, 1812. With this mission as the board's first attempt to convert its vision of evangelism abroad into reality, it dispatched a large number of missionaries from America to many other parts of the world.

The organization was also responsible for evangelism in the Hawaiian Islands, or Sandwich Islands as Captain John Cook named the islands after his benefactor, the Earl of Sandwich. Sometime in 1815 the board assumed responsibility for caring for four natives of the Hawaiian Islands, one of whom was Henry Opukahaia. In the following year the board established an institution to train these four youths; another native of Hawaii, Prince Tamoree, son of an Hawaiian chief, was to join the group. The institution, the Foreign Mission School, was established, and the first class was held in May 1817. In addition to the five natives of Hawaii, seven others joined the student body. Even though a tragedy struck the school when Opukahaia died of typhus fever on February 17, 1818, the rest of the students as well as the townspeople resolved to carry on the task of sending missionaries to the islands for Christian evangelism. In fact, the number of students as well as the number of mission projects continued to grow. Before the school was closed in 1826, it had approximately 100 students of different nationalities in attendance—Chinese, Malayans, Greeks, Hawaiians, and American Indians.

One outstanding result of this institutional effort to train missionaries for foreign evangelism was the establishment of a mission on the Hawaiian Islands. In 1818 the board received a request that a missionary company be dispatched immediately to the Hawaiian Islands, but the board was not able to organize such a group until the latter part of 1819. Finally, a group of twenty-two persons— two ordained ministers, a physician, a farmer, teachers, wives, and children— were found, and they were sent to Hawaii along with three native Hawaiians— Thomas Hopu,* William Kanui, and John Honolii—and Prince Tamoree on October 23, 1819, on the *Thaddeus* which reached Hawaii in March 1820. The two ordained ministers, who were the leaders of this first missionary expedition, Asa Thurston and Hiram Bingham, were recent graduates of Andover Seminary. Bingham moved from Kailua, their original port of entry to Honolulu where he established a mission in a seaport village. Bingham (1789–1869), author of a book, called *Residence of Twenty-One Years of the Sandwich Islands; Or the Civil, Religious, and Political History of these Islands* (1848) went to Hawaii at the age of forty and spent the next twenty-one years working to convert

Hawaiian natives to Christianity. He was the first to preach in Hawaii, and he launched the ambitious project of translating the Bible into the native language. By 1828 he was able to translate the four Gospels into native Hawaiian and put them in circulation. In 1840 he was forced to leave the islands when his wife became ill. He never gave up hope of returning to Honolulu Kawaiahao Church, but he was not able to realize it.

FURTHER READING: Hiram Bingham, *Residence of Twenty-One Years of the Sandwich Islands; Or the Civil, Religious, and Political History of these Islands*, New York: Sherman Converse, 1848; Gavan Daws, *Shoal of Time*, Honolulu: University Press of Hawaii, 1968; Clifton J. Phillips, *Protestant America and the Pagan World*, Cambridge, Mass.: Harvard University Press, 1969; William E. Strong, *The Story of the American Board*, Boston: Pilgrim Press, 1910.

AMERICAN FACTORS. *See* Big Five.

AMERICAN LOYALTY CLUB, a Nisei* organization established in San Francisco in the fall of 1919, when a small group of Nisei Americans gathered together to discuss the question of their citizenship and identity. During their bull sessions, according to William K. Hosokawa,* questions such as "What is Japan like?" "What good is our citizenship?" and "What should we, as Nisei, do?" were raised. Among these people were Thomas T. Yatabe, Tom Okawara, Hiyashi Tokutaro, Hiyashi Hideki, Kay Tsukamoto, and George Kiyoshi Togasaki,* who had just returned to San Francisco from service with the U.S. Army in Europe after the Armistice. The Club was established to achieve two goals: (1) to provide the American public with a speakers' bureau so that Japanese Americans and their problems would be known; and (2) to review political candidates for an upcoming election and to encourage Japanese Americans to register to vote.

The name of the organization was changed to American Loyalty League in 1919. After Thomas T. Yatabe, one of the organization's most active members, moved to Fresno in 1923, the league became inactive.

FURTHER READING: Bill Hosokawa, *Nisei*, New York: William Morrow and Co., 1969; Bill Hosokawa, *JACL in Quest of Justice*, New York: William Morrow and Co., 1982.

AMERICAN LOYALTY LEAGUE. *See* American Loyalty Club.

AMERICAN LOYALTY LEAGUE OF FRESNO, a civic organization established by Nisei* Americans in Fresno, California, on March 5, 1923, with Thomas T. Yatabe as president. The league was established as one of many chapters of the American Loyalty League, the idea of which was proposed by an Issei,* Takimoto Tamezo, who served as secretary of the Japanese Association of North America. Takimoto strongly believed that an organization consisting of Americans of Japanese descent would be advantageous to Japanese Americans in promoting their interests. Takimoto called for a meeting of older Nisei from different parts of California and invited Yatabe to address the meeting. During the conference, delegates from San Francisco, Sacramento, Stockton, Livingston, San Jose, and Fresno agreed to establish chapters of the American Loyalty League. All other chapters, however, were stillborn, except one in Fresno. Yatabe and his organization became one of the most crucial catalysts in creating the Japanese American Citizens League* in 1930.

FURTHER READING: Bill Hosokawa, *Nisei*, New York: William Morrow and Co., 1969; Bill Hosokawa, *JACL in Quest of Justice*, New York: William Morrow and Co., 1982.

ANGEL ISLAND DETENTION CENTER, processing center for newly arrived Chinese immigrants. With passage of the Chinese Exclusion Act of 1882,* there was a need to establish an immigration station on the West Coast to process Chinese immigrants for admission to the United States. Consequently, an old warehouse at the Pacific Mail Steamship wharf in San Francisco was converted into a processing station where new Chinese immigrants were corralled before immigration inspectors could examine them to determine their admissibility. Because of crowding as well as other inhuman conditions at the center, local Chinese leaders complained and sent letters of protest both to American authorities and to the Chinese government in Peking. In response to the complaints by local Chinese leaders, Immigration Commissioner General Frank Pearce Sargent* toured the facility and declared it unfit for human habitation. In the meantime the inhuman conditions prevailing at the processing station were reported back to China, and there began a general boycott of U.S. imports that spread from Shanghai to Canton in protest against the treatment of Chinese immigrants at the center.

As a result of the recommendations Sargent made in 1903, Congress appropriated $200,000 for construction of a new processing station on the island. Construction, which began in 1905, was interrupted by the 1906 earthquake and resumed in 1907. The new station was finally completed in October of 1908, but the center was not open until January 1910, when 101 passengers of the *S.S. Siberia*, most of whom were Chinese, were refused admission and were transferred to the island.

The process used to determine the admissibility of Chinese claiming to have the right to land on American soil was long and tortuous. The immigration officials responsible for examining them were instructed to give the benefit of the doubt to the U.S. government when there was a question about the Chinese claim. As a result of the U.S. government's immigration policy, many Chinese languished on the island for months and sometimes years before their cases were settled. Some could not bear the loneliness or humiliation and committed suicide.

The detention center on Angel Island, called the Ellis Island of the West, was known to Chinese detainees as "the Isle of the Immortals." The center was closed on November 4, 1940, when the last 144 Chinese detainees were tranferred to other facilities in San Francisco.

In 1976 the California State Legislature decided to allocate $250,000 for the preservation of the building as well as the historical interpretation of the building, on whose walls Chinese detainees wrote to express their feelings and frustrations. FURTHER READING: Jack Chen, *The Chinese of America*, New York: Harper and Row, 1980; H. M. Lai, "Island of Immortals: Chinese Immigrants and the Angel Island Immigration Station," *California Historical Society* 1 (Spring 1978), pp. 88–103; Delber L. McKee, *Chinese Exclusion Versus the Open Door Policy, 1900–1906*, Detroit: Wayne State University Press, 1977; Him Mark Lai, Genny Lim, and Judy Yung, *Island: Poetry, and History of Chinese Immigrants on Angel Island, 1910–1940*, San Francisco: Hoo Doi, 1980.

ANNEXATION CLUB, a political and conspiratory organization established by Lorrin Thurston in collusion with Henry E. Cooper. The club was organized early in 1892, and its founder, Lorrin Thurston, traveled to Washington, D.C., to see if the government was willing to annex the Hawaiian Islands as a U.S. territory. Although James H. Blount,* chairman of the House Committee on Foreign Relations, was not very receptive to the idea, Secretary of State James Blaine was friendly and President Benjamin Harrison sent his words to Thurston through Secretary of the Navy Benjamin Tracy, saying that "if conditions compel you to act as you have indicated, and you come to Washington with an annexation proposal, you will find an exceedingly sympathetic administration here." Upon returning to Hawaii, Thurston continued to seek the annexation of the island by hook or by crook; first, he thought about staging a coup d'etat to overthrow the government of Queen Liliuokalani*; second, he tried to influence the legislature by having many of his sympathizers elected to that body. In 1893 most members of the club became members of the Committee of Safety that was formed in the law office of William O. Smith, a catalyst to the annexation of Hawaii to the United States as a territory. (*See also* Committee of Safety.)
FURTHER READING: Gavan Daws, *Shoal of Time*, Honolulu: University Press of Hawaii, 1968.

ANPING. *See* Sze Yap (Sze-I).

ANTICIPATORY REFUGEES, a sociological concept developed by E. F. Kunz, who suggests that the movements of refugees can be divided into two separate patterns: the flight-arrival pattern and the associative pattern. The flight-arrival pattern is further divided into two types: the acute and the anticipatory. According to Kunz, anticipatory refugees are those who have actually prepared themselves to leave their home country. Consequently, they are well informed, and many of them are well-to-do and well educated. They tend to do well in their host society as they adjust satisfactorily to a new life.

Kunz offers a caveat, however: highly educated refugees, after they have adjusted with ease to the new environment, may offer more resistance to the assimilationists' pressures than less educated refugees. (*See also* Acute Refugees.)
FURTHER READING: E. F. Kunz, "The Refugee in Flight: Kinetic Models and Forms of Displacement," *International Migration Review* 7 (Summer 1973); E. F. Kunz, "Part II: The Analytic Framework," *International Migration Review* 15 (Spring-Summer 1981); Darrel Montero, *Vietnamese Americans: Patterns of Resettlement and Socioeconomic Adaptations in the United States*, Boulder, Colo.: Westview Press, 1979.

ANTI-COOLIE CLUBS, organizations or groupings of people who used legal or illegal, peaceful or violent means to drive out the Chinese from their community and to expel them from the United States. It is extremely difficult to pinpoint the date when the first anti-coolie club was established in California. The state's historiography is of no help in this research problem. Alexander Saxton claims that groups of people who drove Chinese miners out of their diggings served, for all practical purposes, as anti-coolie clubs. These clubs used not only peaceful, but also violent means when necessary to achieve their goals of excluding and expelling Chinese laborers from jobs and competition. In addition, they often resorted to boycotting as their major public weapon.

The anti-coolie club was basically patterned on the trade-based club. In San Francisco, a spontaneous gathering of people who were against Chinese developed into a legal defense committee; out of this committee developed an organizational structure similar to that of a political party. A central committee of leaders was then charged with organizing anti-coolie clubs in each of the city's twelve wards. Later, this organization was called the Central Pacific Anti-Coolie Association.* Elmer C. Sandmeyer points to the year 1862 as the founding year of the first "official" anti-coolie club in California. The number of such organizations grew rapidly, and in 1876 they were combined under the name of the Anti-Chinese Union. Each member of the union was required to make four pledges: to uphold the constitution of the club, to refuse to employ Chinese, to refuse to buy things from employers of Chinese, and to refuse to support Chinese or the employers of Chinese. The union had many prominent members, including U.S. senators, congressmen, and well-known politicians.
FURTHER READING: S. W. Kung, *Chinese in American Life*, Seattle: University of Washington Press, 1962; Elmer C. Sandmeyer, *The Anti-Chinese Movement in California*, Chicago: University of Illinois Press, 1939; Alexander Saxton, *The Indispensable Enemy*, Berkeley: University of California Press, 1971; M. B. Starr, *The Coming Struggle; On What the People of the Pacific Coast Think of the Coolie Invasion*, San Francisco: Excelsior Office, Bacon and Co., 1873.

ANTI-MISCEGENATION LAWS, laws which in the United States go back as far as 1661. The Colony of Maryland was the first state to forbid intermarriage between individuals of two different races. In the State of Virginia, anti-miscegenation laws dated from 1691. By 1932 thirty states had passed anti-miscegenation laws. The penalties for violating these laws varied from imprisonment for a few months to prison terms of up to ten years and fines of up to $20,000. The marriages were also declared null and void and were therefore not recognized by the state. As of 1949, miscegenation was a felony in eleven states: Alabama, Florida, Georgia, Texas, Indiana, Maryland, Mississippi, Missouri, Oregon, South Dakota, and Tennessee.

Although anti-miscegenation laws in these states did not affect Asian immigrants and their descendants, anti-miscegenation laws in such states as California and Washington prevented them from marrying whites. The California anti-miscegenation law was in force until 1948 when it was repealed. Until 1948 no state or federal court had found an anti-miscegenation law unconstitutional on any ground. In 1954 the Supreme Court of the United States refused to review a conviction of miscegenation in Alabama. The Court turned aside the case of Naim, Ham Say v. Naim, Ruby Elaine.* In the case of McLaughlin v. Florida, the Supreme Court ruled in 1964 that "It is not possible for a state law to be valid under our constitution which makes the criminality of an act depend on the color of the actor," but the Court again avoided the question of the constitutionality of an anti-miscegenation law. It was only in 1967 when the Supreme Court deemed it necesesary to rule on the constitutionality of an anti-miscegenation law, in relation to the case of Loving v. Virginia, that anti-miscegenation laws became unconstitutional in America.

Richard and Mildred Loving were born in Carolina County, Virginia, and grew up as friends. In Central Point, racial lines were less noticed than in other parts of the South. They fell in love and decided to marry. If they married in Virginia, they could be fined $200 as well as being outside the law. In the District of Columbia they could marry without any legal impediment. They were married there on June 2, 1958, and returned to Carolina County. On July 11, 1958, the Justice of the Peace issued arrest warrants on the complaint of the county prosecutor. Each had to post a $1,000 bond to assure their appearance in court. Each entered a plea of not guilty, but the judge charged them with a felony and ordered them held for action of grand jury. The grand jury indicted them, and the trial was held before the Carolina County Court judge without jury, which was waived by the Lovings. They were induced to change their pleas to guilty. On January 6, 1959, the judge sentenced each to a year in jail, suspended if they would leave Virginia and not return for a period of twenty-five years. They paid court costs and went to the District of Columbia to live.

In 1963 the Lovings wrote to Attorney General Robert F. Kennedy asking for his help. He referred their letter to the American Civil Liberties Union (ACLU) and to two Alexandria, Virginia, attorneys, Bernard Cohen and Philip Hirschkop, who decided to represent the Lovings. They filed a motion in the Virginia courts to vacate judgment and set aside the sentence. The motion was denied on December 22, 1965. The next step was to appeal to Virginia's highest court. The state court found no violation of the equal protection or due process clauses of the Constitution, and subsequently the ACLU attorneys filed notice of appeal to the United States Supreme Court on May 31, 1966. The Court accepted the case for review, with a probable date of December 1966 for argument. The ACLU was joined by a number of other organizations interested in minority rights: the Japanese American Citizens League,* the National Association for the Advancement of Colored People (NAACP), the NAACP Legal Defense and Educational Fund, and various Catholic organizations. These groups filed as *amicus curiae*.

The Japanese American Citizens League noted that their organization was open to all, regardless of race and national origin, and was made up of some 20,000 persons of Japanese ancestry across the nation. The group noted that of the 464,332 Japanese Americans counted in the 1960 Census, 17,911 were in states with anti-miscegenation laws, including 1,733 in the State of Virginia. Many of the 17,911 would be affected by state laws forbidding white-Asian marriages.

Chief Justice Earl Warren* delivered the opinion of the unanimous court which found the Virginia law unconstitutional, as it violated due process of law guaranteed by the Fourteenth Amendment. He stated that "the Fourteenth Amendment requires that the freedom of choice to marry not be restricted by invidious racial discrimination. Under our Constitution, the freedom to marry, or not marry, a person of another race resides with the individual and cannot be infringed upon by the State."

FURTHER READING: James H. Johnston, *Miscengenation in the Ante-Bellum South*, Chicago: AMS Press, University of Chicago, 1972; Robert J. Sickels, *Race, Marriage, and the Law*, Albuquerque: University of New Mexico Press, 1972; *Supreme Court Reporter* 75, 348 U.S. 888.

AOKI v. DEANE. *See* San Francisco School Board Segregation Order of 1906.

ARAI, CLARENCE. *See* Seattle Progressive Citizens League.

ARIYOSHI, GEORGE (1926–), politician, business executive, civic leader, and lawyer. Born on March 12, 1926, Ariyoshi attended the University of Hawaii from which he graduated in 1947 with a B.A. degree. He received a law degree and was admitted to the Hawaii bar in 1953. He practiced law between 1953 and 1970. During these years he also served in the Territory of Hawaii House of Representatives between 1954 and 1958, and in 1958 he was elected to the Territory of Hawaii Senate. When the Hawaiian Islands became a state and was admitted to the Union, Ariyoshi was elected to the Hawaii State Senate in 1959 where he served until 1970. In the Senate he served as chairman of the Ways and Means Committee for one year and became Senate majority leader. Between 1970 and 1973 he served as lieutenant governor of Hawaii before he became acting governor in 1973. In the following year he was elected governor of Hawaii, riding on the coattails of the Burns-Inouye coalition. John Anthony Burns,* who took Ariyoshi under his political wings, has been a dominant political figure in Hawaiian politics ever since he engineered the 1954 general election which brought the legislature of Hawaii under the Democratic Party's control. (*See also* Burns, John Anthony.)

ARKANSAS RIVER VALLEY IMMIGRATION COMPANY, a company organized on June 19, 1869, as a joint stock immigration society. Prior to the establishment of this company, there already had been two commercial conventions in the Mississippi Valley, one at Memphis on May 18, 1869, and the other on May 25, 1869. During both of these conventions proposals to import Chinese laborers were submitted for the consideration of the delegates. Delegates at both conventions voted down the proposals. Cotton planters in the Arkansas Valley met at Garretson's Landing, Pine Bluff, to discuss the need for additional labor. Testimonies of people who were familiar with Chinese labor situations in China and on the Pacific Coast were heard at the meeting, and a decision was made to form a joint stock company to be called the Arkansas River Valley Immigration Company. It was decided that each subscriber would invest with a minimum of 300 bales of cotton by November 1 of that year. The company then dispatched George Washington Gift, a former lieutenant commander of the Confederate Navy and a native of Tennessee, to China to bring Chinese laborers. He left San Francisco on September 4, 1869, and arrived in Hong Kong on October 7. He worked diligently and was able to recruit 189 Chinese for the company.

The laborers recruited by Gift arrived in New Orleans on June 1, 1870. Upon arrival, they were examined by V. A. King, commissioner and physician to the Louisiana Board of Immigration, who reported that twenty Chinese had died at sea and that one had died since arrival. The rest of the Chinese laborers were sent to Arkansas and Mississippi where they worked in the cotton fields.

FURTHER READING: Gunther Barth, *Bitter Strength*, Cambridge, Mass.: Harvard University Press, 1964; Lucy Cohen, *Chinese in the Post-Civil War South: A People Without a History*, Baton Rouge: Louisiana State University Press, 1984; Robert Seto Quan, *Lotus Among the Magnolias: The Mississippi Chinese*, Jackson: University Press of Mississippi, 1982; Shihshan Henry Tsai, "The Chinese in Arkansas," *Amerasia Journal* 8, No. 1 (Spring-Summer, 1981), pp. 1–18.

ASAKURA v. CITY OF SEATTLE ET AL. (known as the "Pawnbroker Case), a suit involving R. Asakura, a lawful alien resident of Seattle, Washington, and subject of the emperor of Japan, who came to America in 1904 as a legal pawnbroker. On July 2, 1921, the city of Seattle passed an ordinance, the sole purpose of which was to prevent aliens from obtaining a license to engage in business as pawnbrokers in the city. Asakura appealed to the Superior Court of King County asking to restrain the city from enforcing the ordinance, on the grounds that the ordinance violated the treaty between the United States and Japan, and that it also violated the due process and equal protection clauses of the Fourteenth Amendment. The Superior Court of King County ruled in favor of Asakura by issuing a decree that restrained the city from preventing aliens from obtaining a license. The city of Seattle appealed to the Supreme Court of the State of Washington, and the state's highest court ruled in favor of the city and reversed the Superior Court's decision.

The Asakura case went to the U.S. Supreme Court as a writ of error so that a review of the State Supreme Court's judgment could be made. The case was heard on February 25, 1924, and was decided on May 26, 1924. Justice Butler delivered the opinion of the Court. The question before the Court was whether or not the ordinance passed by the city was in violation of the treaty signed between the United States and Japan in 1911. The Court considered the case solely on the basis of this question and did not address itself to whether or not the ordinance was in violation of the due process and equal protection clauses of the Fourteenth Amendment of the Constitution. In the opinion of the Court, which Justice Butler delivered, a treaty made under the authority of the United States was the supreme law of the land and the judges in every state had to be bound by the treaty. Furthermore, the treaty that was made in order to strengthen friendly relations between the United States and Japan and to protect citizens of one country residing in the territory of another could not be ruled null and void by municipal ordinances or state laws. The Supreme Court ruled against the city and reversed the decision made by the state's Supreme Court.

FURTHER READING: Consulate-General of Japan, *Documental History of Law Cases Affecting Japanese in the United States, 1916–1924*, San Francisco: 1925; 265 U.S. 332, 1924.

ASIA PACIFIC TRIANGLE, a term used in legislating the Immigration and Naturalization Act of 1952,* known as the McCarran-Walter Act. The term appears in Section 202 (a) of the act, and it defines a section of the world that includes the Asian continent and almost the entire Pacific Ocean. In terms of longitude and latitude, the area specified as the Asia-Pacific triangle included all of the earth's surface between 60 degrees east and 165 degrees west longitude and from the North Pole south to 25 degrees south latitude. At the time the act was passed there were twenty independent nations within this triangle, and each of them was given a special quota of 100 per annum for entry into the United States.

Although the McCarran-Walter Act was discriminatory against people of Asian ancestry, it liberalized naturalization laws by permitting people of all races to be eligible for U.S. citizenship. Because of this particular proviso which allowed many Issei* immigrants to become U.S. citizens, the Japanese American Citizens League* lobbied for passage of the act.

FURTHER READING: Robert A. Divine, *American Immigration Policy, 1924–1952*, New Haven, Conn.: Yale University Press, 1957; Frank F. Chuman, *The Bamboo People*, Del Mar, Calif.: Publisher's Inc., 1976; E. P. Hutchinson, *Legislative History of American Immigration Policy, 1798–1965*, Philadelphia: University of Pennsylvania Press, 1981.

ASIAN AMERICAN ASSEMBLY, established as a research project in the Department of Asian Studies at the City College of New York in 1973, when the college received a $25,000 grant from the Field Foundation of New York.

The money was to be spent on developing a community service program to be run by the college. The college added $6,000 to the original grant, and it received another $25,000 from the same foundation. With these three separate grants, the Department of Asian Studies was able to conduct a number of community-related projects and created the Asian American Assembly for Policy Research. Between 1976 and 1978 it held numerous seminars and workshops in an attempt to identify major problems confronting Asian immigrants in America and to recommend solutions to these problems.

ASIAN AMERICAN STUDIES, a branch of academic studies initiated by a group of students of Asian ancestry at San Francisco State College (now California State University at San Francisco) and at the University of California at Berkeley. The beginning of Asian American Studies may be attributed to the civil rights movement of the late 1950s and early 1960s when Third World students presented their demands for recruitment and for the admission of more Third World students into colleges and universities, as well as for the introduction of Black Studies to be controlled by black students and faculty.

When Asian American Studies began at a small number of higher educational institutions, there were probably as many goals as there were programs offering Asian American Studies. The need still exists for a coherent and well-articulated philosophy of Asian American Studies that would present the clear purposes and objectives of the studies to students, higher educational institutions, and Asian American communities. In a survey completed in 1978, Don Nakanishi and Russell Leong pointed out that the goals of Asian American Studies programs remain diverse, although some general goals do run through most existing programs. These goals were identified as the following: to provide students with an alternative educational perspective, to give them opportunities to participate in decision-making processes and to plan programs, and to provide students with a progressive framework for servicing Asian American communities.

Asian American Studies programs remain small. To date only fourteen institutions of higher education offer these programs, and ten of these are located in California.

FURTHER READING: Russell Endo, "Whither Ethnic Studies: A Re-examination of Some Issues," in Stanley Sue, ed., *Asian-Americans: Psychological Perspectives*, Ben Lomond, Calif.: Science and Behavior Books, 1973; Emma Gee, ed., *Counterpoint: Perspectives on Asian America*, Los Angeles: Regents of the University of California, 1976; Don Nakanishi and Russell Leong, "Toward the Second Decade: A National Survey of Asian American Studies Programs in 1978," *Amerasia Journal* 5, No. 1 (1978) pp. 1–19; Amy Tachiki et al., eds., *Roots: An Asian American Reader*, Los Angeles: Regents of the University of California, 1971.

ASIAN AMERICAN WRITERS, authors of creative writing in English who are Americans of Asian ancestry, particularly those whose ancestors came from China, Japan, Korea, and the Philippines. This is a narrow, restricted definition, for it tends to ignore authors of Asian ancestry other than the four countries mentioned and it excludes authors of Asian ancestry who have published in Asian languages. Nonetheless, authorities in the field of Asian American literature have endorsed this definition.

Asian American literature is a rather recent addition to American literature. Although some creative pieces of writing were written by and about Asians in America even before the turn of the century, more perceptive writing on the collective or personal experiences of Asians in America by persons of Asian ancestry did not emerge until the 1950s. An important catalyst in this new development in American literature was the civil rights movement of the 1960s when young people, particularly minority youths, began to question their places in a white American society.

Before Asian American literature could become a viable phenomenon, a community of readership had to be developed, and a forum had to be created for discussing and debating the Asian American experience in America. The civil rights struggle generated the general public's interest in the minority experience, thus creating readership for minority literature. The civil rights movement also produced spin-off interests in the minority experience in America's past, as well as in contemporary times. Asian American Studies programs were established at various colleges and universities across the country in order to create that forum.

Since the 1960s, numerous Asian American writers have taken up the theme of identity in a capitalist, racist, and sexist society. Among these writers are Frank Chin, author of *The Chickencoop Chinaman* (1972) and *Goong Hai Fot Choy*; Janice Mirikitani, author of several poems, including "Attack the Water," "Lullabye" and "Sing with Your Body"; and Lawson Fusao Inada, author of *Before the War* (1971).

Asians in America began to publish their writings as early as the 1900s; many of their works were biographical. Representative of this group are Lee Yan Phou, *When I Was a Boy in China* (1887); New Il-Han, *When I Was a Boy in Korea* (1928); Sugimoto Etsu, *A Daughter of the Samurai* (1925); Lin Yutang, *My Country and My People* (1937) and *Chinatown Family* (1948); Kang Younghill, *The Grass Roof* (1931) and *East Goes West* (1937); and Carlos Bulosan,* *Laughter of My Father* (1944), *The Dark People* (1944), and *America Is in the Heart* (1946).

Beginning in the 1940s, second-generation Asian American writers began to write about their own experiences in American society. A recurring theme in their works was the cultural conflict between the culture of their family and that of the larger society. Representative works are Pardee Low, *Father and Glorious Descendant* (1943), Jade Snow Wong, *Fifth Chinese Daughter* (1945), and Monica Sone,* *Nisei Daughter* (1953).

Some writers have portrayed the community life of Chinese and Japanese Americans with moderate success. Examples are Chin Yang Lee, *Flower Drum Song* (1957), and Louis Chu, *Eat a Bowl of Tea* (1961), both of which depict life in Chinatown* and the Chinese family. The internment experiences of Japanese Americans during World War II are examined in John Okada,* *No-No Boy* (1957). Toshio Mori portrays Japanese community life in *Yokohama, California*, (1949) and *The Chauvinist and Other Stories* (1979).

Other contemporary writers who have successfully interpreted the Asian American experience are Jeffrey Paul Chan in *Jackrabbit* (1974); Shawn Hsu Wong in *Homebase* (1979); and Maxine Hong Kingston in *The Woman Warrior* (1975) and *China Men* (1980).

FURTHER READING: Frank Chin et al, eds., *Aiiieeeee!*, Garden City, N.Y.: Anchor Press, 1975; Kai-yu Hsu and Helen Palubinskas, *Asian-American Authors*, Boston: Houghton Mifflin Co., 1972; Elaine Kim, *Asian American Literature*, Philadelphia: Temple University Press, 1982; and David Hsin-Fu Wand, *Asian American Heritage*, New York: Washington Square Press, 1974.

ASIATIC BARRED ZONE ACT OF 1917. *See* Immigration Act of February 5, 1917.

ASIATIC EXCLUSION LEAGUE, an organization established on May 14, 1905, as an anti-Japanese and anti-Korean group and originally called the Japanese and Korean Exclusion League. The organization used its original title as late as December 8, 1907, when its president, O. A. Tveitmoe, called for a meeting under the league's original name. In 1907, the league published a report based on U.S. government reports on occupations and wages; the report was entitled "Japanese Immigration: Occupations, Wages, etc."

In 1908 the organization changed its name to the Asiatic Exclusion League, though its major objective remained the same. The league, which originally developed out of labor union halls in San Francisco, argued for the exclusion of Japanese and Koreans on both racial and economic grounds. It enumerated several charges against the Japanese and Koreans: they could not be assimilated without bringing injury to whites; they were so distinctively different in terms of race and social heritage that they could not live with whites without doing harm; competition against them was impossible because of their low standard of living; white women were vulnerable to them, and so they should be prohibited from intermarrying; they should not be allowed to become citizens; and finally, if Japanese were allowed to come, Chinese exclusion would be endangered.

Although the league claimed to have a large membership, it must in fact have been rather small inasmuch as it was not able to increase its annual financing beyond $5,000 for any year. Nevertheless, the organization was able to incite enough agitation to goad people into mob action. On September 7, 1907, the league sponsored a parade in which more than 5,000 people marched to Vancouver's City Hall in British Columbia. There they demanded the exclusion of Japanese, and they went through the Japanese section of town, vandalizing and destroying shops and other properties owned by Japanese. Altogether they destroyed fifty-nine shops that day.

The league, drawing its strength from the rank-and-file members of labor unions, continued to agitate for the exclusion of Japanese and Koreans even after the end of World War II.

FURTHER READING: Asiatic Exclusion League, *Proceedings of the Asiatic Exclusion League, 1907–1913*, San Francisco, 1907–1913 (Reprinted in 1977 by Arno Press, New York); Roger Daniels, *The Politics of Prejudice*, New York: Atheneum, 1972; Tricia Knoll, *Becoming Americans*, Portland, Oreg.: Coast to Coast Books, 1982; H. Brett Melendy, *The Oriental Americans*, New York: Hippocrene Books, 1972.

ASSEMBLY CENTERS, temporary detention camps established by the Wartime Civil Control Administration (WCCA) on March 11, 1942. John L. DeWitt,* commanding general of the Western Defense Command, established the WCCA, with Colonel Karl R. Bendetsen* as its director, to carry out the evacuation of Japanese Americans. Soon after the Japanese surprise attack on Pearl Harbor, public sentiment for evacuating persons of Japanese ancestry was expressed. On December 15, 1941, Secretary Frank Knox* of the U.S. Navy claimed that the most effective fifth column work was done in Hawaii. As if they had waited for a signal, radio commentator John B. Hughes called for the evacuation of Japanese Americans and Walter Lippmann* wrote on the topic of "The Fifth Column on the Coast." On February 13, 1942, just one day after Lippmann's syndicated column appeared, the West Coast congressional delegation sent a letter to President Franklin Roosevelt recommending that persons of Japanese ancestry be removed from the entire strategic area of California, Washington, and Oregon.

On February 19, Roosevelt signed Executive Order 9066* which authorized the Secretary of War, or any military commander designated by the Secretary, to establish "military areas" and to exclude "any or all persons." On March 21 Roosevelt strengthened Excecutive Order 9066 by signing Public Law 503, which made it a federal offense to violate any order issued by the military commander under authority of Executive Order 9066. On the following day, a large group of Japanese Americans was evacuated from Los Angeles to the Manzanar Assembly Center. At this time the western half of the three Pacific Coast states and the southern third of Arizona came under a military area in accordance with Public Proclamation* No. 1 which had been issued by General John L. DeWitt on March 2, 1942, stipulating that all persons of Japanese ancestry be evacuated from the area.

On March 24 Civilian Exclusion Order* No. 1 was issued by General DeWitt who ordered all people of Japanese ancestry evacuated from Bainbridge Island in Puget Sound to the Puyallup Army Assembly center by March 30. This evacuation would be repeated many times until a total of 110,000 persons of Japanese ancestry were shifted to assembly centers before their final removal to relocation centers. There were twelve assembly centers in California alone: in Marysville, Sacramento, Tanforan, Stockton, Turlock, Merced, Pinedale, Fresno, Salinas, Santa Anita, Pomona, and Tulare. An Army assembly center was established in Puyallup, Washington, to which the evacuees from Bainbridge

Island were sent. Oregon's assembly center was in Portland, and Arizona's in Mayer. By September 15, 1942, the evacuation of persons of Japanese ancestry to these assembly centers was completed. (*See also* Relocation Centers.)

FURTHER READING: John L. DeWitt, *Final Report: Japanese Evacuation from the West Coast*, Washington, D.C.: U.S. Government Printing Office, 1943; Tricia Knoll, *Becoming Americans*, Portland, Oreg.: Coast to Coast Books, 1982; Dillon S. Myer, *Uprooted Americans*, Tucson: University of Arizona Press, 1971; Michi Weglyn, *Years of Infamy*, New York: William Morrow and Co., 1976.

ASSOCIATION FOR ASIAN PACIFIC AMERICAN STUDIES, an academic, professional, non-profit, and non-political organization established in 1980 to serve the special needs and interests of students, scholars, teachers, and other professionals in the field of Asian Pacific American Studies in the United States.

Preparatory steps toward establishing the association were taken during the summer of 1979 under the leadership of Douglas W. Lee, who was then teaching at the University of Washington in Seattle. By the end of August 1979, the constitution and by-laws of the association drafted by Douglas Lee were agreed on by members of the Steering Committee. Among its members were Steve Fugita, Gary R. Hess, Hyung-chan Kim, Stanford Lyman, and Franklin Odo. The constitution had eight articles, and Article II listed eight different purposes of the association. These purposes reflected its professional and academic orientation, although one of its goals was to educate American society and government concerning the history of Asian Pacific Americans and the contemporary issues and problems they face.

The association held its first annual conference at the University of Washington in Seattle on November 6–8, 1980. The conference began with the presidential address by Douglas Lee, and subsequently twenty different panels were held to discuss the issues and problems important to Asian Pacific Americans in America. The association continues to hold its once every two years conference, but the initial enthusiasm dissipated when Lee left the association.

ASSOCIATION OF INDIANS IN AMERICA, an organization of Asian Indians founded in the late 1960s by concerned leaders of Asian Indians in New York and New Jersey. Leaders of the Asian Indian communities in these states were keenly aware of the proliferation of social groups among them, which were organized on the basis of linguistic affinity and the state of origin in India. The organization felt that the joining of groups was symptomatic of their tendency to avoid contacts with the larger American society. In order to participate more fully in the larger American society, the association was formally chartered in 1971, with affiliate chapters established in various cities and states in the United States. The membership today includes people from almost all Indian states and states in the United States.

The association has endeavored to bring together Asian Indians of diverse religious and linguistic origins during the past decade, and it has created subsidiary organizations based on professional interests. Among these organizations are the Council on Medical Affairs, the Engineers Council of the association, the Council on Trade, and the Council on Travel and Tourism.

The association has been successful in its campaign to have the federal agencies responsible for collecting data on Asian Indians reclassifying them as Asian Indians rather than Caucasian/white. The term ''Asian Indians'' was used for the first time in American history in the 1980 Census questionnaire.

FURTHER READING: Parmatma Saran and Edwin Eames, *The New Ethnics*, New York: Praeger, 1980.

B

BANGO, a copper disc distributed to each plantation worker in Hawaii for the purpose of identification. On paydays, plantation police would check each worker's bango before the paycheck, which was sealed in an envelope, was given to the right person. The origin of the term may be related to the Japanese word for number.

BAY DISTRICT PLAN, a plan developed by the Equal Committee* of the Los Angeles Japanese American Citizens League* before the outbreak of the Pacific War. Nisei* leaders of Los Angeles, concerned about the possible adverse effects on their people of a war between the United States and Japan, arranged to have a meeting with Kenneth Ringle, a lieutenant commander of the U.S. Navy who was dispatched to size up the Nisei in Los Angeles. Ringle sent a report to the chief of Naval Operations, asking him to "take measures to restrain agitators . . . who are attempting to arouse sentiment . . . against these people on the basis of race alone." Sheriff Eugene Biscailuz was also invited to the Los Angeles meeting held in March 1941 between Ringle and the Nisei leaders. After the meeting the so-called Bay District Plan was announced. According to the plan, the Nisei were to report disloyal acts committed by their community members, presumably by their parents' generation; to advise against suspicious members; and to translate and investigate any cases which authorities might turn over to them. (*See also* Equal Committee.)
FURTHER READING: Bill Hosokawa, *JACL in Quest of Justice*, New York: William Morrow and Co., 1982; John Modell, *The Economics and Politics of Racial Accommodation: The Japanese of Los Angeles, 1900–1942*, Urbana: University of Illinois Press, 1977; Michi Weglyn, *Years of Infamy*, New York: William Morrow and Co., 1976.

BEAVER FALLS CUTLERY COMPANY, a manufacturing company that employed a group of seventy Chinese laborers who had been recruited by John Reeves, secretary and treasurer of the cutlery company. Reeves had gone to San

Francisco expressly to recruit Chinese laborers, but was unable to do so. Learning that a group of Chinese had just completed a railroad job in the vicinity of New Orleans, he hastened to the area with an interpreter and recruited the entire group. These Chinese laborers were brought to Beaver Falls, Pennsylvania, on July 1, 1872, to work at the cutlery as strike-breakers.
FURTHER READING: Gunther Barth, *Bitter Strength,* Cambridge, Mass.: Harvard University Press, 1964.

BELLINGHAM ANTI-HINDU RIOT, an incident in 1907 in which mob action was taken to drive out several hundred "Hindus" from the city of Bellingham, a town located about fifty miles south of Vancouver, British Columbia, in the corner of the Pacific Northwest, in the State of Washington.

In May 1907 two Asian Indians, Linah Singh and Allah Sing, entered the United States via Vancouver illegally and were sent back home to India. Upon their return to India, they spread the word that work was available in Bellingham. This precipitated a large influx of Asian Indians into the border city. As the number of Asian Indians increased, the townspeople began to object to their presence. They claimed that the "Hindus" were unsanitary and that they would not adapt to white culture. On the night of September 4, 1907, a mob of 400 to 600 men began to riot and attacked the homes of the Hindus. The mob action was intended to drive them out of Bellingham. As a result of the mob action, six Hindus were hospitalized, 410 were placed under custody in the Bellingham jail, and 750 fled from the city into Canada.

Bellingham Mayor Alfred L. Black was outraged by the riot and was determined to take proper measures against any further incident. Nonetheless, he maintained that the Hindus were responsible for bringing the action on themselves because of their conspicuous dress. Had they not been so conspicuous, he said, they would not have been victimized. One of the City Council members, called into an emergency meeting to discuss the incident, suggested that the Hindus' refusal to assimilate into the local culture was responsible for the mob action. The mill owners unanimously denounced their Hindu employees, but refused to fire any of them.

A formal investigation into the role of the police during the riot suggested that police chief Lewis A. Thomas had known that the riot was planned but chose non-intervention under the condition that no bloodshed would occur. Some observed that the police were sympathetic with the rioters and therefore chose not to act. Although the resignation of Police Chief Thomas was called for, he was not forced to resign. Little substantial action was taken to correct the wrongdoings, and only a few arrests followed. About a week later, Asian Indians in Everett, Washington, asked for police protection as they anticipated mob actions against them.
FURTHER READING: Norris Hundley, Jr., ed., *The Asian American: The Historical Experience*, Santa Barbara, Calif.: ABC-CLIO Press, 1976; H. Brett Melendy, *Asians in America*, Boston: Twayne Publishers, 1977; Robert E. Wynne, "American Labor

Leaders and the Vancouver Anti-Oriental Riot,'' *Pacific Northwest Quarterly* 57, No. 4 (October 1966), pp. 172–179.

BENDETSEN, KARL R. (1907–), lawyer, government official, and business executive. Bendetsen was born on October 11, 1907, in Aberdeen, Washington, and went to Stanford University, from which he received an A.B. in 1929 and an LL.B. three years later. Around 1932 he entered the Officers Reserve Corps, in which he stayed until 1940 when he was admitted to practice in the courts of California, Oregon, and Washington. In 1934 he opened his law office in Aberdeen and continued to practice until he was appointed to the office of the Judge Advocate General for the Army, Washington, D.C., with the rank of captain. His promotion in the army came rapidly as he became a major in 1941 and a colonel in the following year. As head of the Aliens Division of the Provost Marshal General, he was directly involved in planning the evacuation and relocation of persons of Japanese ancestry during World War II. He proudly claimed that he ''conceived the method, formulated details and directed evacuation of 120,000 persons of Japanese ancestry from military areas.'' For his service to the nation, the government awarded him the Distinguished Service Medal. He retired from public service briefly in 1946, but was recalled when he was nominated to become Assistant Secretary of the Army by President Harry S. Truman on January 20, 1950. Many Nisei* Japanese Americans sent letters of protest to the President expressing their bitter feelings about Bendetsen and his involvement in the evacuation decision. Nonetheless, he was appointed and served as Undersecretary of the Army for a brief period between May and September 1952.
FURTHER READING: Roger Daniels, *Concentration Camps U.S.A.: Japanese Americans and World War II*, New York: Holt, Rinehart and Winston, 1971; Audrie Girdner and Anne Loftis, *The Great Betrayal: The Evacuation of the Japanese-Americans During World War II*, New York: Macmillan Co., 1969; Peter Irons, *Justice at War*, New York: Oxford University Press, 1983; Anna Rothe, *Current Biography 1946*, New York: H.W. Wilson Co., 1947; Michi Weglyn, *Years of Infamy*, New York: William Morrow and Co., 1976.

BERGER v. BISHOP, a lawsuit filed in a U.S. District Court against E. Faxon Bishop by Frederick V. Berger for violation of the act of March 3, 1903, entitled ''An Act to Regulate Immigration of Aliens into the United States,'' which had been introduced by Representative William B. Shattuc of Ohio. This law prohibited anyone from bringing to the United States and its territories a contract laborer who had been paid to come before his arrival in the United States.

There had already been a law on the books against bringing contract laborers to the United States, but the act of March 3, 1903, strengthened the Foran Act of February 26, 1885,* by inserting two important provisions. First, the law required an examination of whether or not the alien, upon arrival, had paid his own passage or whether it had been paid by another person, corporation, or society and by whom. Second, the law provided that any private citizen could bring suit against a person, corporation, or society to ferret out the illegal immigration of contract laborers and to receive monetary rewards for doing so. Furthermore, the law permitted a lawsuit for each violation of the provision, and each violation carried with it a $1,000 reward.

E. Faxon Bishop had begun to work for C. Brewer and Company in 1883 and became its secretary in 1891. Two years later he also assumed the position of company treasurer and ultimately became president of the company in 1909. Later he served three terms as president of the Hawaiian Sugar Planters' Association* (HSPA). He was also elected to the Senate of the Territory of Hawaii in 1904, becoming its president in 1907.

After the initial negotiations were completed between the HSPA and Horace N. Allen* for bringing Korean laborers to Hawaii to work on plantations, the HSPA sent Bishop to work out various details of the plan with David W. Deshler,* who had been given the job of recruiting Koreans in Korea. Bishop left for Asia on September 9, 1902, arriving in Japan on September 16, where he arranged for the transportation of Korean laborers and familiarized himself with Japanese immigration regulations.

During the first week of October, Bishop arrived in Korea and made contact with Horace Allen, while staying at the home of David Deshler in Inchon, which was the port of departure for Korean laborers between 1902 and 1905. Bishop negotiated with Deshler on the terms of contract for recruiting Koreans for the HSPA and deposited $25,000 in a bank created by Deshler for the sole purpose of financing the HSPA's immigration project. Every Korean laborer was then paid a sum of $100, half of which went for passage and the other half for incidental expenses. Thus, the HSPA violated the act of March 3, 1903, for it prepaid passage for Korean laborers and gave them pocket money to spend.

The first few shiploads of Korean laborers to Hawaii did not cause any problems for the HSPA, but when the *Nippon Maru*, carrying 113 Koreans, arrived at Honolulu on April 30, 1903, it was not allowed to unload its passengers until May 6, when the Board of Special Inquiry determined that the Koreans were being brought in legally. But during the investigation Bishop admitted that some Koreans had been assisted with money for their passage. This admission became the legal bone of contention between Berger and Bishop. The case was heard by Judge Morris M. Estee who decided on September 19, 1903, that because all Korean laborers aboard the *Nippon Maru* had been recruited before March 3, 1903, the date of passage of the affected law, Bishop was not guilty. Thus, Bishop and the HSPA were found not guilty on a technicality. (*See also* Allen, Horace N.; Deshler, David W. and Foran Act of 1885.)

FURTHER READING: Bong-youn Choy, *Koreans in America*, Chicago: Nelson-Hall Press, 1979; Wayne Patterson, "The Korean Frontier in America: Immigration to Hawaii, 1896–1910," Ph.D. diss., University of Pennsylvania, 1977.

BERTILLON SYSTEM, a system invented by a French anthropologist, Alphonse Bertillon (1853–1914) in 1883 as a means of identifying criminals. It was based on the assumption that there were twelve measurements on an adult that were subject to little change. This system was adopted as the standard method for identifying criminals in the United States and in 1904 it was applied to the examination of incoming Chinese, whose body parts were measured and recorded by immigration officials at the port of entry.

This method was later replaced by the fingerprinting system as an identification method.

BETHEL MISSION SCHOOL, a school established in 1869 as an evening school where Chinese-born adolescents and young adults were taught how to speak, read, and write English. This institution was a precursor of the Chinese language schools in Hawaii. It was said that between 1870 and 1881 a total of 265 students went through this school, 248 of whom were Chinese. (*See also* Language Schools.)

FURTHER READING: Clarence E. Glick, *Sojourners and Settlers: Chinese Migrants in Hawaii*, Honolulu: University Press of Hawaii, 1980.

BIDDLE, FRANCIS (1886–1968), lawyer, government official. Biddle was born into a well-to-do Philadelphia family on May 9, 1886, in Paris. He received a B.A. degree from Harvard University in 1909 and obtained his law degree from Harvard in 1911. He opened his first law office in his hometown, Philadelphia, and was later involved in Democratic Party politics. After changing his loyalty from the Republican Party to the Democratic Party, he was considered an ardent New Dealer. Between 1934 and 1935 he served as chairman of the National Labor Board and became a chief counsel to a joint congressional committee investigating the Tennessee Valley Authority in 1938. Before being appointed Attorney General in September 1941, he served as judge on the U.S. Third Circuit Court as well as U.S. Solicitor General.

Biddle was initially opposed to the Department of War plan to have all persons of Japanese ancestry evacuated and relocated. He felt that there was no need for a mass evacuation of all persons of Japanese ancestry inasmuch as precautionary measures had already been taken to control suspicious alien enemies. He also believed that the removal of all West Coast Japanese, regardless of their citizenship, would be in violation of the constitutional guarantee.

On February 17, 1942, eleven days after Secretary of War Henry Lewis Stimson* had decided on the evacuation and relocation of persons of Japanese ancestry on the West Coast, Biddle sent a memorandum to President Franklin Roosevelt in an effort to stop the plan. But his action was not strong enough. President Roosevelt had already given Stimson permission to carry out the plan with a word of caution to his aides, who were advised to be "reasonable." Many years later, in his memoirs *In Brief Authority* (1962), Biddle expressed deep regret over the entire affair. Perhaps as a reaction to his role in depriving Americans of their constitutional rights, he later became a champion of civil liberties. In 1950 he was elected national chairman of Americans for Democratic Action (ADA), and under his leadership the organization strongly supported civil rights legislation. In his book *The Fear of Freedom* (1952), Biddle spoke out against the anti-Communist hysteria in the early 1950s and severely criticized the House Un-American Activities Committee, publicly condemning Senator Joseph R. McCarthy. After he resigned the ADA chairmanship, Biddle served as advisor to the American Civil Liberties Union. He died in October 1968.

FURTHER READING: Francis Biddle, *In Brief Authority*, New York: Doubleday, 1962; Francis Biddle, *The Fear of Freedom*, New York: Doubleday, 1952; Roger Daniels, *Concentration Camps U.S.A.*, New York: Holt, Rinehart and Winston, 1971; Bill Hosokawa, *Nisei*, New York: William Morrow and Co., 1969.

BIG FIVE, the five major sugar agencies or corporations in Hawaii that controlled not only the sugar economy, but also all other aspects of the Hawaiian economy, including pineapple production, the retail merchandise business, electric power, telephone communication, railroad transportation, steamship lines, banking, and the tourist industry. The five were Castle and Cooke,* C. Brewer and Company, Theo H. Davies and Company, American Factors, and Alexander and Baldwin.

Ever since the introduction of sugar plantations on the Hawaiian Islands by William Hooper in 1835, sugar has been a dominant economic force in Hawaii's economy, transforming not only the lives of Hawaiian natives and those engaged in the industry, but also the relations between the islands and the mainland. The sugar industry in Hawaii grew rapidly under various influences created by the Great Mahele,* the California Gold Rush of 1849,* the American Civil War, and the Reciprocity Treaty of 1875.* Sugar production jumped from 30 tons in 1838 to 556,871 tons in 1920. When measured in dollars, the exported sugar amounted to $119,490,666 in 1920. Between 1875 and 1910 the work force employed in sugar production increased more than thirteen times, from 3,260 to 43,917. Many of these workers were brought to Hawaii from China, Japan, Korea, and the Philippines.

The influence of the five corporations on the sugar economy was dominant. For instance, from the total of 556,871 tons of sugar produced in 1920, American Factors controlled 29 percent, C. Brewer 26 percent, and Alexander and Baldwin 23 percent. Castle and Cooke controlled 10 percent, and Theo H. Davies and Company 6 percent.

After World War II the Big Five corporations began to diversify their investments and interests, as sugar became less dominant in Hawaii's overall economy. Castle and Cooke, the biggest of the five, began to diversify its investments as early as 1946 when it decided to go into macadamia nut orchards by purchasing 1,000 acres of land near Hilo. It acquired major controlling interest in Hawaiian Tuna Packers, Ltd. In 1956 the company organized Hawaii's first electronics firm. Later, Castle and Cooke, the Hawaiian Pineapple Corporation, and the Columbia River Packers Association merged to become the largest business corporation in Hawaii.

C. Brewer and Company, the oldest firm established by non-Hawaiians in 1826, began to expand its sugar interests in new and unusual ways under the leadership of Boyd MacNaughton, who succeeded Alan Davis in 1959, the year Hawaii was admitted into the Union. MacNaughton helped to establish the Hawaiian Agronomics Company in hopes of exporting sugar technology and of managing sugar plantations throughout the world.

C. Brewer and Company received its first international contract from the government of Iran to supervise land development and the operation of sugar mills in that country. The company also purchased all the common stocks of the Hawaiian Insurance and Guarantee Company, showing its interests in fields other than sugar and agriculture.

Theo. H. Davies and Company had begun to diversify its investments long before other major companies did. It had to probably in order to compete with bigger corporations. (It was the smallest of the five.) The company had engaged in shipping, insurance, and wholesale as well as retail merchandising for many years. Under the leadership of James H. Tabor, it acquired the Orient and Pacific lines, with its six passenger ships and ships of four other freighter companies.

American Factors, Hawaii's largest company, went through some radical changes in 1959 under the new leadership of C. Hutton Smith who succeeded George W. Sumner. American Factors made heavy investments in four areas—wholesaling, plantations, land, and insurance. Because of the company's lack of land policy, as well as lack of vision on employer-employee relations, the company began to lose its competitive edge in the wholesale as well as other markets. As soon as Smith became president of the company, he created a public-employee relations department and began to improve employer-employee relations that were competitive with other companies. In order to correct past land policies, he created a new division that was in charge of a $36 million development plan for tourism. American Factors also began to export sugar technology by cooperating with its subsidiary, American Factors Associates, and the Hawaiian Dredging and Construction Company to found a new organization, called Sugar International. It was to design, construct, and operate all sugar industries located in sugar belts the world over. It also invested heavily in foreign land development by agreeing to convert 1.3 million acres in western Australia into pasture land, as well as into land suitable for raising crops such as oats and barley.

Alexander and Baldwin, the second largest of the sugar factors, was least sensitive to changing economic realities in Hawaii. Nevertheless, it also had to undergo some changes in order to stay in business. In 1959, under the leadership of J. W. Cameron, the company began to diversify its overall interests by obtaining one-third ownership of the Matson Navigation Company, 25 percent of the new Kentron Hawaii Electronics firm, in addition to small interests in the Hawaiian Cement Corporation and Hawaiian Western Steel Company.

FURTHER READING: Edwin Burrows, *Hawaiian Americans*, New Haven, Conn.: Yale University Press, 1947; Gavan Daws, *Shoal of Time*, Honolulu: University Press of Hawaii, 1968; Lawrence H. Fuchs, *Hawaii Pono: A Social History*, New York: Harcourt, Brace and World, 1961; J. G. Smith, *The Big Five*, Honolulu: Advertiser Publishing Co., 1944; Ronald Takaki, *Pau Hana: Plantation Life and Labor in Hawaii*, Honolulu: University of Hawaii Press, 1983.

BIGGERS, EARL DERR (1884–1933), author of the Charlie Chan novels. Biggers was born in Warren, Ohio, and developed an interest in writing early in life. He entered Harvard University in 1903, majoring in journalism. After graduating in 1907, he went to work for the *Boston Traveller* as a columnist and theatre critic. Because of his vivid imagination and his tendency to sensationalize facts, he was soon dismissed, at which point he decided to pursue a career as a freelance writer.

Biggers' first attempt at freelance writing was unsuccessful, but it was not long before his style caught the public eye. *Seven Keys to Balkpate* (1913), a novel, was Biggers' initial success and was later adapted to stage and screen. It would be another twelve years before his next success, this time with the novel, *The House Without a Key*, the first of the Charlie Chan series, written in 1925. He continued writing the Charlie Chan novels at the rate of about one a year until his death in 1933. A year before his death he wrote *The Keeper of the Keys*.

The character of Charlie Chan in Biggers' novels was based on a Chinese American detective from Hawaii, Chang Apana. Biggers was even visited once by Apana in his Honolulu home, a visit that undoubtedly influenced his opinion of Asians. Biggers would later be quoted as saying, ''Sinister and wicked Chinese are old stuff in mysteries, but an amiable Chinese on the side of law and order has never been used.'' (Kunitz, p. 62) Evidently, Biggers was interested in improving the image of Asians by changing the prevailing stereotypes associated with Asians. However, he unknowingly created another stereotype of the Chinese in Charlie Chan by depicting them as bowing, self-effacing creatures who live by the writings of Confucius from which they quote frequently.

FURTHER READING: Elaine Kim, *Asian American Literature*, Philadelphia: Temple University Press, 1982; Stanley Kunitz, ed., *Authors Today and Yesterday*, H.W. Wilson Col. 1934; John Reilly, *Twentieth Century Crime and Mystery Writers*, New York: St. Martin's Press, 1980.

BIGLER, JOHN (1805–1871), politician, diplomat. Bigler was born on January 8, 1805, near Carlisle, Pennsylvania, the son of Jacob Bigler, a farmer of German ancestry. He entered Dickinson College but could not complete his education there because his family moved to Mercer County, where he became an apprentice to a printer. In 1827 Bigler's apprenticeship was terminated, and he moved to Bellefonte County to edit the *Centre County Democrat* until 1832. Next he took up the study of law and was admitted to the bar in 1840. Caught by the fever of the California Gold Rush of 1849,* he left Mount Sterling, Illinois, in April 1849 with his wife and daughter, and traveled overland to Sacramento, arriving there in August.

In 1849 Bigler was elected to the Assembly of the first state legislature which convened at San Jose on December 16, 1849. He served as assemblyman for two terms and was twice chosen as speaker of the Assembly. In 1851 he was elected governor on the Democratic ticket and was reelected two years later.

As governor, Bigler sent three special messages to the 1852 legislature, one of which had to do with his proposal to restrict Chinese immigration. This proposal reflected his stand on major policies. In his special message he declared that the unrestricted immigration of Chinese coolies and contract labor was a danger to the state. He believed that the Chinese could not become good citizens. Three years later he took up the same theme, declaring that the state had a right to regulate immigration. He asked for a head tax on Asian immigration to use as a check against the Chinese and as revenue for the state treasury. The legislature followed Bigler's leadership by enacting a $50 tax on all immigrants who could not become citizens.

Bigler ran for a third term but he was defeated. As a reward for his active campaign for the nomination of James Buchanan for President, he was appointed Minister to Chile in April 1857. He was replaced after the election of Abraham Lincoln, however. Upon his return he ran for Congress but was roundly defeated. He was appointed to the office of federal assessor of internal revenue for the Sacramento district by President Andrew Johnson in October 1866, but the U.S. Senate refused to confirm him. He never again held public office.

FURTHER READING: Mary R. Coolidge, *Chinese Immigration*, New York: Henry Holt and Co., 1909; H. Brett Melendy, *The Oriental Americans*, Boston: Twayne Publishers, 1972; H. Brett Melendy and Benjamin F. Gilbert, *The Governors of California*, Georgetown, Calif.: Talisman Press, 1965.

BINGHAM, HIRAM (1789–1869). *See* American Board of Commissioners for Foreign Missions.

BISHOP, E. FAXON. *See* Berger v. Bishop.

BLOUNT, JAMES H. (1837–1903), lawyer, congressman, diplomatic envoy. Born on September 12, 1837, in Jones County, Georgia, Blount attended the University of Georgia, from which he graduated in 1857. He studied law and was admitted to the Macon bar. During the Civil War he served in the Confederate Army. In 1872 he was elected to the House of Representatives and maintained his seat until 1893, when he declined to run for public office. While in Congress, he served on the Appropriations and the Ways and Means committees, and chaired the Committee on Foreign Affairs.

Blount's experience with foreign relations in Congress led President Grover Cleveland to appoint him as a special commissioner with paramount authority to represent the government of the United States and to investigate conditions in Hawaii which led to the establishment of the provisional government there on January 17, 1893 after the revolution that deposed Queen Liliuokalani.* With the President's instruction of March 11, 1893, to find out why the revolution took place and what part American Minister John Leavitt Stevens played, Blount promptly arrived in Hawaii. Blount's thorough investigation led him to conclude that Stevens had taken an active part in the whole affair, and he ordered the

U.S. Marines to withdraw. When Stevens resigned, he served in Stevens' place until August; at that time he returned to Washington to submit his report to the President who accepted it with praise and gratitude.

Although his report clarified the role Minister Stevens played in overthrowing the government of Queen Liliuokalani, it did not stop Sanford Ballard Dole* and his associates from declaring the inauguration of the Hawaiian Republic on July 4, 1894. (*See also* Annexation Club.)
FURTHER READING: Gavan Daws, *Shoal of Time*, Honolulu: University Press of Hawaii, 1968.

BOAT PEOPLE, refugees from Vietnam who fled from that country in boats after the American debacle in 1975. Most of these refugees who risked their lives to escape from Vietnam were ethnic Chinese, whose ancestors had come to Vietnam to establish themselves as businessmen and small traders. A steady flow of Chinese from southern China to Vietnam grew until the number reached 200,000 in 1921. By 1975, 2 million Vietnamese of Chinese ancestry, or ethnic Chinese, called Vietnam their home.

Race or ethnic relations between Vietnamese and ethnic Chinese remained tenuous, as native Vietnamese resented Chinese success in small business and trade. Although the Chinese population in Vietnam constituted 7 percent of the total population, they controlled almost 80 percent of business. In addition, the religious difference between Chinese who held Taoist and Confucian ideas and Vietnamese who were Buddhists aggravated race relations between the Chinese and Vietnamese.

Two factors seemed to have influenced the exodus of ethnic Chinese from Vietnam. First, the victorious government of North Vietnam began to socialize the economy of South Vietnam as early as 1975. But a full-scale socialization was undertaken by the government in 1978, when more small shops owned and operated by ethnic Chinese were ordered closed. Many shop owners who had never worked in the rice fields were marched off to work in the countryside. Second, the international relations between Vietnam and the People's Republic of China went from bad to worse, and eventually, in 1979, the two nations went to war. Before the Chinese invasion of Vietnam, the government of Vietnam encouraged ethnic Chinese to immigrate to other countries. It is not clear why the government took this position, although there has been speculation that the government wanted to take over business interests held by ethnic Chinese.

When the exodus of Chinese businessmen began in 1978, it was arranged through middlemen who charged between $1,000 to $3,000 for each refugee who wanted to get a place on the boat. Nevertheless, it was more orderly than the exodus of large numbers of Chinese who were forced out of Vietnam between March and July 1979. As the Vietnamese government increased its propaganda of fear against all ethnic Chinese during the Chinese invasion, what had been a trickle of ethnic Chinese and Vietnamese wanting to leave Vietnam was turned into a flood of people leaving with no known destination. No accurate records were kept on how many refugees perished at sea. Estimates are as high as 200,000. In July 1979 a conference of sixty-five nations was held in Geneva to consider the problem of caring for these refugees who had not been allowed to land by a number of governments. Finally, under international pressure the Hanoi regime agreed to halt the flight of refugees, while the governments of Australia, France, Canada, the People's Republic of China, and the United States agreed to accept refugees.

FURTHER READING: James Haskins, *The New Americans: Vietnamese Boat People*, Hillside, N.J.: Enslow Publishers, 1980; Tricia Knoll, *Becoming Americans*, Portland, Oreg.: Coast to Coast Books, 1982.

BOGARDUS, EMORY STEPHEN (1882–1973), teacher, scholar, writer, and pioneer in social research. Bogardus was born on February 21, 1882, in Belvidere, Illinois and he received a B.A. degree from Northwestern University in 1908. After earning his Ph.D. from the University of Chicago in 1911, he was appointed to the University of Southern California as assistant professor, rising rapidly to the rank of full professor in 1915. While teaching there, he came to know the problems and issues facing university students from the Philippines and became involved in their plight. He studied and researched Filipino community problems and published numerous articles in an attempt to bring American public attention to Filipinos in America. Among these are "American Attitudes Toward Filipinos," *Sociology and Social Research*, Vol. 14, No. 1 (September-October 1929), pp. 59–69; "Filipino Immigrant Attitudes," *Sociology and Social Research*, Vol. 14, No. 5 (May-June 1929), pp. 472–479; "The Filipino Immigration Situation," *Pan-Pacific Progress*, Vol. 12 (January 1930), pp. 17–19; "The Filipino Press in the United States," *Sociology and Social Research*, Vol. 18, No. 6 (July-August 1934), pp. 581–586; "The Filipino Repatriation Movement in the United States," *Sociology and Social Research*, Vol. 21, No. 1 (September-October 1936), pp. 67–71; and "Citizenship for Filipinos," *Sociology and Social Research*, Vol. 29, No. 1 (September-October 1944), pp. 51–54.

Bogardus is known for his pioneering studies on social distance, race relations, and social psychology.

BOO HOW DOY, a term used to refer to hired or paid soldiers of the *tongs*,* or Chinese secret societies, who were paid to fight frequent *tong* wars against opposition *tongs*. These mercenaries, also known as hatchetmen or highbinders to white citizens, protected the illicit business activities of their *tongs*, which engaged in gambling, prostitution, and smuggling. Chinese secret societies were organized between 1850 and 1860 in San Francisco's Chinatown.* But their presence in Chinese California was not known to the American public until the summer of 1862 when a Sacramento newspaper ran a story on disputing Chinese associations. (*See also Tongs.*)

FURTHER READING: Richard H. Dillon, *The Hatchet Men: The Story of Tong Wars in San Francisco's Chinatown*, New York: Coward-McCann, 1862; Stanford M. Lyman,

The Asian in North America, Santa Barbara, Calif.: ABC-Clio Press, 1970; Tricia Knoll, *Becoming Americans*, Portland, Oreg.: Coast to Coast Books, 1982.

BOSE, SUDHINDRA NATH (1883–1946), teacher, scholar, and professor who taught at the State University of Iowa from 1913 until his death in 1946. When the Congress of the United States began to debate the Immigration Act of February 5, 1917,* also known as the Asiatic Barred Zone Act of 1917, Bose wrote British Ambassador Cecil Spring-Rice, asking what steps had been taken to lodge a protest against the discriminatory bill under debate. In his reply to Professor Bose's inquiry, the British ambassador stated that, because the debate on the bill was considered a domestic matter, it was not proper to interfere with it. (*See also* Immigration Act of February 5, 1917.)
FURTHER READING: H. Brett Melendy, *Asians in America*, Boston: Twayne Publishers, 1977; Haridas T. Muzumdar, *America's Contributions to India's Freedom*, Allahabad, India: Central Book Depot, 1962.

BOW ON GUK (SELF-DEFENSE SOCIETY), an organization of Chinese in Hawaii established in 1887 to help protect the interests of the Chinese community in Hawaii. The organization was established to raise money from within the Chinese community to carry out measures to protect the life and property of Chinese residents in Hawaii. The fund raising was done in response to the rising criticism and outcries of white residents supported by the Anti-Asiatic Union and the Workingmen's Party of California,* which protested against the unfair Chinese competition.

The Society asked its members to contribute a dollar or more, and Chinese merchants were asked to contribute 25 cents for each $100 their business transacted. With the funds raised, the society purchased a two-story building in Chinatown which was used as its headquarters.
FURTHER READING: Clarence Glick, *Sojourners and Settlers: Chinese Migrants in Hawaii*, Honolulu: University Press of Hawaii, 1980.

BOWRON, FLETCHER (1887–1968), lawyer, newspaper reporter, government official, and mayor of Los Angeles. Bowron was born on August 13, 1887, in Poway, San Diego County, California, where he went to school until 1902. He studied law at the University of Southern California, but did not complete his study. He next entered into newspaper reporting and continued to work for the next six years. He got his law degree finally, and in 1917 he was admitted to the California bar but did not have time to practice as he entered the wartime U.S. Army, rising to the rank of second lieutenant before his discharge. Returning to Los Angeles in 1919, he formed a law partnership with Z. B. West and continued to practice until 1923 when he was appointed deputy state corporation commissioner. Later he was appointed to a vacancy on the bench of the Superior Court of Los Angeles County, a position he held for twelve years before he was elected mayor of Los Angeles on September 16, 1938.

After the Japanese attack on Pearl Harbor, Bowron, who had been supported in his mayoral compaign by the Japanese American community in Los Angeles, urged the federal government to take immediate action to remove Japanese Americans. Insisting that people with a sick sentimentality would not want to see all Japanese removed, he called for a total evacuation of all persons of Japanese ancestry—regardless of their citizenship. Federal authorities heeded Bowron's statements and appointed him U.S. Coordinator of Civilian Defense for the Los Angeles Metropolitan Area between 1942 and 1945. He died on September 11, 1968.

FURTHER READING: John Modell, *The Economics and Politics of Racial Accommodation: The Japanese of Los Angeles, 1900–1942*, Urbana: University of Illinois Press, 1977; William Peterson, *Japanese Americans*, New York: Random House, 1971.

BRAIN DRAIN, a term used to refer to the flow of well-educated and highly skilled persons from less economically and technologically developed regions of the world to the United States. The magnitude of the loss of technological and scientific manpower from Asian countries, particularly from Taiwan, the Philippines, Korea, Japan, and India, to the United States through emigration is considered significant, as thousands of students from these countries have decided to stay in the United States after their education and training in America. The draining of the talented and skilled manpower from these nations to the United States will have a lasting impact on the future development of their respective countries.

Tens of thousands of people with scientific and technological know-how have moved to the United States. For instance, between 1953 and 1966 a total of 6,368 Korean students came to the United States for their study, as reported by the Ministry of Education of that country. As of 1967, only 6 percent of them had returned home after their studies. The corresponding figure was 12 percent for students from India and 22.2 percent for students from Hong Kong, China, Formosa, Japan, and India, as of 1966.

FURTHER READING: Walter Adams, *The Brain Drain*, New York: Macmillan Co., 1968; Committee on the International Migration of Talent, New York: Praeger, 1970; Herbert G. Grubel and Anthony Scott, *The Brain Drain*, Waterloo, Ontario, Canada: Wilfried Laurier University Press, 1977; Tai K. Oh, *The Asian Brain Drain: A Factual and Casual Analysis*, San Francisco: R. & E. Research Associates, 1977.

BROWN, L. DEAN. *See* Interagency Task Force.

BRYAN, WILLIAM JENNINGS (1860–1925), lawyer, newspaper reporter, congressman, presidential candidate at the age of thirty-six, and Secretary of State under President Woodrow Wilson. Bryan was born on March 19, 1860, in Salem, Illinois, and went to Illinois College, graduating in 1881. Upon graduation he studied law with Lyman Trumbull and practiced in Jacksonville, Illinois, between 1883 and 1887, when he moved to Lincoln, Nebraska. In 1890 he ran successfully for Congress as a Democratic candidate; he was reelected in 1892. After two terms in Congress, he ran for the Senate but was defeated. Twice, in 1896 and 1900, Bryan was nominated by the Democratic Party as its presidential candidate but was defeated. He supported Woodrow Wilson in Wilson's bid for the Presidency. When Wilson was elected and inaugurated as the first Democratic President of the twentieth century on March 4, 1913, Bryan was named Secretary of State, an office he served until June 9, 1915.

Even before Wilson was elected President, the California Legislature began to discuss a bill drafted by State Attorney General U. S. Webb, which was designed to prohibit aliens ineligible for citizenship from owning land in the State of California.

On March 5, one day after the inauguration, while the California State Legislature was in recess, Japanese Ambassador Chinda Sutemi* called the President to discuss the pending legislation in California. In his reply, President Wilson stated that the federal government could not interfere with state rights in accordance with the Constitution, but that he would do what he could to influence the state legislature so that discriminatory laws would not pass. Wilson then sent Bryan to California for the purpose of consultation and cooperation with the state legislature on the proposed bill. Bryan arrived in California after a four-day trip and delivered an address before the legislature asking its members to respect the President's wishes. Although members of the legislature were cordial to Bryan, they passed the bill while Bryan was still in California. Governor Hiram W. Johnson* signed the bill on May 19, 1913. (*See also* Johnson, Hiram W.; Chinda Sutemi; and Alien Land Act of California, 1913.)

FURTHER READING: Roger Daniels, *The Politics of Prejudice*, Berkeley: University of California Press, 1962; Paul W. Glad, *William Jennings Bryan: A Profile*, New York: Hill and Wang, 1968; Louis W. Koenig, *Bryan*, New York: G.P. Putnam's Sons, 1971; George M. Stephenson, *A History of American Immigration, 1820–1924*, New York: Russell and Russell, 1964.

BUAKEN, MANUEL (1911–   ), writer. Buaken was born in the Philippines in April 1911 to Nicholas Buaken and Anna Biteng whose ancestors had migrated to the Philippines from India. His parents were highly educated, his father being a Methodist minister and his mother a scholar of Sanskrit literature. Manuel grew up in the Philippines and was sent to the United States on September 17, 1927, for his education at Princeton University. Although he had a church scholarship, he decided to give it up and instead began to work as a dishwasher, berry picker, janitor, houseboy, and kitchen helper in order to finance his education. Through his work connections, he came to know much about the life of Filipino workers in America. Later he described his experience with Filipino workers in his book, *I Have Lived with the American People* (1948).

During World War II Buaken served with the Third Battalion, First Filipino Infantry Regiment* at Hunter Liggett Military Reservation, Camp Roberts, California, before the Infantry was sent to Australia on January 13, 1943.

FURTHER READING: Manuel Buaken, *I Have Lived with the American People*, Caldwell, Idaho: Caxton Printers, 1948.

BUDDHIST CHURCHES OF AMERICA, established on September 2, 1899, when the Buddhist missionaries Sonoda Shuyei and Nishijima Kukuryo arrived in America to carry out their mission of caring for the followers of Buddhism among the early Japanese immigrants from Hiroshima, Kumamoto, Yamaguchi, and Fukuoka prefectures. These two missionaries were dispatched by the leader of Nishi Hongwanji (West School of the Original Vow to Amita Buddha) of Jodo Shinshu, Kenjyo Akamatsu. The Nishi Hongwanji branch of Jodo Shinshu is one of ten branches of Buddhism; it has been estimated that 70 to 90 percent of Japanese Buddhists in America belong to this branch.

The Buddhist Churches of America has a membership of fifty-seven churches with eighty ministers.

FURTHER READING: Bill Hosokawa, *Nisei*, New York: William Morrow and Co., 1969; Tetsuden Kashima, *Buddhism in America: The Social Organization of an Ethnic Religious Institution*, Westport, Conn.: Greenwood Press, 1977.

BULOSAN, CARLOS (1913–1956), migrant farm worker, labor organizer, union activist, and writer. Bulosan's date of birth is as controversial as his writings. *Current Biography* for 1946, published in 1947, states that Bulosan was born on November 24, 1914, but a more recent publication gives his date of birth as November 24, 1913. At any rate, these two sources agree on his birthplace. He was born in the town of Binalonan, Pangasinan, in the central Philippines. He completed his high school education in the Philippines and followed his older brother, Aurelio, to the United States, arriving in Seattle on July 22, 1930.

Bulosan began working at the age of eleven. At twelve, he went to work at a bakery shop and at fourteen in an ice factory. Upon arriving in the United States, he was kidnapped and sold for $5 to work in Alaska as a cannery worker. He later followed various crops during harvest season in California, Oregon, Washington, and Idaho. In order to improve living conditions for the Filipinos, he began to help organize Filipino cannery and packing-house workers into a union in 1934. He worked toward this goal for two years before he was hospitalized in 1936 at Los Angeles County Hospital, where he stayed for two years. During this period he developed friendships with two young literary women, one of whom was Dorothy Babb; she would bring various literary classics for him to read.

Bulosan's writing career began when he wrote for a union magazine, *New Tide*. He continued to write, publishing his first book of poems, *Letter from America*, in 1942. *Chorus for America* was published that same year and *The Voice of Bataan* followed in 1943.

Bulosan's autobiographical work, *America Is in the Heart* (1946), is his best known book. It describes not only Bulosan's life and the bitter and cruel experience he underwent in America, but also the lives of hundreds and thousands of Filipinos who struggled to eke out a living at canneries and on farms. As Ruben Alcantara states, *America Is in the Heart* should be the single most important primer for any student wanting to know and study the Filipino experience in America. Bulosan died in Seattle in 1956.

FURTHER READING: Carlos Bulosan, *America Is in the Heart: A Personal History*, New York: Harcourt, Brace and Co., 1946; Susan Evangelista, *Carlos Bulosan and His Poetry: A Biography and Anthology*, Seattle: University of Washington Press, 1985; Elaine H. Kim, *Asian American Literature*, Philadelphia: Temple University Press, 1982; *Amerasia Journal* 6, No. 1 (May 1979), pp. 1–154.

BUREAU OF KOREAN INFORMATION, a political organization established on the last day of the three-day conference held from April 14 to 16, 1919, in Philadelphia, under the leadership of So Jae-p'il (Philip Jaisohn)* and Syngman Rhee,* leaders of the Korean independence movement. The first Korean Liberty Congress, as the conference was officially named, was held in order to carry out propaganda activities aimed at people of the Western world—particularly Americans—whom Philip Jaisohn felt needed to be informed that Koreans were victims of Japanese rule. Twenty-seven organizations of Koreans in the United States and Mexico sent their representatives to this Congress.

At the end of the Congress, a ten-point resolution was passed to express the Koreans' ardent desire for freedom and independence, and to proclaim to the world their belief in democratic ideals. The resolution called for the recognition of the Korean provisional government in Shanghai by the League of Nations.

On the final day of the Congress, the Bureau of Korean Information was created to carry out propaganda activities for Korean independence. Shortly after the Congress adjourned, the bureau published the Proceedings of the First Korean Congress, and a monthly magazine, the *Korea Review*, which was published regularly from April 1919 until 1922. The bureau also published pamphlets informing people around the world of Japanese atrocities committed in Korea. The bureau ceased to function after Syngman Rhee established the Korean Commission in Washington, D.C. to carry out diplomatic and propaganda activities for Korean independence.

FURTHER READING: Bong-youn Choy, *Koreans in Korea*, Chicago: Nelson-Hall, 1979; Chong-sik Lee, *The Politics of Korean Nationalism*, Berkeley: University of California Press, 1965.

BURKE, THOMAS (1886–1945), writer. Burke was born in London and orphaned at an early age. After living with an uncle for several years, he spent four years in an orphan asylum. At fifteen he entered a commercial office but disliked the work. Burke's interests centered on the arts, for he wanted to be a violinist but could not afford lessons. He turned to writing and sold his first story by the time he was sixteen. At age nineteen, he became an assistant to a second-hand bookseller and later entered the office of a literary agent. During his seven years there, Burke privately published two volumes of verse, as well as several anthologies. In 1914 he worked in the American Division of Ministry of Information. His first principal work, *Limehouse Nights*, was published in 1916. Later, one of his stories from the volume, *The Chink and the Child*, was adapted for the screen under the title of *Broken Blossoms*, with film stars Lillian Gish and Richard Barthelmess (1895–1963). His novel, *The Wind and the Rain* (1924), is autobiographical. Charlie Chaplin, who read the book and noticed a similarity in their backgrounds, wrote to Burke, and they established a firm friendship.

Burke is best remembered as an excellent interpreter of life in London's East End. Despite this description, Burke could have related to the people in London in only a superficial way. He made blatantly racist remarks and derogatory, offensive descriptions. Perhaps what is most surprising is that Burke was a very close friend of Quong Lee, a Chinese philosopher; yet Burke continued to create racist stereotypes, depicting the Chinese as "yellar Chinks" or "dirty Chinks" with "flat faces," "long eyes" and "long eyebrows."

There is little doubt that Burke wrote to entertain his readers and did so by overplaying the mysterious to set a pace of high adventure, describing the Chinese with such words as "creeping, sly cat, treacherous, sneaky, and having evil odors." All he really entertained were notions of the unbridgeable gap between peoples.

FURTHER READING: Thomas Burke, *Nights in London*, New York: Henry Holt and Co., 1919; Elaine H. Kim, *Asian American Literature*, Philadelphia: Temple University Press, 1982; Stanley J. Kunitz, *Authors Today and Yesterday*, New York: H. W. Wilson Co., 1934.

BURLINGAME, ANSON (1820–1870), politician, diplomat. Burlingame was born in New Berlin, New York, on November 14, 1820, the son of Joel Burlingame, who was a Methodist and lay preacher. The family later moved to Ohio and then to Detroit. Burlingame attended the Detroit branch of the University of Michigan, and at the age of twenty-three he entered Harvard Law School. Upon completion he became a junior law partner of George P. Briggs, son of Ex-Governor George Nixon Briggs. In 1847 he married Jane Livermore. Burlingame was elected to the Massachusetts Senate in 1852, and three years later he was elected to Congress, where he served three terms before he was unseated in 1860 by William Appleton. For his service to the Republican Party, Burlingame was appointed in 1860 to become America's Minister to Vienna; later he was appointed to represent America in Peking. He served his country well for six years. He resigned in November 1867, when the Chinese government asked him to become head of an official delegation to visit the Western powers, both to observe Western civilization and to establish better diplomatic relations with Europe and the United States. In America Burlingame negotiated with William H. Seward for the treaty known as the Burlingame Treaty of 1868.*

After a successful diplomatic assignment in Washington, Burlingame went to London where he was assured that London would not support the excessive demands of foreign merchants in China. From London he went to Paris, Berlin, and other European capitals. He reached St. Petersburg in February 1870, where he died of pneumonia on February 23, 1870.

As one of his biographers points out, few Americans served their country as well and no one has surpassed him in his service to China based on a policy of justice and friendship. (*See also* Burlingame Treaty of 1868).

FURTHER READING: Jack Chen, *The Chinese of America*, New York: Harper and Row, 1980; Mary R. Coolidge, *Chinese Immigration*, New York: Henry Holt and Co., 1909; Frederick Wells Williams, *Anson Burlingame and the First Chinese Mission to Foreign Powers*, New York: Charles Scribner's Sons, 1912.

BURLINGAME TREATY OF 1868, a treaty negotiated between the United States and the Ch'ing Dynasty of China to add certain articles to a treaty concluded on June 18, 1858. The individuals responsible for laying the groundwork for the treaty were Secretary of State William H. Seward for the United States and Anson Burlingame* and two Chinese officials for China. The treaty added eight articles to the already existing Reed Treaty of 1858, which is called the Treaty of Tientsin. Although several of the articles simply amplified the agreements between the two governments in 1858, the first and second and fifth articles were crucial, for they were related to Chinese immigrants in the United States.

The first article stated that the United States and the people of the United States in China would respect the territorial integrity of China. The emperor of China would by no means relinquish his right of eminent domain over land and water which foreign parties might be occupying. The article also stated that any land or water granted by China to the United States for trade or commerce would remain under the jurisdiction of the Chinese government. Article Two stated that in respect to trade or navigation within the Chinese dominion the Chinese government would make the final decisions and regulations when they were not stipulated in the treaty, but these regulations had to be made in good faith and in accordance with the rules laid down in the treaty. Article Five, the most important part of the Burlingame Treaty, stated that the two governments recognized the mutual advantage of free migration for the purpose of trade, curiosity, and taking up residence in the United States and China. Thus, citizens of either country could at any time voluntarily change their home and allegiance to the other country. This movement was also to be voluntary, and any removal of citizens from either country to the other against their will would be made a penal offense.

In summary, the Burlingame Treaty was important because it put America's traditional policy of respect for China's territory and law on record and opened migration between the two countries. In applying this treaty through the years, the United States has acted in two sharply contrasting ways: the United States has remained courteous and respectful of the territorial rights of the Chinese in its diplomatic actions, but has ignored and discarded the part of the agreement dealing with free immigration policy.

FURTHER READING: Mary Roberts Coolidge, *Chinese Immigration*, New York: Henry Holt and Co., 1909; James Whitney, *The Chinese and the Chinese Question*, New York: Tibbals Book Co., 1888; Frederick Wells Williams, *Anson Burlingame and the First Chinese Mission to Foreign Powers*, New York: Charles Scribner's Sons, 1912.

BURNS, JOHN ANTHONY (1909–   ), police officer, small business operator, and governor of Hawaii in 1962. Burns was born on March 20, 1909, in Fort Assinneboine, Montana, but moved to Hawaii where he attended the University of Hawaii.

Burns launched his political career in 1948 when he participated in the Territory of Hawaii Democratic Party Convention. Until that time, Hawaii's politics had been dominated by the Republican Party. In spite of repeated efforts, the Democratic Party was not able to capture the legislature because of its weak leadership and factionalism. The party's factionalism was more pronounced during the 1948 convention when conservatives and members of the International Longshoremen's and Warehousemen's Union* (ILWU) fought hard against each other for control of the party. Those convention delegates who considered themselves independent rallied around the future leaders of Hawaii's Democratic Party such as John Burns, Vincent Esposito, and John Wilson. Burns had a more active part in the 1952 territorial Democratic convention when he supported Frank F. Fasi as the party's leader.

Burns developed compassion and sympathy for the downtrodden while working as a police officer in Hawaii. During the war he had learned of the Japanese community's resentment of Hawaii's power-wielding oligarchy, whose members were mostly white. He listened to their complaints and learned their frustrations and worked toward the betterment of Hawaii's Japanese community. When Daniel Inouye* asked him to talk before the 442nd Veterans' Club, in 1948, he urged its members to turn the club into power for political action to improve the lives of Japanese Americans.

Many Nisei* and Sansei* Japanese Americans who were inspired by his dedication to rebuild the Democratic Party and to work for the betterment of the Japanese community associated themselves closely with Burns. Among them were Daniel Inouye, Takabuki Matsuo, Mike Tokunaga, and Bill Richardson. With the help of the Japanese community and the members of the ILWU, Burns achieved an overwhelming victory in the 1956 election. The election sent twelve Democrats and only three Republicans to the territorial Senate. Two-thirds of the House members were Democrats. Burns became a delegate to Congress from Hawaii and remained in that capacity until 1959, when Inouye persuaded him to run for the governorship of Hawaii, the fiftieth state to be admitted into the Union in 1959. Burns lost his bid to William F. Quinn. But in his second attempt, Burns won the governorship, a position he held until 1974.

FURTHER READING: Gavan Daws, *Shoal of Time*, Honolulu: University Press of Hawaii, 1968; Lawrence H. Fuchs, *Hawaii Pono: A Social History*, New York: Harcourt, Brace and World, 1961; Dennis H. Ogawa, *Kodomo no tgame ni* (For the Sake of the Children), Honolulu: University Press of Hawaii, 1978; Paul C. Phillips, *Hawaii's Democrats: Chasing the American Dream*, Washington, D.C.: University Press of America, 1982.

BUSINESS PROMOTION CORPORATION (HUNGOP CHUSIK HOESA), a small business company organized by Ahn Sok-jung in Redlands, California, in February 1910. A total of $3,000 was to be created from issuing sixty stock certificates, each of which was to be sold for $50. This was one of the first small business firms established by Koreans in the continental United States. There is no record indicating how long Ahn stayed in business.

FURTHER READING: Bong-youn Choy, *Koreans in America*, Chicago: Nelson-Hall, 1979; Hyung-chan Kim, *The Korean Diaspora*, Santa Barbara, Calif.: ABC-Clio Press, 1977.

C

C. BREWER AND COMPANY. *See* Big Five.

CABALLEROS DE DIMAS-ALANG, founded on February 22, 1921, in San Francisco, one of the three major Filipino fraternal organizations. The other two were Legionarios del Trabajo* and Gran Oriente Filipino.* Dimas-Alang was the pen name of Jose Rizal,* the Philippine national hero during the last days of Spanish colonial rule, who was executed by a Spanish firing squad for his revolutionary activities. The organization adopted Dimas-Alang as its name and established more than 100 lodges in Filipino communities across the United States. The membership of the organization reached more than 2,000 men and women.
FURTHER READING: Fred Cordova, *Filipinos: Forgotten Asian Americans*, Dubuque, Iowa: Kendall and Hunt Publishing Co., 1983.

CABLE ACT OF 1922, a law passed by the Congress of the United States on September 22, 1922, in order to restrict the naturalization and citizenship of married women. Some of the major provisions included in the act were highly discriminatory against persons of Asian ancestry. Section Three stipulates that any female citizen who marries an alien ineligible for citizenship "shall cease to be a citizen of the United States. If at the termination of the marital status she is a citizen of the United States she shall retain her citizenship, regardless of her residence." This meant that any Asian woman citizen who married an Asian man ineligible for U.S. citizenship lost her citizenship, and if she was divorced or widowed, she could not regain her original legal status because she would be ineligible for citizenship. However, a Caucasian woman under the same circumstances would be able to apply for and regain her citizenship. This law was amended in 1931 as a result of the lobbying effort of Suma Sugi, who was sent to Washington, D.C., by the Japanese American Citizens League.*

Section Two, which had an impact on Asian women marrying U.S. citizens, stated that any woman who married a citizen of the United States could not become a citizen of the United States by reason of such a marriage. She had to be ruled eligible for citizenship before she could apply. Because persons of Asian ancestry were ruled ineligible for U.S. citizenship, any Asian woman marrying a U.S. citizen was denied her right to become a citizen of the United States.

FURTHER READING: Bill Hosokawa, *Nisei: The Quiet Americans*, New York: William Morrow and Co., 1969; Yamato Ichihashi, *Japanese in the United States*, Stanford, Calif.: Stanford University Press, 1932; Rose Hum Lee, *The Chinese in the United States of America*, Hong Kong: Hong Kong University Press, 1960.

CALIFORNIA CAPITATION TAX, a law passed on April 28, 1855, by the California State Legislature requiring the master, owner, or consignee to pay $50 for every person on his ship who was ineligible to become a U.S. citizen before they could enter California. The law was ruled unconstitutional, when challenged by the owners of the ship *Stephen Baldwin*, which had brought 250 Chinese passengers in 1857. (*See also* People v. Downer.)

FURTHER READING: Mary Roberts Coolidge, *Chinese Immigration*, New York: Henry Holt and Co., 1909; Stanford M. Lyman, *Chinese Americans*, New York: Random House, 1974.

CALIFORNIA CONSTITUTIONAL CONVENTION OF 1849, California's first constitutional convention, which among other issues tackled the problem of slavery and the property rights of foreigners. In the mid-nineteenth century when a military government replaced the alcalde system of government in California, the people demanded an elected government. On June 3, 1849, Governor Bennett Riley, who had succeeded Military Governor Richard Barnes Mason on April 13, 1849, issued a proclamation by which he called for a constitutional convention. Two days earlier he had learned that Congress had adjourned without taking action on the question of California statehood.

At first, the proclamation was not well received throughout the state, particularly in San Francisco, but in California's rapidly expanding economy the need for law and order had accelerated. A total of forty-eight delegates was elected throughout the state, and they gathered at Monterey to open the First Constitutional Convention on September 1. The convention covered many topics of discussion, including (1) the development of three departments of government; (2) the establishment of corporations, banks, schools, and taxes; (3) possible eastern boundaries for California, (4) miscellaneous provisions such as possible designs for the state seal, compensation for travel, and the constitution, and (5) the free-Negro controversy.

The controversial issue of abolishing slavery in California produced a long and heated discussion. The eight delegates from San Francisco argued strongly against Negro slavery. William E. Shannon, a delegate from San Francisco, presented a resolution stating that "Neither slavery nor involuntary servitude, unless for the punishment of crimes, shall ever be tolerated in this State.'' After much debate and discussion, the convention delegates finally adopted the resolution. The convention also adopted a motion allowing foreigners who were bona fide residents to have the same rights of property as native-born citizens. The constitution adopted by the delegates was then ratified by the people on December 20, and a civil governor, Peter H. Burnett, was sworn in as the first governor of the State of California on the same day. California was admitted on September 9, 1850, as the thirty-first state of the Union, and, more importantly, it joined the union as a free state.

The constitution that allowed foreigners to enjoy the rights of property as native-born citizens on paper did not guarantee that it actually happened in practice. Racial antipathy increased to pit one race against another, and foreigners were blamed for unfair competition.

As competition in the mines became intensified, the Chinese became the object of persecution by white citizens. Various legal and extralegal methods were used to persecute, harass, intimidate, and exclude Chinese from the state between 1870 and 1878, when the Second Constitutional Convention was called to deal with the Chinese question. (*See also* California Constitutional Convention of 1878.)

FURTHER READING: Cynthia E. Browne, *State Constitutional Conventions*, Westport, Conn.: Greenwood Press, 1973; J. Ross Browne, *Report of the Debates in the Convention of California, on the Formation of State Constitution*, Washington, D.C.: 1850; Cardinal Goodwin, *The Establishment of State Government in California*, New York: Macmillan Co., 1914; H. Brett Melendy, *The Oriental Americans*, Boston: Twayne Publishers, 1972.

CALIFORNIA CONSTITUTIONAL CONVENTION OF 1878, California's second constitutional convention, called primarily to deal with the question of Chinese labor. The need for a second constitutional convention in California began to emerge from the murky and confused social, economic, and racial backgrounds of the state's people. Hundreds of thousands of people had moved to California from elsewhere in the nation and the world, all drawn by the quest for gold. In 1879 Californians had a good reason to be disillusioned and frustrated; mining was on the decline, economic depression had struck hard at the farmer, with much of the land in the hands of a few people, and there was a business slump and widespread unemployment. ''Bust and boom'' was not unknown to Californians, and these problems would not have added anxiety to their lives had it not been for the unresolved question of what to do with Chinese laborers and Chinese immigration. The Chinese question became the focal point of the Second Constitutional Convention, which convened on September 28, 1878, and lasted until March 3, 1879.

The convention had 152 delegates: 11 Republicans, 10 Democrats, 77 non-partisans, 3 independents, and 51 Workingmen. The main goal of the

Workingmen's Party of California* during the convention was to drive out the Chinese, as summarized in their slogan, "Chinese must go!"

The Workingmen's Party, led by an Irish immigrant, Denis Kearney,* gained one-third of the seats at the convention and took the lead in writing a set of racist anti-Chinese clauses into the constitution. From the beginning of the convention the question of Chinese laborers in California and of Chinese immigration drew much attention from the delegates, although there were other issues of major importance such as what to do with coralling corporations and the burden of taxes. A standing committee was appointed to draft a section dealing with Chinese laborers, and John F. Miller of San Francisco, president of the Alaska Commercial Company, was made chairman of the committee which wrote provisions dealing with (1) exclusion of the Chinese from California, (2) the right to sue or be sued in the courts, (3) employment, (4) the right of settlement in the state, (5) the right to catch fish in the state, and (6) the right to purchase or hold real property. The committee also stated that any person employing the Chinese should be disfranchised.

Emotions ran high as the delegates debated the issues and feelings were stirred up, but when the dust finally settled, the new constitution allowed the legislature to prescribe conditions under which aliens could be admitted to the state. It prohibited corporations from employing Chinese in any capacity and prevented any Chinese from being hired to work in any state, county, municipal, or other public sector, except in punishment for crime, and authorized the legislature to discourage Chinese immigration to the state.

In view of the Supreme Court's ruling on the Chy Lung v. Freeman* case, the convention delegates felt that the Court should not interfere with the federal government's exclusive right to regulate immigration. Rather, they recommended that a memorial be sent to Washington asking Congress to stop Chinese immigration. Requests also went to the governors of Oregon, Nevada, Montana, Washington, Idaho, and Arizona, urging them to make a similar appeal to the federal government. Three years after the convention, Congress passed the Chinese Exclusion Act of 1882.* (See also California Constitutional Convention of 1849; Chinese Exclusion Act of 1882; In Re An Chong: and In Re Tiburcio Parrott).
FURTHER READING: Mary R. Coolidge, Chinese Immigration, New York: Henry Holt and Co., 1909; Elmer C. Sandmeyer, The Anti-Chinese Movement in California, Urbana: University of Illinois Press, 1939; Alexander Saxton, The Indispensable Enemy, Berkeley: University of California Press, 1971; State Senate, Chinese Immigration: Its Social, Moral, and Political Effect—Report to the California State Senate of Its Special Committee on Chinese Immigration, Sacramento, Calif.: State Office, 1878; Carl Swisher, Motivation and Political Technique in the California Constitutional Convention, 1878–1879, New York: Da Capo Press, 1969.

CALIFORNIA FOREIGN MINERS' TAX (also known as Foreign Miners' License tax), a tax passed in 1850 requiring that all persons who were not native-born citizens of the United States take out a license to mine at $20 per month.

This law was repealed in the following year as it created a negative effect in reducing the number of foreign miners willing to pay. Mexican miners resorted to violence as they took up arms to challenge collectors who were allowed to receive $3 for each license issued.

Spanish and Mexican miners had been driven out of mining by the end of 1852, and the Chinese became the object of economic exploitation. In 1852 the legislature renewed its license and required that all persons who were not native-born citizens of the United States pay $3 per month in order to mine in California. In 1855 the license tax was raised to $4 per month, and it was to increase $2 per month every year after 1855. This law had the same effect on Chinese as the 1850 law had on Mexicans. The income from issuing licenses decreased. Several attempts were made to collect the taxes more effectively by raising the collector's share, but finally the Foreign Miners' Tax was ruled unconstitutional in 1870.

FURTHER READING: Gunther Barth, *Bitter Strength*, Cambridge, Mass.: Harvard University Press, 1964; Mary R. Coolidge, *Chinese Immigration*, Henry Holt and Co., 1909; Stanford M. Lyman, *Chinese Americans*, New York: Random House, 1974.

CALIFORNIA GOLD RUSH OF 1849, the rush to California after the discovery of gold at Sutter's Creek on January 24, 1848. Following the discovery people—not excepting the Chinese—began to rush into California from all directions. Gold was a strong incentive for the Chinese to come to California, but there was a stronger enemy that pushed them out of their ancestral homeland in search of a better life. For many centuries Chinese in the southeastern part of China had fought hunger and starvation. The reality of present misery, coupled with the prospect of future wealth, was strong enough to send many adventure-seeking Chinese on their journey to the "Mountain of Gold," as California was then called by the Chinese.

Before 1849, there were few Chinese in America, but Chinese infected by gold fever rushed into California, and their number grew substantially after 1849. By 1855 there were 20,000 Chinese and in 1861, 100,000—most of whom were in California.

By the time the Chinese reached the "Mountain of Gold," the gold yields were decreasing. Even so, they continued to mine. The independent Chinese usually had to start their digging in the already overworked southern mines in Toulumne, Calaveras, Mariposa, and Sonora, although they could be found anywhere from which they were not driven away. The Chinese were usually found at placer mines, while white miners followed richer mines in the north. Chinese also replaced white miners and were paid $1.00 to $1.25 per day. By 1860 the Chinese were the largest immigrant group of miners in California, each of the more important mining counties having at least 2,000 Chinese.

The Chinese who mined independently usually lived and worked in their own band unwilling to interact with white miners, going to their own merchants and to the Six Companies for goods. As the gold yields continued to decrease, more and more Chinese left the mines in search of other forms of employment in large cities. Because of the shortage of women in California at this time, they took the jobs that were usually relegated to women and that few white men wanted: cooking, laundry work, and domestic service.

FURTHER READING: Emil W. Billeb, *Mining Camp Days*, Berkeley, Calif.: Howell-North Books, 1968; Donald Jackson, *Gold Dust*, New York: Alfred A. Knopf, 1980; Margaret Sanborn, *The American: River of El Dorado*, New York: Holt, Rinehart and Winston, 1974; Stewart White, *The Forty-niners: A Chronicle of the California Trail and El Dorado*, New Haven, Conn.: Yale University Press, 1918.

CALIFORNIA JOINT IMMIGRATION COMMITTEE. See McClatchy, Valentine Stuart.

CALIFORNIA ORIENTAL EXCLUSION LEAGUE, an organization established in September 1919 as a result of a meeting held by anti-Asian exclusionists in the office of State Controller John S. Chambers. The league, founded with Senator J. M. Inman as its president, proposed a five-point program: cancellation of the Gentlemen's Agreement,* exclusion of "picture-brides,"* exclusion of Japanese as immigrants, denial of citizenship to Asians, and passage of a constitutional amendment limiting U.S. citizenship to children born of both parents who were eligible for U.S. citizenship.

CALIFORNIA POLICE TAX, another capitation tax passed by the California State Legislature in 1862 which required that all Mongolians over eighteen years of age pay $2.50 per month, if they were not engaged in the production of rice, sugar, tea, or coffee, or had not already paid the California Foreign Miners' Tax.* This law was ruled unconstitutional by the Supreme Court of California in the following year, when the highest court of the state ruled on the case of Lin Sing v. Washburn.* (*See also* Lin Sing v. Washburn.)

CALIFORNIA SENATE ADDRESS AND MEMORIAL OF 1876, the result of a California state committee's investigation of Chinese immigration in the state. The question of the Chinese problem was revived in California when the Democratic Party in control of the legislature decided to use the Chinese issue to its advantage in the upcoming election of 1876. Creed Haymond of Sacramento offered a resolution in the Senate on April 3, 1876, calling for a committee to investigate the number of Chinese immigrants and their impact on the social, political, and economic conditions of the state as well as the possible means of excluding them. The Senate appointed the committee, with Haymond serving as its chairman.

The committee received $2,000 for its investigation expenses and spent $1,840.01 on its task; it published its report under the title *Chinese Immigration: Its Social, Moral, and Political Effect*. The report consisted of three major sections: (1) An Address to the People of the United States upon the Evils of

Chinese Immigration, (2) Memorial of the Senate of California to the Congress of the United States, and (3) Proceedings of the Commission. The first two sections emphasized five aspects of Chinese life in California; prostitution, criminality, inability or refusal to be assimilated, competition, and coolie* slavery. In the memorial to Congress, it recommended that Congress take action on three matters: that the government cooperate with Britain in prohibiting the coolie trade,* that all treaties made with the Chinese government be made null and void, and that Congress legislate a law prohibiting more than ten Chinese from entering the United States at any one time.

As Theodore Hittell, an acknowledged authority on the history of California, states, the committee provided ''anti-Chinese thunder for the demagogues of San Francisco.'' (Coolidge, p. 95.) It also provided much misinformation for those in Congress who wanted to exclude the Chinese. Congress passed the Chinese Exclusion Act in 1882.*

FURTHER READING: Mary R. Coolidge, *Chinese Immigration*, New York: Henry Holt and Co., 1909; State Senate, *Chinese Immigration: Its Social, Moral, and Political Effect*, Sacramento, Calif.: State Office, 1878.

CALIFORNIA SENATE BILLS NO. 175 AND NO. 176, laws classifying the Malay race as non-white. While the judicial decision on the case of Salvador Roldan v. Los Angeles County* was pending, Herbert C. Jones,* state senator from Santa Clara County, introduced Senate Bills No. 175 and No. 176, both of which proposed to amend Sections 60 and 69 of the Civil Code by classifying the Malay race as non-white. Mongolians were already prohibited from marrying whites in accordance with the anti-miscegenation law,* as stipulated in Sections 60 and 69. While these bills were placed on the agenda for debate, the Court of Appeals ruled on January 27, 1933, that Filipinos were not prohibited from marrying whites in California because the Filipinos were not Mongolians. The marriage between Salvador Roldan and Marjorie Rogers was permitted.

But this liberalization of the Law was to be short-lived. The California State Legislature passed both bills on April 5, 1933, and sent them to Governor James Rolph for his signature. Rolph signed the bills into law on April 20, to be effective August 21, 1933.

CALIFORNIA THESIS, a theory advanced by Mary Roberts Coolidge in her book, *Chinese Immigration* (New York: Henry Holt and Co., 1909), which examines why U.S. government policy excluded Chinese laborers from the United States in 1882. According to Coolidge, Chinese immigrants had been readily accepted during the first phase of their immigration to California, and no major racial disturbances had been directed against the Chinese until 1869, when a commercial depression drove the unemployed to San Francisco where they fanned anti-Chinese sentiment. Although anti-Chinese legislation was passed in California in 1870 and 1876, it was ruled unconstitutional. As a result, the anti-Chinese movement in California had to seek alliance not from Sacramento, but from Washington. In essence, the California Thesis claims that political events stirred up by working people of Irish descent in California led to the adoption of a national policy that committed the U.S. government to the exclusion of Chinese laborers. This theoretical position has been challenged by a number of scholars, incuding Stuart C. Miller, author of *The Unwelcome Immigrant* (1969).

FURTHER READING: Stuart C. Miller, *The Unwelcome Immigrant: The American Image of the Chinese, 1785–1882*, Berkeley: University of California Press, 1969.

CAMERON, DONALDINA (1869–1968), teacher and social worker who spent her lifetime in San Francisco Chinatown* rescuing, helping, and guiding Chinese immigrants who were exploited not only by their white masters, but also by their countrymen working for *tongs*.* Cameron was born on July 26, 1869, in New Zealand and came to California with her father who was a sheep rancher. She grew up on a ranch close to Merced, California, and later followed her father when he came to the Willows, a suburb of San Jose, to work for another sheep rancher. She completed her high school education in Oakland and started a teacher training course, but was unable to complete her training after her father's death. At nineteen, she had planned to marry a friend of her brother but decided against it. Instead, she went to work for Margaret Culbertson in April 1895 at the Chinese Presbyterian Mission Home on Sacramento Street in San Francisco.

After Culbertson's death in 1897, Cameron took over the management and daily operation of the Home, although she refused to accept the superintendency when it was offered to her. The Home was not only a rescue center to which Chinese prostitutes and slave girls were brought after they were rescued from their masters, but also an educational institution where Chinese women were taught useful occupations for their economic independence.

Because of her lifetime work in rescuing and helping unfortunate Chinese women enslaved by their men and employers, she was both loved and hated. Cameron was loved by those who were rescued through her efforts; they called her "Lo Mo," or old mama. She was hated by those who controlled Chinese *tongs*; they called her Fahn Quai, or White Devil. Cameron decided to accept the superintendency in 1900. Over a period of forty years during which she devoted herself to helping Chinese women in trouble, it is estimated that she rescued more than 3,000 of them. Lorna Logan took over the directorship of the Home in May 1934, when Cameron reached the retirement age of sixty-five. But Cameron continued to work at the Home until her death on January 4, 1968. The California State Legislature recognized her lifetime work and contribution to the Chinese community in San Francisco by passing a resolution after her death submitted by Assemblywoman March Fong.

FURTHER READING: Jack Chen, *The Chinese of America*, New York: Harper and Row, 1980; Rose Hum Lee, *The Chinese in the United States of America*, Hong Kong: Hong Kong University Press, 1960; Mildred Martin, *Chinatown's Angry Angel*, Palo

Alto, Calif.: Pacific Books, 1977; Carol Green Wilson, *Chinatown Quest*, Stanford, Calif.: Stanford University Press, 1931.

CAMINETTI, ANTHONY (1854–1923), lawyer, district attorney, congressman, and U.S. Commissioner of Immigration. Caminetti was born on July 30, 1854, in Jackson, Amador County, California. He studied law at the University of California at Berkeley and was admitted to the bar in 1877. For a period of four years, between 1877 and 1882, he served as district attorney in his hometown. In 1883 he was elected to serve in the State Assembly and in 1885 to the State Senate where he served until 1887. He was elected to the 52d and 53d Congress as a Democrat between March 4, 1891, and March 3, 1894. Caminetti failed in his bid for a third term and returned to his home state to serve as a public official. President Woodrow Wilson appointed him U.S. Commissioner of Immigration in 1913; he continued to work as commissioner until 1921, just two years before his death on November 17, 1923.

Caminetti was an active member of the Native Sons of the Golden West, an organization committed to the total exclusion of all Asians. In 1914, while testifying before Congress, he advocated and worked toward the exclusion of Hindus. When the Asiatic Barred Zone Act of 1917 passed through Congress, he praised the concept and urged strongly that it should also include Africa and other parts of Asia.

FURTHER READING: S. Chandrashekhar, *From India to America*, La Jolla, Calif., A Population Review Book, 1982; H. Brett Melendy, *Asians in America*, Boston: Twayne Publishers, 1977.

CANNERY WORKERS, seasonal workers, many of whom were Asian immigrants. The Chinese in America began to fish along the West Coast as early as the 1850s. It is estimated that by 1888 there were approximately 3,000 Chinese in thirty fishing camps in California. They fished mainly sturgeon and squid, although they also harvested shrimp and abalone. Because of intense competition between white and Chinese fishermen, bitter feelings and animosity were created, and soon Chinese fishermen became the targets of legislative discrimination in California. The number of Chinese fishermen began to decline as formal and informal discriminatory measures were used to drive them out of the fishing industry. In addition, the Chinese Exclusion Act of 1882* contributed to a further decline in the number of Chinese engaged in the fishing industry. By the 1900s Chinese were virtually eliminated from the fishing industry, except for work as fish cleaners.

In the cannery industry the Chinese were the first group of Asian immigrants employed to clean fish—mainly salmon. It is said that R. D. Humeat employed Chinese at his Rogue River plant, and later, Chinese cannery workers were hired to work at canneries on the Sacramento and Columbia rivers. After the Pacific Northwest and Alaska became the center of the salmon fishing industry in later years, Chinese and other Asian immigrants followed wherever they could find employment. The use of Chinese salmon butchers was so widespread in the Pacific Northwest and Alaska that when a new machine was introduced to the salmon fish industry in 1905, replacing many Chinese cannery workers, the machine was called "Iron Chink."*

Although the Chinese were the first group of Asian immigrants to work as cannery workers, they were by no means the only group. Filipino seasonal workers were also hired at the canneries in the Pacific Northwest and Alaska during the fishing season. By 1928 Filipino cannery workers, otherwise known as "Alaskeroos," constituted the largest single Asian immigrant group in Alaska. As Filipino predominance in the Alaska salmon cannery industry became evident and as Filipinos began to struggle to improve their living conditions, they went into labor union activities. They finally established the Cannery Workers' and Farm Laborers' Union Local 18257 on June 19, 1933, under the leadership of a twenty-three-year-old native of the Philippines, Antonio Gallego Rodrigo. It was chartered in the following year by the American Federation of Labor. Six years later, the union was recognized as the sole and exclusive bargaining agent for cannery workers bound for Alaska. (*See also* Alaska Cannery Workers.)

FURTHER READING: Fred Cordova, *Filipinos: Forgotten Asian Americans*, Dubuque, Iowa: Kendall and Hunt Publishing Co., 1983; Hyung-chan Kim, ed., *The Filipinos in America, 1898–1974*, Dobbs Ferry, N.Y.: Oceana Publications, 1976; Him Mark Lai et al., *The Chinese of America, 1785–1980*, San Francisco: Chinese Culture Foundations, 1980; Bruno Lasker, *Filipino Immigration*, Chicago: University of Chicago Press, 1931.

CAPITAL INVESTMENT COMPANY, a corporation founded in 1945 by Ho Chinn* who started the company with less than $200,000 in capital. In anticipation of a land boom in Oahu, he purchased 9,000 acres of a former plantation and divided it for small homes and farm lots. By 1950 the company, with total assets amounting to $2 million, began to expand its business interests into other areas such as automobile distributorship and banking. (*See also* Ho Chinn.)

CASTLE AND COOKE, one of the five major sugar agencies or corporations in Hawaii, founded by Samuel N. Castle and Amos Starr Cooke. (*See also* Big Five.)

FURTHER READING: Ralph S. Kuykendall, *The Hawaiian Kingdom, 1854–1874: Twenty Critical Years*, Honolulu: University of Hawaii Press, 1953; Merze Tate, *The United States and the Hawaiian Kingdom*, New Haven, Conn.: Yale University Press, 1965.

CELLER, EMANUEL (1888–1981), lawyer, business executive, and congressman from Brooklyn, New York. Celler was born on May 6, 1888, in Brooklyn of Jewish background. He graduated from Columbia University in 1910 with a B.A. degree, and continued his law study at the university, receiving his law degree two years later. He began his law practice in New York before he ran for the U.S. House of Representatives from New York's 10th Congressional District. Celler was elected to Congress in 1922 and served there until his defeat in 1972. During his fifty years of service in Congress, he was known as a liberal who fought for various causes. He supported the Marshall Plan, the establishment of the North Atlantic Treaty Organization, Truman's veto of the McCarran Internal Security Act of 1950, and the Civil Rights Acts of 1957. He was one of the strongest opponents of McCarthyism and attempted to insert an anti-McCarthyism plank in the Democratic Party platform during the party's convention in 1952.

Celler opposed the British policy of limiting Jewish immigration to Palestine to 15,000 per year and consequently voted against post-war aid to Britain. Because of his intense dislike of the British policy toward India, Ireland, and Palestine, he supported the Indian revolutionaries' struggle for India's independence and strongly advocated the establishment of a Jewish state in Palestine.

Celler's support of the right of Asian Indians to naturalization in the United States and of passage of the Immigration Act of October 3, 1965* influenced the United States' general immigration policy with regard to persons of Asian ancestry.

In 1944 Celler and Claire Luce sponsored a bill that would allow natives of India to be admitted to America and to be naturalized. The bill was finally discussed, amended, and passed during the second session of the 79th Congress, with a provision that authorized persons of Filipino descent be naturalized. The bill was signed into law on July 2, 1946.

Celler also supported the Immigration Act of 1965, which eliminated the national origins quota for immigration from Asia. After he was defeated in his bid to return to Congress in 1972, Celler continued to practice law. He died on January 15, 1981.

CENTRAL CALIFORNIA LAND COMPANY. *See* Abiko Kyutaro.

CENTRAL JAPANESE ASSOCIATION OF SOUTHERN CALIFORNIA, an organization established in 1915, with headquarters in Los Angeles, to coordinate the organizational efforts of local Japanese associations for the purpose of protecting the general interests of the Japanese people in America. Although members of the organization were local Japanese associations, it was greatly influenced by the government of Japan through its Los Angeles consulate office. FURTHER READING: John Modell, *The Economics and Politics of Racial Accommodation: The Japanese of Los Angeles, 1900–1942*, Urbana: University of Illinois Press, 1977.

CENTRAL JAPANESE LEAGUE. *See* Reform Society.

CENTRAL PACIFIC ANTICOOLIE ASSOCIATION. *See* Anti-coolie Clubs.

CENTRAL PACIFIC RAILROAD COMPANY, established by the Big Four, who completed the transcontinental railway in 1869. The introduction of the railroad in the eastern half of the United States prompted dreams of linking the

West with the East by rail. These dreams became speculative talk, and with the outbreak of the Civil War, talk was converted into concrete projects. Abraham Lincoln believed that a transcontinental link with the West would draw support from the West for his war effort. Vast funds would be required to get the project off the drawing board and into action. It was estimated that it would cost twice the federal budget of 1861.

Talk of a transcontinental railroad was initiated with a civil engineer named Theodore Judah, who believed it was possible to cross the Sierra Nevada with rails. Unable to raise the necessary capital for such a vast undertaking, he sought cooperation with prominent businessmen in California. The people who established the Central Pacific Railroad with Judah were Leland Stanford,* C. R. Huntington, Mark Hopkins, and Charles Crocker,* commonly known as the Big Four. Later, after a disagreement with the Big Four, Judah left the company, obtaining $100,000 for his share.

Because of manpower and material shortages during the war, it was difficult to make much progress. After the end of the Civil War, however, many veterans and Irish immigrants were hired and the work began again. Even with the additional labor, however, progress was slow, as many laborers refused to work on a regular basis and many of them left for better opportunities in California. Moreover, Irish immigrant workers were sometimes unruly; many of them did not stay long, and those who did protested this arduous labor through work slowdowns and strikes. After two years, the company had laid only fifty miles of track. A drastic solution was needed to make more progress on the project. Charles Crocker, the construction foreman, began to think about using Chinese labor, even though Chinese labor had never been used in building the railroad. Under the protest of his partner, he hired fifty Chinese on a trial basis. James Strobridge, his partner and the superintendent of construction, said that he did not want to become boss of Chinese laborers.

The Chinese came with no knowledge of how to build a railroad, but soon they excelled the whites. They were paid $26 a month, out of which they paid for their own rations, unlike the whites whose rations were paid for them. The Chinese exceeded Crocker's expectations, and in a short period of time over 15,000 Chinese laborers were hired.

The Chinese who worked on the Central Pacific Railroad were divided into groups of about thirty, with an Irishman as their foreman. At first it was feared that the Irish and the Chinese would not get along because the Irish would have to compete with the Chinese for their jobs. But this fear did not materialize as the Chinese workers took the hard menial work off the backs of the Irish, and the Irish, now given responsibility, enjoyed the newfound respect.

Their employers appreciated the Chinese laborers as reliable workers who did not drink, fight, or strike. The Chinese learned all parts of the work easily and worked well from sunup to sundown under Crocker's strict leadership. Curtis, the engineer in charge, described them as "the best roadbuilders in the world."

Even Strobridge agreed with these comments. Leland Stanford described them as quiet, peaceful, patient, and industrious.

The Chinese won their respect the hard way. On one tough section of work in the Sierra Nevadas, the workers were lowered on ropes off cliffs to chip away at the granite walls to form a narrow ledge, which could later be deepened. The most difficult section was the ten summit tunnels on the twenty-mile stretch from Cisco to Lake Ridge. It was estimated that 90 percent of the track laid from Sacramento, California, to Promontory, Utah, was laid by Chinese. The joining of the Central Pacific Railroad and the Union Pacific Railroad at Promontory, Utah, occurred on May 10, 1869. During the ceremony Crocker was the only person who acknowledged the contribution of the Chinese to the completion of the transcontinental railway. The completion of the transcontinental railway was the greatest engineering marvel of the nineteenth century. But railroad construction proved to be a knife in the side of the Chinese. The many immigrants who had entered California looking for work added to the unemployment. Californians soon began to look for someone to blame, and the Chinese became their scapegoats.

FURTHER READING: Sarah Pratt Carr, *The Iron Way*, Chicago: A.C. McClurg and Co., 1907; J. R. Perkins, *Trails, Rails and War*, Indianapolis, Ind.: Bobbs-Merrill Co., 1929; Glenn Chesney Quiett, *They Built the West*, New York: Appleton-Century, 1934; Edwin L. Sabin, *Building the Pacific Railway*, Philadelphia: J.B. Lippincott Co., 1919.

CHAE CHAN PING v. UNITED STATES, a case involving a Chinese laborer who lived in California from 1875 to 1887. In June 1887 Chae Chan Ping left for China with a certificate permitting his return to the United States. In October 1888 he returned to California, asked permission to land, but was refused by the port collector on the grounds that the congressional act of October 1, 1888, known also as the Scott Act of 1888,* made null and void the certificate of identity issued under the Chinese Exclusion Act of May 6, 1882.* The certificate was considered a mere license and was revocable at any time. He was detained on board the steamer *Belgic* and forbidden to enter the United States.

A petition on Chae Chan Ping's behalf was presented to the Circuit Court of the United States alleging that he was unlawfully restrained of his liberty, but the court ruled that his detention was lawful. An appeal challenged the validity of the act of October 1, 1888, criticizing it as being in violation of the then existing treaties between the United States and China. The Supreme Court decided in favor of the U.S. government, arguing that nothing in the treaties between the United States and China impaired the validity of the act of 1888. It pointed out that the U.S. government had the right to exclude aliens from its territory, as jurisdiction over one's territory was part of a nation's independence. If the government could not exclude aliens, it would be, to that extent, subject to the control of another power. Furthermore, the Court stated, it was the highest duty of every nation to preserve its independence and to maintain its security against any foreign aggression. Thus, if the government considered the presence of foreigners to be dangerous to peace and security, exclusion was the only answer.

It was a power the government could not abandon. The Court therefore ruled that whatever license Chinese laborers may have obtained to return before passage of the Scott Act, it was held at the will of the government and was revocable at any time at its pleasure.

FURTHER READING: Milton R. Konvitz, *The Alien and the Asiatic in American Law*, Ithaca, N.Y.: Cornell University Press, 1946; *Supreme Court Reporter* 9, 130 U.S. 581, October Term, 1888, pp. 623–32.

CHANDLER, ALBERT BENJAMIN (1898–   ), jazz musician, basketball coach, public official, and senator. Chandler was born on July 14, 1898, in Corydon, Kentucky, and received his B.A. degree from Transylvania College in 1921. He got his law degree at the University of Kentucky in 1924. During that year he opened his law practice in Versailles, Kentucky, while continuing to coach at Centre College in Danville. He was elected to the Kentucky State Legislature and was made lieutenant governor in 1931. Four years later, as a strong supporter of the New Deal, he ran for the office of governor of Kentucky and was elected. In 1939 he resigned the governorship in order to become a senator to replace Senator William Logan who had died in October. In December he was sworn in, and in November 1940 he was elected to serve out the remainder of the term to January 1943.

Chandler became the spokesman in the Senate for the Beat Japan First bloc and chairman of the Senate's Military Affairs Subcommittee in charge of investigating Alaskan and West Coast bases. In 1943 he was made head of another Military Affairs Subcommittee to investigate relocation centers that housed persons of Japanese ancestry who had been evacuated from the West Coast.

In January 1943 the Military Affairs Subcommittee of the Senate began to hold a series of hearings on a bill that proposed transfer of relocation centers under the War Relocation Authority* to the War Department. The bill was introduced by Senator Monrad Charles Wallgren of Washington and was designed to turn the relocation centers over to the army so that the administration of these centers might become more austere. Senator Chandler, as head of the subcommittee, visited a number of relocation centers and issued a critical statement implying that 60 percent of the internees were disloyal to America. The report submitted by the subcommittee in May 1943 recommended that the evacuees who had answered "no" to the loyalty question on Application for Leave Clearance* be segregated from other Japanese evacuees and be interned, that all loyal and able-bodied Japanese be given an opportunity to work in areas where they would be accepted, and that the military draft be applied to all Nisei* Japanese as it applied to all citizens.

Dillon S. Myer,* who served as director of the War Relocation Authority, states in his book, *Uprooted Americans* (1971), that Chandler was one of several congressmen antagonistic toward persons of Japanese ancestry, particularly during the time of evacuation and relocation.

Chandler resigned from his Senate seat on November 1, 1945, when he was made commissioner of organized baseball. He served in that capacity until 1950. He returned to law practice and now lives in Versailles, Kentucky.

CHANDRA, RAM (?–1918), editor of *Aftab* and *Akash,* two nationalist papers in Delhi. Ghandra was brought to San Francisco by Har Dayal* to help publish the *Hindustan Gadar,* or *Chadar* in 1913. The first issue of the newspaper was published on November 1, 1913, and Chandra soon replaced Dayal as editor. When war broke out between England and Germany, Asian Indian revolutionaries in America saw an opportunity to work for India's independence from England by obtaining military assistance from Germany. One of the revolutionary projects proposed was to ship men and arms to India for revolutionary activities. Chandra was known to have boasted of his ability to finance such a project, saying that he could get as much money as he wanted from the Germans. On August 29, 1914, the steamship *Korea* left San Francisco with sixty-two aboard, and it stopped at various ports on its way to Calcutta. Upon arrival the revolutionaries were arrested and imprisoned. Similar projects were aborted because they were badly planned.

When the United States later declared war on Germany in 1917, members of the Ghadar Revolutionary Party* were arrested on suspicion of conspiracy. Chandra was one of the revolutionaries put under arrest. During the trial in San Francisco, Chandra was shot to death, on April 23, 1918, by Ram Singh, another suspect accused in the case.

FURTHER READING: Kalyan Kumar Banerjee, *Indian Freedom Movement: Revolutionaries in America*, Calcutta: Jijnasa, 1969; R. C. Majumdar, ed., *Struggle for Freedom*, Bombay, India: Bharatiya Vidya Bhavan, 1969; H. Brett Melendy, *Asians in America*, Boston: Twayne Publishers, 1977.

CHANDRASHEKHAR, SUBRAHMANYAN (1910–   ), physicist, scholar, and Nobel laureate. Chandrashekhar was born in Lahore, India, now a part of Pakistan, on October 19, 1910. He came from a prominent Hindu family; his uncle was a Nobel laureate in 1930. He completed his B.A. degree at the University of Madras and his Ph.D. degree in physics at Cambridge University. He began his teaching career in 1933 at Trinity College, Cambridge.

Chandrashekhar joined the University of Chicago faculty in 1936 as an assistant professor and was promoted to associate professor in 1945. The following year he was made Distinguished Service Professor at the university. He became a U.S. citizen in 1953.

In 1983 Chandrashekhar was awarded the Nobel Prize in physics which he shared with Professor William A. Fowler of the California Institute of Technology. Professor Chandrashekhar received the Nobel Prize "for his theoretical studies of the physical processes of importance to the structure and evolution of the stars."

CHANG CHAN et al. v. JOHN D. NAGLE, a case heard in 1925 regarding the admission of alien Chinese wives of U.S. citizens. In 1924 Chang Chan and three others petitioned for release from detention four Chinese women whom they claimed were their lawful wives. These women were held under detention by John D. Nagle, commissioner for the port of San Francisco. The petitioners, all native-born citizens of the United States, married the four women before July 1, 1924. These women boarded the *President Lincoln* in China and arrived at San Francisco on July 11, 1924, without immigration visas. They were denied admission and were detained. The Secretary of Labor denied the women permanent admission because "Section 13 of the Act of 1924 mandatorily excluded the wives of U.S. citizens of Chinese race if such wives are of a race or persons ineligible for citizenship." The Department of Labor had no alternative but to recommend exclusion.

The petitioners then appealed to the Circuit Court of Appeals which certified the question to the Supreme Court. The case was heard between April 17 and 20, 1925, and the highest court made its decision on May 25, 1925. Justice James C. McReynolds delivered the opinion of the court: Chinese women ineligible for citizenship did not become citizens by marriage to citizens and remained incapable of naturalization (under Rev. St. 2169 and Chinese Exclusion Act May 6, 1882), and alien Chinese wives of U.S. citizens were not entitled to admission to the United States (under Immigration Act, May 26, 1924 and the Cable Act, September 22, 1922).

FURTHER READING: Milton R. Konvitz, *The Alien and the Asiatic in American Law*, Ithaca, N.Y.: Cornell University Press, 1946; *Supreme Court Reporter* 45, 268 U.S. 346, 1925, October Term 1924, 1926, pp. 540–41.

CHANG IN-HWAN (1875–1930), a sugar plantation worker, Alaska cannery worker, member of the Great Unity Fatherland Protection Association, which was a patriotic organization devoted to Korea's independence from Japan. Chang was born on March 30, 1875, in North P'yongan Province, Korea, and came to Hawaii to work as a sugar plantation worker after he was recruited by a Hawaiian Sugar Planters' Association* agent. He arrived in Hawaii in February 1905 to work on the Island of Maui and moved to the mainland in the following year.

In 1905 the Japanese government hired an American, Durham White Stevens, to justify Japanese policy toward Korea. Stevens was reported to have said that the Japanese takeover of Korea was good for Koreans. When the news reached Koreans in the Bay Area that Stevens had been dispatched by the Japanese government to the United States to defend Japan's policy toward Korea, many concerned Koreans held a number of meetings to discuss their reactions. In one of the meetings held between March 22 and 23, 1908, Chon Myong-wun, a member of the Mutual Assistance Association,* said that he would take care of the pro-Japanese American in his own way, but Chang kept his silence. Chon acquired a toy gun with which to attack Stevens, but Chang managed to procure a real gun from his roommate. On March 23, 1908, Chang shot Stevens twice, and Stevens died at St. Francis Hospital two days later. Chang was arrested, tried for the assassination committed in "patriotic passion" in December of that year, and convicted of murder of the second degree. He served ten years in San Quentin, was released on January 17, 1919, and returned to Korea to start a small business. His business failed because of Japanese persecution, and Chang returned to San Francisco. He held odd jobs before he committed suicide on May 22, 1930, after a long illness, which was a result of his imprisonment.

Chang was considered a patriot who fought for Korea's independence from Japan. Accordingly, his corpse was taken to Korea on August 3, 1975, to be buried in the National Cemetery. (*See also* Stevens Incident.)

FURTHER READING: Bong-youn Choy, *Koreans in America*, Chicago: Nelson-Hall, 1979; Hyung-chan Kim, *The Korean Diaspora*, Santa Barbara, Calif.: ABC-Clio Press, 1977.

CHANG YIN-HUAN (1837–1900), scholar, poet, diplomat. Chang was born on February 8, 1837, in Fo-shan or Fatshan in the District of Nan-hai, or Canton, China. He failed to pass a state-administered *hsiu-ts'ai* (prefectural) examination but purchased the title of a student of the Imperial Academy and later the rank of magistrate. He went to work with Li Hung-chang in 1875 to fortify Chinese ports following the Japanese invasion of Formosa. In 1885 Chang was appointed Minister to the United States of America, Peru, and Spain, and came to America in March 1886 to serve his country. In the summer of 1889 Chang was recalled to Peking, and he was given the post of senior vice-president of the Board of Revenue in 1892.

During his more than three years of service as Chinese Minister in Washington, D.C., Chang successfully negotiated for full payment of damages inflicted against Chinese lives and property in the Rock Springs Massacre of 1885* as well as at the Log Cabin Bar near the Snake River. The U.S. government agreed to pay $147,748 to the Chinese government for the deaths of twenty-nine Chinese miners and for damage to their properties at Rock Springs, Wyoming. According to the treaty which Chang Yin-huan was to negotiate with Secretary of State Thomas Francis Bayard, China was to receive $276,619 from the American government for the Snake River massacre. Chang then began to negotiate for a more equitable treaty with the United States for the immigration of Chinese laborers. However, he felt strongly that China needed to impose voluntary restrictions on its immigrants in order to avoid much stricter restrictions by the U.S. government. He successfully negotiated with Secretary Bayard on February 29, 1888, for a treaty that would, among other things, prohibit the immigration of Chinese laborers to the United States for a period of twenty years, require payment by the American government for loss of life and property among Chinese miners at the Log Cabin bar, and obtain the U.S. government's promise to protect Chinese from mob action.

Because of the clause prohibiting Chinese immigration for twenty years, many people in Canton were opposed to the treaty and put pressure on the government not to ratify it. The government in Peking hesitated to ratify the treaty, a delay which the U.S. government misinterpreted as an outright Chinese rejection of the treaty. This misunderstanding gave members of Congress additional ammunition to pass William L. Scott's bill, which proposed to exclude all Chinese laborers from returning to the United States after visiting in China, regardless of whether they possessed the certificate of identity issued by the U.S. government giving them a right to reentry.

Chang Yi-huan served his country in other public offices, but when anti-foreign conservatives gained power in China he was first banished to Sinkiang, and then, in 1900, executed. (*See also* Scott Act of 1888.)

FURTHER READING: Arthur W. Hummel, *Eminent Chinese of the Ching Period (1644– 1912)*, Washington, D.C.: U.S. Government Printing Office, 1943; Shih-shan Henry Tsai, *China and the Overseas Chinese in the United States, 1868–1911*, Fayetteville: University of Arkansas Press, 1983.

CHEE KUNG TONG, an organization commonly called the Chinese Free Masons, established in San Francisco in 1879. The Chee Kung Tong helped Dr. Sun Yat-sen* in his struggle to overthrow the Manchu Dynasty. According to an authority on the Chinese Free Masons, the first *tong* was organized by a group dissatisfied with the way the Chee Kung Tong was managed. Subsequently, other *tongs* were established among the Chinese in America. At the time Rose H. Lee* studied the Chinese community in America, there were six major *tongs*: Hip Sing, Bing Kung, Sui Ying, Ying On, On Leong, and Chee Kung Tong. (*See also* Tongs.)

FURTHER READING: Rose H. Lee, *The Chinese in the United States of America*, Hong Kong: Hong Kong University Press, 1960.

CHEMULP'O, TREATY OF (1882), also known as the Treaty of Amity and Commerce, and the Korean-American Treaty of 1882, an agreement that established diplomatic relations between Korea and the United States, the first Western nation to recognize Korea diplomatically. The treaty had been negotiated between Li Hung-chang of China and Robert W. Shufeldt of the United States in Peking before Korea was advised by Li to conclude a commercial treaty with the United States. Li had been concerned with Japan's advance into the Korean peninsula which had been China's exclusive domain, and he felt that a Western power, namely, the United States, would serve in Korea as a counterforce against Japan.

The treaty, formalized on May 22, 1882, had a number of important provisions for the future development of Korean-American relations, particularly in the area of emigration. Article Five of the treaty allowed Koreans to visit the United States and to reside, to rent premises, and to purchase or construct residences of warehouses in all parts of the country.

Although the treaty allowed Koreans to come to the United States to live, the first group of Korean immigrants did not leave for the United States until 1902.

CH'EN LAN-PIN. *See* United Chinese Society.

CHEUNG SUM SHEE et al. v. NAGLE, COMMISSIONER OF IMMIGRATION FOR THE PORT OF SAN FRANCISCO, a case heard in 1925 regarding the admission to the United States of families of Chinese merchants. In 1924 Cheung Sum Shee and other wives and children of resident Chinese merchants who were lawfully domiciled within the United States were denied entry into the United States by the Secretary of Labor. They appealed, and the Supreme Court heard the case on April 17 and 20, 1925, handing down its decision on May 25, 1925. The main question raised by this case was whether the petitioners, not being merchants themselves, should be prohibited from entering the United States under the restriction of the Immigration Act of 1924.*

Having departed from China, Cheung Sum Shee and her children arrived in the United States on July 11, 1924, and sought permanent admission. The Secretary of Labor denied their applications on the basis that the mercantile status of the husband did not guarantee permission for wives and children as a matter of law. The Court delved into the question: Were the alien Chinese wives and minor children of Chinese merchants who were lawfully domiciled within the United States prior to July 1, 1924 mandatorily excluded from the United States as provided by the Immigration Act of 1924?

Justice James Clark McReynolds delivered the opinion of the Court. In his view the Immigration Act of 1924 should be interpreted in context of preserving the prior treaty rights of aliens unless clearly annulled. Consequently, alien wives and minor children of Chinese merchants lawfully domiciled in the United States could not be excluded by the Immigration Act of 1924.

Although Cheung Sum Shee would not enter the United States solely to "carry on trade," she was nevertheless allowed to enter on the theory that a treaty provision that allowed merchants to enter the United States extended to their immediate families. The Court felt that Congress must have known this when considering the act and would have specifically noted the exclusion of these people, had exclusion been the intent.

FURTHER READING: *Supreme Court Reporter* 45, 268, U.S. 336, 1924.

CHEW HEONG v. UNITED STATES, a case that went to the Supreme Court in error from the Circuit Court of the United States for the District of California. The question before the Court was whether Section 4 of the Chinese Exclusion Act of 1882* approved by Congress on May 6, 1882, as amended on July 5, 1884, requiring all Chinese laborers to produce the certificate of residence as the only evidence acceptable for their reentry into the United States was applicable to Chinese laborers who, residing in the United States on November 17, 1880, departed prior to May 6, 1882, and remained out of the country after July 5, 1884.

Chew Heong was a Chinese laborer who resided in the United States until June 1881, when he left the United States for Hawaii. He left before the Chinese

Exclusion Act was passed. He remained there until September 15, 1884, when he was aboard a vessel bound for the port of San Francisco. Upon arrival he asked to leave the ship but was denied permission under the Chinese Exclusion Act of May 6, 1882. The law required that all Chinese laborers possess a certificate of residence for reentry into the United States. Because he had left before passage of the relevant law, Chew did not have his certificate.

In their argument on behalf of Chew Heong, Attorneys H. S. Brown and Thomas D. Riordan stated that the treaty of 1880 between China and the United States gave Chew Heong, at the time of his departure for Hawaii, the right to go from and return to the United States, without being restricted to regulations adversely affecting that right. The argument was heard, and the decision was made in favor of Chew Heong on December 8, 1884. In delivering the opinion of the Court on this first test case on the Chinese Exclusion Law of 1882, Justice John M. Harlan stated:

> It would be a perversion of the language used to hold that such regulations apply to Chinese laborers who had left the country with the privilege, secured by treaty, of returning, but who, by reason of their absence when those legislative enactments took effect, could not obtain the required certificate.

Justice Stephen J. Field, in his dissenting opinion, disagreed with Justice John M. Harlan, upholding the absolute power of Congress to exclude Chinese. Justice Joseph P. Bradley concurred with Justice Field.

FURTHER READING: Milton Konvitz, *The Alien and the Asiatic in American Law*, Ithaca, N.Y.: Cornell University Press, 1946; *Supreme Court Reporter* 5, 112, U.S. 536, 1884.

CHEW YICK KUNG SHAW (also known as Chao-i Kung-so, or the Luminous Unity Office), organized on November 19, 1849 to protect and promote Chinese interests. Three hundred Chinese representing 789 Chinese men and 2 Chinese women met at the Canton Restaurant on Jackson Street in San Francisco to select a committee of four: Ahe, You-ling, Atung, and Attoon. This first Chinese organization was dissolved quickly as Chinese immigrants from different districts of Kwangtung Province of China began to establish their own district offices.

FURTHER READING: Gunther Barth, *Bitter Strength*, Cambridge, Mass.: Harvard University Press, 1964.

CHIEF'S CHILDREN'S SCHOOL, founded in 1839 in Honolulu to educate the children of the higher chiefs. The school was founded by Mr. and Mrs. Amos Starr Cooke, who were financially supported by the chiefs. By the Organic Act of 1846, the school for young chiefs was called the Royal School and was placed under the direct control of the minister of public instruction. From the school's beginning English was the language of instruction, and ten years later a plan was adopted to admit the children of white residents of Honolulu. This change drastically affected the nature of the institution: after the new plan was adopted, it became exclusively a select English school. In 1851 Edward G. Beckwith became principal, and two years later the school reported 121 students, 95 of whom were white, 8 Hawaiian, and 18 part-Hawaiian.

The Royal School played an important role in educating the future leaders of the Hawaiian Kingdom. Every future Hawaiian king after Kamehameha III as well as many high chiefs received their education at the school between 1839 and 1850. For instance, Kamehameha IV, a student of the Royal School, had a good command of English and was known to have been more European than Hawaiian in ideas and tastes.

FURTHER READING: Ralph S. Kuykendall, *The Hawaiian Kingdom, 1778–1854: Foundation and Transformation*, Honolulu: University of Hawaii Press, 1947; Ralph S. Kuykendall, *The Hawaiian Kingdom, 1854–1874: Twenty Critical Years*, Honolulu: University of Hawaii Press, 1953.

CHIN BAK KAN v. UNITED STATES, a case that went to the Supreme Court in 1902 as an appeal from the District Court of the United States for the Northern District of New York to review a judgment that affirmed a commissioner's decision to deport a Chinese laborer by the name of Chin Bak Kan. The appellant entered the United States on or about May 13, 1901, from Canada, and was aware that he had entered illegally. On May 13, 1901, he was apprehended and brought before the commissioner, who ordered him deported after a hearing. The judgment of the commissioner was then appealed to the District Court which affirmed the deportation of the appellant.

The question before the Supreme Court was whether a commissioner had the authority to order deportation of a Chinese laborer who was found to be in the United States illegally, and whether a Chinese who claimed to be a citizen of the United States had the burden of proving his citizenship. The case was argued on March 13 and 14, 1902, and was decided on June 2, 1902.

Chief Justice Melville W. Fuller, in his opinion affirming the deportation of Chin Bak Kan, ruled that a commissioner was duly authorized to conduct deportation proceedings and the commissioner who ordered Chin Bak Kan deported acted in conformity with the Chinese Exclusion Act of May 6, 1882.* Furthermore, although the appellant claimed that he was a citizen of the United States, he had the burden of proving he was in fact a U.S. citizen.

By this decision the Court strengthened the power of the executive branch of government in dealing with aliens. The Court had already empowered the executive branch to require Chinese laborers to produce credible white witnesses in the case of Fong Yue Ting v. United States,* and in the case of Li Sung v. United States.* In the second case, the Court ruled that an alien could not take advantage of the constitutional guarantee against unreasonable search and seizure. In this case, the Court ruled that a Chinese laborer claiming his U.S. citizenship had the burden of proof.

FURTHER READING: Milton R. Konvtiz, *The Alien and the Asiatic in American Law*, Ithaca, N.Y.: Cornell University Press, 1946; *Supreme Court Reporter* 22, 186 U.S. 193, 1901.

CHIN HUNG WO (1912–   ), businessman. Chin obtained a B.A. degree from Utah State in 1935 and a Ph.D. from Cornell University in 1945. Upon returning to Hawaii, he was asked to become president of the financially troubled Trans-Pacific Airlines, with power to negotiate with its competitor, Hawaiian Airlines, for a merger or to dispose of the airlines. When the negotiations for a merger failed, Chin decided to change the name of the airlines to Aloha Airlines and worked hard to bring in $2 million in new capital through two stock issues. His success in the air transport business enabled him to diversify his interests in other businesses. He invested in real estate, banking, and insurance. Today he owns a number of major financial establishments in Hawaii and serves as chairman of Aloha Airlines, Inc.

CHIN MURDER CASE, a case involving a Chinese American, Vincent Chin, a twenty-seven-year-old draftsman for an engineering firm in Detroit, who was beaten to death by two assailants, Ronald Ebens, and his stepson, Michael Nitz in 1982. Ebens, a former automaker who was laid off from his job, and his son, taunted Chin at a local pub, the Fancy Pants Club, on June 19, 1982, calling Chin a "Chink" and a "Nip." Ebens later got a baseball bat out of his car, chased Chin down the street, and with his stepson, administered the fatal beating in a nearby parking lot. Chin died on June 22, just two days before his planned marriage.

The assailants were charged and prosecuted, but after plea bargaining, they pleaded guilty of manslaughter and were freed on probation and fined $3,780 each. The sentencing judge, Charles Kaufman, defended his decision on the grounds that Ebens had worked for a well-known company for eighteen years, that his stepson was a part-time student who was also employed, and that they would not go out and hurt other people. He claimed that punishment should fit the criminals, not the crime.

Outraged by this decision, the local Chinese American community was mobilized to protest against the injustice of the case, and the American Citizens for Justice was successful in rallying support from civil rights groups in major cities across the nation.

When Asian Americans charged that the decision was one of legalized murder, the Justice Department asked the Federal Bureau of Investigation to conduct an investigation on April 29, 1983. As a result, the two assailants were indicted on charges that they violated the civil rights of Vincent Chin. They were charged with two counts of violating Chin's civil rights: the first for preventing Chin from enjoying the accommodations of the bar, and the second for the actual attack. In 1984, the jury deliberated twelve hours over a total of three days before finding Ebens guilty of having violated Chin's civil rights, although it was not able to find Nitz guilty as charged. On September 18, 1984, Federal District Judge Anna Diggs Taylor sentenced Ronald Ebens to twenty-five years in prison for violating Chin's civil rights. Ebens had been free on a $20,000 bond while his case was on appeal.

FURTHER READING: *New York Times*, June 6, 29, 1984; September 19, 1984.

CHIN YOW v. UNITED STATES, a case submitted to the U.S. Supreme Court on December 13, 1907, as an appeal from the District Court of the United States for the Northern District of California to review an order denying Chin Yow the petition for a writ of habeas corpus. Chin claimed that he was a citizen of the United States and a legal resident of San Francisco, and had been denied his right to enter the United States by the Department of Commerce and Labor. He stated that he had left the United States in 1904 for a temporary visit to China, and upon his return he was prevented from entering his own country. He alleged that he was prevented from obtaining testimony from witnesses who, had they been given the opportunity, could have produced evidence of his U.S. citizenship.

The question before the Court was whether Chin was entitled to a writ of habeas corpus. The Chinese Exclusion Act of 1882* prevented the immigration of Chinese laborers and excluded Chinese from citizenship by naturalization. The intent of the law was to exclude aliens only and to allow U.S. citizens to return to the United States.

Chin had been placed in custody of the Pacific Mail Steamship Company to be returned to China. Therefore, the question was whether he was illegally imprisoned and was to be deported against his will. Although Chin did not prove that he was a U.S. citizen, he should have been given the opportunity to prove that he was in fact a U.S. citizen who was entitled to his rights. If Chin could not prove this, then his deportation would remain in force.

Justice Oliver Wendell Holmes delivered the opinion of the Court on January 6, 1908, which in essence stated that Chin had been imprisoned without due process of law and should be granted a writ of habeas corpus.

FURTHER READING: Milton R. Konvitz, *The Alien and the Asiatic in American Law*, Ithaca, N.Y.: Cornell University Press, 1946; *Supreme Court Reporter*, 208 U.S. 8, 1907.

CHINA-AID SOCIETY. *See* Korean National Revolutionary Party.

CHINA AREA AID ACT OF 1950, a law enacted by the U.S. Congress on June 5, 1950, authorizing the President to extend economic assistance to any place in China that was not under Communist control. The act authorized the President to spend the maximum of $40 million for general relief purposes and $8 million for relief on humanitarian grounds. The law, which was to be in effect until June 30, 1951, was important to Chinese students in America because it authorized the Secretary of State to spend the maximum amount of $6 million for tuition, transportation, and emergency medical care for citizens of China who were in the United States for study, teaching, or research. The law also allowed Chinese students to work for money, provided they received permission from the Commissioner of Immigration and Naturalization.

FURTHER READING: Rose Hum Lee, *The Chinese in the United States of America*, Hong Kong: Hong Kong University Press, 1960; U.S. Statutes at Large, 64 Stat 202, 22 U.S.C. 1547; Public Law 535, 81st Congress.

CHINA FIRE ENGINE COMPANY, an organization established in February 1878 in Honolulu, Hawaii, by a group of fifty Chinese who were responsible for bringing a steam fire engine to the island. Prior to 1878, there had been a number of fires, which had destroyed the properties of Chinese merchants in Honolulu's Chinatown.* Concerned with the problem of protecting their lives and properties, Chinese merchants decided to procure a steam fire engine so that they would not be forced to depend on the Caucasian fire engine companies in Honolulu.

Initially, a group of Caucasian residents in Honolulu had ordered a steam fire engine which had been purchased by money appropriated by the legislature. Thus, a fire fighting company of Caucasians known as Honolulu Fire Engine Company, No. 1, was created. The Chinese then organized themselves into a Chinese fire fighting company and requested that it be recognized as part of the Honolulu Fire Department. Upon winning recognition, it was known as China Fire Engine Company, No. 2.

The experience of organizing this company was valuable, for the Chinese had to write a constitution and by-laws and had to administer the company in accordance with these formal provisions. When the Chinese decided to establish their community organizations, the experience gained from establishing the China Fire Engine Company proved indispensable.

FURTHER READING: Clarence E. Glick, *Sojourners and Settlers*, Honolulu: University Press of Hawaii, 1980.

CHINATOWN, both a concept and a physical presence of Chinese immigrants and their descendants in the United States and in other parts of the world. These immigrants live in a geographically designated area and share community life with a culture separate from that of the dominant society. As a concept, it refers more to a state of mind than to the physical presence of old and new immigrants who strongly feel that they are different socially and culturally and that they are not an integral part of the dominant society. They perceive themselves as being different and alienated from the main current of the dominant society, which discriminates and persecutes them because of their racial or cultural characteristics. This sense of alienation is accompanied by the need for identity, which is partially met as they come to associate themselves with other immigrants of the same ethnic or cultural origin. Chinatown as a concept may be said to exist not only in the minds of Chinese immigrants, old and new, but also in the minds of Japanese, Filipino, Korean, Asian Indian, Southeast Asian, and other immigrants, particularly those who are racially identifiable.

The concept of Chinatown delineated above is not commonly used, however. Chinatown is more generally understood as the physical presence of Chinese ghettos established in the United States and in other parts of the world where old and new Chinese immigrants move to find housing, employment, social and educational services, and social affiliations with their countrymen. The new immigrant's need for cultural and economic survival is not restricted to the Chinese; it is applicable to Korean, Filipino, Japanese, Asian Indian, and Southeast Asian immigrants as well. These immigrant groups also have their respective ghettos which are called Koreatown, Japantown or "Little Tokyo," "Manilatown," and "Little Saigon."

Chinatown developed almost simultaneously with the arrival of Chinese immigrants in California in 1847. The first Chinatown in the United States was established in San Francisco, but as the Chinese began to move to other parts of the country in search of work and new opportunities, other major American cities such as Chicago, Los Angeles, and New York also began to see the establishment of Chinatowns.

Traditionally, Chinatown was associated with an overabundance of Chinese males over females, *tong* wars, opium dens, prostitution, and a general state of poverty. This distorted image of Chinatown was portrayed in story books and films which perpetuated the stereotypes of the Chinese among Americans. Today Chinatown is also viewed as a tourist attraction, giving curious tourists the sounds and sights of an alien culture in their midst.

Chinatown has served many useful purposes to old and new Chinese immigrants for many years. When Chinese immigrants did not have any organization or institution to turn to for help, Chinatown's network of community organizations extended its assistance by finding housing, employment, and social services. As immigrants began to look for psychological and spiritual support, Chinatown also provided a place of worship or meditation. Chinatown also serves Chinese immigrants as a center of business where they purchase their daily necessities.

Whether or not Chinatown will continue to exist among Chinese immigrants is open to question. Rose Hum Lee* suggests that Chinatown may disappear as Chinese immigrants become economically and socially successful and assimilate into and are accepted by the dominant society.

FURTHER READING: Elaine H. Kim, *Asian American Literature*, Philadelphia: Temple University Press, 1982; Peter Kwong, *Chinatown, N.Y.: Labor and Politics, 1930–1950*, New York: Monthly Review Press, 1979; Calvin Lee, *Chinatown, U.S.A.*, Garden City, N.Y.: Doubleday and Co., 1965; Rose Hum Lee, *The Chinese in the United States of America*, Hong Kong: Hong Kong University Press, 1960; Bernard P. Wong, *Chinatown: Economic Adaptation and Ethnic Identity of the Chinese*, New York: Holt, Rinehart and Winston, 1982.

CHINDA SUTEMI (1856–1929), diplomat and Japanese government official who served as Japanese ambassador to Washington, D.C., during the Wilson administration. Chinda was born in Hirosaki Aomori Prefecture, studied in the United States, and joined Japan's diplomatic service in 1885. In 1891 when Chinda was working as Japan's consul in San Francisco, he recommended in his report to his superior that Japan carefully select those Japanese immigrants coming to America by excluding prostitutes, contract laborers, unhealthy persons, and men of no means. He felt that the issues surrounding the immigration of Japanese workers to America would someday become a bone of contention between the two nations.

In 1913 Ambassador Chinda met with President Woodrow Wilson and Secretary of State William Jennings Bryan* and asked them to use their political influence to block the passage of the Alien Land Act of California, 1913,* known also as the Heney-Webb Alien Land Law. In spite of Japan's protest against the bill and President Wilson's effort to prevent a discriminatory law from passing through the California State Legislature, it was approved and went into effect on August 10, 1913.

CHINESE AMERICAN BANK, organized in 1916 in Hawaii. Because it was established as an independent bank, the Chinese American Bank had difficulty from the beginning. It had to compete with other banks for small deposits from Chinese workers in Hawaii. The bank closed its business in 1932 but reopened on April 20, 1935.

FURTHER READING: Clarence E. Glick, *Sojourners and Settlers*, Honolulu: University Press of Hawaii, 1980.

CHINESE AMERICAN CITIZENS ALLIANCE. *See* Native Sons of the Golden State.

CHINESE BOYCOTT OF 1905, organized to persuade the United States to change its immigration policy on China. With the expiration of the Gresham-Yang Treaty* on December 7, 1904, the Ch'ing government made an effort to negotiate with the Roosevelt administration for another treaty. Between August 1904 and January 1905 the Ch'ing government presented two treaty drafts to the Roosevelt administration, but both were rejected. Rigid and tight restrictions on Chinese had already been in existence, and more restrictions were predicted. In the meantime, treaty negotiations were not making any progress. Under these circumstances, Chinese merchants in Shanghai, when their help was requested by their fellow countrymen in the United States, organized to boycott American products in 1905. The boycott was organized under the leadership of Tseng Shao-ching, who sent telegrams to the Chambers of Commerce of twenty-two treaty ports and asked them to refuse to purchase American goods unless the American government agreed to modify its Chinese immigration policy.

The boycott movement spread quickly to other major cities in China as well as to overseas Chinese communities in the Philippines and the United States. The boycott was particularly strong in Canton, for many Chinese immigrants in the United States were from this part of China.

Contemporary historians disagree on the causes of the boycott. Some believe that the boycott was spearheaded by Chinese merchants who feared American competition in a limited market. Others believe that the boycott was a natural result of the Chinese' nationalistic feelings against America's racist immigration policy.

The boycott was initially very successful as the Ch'ing government adopted a neutral attitude at the beginning. But the Ch'ing government later decided to oppose the boycott because it feared that the movement might develop into a political threat to its very survival. Leading the opposition to the boycott movement was Yuan Shih-k'ai, who ordered all the provincial governments of the east coast and along the Yang-tse River to prohibit merchants from boycotting American products. In addition to government pressure on the boycott movement, the rivalry between the followers of K'ang Yu-wei* and Sun Yat-sen* created disharmony and lack of coordination among boycott leaders. The American government's firm protest and threat against the Ch'ing government, along with a conciliatory gesture by President Theodore Roosevelt toward Chinese immigration, also helped to end the boycott movement.

FURTHER READING: Delber L. McKee, *Chinese Exclusion Versus the Open Door Policy, 1900–1906: Clashes over China Policy in the Roosevelt Era*, Detroit: Wayne State University Press, 1977; Shih-shan Henry Tsai, *China and the Overseas Chinese in the United States, 1868–1911*, Fayetteville: University of Arkansas Press, 1983.

CHINESE CHAMBER OF COMMERCE, a Chinese merchants' organization founded in August 1911 in accordance with the Ch'ing Dynasty's advice given to overseas Chinese merchants. The Ch'ing Dynasty recognized the importance of overseas Chinese and desired to develop close relations with them. Consequently, the government encouraged them to organize an institution by sending them money and by-laws. In response to the government's proposal, the leaders of the United Chinese Society* established the Chinese Merchants' Association, known in Chinese as Chung Wah Chung Seong Wui. After the Ch'ing Dynasty was overthrown, another Chinese merchants' association, the Overseas Chinese Merchants' Association, or Wah Kiu Seong Wui, was created by followers of Dr. Sun Yat-sen.* This latter organization was quickly dissolved, however, when General Yuan Shih-k'ai took over the reins of power in China. Although there were some differences and conflicts between the United Chinese Society and the Chinese Merchants' Association, by July 1915 the United Chinese Society was under the control of those who were in charge of the Chinese Merchants' Association. In 1926 the Merchants' Association acquired a new name, the Chinese Chamber of Commerce of Honolulu. (*See also* United Chinese Society.)

CHINESE CIVIC ASSOCIATION, an organization of Hawaiian-born Chinese youth, most of whom attended colleges and universities in mainland United States. Established in 1925, the organization was distinctively different from other traditional Chinese organizations because it sought to garner broader support from the local Chinese community for its struggle against discrimination and economic exploitation. Members of the organization entered into and fought against the so-called English Standard schools which discriminated against children who had limited proficiency in English. Through the organization, the English Standard schools were abolished by 1955. The organization then began to concentrate on raising scholarship money for the University of Hawaii, which many students of Chinese descent attended.

FURTHER READING: Tin-Yuke Char, ed., *The Sandalwood Mountains*, Honolulu: University Press of Hawaii, 1975; Lawrence H. Fuchs, *Hawaii Pono: A Social History*, New York: Harcourt, Brace and World, 1961.

CHINESE COMMERCIAL AGENT'S CERTIFICATE (also known as the Chinese Benevolent Society's Ticket as well as the Chinese passport), issued by C. Alee, the president of the United Chinese Society,* to any Chinese desiring to obtain a passport to come to Hawaii. This arrangement was negotiated between the government of the Kingdom of Hawaii and the United Chinese Society in order to prevent Chinese emigrants from obtaining fraudulent passports in Hong Kong. The consul general of Hawaii stationed in Hong Kong was informed that the Chinese commercial agent charged $3 for the certificate and that $2 of this fee would be paid to the Chinese Benevolent Society.

FURTHER READING: Clarence E. Glick, *Sojourners and Settlers; Chinese Migrants in Hawaii*, Honolulu: University Press of Hawaii, 1980.

CHINESE CONSOLIDATED BENEVOLENT ASSOCIATION. *See* Chinese Six Companies.

CHINESE EDUCATIONAL MISSION, organized in May 1872 as a result of the efforts of Yung Wing,* who had been brought to America for education by an American missionary, Samuel Robbins Brown. Yung Wing graduated from Yale University in 1854 and returned to China. With help from government officials such as Li Hung-chang and Tseng Kuo-fan, he was able to persuade the government of the Ch'ing Dynasty to send young Chinese students to America for training and education. Through Yung's efforts, 120 young students were recruited between 1872 and 1875, and they were sent to American colleges and universities at a cost of $1,200 per student per year. The mission was to be supervised by Ch'en Lan-pin, a conservative official who devoted himself to Chinese learning. Yung Wing was appointed assistant commissioner for the mission. The Educational Mission established its headquarters at Hartford, Connecticut, where a building was erected in 1874 for the use of the mission.

Because of the difference in educational philosophy between Yung Wing and Ch'en Lan-pin, the mission was recalled in 1881 as it came under increasing criticism in China for its educational program. At the time the mission was recalled, only two students graduated from college, and several were enrolled in college courses. Some students married American girls in violation of the mission's regulations.

Among those who returned to China and later achieved great prominence were T'ang Saho-i, first premier of the Republic, Chan T'ien-yu, chief engineer of the Peking-Kalgan Railroad, Liang Tun-yen, onetime Foreign Affairs Minister, and Admiral Ts'ai T'ing-kan and Jung K'uei. Jung was connected with the Chinese Legation in Washington for more than forty years.

FURTHER READING: Thomas E. LaFargue, *China's First Hundred*, Pullman: Washington State University, 1942; Rose Hum Lee, *The Chinese in the United States of America*, Hong Kong: Hong Kong University Press, 1960; Y. C. Wang, *Chinese Intellectuals and the West, 1872–1949*, Chapel Hill: University of North Carolina Press, 1966; Edmund H. Worthy, Jr., "Yung Wing in America," *Pacific Historical Review* 34 (1965), pp. 265–287; Yung Wing, *My Life in China and in America*, New York: Henry Holt and Co., 1909.

CHINESE EXCLUSION ACT OF 1882, a law prohibiting the immigration of Chinese laborers for ten years and the naturalization of Chinese residents of the United States. Although the initial response of whites in California to Chinese immigration was friendly, anti-Chinese sentiments soon developed among whites who felt the Chinese were the cause of California's economic problems. As early as April 1855, the state legislature enacted a law in order to discourage Chinese immigration to California. Finally, the legislature passed an anti-Chinese state constitution in 1879. It prohibited business firms formed under the laws of California from employing any Chinese, either directly or indirectly. The Chinese were prevented from being hired on any state, county, municipal, or other public works, except in punishment for a crime.

In 1879 the U.S. Congress passed a measure forbidding ships from bringing more than fifteen Chinese at one time, but the measure was vetoed by President Rutherford B. Hayes because it contradicted the provisions of the Sino-American Treaty of 1868, also known as the Burlingame Treaty of 1868.* The Treaty of 1880 between Chinese representatives and U.S. commissioners, including James Angell, American ambassador to Peking, was negotiated and signed by the two countries on November 17. According to the provisions of the treaty, China agreed to the regulation, limitation, and suspension, but not absolute prohibition, of Chinese laborers immigrating to the United States. In return, the U.S. government promised to take measures to protect the Chinese already in the country and to secure for them the same rights and privileges accorded nationals of other countries enjoying most-favored-nation treatment. This renegotiated treaty enabled people in Congress to pressure for an exclusion law, and in 1881 Congress passed a measure to exclude the immigration of Chinese laborers for twenty years. However, President Chester A. Arthur, who believed a twenty-year suspension of Chinese immigration would be tantamount to prohibition, vetoed it on the grounds that it was unreasonable and unjustified. Following the presidential veto, a flurry of other bills called for the suspension of Chinese immigration for a longer period of time than that of the original bill. Finally, Congress decided to compromise with the President and sent him a measure to suspend Chinese immigration for a period of ten years. The bill was signed on May 6, 1882, by President Arthur.

In its final form, the act prohibited the immigration of Chinese laborers, both skilled and unskilled, and denied Chinese residents in the United States the right to become American citizens. It also denied entry to wives of Chinese laborers already in the United States. Chinese residents were required to carry valid passports after they had been duly registered. In 1892 the act was renewed in the form of the Geary Act* and extended for another decade. The exclusion was made "permanent" in 1902.

FURTHER READING: Jack Chen, *The Chinese of America*, New York: Harper and Row, 1980; Mary Roberts Coolidge, *Chinese Immigration*, New York: Henry Holt and Co., 1909; Shien-woo Kung, *Chinese in American Life*, Seattle: University of Washington Press, 1962; Delber L. McKee, *Chinese Exclusion and the Open Door Policy*, Detroit: Wayne State University Press, 1977.

CHINESE HAND LAUNDRY ALLIANCE, a trade organization established among Chinese laundrymen in New York City on April 26, 1933, in response to the action taken by the Board of Aldermen of New York City that required all Chinese laundrymen to post a $1,000 bond to operate a one-person laundry and to pay $25 for the annual registration fee. This action taken by the board in the form of a city ordinance was instigated by New York's non-Chinese laundry operators who feared competition from Chinese laundrymen who had established themselves in the business long before washing machines and steam presses were introduced. In fact, laundries employ large numbers of people and represent the oldest business among the Chinese in America. The Chinese had been engaged in the business long before the famous case, Yick Wo v. Hopkins,* was brought to the Supreme Court of the United States in 1886. According to the 1920 U.S. Census, 30 percent of all Chinese were engaged in laundry work, and there were 3,350 Chinese hand laundries in New York City during the 1930s.

Chinese hand laundrymen did not organize themselves into a trade union until 1933, when the Chinese Hand Laundry Alliance was established. Until then, they were organized in various guilds, which were basically established along clan, district, or family lines. As a result, they lacked a strong organization to promote their own interests.

Once the organization was established to combat discrimination against Chinese hand laundrymen, it fought against the action taken by the board and had the bond reduced to $100. It also fought against the requirement of being fingerprinted which the commissioner of the New York City License Bureau had imposed on the Chinese operating small-scale laundries.

The Chinese Hand Laundry Alliance also helped to establish social clubs in New York's Chinatown.* One of them, the Quon Shar or Mass Club, is one of the most successful social clubs in Chinatown.

FURTHER READING: Peter Kwong, *Chinatown, N.Y.: Labor and Politics, 1930–1950*, New York: Monthly Review Press, 1979; S. W. Kung, *Chinese in American Life*, Seattle: University of Washington Press, 1962.

CHINESE HISTORICAL SOCIETY OF AMERICA, a non-profit organization established in San Francisco on January 15, 1963, when a first formal meeting was held with thirty-one persons in attendance. The meeting was the outgrowth of a previous discussion held by a group of five men to explore the feasibility of forming a Chinese historical society. The name "Chinese Historical Society of America" was approved at the end of the first meeting, and the society was duly registered in the State of California on March 15, 1963.

The society's first president was Thomas W. Chinn, and its headquarters is now located at 17 Adler Place, San Francisco. (The society has a small museum open to the public free of charge every day from 1:00 to 5:00 p.m. except Sundays and Mondays.)

During its brief existence, the society has contributed greatly to an understanding of Chinese American history by means of public lectures. The society has published a number of books, including *A History of Chinese in California*, published in 1969, and it still publishes a monthly bulletin to inform its members of the latest developments in scholarship on Chinese American history.

CHINESE LABOR CONVENTION IN MEMPHIS, a convention held on July 13, 1869, in the Greenlaw Opera House in Memphis, Tennessee, in an attempt to find the best and cheapest ways of getting Chinese laborers to work for cotton planters, railroad companies, and other Southern industrialists in Alabama, Georgia, Kentucky, Mississippi, South Carolina, Louisiana, Arkansas, Tennessee, and Missouri.

The convention had been planned and organized by George Washington Gift and some thirty members of the Chamber of Commerce in Memphis who met on June 30, 1869. Before this group adjourned, they adopted resolutions calling for the importation of Chinese laborers directly from China, calling a convention on July 13, and inviting newspapers in the South to publish the proceedings of the convention.

As planned, the convention was held on July 13 with approximately 200 delegates from eight Southern states and California in attendance, who chose Isham G. Harris as their permanent chairman. They listened to a series of encouraging speeches and reports. The first guest to address the delegates of the convention was a Chinese by the name of Tye Kim Orr, who gave them some practical suggestions and sound advice about importing Chinese laborers. Cornelius Koopmanschap* arrived on the second day of the convention and was surprised to find so many people interested in procuring Chinese laborers in the South.

At the end of the convention, almost all delegates of the convention supported General Gideon S. Pillow's proposal to incorporate a company to be called the Mississippi Valley Immigration Labor Company.* It was to be capitalized at $1 million, with each share of stock to cost $100. Although the Tennessee State Legislature approved the incorporation of the company in December 1869, the legislature prohibited the company from bringing in Chinese immigrants. The Memphis Convention had hoped to bring to the South many thousands of Chinese laborers, but only a trickle of the expected number came to work on railroads and plantations. (*See also* Mississippi Valley Immigration Labor Company; Koopmanschap, Cornelius.)

FURTHER READING: Gunther Barth, *Bitter Strength*, Cambridge, Mass.: Harvard University Press, 1964; Lucy M. Cohen, *Chinese in the Post-Civil War South: A People Without a History*, Baton Rouge: Louisiana State University Press, 1984; Alexander Saxton, *The Indispensable Enemy: Labor and the Anti-Chinese Movement in California*, Berkeley: University of California Press, 1971.

CHINESE SIX COMPANIES (known as Chung Wah Kung Saw in Chinese), was created in the 1850s as a coordinating council responsible for the general affairs of the district companies.* The council was administered by the heads of the district companies. Commonly known as the Chinese Consolidated Benevolent Association, the name "Chung Wah Kung Saw" was changed to "Chung Wah Wui Kun" in 1862.

Since its creation in San Francisco, the organization has functioned as the spokesman for all Chinese in America. Although there are Chinese Consolidated Benevolent Associations in many Chinese communities in cities such as Chicago, New York, and Los Angeles, these associations look to the San Francisco organization for leadership.

The association was very important in the lives of Chinese immigrants who found themselves in a hostile environment. It helped them find employment; it facilitated their relations with the U.S. government; it functioned as a quasi-judicial institution in settling individual and community disputes referred to the association for arbitration and solution; and it worked toward the betterment of the life of Chinese in America by petitioning to the U.S government for the protection of Chinese rights and sometimes carrying their litigation to the Supreme Court of the United States.

On the negative side, it also worked to control and limit the opportunities of the average Chinese worker in America. The association's control over the worker was tight: he was not able to free himself from the financial debts he owed to the association. In addition, his physical mobility was restricted as he was not allowed to move unless he was free from all debts, and very seldom did the Chinese worker find himself free from debts.

The power the association has over the Chinese in America today is not as strong as it used to be, and the nature of the Chinese population has changed. Today, Chinese, whether born in America or abroad, are better educated and more affluent and seek to settle their disputes by means of legal institutions. Most of them have moved into suburbia where they mingle with members of the majority society.

FURTHER READING: Gunther Barth, *Bitter Strength*, Cambridge, Mass.: Harvard University Press, 1964; Him Mark Lai et al., *The Chinese of America, 1785–1980*, San Francisco: Chinese Culture Foundation, 1980; Rose Hum Lee, *The Chinese in the United States of America*, Hong Kong: Hong Kong University Press, 1960.

CHINESE TIMES, THE, a newspaper founded in 1921 by the Chinese American Citizens Alliance, a group that changed its original name, the Native Sons of the Golden State,* in 1915. The alliance was established in 1895 in San Francisco, and its membership was almost exclusively made up of persons born in America of Chinese ancestry. The Alliance established local chapters in Chicago, Detroit, Pittsburgh, Boston, Houston, San Antonio, Albuquerque, Los Angeles, Fresno, San Diego, Salinas, Portland, and Oakland. *The Chinese Times*, as the official publication of the Alliance, had the largest circulation of any Chinese language newspaper in the United States.

CHING KING CHUN. *See* United Chinese Society.

CHINK, CHINK, CHINAMAN, a pejorative term for the Chinese. The term ''Chink'' must have been derived from the dynastic title, Ch'ing, for Chinese immigrants came from the Ch'ing Dynasty. Other pejorative terms used for the Chinese were ''John Chinaman,''* ''Heathen,'' ''Celestials,'' or ''Chinee.'' Seldom were Chinese in America called by their own names.

CHON MYONG-WUN. *See* Chang In-hwan.

CHONG CHUM v. KOHALA SUGAR COMPANY, a case decided by the Supreme Court of Hawaii on February 26, 1892, testing the constitutionality of the act of 1890, which allowed employers to withhold their employees' wages. The plaintiff, Chong Chum, a native of China, was employed by the Kohala Sugar Company after he came to Hawaii under the sponsorship of the company which had obtained a permit to bring him. Before his departure for Hawaii, he was told to sign a written contract that would pay him $15 per month as a plantation worker and would allow the company to withhold $3.75 every month until a sum of $75 was collected. The money collected was then to be turned over to the Board of Immigration for Chong's return trip to China. He signed the contract because he was told he would not be able to land unless he signed it.

Chong Chum brought suit against the company and asked the court to declare the requirements of the permit of entry and residence unconstitutional and to prevent the company from withholding $3.75 from his wages every month. Justice Sanford Ballard Dole,* who had ruled on the case while on circuit, was now faced with an appeal from his ruling.

The Supreme Court of Hawaii did not agree with Justice Dole's decision made while on circuit, when he ruled that the requirements of permit entry as well as residence were in violation of the plaintiff's constitutional rights. The highest court of Hawaii, however, agreed with Justice Dole's previous ruling that the portion of the act of 1890 allowing employers to withhold their employees' wages was unconstitutional. (*See also* Dole, Sanford Ballard.)

FURTHER READING: Ethel M. Damon, *Sanford Ballard Dole and His Hawaii*, Palo Alto, Calif.: Pacific Books, 1957; Ralph S. Kuykendall, *The Hawaiian Kingdom*, Vol. 3, Honolulu: University of Hawaii Press, 1967.

CHOY, HERBERT Y.C. (1916–), the first Asian American to be appointed to a U.S. federal court. Choy was born on January 6, 1916, to Choy Du-wuk, who had come to Hawaii as an immigrant. Choy was born in the sugar plantation village of Hakaweli but grew up in Honolulu. He received his B.A. degree from the University of Hawaii and his J.D. from Harvard in 1945. He served in the military during World War II.

In 1975 Choy joined the law firm of Fong and Miho as a partner, and the following year he was appointed to the U.S. Court of Appeals for the Ninth Circuit by President Richard M. Nixon.

CHUNG KUN-AI (1865–1958), an early Chinese immigrant who came to Hawaii with his parents, who were merchants. Chung grew up in Hawaii and attended Iolani College, better known as Bishop's School. Upon completion of his schooling, he went into business and established a tailor shop, but his business failed. He then went to work for James Dowsett, a ranch businessman. After the death of his employer, he and several of his friends incorporated a business that was capitalized at $60,000. The business firm called City Mill Company prospered, and Chung was able to give generous donations to various causes of the Honolulu Chinese community. In 1953 he founded the Chung Kun-ai Foundation in order to encourage Christian stewardship.

FURTHER READING: Tin-Yuke Char, *The Sandalwood Mountains*, Honolulu: University Press of Hawaii, 1975.

CHUNG MEI HOME FOR YOUNG BOYS, a home for Chinese children established in 1923 by the Reverend Charles Shepherd, who had struggled to found a children's home for many years. Through his efforts, a two-story building was acquired. A ceremony dedicating Chung Mei Home at 3000 Ninth Street, Berkeley, California, was held on October 7, 1923.

CHUNGSHAN. *See* Hiangshan.

CHUNG WAH CHUNG SEONG WUI (Chinese Merchants' Association). *See* Chinese Chamber of Commerce.

CHUNG WAH KUNG SAW. *See* Chinese Six Companies.

CHUNG WAH TUNG MING WUI, a revolutionary organization that replaced the Hing Chung Wui* in 1903. During the absence of Dr. Sun Yat-sen* in Honolulu, Hawaii, some members of the Hing Chung Wui left the organization to join its rival group, Bow Wong Wui or Pao-huang Hui* (Society to protect the Emperor)* established by Liang Chi'i-ch'ao.*

After his return to Honolulu in 1903, Sun began to stress the difference between his organization and Pao-huang Hui, and explained to his followers his revolutionary political program which emphasized driving out the Manchus, restoring China, and establishing a republic. Because of his efforts to reestablish the revolutionary base among overseas Chinese in Hawaii, many Chinese in Hawaii withdrew their membership from the Pao-huang Hui and joined Sun's organization.

FURTHER READING: Hao Chang, *Liang Ch'i-ch'ao and Intellectual Transition in China*, Cambridge, Mass.: Harvard University Press, 1971; Clarence Glick, *Sojourners and Settlers*, Honolulu: University Press of Hawaii, 1980.

CHUNG WAH WUI KUN. *See* Chinese Six Companies.

CHURCH, DENVER SAMUEL (1862–1952), a congressman from California. Church was born on December 11, 1862, in Folsom City, Sacramento County, California. He graduated from Healdsburgh College in 1883 and studied law. Upon admission to the bar Church began practice in Fresno, California, and later became a district attorney in 1907, serving until 1913. In the same year he was elected to Congress and served until 1919. In Congress, Church led a strong campaign to exclude all Hindu laborers from America. In 1914 he introduced a bill to exclude Hindu laborers, with support from Senator Ellison DuRant Smith of South Carolina, as well as from Representative John Burnett of Alabama, who then served as chairman of the House Committee on Immigration and Naturalization. After much debate, the Church bill was tabled. By that time, other measures had been taken to effectively control the immigration of Hindu laborers to America. Church died on February 21, 1952.

FURTHER READING: S. Chandrashekhar, *From India to America*, La Jolla, Calif.: A Population Review Book, 1982; H. Brett Melendy, *Asians in America*, Boston: Twayne Publishers, 1977.

CHY LUNG v. FREEMAN, a case argued before the U.S. Supreme Court on January 14, 1876. This case can be viewed as a general test of the constitutional limits of states to pass laws regulating immigration, where no such laws existed previously. It can also be viewed as a case against discriminatory procedures incorporated into law, as a state statute. Enacted in California, this law had the stated purpose of protecting California soil from those immigrants considered unworthy of passage. The legal method utilized for this purpose was an arrangement allowing the state commissioner of immigration, upon his inspection, to levy a bond requirement on the captain of an arriving ship for every passenger decreed unworthy of entrance. In practice, the looseness of the standards upon which immigrants could be judged (including criminals, paupers, the diseased, and lewd and debauched women) provided the state with a framework for extortion and allowed the legalization of discrimination.

Chy Lung was a Chinese woman who found herself categorized as a debauched woman, and thus unable to land on American soil because the captain refused to give the prescribed bond. She then sued for a writ of habeas corpus resulting in her detention in San Francisco, pending the trial, after which she filed a writ of error with the Supreme Court, to test the constitutionality of the act under which she was held. The case which Chy Lung presented to the Supreme Court contained the reality of legalized discrimination but rested on the legal ground of direct constitutional violations.

In his opinion for the Court, Justice Samuel F. Miller stated that a state's right to pass laws to protect itself from undesirable foreigners was very limited, and it could not extend so far as to prevent or obstruct other classes of people from the right to hold personal and commercial relations with the people of the United States. In his opinion the statute of California violated the power of Congress, which has the responsibility to regulate and carry on commerce with other nations. The Supreme Court, however, did not specify what limits should be imposed on state legislation regulating the entry of aliens, and it left the question open until Congress passed the Immigration Act of August 3, 1882* to fill the void. (*See also* In Re Ah Fong.)
FURTHER READING: Frank F. Chuman, *The Bamboo People*, Del Mar, Calif.: Publisher's Inc., 1976; Milton Konvitz, *The Alien and the Asiatic in American Law*, Ithaca, N.Y.: Cornell University Press, 1946; *United States Supreme Court Reports*, 23 Lawyer Edition, U.S. 90–93, October Term, 1875, pp. 550–52.

CIGAR MAKERS' INTERNATIONAL UNION, a nationwide labor organization originally established under the name, the National Cigarmakers Union, in 1864 with a membership of approximately 1,000. It was renamed the Cigar Makers' International Union in 1867, with an increased membership of 5,800. As a result of the depression of 1873–1879, the cigar business, which was considered a luxury business, declined drastically and a number of union members dropped out. In 1875 the union went through a further organizational change, and elected Samuel Gompers* as president and Adolph Strasser as financial secretary.

Under Gompers' leadership, the union launched a vicious anti-Chinese campaign to drive out Chinese from the cigar-making business. Specifically, Local 228 of the Cigar Makers' International Union, established in San Francisco in 1884, did not require its members to refuse to work for employers who had Chinese workers in their shops; instead, the union encouraged its members to work for shops with Chinese workers and did everything to place union members in white-owned factories. This was the beginning of the end of Chinese employment in the cigar business.
FURTHER READING: John R. Commons et al., *History of Labour in the United States*, 4 vols., New York: Macmillan Co., 1918; Jack Chen, *The Chinese of America*, New York: Harper and Row, 1980; Bernard Mandel, *Samuel Gompers*, Yellow Springs, Ohio: Antioch Press, 1963; Alexander Saxton, *The Indispensable Enemy*, Berkeley: University of California Press, 1971.

CIVILIAN EXCLUSION ORDERS, a series of orders issued by General John L. DeWitt,* commanding general of the Western Defense Command, to exclude persons of Japanese ancestry from certain strategic areas on the West Coast considered critical for the military. The general plan for the evacuation and relocation of persons of Japanese ancestry was put into operation immediately after the President signed the now famous Executive Order 9066,* on February 19, 1942. It was claimed that the removal of all persons of Japanese ancestry from the West Coast was for military necessity,* and civilian exclusion orders were issued in the order of their relative military importance.

Civilian Exclusion Order No. 1, issued on March 24, 1942, excluded all persons of Japanese ancestry from Bainbridge Island on Puget Sound to the Bremerton Naval Yard and ordered them to assemble at the Puyallup Army Assembly Center by March 31, 1942. Civilian Exclusion Order No. 2 and No. 3 ordered all persons of Japanese ancestry removed from San Pedro, Long Beach, and other areas in Los Angeles County, California. Exclusion Order No. 4 covered the city and most of the county of San Diego, California, whereas Exclusion Order No. 5 removed persons of Japanese ancestry from most dock areas and the waterfront of San Francisco.

FURTHER READING: John L. DeWitt, *Final Report: Japanese Evacuation from the West Coast, 1942*, Washington, D.C.: U.S. Government Printing Office, 1943; Dillon S. Myer, *Uprooted Americans*, Tucson: University of Arizona Press, 1971; Michi Weglyn, *Years of Infamy*, New York: William Morrow and Co., 1976.

CLARK, MARK W. (1896–1984), general of the U.S. Army. Clark was born into a military family on May 1, 1896. He graduated from West Point in 1917 and served in France as a captain. Upon returning home he attended Infantry, General Staff and War College. When World War II began, he was assigned to the General Staff and was instructed to write a memorandum for the President on the subject of enemy aliens. He recommended that no memorandum be sent to the President on the subject and that only a small number of enemy aliens be moved by force, if necessary. No mention was made of removing citizens of the United States. When Clark visited General John L. DeWitt* on February 12, 1942, he was told that an evacuation of all persons of Japanese ancestry was in the works. He showed dismay because he had already recommended in his memorandum that no major evacuation be carried out indiscriminately.

FURTHER READING: Roger Daniels, *Concentration Camps U.S.A.*, New York: Holt, Rinehart and Winston, 1971; Bill Hosokawa, *Nisei*, New York: William Morrow and Co., 1969.

CLARK, TOM CAMPBELL (1899–1977), U.S. Supreme Court Justice. Clark was born on September 23, 1899, in Dallas, Texas. He received his B.A. and law degrees from the University of Texas in 1921 and 1922, respectively. He worked as civil district attorney of Dallas between 1927 and 1932, and was named to a Justice Department post in 1937, specializing in antitrust cases. In

January 1942 he was appointed coordinator of the Alien Enemy Control Program within the Western Defense Command. He unquestionably followed and supported Attorney General Francis Biddle's* order and general plan to evacuate and relocate all persons of Japanese ancestry from the West Coast. In 1945 Clark was appointed Attorney General and nominated to the Supreme Court of the United States in 1949. He served on the Court until his retirement in June 1967. His son, Ramsay Clark, also served as U.S. Attorney General. Clark later regretted the role he had played in evacuating and relocating persons of Japanese ancestry.

FURTHER READING: Roger Daniels, *Concentration Camps, U.S.A.*, New York: Holt, Rinehart and Winston, 1971; Bill Howokawa, *Nisei*, New York: William Morrow and Co., 1969.

CLEVELAND, GROVER. *See* Scott Act of 1888.

COBOY-COBOY, a term used to describe the abduction of the wife by other Filipinos in Hawaii in the early days of the Filipino immigration. The origin of the term is not known, although it might have been derived from American cowboy movies in the 1920s in which the heroine is often saved or abducted by her secret admirer. Although wife abduction occurred only rarely among Filipinos in Hawaii, coboy-coboy was feared and it was even known among Filipinos in the Philippines.

FURTHER READING: Ruben R. Alcantara, *Sakada: Filipino Adaptation in Hawaii*, Washington, D.C.: University Press of America, 1981; Robert N. Anderson et al., *Filipinos in Rural Hawaii*, Honolulu: University of Hawaii Press, 1984; Luis V. Teodoro, Jr., ed., *Out of This Struggle: The Filipinos in Hawaii*, Honolulu: University Press of Hawaii, 1981.

COCKRILL et al. v. PEOPLE OF STATE OF CALIFORNIA, one of the major court cases challenging the constitutionality of the California Alien Land Act of 1913* as amended in 1920. The case involved W. A. Cockrill, a practicing attorney of Santa Rosa, and S. Ikada, one of Cockrill's clients, both of whom were found guilty of conspiring to effect a transfer of real property in violation of the alien land law. W. A. Cockrill made a contract with Mr. and Mrs. Souza, who agreed to sell Cockrill five acres of agricultural land situated in Sonoma County. The first payment, $150, was paid by S. Ikada, a citizen of Japan, who intended to purchase the land for his American-born children. On August 26, 1921, the Souzas testified to the effect that they knew that Cockrill made the contract to buy the land for S. Ikada's children. On November 14, 1921, the grand jury of Sonoma County returned an indictment against Cockrill and Ikada, charging them with conspiracy to violate the alien land law. Subsequently, the two were found guilty as charged, and each defendant was fined $750. On appeal the District Court of Appeal affirmed the decision of the Superior Court of Sonoma County, and the defendants then brought error to the Supreme Court of the United States. The attorneys for Cockrill and Ikada made their arguments on two legal grounds. First, they argued that the prima facie presumption created by the alien land law was in violation of the due process and equal protection clauses of the federal Constitution and that the same presumption was a violation of Article 1 of the 1911 Treaty between Japan and the United States.*

The Court heard the argument on March 6, 1925, and decided the case on May 11. In delivering the opinion of the Court, Justice Pierce Butler stated that the rule of evidence was applied equally to citizens and eligible aliens as well as to persons ineligible for U.S. citizenship, and therefore the alien land law was not inconsistent with the due process and equal protection clauses of the federal Constitution. It was also ruled that the 1911 treaty was not violated inasmuch as it did not give Japanese subjects any protection that was not given them by the due process and equal protection clauses of the Fourteenth Amendment.

FURTHER READING: Consulate-General of Japan, *Documental History of Law Cases Affecting Japanese in the United States, 1916–1924*, Vol. 2, San Francisco: 1925; Frank F. Chuman, *The Bamboo People*, Del Mar, Calif.: Publisher's Inc., 1976.

COLLINS, WAYNE MORTIMER (1899–1974), a militant San Francisco attorney who fought for the civil rights of Japanese Americans during and after World War II. Collins represented Fred Toyosaburo Korematsu in the legal battle to free Korematsu from the conviction resulting from a violation of an evacuation order during World War II. Collins also represented Endo Mitsuye in her legal battle to gain a habeas corpus.

After World War II Collins represented Iva Ikuko Toguri d'Aquino,* better known among Americans as Tokyo Rose, as her legal counselor to have her exonerated from charges that she had collaborated with the Japanese military during the Pacific War.

Collins scorned the Japanese American Citizens League* (JACL) for its acquiescence to, if not active cooperation with, the U.S. government's decision to remove, evacuate, and relocate all persons of Japanese ancestry during World War II. He referred to members of the JACL as "a bunch of jackals." (*See also* Korematsu v. United States; Endo, Ex Parte; and d'Aquino, Iva Ikuko Toguri.)

FURTHER READING: Bill Hosokawa, *JACL in Quest of Justice*, New York: William Morrow and Co., 1982; Clifford I. Uyeda, "The Pardoning of 'Tokyo Rose': A Report on the Restoration of American Citizenship to Iva Ikuko Toguri," *Amerasia Journal* 5, No. 2 (1978): 69–93.

COLUMBIA MINERS' CONVENTION, a meeting held on May 8, 1852, in Columbia, Toulumne County, California, which passed an anti-Chinese resolution. Before 1852 there had been anti-foreign sentiment among white miners in California. This sentiment had contributed directly to the passage of the California Foreign Miners Tax* law, which required that all persons who were not native-born citizens of the United States pay $20 per month for their right to mine in California. But this requirement was generally considered to be directed against

Mexicans, South Americans, Spanish Americans, and Kanakas. Chinese miners were not the target of the intense anti-foreign feelings before 1852. Scholars such as Chiu Ping and Mary Coolidge claim that the organized campaign against Chinese labor originated from Columbia after the convention passed its resolution calling for the expulsion of Chinese miners from California mines.

Although the white miners' fear of Chinese competition might have instigated the call for the expulsion of Chinese miners, the real reason for the anti-Chinese campaign had a great deal to do with the white miners' desire to remain independent miners whose interests were directly threatened by a new water project. The project put into operation by the Toulumne County Water Company was about to gain a monopoly on water, which was essential for mining techniques used in California. It seems that white miners wanted to drive out the Chinese because they believed the Chinese would have better bargaining power with the water company. If this was indeed their reason, it was to no avail because after the Chinese were expelled from Columbia and the ditches were completed, the water rates were too high and many of the miners were forced to abandon the claims they had staked out.

FURTHER READING: Ping Chiu, *Chinese Labor in California, 1850–1880*, Madison: State Historical Society of Wisconsin, 1963; Mary R. Coolidge, *Chinese Immigration*, New York: Henry Holt and Co., 1909; Alexander Saxton, *The Indispensable Enemy*, Berkeley, Calif.: University of California Press, 1971.

COLUMBIA RESOLUTION. *See* Columbia Miners' Convention.

COMBINED ASIAN-AMERICAN RESOURCES PROJECT, founded in April 1969 in San Francisco by a group of concerned Asian American writers. Among the people actively involved in this organization were Lawson Inada, author of *Before the War* (1971); Jeffery Chan, author of *Jackrabbit* (1974) and other short stories; Frank Chin, author of a play called *The Chickencoop Chinaman* (1972); and Shawn Wong, author of a short story, "Homebase" (1979), and other stories.

The Combined Asian-American Resources Project, Inc. was originally engaged in three major areas of interest. First, members were interested in carrying out oral history projects focusing on the rural Chinese population and Asian American professionals. Second, the organization served as a catalyst, organizing in-service workshops for teachers in the field of Asian American Studies. Third, the organization devoted its energies to publishing books worthy of attention. The group was responsible for making arrangements to have John Okada's* *No-No Boy* (1957), published by the University of Washington Press. The group also encouraged the press to issue new editions of Carlos Bulosan's* *America Is in the Heart* (1946), Louis Chu's *Eat a Bowl of Tea* (1961), and Monica Sone's* *Nisei Daughter* (1953).

Jeffery Chan of San Francisco State University is the current president of the organization.

COMMISSION ON WARTIME RELOCATION AND INTERNMENT OF CIVILIANS, created on July 31, 1980, by the 96th Congress charged mainly with gathering facts to determine whether any wrong was committed against those American citizens and permanent resident aliens affected by Executive Order 9066* signed into law by President Franklin D. Roosevelt.

The bill establishing the commission was sponsored by Norman Y. Mineta* of California and Daniel Inouye* of Hawaii. The commission was originally composed of seven members but two more members were added: Joan Bernstein, chair and a former general counsel for the Department of Health, Education and Welfare; Representative Dan Lungren, vice-chair, a Republican from California; Edward Brooke of Massachusetts, former U.S. senator; Robert F. Drinan, former U.S. Representative from Massachusetts; Arthur S. Flemming, former Secretary of Education; Arthur Goldberg, former Associate Justice of the Supreme Court of the United States; the Reverend I. V. Gromoff; Judge William M. Marutani; and Hugh B. Mitchell of Washington. Two more members were added during the Reagan administration.

The commission was to hold public hearings in appropriate cities in the United States and was to submit a written report of its findings and recommendations to Congress no later than January 15, 1982. The commission was authorized to spend $1.5 million to carry out the provisions of the act known as Public Law 96–317.

The commission fulfilled the first two mandates of the act by submitting to Congress a unanimous report, *Personal Justice Denied*, which extensively reviews the history of the exclusion and detention of all persons of Japanese ancestry during World War II. The report, submitted to Congress to remedy the wartime treatment of American citizens of Japanese ancestry and permanent resident aliens of Japanese extraction, placed the blame squarely on President Roosevelt, who delayed the release of the Japanese Americans until after the 1944 presidential election for political reasons. The commission made five recommendations:

1. That Congress pass a joint resolution, to be signed by the President, which recognized that a grave injustice was done and offered the apologies of the nation for the acts of exclusion, removal, and detention;

2. That the President pardon those who were convicted of violating the statutes imposing curfew on American citizens of Japanese descent;

3. That Congress direct the agencies to which Japanese Americans might apply for the restitution of positions, status, or entitlements lost in whole or in part because of acts or events between December 1, 1941, and 1945 to review such applications without liability, giving full consideration to the historical findings of this commission;

4. That Congress demonstrate official recognition of the injustice done to American citizens of Japanese ancestry and Japanese resident aliens, and that it recognize the nation's need to make redress for these events, by appropriating monies to establish a special foundation;

5. That Congress establish a fund that would provide personal redress to those who were excluded, as well as serve the purposes set out in Recommendation 4. Appropriation of $1.5 billion would be made to the fund over a reasonable period to be determined by Congress. This fund would be used first to provide a onetime per capita compensatory payment of $20,000 to each of the approximately 60,000 surviving persons excluded from their places of residence pursuant to Executive Order 9066. The burden would be on the government to locate survivors. Payment would be made to the oldest survivors first. Congressman Dan Lungren opposed the idea of paying $20,000 to each surviving evacuee and so dissented on this particular recommendation.

FURTHER READING: Commission on Wartime Relocation and Internment of Civilians, Vol. 2, Washington, D.C.: U.S. Government Printing Office, 1982 and 1983; Bill Hosokawa, *JACL in Quest for Justice*, New York: William Morrow and Co., 1982; Peter Irons, *Justice at War: The Story of Internment Cases*, New York: Oxford University Press, 1983; *New York Times*, February 25, 1983, and June 17, 1983.

COMMITTEE OF SAFETY, organized in Honolulu, Hawaii, on January 14, 1893, at the law office of William O. Smith, an active member of the Annexation Club* founded in 1892. All except one of the thirteen committee men were former members of the Annexation Club. The committee was composed of the chairman, H. E. Cooper, F. W. McChesney, T. F. Lansing, and J. A. McCandless, who were American citizens; W. O. Smith, L. A. Thurston, W. R. Castle, and A. S. Wilcox, who were Hawaiians born of American parents; W. C. Wilder, American; C. Bolte and H. F. Glade, Germans; Henry Waterhouse, Tasmanian; and Andress Brown, a Scot. Glade and Wilcox resigned after two days; they were replaced by Ed Suhr, a German, and John Emmeluth, an American.

The members of the committee conspired to overthrow the legitimate government of Queen Liliuokalani* after her statement on January 14, 1893, that she would alter the constitution. The committee members felt that the queen had committed a revolutionary act and that they had every right to take the task of "restoring law and order" into their own hands.

The committee members were very active in making arrangements to create a new government. The government was established on July 4, 1894, with Sanford Ballard Dole* as its president. President Grover Cleveland later sent a letter of recognition to the new regime. Thus, a further step toward the annexation of Hawaii by the United States was taken.

FURTHER READING: Gavan Daws, *Shoal of Time*, Honolulu: University Press of Hawaii, 1968; Ralph S. Kuykendall, *The Hawaiian Kingdom*, Vol. 3, Honolulu: University of Hawaii Press, 1967; Sylvester Stevens, *American Expansion in Hawaii*, New York: Russell and Russell, 1945; Merze Tate, *Hawaii: Reciprocity or Annexation*, East Lansing: Michigan State University Press, 1968.

COMMITTEE OF THIRTEEN, organized on July 20, 1853, at the height of the smallpox epidemic. The committee was comprised of businessmen and others who were concerned with the ravages of the epidemic and its possible effects

on the economy in Hawaii, particularly on the fall visit of whaling fleets. A number of public meetings were held between July 18 and 19, and seven resolutions were adopted and forwarded to the Privy Council. The resolutions called for the burning of the contaminated houses, improved vaccination, and the appointment of volunteers to carry out preventive measures against the possible outbreak of the epidemic. Other meetings were held to place the blame on people responsible for lack of preventive measures taken by the government. At one of these meetings, George Lathrop read a series of resolutions accusing physicians Gerrit Parmele Judd* and Richard Armstrong of negligence in the early stages of the epidemic. At yet another meeting a resolution was passed calling for their resignation. Then a Committee of Thirteen was created to circulate petitions for their resignation. Judd and Armstrong stayed on as Ministers until they were dismissed by Kauikeaouli (King Kamehameha III), who reappointed every minister except Judd.
FURTHER READING: Gavan Daws, *Shoals of Time*, Honolulu: University Press of Hawaii, 1968; Ralph S. Kuykendall, *The Hawaiian Kingdom*, Vol. 1, Honolulu: University of Hawaii Press, 1947.

COMPADRAZGO, a system of establishing a ritual kinship that originated from the Roman Catholic ceremonies of marriage and baptism. This formalized system of ritual kinship was intended to provide someone beyond the immediate family with an obligation for the child's or couple's welfare. Although the system was originally intended to provide someone with moral and spiritual support, financial and even political support became part of the overall obligation as the system changed. The *compadrazgo* filled the void in the Filipinos' alliance system in the absence of extended families among Filipinos in Hawaii. Filipino immigrants in Hawaii took the system very seriously, and wedding and baptismal parties became important occasions for communal festivities.
FURTHER READING: Robert N. Anderson et al., *Filipinos in Rural Hawaii*, Honolulu: University of Hawaii Press, 1984.

COMRADE INVESTMENT COMPANY (TONGJISIKSAN HOESA), a business firm created by the Comrade Society (Tongji-hoe)* established by Syngman Rhee,* who wanted to put into practice one of the Three Great Principles of the Comrade Society, which read: "the economic freedom is the life of a nation; let us promote self-reliance together." Thus, the Comrade Society incorporated a business firm in 1924 by selling $100 shares to subscribers, to last for twenty-five years under the laws of the Territory of Hawaii. Syngman Rhee became the company's director.
FURTHER READING: Bong-youn Choy, *Koreans in America*, Chicago: Nelson-Hall, 1979; Hyung-chan Kim, *The Korean Diaspora*, Santa Barbara, Calif.: ABC-Clio Press, 1977.

COMRADE SOCIETY (TONGJI-HOE), a patriotic organization among Koreans in Hawaii and the U.S. mainland that was established by Syngman Rhee,* who wanted to use the organization to support the Korean provisional government in Shanghai in its work toward Korea's independence. Two separate dates are given as the founding date of the group. Kingsly K. Lyu claims that it was founded in November 1920, whereas Kim Won-yong believes it was organized on July 21, 1921. The purposes of the organization are well described in its Three Great Principles:

> 1. The three pledges proclaimed in the 1919 Declaration of Independence shall be observed. Let us carry out our great mission in a spirit of non-violence and self-sacrifice.
> 2. Systematic action is the mother of success. We shall therefore forsake acts of individualism, respect order within the organization and obey the leadership.
> 3. Economic freedom is the life of a nation. Let us promote self-reliance together.

After Syngman Rhee became president of Korea in 1948, the organization worked to support his regime. After he was ousted from office, the organization became defunct.

FURTHER READING: Bong-youn Choy, *Koreans in America*, Chicago: Nelson-Hall, 1979; Hyung-chan Kim, *The Korean Diaspora*, Santa Barbara, Calif.: ABC-Clio Press, 1977.

CONFESSION PROGRAM, established by the Department of Justice and State Department in 1955 to flush out from among Chinese residents in the United States illegal immigrants who had come to America through various ruses such as "paper sons"* and the "slot cases."* The Chinese in America were called on to confess their true identity. Those who had entered the country by illegal means were granted immunity from prosecution when their confession was given within a specified period of time, but those who had become U.S. citizens lost their citizenship, although they were given a chance to reapply for citizenship.

For some time fear ran high among Chinese residents in America that they would be forced to confess or to undergo intensive interrogation by government officials.

FURTHER READING: Jack Chen, *The Chinese of America*, New York: Harper and Row, 1980; B. L. Sung, *The Story of the Chinese in America*, New York: Macmillan Co., 1967.

CONSTITUTIONAL MONARCHY SOCIETY (DAI KWOCK HIN JING WUI). *See* Pao-huang Hui (Society to Protect the Emperor).

CONTRACT LABOR SYSTEM, a method widely used in the 1850s, 1860s, and 1870s, to recruit Chinese laborers to go abroad to work for pay. Chinese looking for work abroad were given passage to their destination by Chinese merchants who were reimbursed by relatives of the laborers or by their future employers. Laborers recruited under this system were no different from indentured servants; both groups had to work to pay off their debt, although they did agree to do it by their own volition. In Hawaii indentured servitude was not to exceed five years, providing the contract was made in Hawaii. If a contract laborer was absent or refused to work, he was subject to arrest and a fine not to exceed double the time absent.

Contract labor relied heavily on the credit-ticket system as merchants extended credit to Chinese who were willing to come to America in order to earn wages, and merchants were assured a handsome profit for their investment.
FURTHER READING: Gunther Barth, *Bitter Strength*, Cambridge, Mass.: Harvard University Press, 1964; Ta Chen, *Chinese Migrations, with Special Reference to Labor Conditions*, Washington, D.C.: U.S. Government Printing Office, 1923; Clarence Glick, *Sojourners and Settlers*, Honolulu: University Press of Hawaii, 1980.

CONVENTION OF 1886 BETWEEN JAPAN AND HAWAII. See Irwin, Robert W.

COOLIDGE, CALVIN. *See* Immigration Act of 1924; Johnson, Albert; *and* Lodge, Henry Cabot.

COOLIE, a term used to refer to all types of menial laborers. The term may have originated from the word "koli," an aboriginal race in western India. There is a Chinese term, *k'u-li*, meaning "bitter strength" or "bitter labor," rather than "one who does bitter labor," as is often misunderstood by Westerners. Sometimes the term "coolie" was related to laborers who were transported from China to other parts of the world in the coolie trade,* thereby creating confusion that links the term "coolie" with Chinese laborers. The Chinese, however, used a different term referring to Chinese laborers, who were called *hua kung* or they were simply called *chu-tsai*, meaning literally "human pigs."

Foreigners seem to have used the word "coolie" for Chinese laborers in China, and the Chinese gradually adopted its use. (*See also* Coolie Trade.)
FURTHER READING: Gunther Barth, *Bitter Strength*, Cambridge, Mass.: Harvard University Press, 1964; Jack Chen, *The Chinese of America*, New York: Harper and Row, 1980; Robert L. Irick, *Ch'ing Policy Toward the Coolie Trade, 1847–1878*, San Francisco: Chinese Materials Center, 1982.

COOLIE BILL, a bill introduced to the California State Legislature by George B. Tingely on March 6, 1852, in order to ease the problem of labor shortage in California. His bill was offered as a measure to enforce the contracts made in China to perform work in California for periods of ten years or less at fixed wages. Although it was intended to solve the state's labor problem, it set off a great deal of controversy over Chinese contract laborers and acrimonious attacks against the Chinese, who were considered highly undesirable people.

On April 23, 1852, Governor John Bigler,* siding with the anti-Chinese agitators in California, proposed to the legislature to use the state's taxing power to limit Chinese immigration to the state and to ask Congress to exclude Chinese laborers. The California Senate Committee reported out the Tingely bill, but it called for Chinese exclusion. The political opposition to this scheme of financing Chinese immigration was strong during the 1852 Democratic State Convention which adopted a resolution disapproving the Tingely Bill.

As a result, the Tingely Bill did not pass, and many Chinese laborers who wanted to come to America to work were left with little choice but to use the credit-ticket system.

FURTHER READING: Mary R. Coolidge, *Chinese Immigration*, New York: Henry Holt and Co., 1909; H. Brett Melendy, *The Oriental Americans*, Boston: Twayne Publishers, 1972.

COOLIE TRADE, a cruel and inhuman form of business transaction involving the selling and buying of Chinese laborers who were shipped from China to many parts of the world to be employed in raising coffee, sugar, and other agricultural crops. Many scholars equate the coolie trade with the slave trade of Chinese laborers. Therefore, the coolie trade as a means of sending Chinese laborers abroad should be clearly separated from the contract labor system* through which Chinese obtained their entry into Hawaii, the U.S. mainland, and other parts of the world.

The Western imperialistic powers began to have labor shortage problems as native populations in their colonies either refused to cooperate with them or were wiped out. The labor shortage problem was exacerbated in 1862 when the slave trade was banned internationally. Westerners then looked to China as a source of cheap labor. The coolie trade then was a means of replacing black slave laborers with Chinese.

As early as 1810 Chinese laborers were shipped to the Western Hemisphere— but they were small in number. The large-scale migration of Chinese to the Western Hemisphere occurred in the late 1840s, as a result of the discovery of gold in California in 1848 and the need for cheap labor in South America. Chinese laborers who were drawn to California were voluntary immigrants who came as contract laborers and acquired their passage to California on credit to be paid off through their hard labor. Although a minority of them worked in gold mines, the majority of them held domestic or menial jobs.

The coolie trade, the business of selling and buying Chinese laborers who were deceived into signing work contracts that made them no better than slaves, began in earnest in 1847, when the first shipment of Chinese laborers to Peru left Macao. Macao served as a center of Chinese immigration to Southeast Asia, and subsequently in the next twenty-nine years, Cuba imported 150,000 and Peru 74,000 Chinese coolies.

The Ch'ing government did not approve of the emigration of its subjects and made every effort to stop the coolie trade. However, its effort did not prevent native Chinese and foreigners from engaging in the coolie trade. The American government gradually began to become concerned about its citizens' participation in the coolie traffic across the Pacific. Some of the American ships engaged in transporting coolies for monetary gain were the American brig *Eagle*; the *Honolulu*; the American schooner *Anonyma*; the *Game Cock*; the *Flying Cloud*; the *Witchcraft*; the *Challenge*; and the *Mermaid*. American concerns did not promote action to prevent the trade; a decisive action to halt the inhuman traffic came about only after the *Robert Bowne* Mutiny on March 30, 1852. The ship, with its 410 Chinese laborers aboard, left Amoy on March 21, 1852, to bring them to San Francisco, but because of an unexpected tragedy, it sailed to Yaeyama Islands. After eight days into the voyage, the captain of the ship ordered the Chinese aboard be scrubbed with brooms and their queues cut off as he believed that the Chinese did not, or could not, keep themselves clean. This order immediately set off a rebellion among the Chinese who felt disgraced by the captain's orders. The mutineers killed the captain, his first and second officers, four crewmen, and ten Chinese.

After this incident, Chinese laborers were put into barracoons until they were ready to board ships that carried them as human cargo—at ten times more than the vessels' capacity. This inhuman and cruel business of buying and selling Chinese laborers began to draw the attention of American officials in both China and Washington, D.C. American authorities were embarassed by the participation of American ships in transporting Chinese laborers, and Congress passed a law prohibiting the participation of American ships and citizens in the coolie trade in February 1862. However, American ships continued to engage in the trade even after this law was passed. The coolie trade continued until the early 1870s, when Yung Wing* was appointed to investigate the coolie traffic; he presented some damning pictures of mistreated Chinese laborers to the Peruvian commissioner. The Ch'ing government banned the coolie traffic, and the Portuguese authorities in Macao also outlawed it in 1874.

FURTHER READING: Gunther Barth, *Bitter Strength*, Cambridge, Mass.: Harvard University Press, 1964; Jack Chen, *The Chinese of America*, Harper and Row, 1980; Robert L. Irick, *Ch'ing Policy Toward the Coolie Trade, 1847–1878*, San Francisco: Chinese Materials Center, 1982; M. B. Starr, *The Coming Struggle: On What the People on the Pacific Coast Think of the Coolie Invasion*, San Francisco: Excelsior Office, Bacon and Co., 1873; Sing-wu Wang, *The Organization of Chinese Emigration, 1848–1888*. San Francisco: Chinese Materials Center, 1978.

CORPS FOR THE ADVANCEMENT OF INDIVIDUALS, a patriotic organization established on May 13, 1913 by Ahn Chang-ho* in San Francisco. Ahn believed that Korea could achieve national independence only through national regeneration, based on truth-seeking, deeds, loyalty, and courage. Ahn's organization continued to train and educate Korean youth during the period of Japanese colonial rule in Korea. After World War II, the Corps became an educational organization in South Korea. (*See also* Ahn Chang-ho.)

CREDIT-TICKET SYSTEM. *See* Contract Labor System.

CROCKER, CHARLES (1822–1888), railroad builder, one of the Big Four. Crocker was born in Troy, New York, on September 16, 1822. An enterprising youth, at the age of twelve he quit school, borrowed $200 to purchase the agency for a New York newspaper in Troy, and worked to support his mother and sister. In 1836 he sold his business for a $100 profit and with his mother and sister went to live with his father and brothers in Marshall County, Indiana. At seventeen he left home to work first as a farm hand, then in a sawmill, and later in the iron mines.

In 1849, with the hopes of finding a more valuable metal, Crocker ventured to California with two of his brothers, as many "forty-niners" did. Crocker gave up mining in 1852 and opened an extremely successful store in Sacramento. In 1855 he was elected to the City Council, and five years later he was elected to the California State Legislature. There he developed friendships with Leland Stanford,* Collis P. Huntington, and Mark Hopkins and later went into railroad building with them.

From 1863 (when the work commenced to build the Central Pacific Railroad) to 1869 (when it was completed at Promontory, Utah), Crocker actively supervised the building of the railroad. He lived and worked without rest. When the work commenced, Crocker and James Strobridge, his superintendent, employed white laborers, but they soon found the white workers indolent and unproductive. However, Strobridge and Crocker were reluctant to employ Chinese because of their prejudice against the Chinese. Strobridge was later remembered for his statement, "I will not boss Chinese." Because of severe labor shortages, however, Crocker and Strobridge decided to employ Chinese. Fifty Chinese were first tried out to see if they could do hard work. After the initial fifty were proven successful, more and more Chinese were hired until there were between 10,000 and 12,000 Chinese working full time on the railroad.

In his testimony given before a congressional hearing on the Chinese immigration, Crocker observed that the Chinese were equal to the best white men in their ability to work. Crocker died in a diabetic coma on August 14, 1888.

FURTHER READING: Oscar Lewis, *The Big Four*, New York: Alfred A. Knopf, 1938; Alexander Saxton, *The Indispensable Enemy*, Berkeley: University of California Press, 1971; George F. Seward, *Chinese Immigration*, New York: Charles Scribner's Sons, 1881.

CROCKER'S PETS, a nickname given to Chinese workers who built railroads for the Central Pacific Railroad Company* under the supervision of Charles Crocker,* who testified in a Senate hearing on Chinese immigration to the effect that Chinese were equal to the best white men in terms of their power for endurance, when such a statement from a white man was not popular. It is estimated that Crocker had as many as 12,000 Chinese on his payroll. (*See also* Crocker, Charles.)

FURTHER READING: Jack Chen, *The Chinese of America*, New York: Harper and Row, 1980; George F. Seward, *Chinese Immigration*, New York: Charles Scribner's Sons, 1881.

CUBIC AIR ORDINANCE, passed by the San Francisco Board of Supervisors on July 29, 1870, requiring that every house, room, or apartment within the city of San Francisco and the county have within its walls at least 500 cubic feet for each adult dwelling or sleeping therein. Any violation of the ordinance was considered a misdemeanor, and for every offense a fine of $10 to $500 and a term of imprisonment not lasting more than three months was to be imposed. This ordinance was passed with Chinese laborers as its targets, as they were known to live in boardinghouses and apartments. In 1873 the ordinance was declared void by the county court.

FURTHER READING: Stanford M. Lyman, *Chinese Americans*, New York: Random House, 1974; Cheng-Tsu Wu, "*Chink!*," New York: World Publishing, 1972.

D

DAIHYO SHA KAI (REPRESENTATIVE BODY), an organization established by pro-Japan evacuees at the Tule Lake Segregation Center,* to which "disloyal" Americans of Japanese ancestry were brought from other relocation centers after they had either refused to answer or negatively answered Question 28 listed on Application for Leave Clearance.* Because these people refused to foreswear their allegiance to the Japanese emperor, the American government considered them disloyal and decided to segregate them from other evacuees who answered the question affirmatively. What government authorities did not realize was that by asking the Japanese to foreswear their allegiance to the Japanese emperor and to swear unqualified allegiance to the United States, they were forcing them to become stateless persons; by foreswearing their allegiance to the emperor they would lose their Japanese citizenship, but pledging allegiance to the United States would not make them American citizens, for persons of Asian ancestry were not eligible for U.S. citizenship.

The organization was established on October 16, 1943, after an election was held to select a representative from each of the sixty-four blocks at the center. The purpose of the election was to choose representatives who could improve living conditions at the center after a consultation with the relocation authorities. A demand for better living conditions was made after two incidents occurred on October 13 and 15, 1943, when some evacuees were hurt and one eventually died after they had been involved in separate automobile accidents.

On October 17, the day after the election, representatives held the first meeting and chose George Kuratomi as chairman and H. Doi as vice-chairman of the organization. On October 18 the organization appointed a seven-member Negotiating Committee to deal with the administration on questions related to improving living conditions at the center. A number of meetings were held between the administration and members of the Negotiating Committee to work out a plan of action to improve living conditions, but violence between some

young evacuees and administrative officers marred the negotiation. Finally, on November 4, 1983, the army entered the Tule Lake Center with tanks and guns to take over the administration. Martial law was declared and was not lifted until January 15 of the following year. (*See also* Leave Clearance.)
FURTHER READING: Audrie Girdner and Anne Loftis, *The Great Betrayal*, New York: Macmillan Co., 1969; Dorothy Thomas and Richard Nishimoto, *The Spoilage* Berkeley: University of California Press, 1969.

DAI KWOCK HIN JING WUI (CONSTITUTIONAL MONARCHY SOCIETY). *See* Pao-huang Hui (Society to Protect the Emperor.)

DANIELS, ROGER (1927–   ), professor of history and chairman of the Department of History at the University of Cincinnati. Daniels has made major contributions to the field of Asian American Studies by developing some important concepts as well as writing a number of books on the general topic of Asian American history. His scholarship in the area of Japanese evacuation and relocation during World War II is especially noteworthy.

One of the key concepts which Daniels has developed in the field of race relations is the theory of the two-category system, on which he collaborated with Harry H. L. Kitano.* According to Daniels and Kitano, race relations are based on a two-category system that stratifies the division between whites and non-whites. In this system whites are recognized as superior to non-whites. This stratification is maintained through social and psychological mechanisms of stereotyping of those who are considered inferior, formal rules that separate the superior from the inferior, violence against the inferior when they are not in line with what the superior expect, and genocide. According to Daniels and Kitano, prejudice, which is incipient in race relations between whites and non-whites, may degenerate into discrimination, segregation, apartheid, expulsion, and, finally, extermination, which the superior people may employ against the so-called inferior.

The boundary line that preserves the division between the superior and the inferior may change in favor of the inferior, depending on their affinity with the superior in nationality, color, religion, culture, political ideology, and other sociocultural factors.
FURTHER READING: Roger Daniels and Harry Kitano, *American Racism: Exploration of the Nature of Prejudice*, Englewood Cliffs, N.J.: Prentice-Hall, 1970.

D'AQUINO, IVA IKUKO TOGURI (1916–   ), Tokyo Rose. D'Aquino was born of Japanese parents on July 4, 1916, in Los Angeles, attended UCLA, and received a B.A. in zoology. She planned to go into graduate work and took premedical classes. In June 1941, while Japan and the United States were negotiating to stave off a possible war, Iva's mother received news that her sister was ill and that the sister wanted to see Iva's mother in Japan. She was not able to go, but the family decided to send Iva.

Iva left for Japan on July 5, 1941, with a certificate of identification which simply stated that she was leaving the United States temporarily. This certificate was not issued by the Immigration Office; rather, it was a simple statement notarized by a local notary office. In Japan, while visiting with her aunt, Iva applied for a U.S. passport to get back to the States, but was denied one because her citizenship had not been proven. In September 1942, ten months after the Pearl Harbor attack, she applied for evacuation through the Swiss legation but did not have enough money to pay for the trip. She was often visited by Japanese Special Security Police officers and was told that she should change her citizenship to Japanese to make things easier for her. She refused. While working for the Domei News Agency, she met Filipe J. d'Aquino and married him on April 19, 1945.

Iva was employed at various places in 1942 and in the early part of 1943. On August 23, 1943, she began working as a part-time typist for the Overseas Bureau at the NHK (Japan Broadcasting Corporation) and took her first step to becoming the legendary Tokyo Rose. The NHK recruited radio professionals among the Allied prisoners of war to broadcast anti-American propaganda material written for them, and Iva became acquainted with the POWs, among whom were Charles Cousens, Wallace E. Ince, and Norman Reyes. Cousens started writing his own scripts for the "Zero Hour" program, for which he wanted a comical voice, and Iva became that voice. By mid-November 1943 Iva started her broadcasts. Cousens left as a result of an illness, leaving Iva to use his old scripts. At this point Iva started taking long and frequent vacations and discontinued coming on Saturdays.

August 15, 1945, brought Japanese surrender. By August 31, 1945, journalists were all over Japan looking for big stories. Two reporters from the Hearst paper organization, Clark Lee and Harry Brundidge, began to delve into the story of Tokyo Rose, as their home office became interested in publishing a story on Tokyo Rose.

On August 31, 1945, Lee and Brundidge sent Leslie Nakashima, a friend of Clark Lee, to the NHK offices with the assignment of learning the identity of Tokyo Rose. Nakashima was given Iva's name by Oki Kenkichi, who told Nakashima that there were five or six female announcers on the "Zero Hour" program. On September 1, 1945, the two reporters interviewed Iva and had her sign a contract saying that she was the one and only Tokyo Rose. There are a number of speculations as to why she signed the contract. One of the reasons, as Iva explained later, was that she felt she would be known in the United States and all over the world as a result of the interview. The interview was to be published in *Cosmopolitan*, which promised to pay her $2,000 for her story. Iva did not see the promised $2,000. By October 17, 1945, Iva's name was known worldwide. Also on this date, she was arrested for trying to demoralize American troops. On November 16, she was moved to Sugamo Prison, where Japanese war criminals were held, and she was questioned several times while interned there. The Eighth Army Counter Intelligence Corps put together an investigative report on her, which was transmitted to the Department of Justice. On April 27, 1946, the Justice Department said it had no interest in the case. She was not released until October 1946; the reasons her release took so long were the bureaucratic complications and problems with journalists.

Walter Winchell and a California anti-Oriental organization, the Native Sons of the Golden West, began to pressure the Justice Department and Congress for not prosecuting Tokyo Rose for the act of treason. Iva was arrested again by the CIC on August 26, 1948, and was again taken to Sugamo Prison. On September 3 she boarded a ship to San Francisco, arriving there on September 23, where she was arraigned the same day. She was indicted on October 8, 1948, on eight counts of overt acts for various broadcasts she had made over Radio Tokyo between November 1, 1943, and August 13, 1945.

The jury trial lasted fifty-six days and was the most expensive trial on record at that time. The jury, after four days of deliberation, was unable to reach a verdict—but after being admonished by the judge to remember the time and money spent on the trial, the jury reached a verdict, finding Iva guilty on one count. Iva was found guilty on Count VI which read: "On a day during October 1944 the defendant did speak into a microphone concerning the loss of ships." For this she was sentenced to ten years in a federal prison and was fined $10,000 by Judge Michael J. Roche. She was released from prison on January 18, 1956 but was immediately harassed by the district office of the Immigration Service, which ordered her to leave the United States by April 13, 1956; in the event she failed to comply with the order she was to face deportation proceedings. She would have been deported to Japan, had it not been for Wayne Mortimer Collins,* her lawyer during the trial, who supported Iva's strong will to fight against deportation.

Friends of Iva worked very hard to have her pardoned by three presidents; first, by President Dwight D. Eisenhower; second, by President Lyndon B. Johnson; and third, by President Richard M. Nixon. Finally, with the help of Senator S. I. Hayakawa* and Dr. Clifford I. Uyeda, who organized a Japanese American Citizens League* committee to campaign for a presidential pardon for Iva, she was pardoned by President Gerald Ford on January 19, 1977.

FURTHER READING: Frank F. Chuman, *The Bamboo People*, Del Mar, Calif.: Publisher's Inc., 1976; Masayo Duus, *Tokyo Rose: Orphan of the Pacific*, Tokyo, Japan: Kodansha, 1979; 180 *Federal Reporter*, 2d Series, Iva Ikuko Toguri d'Aquino v. United States (cited as 180 F. 2d 271), West Publishing Co., 1951; 192 *Federal Reporter*, 2d Series, Iva Ikuko Toguri d'Aquino v. United States; *United States Supreme Court Reports*, 96 Lawyer Edition, October 1951 term U.S. 342–343; Clifford I. Uyeda, *A Final Report and Review: The Japanese American Citizens' League National Committee for Iva Toguri*, Seattle: University of Washington Occasional Monograph Series, 1980.

DAS, TARAK NATH. *See* Friends of Freedom for India.

DAYAL, HAR (1884–1939), Indian nationalist. Dayal was the youngest of the four sons of Lala Gauri Dayal, an employee of the British who worked as a reader in the District Court at Delhi. At the age of seventeen Dayal was married to Sundar, who bore a son two years after their marriage. The son died shortly after his birth, and their daughter, Shanti, was born in 1908. Har Dayal attended Christian mission schools in Delhi where he completed his Bachelor of Arts degree at Saint Stephen's College. After graduation, he was selected for a state scholarship given to promising young Indians to be sent to England for their education before they were to join the government service. He left India in 1905 for Saint John's College, Oxford, where he planned to study European history and British India. He returned to India for a brief period to bring his wife with him to Oxford. In England he met a number of his countrymen who later played prominent roles in India's independence movement. Dayal's nationalism and desire for India's freedom grew while he was at Oxford. Because of his negative feelings toward British colonialism (to which he could not give allegiance), he forfeited his scholarship and returned to India in 1908 in order to work toward India's independence.

Prevented by British surveillance from continuing his activities in India, Dayal in September 1908 again returned to England where he set himself up to distribute the Lahore newspapers. He joined a number of Indian nationalists in Paris, where he came in contact with Egyptian nationalists and Russian revolutionaries. He came to America in February 1911 in order to continue his study of Buddhism at Harvard University, which gave him permission to use its university library. But Dayal's study was interrupted by a plea from a fellow Punjabi, Bhai Teja Singh, who told Dayal that a great number of Sikhs and other Punjabi laborers in California were in need of a leader for their struggle against prejudice and discrimination.

Dayal agreed to go to California and came to Berkeley in the spring of 1911. He was offered a position at Stanford University by its president, David Starr Jordan, to lecture without pay on Indian philosophy, but he was not allowed to teach after he was accused of having conspired with a German during World War I. While at Stanford, he founded a club called the Radical Club, and he continued to write about his political philosophy.

In May 1913 Dayal founded the Hindu Association of the Pacific Coast* in Portland, Oregon, and on November 1 of that year he declared the existence of the Ghadar Revolutionary Party.* The party established a propaganda program to inform people in the West of India's fight for freedom and hatched up a number of schemes to smuggle arms into India. It also developed a plan of action to collaborate with Germany to stir up armed insurrection in India.

In March 1919 Dayal declared himself converted to the "principle of Imperial unity," recanted his radical political philosophy, and moved to Sweden during that same year, remaining there for the next decade. In the later years of his life he devoted most of his time to studying and lecturing on Indian culture.

FURTHER READING: Emily C. Brown, *Har Dayal*, Tucson: University of Arizona Press, 1975; L. P. Mathur, *Indian Revolutionary Movement in the United States of America*, Delhi: S. Chand and Co., 1970; Khushwant Singh, *Gadhar 1915: India's First Armed Revolution*, New Delhi: R and K Publishing House, 1966.

DECLARATION OF ALL-KOREAN CONVENTION, announced on April 28, 1941, when a nine-point program was adopted by representatives from nine social and political organizations who gathered together to form a united front against Japanese colonial rule in Korea. These representatives founded an organization called the United Korean Committee* in support of the Korean provisional government-in-exile in Shanghai, China. The founding of this organization was a remarkable achievement inasmuch as factionalism had plagued many Korean organizations in the United States. The nine organizations decided to maintain their organizational status quo, but they decided to give the United Korean Committee exclusive charge of diplomatic and political activities for Korea's independence. All contributions in support of Korean independence were sent to the United Korean Committee, and Syngman Rhee* was appointed chairman of the committee.

FURTHER READING: Chong-sik Lee, *The Politics of Korean Nationalism*, Berkeley: University of California Press, 1965.

DESHLER, DAVID W., recruiter of Korean workers for Hawaii. Deshler was born to a distinguished family in Columbus, Ohio. His father worked as a bank teller in a family bank, the National Exchange Bank, before he died in 1880. His mother was remarried in April 1882 to George Kilhon Nash (1842–1904), who became governor of Ohio in 1899. Deshler's stepfather, Nash, was a strong supporter of the Sherman-Hanna-McKinley wing of the Republican Party, which was in competition with the Foraker faction. The friendship between Governor Nash and President-elect William McKinley later became a very important factor in Deshler's career.

In 1896 Deshler went to Korea seeking opportunities to invest in business and later entered the mining business with an American businessman.

When Horace N. Allen,* an American missionary in Korea, needed political influence to obtain an appointment as American Minister to Korea, Deshler was able to put in a good word to McKinley on Allen's behalf. After Allen became Minister, he devised a scheme whereby Korean workers would be sent to Hawaii as the Hawaiian Sugar Planters' Association* had requested. Allen believed that if American businessmen invested heavily in Korea Washington would commit America's power and prestige to the protection of the Korean peninsula. When Emperor Kojong* of the Yi Dynasty approved the immigration scheme, Allen asked Deshler to help recruit Korean workers willing to go to Hawaii. In this way Allen paid off his political debt to Deshler.

Deshler accepted Allen's offer and created the necessary infrastructure to bring the immigration scheme to its successful conclusion. He also made a fortune as he was paid $54 for every male adult worker he recruited and sent to Hawaii.

FURTHER READING: Wayne Patterson, *The Korean Frontier in America: Immigration to Hawaii, 1896–1910*, Ann Arbor, Mich.: University Microfilms International, 1979.

DEWITT, JOHN LESESNE (1880–1962), commanding general of the Western Defense Command in World War II. Dewitt was born on January 9, 1880 at Fort Sidney, Nebraska, and attended Princeton University before leaving to fight in the Spanish-American War. He was commissioned a second lieutenant in the Regular Army in 1898. After he was promoted to the rank of first lieutenant, he was sent to the Philippines to fight against the Philippine independence fighters. He was stationed in the Philippine Islands between 1899 and 1902, when he was sent to Columbus Barracks, Ohio. In 1903 he was sent back to the Philippines, where he stayed until 1905. After World War I, during which time he served on the Infantry Equipment Board responsible for devising equipment used by soldiers, DeWitt was again assigned to another service in the Philippines. In December 1939 he was sent to San Francisco, with the rank of lieutenant general, to be in charge of the Fourth Army and the Ninth Corps Area.

Two days after the Japanese attack on Pearl Harbor, DeWitt was appointed Western Defense commander, with wide discretionary authority not only on military but also on civil affairs on the entire Pacific Coast. U.S. Attorney General Francis Biddle* gave DeWitt unprecedented authority to designate security zones in which the movement of all persons of Japanese ancestry would be controlled and restricted. DeWitt was empowered by Executive Order 9066* to exclude all persons of Japanese ancestry from the areas designated as military zones. As a commander in charge of a theatre of war, he was charged with devising security measures to be taken against possible invasion of the U.S. mainland. However, the measures he undertook—the exclusion, evacuation, and relocation of all persons of Japanese ancestry—violated the civil rights of American citizens as guaranteed by the Constitution. His personal feelings toward Japanese might have influenced his decision to exclude all persons of Japanese descent from the Pacific Coast.

FURTHER READING: Frank F. Chuman, *The Bamboo People*, Del Mar, Calif.: Publisher's Inc., 1976; Roger Daniels, *Concentration Camps U.S.A.*, New York: Holt, Rinehart and Winston, 1971; Jacobus ten Broek, Edward N. Barnhart, and Floyd W. Matson, *Prejudice, War and the Constitution*, Berkeley: University of California Press, 1954; Michi Weglyn, *Years of Infamy*, New York: William Morrow and Co., 1976.

DE YOUNG, MICHEL HARRY (1847–1925), journalist. DeYoung, the son of Michel H. and Amelia de Young, was born on September 30, 1849. He followed his family to a California mining town at the age of five and later moved to San Francisco. He and his brother founded a newspaper known as the *Daily Dramatic Chronicle* in January 1865, when they were sixteen and eighteen, respectively. Among the contributors to their newspaper were Mark Twain,* Bret Harte,* Prentice Mulford, and Charles Warren Stoddard. On September 1, 1868, the name of the newspaper was changed to the *Daily Morning Chronicle*, and still later (1869) to the *San Francisco Chronicle*. In 1880 de Young's brother died, and he assumed responsibility for the paper as owner and editor-in-chief.

As an influential journalist, de Young launched vicious attacks against Japanese in America. Beginning on February 23, 1905, his *Chronicle* printed racist headlines such as "Brown Men Are Made Citizens Illegally," "Japanese a Menace to American Women," and "Brown Men an Evil in the Public Schools." He died on February 15, 1925, after a career that involved service to various national committees and civic organizations.

DIES COMMITTEE, established in 1938 in the U.S. House of Representatives with an appropriation of $25,000 as a Committee to Investigate Un-American Activities. The chairman of the committee, Martin Dies of Texas, was a sensational headline-seeking politician who saw "Reds" anywhere along the political spectrum once he made up his mind to do so. He launched a number of investigations alleging that many labor and civic organizations in America had been infiltrated by Nazis and Communists. Among the organizations whose activities were investigated for possible involvement with Nazis and Communists were the Department of Labor, the Works Progress Administration Federal Theatre and Writers' Project, the National Labor Relations Board and the Wages and Hours Board, the American League for Peace and Democracy, as well as the Workers' Alliance. Both Eleanor Roosevelt and the President characterized as sordid Dies' investigation of the Milk Consumers' Protective Committee, the League of Women Shoppers, Consumers' Union, and the Consumers' National Federation for their possible involvement in Communist activities.

After the Japanese attack on Pearl Harbor, Dies claimed that the tragedy could have been avoided had his committee been allowed to "reveal the facts"— presumably the "facts" relating to Japanese Americans in September 1940. Dies charged that sentimental attitudes toward Fifth Columnists were responsible for Pearl Harbor. In a speech delivered on January 28, 1942, he claimed that an even more serious tragedy than the Pearl Harbor tragedy would occur on the West Coast, if the government continued to ignore the Japanese American "problem."

After all persons of Japanese ancestry were incarcerated in relocation centers,* the Dies Committee appointed a subcommittee to investigate the War Relocation Authority* (WRA). The subcommittee, comprised of John Costello of Los Angeles, Karl E. Mundt of South Dakota, and Herman P. Eberharter* of Pennsylvania, seized Japanese American Citizens League* records in Washington and held public hearings in Los Angeles with carefully selected witnesses, who claimed that the federal government had mishandled dangerous Japanese Americans. The subcommittee members also visited a number of relocation centers in Western states in preparation for the hearings in Washington, D.C., that were held on July 6, 1943. One witness in the hearings, Dillon S. Myer,* then director of the War Relocation Authority, challenged the committee to prove and substantiate its claims that the WRA was lax and that it had released information to the Japanese American Citizens League that was not made available to the government, that it had provided liquor to internees, and that it had released known saboteurs. When the committee was unable to prove its claims, the subcommittee chairman called off the investigation after only three days of hearings. The Dies Committee again investigated the WRA after the incident at the Tule Lake Segregation Center* on November 1 and 3, 1943, charging the WRA with laxness and inefficiency.

FURTHER READING: Bill Hosokawa, *JACL in Quest of Justice*, New York: William Morrow and Co., 1982; Dillon S. Myer, *Uprooted Americans*, Tucson: University of Arizona Press, 1971; Jacobus ten Broek et al., *Prejudice, War and the Constitution*, Berkeley: University of California Press, 1954.

DISPLACED PERSONS ACT OF 1948, passed by the U.S. Senate on June 2, 1948, and by the House on June 11, 1948. The Senate and House bills then went to conference for a compromise. The final version was sent to President Harry S Truman who signed it into law on June 25, 1948. The bill was the result of the President's concern about displaced persons (DPs) in Europe during World War II. It was estimated that the war had displaced 6 million people in Europe. One million were resettled in various parts of the world, and the United States admitted 2,551 DPs from Europe in 1945 in line with a Truman directive. However, a long-term solution was lacking, and so President Truman urged Congress to turn its attention to the problems of DPs.

In its final form, the bill allowed the admission into the United States of up to 205,000 DPs for a period of two years. The original act affected only Europeans, but an amendment added to the 1948 act on June 16, 1950, allowed the Chinese already in America to remain in the United States, for many Chinese were reluctant to return to a China controlled by Communists. As many as 15,000 Chinese in America were allowed to adjust their status.

FURTHER READING: Marion T. Bennett, *American Immigration Policies*, Washington, D.C.: Public Affairs Press, 1963; Robert A. Divine, *American Immigration Policy, 1924–1952*, New Haven, Conn.: Yale University Press, 1957; S. W. Kung, *Chinese in American Life*, Seattle: University of Washington Press, 1962.

DISTRICT COMPANIES, social organizations established among Chinese immigrants in the 1850s. Chinese immigrants to the United States came primarily from eight of the ninety districts in Kwangtung Province of China: Nanhai (Namhoi), Panyu (Punyu), Shunde (Shuntak), Enping (Yangping), Kaiping (Hoiping), Taishan (Toishan), Xinhui (Sunwui), and Zhongshan (Chungshan).

The first three districts were commonly called Sam Yap,* meaning three districts, and the next four districts were known as Sze Yap (Sze-I),* meaning four districts. The overwhelming majority of these immigrants spoke either Sze Yap or Sam Yap dialects of the people living in these districts, and few Mandarin-speaking Chinese came to America before 1950. Immigrants from the first seven districts mentioned above organized themselves into their respective district associations, which were then grouped into two district associations, namely, the Sam Yap District Association, consisting of the Nanhai, Panyu, and Shunde, and the Sze Yap District Association, composed of the Enping, Kaiping, Taishan, and Xinhui.

According to Rose Hum Lee, 57 percent of the Chinese population in America belonged to the Sze Yap District Association, only 8 percent were under the jurisdiction of the Sam Yap District Association, and the rest were from the Zhongshan District. The Sze Yap group developed four associations under its jurisdiction (Ning Yung, Hop Wo, Kong Chow, and Sue Hing), and the Sam Yap group controlled two (Yeong Wo and Yan Wo). These six associations are commonly called the Chinese Six Companies,* also known as the Chinese Consolidated Benevolent Association. The Chinese Six Companies in San Francisco served as spokesmen for the Chinese people in America and ruled supreme over all other local Chinese Consolidated Benevolent Associations. This was, however, more true thirty years ago than it is today.

FURTHER READING: Gunther Barth, *Bitter Strength*, Cambridge, Mass.: Harvard University Press, 1964; Him Mark Lai, *The Chinese in America, 1785–1980*, San Francisco: Chinese Culture Foundation, 1980; Rose Hum Lee, *The Chinese in the United States of America*, Hong Kong: Hong Kong University Press, 1960.

DOHO, a Japanese term sometimes pronounced *dobo*. Used to signify all ethnic Japanese at home and abroad, regardless of their citizenship. It was customary to place the word *doho* after the name of the country where they were found. If they lived in Hawaii, they were called Hawaii *doho*.

DOLE, SANFORD BALLARD (1844–1926), president of Republic of Hawaii, governor of the Territory of Hawaii. Dole was born on April 23, 1844, to Daniel and Emily Dole, both of whom had come to Hawaii from Maine to become missionaries. The American Board of Commissioners for Foreign Missions* sent the Doles to Hawaii in 1840 when Daniel and his wife were both thirty-two years of age. Four years later Emily Dole died while giving birth to Sanford.

Sanford attended the school at Punahou, an institution which his father labored long and hard to establish. By 1850 there were twenty-one children at Punahou, one of whom was Sanford Dole. In 1866 he was sent to Massachusetts for education at Williams College, where he studied to be a lawyer. Two years later he was admitted to practice law at the Suffolk County bar. Upon his return to Hawaii he practiced law in Honolulu, finally becoming Associate Justice of the Supreme Court of Hawaii on December 28, 1887.

Dole was active in local politics, particularly the politics of annexation of Hawaii to the United States. In 1886 he joined the Hawaiian League,* which had been established to secure efficient, honest, and decent government; members of the league pledged their property, lives, and honor for the purpose of carrying out their objectives. But Dole resigned from the league after he became embroiled in the radical faction of the secret society which advocated the overthrow of the monarchy. In 1893 he participated in various meetings held to discuss the overthrow of the Hawaiian monarchy but advised conspirators not to take a radical step.

He felt that his duty was to work toward maintaining a stable government. This was his belief until January 16, 1893, one day before the revolution that overthrew the Hawaiian monarchy. On July 4, 1894, Dole was inaugurated as the first and only president of the Republic of Hawaii. When Congress made Hawaii a Territory of the United States, effective midnight, June 13–14, 1900, Dole was sworn in as the first governor of the U.S. Territory of Hawaii. In 1903 he resigned the governorship to become a judge of the Federal District court, an appointment made by President Theodore Roosevelt.

During his long career as judge of the Supreme Court of Hawaii, president of the Republic of Hawaii, and governor of the Territory of Hawaii, Dole made a number of decisions affecting the immigration of Asians to the Hawaiian Islands, notably, he vetoed a bill passed by the Hawaiian Legislature that would have restricted importation of *sake* from Japan, and he advised the legislative chamber to come up with a less discriminatory bill; he ruled in favor of a Chinese laborer in the case of Chong Chum v. Kohala Sugar Company,* which was decided on February 26, 1892; and he encouraged the immigration of Korean laborers to the Hawaiian Islands by approving the request made by the Hawaiian Sugar Planters' Association* to bring Koreans to work on their plantations.

FURTHER READING: Francis Hilary Conroy, "The Japanese Expansion into Hawaii, 1868–1898," Ph.D. diss., University of California, 1949; Ethel M. Damon, *Sanford Ballard Dole and His Hawaii*, Palo Alto, Calif.: Pacific Books, 1957; Wayne Patterson, *The Korean Frontier in America*, Ann Arbor, Mich.: University Microfilms International, 1979; Merze Tate, *The United States and the Hawaiian Kingdom*, New Haven, Conn.: Yale University Press, 1965.

DONALDINA CAMERON HOME, originally called the Chinese Presbyterian Mission Home, founded by Margaret Culbertson in 1873 on 920 Sacramento Street in San Francisco's Chinatown. The Home was used as a center for aiding and educating Chinese slave girls and prostitutes so that they could earn a living. The building that housed the Home was destroyed during the San Francisco earthquake in 1906, but it was again raised in 1907. Donaldina Cameron* came to work at this Home for Chinese girls in trouble on April 1895 and continued there until she died in 1968. In recognition of her lifetime devotion to the welfare of the Chinese community in San Francisco, the Home was renamed the Donaldina Cameron Home on June 7, 1942, and is still used as a Chinese community center. (*See also* Cameron, Donaldina.)

DRAVES, VICTORIA MANALO (1924–   ), Olympic swimmer. Draves was born in San Francisco to an English mother and a Filipino father. She was offered a number of roles in movies, but she was determined to be a professional swimmer. She refused four movie offers to become a professional in the swimming troupe headed and coached by Buster Crabbe, a 1932 Olympic champion. Shortly after she married Crabbe, she performed in the Olympics in London in 1949, winning two individual titles in platform and springboard diving.

DUAL CITIZENSHIP, the legal status of persons who have citizenship in two countries. Because nations do not employ uniform legal principles in conferring citizenship, persons born in the United States whose parents came from Japan, China, and Korea could have dual citizenships. In the case of Japan, that country applied the principle of *jus sanguinis** to confer its citizenship; hence, children born of Japanese parents, regardless of where they were born, were recognized as citizens of Japan. Korea and China used the same principle. Because the United States applied the principle of *jus solis** in granting citizenship, it was possible for persons born in the United States of Japanese, Chinese, or Korean parentage to hold two different citizenships.

This situation was somewhat cleared for Japanese Americans when the Imperial Diet of Japan passed a law on December 1, 1924, allowing Nisei* born before that date to declare their Japanese citizenship null and void by filing formal notification with the Home Minister of Japan. It also allowed Nisei born after December 1, 1924, to acquire Japanese citizenship if their parents had their children's names registered at a Japanese consulate. Those Nisei whose parents did not register their names with Japanese authorities within the first two weeks of their birth lost their Japanese citizenship.

FURTHER READING: Frank F. Chuman, *The Bamboo People*, Del Mar, Calif.: Publisher's Inc., 1976; John J. Stephen, *Hawaii Under the Rising Sun*, Honolulu: University of Hawaii Press, 1984.

E

EAST INDIA STORE, established by two brothers from India, Jhamandas and Gobindram Watumull, both of whom were born in Hyderabad, Sind Province, India. Jhamandas left India for the Philippines when he was sixteen years of age, and by 1909 he had a small store in Manila. In 1913 his business followed American troops to Hawaii and was open on Fort Street. The business prospered and by 1957 the East India Store in Honolulu had ten stores, an apartment house in Waikiki, and mercantile developments both in Waikiki and Kailua.

EAST-WEST DEVELOPMENT COMPANY (Tong-So Kaebal Hoesa), a company established by David W. Deshler* in 1902 and used exclusively to process Korean laborers going to Hawaii. Deshler, who had come to Korea for business prospects, was asked by Horace N. Allen* to become a recruiter for the Hawaiian Sugar Planters' Association* to send Korean laborers to Hawaii in the spring of 1902. It was for this reason that he created the East West Development Company. The company was closed after Korean immigration to Hawaii was halted by the Japanese in 1905. (*See also* Deshler, David W.)
FURTHER READING: Wayne Patterson, *The Korean Frontier in America*, Ann Arbor, Mich.: University Microfilms International, 1979.

EBERHARTER, HERMAN P. (1892–1958), U.S. congressman, member of Dies Committee.* Eberharter was born on April 29, 1892, in Pittsburgh, Pennsylvania, and attended Holy Trinity Parish School, Morehead School, and Fifth Avenue High School. Upon graduation from Duquesne University Law School, he was admitted to the bar in 1925 and began to practice law in his hometown. Between 1935 and 1936 he served as a representative in the Pennsylvania State Legislature. In 1936 he ran for Congress as a Democrat and was elected to the 75th Congress, serving in the ten succeeding congresses until his death on September 9, 1958, in Arlington, Virginia.

Eberharter was a member of the subcommittee of the Dies Committee,* formally known as the House Special Committee to Investigate Un-American Activities. Among other tasks the subcommittee investigated the War Relocation Authority* and set out in 1943 to prove the disloyalty of Japanese Americans. Eberharter was very critical of the committee report that was released after the Dies Committee held public hearings on the West Coast as well as in Washington, D.C. He maintained that the conclusion reached by the majority on the committee was prejudiced and that most of the statements included in the majority's report were not proven. The Dies Committee was unable to prove the Japanese disloyal. (*See also* Dies Committee.)

EDO, TREATY OF (1858), an agreement signed on board the American war vessel, *Powhatan*, on July 29, 1858, as a Treaty of Commerce and Navigation, and proclaimed on May 23, 1860. The treaty provided for the opening of other ports for ships from the United States and made void all provisions of the treaty signed at Kanagawa on March 31, 1854, which were in conflict with the present treaty. Through this treaty, Japan recognized the right of Americans to reside in Japan and the government of the United States gave Japan's citizens the right to go to America. But Japan did not allow its people to leave the country until 1866. Americans obtained extraterritoriality and most-favored-nation status from Japan.
FURTHER READING: Roger Daniels, *Three Short Works on Japanese Americans*, New York: Arno Press, 1978; Foster R. Dulles, *Yankees and Samurai*, New York: Harper and Row, 1965; Yamato Ichihashi, *Japanese in the United States*, Stanford, Calif.: Stanford University Press, 1932.

EISENHOWER, MILTON STOVER (1899–   ), director of the War Relocation Authority,* college president. Eisenhower was born on September 15, 1899, in Abilene, Kansas. The younger brother of Dwight D. Eisenhower received his B.S. degree in industrial journalism from Kansas State University in 1924. Upon graduation he entered the Foreign Service and became vice consul in Edinburgh where he continued his university studies. In 1926 he was appointed an assistant to the Secretary of Agriculture, and two years later he became information director of that department.

Eisenhower was appointed director of the War Relocation Authority on March 18, 1942, by President Franklin Roosevelt until he was replaced by Dillon S. Myer* on June 17, 1942. As director of the WRA, Eisenhower supervised the work of relocating persons of Japanese ancestry from the West Coast to relocation centers* designated by the government.

Eisenhower served as president of Kansas State College of Agriculture and Applied Science from 1943 to 1950 when he was named president of Pennsylvania State University.
FURTHER READING: Dillon S. Myer, *Uprooted Americans*, Tucson: University of Arizona Press, 1971.

ELDRIGE, JOHN v. SEE YUP COMPANY, one of the earliest court cases involving Chinese in America. This case was brought to the Supreme Court of the State of California in the spring of 1859 as a result of a dispute in May 1853 over who held a piece of property on which a Chinese Buddhist Temple had been erected. The case also addressed the issue of where Chinese worshiped and carried out their moral instruction. When the issue of whether or not Chinese could practice their ''heathenish or superstitious religious'' rites in the temple was taken to the state's highest court, Justice Joseph G. Baldwin ruled that the Court had no authority to determine whether or not the practice of ''heathenish or idolatrous'' rites by the Chinese was against public policy or morals. He confined his opinion on the case strictly to the question of who held the title. The Court overturned the lower court's decision and remanded with instructions for a new trial.

FURTHER READING: Gunther Barth, *Bitter Strength*, Cambridge, Mass.: Harvard University Press, 1964; 17 Cal. 45, October 1860.

ELIZALDE, JOAQUIN M., resident commissioner of the Philippines to the United States. Elizalde was sworn in as commissioner on January 3, 1939. In testimony he gave before Congress in 1939 concerning the Merchant Marine Act, he unsuccessfully tried to defend the rights of Filipinos. The act required that crews on fishing vessels carrying the American flag be 75 percent American, either born or naturalized.

EMERGENCY DETENTION ACT OF 1950 (also known as the Internal Security Act of September 23, 1950), a law designed to impose stringent restrictions on and exclusion of Communists and other classes of people considered dangerous to the internal security of the United States. The act was passed over President Harry S Truman's veto. Originally introduced to the Senate by Patrick Anthony McCarran of Nevada, chairman of the Judiciary Committee, the Detention Act incorporated various parts of earlier Senate bills. Title II of the act empowered the President of the United States to apprehend and detain ''each person as to whom there is reasonable ground to believe that such person probably will engage in, probably will conspire with others to engage in, acts of espionage or of sabotage.'' In justifying this provision in the act, it was claimed that the court decisions that upheld the validity of the Japanese relocation programs during World War II gave sufficient ground for enactment of the law.

During its biennial convention on August 23, 1968, the Japanese Americans Citizens League* decided to work toward the repeal of Title II and campaigned vigorously for the repeal. Senator Daniel K. Inouye* of Hawaii, a Nisei* World War II veteran, introduced S. 1872 to repeal Title II, and in 1971 his colleagues in Congress approved the bill. President Richard M. Nixon signed the bill on September 25, 1971, thereby eliminating the threat of reactivating concentration camps in America.

FURTHER READING: Frank F. Chuman, *The Bamboo People*, Del Mar, Calif.: Publisher's Inc., 1976; E. P. Hutchinson, *Legislative History of American Immigration Policy, 1798–1965*, Philadelphia: University of Pennsylvania Press, 1981.

EMMONS, DELOS C. (1888–1965) military governor of Hawaii in 1941. Emmons was born on January 17, 1888, in Huntington, West Virginia, and graduated from West Point in 1909. He was commissioned in the infantry in that year and served with the 30th Infantry in San Francisco, Alaska, New York, and on the Mexican border. Emmons was later transferred to the aviation section. In 1934 he reached the rank of lieutenant colonel and was assigned to the 18th Composite wing in Hawaii as commander. In October 1940 Emmons was made temporary lieutenant general and was assigned to the Air Force Combat Command as its commander. In December 1941, just ten days after the Japanese attack on Pearl Harbor, he was named commander of the Hawaiian Department, which also made him military governor of Hawaii. On December 21, two weeks after the Japanese attack, Emmons assured the Japanese American population in Hawaii that they should not fear as long as they remained loyal to the United States. No mass evacuation of persons of Japanese ancestry was undertaken in Hawaii during World War II.

ENDO, EX PARTE, a case argued in the U.S. Supreme Court in 1944 involving Endo Mitsuye, an evacuee at Tule Lake, who filed for a writ of habeus corpus. After the Japanese attack on Pearl Harbor on December 7, 1941, President Franklin Roosevelt issued Executive Order 9066* on February 19, 1942, authorizing the Secretary of War or his designated military commander to establish military areas and to exclude people from them. On the following day, Secretary Henry L. Stimson* ordered General John L. DeWitt* to carry out the evacuation of persons of Japanese ancestry from the West Coast. Accordingly, General DeWitt issued Proclamation No. 1* establishing Military Areas Nos. 1 and 2, from which all persons of Japanese ancestry were to be removed. This was on March 2, 1942. Sixteen days later President Roosevelt issued Executive Order 9102* establishing the War Relocation Authority* (WRA), which was to look after the evacuees from the West Coast. Milton S. Eisenhower* was appointed as its director on March 21, 1942. The President signed Public Law No. 503, making any violation of an order of the military commander, as specified under Executive Order 9066, a misdemeanor. On March 24 General DeWitt issued a general curfew order for all persons of Japanese ancestry within Military Area No. 1, confining them to their homes between 8:00 P.M. and 6:00 A.M. All these measures were taken for the ostensible purpose of protection against espionage and sabotage of national defense areas.

In June 1942, Miss Endo Mitsuye, a person of "conceded loyalty" to the United States, was evacuated from Sacramento to the relocation center at Tule Lake. Within a month she filed for a writ of habeas corpus. One year later, in July 1943, the District Court denied the request, and an appeal was immediately filed with the Circuit Court of the same area. However, Miss Endo was subsequently transferred from Tule Lake to a relocation center in Utah, where she remained while her case was on appeal and the laws surrounding her detention were questioned.

Although the Justice Department and the WRA readily admitted Miss Endo was in no way a threat to the U.S. war effort, they attempted to justify her detainment on the grounds that it took time to relocate evacuees into areas where they would be well received by the community. They argued that the WRA's supervised, orderly control of resettlement was essential to the safety and well-being of all citizens.

Although not clearly stated within the case, the denial of writ of habeas corpus to Miss Endo and the excessive length of her detention seem to have resulted in part from bureaucratic red tape. When she was evacuated to an area outside the district where the writ had been originally filed, questions of who held jurisdiction over the case and who should have been regarded as respondent were left undecided. In addition, Endo did not follow precise WRA procedures for attaining a "leave permit," and failure to follow procedures seemed to have had adverse legal ramifications on her request for the writ and, ultimately, her release.

The American Civil Liberties Union filed a brief on Endo's behalf, which argued that the government had no power to detain a citizen against whom there were no criminal charges, that the classification of citizens based only on ancestry was a denial of due process and was forbidden by the Fifth Amendment, and that because the petitioner was detained against her own will and without judicial process, she was entitled to relief in the courts without showing compliance with WRA regulations.

The Supreme Court ruled on the case on December 18, 1944, and decided unanimously in favor of the petitioner. Justice William O. Douglas, who wrote the opinion of the Court, stated that "whatever power the War Relocation Authority may have to detain other classes of citizens, it has no authority to subject citizens who are conceded loyal to its leave procedure." Although Endo was deprived of her constitutional rights under the Fifth and Fourteenth Amendments for over two years, the Court evaded the constitutional questions surrounding her detention and ruled on the basis of a minor technicality. Perhaps Justices Frank Murphy and Owen J. Roberts reflected the conscience of the Court when they filed their separate concurring opinions. Justice Murphy stated that the detention was not only unauthorized, but it was also "another example of the unconstitutional resort to racism inherent in the entire evacuation program." Justice Roberts also pointed to the constitutional question when he concluded that the Court was faced with a serious question as to whether the relator's detention violated the guarantees of the Bill of Rights of the Constitution, especially the guarantee of due process of law.

FURTHER READING: Frank F. Chuman, *The Bamboo People*, Del Mar, Calif.: Publisher's Inc., 1976; Roger Daniels, *Concentration Camps U.S.A.*, New York: Holt, Rinehart and Winston, 1971; Milton R. Konvitz, *The Alien and the Asiatic in American*

Law, Ithaca, N.Y.: Cornell University Press, 1946; Jacobus ten Broek et al., *Prejudice, War and the Constitution*, Berkeley: University of California Press, 1970; *Supreme Court Reporter* 65, 323 U.S. 283, 1944, pp. 208–222.

ENRYO, one of the norms considered important in influencing the behavior of Japanese. *Enryo* is commonly translated into English as deference, reserve, or diffidence, and is often observable among Japanese in public meetings or in social situations where they are not willing to speak out to express their feelings and opinions, or where they hesitate to ask questions. Harry Kitano* claims that because the Japanese were so meek and humble, so traditionally obedient to authority, they followed the evacuation order during World War II without protest.

Enryo has other behavioral characteristics which are collectively termed the enryo syndrome; these characteristics include *Ha zu ka shi, Hi-ge*, and *Amae.* * *Ha zu ka shi* refers to Japanese unwillingness to take a risk or consideration for others' feelings. *Hi-ge* refers to Japanese modesty or humility as observed in their interaction with others.

FURTHER READING: Bill Hosokawa, *Nisei*, New York: William Morrow and Co., 1969; Harry H. L. Kitano, *Japanese Americans*, Englewood Cliffs, N.J.: Prentice-Hall, 1969; Dennis M. Ogawa, *Kodomo no tame ni* (For the sake of the children), Honolulu: University Press of Hawaii, 1978.

EQUAL COMMITTEE, created in 1940 within the Los Angeles Japanese American Citizens League* in response to the City Council's refusal to accept the city engineer's recommendations for a new housing development plan. The housing plan, known as the Jefferson Park Development, was undertaken in 1938, and by February 1940 the planners submitted to the Los Angeles city engineers a 191-lot area, which would have excluded people of all racial origins except Japanese and Caucasian. The committee pressured the City Council to approve the plan because it had no right to refuse the city engineers' favorable recommendations. Although the project was finally approved, not many Japanese were interested in buying lots, and the project eventually failed. The committee continued to function, and by 1941 it evolved into a permanent group devoted to bettering relations with the white community. After the Japanese attack on Pearl Harbor, the same leaders on the committee became members of the Anti-Axis Committee of the Japanese American Citizens League.

FURTHER READING: John Modell, *The Economics and Politics of Racial Accommodation: The Japanese of Los Angeles, 1900–1942*, Urbana: University of Illinois Press, 1977.

ESTATE OF TETSUBUMI YANO. *See* State of California v. Hayao Yano and Tetsubumi Yano.

EU, MARCH KONG FONG (1927–   ), Secretary of State, California. Eu was born in Oakdale, California, on March 29, 1927. She attended Salinas Junior College and later earned a B.S. degree from the University of California at Berkeley. Eu worked her way through school as a dental hygienist. She went on to Mills College where she received a Master's degree in education, and she obtained her doctorate from Stanford University in 1956. She was elected to the California State Legislature in 1966; she ran again in 1970 and 1972 and won both times. Eu won her bid for the post of Secretary of the State of California in 1975, thereby becoming the first woman of Asian American ancestry to become California's Secretary of State. Eu claimed that she represented the needs, wishes, and aspirations of all the population. At the same time, she serves as a role model for people of Chinese ancestry, as well as other minorities.

EUREKA EXPULSION OF CHINESE, an incident touched off in Eureka, California, by the fighting of rival Chinese factions in February 1885. During the gun fights between rival factions of Chinese, a city councilman was shot and killed, and a boy was wounded. After the incident, a thousand men gathered in Centennial Hall and elected a committee charged with the responsibility of notifying the city's Chinese residents to leave the city within twenty-four hours upon notice. After citizens began to set up gallows at the main entrance the next day, the Chinese did not offer any resistance. They packed and left the town on two steamers that took them to San Francisco.

EXCLUSION LAW OF 1924. *See* Immigration Act of 1924.

EXCLUSION LAWS, all the legislative actions taken by the U.S. Congress to restrict and ban the immigration of Asians to America. There are too many laws to mention them one by one. The U.S. government instituted the Alien Act in 1798 which empowered the President to expel any alien whom he considered dangerous to the peace and security of the nation. But this act did not specify any racial or national group to be excluded as a class or group. Immigration to America was not subject to strict control; in fact, in its ruling on the Henderson v. Mayor of New York case the Supreme Court of the United States declared all state statutes restricting immigration unconstitutional.

The immigration of the Chinese people was not restricted until after 1879. In 1880 the U.S. government prohibited the entry of Chinese laborers into its territory, and two years later, the U.S. Congress passed the Chinese Exclusion Law prohibiting the immigration of Chinese workers. The Chinese were, therefore, the first national or racial group to be identified as a group of people undesirable for immigration by the U.S. government.

With Chinese exclusion achieved, American exclusionists turned their attention to Japanese immigration. The Japanese were allowed to come into America with no restriction until 1907 when the U.S. and Japanese governments reached an agreement to restrict Japanese immigration. This initial step led to the complete

exclusion of all Asians in 1924 when Congress passed the National Origins Act.*
These exclusion laws are now a source of embarrassment and shame for all
believers in equality of opportunity for everyone under law.
FURTHER READING: Delber L. McKee, *Chinese Exclusion Versus the Open Door
Policy*, Detroit: Wayne State University Press, 1977; Fred W. Riggs, *Pressures on
Congress: A Study of the Repeal of Chinese Exclusion*, New York: King's Crown Press,
1950.

EXECUTIVE ORDER 9066, a presidential order issued on February 19, 1942,
empowering the Secretary of War and his designated military commanders to
prescribe military areas from which any or all persons might be excluded. This
order was signed by President Franklin D. Roosevelt after a casual conversation
with Henry Lewis Stimson,* Secretary of War, and with John J. McCloy,
Assistant Secretary of War. The President asked them to do anything necessary
under the circumstances, though he cautioned them to be reasonable. Although
Executive Order 9066 did not mention the Japanese or Japanese Americans
specifically, it was used exclusively against persons of Japanese ancestry. A
mass removal of German and Italian Americans was authorized, but no such
evacuation was ever carried out.

In order to add teeth to Executive Order 9066, Congress passed Public Law
503* on March 21, 1942, making violation of the order a misdemeanor carrying
a fine not to exceed $5,000 or imprisonment for not more than one year, or both,
for each offense.
FURTHER READING: Roger Daniels, *The Decision to Relocate the Japanese Americans*,
New York: J. B. Lippincott Co., 1975; Dillon S. Myer, *Uprooted Americans*, Tucson:
University of Arizona Press, 1971.

EXECUTIVE ORDER 9102, signed by President Franklin D. Roosevelt on
March 18, 1942, in order to create the War Relocation Authority* (WRA). On
the same day, Milton Stover Eisenhower* was appointed director of the WRA.

EXECUTIVE ORDER 9814, signed by President Harry S Truman on December
23, 1946, establishing the President's Amnesty Board to examine and consider
the cases of all persons convicted of violating the Selective Training and Service
Act of 1940 as amended. This board was asked to report its findings and
recommendations to the Attorney General with regard to whether or not executive
clemency should be granted. Upon the board's recommendations, President
Truman issued Presidential Proclamation 2762 on December 12, 1947, granting
full pardon to those convicted of violating the law, including 265 Nisei* Japanese
Americans.

F

FA'A SAMOA, a term used to refer to Samoan traditional folklore and mores. Many anthropologists claim that this is based on their kinship relations. According to some, Samoans who have immigrated to the mainland United States use it as a survival strategy to maintain native culture.

FURTHER READING: Cluny MacPherson, Bradd Shore, and Robert Franco, eds., *New Neighbors . . . Islanders in Adaptation*, Santa Cruz: Center for South Pacific Studies, University of California, Santa Cruz, 1978; Robert Trumbull, *Tin Roofs and Palm Trees: A Report on the New South Seas*, Seattle: University of Washington Press, 1977.

FAGEL, ANTONIO, a Filipino labor union leader who succeeded Pablo Manlapit* and Epifanio Taok as the leader of the Filipino Federation of Labor* when Malapit and Taok were jailed after the 1924 strike in Hawaii. Fagel renamed the organization Vibora Luviminda. (*See also* Filipino Federation of Labor.)

FAIR PLAY COMMITTEE OF ONE, a committee established by Okamoto Kiyoshi at Heart Mountain relocation camp in November 1943. Okamoto was born in Hawaii and later moved to Los Angeles, where he received a good education. He became an engineer before he was ordered to evacuate and relocate at Heart Mountain, Wyoming, during the Pacific War. He opposed the War Relocation Authority* (WRA) from the beginning, claiming that the evacuation and relocation of persons of Japanese ancestry were illegal actions. Even though the so-called disloyal Japanese who had answered "no" to the loyalty question on the Application for Leave Clearance* had been segregated in the Tule Lake Segregation Center,* many Japanese internees protested against evacuation. Many of them were particularly opposed to the registration for draft and volunteer programs. Okamoto became a leader among these Nisei* who believed that the entire evacuation program was illegal and that it should be tested in court. By the end of February 1944 there were as many as 275 dues-paying members of the committee, and they continued to agitate the WRA with their charges that the evacuation was illegal and with their resistance against draft registration. Finally, the WRA decided to send Okamoto to Tule Lake on March 27, 1944.

Okamoto's removal did not discourage the members of the committee. Okamoto was replaced by Paul T. Nakadate, a twenty-seven-year-old Nisei, whose loyalty to the United States was recognized even by the WRA. Nakadate believed that the rights of the Nisei Americans had been violated, and he did not give an unequivocal answer to whether he would serve in the U.S. Army. Because of his attitude, Nakadate was sent to Tule Lake. After his transfer, other leaders of the committee were also removed from Heart Mountain, and draft resisters were put under arrest by Carl L. Sackett, a U.S. attorney based in Cheyenne, Wyoming, after they refused preinduction orders in late March and early April 1944. (*See also* Okamoto Kiyoshi v. United States.)

FURTHER READING: Frank F. Chuman, *The Bamboo People*, Del Mar, Calif.: Publisher's Inc., 1976; Douglas W. Nelson, *Heart Mountain: The History of an American Concentration Camp*, Madison: Department of History, University of Wisconsin, 1976.

FARRINGTON, GOVERNOR, et al. v. T. TOKUSHIGE et al., a case argued on January 21, 1927, and decided on February 21, 1927, by the U.S. Supreme Court, which ruled in favor of the respondents. The petitioners, represented by their lawyer, William B. Lymer, claimed that the provisions of the law entitled "An Act Relating to Foreign Language Schools and Teachers Thereof," as amended by Act 171 of 1923 and Act 1952 of 1925, were lawful as they were enacted by the Hawaii Legislature, and the petitioners, Governor, Attorney General, and Superintendent of Public Instruction of the Hawaiian Territory, should be able to enforce lawful regulations. According to the law, no foreign language schools were allowed to operate unless they received a written permit from the Department of Public Instruction and unless a fee of $1 per pupil had been paid. Respondents, one of whom was T. Tokushige, represented by his lawyer, Joseph Lightfoot, claimed that enforcement of the law would deprive him of his liberty and property without due process of law which would be in violation of the Fifth Amendment of the Constitution.

At the time of the litigation, there were 163 foreign language schools in Hawaii, nine of which were conducted in Korean, seven in Chinese, and the remainder in Japanese. These Japanese language schools enrolled a total of 20,000 pupils taught by 300 teachers, and the property used in this endeavor was valued at $250,000. These schools received no financial assistance from public funds.

Justice James C. McReynolds delivered the opinion of the Court, which affirmed the decree made by the Circuit Court of Appeals. The Justice stated that "the Japanese parent has the right to direct the education of his own child without unreasonable restrictions; the Constitution protects him as well as those who speak another language." Grounding the unanimous decision of the Court on the Meyer v. Nebraska, Bartels v. Iowa, and Pierce v. Society of Sisters decisions, the Justice maintained that the grave problems facing the Hawaiian territorial

government with regard to educating the large alien population should not transcend the limitations of the Constitution.
FURTHER READING: Milton R. Konvitz, *The Alien and the Asiatic in American Law*, Ithaca, N.Y.: Cornell University Press, 1946; *The Supreme Court Reporter*, Vol. 47, 273 U.S. 284 October Term, 1926.

FIFTEEN PASSENGERS BILL, a bill which proposed to limit Chinese immigration by requiring ships to carry no more than fifteen passengers at one time. Although President Rutherford B. Hayes' message to the 45th Congress did not call for any legislative measures to be taken against Chinese immigration, Congress gave attention to the question of Chinese immigration as a result of a memorial from the Oregon Legislature. For a while some congressmen resisted the demands of West Coast congressmen, but eventually the House took up the Wren Bill, which proposed to restrict Chinese immigration, and later passed it by a vote of 155 to 72 on January 18, 1879. The Senate took up the bill and passed it, with a number of amendments, by a vote of 39 to 27. The bill, as passed by both the House and the Senate, restricted Chinese immigration as it required that no ship should carry more than fifteen Chinese passengers. President Hayes vetoed the bill on the ground that it violated the Burlingame Treaty of 1868.*
FURTHER READING: E. P. Hutchinson, *Legislative History of American Immigration Policy, 1798–1965*, Philadelphia: University of Pennsylvania Press, 1981; S. W. Kung, *Chinese in America*, Seattle: University of Washington Press, 1962, 1973.

FILIPINO AGRICULTURAL WORKERS ASSOCIATION, an association of Filipino asparagus workers in the Stockton and Sacramento valleys founded in April 1939 under the leadership of Macario Bautista, president of the association.

FILIPINO AMERICAN POLITICAL ASSOCIATION, an association founded in 1969 by delegates of local Filipino communities in the area stretching from San Diego to the Bay Area in California whose members met to work on human rights issues. The first annual convention of the association was held in 1969 when Cesar Chavez was invited to address the delegates, and Larry Dulay Itliong* was elected president of the association. (*See also* Itliong, Larry Dulay.)

FILIPINO FEDERATION OF AMERICA, organized on March 30, 1927, in Hawaii, when a group of Filipinos met to create an organization to promote friendly relations between Americans and Filipinos. The organization made an effort to gain rights of U.S. citizenship for the Filipinos. Hilario Camino Moncado was president of the organization.
FURTHER READING: Hyung-chan Kim and Cynthia C. Mejia, eds., *The Filipinos in America*, Dobbs Ferry, N.Y.: Oceana Publications, 1976.

FILIPINO FEDERATION OF LABOR, organized in 1919 under the leadership of Pablo Manlapit,* who came to Hawaii in 1910 from the Philippines. Manlapit launched a vigorous campaign to organize Filipinos working on Hawaii's sugar cane fields in order to improve their lives. He hoped to discourage Filipinos in the Philippines from coming to Hawaii by informing them of the true working conditions on Hawaii's plantations. The strength of the newly organized labor union was tested when the Filipino workers on Oahu went on strike after the Hawaiian Sugar Planters' Association* rejected the union's demands on January 19, 1920. The union members were on strike for three weeks, but they were not able to sustain their strength. Consequently, Manlapit called off the strike, only to resume it after five days. The Hawaiian Sugar Planters' Association responded swiftly to the strike, expelling 12,000 workers, most of whom were Japanese, from plantation housing. It also made an extra effort to recruit more Filipino workers from the Philippines.

In spite of the setback he suffered, Manlapit launched another campaign, this time under the name of the Higher Wage Movement, with cooperation from Japanese labor organizers. The movement strove for better working conditions and higher wages for plantation workers, demanding that they be paid $2 per day for a forty-hour week. The Hawaiian Sugar Planters' Association refused to honor the demands, and Manlapit called for a strike on April 1, 1924. Although Manlapit claimed that 12,000 workers went on strike, about 3,000 workers, 25 percent of all those employed in the plantations, were out on strike by June. The strike was unsuccessful however, as fresh workers from the Philippines were brought to be used as strike-breakers.

The conflict between striking workers and their employers resulted in one of the bloodiest incidents in the history of the labor movement in Hawaii, when sixteen striking union members and four policemen died on September 9, 1924, at Hanapepe, Kauai. This incident is commonly known as the Hanapepe Massacre.* Because of the violence that erupted during the incident, Manlapit and sixty others were convicted of conspiracy, and each was sentenced to two years in prison. Manlapit was given the choice of becoming an exile but returned to Hawaii in 1932 when he organized another labor union, the Filipino Labor Union, with the help of Epifanio Taok and Antonio Fagel.* Taok was later imprisoned, and Manlapit was banished to the Philippines in 1935. Fagel then took the union underground and renamed it Vibora Luviminda. The first word of the organization's name came from the "nom de guerre" of Artemio Ricarte, who was sent into exile from the Philippines by American authorities because he had refused to take an oath of allegiance to America at the conclusion of the Filipino-American War; the second word is a combination of the first syllables of Luzon, Visayas, and Mindanao, areas from which the majority of Filipino laborers in Hawaii came.

Under Fagel's leadership, the Filipino Labor Union organized Filipino workers who went on strike in June 1936 at four plantations on Maui, demanding higher wages and the dismissal of five foremen. The Hawaiian Sugar Planters' Association decided to give a 15 percent pay increase, but this small victory was overshadowed by the imprisonment of Fagel and other labor union leaders in September 1937. After Fagel was imprisoned, the union fell into disarray and collapsed.

The Filipino Federation of Labor arose out of the ashes of the Filipino Labor Union, establishing itself as a duly registered labor union in California. On March 31, 1927, it registered as a labor union in the State of California.

FURTHER READING: Robert N. Anderson et al., *Filipinos in Rural Hawaii*, Honolulu: University of Hawaii Press, 1984; Lawrence H. Fuchs, *Hawaii Pono: A Social History*, New York: Harcourt, Brace and World, 1961; Hyung-chan Kim and Cynthia C. Mejia, eds., *The Filipinos in America, 1898–1974*, Dobbs Ferry, N.Y.: Oceana Publications, 1976.

FILIPINO HIGHER WAGE MOVEMENT. *See* Filipino Federation of Labor.

FILIPINO LABOR SUPPLY ASSOCIATION OF MONTEREY COUNTY, organized on January 27, 1933, at Rufo Canete's camp near Salinas, California. Canete was elected president of the association.

In the 1930s labor contractors began to feel increasing pressure from Filipino workers as competition for employment began to intensify. They had to compete against each other in order to have a bigger share of labor supply. The labor contractor as the middleman between growers and workers played a significant role in Western agriculture. Workers depended on the labor contractor as he knew where the work was and how to negotiate wages and hours for them. Growers depended on contractors, for they did not have to burden themselves with recruiting workers and making all the necessary arrangements for them, including housing, transportation, wages, and other accommodations.

When there was severe competition among labor contractors, they had to accept lower wage rates for their workers. Workers, therefore, received less as there was less to go around. The labor contractor was responsible for housing, food, and other necessities which the workers under his supervision needed. For every service provided, a service charge was imposed.

FILIPINO LABOR UNION, a union organized on December 10, 1933, when a group of Filipino labor contractors met in the gymnasium of the Salinas Athletic Club. Rufo Canete, president of the Filipino Labor Supply Association of Monterey County,* was elected president of the union. This union was different from the Filipino Labor Union which was established by Pablo Manlapit*, Epifanio Taok, and Antonio Fagel* in Hawaii; the two had no significant relationship to each other.

The Filipino Labor Union in Salinas, California, was established by a group of labor contractors motivated by self-interest. The contractors foresaw their future in terms of the availability of field work and the increasing interest of the American Federation of Labor in agricultural unionization. They believed that they could not only attract the interest of the American Federation of Labor in organizing Filipino workers, but could also occupy major administrative positions in the labor union once it was organized. The labor contractors' interests sometimes collided with those of Filipino workers, making the labor movement among the Filipino workers quite shaky.

The Filipino Labor Union led a successful strike against growers on August 27, 1934, in Salinas. (*See also* Salinas Lettuce Strike of 1934.)

FURTHER READING: Howard A. DeWitt, "The Filipino Labor Union: The Salinas Lettuce Strike of 1934," *Amerasia Journal* 5, No. 2 (1978): 1–21; Hyung-chan Kim and Cynthia C. Mejia, eds., *The Filipinos in America, 1898–1974*, Dobbs Ferry, N.Y.: Oceana Publications, 1976.

FILIPINO LEAGUE (LA LIGA FILIPINA), organized by Jose Rizal* in the Philippines on July 3, 1892, in order to protect all Filipinos against violence and injustice. The organization developed a social reform program under Rizal's leadership. After he was executed, more radical revolutionaries took over the league's leadership.

FILIPINO NATURALIZATION ACT, a bill extending American citizenship to Filipino residents of America who had come to the United States before March 24, 1943. During the second session of the 79th Congress, Emanuel Celler* of New York introduced a bill designed to grant admission and naturalization to natives of India. This bill was reported back by the committee, debated, and passed by the House, but the Senate did not act on it until the second session. During the second session the Senate added the Ball (Minnesota) amendment to extend the bill to include Filipino persons or persons of Filipino descent. With the House agreement and presidential signature, the bill became law on July 2, 1946, to be known as the Filipino Naturalization Act*.

FILIPINO REPATRIATION ACT OF 1935, a bill passed in the midst of the Great Depression in order to send back to the Philippines those Filipino residents in America who were willing to go home at the U.S. government's expense. Between 1930 and 1933, 3 to 15 million people were unemployed in America, and unemployment among Filipino residents was high. In 1933 of the 12,000 Filipinos living in Los Angeles County, 75 percent were unemployed. Because of the high rate of unemployment among Filipinos and the unavailability of social relief resources to them, Filipinos wrote President Franklin Roosevelt asking him for relief and how they could return to the Philippines at the U.S. government's expense. This relief came in the form of congressional action.

In 1933 Samuel Dickstein of New York introduced a bill known as House Joint Resolution 549, but it was not debated, as it was presented to the resolution committee for its consideration. Later that year it was reintroduced in modified form and was known as House Joint Resolution 118. In explaining the purpose of the bill, Dickstein indicated that it was intended to help homeless and unemployed Filipino residents in America. He stated that they were the burden of charity organizations. One of the provisions in his proposed bill was to deport Filipinos at government expense. After their return to their native country, they would not be able to reenter the United States because they had used government money to go home. The bill did not receive much support from members of Congress and consequently did not pass.

Two years later Richard Welch of California introduced a bill that was designed to repatriate Filipino residents at the government's expense. Although his bill also required that no Filipino would be allowed to come back to the United States if he or she received the benefits of the act in returning to the Philippines, that section was amended to comply with the immigration provisions of the Tydings-McDuffie Act of 1934.* Hence, those who were repatriated to the Philippines were allowed to come back to America as part of the annual quota of fifty immigrants which the Philippines received. During the first year of operation, a total of 533 Filipinos were sent back to their native land, at an average cost of $116 per person. By the end of the program in December 1940, a total of 2,190 Filipinos had been repatriated to the Philippines.

FURTHER READING: Casiano Coloma, *A Study of Filipino Repatriation Movement*, San Francisco, R. and E. Research Associates, 1974; Hyung-chan Kim and Cynthia Mejia, eds., *The Filipinos in America, 1898–1974*, Dobbs Ferry, N.Y.: Oceana Publications, 1976.

FILIPINO UNEMPLOYMENT ASSOCIATION, organized by Pablo Manlapit* between 1913 and 1914, after he had been fired by the Hawaiian Sugar Planters' Association* for his involvement in a labor strike. (*See also* Manlapit, Pablo.)

FILIPINOS IN THE U.S. NAVY, members of a special community of Filipinos in America as a result of their service in the U.S. Navy. Although Filipinos were generally not allowed to petition for their U.S. citizenship, those Filipinos who had served in the U.S. Navy for a period of three years were permitted to petition for their U.S. citizenship in accordance with a law passed in May 1918. Of course, this meant that there was a considerable group of Filipinos who had already begun to serve in the Navy or who had completed their service. These Filipinos had been recruited in many parts of the Philippines and were inducted into the Navy at the U.S. Naval Station at Sangley Point in Cavite City in the Province of Cavite. Filipinos served in the U.S. Navy as early as 1914 before World War I, and by 1917 there were approximately 2,000 Filipinos in the Navy. During World War I, a large number of Filipinos joined the Navy, and by 1919 there were 6,000 Filipinos. Although blacks were not allowed to join the Navy, Filipinos were highly represented.

After the Philippines became independent in 1946, a treaty was concluded between the United States and the Philippines which enabled Filipinos to enlist in the U.S. navy without losing their Philippine citizenship. The Military Bases Agreement signed in 1947 established special relations between the Philippines and the United States, which allowed up to 2,000 men a year to enlist for military and professional training, which usually meant steward jobs. These included cooks, waiters, pantrymen, dishwashers, custodians, bedmakers, and valets whose duties were to serve officers. Because of economic conditions in their native land, an abundance of people were willing to enlist in the U.S. Navy, even though their opportunity for upward mobility was limited. Most Filipinos enlisted in the Navy with steward rating and remained there, although some did move into other naval occupational areas after training.

It is estimated that as many as 22,000 Filipinos joined the Navy between 1944 and 1973. According to one report, there were 16,669 Filipinos in the U.S. Navy as of 1970 and 80 percent of them were stewards.

FURTHER READING: Fred Cordova, *Filipinos: Forgotten Asian Americans*, Dubuque, Iowa: Kendall/Hunt Publishing Co., 1983; Jesse Quinsaat, ed., *Letters in Exile*, Los Angeles: Regents of the University of California, 1976; Stanley Sue and Nathaniel N. Wagner, eds., *Asian-Americans: Psychological Perspectives*, Ben Lomond, Calif.: Science and Behavior Books, 1973.

FIRST FILIPINO INFANTRY REGIMENT, a military unit composed exclusively of Filipinos in America soon after the Japanese attack on Pearl Harbor in 1941, which sent many Filipinos to army recruiting centers near their communities. Many Filipinos wanted to help the United States fight Japan, but they were not allowed to enlist in the U.S. Army because of a technicality: they were not U.S. citizens. As nationals of the United States they were classified as 4-C, a class of people who were not permitted to serve in the U.S. military forces.

On January 3, 1942, the day after Manila was occupied by Japanese troops, the War Department changed its policy and enabled Filipinos in America to serve in U.S. military forces. On February 19, 1942, Secretary of War Henry L. Stimson* announced the formation of the First Filipino Infantry Battalion, which was activated on April 1, 1942, to be stationed at Camp San Luis Obispo, California. On July 3, 1942, the unit was inactivated and reorganized into the First Filipino Infantry Regiment* under order of the commanding general of the Eighth Army. All personnel and equipment were transferred to Salinas, California, on July 13, 1942, which became the unit's Organization Day.

Filipino enlisted men were trained at Fort Ord, Camp Cooke, San Luis Obispo, the Presidio of Monterey Language School, and Salinas Garrison in a wide range of skills and techniques of warfare under the leadership of white officers, although there were some Filipino noncommissioned officers. After training, enlistees were sent overseas. The First Filipino Infantry Regiment was shipped to Australia on January 13, 1943, and then to Oro Bay, and to New Guinea, where they saw their first action against the Japanese in overtaking airbase sites. They were moved on to northern Luzon, the Visayas Islands, and southern Mindanao where they displayed their courage, their skill in warfare, and their ability to fight against the enemy under adverse conditions.

FURTHER READING: Lorraine Jacobs Crouchett, *Filipinos in California*, El Cerrito, Calif.: Downey Place Publishing House, 1982; Brett Melendy, *Asians in America*, Boston: Twayne Publishers, 1977.

FIRST KOREAN LIBERTY CONGRESS, a political conference of Koreans in America that was held in Philadelphia under the leadership of So Jae-p'il (Philip Jaisohn)* from April 16 to 19, 1919. (*See also* Bureau of Korean Information.)

FONG, HIRAM LEONG (1907–   ), U.S. senator. Born on October 1, 1907, the son of indentured plantation workers from China, Fong worked his way through the University of Hawaii after graduation from McKinley High School. After he received his B.A. degree from the University of Hawaii in 1930, he went on to Harvard Law School. Upon graduation in 1935, he was admitted to the bar and commenced his law practice in Honolulu. Fong was the first person in Hawaii to found a multiracial law office. His talents were diverse; while practicing law, he also invested in business and created a firm called Finance Factors, which had several million dollars in assets by 1960.

Fong was elected as a Republican to the Hawaiian Territorial Legislature in 1938 and served there until 1954. While serving in the legislature, he developed good working relations with the International Longshoremen's and Warehousemen's Union* (ILWU), which supported his candidacy for the U.S. Senate in 1958. Fong was the first Republican to be supported by the normally Democratic ILWU. As a senator, he took more liberal stands on domestic issues than on foreign policy. He won reelection in 1964.

During his second term in office, Fong supported the 1965 Voting Rights Act and wrote a key amendment to include poll watchers. As a member of the Judiciary Committee's Immigration and Naturalization Subcommittee, he worked to eliminate the traditional immigration restrictions which were unfavorable to Asians. During the Nixon years, he became more conservative and voted for large defense spending which earned him a 100 percent rating from the American Security Council. Fong's support for the Nixon policies in Vietnam hurt his popularity in Hawaii and contributed to a weakening relationship between him and the ILWU, but he was reelected in 1970 on the basis of his organization. Fong retired from politics at the end of his third term in 1976.

FONG YUE TING v. UNITED STATES, a case argued in the U.S. Supreme Court in 1893 involving Chinese workers ordered deported for not having certificates of residence. In 1868 the United States and China signed the Burlingame Treaty,* which allowed a citizen of each nation to change his home and allegiance, to have the right to emigrate, and to enjoy the same rights and privileges of the citizens of the other nation. In 1880 the United States renegotiated for a new treaty in order to regulate, limit, and suspend the immigration of Chinese to the United States. In 1882 the Chinese Exclusion Act* prohibited the immigration of Chinese laborers, both skilled and unskilled, and required that all Chinese residents in the United States acquire a certificate for reentry into the United States. In 1884 Chinese were required to carry certificates not only to reenter, but also to leave the country. Those who did not carry certificates were expelled from the country. The Geary Act of 1892* required all Chinese laborers in the United States to apply for a certificate of residence within one year from the time of passage. If after one year any Chinese was found without a certificate, he was arrested, brought before a judge, and deported unless he could prove to the judge that his failure to obtain one was due to accident, sickness, or an unavoidable cause or that he had lost his card.

This case before the Supreme Court involved the appeal of three Chinese laborers who had been ordered deported in 1892 for not having certificates of residence in accord with the Geary Act. The first defendant, Fong Yue Ting, had resided in the United States since 1879 and intended to remain, but he had failed to apply for a certificate within one year and was therefore arrested. The second man was arrested under similar conditions, brought before a judge, and ordered deported. Although the petition said the order was "without any hearing of any kind," that claim was shown to be false, as a record of hearing was attached to the petition. He was ordered deported because he failed to prove to the judge that he had a legal right to be in the United States. The third defendant had applied for a certificate. However, Chinese had to have at least one credible white witness who would testify that they were legal residents. The third defendant was unable to provide a credible white witness because he lived in Chinatown,* had little contact with whites, and therefore did not know a white who could testify in his behalf. He was arrested, brought before a judge, and, although he proved he did not have a certificate due to an unavoidable cause, he was ordered deported.

The Supreme Court upheld the rulings of the lower court. Justice Horace Gray, for a majority of the Court, said that the right to forbid or limit immigration was inherent in a nation's sovereignty, that the defendants were not citizens but aliens, and that excluding them was a part of U.S. jurisdiction over its territory. The Court made a reference to the unassimilable character of the Chinese, who would not adapt to American society, who were considered dangerous to peace and security, and who would create religious disturbances.

The Geary Act required a white witness, the Court claimed, because Chinese witnesses did not fully understand the implications of the oath they took. This requirement was similar to the one required of all people, seeking naturalization as American citizens. However, any U.S. citizen could fill the latter requirement, whereas the Geary Act specifically required a white witness.

Justices David J Brewer, Stephen J. Field, and Melville W. Fuller dissented from the majority opinion and wrote strong opinions condemning the decision made on May 15, 1893. Basically, the three dissenting Justices argued that (1) the defendants were lawfully residing in the United States and were, therefore, protected by the Constitution, (2) if the certificate could be required of one

group, it would soon be required of other groups, and (3) the defendants were subject to unreasonable search and seizure and were deprived of liberty because deportation, a form of punishment, was imposed on them when they had done no wrong.
FURTHER READING: Milton R. Konvitz, *The Alien and the Asiatic in American Law*, Ithaca, N.Y.: Cornell University Press, 1946; *Supreme Court Reporter* 13, 149 U.S. 698, 1893, pp. 1016–41; William L. Tung, *The Chinese in America, 1820–1973*, Dobbs Ferry, N.Y.: Oceana Publications, 1974; Cheng-Tsu Wu, *"Chink!"* New York: World Publishing, 1972.

FORAN ACT OF 1885, a legislation passed by the 48th Congress of the United States to forbid contract labor. During the first session of the 48th Congress, Representative Martin A. Foran of Ohio introduced a bill in the House of Representatives, H.R. 2550, the major goal of which was prohibit prepayment for transportation or assistance of any foreign aliens under contract for labor or service prior to emigration. The Senate had a similar bill, Senate Report 820. During the second session, Congress passed the bill on February 26, 1885, and the law went into effect immediately. Because of this law, labor recruiters used various methods to circumvent legal requirements and continued to subsidize transportation of laborers coming to Hawaii as well as to the U.S. mainland. (*See also* Berger v. Bishop.)
FURTHER READING: U.S. Statutes at Large, Vol. 23, Chapter 164, 1885.

FOREIGN COMMISSION OF THE KOREAN OVERSEAS ASSOCIATION (also known as the United Korean Committee in America*), founded on April 20, 1941, when fourteen representatives from nine social and political organizations of Koreans attended an all-Korean representatives convention in Honolulu, Hawaii. The committee was created in order to support the Korean provisional government-in-exile in Shanghai, China, in its effort to gain Korea's independence. The committee was to become the only diplomatic agent of the government, and Syngman Rhee* was elected to chair the committee. (*See also* Rhee, Syngman.)
FURTHER READING: Bong-youn Choy, *Koreans in America*, Chicago: Nelson-Hall, 1979; Chong-sik Lee, *The Politics of Korean Nationalism*, Berkeley: University of California Press, 1965.

442ND REGIMENTAL COMBAT UNIT, a special military unit made up of Nisei* American citizens of Japanese ancestry. The unit was organized after the War Department announced its plan to accept Nisei volunteers on January 28, 1943. Before December 7, 1941, there were already more than 1,500 men of Japanese ancestry from Hawaii who had been inducted into the army. Previously, Mike Masaoka,* as a representative of the Japanese American Citizens League,* suggested to the War Department that a "suicide battalion" be created with Nisei volunteers who would be held as hostages to show the American government that they were loyal to America. The military authorities turned down the suggestion on the ground that it ran counter to American policy not to create racially segregated military units except in the case of blacks.

The 442nd Combat Unit was activated on February 1, 1943, and preparations were immediately made to train Nisei volunteers at Camp Shelby, Mississippi, where a small group of Nisei non-commissioned officers had been dispatched to undertake the task of training them. The unit was made up of the 442nd Infantry Regiment, the 552nd Field Artillery Battalion, the 232nd Combat Engineer Company, and the 206th Army Ground Forces Band. Colonel Charles W. Pence, its first commander, was assisted primarily by white officers, although some Nisei who had been trained in college Reserve Officer programs were made lieutenants and captains. The unit consisted of 1,500 volunteers from the U.S. mainland and 2,686 from Hawaii.

The 100th Infantry Battalion, made up of 1,500 men of Japanese ancestry in Hawaii, completed its training earlier and was sent to Oran in North Africa on August 21, 1943. After landing at Salerno, Italy, on September 22, 1943, it saw military action at Volturno, the Rapido River, and Monte Cassino. On June 11, 1944, the 100th Infantry Battalion became the 1st Battalion of the 442nd Combat Unit, although it was allowed to retain its original name.

The 442nd Combat Unit is renowned for its mission and its success in rescuing the Lost Battalion (the 1st Battalion of the 141st Infantry Regiment made up largely of Texans) from German encirclement. In this rescue operation, however, the unit suffered a great number of casualties: 140 dead and 660 wounded.

For their courage and achievement, the unit was awarded forty-three Division Commendations, thirteen Army Commendations, two Meritorious Service Unit Plaques, and seven Presidential Distinguished Unit Citations. More than 18,000 individual decorations were given to members of the unit, including 1 Congressional Medal of Honor, 52 Distinguished Service Crosses, 1 Distinguished Service Medal, and 560 Silver Stars. Among the prominent Americans who served in the 442nd Combat Unit were Senator Daniel K. Inouye* and Mike Masaoka.

FURTHER READING: Bill Hosokawa, *Nisei*, New York: William Morrow and Co., 1969; Daniel Inouye, *Journey to Washington*, Englewood Cliffs, N.J.: Prentice-Hall, 1967; John A. Rademaker, *These Are Americans: The Japanese Americans in Hawaii in World War II*, Palo Alto, Calif.: Pacific Books, 1951; Orville C. Shirey, *Americans— The Story of the 442nd Combat Team*, Washington, D.C.: Infantry Journal Press, 1946; Chester Tanak, *Go For Broke*, Richmond, Calif.: Go For Broke, Inc., 1982; Robert A. Wilson and Bill Hosokawa, *East to America*, New York: William Morrow and Co., 1980.

FREEDMAN'S HYPOTHESIS, the idea that Chinese secret societies developed in China in response to the need for an organization that would bring together people (who were otherwise divided by blood, geographic, and language affiliations) against the state and local governments. Immigrant Chinese willingly joined secret societies for protection.

FURTHER READING: Maurice Freedman, *Lineage Organization in Southeastern China*, London: Athlone, 1958; Maurice Freedman, *Chinese Lineage and Society: Fukien and Kwantung*, New York: Humanities Press, 1966; Stanford M. Lyman, *Chinese Americans*, New York: Random House, 1974.

FRICK v. WEBB, a suit brought by appellants Raymond L. Frick and N. Satow in order to prevent U. S. Webb, Attorney General of California, and Matthew Brady, District Attorney of the city and county of San Francisco, from enforcing the California Alien Land Law, which was approved by the electors on November 2, 1920. According to the California statute, aliens ineligible for citizenship could acquire shares of stock in any corporation that was authorized to acquire, possess, or convey agricultural land only if such acquisition was permitted by treaty. Appellants claimed that this statute was in violation of the due process and equal protection clauses of the Fourteenth Amendment and of the Treaty of Commerce and Navigation of 1911* between the United States and Japan.

Raymond L. Frick, a citizen of the United States, owned twenty-eight shares of the capital stock of the Merced Farm Company which owned 2,200 acres of farmland in California. Frick wanted to sell his shares to N. Satow, a citizen of Japan who was ineligible for U.S. citizenship. Because he wanted to sell his share to a Japanese, Frick was told that he would be violating the California Alien Land Law and that the government would confiscate his shares. Frick and Satow applied for an injunction to restrain Webb and Brady from enforcing the 1920 Alien Land Law. Their application was heard by three judges who ruled against Frick and Satow, who then appealed to the Supreme Court. The case was heard on April 23 and 24, 1923, and was decided on November 19, 1923.

In delivering the opinion of the Court, Justice Pierce Butler stated that, although the treaty between the United States and Japan allowed Japanese in America to carry on trade, it did not give them the privilege of acquiring such shares of stock. He declared that the California Alien Land Law was not in violation of the treaty between the United States and Japan and that it did not violate the due process and equal protection clauses of the Fourteenth Amendment.

FURTHER READING: Frank F. Chuman, *The Bamboo People*, Del Mar, Calif.: Publisher's Inc., 1976; Consulate-General of Japan, *Documental History of Law Cases Affecting Japanese in the United States, 1916–1924*, San Francisco: 1925; Yamato Ichihashi, *Japanese in the United States*, Stanford, Calif.: Stanford University Press, 1932; *Supreme Court Reporter* 263, U.S. 326, 1923.

FRIENDS OF FREEDOM FOR INDIA, a political organization founded by Tarak Nath Das for the purpose of achieving India's independence from Britain. It was established by Das in cooperation with Sailendra Nath Ghose and B. K. Roy, biographer of Tagore, after Das was released from prison where he had served sixteen months of his twenty-month prison term. He was arrested and convicted for collaborating with America's enemy, Germany, during World War I. The case became known as the Hindu Conspiracy Case.*

The British government attempted to have Das deported to India but could not because he was a citizen of the United States.

When Sailendra Nath Ghose took control of the organization, after Das left for graduate studies at Catholic University in Washington, D.C., the organization later changed its name to India Freedom Foundation.

FURTHER READING: Emily C. Brown, *Har Dayal*, Tucson: University of Arizona Press, 1975; Haridas T. Muzumdar, *America's Contributions to India's Freedom*, Allahabad, India: Central Book Depot, 1962.

FRIENDSHIP SOCIETY (CH'INMOK-HOE), established in 1903 under the leadership of Ahn Chang-ho* in San Francisco in order to promote and protect the interests of Koreans in America. This was the first Korean social organization established in Korea.

FU MANCHU, a fictitious Chinese character created by novelist Sax Rohmer.* In Rohmer's novels Fu Manchu was described as a sinister and diabolical genius bent on dominating the world. (*See also* Rohmer, Sax.)

FUJII SEI v. STATE OF CALIFORNIA, a landmark case decided by the Supreme Court of California on April 17, 1952, in favor of Fujii Sei. Before this case was decided, the Supreme Court of the United States had handed down several major decisions to put a legal stamp on the Alien Land Act of California, 1913.* The decisions that upheld the discriminatory land law's constitutionality were Terrace et al. v. Thompson, Attorney General of Washington,* Porterfield v. Webb,* Morrison et al. v. People of the State of California,* and Cockrill et al. v. People of the State of California.* The constitutionality of the California Alien Land Act was once more challenged in court when the highest court of the land agreed to hear the Oyama v. California* case. The case had already been ruled on by the California Supreme Court, which decided to uphold the constitutionality of the law. The U.S. Supreme Court, however, reversed the decision of the California Supreme Court by six to three. In his opinion for the Court, Chief Justice Fred M. Vinson stated that the Alien Land Act deprived Fred Oyama of the equal protection of California's laws and of his privileges as an American citizen.

Encouraged by the Supreme Court's decision, Fujii Sei, a Japanese alien who had come to America at an early age, bought a piece of land and took title in his own name as a Japanese alien, who was, therefore, ineligible for U.S. citizenship. According to the California Alien Land Act of 1913, an alien ineligible for citizenship was prohibited from holding title to land. Because Fujii Sei was an alien, the State of California took an escheat action to take land away from Fujii, and Superior Court Judge Wilbur Curtis ruled that the state was right in taking such an action. Fujii appealed the Superior Court's judgment to the California Supreme Court, which reversed the Superior Court decision by a four to three decision. The state's highest court ruled that California's Alien Land

Act prohibiting aliens ineligible for U.S. citizenship from holding land was in violation of the equal protection clause of the U.S. Constitution as well as the Constitution of California.

FUJIMOTO, CHARLES K. *See* Hawaii Seven.

FUJITA YOSHIRO, secretary to Japanese Consul Chinda Sutemi,* who was stationed in San Francisco. Fujita's superior asked him to tour the Pacific Northwest in an attempt to investigate living conditions among Japanese immigrants. He set out in July 1891 and headed first for Seattle, which had approximately 250 Japanese. Of these he could find only 40 people who were involved in legitimate businesses or occupations; the rest were involved in gambling, prostitution, or pimping. Upon finding this, he urged local Japanese community leaders to take vigorous actions against the undesirable elements in the community in cooperation with American authorities, but he got little response from either Japanese or local authorities. From Seattle Fujita moved to Port Blakely on Bainbridge Island where he was told that 80 Japanese were among 500 people employed at a local sawmill. Arriving at the sawmill early in the morning, he was able to find only 50 people; the rest were in the bunkhouse gambling. He was very discouraged by what he saw in Seattle and Port Blakely. In Tacoma he was pleasantly surprised to learn that of the 90 Japanese living there, none was involved in either gambling or prostitution. From Tacoma he went to Spokane and Portland where he found local conditions similar to those of Seattle. On his train trip back to San Francisco he discovered Japanese in residence at almost every stop. He regretted learning that almost all of these people were involved in houses of pleasure or gambling.

Fujita's superior, Chinda, submitted the report with no comments to his superior in Tokyo. The report indicated that there were many types of Japanese immigrants from different walks of life. Each was capable of engaging in illegal activities for his survival. Some Japanese were law-abiding citizens, but others were parasites and hoodlums. Sometimes whites only saw the bad elements within the Japanese community and pointed to them as a threat to their way of life.

FUKUNAGA CASE, a case involving the kidnapping and killing of Gill Jamieson in 1928 by Myles Fukunaga, a Nisei* born to Japanese plantation workers in Hawaii. Gill, the son of a prominent banker, Frederick Jamieson, vice-president of the Hawaiian Trust Company, was kidnapped on September 18, 1928, by Myles Fukunaga, who felt he had a score to settle with the Hawaiian Trust Company.

Fukunaga's parents had come to Hawaii only for work and always intended to go back to Japan. Myles, a loyal son, planned the kidnapping so that his parents would have enough money to return to their homeland. Another reason why he kidnapped Jamieson had to do with the treatment his mother received from a representative of the Hawaiian Trust Company who had come to Myles' home to collect rent money for the company. His mother begged the collection agent to wait one more month as she did not have enough money as a result of Myles' illness. But the man refused and demanded immediate payment. After the man left, Myles overheard his mother crying in her room; this hurt him deeply.

Following this incident Myles devised a plan to kidnap Jamieson for ransom money. He demanded $10,000 after Gill was kidnapped, $4,000 of which he received. For reasons unknown, however, Myles killed Gill and left a crude cross made of sticks on top of the boy's body. Myles was apprehended on September 23, and his trial began on October 3.

During the trial the Japanese community in Hawaii was mobilized to assure a fair trial for Fukunaga. The editor of *Hawaii Hochi*, Fred Makino, demanded in his editorials that Myles be given a thorough test for sanity. The Japanese community raised money to send Myles' parents back to Japan and hired a psychologist, J. C. Thompson, to examine Myles. Thompson stated that Myles was insane, but the court decided otherwise. On October 8, only five days after the trial had begun to determine the young man's fate, Judge A. Steadman read his decision, sentencing Myles to death by hanging. A series of unsuccessful court appeals followed, but the U.S. Supreme Court refused to hear his case. Myles was executed on November 19, 1929.

FURTHER READING: Gavan Daws, *Shoal of Time*, Honolulu: University Press of Hawaii, 1968; Lawrence H. Fuchs, *Hawaii Pono*, New York: Harcourt, Brace and World, 1961; Dennis Ogawa, *Jan Ken Po: The World of Hawaii's Japanese Americans*, Honolulu: University Press of Hawaii, 1973.

FUN KUNG, one of two work systems commonly used among the Chinese in Hawaii. *Fun kung*, which literally means "divide work," refers to a cropper arrangement between a landlord and a group of workers organized under a manager, chosen from among the workers and held responsible for making arrangements with the landlord concerning income as well as working conditions. It was said that the landlord demanded 60 percent of the income from a rich rice farm and 50 percent from a less rich farm.

After the annexation of Hawaii, Chinese workers sought to be hired not as individuals but as members of a group, and wanted to share the profits with the landlord. With no major supply of Chinese workers after the annexation, the landlord was often compelled to comply with their demands. (*See also Hop Pun.*)

FURTHER READING: Clarence E. Glick, *Sojourners and Settlers*, Honolulu: University Press of Hawaii, 1980.

FURUYA MASAJIRO (1862–?), businessman who established the Japanese Commercial Bank in Seattle in 1907 and purchased the Oriental American Bank in 1913. Furuya was one of the first enterprising businessmen in the Japanese community of Seattle. (*See also* Japanese Commercial Bank.)

FUSANG, the name of the country which Hui Shen* claimed he discovered on his journey to the East. Hui Shen stated that the land of Fusang was located 20,000 *li*, or 7,000 miles, to the east of China. This historical claim was recorded in the Forty-first Book of Chuan, in the 230th volume of the *Great Chinese Encyclopedia*, compiled between 502 and 556 A.D.

A number of studies have been done on the question of whether or not the Chinese discovered America before Columbus. These studies have not definitively established whether the land discovered by Hui Shen was America. There still remains the question: Who first discovered America? Chinese or Europeans?

FURTHER READING: George Chapman, *History of California*, New York: Macmillan Co., 1951; Stan Steiner, *Fusang: The Chinese Who Built America*, New York: Harper and Row, 1979; Edward P. Vining, *Inglorious Columbus: or, Evidence that Hwui Sahn and a Party of Buddhist Monks from Afghanistan Discovered America*, New York: Appleton, 1885.

G

GA-MAN, a Japanese term meaning ''internalization'' and ''suppression of anger and emotion,'' according to Harry H. L. Kitano.* As a part of the Japanese traditional value system, it helps to explain the behavior of Japanese who endure hardship in life without overtly showing their feelings. This may also help explain the Caucasian view of the Japanese as inscrutable.

GANEN-MONO, a group of Japanese immigrants who came to the Hawaiian Islands on June 19, 1868 to work on sugar plantations after they were recruited by Eugene Van Reed, an agent for the Hawaiian Sugar Planters' Association.* A motley group of 141 Japanese consisting of artisans, ex-samurai, intellectuals, criminals, and a few farmers were recruited off the streets of Yokohama and were sent to Hawaii in 1868, the first year of the Meiji Restoration. The term *Ganen-mono*, which means ''the first year men,'' is derived from the fact that this group of Japanese immigrants were the first Japanese who came to Hawaii during the first year of the Meiji Restoration.
FURTHER READING: Francis Hilary Conroy, *The Japanese Expansion into Hawaii, 1868–1898*, San Francisco: R. and E. Research Associates, 1973; Dennis M. Ogawa, *Kodomo no tame ni* (For the Sake of the Children), Honolulu: University Press of Hawaii, 1978.

GAPITIS, a term originating from the false notion held by many American administrators at Fort Indian Town Gap, Pennsylvania, one of the four Indochinese Refugee Reception Centers* established by the U.S. government in 1975. The administrators believed that the Vietnamese refugees at the center did not want to leave because they had developed a sense of security and they feared life outside the refugee center. The administrators could not understand why so many Vietnamese refugees were refusing the American sponsorship which would help them leave the camp. Many saw their unwillingness as a sign of a pathological

or psychological illness that was not common to Americans. They believed that the refugees fabricated reasons to stay in the camp, unaware of the brighter life that was possible for them outside the camp—a life of freedom, educational opportunity, and potential happiness.
FURTHER READING: Gail P. Kelly, *From Vietnam to America*, Boulder, Colo.: Westview Press, 1977.

GEARY ACT OF 1892, a law passed in the wake of the renewal of the Chinese Exclusion Act of 1882,* one of several bills used to regulate Chinese immigration. Mounting public pressure was applied to Congress and the President for action against the imagined increase in Chinese immigration. Originally, the Chinese Exclusion Act established a conditional time limit of ten years. When this time period elapsed, the same bill was renewed with supplemental regulations. This supplement to the original Chinese Exclusion Act, the Geary Act, was initiated by Thomas Geary, a Democrat from California, who had succeeded in his effort to expel Chinese from Sonoma County. The bill, as submitted by Congressman Geary, sought to prohibit all Chinese (except diplomats and merchants) from coming to the United States. After adding a number of amendments, the House passed the bill by a vote of 178 to 43, with 108 abstentions. Thus, the Chinese Exclusion Act of 1882 was extended for another decade. The Geary Act prohibited the entry of Chinese laborers into the United States, provided for the deportation of any Chinese considered unlawful alien residents in America, denied bail to any Chinese during habeas corpus proceedings, and required that all Chinese carry a certificate of residence.

The last provision was the most critical for persons of Chinese ancestry living in America. All Chinese were required to obtain their certificate of residence within one year after passage of the bill, and they had to produce a white witness willing to testify that they were lawful residents. No person of Chinese ancestry was allowed to serve as a witness for another Chinese. Any Chinese unable to produce the certificate of residence was liable to deportation, and anyone found falsifying a certificate was to be fined $1,000 or imprisoned for not more than five years.

Several Chinese communities challenged the constitutionality of the Geary Act and had it tested in the courts. The Chinese government sent letters of protest against this discriminatory legislation. Nonetheless, the Supreme Court upheld the law in 1893 in the case of Fong Yue Ting v. United States.*
FURTHER READING: Mary R. Coolidge, *Chinese Immigration*, New York: Henry Holt and Co., 1909; Edward P. Hutchinson, *Legislative History of American Immigration Policy, 1798–1965*, Philadelphia: University of Pennsylvania Press, 1981.

GEE KUNG TONG. *See Tongs.*

GENERAL DEFICIENCY APPROPRIATION ACCOUNT ACT OF 1904, a bill extending Chinese exclusion laws. During the 58th Congress, three bills called for revision of the Chinese exclusion laws, and a fourth bill was introduced by Edward James Livernash of California, who wanted to prohibit Chinese from working on vessels carrying the American flag, but this particular bill was not reported out of committee. However, a section strengthening the Chinese exclusion laws was included in a deficiency bill. It was approved by Congress and became the Act of April 17, 1904.

Section 5 of the act was relevant to Chinese exclusion, for it continued and extended, without modification, the limitation and condition of Chinese exclusion laws. According to this section, the Chinese exclusion laws were applicable to the island territory under the jurisdiction of the United States, and Chinese were prohibited from moving to the U.S. mainland from such island territory.

Congress passed this act in response to the Chinese government's decision to terminate the 1894 treaty between China and the United States after the end of its ten-year period. The Chinese government had been under pressure from nationalists in China who demanded that the government end unequal treaties.

GENTLEMEN'S AGREEMENT, a 1907 agreement whereby the San Francisco School Board rescinded its segregation order and Japan agreed to withhold passports from Japanese workers seeking to migrate to the United States. After the Chinese Exclusion Act of 1882,* Japanese immigration to the Western United States began to increase. Because of the racist sentiment of Americans on the West Coast, especially in California, the San Francisco Board of Education ordered the exclusion of Japanese, Korean, and Chinese children from the public schools under its jurisdiction on October 11, 1906. The Japanese government charged that the board's action violated the Treaty of Commerce and Navigation between the two nations, as concluded on November 22, 1894.* In order to avoid a potential international crisis, President Theodore Roosevelt invited the San Francisco School Board to Washington for a conference and concluded an agreement that allowed all aliens in the United States to attend public schools providing the students demonstrated a familiarity with the English language, were under the age of sixteen, and had an educational level that was the equivalent of their grade age. The San Francisco Board rescinded its segregation order in March 1907, and a potential international crisis was avoided. This agreement was not without a price for the Japanese government. In order to placate the Californians, who opposed the immigration of Japanese laborers, President Roosevelt and Secretary of State Elihu Root negotiated the Gentlemen's Agreement with Japanese Foreign Minister Hayashi Tadasu. Talks between Tokyo and Washington had begun in December 1906 in an attempt to negotiate an acceptable level of Japanese immigration to the United States. With the San Francisco school segregation issue out of the way, the two governments were able to reach an agreement in 1908. As part of the agreement, the Japanese government voluntarily withheld passports from Japanese laborers who wanted to go to the United States, with the exception of previous U.S. residents who had returned to Japan, and the wives, children, and parents of current residents in the United States. The agreement also closed Japanese immigration to the United States through Hawaii, Mexico, and Canada.

FURTHER READING: Rodman W. Paul, *The Abrogation of the Gentlemen's Agreement*, Cambridge, Mass.: Harvard Phi Beta Kappan, 1936 (included in Roger Daniels, ed., *Three Short Works of Japanese Americans*, New York: Arno Press, 1978); Yamato Ichihashi, *Japanese in the United States*, Stanford, Calif.: Stanford University Press, 1932; Thomas A. Bailey, *Theodore Roosevelt and the Japanese-American Crises*, Stanford, Calif.: Stanford University Press, 1934.

GEORGE, HENRY (1839–1897), economist. George was born on September 2, 1839, to a middle-class family in Philadelphia. He is best known for his book, *Progress and Poverty* (1879), in which he advocated the idea of a single tax system. His basic premise was that private ownership of land causes unequal distribution of wealth, and, therefore, it should be replaced with common ownership of land.

In his lifetime George was known as a champion of the working man, but this championship was for whites only. He was an outspoken opponent of coolie* labor and Chinese immigration, which became a rallying point for the labor leaders of his time. The Chinese laborers were definitely a convenient scapegoat for California's economic ills in the 1870s, but today's historians have perceived many diverse causes, which were not limited to problems in California.

George sincerely believed that the availability of cheap Chinese labor would drive down wages for all, thereby reducing trade and decreasing sales. George seemed to have had difficulty justifying his anti-Chinese sentiment on purely economic grounds; his claim that Chinese labor hurt the white labor force was, therefore, combined with his notion that the Chinese could not be assimilated into the American culture. His vitriolic racist comments published in the *New York Tribune* on May 1, 1869, stirred up a great deal of emotion in both New York and San Francisco. In his letter he denounced the Chinese as "utter heathens, treacherous, sensual, cowardly, and cruel," who practice "all the unnameable vices of the East."

George died of a stroke on the morning of October 29, 1897. His service was attended by an estimated 100,000 people.

FURTHER READING: Charles A. Baker, *Henry George*, New York: Oxford University Press, 1965; Henry George, *Progress and Poverty*, New York: Robert Schalkenbach Foundation, 1936; "The Chinese in California," *New York Tribune*, May 1, 1869.

GHADAR REVOLUTIONARY PARTY, a political party organized on November 1, 1913, in San Francisco, where representatives of various Asian Indian organizations gathered together to found a Hindu Association of America. According to other authorities, however, the Ghadar Party was founded on the already existing organizational basis provided by the Hindu Association of the Pacific Coast,* which was established in May 1913. The party decided to publish a weekly newspaper, beginning on November 1, 1913, under the name of *Ghadar*, meaning "rebellion," in commemoration of the Sepoy Mutiny of 1857 in Urdu, Marathi, and Gurumukhi.

Asian Indians began to come to the United States by way of Canada at the beginning of the twentieth century. By 1910 there were as many as 30,000 in the three states of the Pacific Coast. Although they were officially classified as Hindus, most of them were Sikhs from Punjab. They were subject to racial discrimination in California where they worked as farmers and cannery workers. A number of events awakened their political sense. First, events in Egypt, China, Ireland, and Turkey gave them hope that they too would attain political freedom from the British Empire. Second, the arrival of young Indian intellectuals intensified their feelings of patriotism and their yearning for liberty. One of these young intellectuals in California was Har Dayal,* who had been given a scholarship to study at Oxford after his graduation from the St. Stephen's College in 1905. He eventually gave up his scholarship and later immigrated to the United States.

In 1911 Dayal was invited to teach at Stanford University but was forced to withdraw because of his political views and activities; he then traveled up and down the Pacific Coast and talked about the need for revolution. He worked hard to found an organization called the Hindu Association of the Pacific Coast in May 1913, and with the help of Tarak Nath Das, Ram Chandra,* and others was able to establish the Ghadar Revolutionary Party. Har Dayal had to flee the United States because of his political activities, which Britain had asked the U.S. government to suppress.

Although Har Dayal provided leadership for the party when it was needed, his flight from the United States in 1914 left the responsibility of caring for the party with such leaders as Baba Sohan Singh Bhakna and Ram Chandra. Chandra had reportedly said that Indians desired nothing less than the establishment in India of a republic, a government of the people, by the people, and for the people of India. Under the able leadership of Ram Chandra, the party was able to smooth over the differences between Muslims and Hindus and embarked on various revolutionary projects. One of the most ambitious projects involved the sending of armed revolutionaries to India to start a revolution. This plan was conceived of and financed by the German government during World War I. In Berlin, a committee called the German Union of Friendly India was organized on September 4, 1914, and it was to orchestrate its plan to send Indian revolutionaries to India through the German embassy in the United States. The Berlin Committee sent Chandra Kanta Chakravarty to the United States to plan for the mission and gave him $50,000. Ram Chandra received $1,000 monthly from the German consulate in San Francisco.

Chakravarty was arrested in New York on March 6, 1917, for violation of the Neutrality Laws, and Ram Chandra was placed under arrest after the United States declared war. Other co-conspirators were arrested in San Francisco and Chicago, and the trial of thirty-five of the original defendants began on November 20, 1917. On the last day of the trial, Ram Chandra was killed by Ram Singh, another defendant, who was in turn killed by a federal marshal. All defendants, except one American, were found guilty.

These incidents dealt a serious blow to the Ghadar Party, which was reorganized in 1919 in an attempt to revitalize its revolutionary activities. Although the party resumed its party publications in 1923, a number of its members deserted the party and joined the international Communist movement by 1925.

FURTHER READING: S. Chandrashekhar, *From India to America: A Brief History of Immigration; Problems of Discrimination; Admission and Assimilation*, La Jolla, Calif.: A Population Review Book, 1982; R. C. Majumdar, ed., *Struggle for Freedom*, Bombay, India: Bharatiya Vidya Bhavan, 1969; H. Brett Melendy, *Asians in America*, Boston: Twayne Publishers, 1977; Haridas T. Muzumdar, *America's Contributions to India's Freedom*, Allahabad, India: Central Book Depot, 1962; G. S. Deol, *The Role of the Ghadar Party in the National Movement*, Delhi: Sterling Publishers, 1969.

GHADAR SYNDROME, the idea that a militant nationalist movement among Asian Indians abroad was an outlet for the frustration they had experienced in their struggle to achieve social and economic justice for themselves and their children. Therefore, it means the infusion of nationalistic pride with ethnic identity among Asian Indians.

GHOSE, SAILENDRA NATH. *See* Friends of Freedom for India.

GIBSON, WALTER MURRAY (1823–1888), advocate of importing agricultural labor to Hawaii from Malaysia. Gibson was born to English immigrants, lived in South Carolina before he came to Hawaii, and arrived in Honolulu on July 4, 1861. He claimed to represent the Church of the Latter Day Saints and collected money to purchase property he had registered in his name on the Island of Lanai. Mormons in Hawaii questioned his claim and asked Brigham Young to send a team of investigators to report on Gibson's conduct. After the investigation he was excommunicated from the church.

Gibson believed that the Hawaiian Kingdom needed a repopulation of the natives. He expressed his major views on repopulation in his ''Address to the Hawaiian People'' in 1876. As editor of *Nuhou Hawaii*, he had a powerful position through which he advocated ''Hawaii for Hawaiians.'' But his extreme nationalism won him many enemies, who finally united to overthrow him. He was forced into exile in San Francisco, where he died on January 21, 1888.

FURTHER READING: Lawrence H. Fuchs, *Hawaii Pono*, New York: Harcourt, Brace and World, 1961; Sylvester K. Stevens, *American Expansion in Hawaii, 1842–1898*, New York: Russell and Russell, 1945; Merze Tate, *The United States and the Hawaiian Kingdom*, New Haven, Conn.: Yale University Press, 1965.

GOKHALE, SHANKAR, LAXMAN v. UNITED STATES, a case involving the question of whether the lower courts could revoke existing citizenship rights. Ever since February 19, 1923, when the U.S. Supreme Court handed down its decision on the question of whether or not an Asian Indian should be eligible for U.S. citizenship in the case of United States v. Bhagat Singh Thind* the government threatened to cancel the citizenship of a number of Asian Indians who had obtained their U.S. citizenship before 1923. In one such case Gokhale of Schenectady, New York, had been working as a research engineer for General Electric since 1912, but his citizenship was canceled by District Appellate Court action. He appealed to the U.S. Supreme Court, which reversed the lower court's decision and ordered it to dismiss the government's bill of complaint. In its decision, the Supreme Court ruled that the lower courts did not have the power to revoke existing citizenship rights.

FURTHER READING: H. Brett Melendy, *Asians in America*, Boston: Twayne Publishers, 1977; Gokhale v. United States, 178 U.S. 662.

GOLDEN MOUNTAIN. *See* California Gold Rush of 1849.

GOLETA, CALIFORNIA, a small town located near Santa Barbara, California, where the only Japanese attack on the U.S. mainland occurred when a Japanese submarine fired a few ineffective volleys on oil installations on February 23, 1942. Although concern with protecting military installations on the Pacific Coast was the dominant reason for the decision to remove and evacuate persons of Japanese ancestry after the Japanese attack on Pearl Harbor, this was the only attack known on the U.S. mainland.

GOMPERS, SAMUEL (1850–1924), labor leader. Gompers was born on January 27, 1850, in a poor section of London, England, where he grew up and attended a Jewish free school. He was soon forced to leave school in order to take up an apprentice job in a shoe-making industry. After working with a local cobbler, he turned to his father's trade of cigar-making. His father, Solomon Gompers, immigrated to New York in 1863 and brought Samuel with him. At an early age he joined the Cigarmakers Union in 1864 because he was convinced that every wage earner should join the union of his trade. Thirteen years later he was elected president of the Cigarmakers Union and worked to improve the economic conditions of his union's members.

Unable to complete his formal education and yet yearning to learn more about the world around him, Gompers attended high school and actively participated in debates at Cooper Union on the East Side of New York. Discussions in the cigar-making shop became early labor forums where many radical labor leaders came to express their views. One of them was Feridant Laurrel, whom Gompers later acknowledged as his best teacher. Laurrel translated Karl Marx's *Communist Manifesto* and taught union members about trade unionism and the history of the struggle to improve laboring class conditions.

Gompers was a champion of Chinese exclusion because Chinese cigarmakers were considered a threat to the members of the Cigarmakers' International Union.* In 1878 it was estimated that there were approximately 40,000 cigarmakers in the United States, and nearly a quarter of them were Chinese, whose standard of living was considered lower than that of white laborers. White cigarmakers strongly felt that they could not compete with their Chinese counterparts, simply because the Chinese were willing to work more for less money. They called for concrete measures to deal with Chinese immigration and pressured politicans to end Chinese immigration.

Gompers and Adolph Strasser organized the American Labor Movement, which was the beginning of persistent unionism in America. Once the movement was unleashed, it became a singular unifying force of American workers who were divided among themselves by their religion, language, political ideology, as well as their ethnic membership.

In 1881 Gompers was instrumental in establishing the Federation of Organized Trade and Labor Unions of the United States and Canada, and was elected president of that body the following year. Four years later the organization changed its name to the American Federation of Labor. Gompers earned the title of "Labor Statesman" because of his conservative and yet work-oriented unionism, the principle of which advocated unionism within the existing economic system.

During World War I President Woodrow Wilson appointed Gompers to serve on the Council of National Defense, an office he used effectively to show the American public that American labor stood behind the government. Although he won many battles for his union members, he suffered many losses toward the end of his life: he lost his wife and daughter, and he lost his health as a result of Bright's Disease, which made him nearly blind. He lost many members of the American Federation of Labor, whose reputation was tarnished when corruption within the organization was revealed.

In 1924 Gompers collapsed while attending a meeting of the Pan-American Federation of Labor in Mexico City. A train rushed to bring him across the border to America. He died on December 13, 1924, in San Antonio, Texas.

FURTHER READING: Jack Chen, *The Chinese of America*, New York: Harper and Row, 1980; Martin H. Greenberg, *The Jewish Lists*, New York: Schocken Books, 1979; Bernard Mandel, *Samuel Gompers; A Biography*, Yellow Springs, Ohio: Antioch Press, 1963; Dave and Inez Morris, *Who was Who in American Politics*, New York: Hawthorn Books, 1974.

GONG LUM et al. v. RICE et al., a case initiated by Gon Lum, father of Martha Lum, who filed for a petition of writ of mandamus to be directed to the trustees of the Rosedale Consolidated High School District, ordering them to admit his daughter, born in the United States, therefore a citizen of America, to a Rosedale high school. The trial court ordered a writ of mandamus, but school officials appealed to the Supreme Court of Mississippi, which heard the case and reversed the decision of the trial court.

The Court heard the arguments on October 13, 1927, and decided on November 21, 1927. In their arguments before the Court, the plaintiffs claimed that Martha was not a member of the colored race and was an educable child, a citizen of the United States who was entitled to attend the schools provided by law in the State of Mississippi. Denying her the right to attend a high school attended by white students was a violation of the Fourteenth Amendment of the Constitution, they argued. The defendants claimed that Martha was a person of Mongolian race, and therefore not entitled to attend the schools provided for the children of the Caucasian race.

The main question before the Court was whether or not the State of Mississippi had the right to deny Martha the right to attend a school attended by white children. Chief Justice William Howard Taft delivered the opinion of a unanimous court. In his opinion he declared that the state had the right to separate white children from children of other races as long as separate facilities were provided for them. In essence, the court upheld the "separate but equal" doctrine that was voiced in the case of Plessy v. Ferguson in 1896.

FURTHER READING: Milton R. Konvitz, *The Alien and the Asiatic in American Law*, Ithaca, N.Y.: Cornell University Press, 1946; *Supreme Court Reporter*, 48, 275 U.S. 78, 1927.

GOO KIM FUI. *See* United Chinese Society.

GOVIL, HARI G. *See* India Society of America.

GRAN ORIENTE FILIPINO ("Great Filipino Lodge"), a communal organization established in 1920 in San Francisco. The group had 700 members, 100 of whom were women. It was known as one of the "Big Three," along with Caballeros de Dimas-Alang* and Legionarios del Trabajo,* and it was imported from the Philippines.

GRAPE STRIKE, DELANO, organized in 1965 by Filipino agricultural workers. The effort of the Filipino Agricultural Laborers Association to organize Filipino workers under the leadership of the American Federation of Labor initially failed, but the Congress of Industrial Organizations continued to increase its Filipino membership. When the two organizations were merged in 1955, its council decided to organize the Agricultural Workers Organizing Committee, and it hired Larry Dulay Itliong,* a Filipino, to serve as an organizer of the new group.

On September 8, 1965, Filipino agricultural workers decided to strike grape growers in Delano, California, under the leadership of Itliong for their union recognition and higher wages. When grape growers brought in Mexican grape pickers soon after the strike, Itliong came to Cesar Chavez, head of the National Farm Workers Association, to seek his help. Chavez, though initially reluctant to support Filipinos, decided to join the strike on September 16. Although it was a labor strike against grape growers in California, it rapidly developed into a cause for the civil rights movement both for Chicanos and Filipinos, thereby raising their consciousness concerning their economic and social status in America.

In order to carry out the strike successfully, the leaders appealed to the conscience of college students, religious leaders, and civil rights workers, many of whom came to Delano to help the striking workers resist local pressure. Chavez and Itliong sought the active assistance of politicians such as Robert Kennedy; the association created a great deal of national publicity for the cause of striking workers.

The strike was long and its struggle bitter, but finally, with the intervention and arbitration of the National Conference of Catholic Bishops, which decided to create an *ad hoc* Delano Committee, major growers decided to recognize the United Farm Workers Organizing Committee* as the bargaining agent in April 1970.

FURTHER READING: Lorraine J. Crouchett, *Filipinos in California*, El Cerrito, Calif.; Downey Place Publishing House, 1982; John D. Dunne, *Delano*, New York: Farrar Straus and Giroux, 1971; Paul Fusco and George D. Horowitz, *La Causa, The California Grape Strike*, New York: Macmillan Co., 1970; Dick Meister and Anne Loftis, *A Long Time Coming: The Struggle to Unionize Farm Workers*, New York: Macmillan Co., 1972.

GREAT EASTERN BUSINESS CORPORATION, a small business firm incorporated by the Korean National Association* of North America on March 1, 1910, when it decided to issue 1,000 stock certificates at $50 to capitalize a model farm in Manchuria. However, as a result of a poor decision in selecting the business site, the whole venture failed, costing the association $3,000.

GREAT MAHELE OF 1848, a new land ownership system undertaken by the Board of Land Commissioners of Hawaii on the recommendations of American advisers. Previously, the king had owned all land, and no foreigners were allowed to buy or lease land to justify capital investment on a large scale.

In accordance with the principles adopted by the Board of Land Commissioners, the lands were divided into three equal parts: one part for the king, another for the chiefs, and the third for the tenants or landowners. A committee was formed to develop seven rules by which the lands were to be divided, and with the adoption of the rules, the mahele, or division, was signed on March 7, 1848. On the following day King Kamehameha III divided his own land into two parts: one part called crown land, which was to be his own property, and the other larger part, which would be known as government land.

As a result of the Great Mahele, foreigners rushed to purchase land from chiefs who were eager to get rich quickly. These foreigners then invested their capital in developing and cultivating land for sugar production. Their sugar production plans were further aided by the passage of the Masters and Servants Act of 1850,* which established a Hawaiian Board of Immigration to import workers for the sugar plantations. The new legislation allowed entrance to Hawaii to all immigrants who carried at least $50 and who could prove they could be self-supporting. Although the Great Mahele and the Masters and Servants Act of 1850 paved the way for sugar production, only through the California Gold Rush of 1849,* the American Civil War, and the Reciprocity Treaty of 1875* did sugar become enthroned as Hawaii's king. In 1897 Hawaii's exports totaled $16.2 million, $15.4 million of which was in sugar export.

FURTHER READING: John J. Chinen, *The Great Mahele*, Honolulu: University of Hawaii Press, 1958; Lawrence H. Fuchs, *Hawaii Pono*, New York: Harcourt, Brace and World, 1961; Theodore Morgan, *Hawaii: A Century of Economic Change, 1778–1876*, Cambridge, Mass.: Harvard University Press, 1948; Sylvester K. Stevens, *American Expansion in Hawaii, 1842–1898*, New York: Russell and Russell, 1945.

GREAT STRIKE OF 1909, a labor action that occurred on May 9, 1909, when several hundred Japanese laborers on the Aiea Plantation went on strike demanding higher wages. The strike spread rapidly: workers on Waialua went on strike on May 19, Kahuku followed suit on May 22, and soon after Waianae, Ewa, and Waimanalo workers joined in. A total of approximately 7,000 Japanese workers went on strike under the leadership of the Higher Wage Association.*

The strike divided the Japanese community, and the Hawaiian Sugar Planters' Association* was quick to use this division against the striking workers. Sheba Sometaro, editor of the *Hawaii Shimpo*, warned the striking workers against using violence and advised them to go back to work. His attitude toward the strike and Japanese workers earned him the sobriquet "Planter's Dog," and he was often associated with the interests of the Hawaiian Sugar Planters' Association. The association hired Chinese, Portuguese, Hawaiians, and Koreans as strikebreakers to replace Japanese, and it refused to negotiate with the striking Japanese workers. The association also used different tactics to break the will of the striking workers. They were evicted from their homes and separated from their leaders, some of whom were arrested and tried on charges of conspiracy.

One of the striking members, Mori Tomekichi, made an attempt on the life of Sheba Sometaro, who was seriously wounded. Two days later, on August 5, 1909, the strike leaders met together and decided to call off the strike. Their struggle for better living conditions and higher wages was not made in vain, however; on November 29, 1909, the Hawaiian Sugar Planters' Association decided to raise the wages of Japanese laborers and abolished the system of wage differentiation on the basis of nationality.

FURTHER READING: Lawrence H. Fuchs, *Hawaii Pono*, New York: Harcourt, Brace and World, 1961; Dennis M. Ogawa, *Kodomo no tame ni* (For the Sake of the Children), Honolulu: University Press of Hawaii, 1978; Ronald Takaki, *Pau Hana: Plantation Life and Labor in Hawaii*, Honolulu: University of Hawaii Press, 1983.

GREAT UNITY FATHERLAND PROTECTION SOCIETY, a patriotic organization established among Koreans in America between 1905 and 1908 dedicated to protecting the political independence of Korea and to eliminating Japanese colonial interests from Korea. On March 23, 1908, a member of the society, Chang In-hwan,* shot and killed Durham Stevens, an American employed by the Japanese to justify their occupation of Korea. (*See also* Chang In-hwan.)

GRESHAM-YANG TREATY. *See* Treaty of 1894 Between China and the United States.

GUBERNATORIAL CAMPAIGN OF 1867 IN CALIFORNIA, a campaign dominated by the racial issue. On June 19, 1867, the Democrats met in convention in San Francisco and elected as their candidate, Henry H. Haight,* who pledged loyalty to the state platform and to the principles of the party. One of these principles was the party's commitment to oppose Chinese suffrage and to protect the Pacific states from Chinese and Mongolian immigration. The post-convention campaign was dominated by issues concerned with the influx of Chinese into California, and the Democrats were strongly opposed to Chinese labor. It could be said that the campaign was decided in favor of the anti-Chinese party and the anti-Chinese candidate.

In comparison with the Democratic Party, the Union Party that had nominated George C. Gorham sent a mixed message to the California voters. During their convention the Unionists adopted a resolution calling for restriction on Chinese immigration but did not address the question of Chinese suffrage. Gorham, however, opposed Chinese suffrage, even though he had previously written to the Anti-Coolie Association in San Francisco, indicating that he favored cheap labor, opposed anti-coolie associations (though he was also against coolieism), and believed in the brotherhood of humankind, implying that the Asiatic brethren should also be included in that brotherhood. In the heat of campaign he was compelled to recant much of his letter and to adopt a more anti-Chinese posture. His switch on Chinese labor came too late, and he lost his gubernatorial bid to Haight. (*See also* Anti-Coolie Clubs.)

FURTHER READING: John Shertzer Hittell, *History of the City of San Francisco*, San Francisco: A. L. Bancroft and Co., 1878; H. Brett Melendy and Benjamin F. Gilbert, *The Governors of California*, Georgetown, Calif.: Talisman Press, 1965; Alexander Saxton, *The Indispensable Enemy: Labor and the Anti-Chinese Movement in California*, Berkeley and Los Angeles: University of California Press, 1971.

GUEY HEUNG LEE v. JOHNSON, a case heard before the U.S. Supreme Court in 1971 involving a Chinese pupil who was reassigned to another public school in San Francisco by the San Francisco Unified School District as part of its comprehensive plan to achieve school desegregation. The plan called for reassigning children of Chinese ancestry who had been attending almost exclusively segregated schools, accommodating pupils of Chinese ancestry. Chinese parents whose children were reassigned applied for a stay for pending appeal, based on the claim that reassignment would mean that their children could not maintain their cultural heritage and could not learn the language of their parents. Justice William O. Douglas, in his opinion for the Court on August 25, 1971, ruled in favor of the San Francisco Unified School District by applying the principles established in Brown v. Board of Education in 1954 and Swann v. Mecklenburg in 1970. He reasoned that, because there had been no evidence that the San Francisco School District had eliminated all discrimination, the Chinese request should be denied.

FURTHER READING: Nicholas Appleton, *Cultural Pluralism in Education*, New York: Longman, 1983; U.S. Reports, Vol. 404, 1215, 1971.

GUILDS, CHINESE, craft and business guilds found among Chinese workers employed in the cigar-making, garment, and shoe-making industries. These guilds were highly protective and monopolistic, carefully guarding their interests against outside competition. Although they were allegedly established to protect the workers' economic interests, they exercised tight control over workers whose income, mobility, and opportunities were strictly regulated.

The Tung Dak Tong was a guild of Chinese employed in the cigar-making industry, whereas the Lei-Shing Tong was a shoe and book manufacturing guild. The garment industry had three guilds among the Chinese: the Tung Yip Tong, the Gwing Yi Hong,* and the Gum Yi Hong.*

FURTHER READING: Gunther Barth, *Bitter Strength*, Cambridge, Mass.: Harvard University Press, 1964; Jack Chen, *The Chinese of America*, New York: Harper and Row, 1980; Stanford M. Lyman, *Chinese Americans*, New York: Random House, 1974; Alexander Saxton, *The Indispensable Enemy*, Berkeley: University of California Press, 1971.

GULICK, SIDNEY L. (1860–1945) professor of theology, writer, promoter of peaceful relations between Japan and the United States. Gulick served as a congressional Minister in Kumamoto, Japan, and taught at Doshisha University in Kyoto for twenty-six years. In his capacity as professor of theology, he became acquainted with Japanese political leaders, delivered many lectures, and wrote about sensitive issues surrounding Japanese immigration to the United States and potential problems between the two nations.

In order to help solve problems relating to Japanese immigration, Gulick accepted the challenge of establishing a council to study the rising tensions between Japan and America. The American Board of Missionaries in Japan asked him to approach the Federal Council of the Churches of Christ in America about establishing such a council. He then became secretary of the council in 1914.

Gulick also served as secretary of the American Branch of the World Alliance for Promotion of International Friendship Through the Churches, the National Committee for Constructive Immigration Legislation, and the National Committee on World Friendship Among Children. He wrote many books, including *American Democracy and Asiatic Citizenship* (1918) and *The American Japanese Problem* (1914).

In his proposal regarding legislation for Asiatic immigration, Gulick suggested that Asiatic immigration be controlled and that Asians be allowed only a certain percentage of those who were already naturalized citizens of the United States or American-born. The National Committee for Constructive Immigration Legislation soon adopted his position, which was written into law, with modifications, as the Immigration Act of 1921 and the Immigration Act of 1924.*

FURTHER READING: Roger Daniels, *The Politics of Prejudice*, Berkeley: University of California Press, 1962; Sidney L. Gulick, *The American Japanese Problem*, New York: Charles Scribner's Sons, 1914.

GULLION, ALLEN WYANT (1880–1946) provost marshal general of the U.S. Army during World War II and participant in Japanese evacuation. Gullion was born on December 14, 1880, at Carrollton, Kentucky, to Edmund A. and Atha Gullion. He graduated from Centre College in 1901 with a B.A. degree and from the U.S. Military Academy in 1905. Upon graduation he was commissioned as second lieutenant of infantry. After two years' service in the Philippines, he taught at the State University at Lexington, Kentucky. In 1914 he received a law degree from that same institution.

Gullion attained the rank of major general and became the judge advocate general of the army on December 1, 1937, and provost marshal general on August 2, 1941. In his capacity as provost marshal general, he was intimately involved in both private and public meetings at which the plan for evacuating all persons of Japanese ancestry was discussed. He supported the general evacuation plan. He was privy to President Franklin Roosevelt's decision and so easily obtained a draft copy of Executive Order 9066.* On the night of February 17, 1942, just two days before Executive Order 9066 was officially proclaimed, he read it to a group of government officials gathered together at the residence of U.S. Attorney General Francis Biddle.* Knowing that the order was forthcoming, he alerted all commanding generals of all corps areas to the impending Japanese evacuation on February 17, 1942.

Gullion advocated the evacuation and removal of all persons of Japanese ancestry on the basis that the writ of habeas corpus was not as important as what he saw as military necessity.*

GUM YI HONG (Guild of Brocaded Clothing), a guild organized in 1880 among Chinese employed in the garment industry making overalls and other work clothes. The guild grew in number and in strength to regulate work hours and to bargain on wages. In 1967 it was the last Chinese garment industry guild to go out of business. (*See also* Guilds, Chinese.)

GUPTA, HERAMBA LAL, a German agent of Asian Indian origin who was sent to the United States in 1915 to plot against the British government in India. (*See* Hindu Conspiracy, 1914–1917.)

GWING YI HONG (Guild of Bright Clothing), a guild organized among Chinese employed in the garment industry making shirts, ladies garments, and undergarments. It disappeared in the 1920s. (*See* Guilds, Chinese.)

H

H. HACKFELD AND COMPANY, the predecessor of American Factors (known today in Hawaii as Amfac), established in Germany in 1849 by Heinrich Hackfeld in order to finance sugar plantations. Its transfer to the Hawaiian Islands proved to be successful, and by the early 1880s it was responsible for financing eighteen major sugar plantations, which constituted more than one-third of Hawaii's total.

In 1897 the company became interested in importing Korean workers. It had been advised to look into the possibility of bringing them to Hawaii by a Russian who claimed to have some influence on the Russian legation office in Korea where King Kojong* was in hiding. This scheme to import Koreans to replace Chinese and Japanese laborers did not materialize, probably because King Kojong left the Russian legation before all the necessary arrangements could be made. FURTHER READING: Wayne Patterson, *The Korean Frontier in America: Immigration to Hawaii, 1896–1910*, Ann Arbor, Mich.: University Microfilms International, 1979.

HAAN KILSOO. *See* Sino-Korean People's League.

HAIGHT, HENRY H. (1825–1878), governor of California. Haight was born on May 20, 1825, in Rochester, New York. He graduated from Yale University with high honors in 1844. He later studied law and was admitted to the Missouri bar in 1847. He followed the gold fever in California, arriving at San Francisco via the Isthmus of Panama on January 20, 1850. He was the Democratic Party's candidate for governor in 1867 and ran hard on an anti-Chinese platform and defeated the Union Party candidate, George C. Gorham.* Throughout his political career he was known for his anti-Chinese stance. (*See also* Gubernatorial Campaign of 1867 in California.)

HAKKA, a term that literally means guest dwellers in Chinese and refers particularly to those Chinese in the southeastern part of China whose ancestors migrated from northeastern provinces in the early thirteenth century. By the turn of the seventeenth century, the Hakkas were found in the mountain regions of the Pearl River Delta,* where they began to acquire land through their diligence and thrift. They spoke their own dialect, and their women refused to bind their feet, which enabled them to work as hard as the men. Because of their distinct cultural differences from the Punti* or native people, a number of conflicts developed, and in 1868 the Hakkas suffered a great loss in their war against the Punti. Their women were captured and sold as servants and prostitutes.

These two peoples continued their conflict in California, where they fought each other with as much violence and vengeance as in their native land. The Hakkas in California developed their own association called the Jenho hui-kuan (the Yan Hop Company).

FURTHER READING: Gunther Barth, *Bitter Strength*, Cambridge, Mass.: Harvard University Press, 1964; Stanford M. Lyman, *Chinese Americans*, New York: Random House, 1974; Shih-shan Henry Tsai, *China and the Overseas Chinese in the United States, 1868–1911*, Fayetteville: University of Arkansas Press, 1983.

HAMADA HIKOZO (1837–1897), first Japanese American citizen. Hamada was born in the Province of Harima, Japan, to a farmer, and his childhood name was Hikotaro. In 1850 he sailed for Edo, but his ship was wrecked in a typhoon and he was rescued by the American sailing ship *Auckland*. He was brought to San Francisco where he attended school and he had a job as the collector of customs. Later he moved to Baltimore where he attended a Roman Catholic school and was eventually converted to Christianity. He was baptized a Catholic and took the Christian name of Joseph Heco. He was the first Japanese American, becoming a naturalized American citizen on July 7, 1858.

In 1860 Hamada went to Japan with E. M. Dorr, the newly appointed American consul in Kanagawa, in order to serve as interpreter, but he resigned and returned to the United States when the anti-foreign feelings rampant among the Japanese posed a threat to his safety. Returning to Japan in 1862, Hamada served in the American Consulate Office briefly before opening a new import-export business in Yokohama. He also published a Japanese newspaper in Yokohama, the *Kaigai Shimbun*, which was the first privately published newspaper in Japan. In 1872 he took a government job in the Ministry of Finance but resigned two years later. In 1895 he published his autobiography, *The Narrative of a Japanese*.

HAMPTON, CHAIRMAN, U.S. CIVIL SERVICE COMMISSION v. WONG MOW SUN, a decision handed down on June 1, 1976, centering on whether a Civil Service Commission policy was constitutional and within the discretionary power of that agency. The Civil Service Commission's policy under question defined those eligible for civil service employment as being ''American citizens.''

The plaintiffs, Wong Mow Sun et al., were all lawfully and permanently residing aliens of Chinese ancestry, each of whom, though qualified, was denied federal employment solely on the basis of race. The defendant was Civil Service Commission chairman Robert E. Hampton. Class-action proceedings began in the North District Court of California. The plaintiffs alleged that the advantage given to citizens applying for federal civil service jobs was arbitrary and violated the due process clause of the Fifth Amendment and a specific executive order which forbids discrimination because of national origin. The district court ruled that "national origin" referred to prohibitive discrimination among citizens, national origin being their cultural heritage. The court therefore held that the Civil Service Commission discrimination was constitutional.

The plaintiffs appealed to the Ninth Circuit Court of Appeals. During the two years pending in that court, the Supreme Court decided two cases that were similar. In Sugarman v. Dougal (413 U.S. 634), a New York civil service law which said, in essence, that only U.S. citizens could hold permanent positions in the state's civil service, was found to violate the equal protection clause of the Fourteenth Amendment. Also in reference to Griffiths (413 U.S. 717), the Supreme Court ruled that the exclusion of aliens from the practice of law as sanctioned by the State of Connecticut was unconstitutional.

The Court of Appeals recognized that the Congress and the President, not the states, had power over immigration and naturalization. The Appeals Court reversed in favor of the plaintiffs. While accepting the argument that citizenship might be required in positions involving policymaking and national security interests, it held that the Civil Service Commission's regulation violated the due process clause of the Fifth Amendment.

The defendants petitioned for certiorari, and the Supreme Court granted it. They also petitioned to change the question: to decide whether the Civil Service Commission regulation was within the constitutional powers of Congress and the President. The defendants argued that reserving the federal services for citizens provided an incentive to aliens to qualify for naturalization and thereby participate more effectively in society. In addition, the citizenship requirement had been in effect in the United States for 100 years and conformed to international law. Most foreign countries require undivided loyalty in sensitive civil service positions. This clearly justifies a citizenship requirement in at least some parts of the civil service, and the broad exclusion of aliens serves an administrative purpose of avoiding the trouble and expense of classifying those positions that are executive or sensitive in nature.

After reviewing various precedent cases, the Supreme Court stated that Congress and the President had the constitutional power to impose the requirement which the Civil Service Commission adopted. The Civil Service Commission assumed that the national interests of the Congress and President adequately supported the policy of their regulation. The Court ruled that because these lawful resident aliens were admitted as a result of decisions made by Congress and the President, due process required that the decision to deprive them of certain liberties be made at a comparable level of government or by the Civil Service Commission if it was properly within their concern; in this case, it was not. It was also the opinion of the Court that by denying employment to the lawful aliens, the Civil Service Commission deprived them of liberty without due process of law. Therefore, the Supreme Court affirmed the judgment of the Court of Appeals. FURTHER READING: A. Peter Mutharika, *The Alien Under American Law*, Vol. 1, New York: Oceana Publications, 1981, pp. 83–100; U.S. Reports, Vol. 426, 426 U.S. 88, 1976.

HANAPEPE MASSACRE, an incident arising in 1924 out of a labor strike called by the members of the Filipino Federation of Labor* under the leadership of Pablo Manlapit.* The massacre occurred on September 9, 1924, when sixteen striking union members and four policemen were killed in a violent confrontation between police and workers at Hanapepe, Kauai. (*See also* Filipino Federation of Labor.)

HANIHARA MASANAO (1876–1932), Japanese ambassador to the United States. Hanihara was born to an aristocratic family in Japan. He entered diplomatic service after his formal education serving in Washington from 1902 to 1911. In 1922 he was appointed Japan's ambassador to Washington, Earlier, from 1902 to 1911, he had served in Washington where he was known as "Hany" to government officials—from the President to State Department clerks.

When Congress began to debate immigration bills introduced by Albert Johnson* in the House of Representatives and Senator Henry Cabot Lodge* in the Senate, Hanihara had an interview with the Secretary of State and voiced his concern about a provision in the proposed bills which excluded aliens ineligible for U.S. citizenship. Congress held public hearings on the bills and summoned witnesses from California, who included such anti-Japanese advocates as Valentine Stuart McClatchy,* James D. Phelan,* and Ulysses S. Webb.

Despite these three men's efforts to influence Congress in favor of excluding Japanese from immigration, the House Committee reported out a bill different from the one proposed, and it left the matter of Japanese immigration to be dealt with under the Gentlemen's Agreement.* Because of the nature of the agreement, however, Hanihara, as Japanese ambassador to America, was asked to clarify various provisions. Instead of making a general summation, Hanihara commented on the pending immigration bill, stating that enactment of the immigration bill with exclusion of Japanese would produce "grave consequences." Senator Lodge, interpreting these two words as a threat to the United States, thereupon influenced his colleagues to vote in favor of Japanese exclusion. FURTHER READING: Yamato Ichihashi, *Japanese in the United States*, Stanford, Calif.: Stanford University Press, 1932; Robert Wilson and Bill Hosokawa, *East to America*, New York: William Morrow and Co., 1980.

HANKA ENTERPRISE COMPANY, a construction company established by Hahn Si-dae, who came to America as an immigrant from Korea in 1905. He and his family established the company in Delano, California, in the early 1920s. At the end of World War I, he bought agricultural land and expanded his company land holdings to 400 acres. His company also went into the apartment construction business in Inglewood, California. The company employed many Koreans, including some Korean students. Hahn sold his business after World War II and returned to Korea.

HAOLE, a Hawaiian term for white Americans or Caucasians. It originally meant "foreigners." Natives are called *kanaka*.
FURTHER READING: Andrew W. Lind, *Hawaii's People*, Honolulu: University Press of Hawaii, 1980.

HARE-HAWES-CUTTING ACT, the first legislation, passed by Congress in 1933, promising political independence to the Philippine Islands, following a ten-year interim period after passage of the act. Historians have proposed several theories as to why this act was passed at a time when no major colonial powers in Europe had even contemplated relinquishing their power over their colonies. The most prevalent theory is that economic factors prevailing in America during the Great Depression pushed the Hare-Hawes-Cutting Bill through Congress.

When the Congress began to discuss Philippine independence, America was already in the throes of the Great Depression. Businessmen and corporations that had invested heavily in the Philippine Islands, fearing the great losses which the independence of the islands would bring, lobbied against any legislation that would grant independence to the islands.

Among those who favored Philippine independence were organizations and associations that basically opposed Filipino immigration to the United States as well as duty-free imports of goods and materials from the islands. When the debates on the Hare Bill in the House of Representatives and on the Hawes-Cutting Bill in the Senate began, people on both sides of the aisle were sharply divided on the question, not only on the basis of economic interests, but also on ideological grounds. Democrats were pro-independence, whereas Republicans were protective of America's interests in the Philippines, and inevitably they voted along this ideological line. When the final tallies were made on the Hare Bill in the House, the votes were 306 to 47 for passage, with all the nay votes coming from Republicans. The Hawes-Cutting Bill did not fare as well in the Senate as the Hare Bill did in the House; nevertheless, it passed after a number of amendments were added to the original bill.

The Hare Bill had a provision granting the Philippine Islands political independence, following an interim period of eight years, and the Senate passed its version of the Philippine independence act, granting political independence to the islands with an interim period longer than the ten-year period the House approved. A conference committee compromised on an interim period of ten years. President Herbert Hoover vetoed the bill, but Congress overrode his veto on January 17, 1933.

Many political leaders in the Philippines, including Manuel Quezon,* viewed the act as disastrous to the islands' economy, for Philippine exports to the United States would face increasing tariff rates at the same time that American exports to the Philippines would be admitted free. Quezon led the opposition to the act, and he came to Washington, D.C., for a conference with the new President, Franklin Roosevelt. Quezon was unable to influence Congress to come up with better legislation, and Congress enacted a bill similar to the Hare-Hawes-Cutting Act. This was the Tydings-McDuffie Act,* which passed in Congress on March 23, 1934, and the President signed it on the following day. On May 1, 1934, the Philippine legislature approved the Tydings-McDuffie Act.

In 1935 the people of the Philippine Islands approved the constitution and elected Quezon as President. He was sworn in on November 15, 1935. Thus, the Commonwealth of the Philippines came into being.

As a result of the Tydings-McDuffie Act, Filipino immigration to the United States was limited to an annual quota of fifty people during the interim period, which was then to be followed by the exclusion of immigrants from the islands to the United States.

FURTHER READING: Theodore Friend, *Between Two Empires: The Ordeal of the Philippines, 1929–1946*, New Haven, Conn.: Yale University Press, 1965; Manuel Gallego, *The Price of Philippine Independence Under the Tydings-McDuffie Act*, Manila: Barristers' Book Co., 1939; E. D. Hester, "Outline of Our Recent Political and Trade Relations with the Philippine Commonwealth," *Annals of the American Academy of Political and Social Science* 226 (1943); Grayson V. Kirk, *Philippine Independence*, New York: Farrar and Rinehart, 1936.

HARRISON, FRANCIS B. (1873–1957), Congressman, governor-general of Philippines. Harrison was born on December 18, 1873, in New York City to Burton Norvell Harrison, who served as private secretary to Confederate President Jefferson Davis. He graduated from Yale University in 1895 and studied law at the New York Law School. He was admitted to the bar in 1898 but did not practice law. Instead, he taught evening classes at the New York Law School before joining the armed services at the outbreak of the Spanish-American War.

In 1902 Harrison won a seat in Congress, and two years later he ran for lieutenant governor of New York but lost. In 1906 he again ran for Congress and was elected to serve three terms. While in Congress, he served on a number of influential committees and became known as a consistent anti-imperialist who criticized official policies toward American colonies, particularly the Philippines. He established himself as a liberal Democrat following in the footsteps of Woodrow Wilson. When Wilson became President in 1913, he appointed Harrison governor-general of the Philippines, and with this appointment a new era between America's colony and its mother country was ushered in: Filipinization. Between 1913 and 1921, when Harrison left the Philippines, he pursued policies established to encourage the rapid transfer to power over the government and economy from Americans to Filipinos, who were increasingly given lower-echelon governmental positions. After the passage of the Jones Act in 1916,* Harrison transferred much of his power to the Filipino Senate, which was created by the 1916 law. His policy of Filipinization incurred the anger and hostility of the American residents who soon began to lose their advantages over the Filipinos. During his term in office as governor-general, the number of Americans in government service decreased from 2,624 to 614, either through forced resignation or unbearable working conditions.

Harrison's contribution to the independence of the Philippine Islands from the United States was so great and far-reaching that when he died on November 21, 1957, he was given a state funeral by the government of the Philippines, where he was buried.

FURTHER READING: Beth Day, *The Philippines: Shattered Showcase of Democracy in Asia*, New York: M. Evans and Comp., 1974; George Farwell, *Mask of Asia*, New York: Frederick A. Praeger, 1966; Joseph Hayden, *The Philippines: A Study in National Development*, New York: Macmillan Co., 1942.

HARTE, BRET (1836–1902), writer. Francis Bret Harte was born in Albany, New York, on August 25, 1836. His father had taught at the Albany Academy and then operated a private school in their home. A year later, during hard times, his father's school failed, and Bret's father became a wandering schoolmaster. The elder Harte moved his family from city to city, while they existed at a bare subsistence level. One amenity the Harte home possessed in all its travels was a small but excellent library. At the age of six, when he was home from school due to ill-health Bret began reading Shakespeare. When Bret was nine years old, his father died and left the family penniless. At this point, Bret's mother turned to Bret's paternal grandfather for assistance. He was a well-to-do man who came through and set the family up in a high style of living. At eleven, Bret made his debut in print with a poem entitled "Autumn Musings," which was published in the *Sunday Morning Atlas*. When he showed the poem to other members of the family, he was ridiculed for the juvenile sentiments expressed in the verse. He continued his schooling until he was thirteen. He worked in a law office for a year and then in a counting house until he was seventeen when he traveled to California with his mother and stepfather.

The years Bret Harte spent in California were vitally important in inspiring much of his life's work. Of particular importance was the year he spent as a Wells Fargo messenger working among the diverse groups of gold-seekers, immigrants, and local ethnic groups (e.g., Chinese, Mexicans, and Indians). This experience provided a sharp contrast both to his earlier years of upbringing with a family of education and culture in the East and to his later years of international fame and foreign service.

Harte lived in California from 1854 to 1871. During this time he was employed by many different periodical publications to which he also contributed much of his own work. Harte frequently used his editorial power to condemn white racism. For example, he was editor of *The Northern Californian* when the Mud River Indian Massacre took place in 1860. He wrote a very strong editorial against the people involved in the massacre, and for this trouble he was run out of town and almost killed. Harte used his writing to make a social statement and placed particular emphasis on the underprivileged in society.

In March, 1854 Harte moved to the San Francisco area where he wrote many of his short stories. One of them, *Tales of the Argonauts*, deals with a Chinese boy in America. Harte later became editor-in-chief of *The Overland Monthly*, through which he developed a reputation for printing the best material possible. This paper published Harte's most famous poem, "Plain Language from Truthful James," better known as "The Heathen Chinee." He wrote the poem as a light parody. He himself did not even like it and did not want to publish it. He finally did have it published, but against his better instincts.

The poem became the rallying point for the anti-Chinese movement, just the outcome Harte had feared. He had consistently opposed racial prejudice and was especially disgusted by the harsh treatment of the Chinese in northern California. The poem was about two white Christian males who invite a Chinese person to play poker with them in hopes of cheating the "ignorant Chinaman." It turns out that Ah Sin, the Chinese, beats the two white men, because Ah Sin was better at their style of poker—cheating! Ah Sin was finally run out of the game because he had more cards up his sleeve than any one of the white players. Harte viewed the success of the poem as a confirmation of the widespread prejudice that the Chinese were notable for "ways that are dark" and "tricks that are vain."

FURTHER READING: Geoffrey Bret Harte, ed., *The Letters of Bret Harte*, New York: AMS Press, 1973; Elaine H. Kim, *Asian American Literature*, Philadelphia: Temple University Press, 1982; Robert McClellan, *The Heathen Chinee*, Columbus, Ohio: Ohio State University Press, 1971; Patrick David Morrow, *Bret Harte*, Boise, Idaho: Boise State College, 1972; George R. Stewart, Jr., *Bret Harte: Argonaut and Exile*, Port Washington, N.Y.: Kennikat Press, 1959.

HASHIMURA TOGO. *See* Irwin, Wallace.

HATCHETMAN. *See Boo How Doy.*

HAWAII, ANNEXATION OF, effected by the U.S. Congress in 1898. Several factors led to the annexation of Hawaii by the United States. During the 1830s Hawaii began to experience international pressure from British, French, German, and American claims. These countries wanted economic privileges, and finally the United States was able to negotiate with the Kingdom of Hawaii for a treaty through James Jackson Jarves, who was appointed by the king of Hawaii to negotiate with the United States. The Jarves-Clayton Treaty of 1849 called for "reciprocal liberty of commerce and navigation," which established between the two countries the principle of mutual tariff arrangements with no discrimination against each other.

The independence of the islands was preserved, and mutual aid and the exchange of goods between the two countries was secured. The already existing relations were strengthened by means of the Reciprocity Treaty of 1875.* The negotiation between the two countries on the question of leasing Pearl Harbor was difficult, but eventually King Kalakaua agreed, thereby extending the reciprocity agreement in 1887 another six years. But the growing American influence in Hawaii caused grave concern for the king, who then decided to strengthen the monarchy.

The kings who followed Kamehameha V (who had advocated Hawaii for the Hawaiians) became increasingly anti-American. Alarmed, a group of American reformers finally decided to take the destiny of the Hawaiian Islands into their own hands by means of a bloodless revolt in June 1887, which forced King Kalakaua to proclaim a new constitution. Peace was once again restored, but the political situation grew worse in the 1870s after the McKinley Tariff Act deprived Hawaii of its economic advantages in the United States. In 1893 a conspiratory organization, the Committee of Safety,* was organized under the leadership of William O. Smith and began to work toward the annexation of Hawaii. On July 6, 1898, the Senate passed the joint resolution for the annexation of Hawaii. Hawaii's sovereignty was handed over to the United States on August 2, 1898, when Congress made Hawaii a Territory of the United States, effective as of midnight, June 13–14, 1900. Annexation brought new opportunities for Hawaii. Although the Chinese Exclusion Act of 1882* was applied to Hawaii, thus excluding Chinese immigration, other people from Asia were allowed to come as laborers for the Hawaiian Sugar Planters' Association.* The demand for more laborers was created as a result of annexation and the Reciprocity Treaty of 1875.

FURTHER READING: Gavan Daws, *Shoal of Time*, Honolulu: University Press of Hawaii, 1968; A. Grove Day, *Hawaii and Its People*, New York: Duell, Sloan and Pearce, 1955; Sylvester K. Stevens, *American Expansion in Hawaii, 1842–1898*, New York: Russell and Russell, 1945; Merze Tate, *Hawaii: Reciprocity or Annexation*, East Lansing: Michigan State University Press, 1968.

HAWAII, REPUBLIC OF. *See* Dole, Sanford Ballard.

HAWAII EMPLOYERS COUNCIL, an organization made up of the five major corporations in Hawaii, the Big Five,* in connection with a number of small business firms. The council was created in 1943 in order to cope with anticipated labor demands, particularly demands to be made by the International Longshoremen's and Warehousemen's Union* which began to organize workers on sugar plantations. The two organizations locked horns to test their strength in a strike in the sugar industry on September 1, 1946, when 21,000 workers on thirty-three plantations walked off the job. During the strike that lasted seventy-nine days, 6,000 Filipino laborers were imported from the Philippines to be used on various plantations. But eventually Castle and Cooke, one of the Big Five, decided to settle its differences with the labor union and other companies fell into line.

FURTHER READING: Gavan Daws, *Shoal of Time*, Honolulu: University of Hawaii Press, 1968; Lawrence H. Fuchs, *Hawaii Pono*, New York: Harcourt, Brace and World, 1961.

HAWAII EQUAL RIGHTS COMMISSION, an organization created before World War II but renamed the Hawaii Statehood Commission in January 1947, when the territorial legislature accepted the proposal made in 1944 by the Equal Rights Commission to change its name. (*See also* Hawaii Statehood Commission.)

HAWAII REHABILITATION ACT (also known as the Hawaiian Homes Commission Act of 1920), passed by the U.S. Congress after the territorial legislature of Hawaii asked that Congress provide public lands for the purpose of rehabilitating native Hawaiians. The rehabilitation movement was led by Prince Jonah Kuhio who advocated Hawaii for the Hawaiians. In 1919 Prince Kuhio and John Wise, a part-Hawaiian member of the territorial Senate, were responsible for pushing through the territorial legislature a resolution asking Congress to provide public lands. Although Kuhio and the Big Five* characterized the act as "a triumph of justice for the Hawaiians," it had very little impact on restoring land for the Hawaiians. The act provided people with at least half-Hawaiian ancestry with homestead rights under a ninety-nine-year leasing agreement for a dollar a year. Approximately 185,000 acres were set aside for this purpose. But the real intention, as the Big Five saw it, was to prevent homesteading on sugar lands by eliminating a section from the Organic Act of 1900* which stated that with the expiration of a lease valuable sugar land could be withdrawn from lease land and be made available for homesteading, provided there were twenty-five applicants for homesteading. Although almost 200,000 acres of land were set aside for homesteading, only a small part of it was good for agricultural purposes, for forest reserves and land used for cultivating sugar were excluded from homesteading.

   High hopes for rehabilitating the Hawaiians through the act were not to be realized, partly because of the overriding sugar interest of the Big Five and partly because of Hawaiians' inability to cope with white institutions.

FURTHER READING: Gavan Daws, *Shoal of Time*, Honolulu: University Press of Hawaii, 1968; Lawrence H. Fuchs, *Hawaii Pono*, New York: Harcourt, Brace and World, 1961; Theon Wright, *The Disenchanted Isles*, New York: Dial Press, 1972.

HAWAII SEVEN, seven Hawaiians charged in 1953 with conspiracy against the U.S. government. Traditionally, Hawaii followed the conservative policies of the ruling Republican Party, which used sordid tactics to retain power, as demonstrated by the party's questionable use of the Smith Act. The law made it a criminal offense to conspire to teach and advocate the overthrow of the government; people in power used it against those who presented a threat to the present political system. On August 28, 1951, the Federal Bureau of Investigation (FBI), acting under provisions of the Smith Act, arrested Charles K. Fujimoto, a self-proclaimed Communist; his wife, Eileen Fujimoto, a member of the Communist Party Executive Board as early as 1946; Ariyoshi Koji, editor of the party-line weekly, *Honolulu Record*; Dwight Freeman; and Jack D. Komoto. These people, along with Jack Hall and John Reinecke, were charged with conspiring to overthrow the government. They became known as the Hawaii Seven.

Most of these seven people, particularly Jack Hall, were well known in Hawaii, and at least five of them were among the so-called Reluctant Thirty-Nine,* who had refused to answer leading questions put to them by the House Committee on Un-American Activities hearings in Honolulu in 1950. The Reluctant Thirty-Nine were later acquitted of all charges.

The Hawaii Seven were given their day in court; they were tried in 1953 and were found guilty as charged. They were sentenced to fines of $5,000 and given jail terms of five years each. They appealed while they were free on bail. In January 1958, the U.S. Circuit Court of Appeals in San Francisco reversed the conviction of the Hawaii Seven when it ruled that the abstract teaching of communism did not constitute conspiracy to overthrow the government by force or violence as defined in the Smith Act.

Hawaii has always been dominated by a single political party. Until 1954, the business establishment used the Republican Party to direct and control Hawaii's society and economy. Following World War II, militant labor organizations pushed their way into "co-equal status" with business, gaining a share of governing power. Along with organized labor which began to challenge the Republican monopoly of power, the incident involving the Hawaii Seven helped to undermine the traditional base of Republican political hegemony. In addition, the independent faction within the Democratic Party, led by John Anthony Burns* and Daniel Inouye* brought about the shift in political power in Hawaii in 1954.

FURTHER READING: Gavan Daws, *Shoal of Time*, Honolulu: University Press of Hawaii, 1968; A. Grove Day, *Hawaii: Fiftieth State*, New York: Meredith Press, 1962; Francine du Plessix Gray, *Hawaii: The Sugar-Coated Fortress*, New York: Random House, 1972; Edward Johannessen, *The Hawaiian Labor Movement*, Boston: Bruce Humphries, 1956; Paul C. Phillips, *Hawaii's Democrats: Chasing the American Dream*, Washington, D.C.: University Press of America, 1982; Theon Wright, *The Disenchanted Isles*, New York: Dial Press, 1972.

HAWAII STATEHOOD COMMISSION, originally created in 1935 as the Hawaii Equal Rights Commission by the territorial legislature. The commission was charged with assuring that Hawaii would receive equality with other states in federal legislation and with studying the feasibility of submitting the issue of Hawaii's statehood to a plebiscite. The commission authorized Governor J. B. Poindexter to work with the congressional delegation on the question of statehood.

Twenty different congressional hearings were held between 1935 and 1958, and during these hearings more than 1,000 witnesses were called to testify on the matter of Hawaii's statehood. In the meantime, the name of the Hawaii Equal Rights Commission was changed to the Hawaii Statehood Commission.

Hawaii's struggle for statehood was a long, hard one. Beginning with its annexation to the United States in 1898, Hawaii's political battle with Congress lasted at least more than half a century before it won admission as the fiftieth state on March 12, 1959. This was the longest period of time any state had to wait in the history of the United States.

There was a marked division between the opponents and supporters of statehood, but finally the supporters began to emerge as the stronger political force. Groups as diverse as the Hawaiian Sugar Planters' Association* and the International Longshoremen's and Warehousemen's Union* (ILWU) were strong supporters of Hawaii's statehood.

The commission was in need of support groups, and it used them effectively to further its cause for statehood. Of course, organizations such as the Hawaiian Sugar Planters' Association donated money to the commission, for it saw monetary benefits that would come its way as a result of Hawaii becoming a state. The commission made elaborate preparations so that the territory's qualifications as a state would not be questioned either by the members of Congress or by others who opposed Hawaii's statehood. By the early 1950s it became evident that Hawaii could no longer be denied the statehood it had been seeking; it was paying more in federal tax than nine of the mainland states, although it had no effective voice in Congress to represent the people of Hawaii.

After Hawaii was admitted to the Union, elections were held to send its representatives to Congress for the first time. One U.S. Senate seat went to Hiram Fong,* the son of an immigrant from China, and Daniel K. Inouye* was elected to serve in the House of Representatives. More surprising to most political observers was the election of Patsy Takemoto Mink,* a woman of Japanese descent, to serve in the House. Her election broke every rule of orthodox American politics.

FURTHER READING: Gavan Daws, *Shoal of Time*, Honolulu: University Press of Hawaii, 1968; Lawrence H. Fuchs, *Hawaii Pono*, New York: Harcourt, Brace and World, 1961; Theon Wright, *The Disenchanted Isles: The Story of the Second Revolution in Hawaii*, New York: Dial Press, 1972.

HAWAIIAN EVANGELICAL ASSOCIATION, organized in 1854 as part of the effort of the American Board of Commissioners for Foreign Missions* to encourage native Hawaiian pastors to participate in church affairs. Once organized, it replaced the Sandwich Island Mission and extended its membership to native pastors. This step was particularly important in view of the fact that approximately one-fourth of the whole population of Hawaii were members of churches under this association. By 1870 there were fifty-eight churches with a membership of 14,850 people.

HAWAIIAN HOMES COMMISSION ACT OF 1920. *See* Hawaii Rehabilitation Act.

HAWAIIAN LEAGUE, established in January 1887 under the leadership of Dr. S. G. Tucker and Lorrin A. Thurston, following their conversation on the need for such a secret and conspiratory organization on December 26, 1886. The organization was established to demand and secure reform in government. During the first meeting, members of the organization drew up a constitution. After they memorized its contents, they destroyed it because they considered it too dangerous to keep. The members pledged their property, lives, and sacred honor to the organization's purpose and swore to keep secret the existence of the organization.

Later, the members of the organization discussed how to reform the government and what to do with King Kalakaua.* Volney Ashford, a member of the organization, suggested that the king be killed and that government offices be filled with members of the organization. This was too radical an alternative to more moderate members like Sanford Ballard Dole* and Peter Jones who resigned from the organization when they realized that its radical members would soon dominate.

The Hawaiian League, together with the Honolulu Rifles Company, pushed through a new constitution which the king (Kalakaua) was forced to proclaim on July 1, 1887.

HAWAIIAN NATIVE CLAIMS SETTLEMENT ACT, presented before a Congressional Subcommittee on Indian Affairs on February 11 through 14, 1975. The subcommittee was chaired by Representative Lloyd Meeds of Washington. The hearings were held on each of the six Hawaiian Islands. These hearings represented an attempt to reimburse the native Hawaiians for the loss of identity and property they experienced as the result of the U.S. intervention in the overthrow of the monarchy in 1893.

The United States government had made an attempt to compensate native Hawaiians through the Hawaiian Homes Commission Act of 1920, known also as the Hawaii Rehabilitation Act,* which provided land for homestead to anyone who could prove they were one-half or more Hawaiian. The Hawaiian Native Claims Settlement Act, H.R. 1944, proposed to go beyond this in order to provide compensation to anyone of Hawaiian blood. H.R. 1944 was sponsored by Representatives Spark Matsunaga* and Patsy Mink* of Hawaii.

The terms of the Settlement Act involved establishing a Hawaiian Native Fund with $1,000,000,000 appropriated from the general fund of the Treasury. This money was to be appropriated as $100,000,000 the year the Act was passed and $100,000,000 per year for nine successive years. The money was to be invested at interest and be administered by a Hawaiian Native Corporation, whose membership would include every Hawaiian native whose name appeared on the roll. Certificate of membership would be cancelled upon the death of a member, but benefits accrued to that time would be distributed to the beneficiaries. The Act, however, died in committee and there has been no attempt to revive it or introduce a bill similar to it.

FURTHER READING: U.S. Congress. House Committee on Interior and Insular Affairs, Hawaiian Native Claims Settlement Act, Part I, Hearings before the Subcommittee on Indians Affairs on H.R. 1944, 94th Congress, 1st Session, Washington, D.C.: U.S. Government Printing Office, 1974.

HAWAIIAN PROVISIONAL INFANTRY BATTALION, created in 1942 expressly for Japanese servicemen in Hawaii. Even before Pearl Harbor, there were Nisei* Japanese in American uniform in Hawaii. The 198th and 299th Infantry Regiments had approximately 1,500 Nisei men guarding shore lines and military installations. The military felt uneasy about integrating servicemen of Japanese ancestry with other servicemen, who complained that they did not want to work with "Japs." As a result of these factors, it was decided in June 1942 to establish the Hawaiian Provisional Infantry Battalion, also known as the 100th Infantry Battalion. It was shipped to Camp McCoy, Wisconsin, and was later transferred to Camp Shelby, Mississippi.

Later, the 100th Infantry became the 1st Battalion of the 442nd Regimental Combat Unit.*

HAWAIIAN REVOLUTION OF 1893. *See* Committee of Safety.

HAWAIIAN SUGAR PLANTERS' ASSOCIATION, originally established as the Royal Hawaiian Agricultural Society on April 29, 1850, when a meeting of all farmers and agricultural workers was held and formed a society to improve and coordinate Hawaiian agriculture. For the first five years, the society was led by Judge William Little Lee, who was later replaced by J. F. B. Marshall. While these two presidents presided over the society, the annual meetings prospered with much enthusiasm. The society even had a limited program of scientific experimentation, including the use of improved strains of plants and animals. Its low financial capability, however, limited this research.

From the beginning of the society, labor shortage was one of the major problems. The California Gold Rush of 1849* lured many potential Hawaiians away to the mainland. At the same time, a need for potatoes and other miscellaneous vegetables prompted many workers to leave regular jobs and become farmers. In addition, with the altered land system, many natives became small-scale landowners. All these factors, when combined with the decrease in the native population, worked to cause a labor shortage. Laborers were badly needed on the plantations.

At a meeting held in early 1850, the society decided to import foreign laborers and made an arrangement with the captain of the British ship, *Thetis*, which brought almost 200 Chinese from Amoy on January 3, 1852. Later that year, the same ship brought more Chinese, and they were employed immediately to work on sugar plantations. After that, importing foreign laborers for plantation work became the society's policy.

In 1850 King Kamehameha III proclaimed the need for foreign capital and labor to aid the need for increased cultivation of the soil. The legislature passed two laws: the first outlawed natives from immigrating to other countries with some special exceptions, and the second law, known as "For the Government of Masters and Servants," made contract labor a legal system. Judge Lee had no problem in passing these laws on the day of their introduction. Apparently, no one realized how big the Hawaiian sugar industry would become, and no one was able to predict the harshness of the Masters and Servants Act of 1850.*

Another major problem facing Hawaii at that time was the need for capital. Judge Lee explained that lack of enough money was the major obstacle to success in the islands. By 1850 the government was forced to stop lending money to business groups; public funds were almost entirely allocated to much needed public improvement projects. Although a bank charter bill was introduced, nothing was done to make it a law. Around 1852 market problems developed for Hawaii as a result of a high import tariff charged on Hawaiian sugar imported to mainland United States. To make matters worse, Manila and China were selling sugar much cheaper to their foreign markets. Consequently, a depression hit Hawaii in 1851–1852. Hawaii needed to be able to sell to the United States without the 30 percent duty tax. The Hawaiian king agreed to free import of flour, fish, coal, and lumber from the United States in exchange for free export of its products, such as sugar, coffee, and syrup, to the United States. This first attempt at a reciprocity agreement by Hawaii was not reciprocated by the United States.

The society merged with the Planters' Society on April 1, 1865, and became known as the Planters' Society. Two years later, it was incorporated, but in 1869 the society was dissolved, and its property and liabilities were turned over to the Hawaiian government.

The Reciprocity Treaty of 1875,* concluded between the United States and Hawaii in 1875, produced a sugar boom in Hawaii. It also created renewed interest in developing an organization among planters who felt their interests would be better protected if they worked together. On March 20, 1882, fifty-five planters, agents, and other persons met and created an organization called the Planters' Labor and Supply Company, which published the *Planters' Monthly*. The organization continued to operate until November 25, 1895, when its name was changed to the Hawaiian Sugar Planters' Association. The main purposes of the association were to improve the sugar industry, to support an experimental station and laboratory, to maintain a sufficient supply of labor, and to develop agriculture in general.

The association maintained one of the strongest lobby groups in Washington, D.C., in order to influence Congress for legislation favorable to its sugar interests. It vigorously worked toward solving labor problems which continued to plague the sugar industry in Hawaii. Through aggressive recruiting efforts undertaken by the association, Japanese, Korean, and Filipino workers, among others, were brought to Hawaii to work on sugar plantations. (*See also* Masters and Servants Act of 1850.)

FURTHER READING: Gavan Daws, *Shoal of Time*, Honolulu: University Press of Hawaii, 1968; Ralph S. Kuykendall, *The Hawaiian Kingdom, 1874–1893*, Honolulu: University of Hawaii Press, 1967; Wayne Patterson, *The Korean Frontier in America: Immigration to Hawaii, 1896–1910*, Ann Arbor, Mich.: University Microfilms International, 1977; Ronald Takaki, *Pau Hana: Plantation Life and Labor in Hawaii*, Honolulu: University of Hawaii Press, 1983.

HAWAIIANOS, Ilocanos* who returned to the Philippines after they had lived in Hawaii or on the mainland.

HAYAKAWA, SAMUEL ICHIYE (1906–   ), scholar, college president, U.S. senator. Hayakawa was born on July 18, 1906, to Japanese parents in Vancouver, British Columbia, Canada. He received a B.A. degree in psychology from the University of Manitoba in 1924, a Master's degree from Magill University in 1930, and the Ph.D. from the University of Wisconsin.

Much of Hayakawa's later scholarship centered on the study of the English language. He is a scholar of world reputation in the field of semantics, a topic in which he is considered a pioneer. He is the author of *Language in Action* (1941), *Language in Thought and Action* (1949), *Language, Meaning and Maturity* (1954), *Our Language and Our World* (1959), *Symbol, Status, and Personality* (1963), and *Through the Communication Barrier* (1979). In addition, he has also done some writing for newspapers. He wrote a column for the Chicago *Defender* for five years (1942–1947), and he was a columnist for the *Register and Tribune Syndicate* from 1970 to 1976.

Hayakawa spent many years on college campuses both as a professor and as a college president. He taught English at the Illinois Institute of Technology (1940–1942), the University of Wisconsin (1936–1939), the University of Chicago (1950–1955), and San Francisco State College (1955–1968). At San Francisco State he made his name as a stern, conservative college president during the late 1960s, when minority students staged a number of protests against the institution.

Hayakawa was elected to the U.S. Senate from California and served as the state's junior senator for six years until his retirement in 1982. As senator, he chaired a subcommittee on Far East Asian and Pacific Affairs in 1982, and in 1981 he helped to push through an amendment to raise the dollar amount of ammunition stored in South Korea from $100,000 to $160,000. This amount was to be used by South Korea in emergency situations. His voting record in Congress reflects his conservatism in both domestic and foreign policy matters. He demonstrated his most insensitive attitude toward Asians in America when he introduced a bill that would have made English the only official language to be used in government and education.

Though a conservative, Hayakawa asked President Gerald Ford to grant a pardon to Iva Ikuko Toguri d'Aquino* (Tokyo Rose). He was also one of the co-sponsors of a bill later known as the Commission on Wartime Relocation and Internment of Civilians* Act.

HAYAKAWA, SESSUE (1889–1973), screen actor. Hayakawa was born on June 10, 1889, in Honshu, Japan, the youngest of five children born to Hayakawa Yoichiro. His father was the governor of Chiba and a firm believer in samurai ideals. Consequently, Kintaro (Sessue's real name) was brought up under the strict warrior code known as Bushido. He was assigned to perform menial chores as a child because his father did not want him to "grow up a soft man with a rich family," as his biographer put it. (*Current Biograph Yearbook, 1962*).

At the age of fifteen, Kintaro enrolled in the Naval Preparatory School of Tokyo, and four years later he was accepted by the Naval Academy in Etajima. In 1908 he was forced to give up his dream of a naval career when he ruptured an eardrum. With the loss of his much coveted career, he became very depressed and attempted to kill himself.

Recovered fully from the self-inflicted injury, Hayakawa came to the United States at the age of nineteen and enrolled at the University of Chicago, from which he graduated with a degree in political science in 1913. On his way back to Japan, he spent a night in Los Angeles where he attended a play in a Japanese theatre. Much to his dismay, the play was directed very poorly, and Hayakawa challenged the owner of the theatre that he could do a far better job of directing the play. The owner accepted Hayakawa's challenge, and he was a smashing success. A year after this event Hayakawa directed his first major stage production, entitled *Typhoon*. Shortly thereafter, *Typhoon* was made into a motion picture featuring Hayakawa in his debut performance on the silver screen. *Typhoon* was followed by other movies starring Hayakawa in such works as *The Wrath of the Gods*, *The Secret Sin*, *The Cheat*, *Tokyo Joe*, *Three Came Home*, and *The Dragon Painter*. The peak of Hayakawa's acting career was his role in *The Bridge Over the River Kwai* (1957).

In 1918, with the financial aid of his parents and a college friend, Hayakawa formed his own company called the Hayworth Pictures Corporation. The corporation netted over $2 million during its first two years of production. Thirty-one years after he began his company, Hayakawa returned to Japan to be reunited with his family. While he was there he also renewed his association with the Zen masters. He was later chosen to be an ordained priest.

A turning point in Hayakawa's life came in 1956, when he was invited back to Hollywood to play the role of a Japanese colonel in the motion picture *The Bridge Over the River Kwai*. After much contemplation concerning his Zen beliefs about war and peace, he decided to accept the invitation. His spectacular portrayal of the rigid Colonel Saito won him the 1957 Golden Globe Award and a nomination for the Oscar as best supporting actor. This image of a stern, rigid disciplinarian that Hayakawa portrayed has been stereotyped by many as the personality characteristic of all Asians.

FURTHER READING: Charles Moritz, ed., *Current Biography Yearbook, 1962*, New York: H. W. Wilson Co., 1962, p. 194.

HEART MOUNTAIN CONGRESS OF AMERICAN CITIZENS, organized among Nisei* evacuees detained in Heart Mountain Relocation Camp located near Cody, Wyoming, in early February 1943. The organization was composed mainly of Nisei who rejected the leadership of the Japanese American Citizens League,* which had argued that cooperation rather than confrontation would reduce prejudice and racism in American public opinion. Nisei internees at Heart Mountain Camp, questioning the wisdom of such a policy of cooperation, decided to organize in order to direct the resistance movement. With regard to registration for the purpose of military draft, the Heart Mountain Congress believed that the government should honor Japanese American citizens' rights, and as long as the government refused to acknowledge their rights, they should refuse to be drafted into the military. The Congress was led by Frank T. Inouye, but he was later taken to Tule Lake Segregation Center* camp where he joined with persons of Japanese ancestry considered disloyal to the United States. Congress leadership was then taken over by Okamoto Kiyoshi, who created the Fair Play Committee of One* in November 1943. (*See also* Fair Play Committee of One.)

FURTHER READING: Frank F. Chuman, *The Bamboo People, the Law and Japanese-Americans*, Del Mar, Calif.: Publisher's Inc., 1976; Douglas W. Nelson, *Heart Mountain: The History of an American Concentration Camp*, Madison: Department of History, University of Wisconsin, 1976.

HEATHEN CHINEE. *See* Harte, Bret.

HECO, JOSEPH. *See* Hamada Hikozo.

HEMET INCIDENT, an incident that occurred in 1913 in Hemet Valley, southern California, where a group of Korean laborers went to pick apricots. They were met by white workers who mistook them for Japanese, and the Korean laborers became the target of mob action. After the incident the consul-general of Japan, which had taken over the Korean peninsula as a colony in 1910, issued a protest and asked for compensation. The president of the Korean National Association,* however, unwilling to have Japan represent the interests of Korean laborers, cabled Secretary of State William Jennings Bryan* informing him that Koreans in America had come to America before Japanese took over Korea and that Japan should not negotiate with the U.S. government on behalf of Koreans in America.

HENEY-WEBB BILL. *See* Alien Land Act of California, 1913.

HENRY LIU MURDER CASE refers to the killing of Henry Liu who refused to bend to accommodate the wishes of the government in Taiwan and lost his life. Overseas Chinese have been encouraged to cooperate with the government established by the Kuomintang, the Nationalist Party of China, ever since it came to power in 1924. The recalcitrants were intimidated into cooperation, or they were eliminated. Henry Liu was one of those overseas Chinese unwilling to cooperate with the government which he once served.

Henry Liu was born in Mainland China where his father, a landlord, was killed by the Communists. Henry fled to Taiwan in 1948 and lived there until 1967. While in Taiwan, he attended a school for political commissioners run by Chiang Ching Kuo, now President of Taiwan, and eventually became a journalist. He moved to Washington, D.C. where he worked as a reporter for the *Taiwan Daily News*. He earned a Master's degree at the American University and then moved to San Francisco in 1978. He was transformed into a leftist, turning against the government in Taiwan by writing critical articles on policies of the government which he once strongly supported.

In the summer of 1978, Liu published an article about a former governor of Taiwan, K. C. Wu, who came to the United States after a falling out with the Chiang family over what he characterized as "their Soviet style of methods." In the article, Wu declared that the younger Chiang had conversed with the secret police to have him killed (*The New York Times*, Nov. 2, 1984, p. A12.). Liu also published a biography of Taiwan President Chiang Ching Kuo that was critical of the government and of the Kuomintang headed by Chiang. This book may have cost Henry Liu his life.

A Chinese scholar warned Liu not to publish the book. However, Liu was believed to have said, "I am not worried. This is the United States. If someone tries to kill me, I'll call the police." (*The New York Times*, Dec. 5, 1984, p. A18.) A representative of Taiwan reported to have offered him a sum of $40,000 if he would cancel publication of his Chiang biography.

Henry Liu, fifty-two years of age, was shot to death in the garage of his own home in Daley City, California, on October 15, 1984. He was apparently shot twice in the chest and once in the face by two hooded Asians who were riding by on bicycles. In November, David Wu, 28 years old, was arrested in San Gabriel, California, on charges of conspiracy and murder in relation to the Henry Liu case. Wu was the driver of the vehicle that took two triggermen to Liu's home and then picked them up after the shooting. The other two triggermen were believed to be Tung Kuei-sen and Wu Tun. Identified as the fourth suspect in the shooting was Chen Chi-li, known also as "the duck." Chen was the leader of a powerful criminal organization in Taiwan known as the Bamboo gang. Mr. Garchick, the lawyer for Liu's family, had evidence that Chen made a long-distance call from San Francisco on October 15, to Chen Hu-men, a Taiwanese official highly placed in the government's intelligence agency. During the call "the duck" reported that his mission had been accomplished.

Chen Hum-men was arrested in Taiwan on January 14, 1985 and was held without bail on suspicion that he had a prior knowledge of the murder. The press reported that Chen Chi-li and Wu Tun confessed to the murder of Henry Liu. The following day, the Taiwan government made a public announcement stating that some of their intelligence officials had been involved in the October 15 shooting of Henry Liu. Investigators of Liu's death believed that there was a political motive in the killing. They were convinced that the murder was a result of the book Liu wrote on Chiang Ching Kuo. There was also a theory that the murder was a result of an extortion plot involving two Bay Area gift shops owned by Henry Liu and his wife, Helen.

As a result of this incident, there has been a number of changes in the U.S. policy towards the government in Taiwan. The shooting has stirred up widespread fear among Chinese intellectuals in the United States to the point where some feel their lives are in danger. Some Chinese did not even attend Liu's funeral because they were concerned about their own safety. One reason for the new uneasiness among the Chinese was the belief that there have been several unsolved murders committed by Kuomintang agents. They are convinced that the government in Taiwan has established an extensive intelligence network to monitor communications between Taiwan and Chinese in the United States.

In April 1985 when Chen Chi-li and Wu Tun were brought to trial at the Taipei District Court, they admitted their involvement in the shooting death of Liu and wept as they begged for their lives.

HIANGSHAN (Chungshan), a district located in Kwangtung Province, China, and very close to Macao, named after Dr. Sun Yat-sen,* a native of Hiangshan, who called himself Chungshan while in Japan. Large numbers of Hiangshan inhabitants immigrated to Hawaii and California. Because of a somewhat distinct dialect, people from this province organized their own district association known as Chungshan Association.

HIGHER WAGE ASSOCIATION (Zokyu Kisei Kai), organized on December 1, 1908, when forty-two individuals concerned with the general welfare of Japanese workers met at the local Japanese YMCA in Honolulu, Hawaii. The association received enthusiastic support from the Japanese community in Hawaii immediately after its organization, and leaders of the association such as Fred Kinsaburo Makino, Soga Yasutaro, and Negoro Motoyuki visited plantations to urge Japanese workers to petition for higher wages and prepare to strike, if necessary. Eleven days later, the association held a mass meeting at the Asahi Theatre in Honolulu. The meeting was attended by 1,700 people and adopted resolutions demanding an increase from $18 to $22.50 per month. The association wrote a letter to the secretary of the Hawaiian Sugar Planters' Association* (HSPA) for a conference, but the HSPA did not respond.

The association established its headquarters at the Yamashiro Hotel in Honolulu and began to organize and plan for a strike, which came in May 1909. (*See also* Great Strike of 1909.)

FURTHER READING: Lawrence H. Fuchs, *Hawaii Pono*, New York: Harcourt, Brace and World, 1961; Ronald Takaki, *Pau Hana*, Honolulu: University of Hawaii Press, 1983.

HILLEBRAND, WILLIAM (WILHELM). King Kamehameha V, aware of labor problems facing Hawaii, proposed that laborers be imported into Hawaii from abroad. After the king recommended that the government take control of this important matter, a law was passed on December 30, 1864, creating a Bureau of Immigration. The bureau was given charge of supervising the importation of foreign laborers, regulating contracts to be made with such laborers, and promoting and encouraging free immigration from abroad.

Hillebrand, who had served as a physician at Queen's Hospital, was appointed commissioner on March 30, 1865, by the king and was instructed to go to China and recruit about 500 Chinese laborers. Arriving in Hong Kong, he engaged the services of a Chinese company, Wohang & Company, and was able to recruit a total of 522 Chinese, including 95 women and 3 children who came to Hawaii aboard the *Alberto* and *Roscote*. The *Alberto* arrived on September 23, and the *Roscote* on October 12, 1865.

HILO MASSACRE, 1938 incident precipitated when Hawaii's labor unions demonstrated against a ship carrying strike-breakers. Before attaining statehood, Hawaii had a long history of labor problems, plaguing its biggest industry, namely, sugar. Although weak labor unions had made numerous attempts to force the Hawaiian Sugar Planters' Association* to recognize them, sugar planters refused to negotiate with them on a regular basis. With the passage of the National Labor Relations Act in 1935, the labor unions were revived, and they began to agitate for better working conditions and higher wages. The major unions involved in this effort were the Honolulu Waterfront Workers' Association, the Inland Boatmen's Union, the Metal Trades Council, and the International Longshoremen's and Warehousemen's Union* (ILWU). These unions gathered forces and decided to test their strength against the Inter-Island Steamship Company, which had the financial backing of the Castle and Cooke and the Matson Navigation Company. Under the leadership of Jack Hall, a strike was called in May 1938 and it continued for four months. On August 1, a group of striking workers protested against the arrival of a ship operated by a group of strike-breakers employed by the Inter-Island Steamship Company. The police warned the protesters not to interfere and were told to break up the demonstration. When they refused, the police used shotguns to disperse the demonstrators. During this incident fifty people were injured, half of them seriously enough to require hospitalization. This incident is known in Hawaiian labor circles as the Hilo Massacre. The strike did not accomplish much as employers refused to give in to the unions. Eventually, waterfront employers in Hawaii were forced to recognize the ILWU, which signed a contract on June 21, 1941, thus ending the six-year struggle for union recognition.

FURTHER READING: Gavan Daws, *Shoal of Time*, Honolulu: University Press of Hawaii, 1968; Lawrence H. Fuchs, *Hawaii Pono*, New York: Harcourt, Brace and World, 1961.

HINDU ASSOCIATION OF THE PACIFIC COAST, an organization established in the early 1900s to promote the publication and free distribution of revolutionary literature for India's independence. As a coalition organization of Hindu intellectuals, Sikh farmers, peasants, and lumber mill workers, it attempted to open its membership to any person from the Indian sub-continent willing to support India's struggle against the British Empire.

It is difficult to chronicle the history of the organization, for the existing accounts are contradictory. It is said that the organization was founded on November 1, 1913, in San Francisco when $15,000 was collected for its support. However, reliable records tend to support the claim that the organization had already been founded toward the end of May 1913. The founding date is less important than the fact that the organization gave birth to a revolutionary movement among Asian Indians in America that was to stun the British. Directly, it was responsible for the founding of the Ghadar Revolutionary Party.* (*See also* Ghadar Revolutionary Party; Dayal, Har.)

FURTHER READING: Emily C. Brown, *Har Dayal*, Tucson: University of Arizona Press, 1975; S. Chandrashekhar, *From India to America*, La Jolla, Calif.: A Population Review Book, 1982; R. C. Majumdar, ed., *Struggle for Freedom*, Bombay, India: Bharatiya Vidya Bhavan, 1969.

HINDU CONSPIRACY, 1914–1917 (also known as the Hindu-German Conspiracy), a revolutionary plot hatched by a group of Indian revolutionaries to overthrow British rule in India. The base for this movement was created on the West Coast of the United States. Indian students in the United States, Sikh peasants, and political refugees from India formed an organization known as the Hindu Association of the Pacific Coast,* which not only offered scholarships to Indian students to come to the United States for their study, but also published a weekly paper called the *Ghadar*, in order to propagandize the organization's effort for India's independence. Soon the association gave rise to the founding of the Ghadar Revolutionary Party,* and the leadership of the party went to a twenty-eight-year-old Oxford-educated Indian, Har Dayal,* who came to America in February 1911. His revolutionary activities in relation to the Ghadar Party made him a *persona non grata* in the eyes of U.S. immigration officials, who placed him under arrest in March 1914. Before government officials could deport him to India where he could be tried for his revolutionary activities, he fled to Switzerland. Another member of the *Ghadar* Party, Ram Chandra,* then assumed party leadership.

The outbreak of World War I in 1914 had a positive effect on the revolutionary activities of the association and the plot to overthrow British colonial rule in India. After much hesitation, Har Dayal went to Berlin in January 1915 where he joined people already working on the Indian Independence Committee, which was founded under the direction of Alfred Zimmerman, who served as director of Foreign Affairs for Germany. Zimmerman sought to gain control of all groups working toward Indian independence.

Meanwhile in California, Ram Chandra, now the leader of the *Ghadar* Party, decided to take action independently of Berlin. He smoothed over the differences between Muslims and Hindus, and recruited Jawala Singh to lead an expedition to smuggle arms and revolutionaries into India. Under Singh's leadership, a group of sixty Indians left San Francisco on the *S.S. Korea*, bound for Calcutta. The ship went first to Canton, China, where it picked up more Indians, bringing the crew up to 150. Upon arrival in Calcutta, Singh and others were arrested, and the expedition ended in failure.

Berlin sent another Indian, Heramba Lal Gupta,* to assume the leadership of the plot in the United States, where he was instructed to recruit Indians and obtain arms to ship to India. First, Gupta negotiated with representatives from the Nationalist Chinese government for arms, but he did not succeed. Then, he went to Japan to seek Japanese cooperation in obtaining arms for India, but Japan tried to turn him in to the British government. Gupta was then replaced by Chandra K. Chakravarty, who organized the Pan Asiatic League as a means of recruiting Indians from Japan and the West Indies. Chakravarty's activities were closely monitored by William Wiseman, chief of British intelligence in the United States, who informed the New York City Police of a bomb plot. Chakravarty's office was raided by police, and he was arrested on March 6, 1917, for violation of U.S. neutrality laws. The plot, hatched with so much hope for India's independence, withered after his arrest. Indian revolutionaries were put under arrest in many parts of the United States, as government officials came to know the names provided by Chakravarty.

FURTHER READING: Kalyan Kumar Banerjee, *Indian Freedom Movement Revolutionaries in America*, Calcutta: Jijnasa, 1969; H. Brett Melendy, *Asians in America*, Boston: Twayne Publishers, 1977; Emily C. Brown, *Har Dayal*, Tucson: University of Arizona Press, 1975.

HING CHUNG WUI (HSING CHUNG HUI), a revolutionary organization founded by Dr. Sun Yat-sen* in Honolulu, Hawaii, in 1894 with the help of his older brother, Sun Mi. Hing Chung Wui, or the Society for the Regeneration of China (now considered to be the origin of the Kuomintang*), was to revitalize China, and for this purpose members of the society raised $6,000 for Dr. Sun Yat-sen before his departure for the continental United States and Europe. (*See also* Chung Wah Tung Ming Wui.)

FURTHER READING: Clarence D. Glick, *Sojourners and Settlers*, Honolulu: University Press of Hawaii, 1980; William L. Tung, *The Chinese in America, 1820–1973*, Dobbs Ferry, N.Y.: Oceana Publications, 1974.

HINODE COMPANY, established in November 1876 in New York by two members of the Oceanic Group,* who came to the United States in March 1876 aboard the *Oceanic*. The Oceanic Group included Arai Ryoichiro, Morimura Toyo, Sato Momotara, Date Chushichi, Masuda Rinzo, and Suzuki Toichi.

Upon arrival in New York, Sato began his business at 97 Front Street, and the business became known as the Japanese and American Agency. Sato also opened another store in collaboration with Morimura, which dealt with Japanese merchandise, including china, lacquer, parasols, fans, scrolls, silk goods, and teas. Morimura left his business with Sato in order to attend Eastman Business College, and Sato's and Morimura's businesses were combined to become the Hinode Company in November 1876. The firm hired a German migrant, Richard von Briesen, as assistant, who soon took over much of Sato's business. This was the beginning of Japanese American trade.

HIRABAYASHI v. UNITED STATES, a case involving Gordon Kiyoshi Hirabayashi, a student at the University of Washington, who on May 9, 1942, failed to return to his residence by 8:00 P.M., in clear violation of the recently established curfew for residents of Japanese ancestry living within Military Area No. 1. General John Lesesne DeWitt* had instituted a curfew law on March 24, 1942, requiring all persons of Japanese ancestry residing or within the limits of Military Area No. 1 to be in their residence between the hours of 8:00 P.M. and 6:00 A.M. On neither May 11 nor May 12 did Hirabayashi report to the Civil Control Station to be registered in anticipation of the impending evacuation and resettlement of persons of Japanese ancestry, as he was required to do under the Civilian Exclusion Order No. 57 of May 10, 1942.

Hirabayashi was arrested and tried and convicted on these misdemeanor charges. His appeal to the Ninth Circuit Court was referred to the U.S. Supreme Court where it was argued on May 11 and 12, 1943. The Court handed down its decision on June 21, 1943, unanimously upholding the decision of the lower court.

Hirabayashi's attorneys raised two specific points in the Court. First, they argued that Congress had unconstitutionally delegated its legislative power by authorizing the military commander to impose a curfew in the defined military area. Second, they argued that, even if the curfew regulation was in all other respects legal, the Fifth Amendment prohibited discrimination between citizens of different races.

Chief Justice Harlan F. Stone, in his opinion for the Court, found nothing unconstitutional about the act of Congress on May 21, 1942, which authorized the curfew order and which ratified and confirmed Executive Order 9066,* issued on February 19, 1942. He found the measures taken by Congress and the President reasonable for the protection of the West Coast against the threat of sabotage and espionage. According to Chief Justice Stone, persons of Japanese ancestry in America during World War II constituted a menace to national safety and defense:

> Whatever views we may entertain regarding the loyalty to this country of the citizens of Japanese ancestry, we cannot reject as unfounded the judgment of the military authorities and of Congress that there were disloyal members of that population whose number and strength could not be precisely and quickly ascer-

tained. We cannot say that the war-making branches of the Government did not have ground for believing that in a critical hour such persons could not readily be isolated and separately dealt with, and constituted a menace to the national defense and safety, which demanded that prompt and adequate measures be taken to guard against it.

According to Chief Justice Stone, Congress had discussed the possible imposition of a curfew by the military commander before it was actually proclaimed. This would be within the limits of his authority. The constitutional mandate that all legislative power be in Congress did not preclude Congress from resorting to the aid of executive or administrative offices. Therefore, it was not unconstitutional for Congress to allow the military commander the power to establish a curfew.

The issue of equal protection under the Fifth Amendment was not treated in depth. The Court's basic argument was that the Fifth Amendment does not include an "equal protection" clause; it guarantees due process under the law. It found that the imposition of a curfew was not a violation of the Fifth Amendment.

In 1981 Hirabayashi, Fred Korematsu, and Yasui Minoru, all of whom had been convicted of violating different laws in connection with the evacuation and removal of Japanese Americans, were informed by Peter Irons, a Harvard-trained lawyer at the University of California at San Diego, that the government had suppressed evidence, known at the time of the evacuation decision, suggesting strongly that the evacuation was not necessary after all. Armed with this new evidence, they petitioned for a writ of error *coram nobis* to have their original convictions overturned. On November 10, 1983, the Korematsu case was dismissed after his original conviction was vacated, and in January of the following year a similar decision was made on Yasui's petition. But U.S. District Court Judge Donald Voorhees, during a court hearing held in Seattle on May 18, 1984, overrode the plea of Justice Department Assistant Attorney Victor Smith to have the case dismissed if the original conviction was vacated.

Gordon Hirabayashi, now a professor emeritus at the University of Alberta, Canada, continued his struggle to have his conviction overturned and to institute a judicial review of the internment of more than 110,000 persons of Japanese ancestry during the Pacific War.

On February 10, 1986, Judge Voorhees handed down his ruling charging the government with concealment of information from the Supreme Court of the United States as well as from the lawyer who represented Gordon Hirabayashi in 1943. According to the ruling, which will have significant impact on other lawsuits pending, the War Department altered General De Witt's original report which stated that the evacuation of Japanese Americans was necessary because it was "impossible" to determine which Japanese Americans were loyal to the U.S. government. The changed report said that the evacuation was necessary because there was "a lack of time" to determine loyalties of Japanese Americans. Had this information been available to Hirabayashi's lawyer, Judge Voorhees continued, he could have pointed out without much difficulty that infants, children of school age, the sick and old were loyal to the U.S. government. Judge Voorhees, however, let stand Hirabayashi's original conviction for violating curfew rules imposed upon persons of Japanese ancestry in 1942.

FURTHER READING: Frank F. Chuman, *The Bamboo People: The Law and Japanese-Americans*, Del Mar, Calif.: Publisher's Inc., 1976; Peter Irons, *Justice at War: The Story of the Japanese American Internment Cases*, New York: Oxford University Press, 1983; Milton R. Konvitz, *The Alien and the Asiatic in American Law*, Ithaca, N.Y.: Cornell University Press, 1946; *Seattle Post-Intelligence*, February 11, 1986, pp. 1, 5.; Jacobus ten Broek et al., *Prejudice, War and the Constitution*, Berkeley: University of California Press, 1970.

HIROSHIMA PREFECTURE, a small administrative unit or district, located in the southwestern part of Honshu Island, Japan, which sent a great number of young Japanese to Hawaii in the late nineteenth and early twentieth centuries. Robert W. Irwin,* an agent for the Hawaiian Sugar Planters' Association* (HSPA) reportedly went to rural districts in Japan in an effort to recruit workers for the HSPA. The HSPA had experienced great difficulty keeping Japanese workers on plantations.

According to Professor Ichihashi Yamato,* the Hiroshima Prefecture supplied a large number of young people to Hawaii primarily because the area was overpopulated. Between 1889 and 1903 over 21,000 inhabitants of Hiroshima Prefecture left for foreign countries. This was slightly more than one-fourth of all Japanese emigrants who left Japan during the same period. Other prefectures that sent their inhabitants abroad as emigrants were Kumamoto, Yamaguchi, Fukuoka, Wakayama, Nagasaki, Okayama, Oita, Saga, and Kagoshima. The District of Sanyodo, made up of Hiroshima, Yamaguchi, and Okayama, sent 35,256 Japanese abroad, which was 41.6 percent of the total emigrants during the period.

FURTHER READING: Yamato Ichihashi, *Japanese in the United States: A Critical Study of the Problems of the Japanese Immigrants and Their Children*, Stanford, CA.: Stanford University Press, 1932.

HMONGS, a major ethnic group in southern China, Vietnam, Laos, and Thailand today. The Hmongs' original homeland was in Central Asia, but they gradually migrated southward until they settled in the mountains of southern China. Driven away from their homes again by the Chinese, they moved southward once more, gradually seeping into their present ethnic enclaves. From before the beginning of the nineteenth century to the present, more than half a million Hmongs have fled from southern China, although 2.5 million Hmongs still live in China. Before the Vietnam debacle in April 1975, there were an estimated 50,000 Hmongs in Thailand, 225,000 in Vietnam, and 350,000 in Laos. Approximately 50,000 of these came to America as refugees in the mid–1970s.

The Hmongs did not choose to become refugees; they were uprooted from their homeland because of foreign invaders. During World War II they fought against the Japanese, and after the war they sided with the Royal Lao in opposition to the Pathet Lao. The two sides fought from 1955 to 1975. It is estimated that about 30,000 Hmongs died in the conflict and that as many as 120,000 Hmong tribesmen became war refugees as of 1974.

HO AH-KOW v. MATTHEW NUNAN, a case settled in California in 1879 involving the Queue Ordinance. In the nineteenth century California led the nation in legislating laws that were anti-Chinese. These laws were passed by various levels of government in order to harass the Chinese and to make their lives intolerable. One of the laws passed by the city and county of San Francisco required that every male prisoner in the city or county jail have his hair cut to a uniform length of one inch from the scalp. This ordinance, better known as the Queue Ordinance of 1876, was ruled unconstitutional in 1879 by the circuit court in California. The case involved Ho Ah-kow, whose hair was cut by Sheriff Matthew Nunan; the court then ordered Nunan to pay Ho $10,000 as compensation.
FURTHER READING: L. S. B. Sawyer, *Reports of Cases Decided in the Circuit and District Courts of the United States for the Ninth Circuit*, vol. v, San Francisco: A. L. Bancroft and Co., 1880.

HO CHINN (1904–), real estate broker, banker, business executive, chairman of the Board of the Gannett Pacific Corporation. Ho was born on February 26, 1905, in Honolulu; he was a grandson of a Chinese rice planter who had immigrated to Hawaii in 1855. He graduated from McKinley High School and went to the University of Hawaii.

Ho founded the Capital Investment Company* in 1944 with less than $200,000 in capital and made it a giant corporation by 1959. For his company board of directors, he selected persons representing each of Hawaii's major ethnic groups. (*See also* Capital Investment Company.)

HOIPING. *See* Sze Yap (Sze-I).

HOKOKU SEINEN-DAN (YOUNG MEN'S ORGANIZATION TO SERVE OUR MOTHER COUNTRY), an organization originally established as the Sokoku Kenkyu Seinen-dan (Young Men's Association for the Study of the Mother Country) at Tule Lake Segregation Center* on August 12, 1944. At that time approximately 500 young men, some older men, and a few women gathered to hear the Reverend Aramaki. Aramaki was known as the founder of the organization, but he was manipulated by radicals at the camp. The organization's expressed aim was to prepare members to become useful citizens of Japan after their repatriation to Japan. The organization, therefore, devoted much time to study of the Japanese language, culture, and history.

This organization was created at Tule Lake in response to the War Relocation Authority's* policy of segregating persons of Japanese ancestry interned during World War II who were considered disloyal to the United States. These so-called disloyal internees had been identified after they had either refused to answer or answered negatively to questions on their willingness to give up their allegiance to Japan and to be loyal to the United States. These questions appeared on the War Relocation Authority Application for Leave Clearance.* Once identified as disloyal, they were then sent to Tule Lake Segregation Center where they were segregated from the rest of the internees.

In spite of extensive efforts to convince their fellow internees at Tule Lake Camp, the organization was not able to create a large membership. Only 500 internees belonged to this organization.

FURTHER READING: Edward H. Spicer et al., *Impounded People*, Tucson: University of Arizona Press, 1969; Dorothy S. Thomas and Richard Nishimoto, *The Spoilage: Japanese-American Evacuation and Resettlement During World War II*, Berkeley: University of California Press, 1969.

HOLT INTERNATIONAL CHILDREN'S SERVICES, an adoption agency with headquarters in Eugene, Oregon. It was founded by Harry Holt (1905–1964) and his wife, Bertha. The agency was officially incorporated in the United States as the Orphan Foundation Fund on October 12, 1956. The Holts had brought eight children born in Korea in October 1955, and *Life* magazine and other mass media publicized their arrival. These children were officially adopted by the Holts in February 1956. Harry Holt went back to Korea in order to start adoption work, and established, with the assistance of David H. Kim, now Executive Director of the agency, an office in a Salvation Army Academy building in Seoul, where their work began officially on March 5, 1956.

The work that began in a very small and humble way grew rapidly and today there are seven regional offices located throughout the United States: Des Moines, Iowa; Omaha, Nebraska; West Trenton, New Jersey; Louisville, Kentucky; Memphis, Tennessee; Lakewood, California; and San Leandro, California. In addition, there are international branch offices in ten nations serving the needs of children as well as those American families wishing to adopt them and nurture them. These nations are Korea, the Philippines, Brazil, Colombia, Bolivia, Thailand, India, Guatemala, Honduras, and El Salvador. Since its establishment in 1956, the agency has brought to the United States approximately 30,000 children from these nations for adoption into American families.

HOME RULE PARTY, political party in Hawaii. Under the provisions of Hawaii's Organic Act,* which became law on June 14, 1900, citizens of the Republic of Hawaii in 1898 automatically became citizens of the Territory of Hawaii in 1898, although Sanford Ballard Dole* and his associates did everything to exclude Hawaiian natives and Asians from citizenship. Congress disagreed with their point of view and allowed natives of Hawaii to vote, provided they were male, of age, and had lived in Hawaii for the required length of time. Asians in Hawaii, however, were excluded from the franchise because they were not considered citizens.

When the first elections were held for the Territory of Hawaii to create the territorial legislature, Robert Wilcox, who was part Hawaiian, advised the Hawaiian natives to vote Hawaiian under the slogan, "Nana i ka ili," or "look at the skin." Hawaiian natives voted for neither Republicans nor Democrats; they voted for candidates of the third party, the Home Rule Party. Fourteen seats of the territorial House went to the Home Rule Party, as against nine for the Republicans and four for the Democrats; the Home Rule Party also won nine of thirteen seats in the Senate.

HONDA, HARRY. *See Pacific Citizens, The.*

HONOLULU CONTRACT, a contract which Francisco Varona* negotiated with plantation owners in Hawaii for the return passage of Filipino workers, who had come to Hawaii to work as plantation workers under contract.

Approximately 2,000 Filipinos came to Hawaii under contract between 1915 and 1919. Because of labor unrest among the Filipino workers in Hawaii, Governor General Francis B. Harrison* sent Prudencio A. Remigio to Hawaii to investigate working conditions among the Filipino workers. Remigio reported his concern about a large number of Filipinos who had come without a guaranteed return passage. Then Harrison sent Varona to Hawaii in 1920 to look into the problem of Filipinos who wanted to come home but were unable to do so for lack of money. Varona worked out an arrangement with plantation owners, who gave Filipinos the opportunity to gain return passage.

HOONG MOON SOCIETIES (HUNG-MEN LEAGUE) (also known as Triad or Three Dots Societies) secret societies or organizations established among overseas Chinese toward the end of the seventeenth century after China was defeated by the Manchus, who established the Ch'ing Dynasty in 1644. The founders of a Hoong Moon society, resentful of the Manchu domination of Chinese, vowed to overthrow the dynasty. Because of this rebellious attitude, the Manchu Dynasty outlawed the organization, and the death penalty was imposed on members of the secret society. During the Taiping Rebellion (1850–1864), members of the society in south China collaborated with the rebels, and the collaborators decided to flee the country when it was clear that the rebellion would fail. Naturally, the Ch'ing court did not look favorably on them and adopted an attitude of indifference toward them. In the absence of their government's interest and concern with their welfare, overseas Chinese were compelled to organize themselves as a means of protecting their self-interest, and this organization took the form of a secret society.

A Hoong Moon society was organized in California after 1879. In Hawaii the Tung Hing Kung Si, another Hoong Moon society, was established in 1869 by the Hakkas,* who felt a greater need for a secret society than the Puntis,* who were more numerous in Hawaii. It is estimated that more than thirty other Hoong Moon societies were organized among overseas Chinese in Hawaii between 1869

and 1910. Although these secret societies had various names, the common name they adopted was the Chee Kung Tong.* (*See* Chee Kung Tong.)
FURTHER READING: Gunther Barth, *Bitter Strength*, Cambridge, Mass.: Harvard University Press, 1964; Clarence E. Glick, *Sojourners and Settlers; Chinese Migrants in Hawaii*, Honolulu: University Press of Hawaii, 1980; Stanford M. Lyman, *The Asian in North America*, Santa Barbara, Calif.: ABC-Clio Press, 1977.

HOOPER, WILLIAM. *See* Ladd and Company.

HOP PUN **(PARTNERSHIP),** one of two systems used by Chinese rice farmers in Hawaii. The other system was called *fun kung*,* a form of "cropper" arrangement between a landlord and a group of rice farmers who rented land from the landlord.

In the *hop pun* system, an independent farm could be established by a small group of Chinese farmers, usually three or four in the group, who would divide the earnings according to the contribution each person made in raising the crop. Usually, one man would be responsible for making arrangements for leasing the land, but everyone in the group would be responsible for food, shelter, and other necessary tools. The *hop pun* system used in Hawaii was similar to the system used in south China, where small rice farms were independently kept.
FURTHER READING: Clarence E. Glick, *Sojourners and Settlers*, Honolulu: University Press of Hawaii, 1980.

HOPU, THOMAS, a boy brought to the United States from Hawaii, along with Opukahaia, by an American sea captain in 1809. Opukahaia later attended Yale University and prepared himself to come to Hawaii for evangelical work among his own people. Unfortunately, he died of typhus before he was able to return to his native land. Hopu, who acquired a Christian name by 1819, was one of four native Hawaiians sent back to Hawaii with Hiram Bingham and Asa Thurston to spread the gospel among his people. (*See* American Board of Commissioners for Foreign Missions.)

HOSHI-DAN. *See* Sokuji Kikoku Hoshi-dan.

HOSOKAWA, WILLIAM K. (1915–), journalist. Hosokawa was born on January 30, 1915, in Seattle, Washington, and graduated from the University of Washington in 1937. The following year he married Alice Tokuko Miyake. Upon graduation he launched his journalism career abroad, taking his first job with the *Singapore Herald* in Singapore in 1938. Leaving the *Singapore Herald* in 1940, he took his second assignment for the *Shanghai Times* and *Far Eastern Review* until 1941. He returned just five weeks before the Japanese attack on Pearl Harbor in 1941 to go through the internment experience as a person of Japanese ancestry. In 1943 he took an editorial position with the *Des Moines Register* in Iowa where he served until 1946, when he moved to Denver to work for the *Denver Post*. He has been recognized as an outstanding journalist, receiving the Outstanding Journalist Award in 1967 from the University of Colorado School of Journalism and again in 1976 from the Colorado Chapter of Sigma Delta Chi.

Hosokawa has made outstanding contributions to an understanding of the Japanese American experience through his books, including *Nisei: The Quiet Americans* (1969); *The Two Worlds of Jim Yoshida* (1972); *Thunder in the Rockies* (1976); *Thirty-Five Years in the Frying Pan* (1978); *East to America* (1980); and *JACL in Quest of Justice* (1982).

HOUSE JOINT RESOLUTION 549. *See* Filipino Repatriation Act of 1935.

HOUSE RESOLUTION 6464. *See* Welch Bill.

HOWE, JAMES WONG (1898–1975), photographer, cinematographer. Howe was born in Canton, China, in 1898 and came to the State of Washington in 1904 with his parents. His original name was Wong Tung Jim, which he continued to use until 1922. He is recognized for his great camera work in the United States and for bringing new, revolutionary techniques to the camera world. Among his best known photographic innovations are the use of the wide-angle lens, deep focus, and ceilinged sets to give the claustrophobic feeling of being aboard ship. In 1947 he was also one of the first cameramen to use a hand-held camera. In his innovative methods of filming he used roller skates and wheelchairs.

Because of his artistic and revolutionary techniques Howe won Oscars for the films *The Rose Tatoo* and *Hud* in 1957 and 1963, respectively. His other acclaimed films include *Come Back Little Sheba*, *The Last Angry Man*, and *The Old Man and the Sea*.

HUA-CH'IAO, a Chinese term referring to all ethnic Chinese living abroad, regardless of their citizenship. The word *hua-ch'iao* is placed after the name of the country where the Chinese live. The Chinese living in Hawaii, for example, are called Hawaii hua-ch'iao.

HUANG TSUN-HSIEN (1848–1905), poet, diplomat. Huang was born in Chia-ying-chou, Kwangtung Province, in China, and was educated in Chinese classics, later becoming a senior licentiate in 1873. In 1876 he was appointed counselor to the legation in Tokyo, Japan, where he stayed until he was appointed consul-general at San Francisco. During his stay in Japan he observed with keen interest the reform measures the Japanese government had undertaken, and he sensed that Japan had ambitious designs on Korea. In his famous book, *A Strategy for Korea* (1880), he recommended that Korea develop friendly relations with Japan and the United States. The conservatives in Korea rejected his suggestions, however. In spite of his busy schedule as counselor to the legation, he found time to write a book on Japan, *Jihpin kuo chih* (A History of Japan), which was published in 1880.

While serving as consul-general in San Francisco, Huang composed a number of poems, some of which described American prejudice against Chinese. Chinese scholars quoted from his poems in their attack against the U.S. exclusion policy.

Huang returned to China in 1885 when his mother died. In 1889 he was appointed counselor to the legation in London but was recalled by Chang Chi-tung, who wanted to use Huang's ideas for reform. As a reformer, Huang was much sought after by many reform-minded Chinese officials. Huang was responsible for establishing Shih-wu Hsueh-t'ang (the Hall for the Study of Current Affairs), where a number of revolutionary leaders discussed reform ideas. Liang Ch'i-ch'ao* once served as dean of Chinese Studies at this school.

FURTHER READING: Shih-shan Henry Tsai, *China and the Overseas Chinese in the United States, 1868–1911*, Fayetteville: University of Arkansas Press, 1983.

HUI (WUI), a term that literally means "association" or "club" in Chinese, but is often translated into English as "rotating credit association" because the Chinese use it both at home and abroad as a means of pooling money. A person in need of a lump sum of money for a business or project would take the initiative in creating a *hui* that would include a number of people, small or large, depending on various conditions. In a *hui* of ten members, if the group decided to create a capital pool of $500 per month, each member would put in $50 per month. The organizer usually received the first lump sum, and others took their turn on the basis of the number they drew in the lottery to decide who received following the first recipient.

Many studies have been undertaken to determine if *hui* as an economic organization has contributed to the development of small enterprises among Chinese abroad, particularly the Chinese in America. One of the major studies done on this question was by Ivan H. Light, who in his book, *Ethnic Enterprise in America* (1972), claimed that the Chinese used this rotating credit association extensively to capitalize their small businesses.

FURTHER READING: Hyung-chan Kim, *The Korean Diaspora*, Santa Barbara, Calif.: ABC-Clio Press, 1977; Ivan H. Light, *Ethnic Enterprise in America: Business and Welfare Among Chinese, Japanese and Blacks*, Berkeley: University of California Press, 1972; Stanford M. Lyman, *Chinese Americans*, New York: Random House, 1974.

HUI KUAN (WUI KUN), district associations among overseas Chinese. (The term literally means "association hall" in Chinese.) Traditionally, the Chinese organized themselves on the basis of kinship, district ties, or special need and interest. Whenever a sufficient number of Chinese immigrate to foreign countries, overseas Chinese developed their organization using a group basis.

The Chinese in the United States were no exception. They, too, organized themselves in kinship associations, district associations, as well as secret societies. Although *hui kuan* were district associations in the strict sense of the words, they took on a wide range of roles and functions in caring for Chinese emigrants and representing their interests to white society. *Hui kuan* served as credit and loan agencies and employment agencies; and as arbiter and mediator between warring individuals and groups for settling disputes. When the government of China was too preoccupied with internal problems, *hui kuan* represented overseas Chinese interests to the various levels of government in the United States. They sent letters of appeals and protest, and memorials in seeking relief from American exclusion policies, notably "Letter of the Chinaman to His Excellency Governor Bigler" in 1852, "Reply to the Message of His Excellency, Governor Bigler" in 1855, a "Remonstrance from Chinese in California to the Congress of the United States" in 1868, a "Memorial from the Six Companies: An Address to the Senate and House of Representatives of the United States" in 1877, and a protest to the President of the United States in 1916 over America's exclusionist practices.

During the first decade of Chinese immigration to the United States between 1847 and 1858, there were five district associations. Because many people from different districts came to America, however, reformation took place until there developed six major district associations known as the Chinese Six Companies,* or the Chinese Consolidated Benevolent Association. (*See also* District Companies.)

FURTHER READING: Jack Chen, *The Chinese of America*, New York: Harper and Row, 1980; Rose Hum Lee, *The Chinese in the United States of America*, Hong Kong: Hong Kong University Press, 1960; Stanford M. Lyman, *Chinese Americans*, New York: Random House, 1974; Six Chinese Companies, "An Address to the Senate and House of Representatives of the United States," San Francisco, December 8, 1877.

HUI SHEN (5th century), a Chinese Buddhist monk who claimed he had discovered people in a land he called Fusang, which is located 7,000 miles east of China. (*See also* Fusang.)

HUIE KIN (1854–1934), writer. Huie Kin came to the United States in 1868 and established in 1885 the first Protestant mission in New York's Chinatown. His book, *Reminiscences*, written in 1868 but not published until 1932 in Peking, describes the suffering which the Chinese immigrants endured during their passage to the United States. "There was no water for washing and passengers collected rain water when it rained," he wrote.

FURTHER READING: Jack Chen, *The Chinese of America*, New York: Harper and Row, 1980; Corinne K. Hoexter, *From Canton to California*, New York: Four Winds Press, 1976.

HULBERT, HOMER B. (1863–1949), diplomat. Hulbert was born on January 26, 1863, in New Haven, Vermont, and attended St. Johnsbury Academy. In 1884 he graduated from Dartmouth College and entered educational service in Korea, where he was chosen as one of the English language teachers requested by the Korean government. He served in Korea from 1886 to 1905 when he entered diplomatic service on behalf of Korea's penultimate king, Kojong,* who sent Hulbert on a secret mission to the United States to try to change America's friendly gesture toward Japanese colonial policy in Korea. His mission failed when the American government refused to accept Korea's plea for diplomatic assistance.

Hulbert was a strong supporter and advocate of Korean immigration to Hawaii as well. When a group of American missionaries criticized Korean immigration, he defended it by stating that Korean immigrants did not go to Hawaii in violation of American laws and that children of Korean immigrants in Hawaii were benefiting from the education provided in Hawaii.

FURTHER READING: Wayne Patterson, *The Korean Frontier in America: Immigration to Hawaii, 1896–1919*, Ann Arbor, Mich.: University Microfilms-International, 1977; Clarence N. Weems, ed., *Hulbert's History of Korea*, New York: Hillary House Publishers Ltd., 1962.

HULUGAN, a formal common savings club used among Filipinos in Hawaii, started in the late 1920s. An economic association similar to Chinese *hui* provided Filipinos in Hawaii with the opportunity to pool their money for various purposes. By rotation, a member could bid and receive his contribution to the club.

HUNG SHUN TONG. *See Tongs.*

HWA CHING, an organization established toward the end of the 1960s in San Francisco's Chinatown,* where a large number of foreign-born Chinese moved after the Immigration Act of October 3, 1965,* went into effect. The members of the organization were primarily foreign-born Chinese youths who challenged the Chinese Six Companies* to provide jobs for unemployed youths in Chinatown. When no answer to this challenge came, members of the organization took to the streets and engaged in disruptive activities. Initially motivated by social idealism for employment for the unemployed and education for the uneducated, some members were later coopted into secret societies.

HYON SUN, a Korean recruited as an interpreter by David W. Deshler* in 1902 when Deshler began to work for the Hawaiian Sugar Planters' Association* to recruit Korean laborers to work on plantations in Hawaii. Hyon came to Hawaii with the second group of Korean immigrants aboard the *Coptic*, which brought them to Honolulu on March 2, 1903. Hyon wrote a book on his experience in Hawaii under the title, *P'owa yuram-ki*, which was published in 1909 in Korea.

In later years, Hyon was involved in the Korean independence movement and served as vice-minister of Foreign Affairs of the Korean provisional government-in-exile in Shanghai.

I

ICHIHASHI YAMATO (1878–1965), professor of history and government at Stanford University for many years. Ichihashi wrote two major books on the problems and issues facing Japanese Americans between 1915 and 1932, when prejudice and discrimination against Japanese Americans ran high in America. His first book on Japanese Americans was *Japanese Immigration: Its Status in California* (1915), and his second was a more thorough study of Japanese Americans, *Japanese in the United States* (1932).

FURTHER READING: Yamato Ichihashi, *Japanese Immigration: Its Status in California*, San Francisco: Marshall Press, 1915; Yamato Ichihashi, *Japanese in the United States: A Critical Study of the Problems of the Japanese Immigrants and Their Children* Stanford, Calif.: Stanford University Press, 1932.

ILOCANOS, a cultural and linguistic group of people found today in the Ilocos region of northwestern Luzon, in the Republic of the Philippines. The major Ilocano provinces, Ilocos Norte, Ilocos Sur, and La Union, experienced economic hardships and overpopulation before recruiting agents from Hawaii arrived to advertise for laborers needed in Hawaii. Many Ilocanos willingly left their homes for Hawaii and the continental United States in search of work.

The Ilocano language, one of the major dialects spoken in the Philippines today, was spoken by approximately 5 million people in 1975.

IMMIGRATION ACT OF AUGUST 3, 1882, the first general federal immigration law to depart from America's traditional policy of encouraging immigrants to come to the United States. As late as May 1862, Congress passed the Homestead Law encouraging Europeans to immigrate to the United States. In 1863 President Abraham Lincoln sent the 38th Congress a message requesting the establishment of a system for the "encouragement of immigration." The 38th Congress went to work on a bill to establish the Office of the Commissioner of Immigration, to be appointed by the President. It also included provisions for federal control over immigrant labor contracts. The bill passed through Congress and, with the President's signature, became the Act of July 1864. This was the beginning of federal control over immigration. But still there was no general federal policy to control and regulate immigration, and in the absence of federal law, many states passed laws regulating and restricting the entry of foreigners into their territory. However, the Supreme Court of the United States in its decision on Chy Lung v. Freeman* ruled that the California State law dealing with regulation of immigrants was unconstitutional because it infringed on the right of Congress to regulate commerce.

After this ruling, the New York Legislature asked Congress to establish federal legislation to protect immigrants as well as cities and towns from convicts who had been allowed to come to the country. Congress was slow in responding to the need for a federal policy, although the 43rd Congress enacted a law known as the Immigration Act of March 3, 1875. The law had five sections, two of which were relevant to the immigration of Chinese to the United States. The first prohibited the importation of any Oriental persons "without their free and voluntary consent," and the second made the contracting to supply coolie* labor a felony.

Congress was asked to take steps beyond the measures provided in the Immigration Act of March 3, 1875, by numerous states which were deprived of head tax revenue, but had the responsibility of caring for unwanted immigrants. The New York members of Congress took the initiative in introducing the bill for the purpose of regulating immigration. Senator John Franklin Miller introduced a bill in the Senate, while Representative Henry Clay Van Voorhis introduced a bill in the House. The House Committee on Commerce reported out its own bill, and the House passed the bill and forwarded it to the Senate, which passed it without debate on July 29, 1882. President Chester A. Arthur signed the bill into law, and it became the Immigration Act of August 3, 1882. The law imposed a head tax of 50 cents on every alien coming by vessel; the money was to be used to defray the expenses of regulating immigration and caring for immigrants in the United States. Another proviso allowed government officials to be aboard the vessel for the purpose of examining immigrants. But the most significant provision in the law was added in Section 4:

> That all foreign paupers, convicts, or accused persons of other than political offenses, or persons suffering from mental alienation, in the United States who are a public charge on their arrival in this country shall be sent back by the United States to the nations to which they belong and from whence they came.

FURTHER READING: E. P. Hutchinson, *Legislative History of American Immigration Policy, 1798–1965*, Philadelphia: University of Pennsylvania Press, 1981; Benjamin B. Ringer, *We the People and Others*, New York: Tavistock Publications, 1983; George M. Stephenson, *A History of American Immigration 1820–1924*, New Haven, Conn.: Yale University Press, 1964.

IMMIGRATION ACT OF FEBRUARY 20, 1907, restrictive law designed to limit Japanese immigration to the United States. In response to President Theodore Roosevelt's annual message to the 59th Congress, which asked for more effective protection for the nation from unwanted immigration through legislation, Congress responded with a burst of legislative activity. Initially, as many as thirty bills were introduced during the session to regulate and restrict immigration in one way or another. One of them, sponsored by Charles William Fulton of Oregon and Francis Wellington Cushman of Washington, was passed by the House and the Senate, and was signed into law on June 14, 1906. The law prohibited aliens from fishing in Alaskan waters, unless they had declared their intention to become U.S. citizens.

Representative Augustus Peabody Gardner of Massachusetts introduced a bill on April 9, 1906, that was prepared by the House Committee on Immigration and Naturalization. This committee had received as many as nineteen immigration bills for its consideration. This bill was later replaced by another bill which retained unchanged ten of the thirty-nine sections of the Immigration Act of March 3, 1903. Meanwhile, the Senate had been working on its own bill submitted by Senator William Paul Dillingham of Vermont on February 14, 1906. The bill he submitted was very much like the House bill. The Senate passed the bill with a number of amendments, one of which included a literacy test for immigrants coming to the United States, and sent it to the House. The House Committee on Immigration and Naturalization recommended that the Senate bill be disregarded in its entirety and be substituted by its own bill. This bill was then reported out on June 11, 1906, and was debated in the House. On June 25, Representative Oscar Wilder Underwood of Alabama spoke in favor of the literacy test which, according to him, "will not only separate the ignorant, vicious, and the lazy from the intelligent and the industrious classes, but to a large extent it will eliminate the lower classes of immigration from the countries that are not of Teutonic and Celtic origin."

The second session of the 59th Congress convened on December 3, 1906, and it immediately went to work on the bill the House had passed at the end of the first session. Because of the Senate's disagreement with the House bill, a conference committee was organized to report. That report was made on February 13, 1907, and omitted the literacy test. It also added two new features before President Roosevelt signed it into law on February 20, 1907.

One of the two features, which was an attempt to further restrict Japanese immigration to the continental United States, was a proviso giving the President authority to refuse entry to a citizen of any nation if he believed that the alien was given a passport to another country or to a U.S. territory with the real intention of allowing him to enter the continental United States. On the basis of this proviso in Section 1 of the Immigration Act of February 20, 1907, President Roosevelt issued an Executive Order prohibiting Japanese and Korean laborers, both skilled and unskilled, from entering the continental United States by way of Mexico, Canada, or Hawaii beginning on March 14, 1907.

FURTHER READING: Frank F. Chuman, *The Bamboo People*, Del Mar, Calif.: Publisher's Inc., 1976; Roger Daniels, *The Politics of Prejudice*, Berkeley: University of California Press, 1962; E. P. Hutchinson, *Legislative History of American Immigration Policy, 1798–1965*, Philadelphia: University of Pennsylvania Press, 1981; Yamato Ichihashi, *Japanese in the United States*, Stanford, Calif.: Stanford University Press, 1932; George M. Stephenson, *A History of American Immigration*, New York: Russell and Russell, 1964.

IMMIGRATION ACT OF FEBRUARY 5, 1917, a restrictive bill containing a literacy test proviso. The Immigration Act of February 20, 1907 established a commission to study immigration. The commission was to consist of three senators, three representatives, and three presidential appointees. On February 22, 1907, members of both the Senate and House were appointed, with William Paul Dillingham chairing the commission. The commission issued nothing of major substance, with the exception of the committee report in 1911, until the debate on the literacy test developed in 1912, when the Dillingham Bill was introduced. The bill was designed to exclude immigrants from Asia by means of a literacy test. The bill, with a number of amendments, passed and was sent to President William Howard Taft for his signature, but he vetoed it because of the literacy test proviso.

With the outbreak of war in Europe an atmosphere of uncertainty hung over America. No one knew how long the war would last, but almost everyone predicted that a new wave of immigration was inevitable. Those who were most devastated by the war could be expected to look to the United States to start their new lives in its industrialized Northern cities. Pressure to restrict the anticipated flow of immigration prompted a number of congressional measures, two of the most controversial being a proposed literacy test and an Asiatic barred zone.

The first session of the 64th Congress lasted from December 1915 to September 1916 and considered thirteen bills, some of which proposed to impose further restrictions on Chinese, Japanese, Hindus, and others. Although ten bills entitled "To regulate the immigration and residence of aliens" were introduced, the bill introduced by Representative John Lawson Burnett of Alabama, with the same title as mentioned above, was reported out on January 31, 1916. The report cited "constitutional, psychopathic inferiority" as a ground for exclusion and proposed the exclusion of "vagrants," "stowaways," "persons suffering from tuberculosis," and "those who advocate or teach the unlawful destruction of property." The most critical measures for Asian immigration, as mentioned previously, were a literacy test and an Asiatic barred zone. The House bill was debated for five days during which numerous amendments were offered, but with the exception of one amendment, all were defeated and the bill was passed by a vote of 307 to 87 on March 30, 1916.

The Senate worked on the Burnett Bill and its committee issued a report that included some minor changes from the original bill passed by the House. The bill was then debated in the Senate for two days, during which time William

Paul Dillingham of Vermont advocated a literacy test in lieu of the percentage plan to be used to restrict immigration to the United States. A Senate amendment proposed to strike out a clause in the Burnett Bill, excluding "Hindus and persons who cannot become eligible, under existing law, to become citizens of the United States by naturalization," and replace it with an Asiatic barred zone defined by latitude and longitude. The Senate passed the bill by a vote of 64 to 7 on December 14, 1916, and sent it to President Woodrow Wilson for his signature, but he vetoed it because of the literacy test proviso. Congress overrode his veto, and the bill was passed to become the Immigration Act of February 5, 1917.

FURTHER READING: Frank F. Chuman, *The Bamboo People*, Del Mar, Calif.: Publisher's Inc., 1976; E. P. Hutchinson, *Legislative History of American Immigration Policy, 1798–1965*, Philadelphia: University of Pennsylvania Press, 1981; George M. Stephenson, *A History of American Immigration, 1820–1924*, New York: Russell and Russell, 1964.

IMMIGRATION ACT OF 1924, restrictive immigration law which through its quota system was particularly discriminatory against Asians. In response to the general demand for a national immigration policy that would regulate and restrict the number and kinds of immigrants admitted to the United States, Congress had passed the Immigration Act of 1907 and the Immigration Act of 1917. The 1907 law placed further restrictions on the immigration of Japanese and Koreans to the continental United States, whereas the 1917 bill created both the Asiatic barred zone and the literacy test to screen out undesirable immigrants. These two congressional acts were considered weak and incapable of preventing undesirable immigrants from coming to the United States by people both within and without Congress who felt there should be further restrictive measures to regulate and control immigration.

During the second session of the 67th Congress, a bill entitled the Immigration Act of 1923 was introduced to establish a quota system. This system would have admitted to the United States only 2 percent of the number of foreign-born residents from that country in the United States at the Census of 1890. The most striking feature of the bill was the series of non-quota classes separated from quota immigrants. But the bill was not considered by the House, and it expired with the end of the session.

Feelings for revising American immigration laws were strong during the first session of the 68th Congress, and a total of fifteen bills were introduced. Because the 1921 Quota Act was slated to expire soon, the House began to work on the bill presented by Albert Johnson* of Washington, while the Senate went to work on the bill introduced by Senator David Aiken Reed of Pennsylvania. The Johnson Bill was reported out by the House Committee in March 1924 and retained the 1917 act as the basic immigration act, but it replaced the 1921 quota formula by establishing national quotas at 2 percent, as proposed in the 1923 Immigration Act mentioned earlier.

The bill, with a number of amendments, passed Congress on April 12, 1924. Upon receipt of the House bill, the Senate decided to replace it with the Reed Bill, which it had been debating. When the bill was debated on April 7, 8, and 9, concerns about Japanese immigration were expressed and Senator Henry Cabot Lodge* of Massachusetts spoke in favor of the Reed amendment which would have set the national origins quota at the 1920 Census level, because he believed it would effectively check Japanese immigration without giving grounds for the accusation that it was discriminatory against Japanese. On April 10, 1924, Japanese Ambassador to the United States, Hanihara Masanao,* wrote a letter to Secretary of State Charles Evans Hughes who transmitted it to the Senate the following day. In the letter Ambassador Hanihara expressed his strong feelings of reservation against the bill and stated that "grave consequences" might be created between the two nations, if the bill prohibiting the immigration of those ineligible for citizenship was to be approved by Congress. This letter was considered as a threat to the United States, and Senator Lodge and others pushed for the passage of the Reed Bill. The Senate gave its approval to the exclusion amendment, as proposed by Senator Reed, and to the entire bill on April 18, 1924. A House-Senate conference was organized to work out minor disagreements between the House and the Senate, and the bill was forwarded to President Calvin Coolidge, who signed it on May 26, 1924.

The Immigration Act of 1924, also known as the Quota Immigration Law, National Origins Act, and the Japanese Exclusion Act, imposed a strict limitation on the number of immigrant visas available per year. The difference between a quota and non-quota immigrant was that non-qota immigrants fit into one or more of the categories specified in the act. In addition, all immigrants from Western Hemisphere countries were classified as non-quota immigrants. The non-quota immigrant had the definite advantage for, not only were non-quota visas unlimited, but a non-quota immigrant could also use a quota immigrant visa. For quota immigrants a specific number of visas per year per nationality was made available. For any nationality the number of visas available equaled 2 percent of the foreign-born U.S. citizens of that nationality residing in the continental United States as determined by the U.S. Census of 1890. The minimum quota of any nationality was set at 100.

The 1924 Immigration Act was discriminatory against Asians for a number of reasons. First, there were not many Asians living in the United States in 1890, the base year used in allocating the number of visas to a nation. Second, Section 13 of the act specified that no alien ineligible for citizenship was to be admitted to the United States. Because Chinese, Japanese, and Koreans were ruled ineligible for U.S. citizenship, they were excluded. (*See also* Immigration Act of 1917.)
FURTHER READING: Robert A. Divine, *American Immigration Policy, 1924–1952*, New Haven, Conn.: Yale University Press, 1957; Frank F. Chuman, *The Bamboo People*, Del Mar, Calif., Publisher's Inc., 1976; E. P. Hutchinson, *Legislative History of American Immigration Policy, 1798–1965*, Philadelphia: University of Pennsylvania Press, 1981; S. W. Kung, *Chinese in American Life*, Westport, Conn.: Greenwood Press, 1973.

IMMIGRATION ACT OF OCTOBER 3, 1965, liberal amendment of the Immigration Act of 1952. The McCarran-Walter Act of 1952, passed over President Harry S Truman's presidential veto on June 25, 1952, was still restrictive and particularly discriminatory against the immigration of Asians, as it included the Asia-Pacific Triangle proviso. After Congress overrode his veto, President Truman appointed a Presidential Commission on Immigration and Naturalization in order to study and evaluate the immigration and naturalization policies of the United States. The commission was created on September 4, 1952, and was asked to report on January 1, 1953, just two days before the 83rd Congress was to convene. The commission report, *Whom We Shall Welcome*, recommended a wide-ranging reform of American policies for immigration and naturalization. Among the measures recommended were abolition of the national origins quota system, an overall ceiling on quota immigration of around 250,000 per year, and the allocation of immigration visas within the quota on the basis of need, overpopulation of the nations sending their citizens as immigrants, and U.S. needs. In response to the commission's report, Senator Herbert Lehman of New York with seven co-sponsors, including Senator John F. Kennedy of Massachusetts, introduced a bill in the Senate to repeal the McCarran-Walter Act of 1952. But no action was taken on the bill. Although some congressmen attempted to revise or repeal the act, the commission's recommendations did not find congressional endorsement until 1965.

Before Congress went to work to revise American policies for immigration and naturalization, however, President Kennedy let his sentiment for a liberal policy be known at a news conference on January 24, 1963, when he said that his administration had been giving attention to immigration questions. This was followed by the President's message to Congress on July 23, 1963, a message that recommended far-reaching revision of the quota system. On the same day Representative Emanuel Celler* of New York, chairman of the House Judiciary Committee, introduced a bill that included much of the Kennedy Administration's recommendations. On the following day Senator Philip Hart of Michigan introduced a counterpart bill in the Senate that was supported by twenty-six of his colleagues. This bill was followed by fifty-one counterpart bills in the Senate. The main features of the Celler and Hart bills reflected the recommended guidelines established by the administration. Among the measures was elimination of the Asia-Pacific Triangle provisions included in the McCarran-Walter Act.

With the assassination of President Kennedy in November 1963, the future of the new legislation was left uncertain, but President Lyndon B. Johnson vowed to carry on the policies of the Kennedy administration; on January 8, 1964, he recommended to the 88th Congress that it consider ways of eliminating bars of discrimination. But because of a group of Southern senators who were against a more liberal immigration policy, the 88th Congress failed to enact any major legislation.

After the 89th Congress convened on January 4, 1965, President Johnson sent his message on immigration on January 13, emphasizing the need to revise the

McCarran-Walter Act of 1952. On the same day Celler of New York introduced the administration bill in the House, and Hart of Michigan introduced the identical bill, supported with thirty-two sponsors, to the Senate. The major provisions of the Celler and Hart bills were essentially the same as those provided in their predecessor bills in the 88th Congress, and they were grouped into twenty sections that were to amend the McCarran-Walter Act of 1952. Two of the most important provisions in the Celler and Hart bills which had major impact on the immigration of Asians to the United States were the elimination of the Asia-Pacific Triangle provisions of the 1952 act and the change of the basis for admission from the national origin to the personal qualifications of the immigrant according to the preference classes.

The House Committee, after extensive hearings, reported out the Celler Bill and recommended strongly that the bill be approved. The House passed the bill, with an amendment from John Edward Fogarty of Rhode Island, by a vote of 318 to 95, with 19 not voting. The Senate committee reported on the House bill on September 15, and it approved the bill by a vote of 76 to 18, with 6 abstaining, on September 22, 1965. A conference committee was appointed to work out differences between the House and Senate versions of the bill, and the conference report was made a week later. The conference draft was accepted by both the House and the Senate, and President Johnson signed it into law on October 3, 1965, during a ceremony that took place at the base of the Statue of Liberty on Liberty Island in New York Bay. This law established a new policy for immigration. The policy was based on the principle of equality, not on the basis of the national origin of individuals who wished to immigrate to the United States.

As mentioned above, the Immigration Act of October 3, 1965, repealed the national origins quota system and eliminated the Asia-Pacific Triangle provisions, but it also included a number of new provisions.

FURTHER READING: Frank F. Chuman, *The Bamboo People*, Del Mar, Calif.: Publisher's Inc., 1976; E. P. Hutchinson, *Legislative History of American Immigration Policy, 1798–1965*, Philadelphia: University of Pennsylvania, 1981; Thomas Kessner and Betty Caroli, *Today's Immigrants*, New York: Oxford University Press, 1981; Tricia Knoll, *Becoming Americans*, Portland, Oreg.: Coast to Coast Books, 1982.

IMMIGRATION AND NATIONALITY ACT OF 1952 (also known as the McCarran-Walter Immigration and Naturalization Act), enacted on June 27, 1952, by the U.S. Congress in order to continue the quota system established by the Immigration Act of 1921 and the Immigration Act of 1924.* The law drafted by Senator Patrick Anthony McCarran and Representative Francis Eugene Walter was 300 pages long, and it introduced a complete codification and revision of U.S. Immigration and Naturalization laws. The McCarran-Walter Act of 1952, which was passed over the veto of President Harry S Truman, eliminated race as a bar to immigration and naturalization, but it retained the principle of national origin which had been American immigration policy since 1924. Included in the act were provisions concerning immigration quotas, regulations of acceptance, exclusions and expulsions of immigrants, passport regulations, travel and control of aliens, detention of aliens for observation and examination, designation of ports of entry, nationality and naturalization, and provisions in the event of war.

Although the law gave Asians the privilege of becoming American citizens through the process of naturalization, it still discriminated against them because they were placed under a quota system for immigration to the United States. When Representative Emanuel Celler* of New York criticized the bill because of its discriminatory nature, McCarran responded by warning against "opening the gates to a flood of Asiatics." The conservative senator from Nevada, who was once characterized as being "silver-haired, silver-tongued and silver-minded" for his aggressive representation of a silver mine region, claimed that he drafted the bill with the security of the United States in mind, because "if this oasis of the world should be overrun, perverted and contaminated, or destroyed, the last flickering light of humanity will be extinguished."

FURTHER READING: Robert A. Divine, *American Immigration Policy, 1924–1952*, New Haven, Conn.: Yale University Press, 1957; Edward P. Hutchinson, *Legislative History of American Immigration Policy, 1798–1965*, Philadelphia: University of Pennsylvania Press, 1981; S. W. Kung, *Chinese in American Life*, Westport, Conn.: Greenwood Press, 1973.

IN RE **AH CHONG,** a judicial decision made on June 9, 1880, at the United States Circuit Court, District of California. The court ruled that a California law prohibiting all aliens who cannot vote in the State of California from fishing in the waters of the state was unconstitutional as it was in violation of the Fourteenth Amendment of the Constitution and of Articles V and VI of the Burlingame Treaty of 1868* between the United States and China.

The new constitution passed by the California Legislature included Article XIX, which prohibited employment of Chinese by any corporation, or on any state, county, municipal, or other public work. Section 4 of the same article authorized the legislature to make appropriate legislation to enforce this law. Accordingly, the legislature passed on April 23, 1880, an act entitled "An Act Relating to Fishing in the Waters of This State," prohibiting all aliens "incapable of becoming electors of this state . . . from fishing, or taking any fish, lobsters, shrimps, or shell-fish of any kind for the purpose of selling or giving to another person to sell."

Ah Chong, the petitioner of this case, was arrested for taking fish in San Pablo Bay and selling them in violation of the law passed on April 23, 1880. He was tried, convicted, and sentenced to spend thirty days in jail. He sued out a writ of habeas corpus and asked to be released on the ground that his imprisonment was in violation of the Burlingame Treaty of 1868 and the Fourteenth Amendment of the Constitution.

Before the U.S. Circuit Court the state's attorney-general claimed that the state has exclusive right to control who can fish, as that right is derived from citizenship. Dismissing the claim of citizenship as a basis for prohibiting Chinese from fishing in California, Chief Justice Lorenzo Sawyer ruled that the right to fish is also a property right and although the state may prohibit all others who are not citizens, it may not single out only Chinese as an excluded class of people. If the Chinese were to be excluded, then the Germans, Italians, English, and Irish also should be excluded. The denial of the right for the Chinese to fish in the waters of the state when that right is given to other aliens is in violation of the Fourteenth Amendment of the Constitution and of Articles V and VI of the Burlingame Treaty. (*See also* California Constitutional Convention of 1879; Burlingame Treaty of 1868).

FURTHER READING: Elmer C. Sandmeyer, "California Anti-Chinese Legislation and the Federal Courts: A Study in Federal Relations," *Pacific Historical Review*, Vol. 5, No. 3, pp. 189-211, 1936; L. S. B. Sawyer, *Reports of Cases Decided in the Circuit and District Courts of the United States for the Ninth Circuit*, Vol. VI San Francisco: A. L. Bancroft and Company, 1882, pp. 451-458.

IN RE **AH FONG,** a judicial decision made by the United States Circuit Court, District of California, on September 21, 1874. The case went to the Circuit Court on petition for a writ of habeas corpus by a Chinese woman representing a group of twenty-one Chinese women who came to California aboard the American steamship *Japan* on August 24, 1873. Their request for permission to land was denied by the commissioner of immigration, who decided to detain them for the purpose of expelling them from the state.

The California State Legislature had passed a law in 1870, authorizing the commissioner of immigration to remove from the state aliens who were considered lewd, idiotic, deaf, dumb, blind, crippled, or infirm, or unable to support themselves. The commissioner considered that these Chinese women belonged to this class of excluded people, and denied them permission to land.

The Pacific Mail Steamship Company,* owner of the steamship, filed petition for a writ of habeas corpus in an attempt to have them released, but the state district court upheld the statute of California and remanded the petitioners to the commissioner. Then the petitioners filed for another writ of habeas corpus with the state supreme court, which ruled that the statute of California in question was neither in violation of the Burlingame Treaty of 1868* between the United States and China nor in violation of the Fourteenth Amendment of the Constitution.

A third habeas corpus was requested and obtained, this time in the United States Circuit Court, which ruled in favor of the petitioners. Presiding Justice Stephen Field recognized the state's police power to exclude paupers and convicts, but claimed that this power was limited. He ruled that the state's statute in question was in violation of the Burlingame Treaty of 1868, of the Fourteenth Amendment of the Constitution, and of the Civil Rights Act of 1870. As a result of this decision all twenty-one women were released except the one whose appeal went to the United States Supreme Court on a writ of error. This was the case of Chy Lung v. Freeman.* (*See also* Chy Lung v. Freeman; Burlingame Treaty of 1868.)

FURTHER READING: Elmer C. Sandmeyer, "California Anti-Chinese Legislation and the Federal Courts: A Study in Federal Relations," *Pacific Historical Review* Vol. 5, No. 3, pp. 189-211, 1936; L. S. B. Sawyer, *Reports of Cases Decided in the Circuit and District Courts of the United States for the Ninth Circuit. Vol III*, San Francisco: A. L. Bancroft and Company, 1877, pp. 144-160.

IN RE **TIBURCIO PARROTT,** a judicial decision made on March 22, 1880 in the United States Circuit Court, District of California. The court declared unconstitutional Section 2 of Article XIX of the Constitution of California, which prohibited corporations formed under the laws of California from employing Chinese. In 1879 the State of California adopted a new constitution which stated that "no corporation now existing, or hereafter formed, under the laws of this state, shall, after the adoption of this constitution, employ, directly or indirectly, in any capacity, any Chinese or Mongolian. The Legislature shall pass such laws as may be necessary to enforce this provision." In accordance with this provision the state legislature passed on February 13, 1880, an act known as "An Act to Amend the Penal Code by Adding Two New Sections Thereto, To Be Known as Sections 178 and 179, Prohibiting the Employment of Chinese by Corporations."

Tiburcio Parrott, president and director of the Sulphur Bank Quicksilver Mining Company, was arrested on charges of having violated Section 2 of Article XIX of the California Constitution. He sued out a writ of habeas corpus in the United States Circuit Court, which ruled that Section 178 and 179 in the penal code, as well as Section 2 of Article XIX of the California Constitution, were in violation of the Burlingame Treaty of 1868* and of the due process clause of the Fourteenth Amendment of the Constitution. (*See also* California Constitutional Convention of 1879.)

FURTHER READING: L. S. B. Sawyer. *Reports of Cases Decided in the Circuit and District Courts of the United States for the Ninth Circuit. Vol. VI*, San Francisco: A. L. Bancroft and Company, 1882, pp. 349-389.

INANAMA, a mutual aid society developed among Filipino workers in Hawaii in the late 1920s. Members of the organization made regular contributions as insurance premiums, and the organization helped its members pay for hospitalization or death expenses.

INDIA HOME RULE LEAGUE OF AMERICA, established by an Indian political leader, Lajpat Rai (1865–1928), in New York City after he returned to the United States in 1914. Rai had visited America in 1906 but soon after returned to India. He supported India's freedom within the framework of the All-India National Congress ideology and rejected the more radical method of gaining independence by means of violent revolution.

Rai founded the league with assistance from a number of Americans, including the Reverend J. T. Sunderland and B. W. Huebsch. Rai gave lectures and published *Young India*, the league's official organ for its public relations. The league collapsed after Rai was deported to India in 1919.

FURTHER READING: H. Brett Melendy, *Asians in America: Filipinos, Koreans, and East Indians*, Boston: Twayne Publishers, 1977; Haridas T. Muzumdar, *America's Contributions to India's Freedom*, Allahabad: Central Book Depot, 1962.

INDIA LEAGUE OF AMERICA, established in the mid–1930s in New York City by a group of concerned Indian community leaders. The founding members included N. R. Checker, V. R. Kokatnur, Anup Singh, and Haridas Muzumdar. Checker was elected president of the league, and plans were made to publish the league's monthly bulletin, *India Today*. Later, J. J. Singh replaced Checker as the league's president. Singh provided the league with the strong enthusiasm and vitality it needed. During World War II the league strove for India's independence as well as for the naturalization rights of Asian Indians in America.

FURTHER READING: Haridas Muzumdar, *America's Contributions to India's Freedom*, Allahabad: Central Book Depot, 1962.

INDIA LEAGUE OF AMERICA, MADISON, WISCONSIN, founded in 1964 when eleven Indian associations in Madison, Wisconsin, were confederated. The league has established numerous local chapters throughout the United States, and it strives to unite immigrants from the Indian subcontinent for the purpose of promoting a common heritage and helping each other in their struggle to "become part of the mainstream of American life," as stated in the league's charter.

FURTHER READING: Parmatma Saran and Edwin Eames, eds., *The New Ethnics*, New York: Praeger, 1980.

INDIA SOCIETY OF AMERICA, a cultural organization established by Hari G. Govil in New York between 1930 and 1931. It was mainly a one-man organization run by Govil, although he was able to attract many people of means who were willing to contribute to the organization. He organized a luxurious reception party in honor of India's great poet, Rabindranath Tagore,* in New York. The society was involved primarily in interpreting India's cultural heritage for interested Americans.

INDIAN AMERICAN CULTURAL SOCIETY, an organization established by the Sikhs in Yuba and Sutter counties in the State of California in 1958, who were formerly members of the Indian Society of Yuba and Sutter Counties.* The organization was principally involved in planning social programs that were related to their religion. One of the main events which they celebrated was Baisakhi Day in honor of the founding of the Sikh religion. They also honored Republic Day, held on January 26 each year to commemorate the adoption of India's 1947 constitution.

INDIAN SOCIETY OF YUBA AND SUTTER COUNTIES, founded in 1945 by Asian Indians who lived along the Feather River and in Yuba City, California. It was basically a social community organization whose primary goal was to revitalize the Asian Indian cultural heritage.

INDOCHINA MIGRATION AND REFUGEE ASSISTANCE ACT OF 1975 (Public Law 94–23), legislation passed by Congress on May 23, 1975 amending the Migration and Refugee Assistance Act of 1962 (MRAA–1962), which authorized the President of the United States to continue membership in the Intergovernmental Committee for European Migration. The President was empowered to assist the movement of refugees and to enhance the economic progress of developing nations by providing selected manpower and money. The government of the United States was to pay its dues for its involvement in the Intergovernmental Committee. In addition, funds were to be appropriated for the High Commissioner of the United Nations for refugee assistance, and funds were to be appropriated whenever the President decided it would be in the interests of the security of the United States to help certain refugee groups. In addition, the President was empowered to assist refugees in the United States, but he was responsible for defining a refugee as being a person who had left his or her country in the Western Hemisphere because of persecution or fear of persecution on account of race, color, religion, or political opinion, and could not return for the same reasons.

The Indochina Migration and Refugee Assistance Act was passed by Congress to redefine the term "refugee" to include people from Vietnam, Laos, and Kampuchea, because MRAA--1962 was applicable only to people in the Western Hemisphere. The law made $455 million available for administering, accommodating, and settling Indochinese refugees, but it also restricted the use of funds to implementation of clauses 3, 4, 5, and 6 of MRAA–1962. According to the law, all funds were to be discontinued after September 30, 1977.

FURTHER READING: Gail Kelly, *From Vietnam to America: A Chronicle of the Vietnamese Immigration to the United States*, Boulder, Colo.: Westview Press, 1977; Darrel Montero, *Vietnamese Americans: Patterns of Resettlement and Socioeconomic Adaptation in the United States*, Boulder, Colo.: Westview Press, 1979; William T. Liu, *Transition to Nowhere: Vietnamese Refugees in America*, Nashville, Tenn.: Charter House Publishers, 1979.

INDOCHINESE MUTUAL ASSISTANCE DIVISION OF THE DEPARTMENT OF HEALTH, EDUCATION AND WELFARE, established on July 12, 1976, in order to provide technical assistance and liaison channels for more than 100 self-help associations found among Indochinese refugees throughout the country.

INDOCHINESE REFUGEE CHILDREN ASSISTANCE ACT OF 1976 (Public Law 94–405), passed by the U.S. Congress to render assistance to states in order to help local educational agencies provide education for Vietnamese and Kampuchean refugee children, among other purposes. In 1976 the task of providing international protection for refugees from Indochina became critical as their physical safety was endangered by the disregard of the refugees' rights both by individuals and governments. During the same year, the so-called boat people,* who had left Indochina in small vessels in quest of a haven in neighboring areas, were reported to have arrived in various parts of Southeast Asia. As the number of people leaving Indochina increased, the attitude of Americans changed toward those Indochinese entering America. Although many boat people suffered greatly in their attempt to leave Indochina, those who arrived in America after their dangerous voyage now faced the additional hardships of prejudice and language and cultural barriers. In an attempt to educate refugee children, the Carter administration introduced the Indochinese Refugee Children Assistance Act, which Congress passed. It went into effect on September 10, 1976, providing educational assistance for elementary-secondary students and adults for the academic year 1976–1977.

INDOCHINESE REFUGEE RECEPTION CENTERS, temporary centers for Indochinese refugees established at U.S. military bases. After the American debacle in Vietnam in 1975, approximately 140,000 Indochinese began to evacuate their homeland. Having helped the American military or diplomatic services or having participated in government programs administered by the South Vietnamese government, many of these people feared for their safety and their lives. Those with middle-class economic status feared that the new Communist regime would force them to reeducate themselves or put them to death. Others feared persecution for their religious beliefs.

The United Nations High Commission on Refugees tried unsuccessfully to work out an agreement between the United States and the new regime. The Ford administration drew up a plan for the evacuation called Operation New Life. Under this plan the refugees would be interviewed, examined, given an identification number, registered with American agencies, introduced to American society, and then given a new place to live and work in the United States.

Once evacuated from Indochina, the refugees were not allowed to immigrate directly to the United States. After evacuation, they were shipped to American overseas bases in Utapo in Thailand, Subic Bay, and Clark Field in the Philippines, Wake, and especially Guam, which held the most overcrowded reception center housing 50,000 in a ninety-day period. The refugees were then transported to mainland reception centers in either Camp Pendleton located near San Diego, California, which held 18,000 refugees, Fort Chaffee in Arkansas which was the largest with 24,000 refugees, Eglin Air Force Base in Florida, which accommodated 5,000, or Fort Indiantown Gap near Harrisburg, Pennsylvania, which held 16,000 refugees.

The U.S. policy with regard to refugee settlement was to move refugees out into American society as quickly as possible through voluntary agencies that usually dealt with immigrants and refugees. Two main reasons seem to have occupied the minds of policymakers at this time. First, they felt that a large concentration of refugee populations in a limited number of communities would create an added financial burden on them. Second, they felt that thinning refugees out across the country would facilitate the assimilation of Indochinese into American life. They did not want to create refugee ghettos or reservations. Whether or not the resettlement of Indochinese refugees has been successful will have to wait for historians to judge. The hard facts that have been made available, however, are not very encouraging. In 1975, after two months out of reception centers, 68 percent of the men found jobs, at low-paying wages. By October 1975, 58 percent were on welfare. But for refugees, loneliness was worse than poverty. The older people and single men suffered more than most. The loss of family was a loss of continuity over the generations.

FURTHER READING: W. T. Liu, *Transition to Nowhere: Vietnamese Refugees in America*, Nashville: Charter House, 1979; Tom Choken Owan, ed., *Southeast Asian Mental Health*, Rockville, Md.: National Institute of Mental Health, 1985.

INOUYE, DANIEL KEN (1924–), U.S. senator. Inouye was born in Honolulu, Hawaii, on September 7, 1924. Upon high school graduation in 1942, he enlisted as a private in the famous 442nd Regimental Combat Unit* and later was commissioned a second lieutenant on the battlefield in 1944. After the war, he graduated from the University of Hawaii in 1950, majoring in government and economics, after which he studied law at George Washington University Law School, where he became a member of the Board of Editors of the *George Washington Law Review*. He received his J.D. degree in 1952 and started his law practice in Honolulu two years later. His driving interest, however, was politics. With assistance from his old friends of the 442nd Regimental Combat Unit, he launched his political campaign when he was elected to the Territorial House of Representatives in 1954. He was reelected in 1956. He served as majority leader in the Territorial House of Representatives for four years and was elected to the Senate in the following territorial election.

When Hawaii became the fiftieth state in March 1959, Inouye ran for and was elected to Hawaii's seat in the House of Representatives. While in the House, he supported attempts to pass civil rights legislation by signing a discharge petition to bring the bill out of the rules committee. In 1962 he ran for one of Hawaii's two Senate seats and was elected to the U.S. Senate, where he became a strong supporter of the Kennedy and Johnson administrations' policies, particularly those concerning civil rights. He served on the Watergate Committee that investigated the campaign activities of the Republican Party and was subjected to a racist characterization by John J. Wilson, a lawyer for John Ehrlichman, who called Senator Inouye "the little Jap." Inouye was one of the first congressmen to ask President Richard M. Nixon to resign.

In the Senate Inouye introduced and sponsored a number of bills to advance the cause of Asian and other minorities in America. He introduced a bill to repeal the Internal Security Act of 1950, which had served as the legal basis for establishing concentration camps in America. This bill was repealed on September 25, 1971, when President Nixon signed the bill which was passed by Congress on September 14. Senator Inouye co-sponsored a bill, S. 1647, better known as the Commission on Wartime Relocation and Internment of Civilians* Act in 1979.

FURTHER READING: Bill Hosokawa, *JACL in Quest of Justice*, New York: William Morrow and Co., 1982; Daniel K. Inouye and Lawrence Elliott, *Journey to Washington*, Englewood Cliffs, N.J.: Prentice-Hall, 1967.

INOUYE, FRANK. *See* Heart Mountain Congress of American Citizens.

INOUYE YUICHI et al. v. CLARK, a case tried in federal court in Los Angeles in 1947, involving four persons of Japanese ancestry who had renounced their U.S. citizenship during the years of their incarceration. Inouye was only seventeen years of age when his father applied for repatriation to Japan. He also renounced his citizenship so that he could be with his parents. Three other renouncers, Marakami Miye Mae, Sumi Tsutako, and Shimizu Mutsu, were incarcerated at the Tule Lake Segregation Center* and were forced to renounce their U.S. citizenship either by their husbands or by others in the camp. Presiding Judge Charles C. Cavanah restored their citizenship and stated that U.S. citizens should not be forced to renounce their citizenship. The government appealed Judge Cavanah's decision to the Ninth Circuit Court of Appeals, but the Circuit court upheld it on August 26, 1949.

INSULAR CASES, a decision handed down by the Supreme Court of the United States on May 27, 1901 on the case of Elias S. A. De Lima et al. v. George R. Bidwell. By the narrow margin of five to four, the Court ruled that the Constitution of the United States cannot be extended to U.S. territories unless Congress decides to extend the Constitution through its legislation. Because of this decision, inhabitants of U.S. territories such as the Philippines and Puerto Rico were denied constitutional protection.

FURTHER READING: W. Cameron Forbes, *The Philippine Islands*, Vol. 2, Boston: Houghton Mifflin Co., 1928; Maximo C. Manzon, *The Strange Case of the Filipinos in the U.S.*, New York: American Committee for Protection of Foreign Born, 1938; *Supreme Court Reporter*, Vol. 21, 1900, 182 U.S. 1.

INTERAGENCY TASK FORCE, created on April 15, 1975, as American withdrawal from South Vietnam became inevitable and President Gerald Ford asked twelve federal agencies to coordinate all U.S. government activities in order to evacuate U.S. citizens, certain Vietnamese citizens, and citizens of other countries from Vietnam. Ambassador L. Dean Brown was named its director. The Interagency Task Force (ITF) then asked civil and military authorities on Guam to make preparations for a group of an estimated 50,000 refugees to be cared for over a period of ninety days. Ambassador Brown returned to his post at the Middle East Institute on May 27, 1975, and was replaced by Julia Taft. In cooperation with one of the military services, the ITF established refugee camps at Fort Chaffee, Arkansas, Eglin Air Force Base, Florida, Camp Pendleton, California, and Fort Indiantown Gap, Pennsylvania. These camps accommodated Vietnamese refugees before they were processed and cleared for relocation in towns and cities across the country.

The ITF completed the first phase of its program of evacuating and resettling Vietnamese refugees in the United States by December 31, 1975, and was replaced by the Refugee Task Force established within the U.S. Department of Health, Education and Welfare.

FURTHER READING: Gail P. Kelly, *From Vietnam to America*, Boulder, Colo.: Westview Press, 1977; Darrel Montero, *Vietnamese Americans: Patterns of Resettlement and Socioeconomic Adaptation in the United States*, Boulder, Colo.: Westview Press, 1979.

INTERMOUNTAIN DISTRICT COUNCIL, organized in 1939 by Mike Masaoka* after he was ejected from a meeting after he criticized the Japanese American Citizens League* during its national convention held in Los Angeles during the summer of 1938. Masaoka pointed out that the league should expand to include Japanese Nisei* in other parts of the country because it was strictly a West Coast organization at that time. He also stated that the league should include not only Nisei, but also anyone who wanted to combat discrimination. Because of this criticism James Yoshinori Sakamoto* asked him to leave. After this unpleasant encounter, Masaoka went home and studied how he could get the league to hear his views. A check of the league's organizational structure revealed that only three chapters would make a District Council, and, more importantly, the chairman of such a council would automatically become a member of the National Board. Masaoka set out to organize chapters in Salt Lake City, Ogden, Boise Valley, Idaho Falls, Mount Olympus, Pocatello, Rexburg, and the Snake River Valley area of eastern Oregon, all of which were grouped into the Intermountain District Council. Masaoka was elected chairman of the council in 1939.

This was the only district council in operation during the internment years of World War II.

FURTHER READING: Bill Hosokawa, *Nisei: The Quiet Americans*, New York: William Morrow and Co., 1969.

INTERNATIONAL LONGSHOREMEN'S AND WAREHOUSEMEN'S UNION (ILWU), established in August 1937 when the Congress of Industrial Organizations (CIO) issued a charter to a group of longshoremen's unions led by Harry Bridges, who became Pacific Coast director of the CIO. Bridges had led a group of local unions which had refused to pay tax to the International Longshoremen's Association established in 1895.

The ILWU is one of the most radical labor unions in the country. Because its president, Harry Bridges, was willing to seek cooperation with groups of different political persuasion, including Communists, the ILWU has not infrequently been harassed by the U.S. government. One of the major government actions taken to weaken the ILWU was the deportation hearings against Bridges, who was ordered deported by the Department of Justice in 1942. The U.S. Supreme Court finally ended the government's persistent pressure on Bridges by deciding in Bridges' favor in 1945.

The ILWU has been very active in organizing minority workers, as is borne out by the history of the ILWU in Hawaii. Hawaii's economy had long been dominated by the Big Five,* and workers found themselves at the mercy of the economic power of the five major corporations on the islands. Despite repeated strikes by weak labor unions, they were not able to get any major concessions from these corporations. In 1940 Kauai longshoremen struck for ten months in order to receive a guarantee of $15 a week. Although their struggle failed, they did not give up their union activities, and finally they organized themselves with the assistance of Jack Hall. They received their charter from the ILWU. This organizational base became the litmus test of ILWU's strength in the islands when it struck on September 1, 1946. It won a minor victory when employers agreed to give a 30-cent wage increase. On May 1, 1949, the ILWU struck again against the Big Five. The strike lasted 157 days and finally ended with a concession from the employers who gave a 21-cent wage increase. The repeated agitation and labor unrest in Hawaii invited strong reactions against the ILWU and its leadership. One of the major efforts to weaken the labor union was the indictment and conviction of Jack Hall in 1954 on violation of the Smith Act. His conviction was later thrown out by the Circuit Court of Appeals in San Francisco in 1958.

The ILWU has played a major role in party politics in Hawaii. Under the leadership of Jack Hall the ILWU continued to recruit its labor union members into the Democratic Party and to support Democratic Party candidates in local elections. The power of the ILWU peaked in 1948, when members of the ILWU were elected to the 1948 Democratic Party Convention Committee. During the convention, Jack Hall challenged the traditional Democratic Party power structure in Hawaii and tried to take over the party. (*See also* Hawaii Seven; Hilo Massacre.)

FURTHER READING: *The ILWU Story: Three Decades of Militant Unionism*, San Francisco: Information Department, International Longshoremen's and Warehousemen's Union, 1963; Charles P. Larrowe, *Harry Bridges*, New York: Lawrence Hill and Co., 1972; Charles A. Madison, *American Labor Leaders*, New York: Harper and Brothers, 1950; Paul C. Phillips, *Hawaii's Democrats: Chasing the American Dream*, Washington, D.C.: Catholic University of America Press, 1982; Maud Russell, *Men Along the Shore*, New York: Brussel and Brussel, 1966; Theon Wright, *The Disenchanted Isles: The Story of the Second Revolution in Hawaii*, New York: Dial Press, 1972.

INTERNMENT OF JAPANESE AMERICANS, the incarceration of more than 110,000 persons of Japanese ancestry, both citizens and resident aliens, during World War II for reasons of national security. (*See also* Civilian Exclusion

Orders, Commission on Wartime Relocation and Internment of Civilians, Executive Order 9066, Japanese American Evacuation Claims Act, Hirabayashi v. United States, Korematsu v. United States, Endo exparte, Tule Lake Segregation Center and War Relocation Authority.)

IRON CHINK, a fish cleaning machine introduced to the cannery industry at the turn of the century. Edmund A. Smith is said to have introduced the machine in 1905, although it had been invented in 1903. The Alaska Packers Association used the machine extensively as a tremendous labor-saving device. One machine replaced fifty-one Chinese laborers, or it was capable of cleaning fifty fish per minute, replacing six Chinese laborers. It was called "Iron Chink" because it largely replaced Chinese workers who had been working in cannery industries on the West Coast and in Alaska.

FURTHER READING: Robert J. Browning, *Fisheries of the North Pacific*, Anchorage: Alaska Northwest Publishing Co., 1980; Hugh W. McKervill, *The Salmon People*, Sidney, British Columbia, Canada: Gray's Publishing, Ltd., 1967; Patrick W. O'Bannon, "Technological Change in the Pacific Coast Canned Salmon Industry, 1900–1925: A Case Study," *Agricultural History* 56, No. 1 (January 1982): 151–66.

IRWIN, ROBERT W. (1844-?), diplomat, recruiting agent. Irwin was born in Copenhagen, Denmark, in 1844 to William Wallace Irwin, the Charge d'Affaires at Copenhagen at that time. With the assistance of his brother Richard, Robert went to Japan in 1866 as the Pacific Mail Steamship Company* agent in Yokohama. Later he helped prominent Japanese businessmen to organize an import-export company, Senshu Kaisha, with Inoue Kaoru who later became Finance Minister of Japan. After Inoue Kaoru left the company for government service, the company was reorganized to become Mitsui Bussan Kaisha.

Irwin married a Japanese woman, Takechi Iki. The legal papers for their marriage were signed on March 15, 1882, thus making the marriage the first such arrangement made on thorough legal grounds between an American and a Japanese. They had six children, all of whom were educated both in Japan and the United States.

Irwin entered Hawaiian affairs in 1880, when the Hawaiian consul-general to Japan, Harlan P. Lillibridge, recommended him as his replacement. Irwin became acting consul general that year, and the following year he was appointed consul general after King Kalakaua of Hawaii visited Japan. When negotiations for a new Japanese immigration to Hawaii began after the Ganen-Mono* affair in 1868, Irwin was asked to help make the necessary arrangements between the government of Hawaii and that of Japan. With the help of his friend, Inoue Kaoru, he went to Yamaguchi Prefecture to recruit Japanese for the Hawaiian Sugar Planters' Association.* He came to Hawaii with the first shipload of Japanese immigrants aboard the *City of Tokyo*, arriving in Honolulu on February 8, 1885. The second group of Japanese immigrants came to Honolulu aboard the *Yamashiro Maru*, arriving there on July 17, 1885. After a formal convention was reached between the government of Japan and the Hawaiian government in 1886, these first two groups of Japanese immigrants came under the provisions made available in that convention. The Convention of 1886 between Japan and Hawaii* became the foundation on which Japanese immigration to Hawaii was built for the following eight years, during which time 28,691 Japanese came to Hawaii. The system Irwin so carefully worked to establish broke down in 1894. FURTHER READING: Francis Hilary Conroy, "The Japanese Expansion into Hawaii, 1868–1898," Ph.D. diss., University of California, 1949.

IRWIN, WALLACE (1875–1959), writer and journalist. Irwin was born in Oneida, New York, on March 15, 1875. He was four years old when his family moved to Cripple Creek, Colorado, in a covered wagon. His father was interested in silver mining and sought work unsuccessfully. Later he tried lumber and cattle but again failed. Irwin never went to school on a regular basis, and when he moved to Denver at fourteen years of age, he started public school. Because of his math deficiency, he was placed as an assayer for a year before he attended Stanford University. In his second year, he wrote the sophomore class play. Irwin became the editor of the university magazine in his junior year. This position ended abruptly when he was expelled from Stanford for his declining scholarship. After his expulsion from Stanford, he began to work as a journalist. His first job was reporting for a Scrippo-Blade paper called the *Report*. That paper soon went bankrupt. He then moved to San Francisco and worked for the *Examiner*. He began as a writer of rhymed headlines and later became a Chinatown* reporter. By thirty-three he was editor of the *Overland Monthly* in San Diego.

During his lifetime Irwin wrote for many other magazines and papers such as *Life, Globe, Saturday Evening Post, Good Housekeeping*, and *Cosmopolitan*. He was later hired by *Collier's Weekly*, where he began writing the "Letters of a Japanese Schoolboy" under the pen name of "Hashimura Togo." The "Letters" were about a young Japanese boy who was wounded in an anti-Japanese riot in Vancouver, British Columbia. Irwin wrote about the enjoyable stay the young boy had in the hospital. The article elicited such an overwhelming response that Irwin continued writing under the name of Togo for two or three more years. The articles were eventually published in a variety of magazines for twenty years. From 1902 to 1936 Irwin wrote books, including *Seed of the Sun* (1921).

Irwin's *Seed of the Sun* is an example of the racist mentality of the time. The author leads the reader to the conclusion that the Japanese are a people who cannot be trusted. He does so by manipulating the reader through character stereotypes. Irwin created the stereotype of the Japanese as being short, sneaky, and deceiving. For instance, Irwin portrays Mr. Shimba, the tenant in the book, as a little man, with a "poker face and wearing the mask of Asia." In contrast, Irwin describes the more fluent and intelligent Japanese as having Anglo-Saxon features. These characters are said to have rounder eyes, and to be better proportioned and taller. For example, Mrs. Awaga, the wife of the Christian minister, being fluent in the English language, is portrayed as "prettier, more helpful, open and human than her Japanese counterpart." Another example is Baron Tazumi, who is said to be a "noble gentleman and a great orator with pale skin and round eyes."

The Japanese in America have faced a multitude of adversities since their immigration. They have faced ridicule, humiliation, and denial of their constitutional rights, these all being a direct result of prejudice and discrimination. This prejudice was conveyed to the public through many means, one of these being the written media. Wallace Irwin, as a journalist and writer, contributed to the creation of conventional stereotypes about the Japanese in America.

FURTHER READING: Wallace Irwin, *Seed of the Sun*, New York: Arno Press, 1978 edition; Elaine H. Kim, *Asian American Literature*, Philadelphia: Temple University Press, 1982; Stanley Kunitz, *Twentieth Century Authors*, New York: H. W. Wilson Co., 1942; *New York Times*, February 15, 1959.

IRWIN, WILLIAM (1827–1886), governor of California. Irwin was born in Butler County, Ohio in 1827 and attended a country school before he was able to go to a private academy near Cincinnati. He graduated from Marietta College in 1848. He taught one year in Mississippi and came back to his Alma Mater where he taught two years. Although he planned to go to law school when he moved to New York in 1851, he changed his mind and went to California where he went into a lumber mill business near Yreka in 1854.

Irwin's political career started in 1862 when he was elected to the 1862 Assembly as a Democrat. In 1869 he was elected to the State Senate for a two-year term, and four years later he became President pro tem of the Senate. Irwin was elected governor of California in 1875 when the state's economy was in deep recession. Because of economic hardships in California, many people agitated for Chinese exclusion from the state. A new political party organized on October 5, 1877, the Workingmen's Party of California,* opposed Chinese immigration and Chinese labor. When a vigilance committee under the leadership of William T. Coleman was organized and began to stir up trouble against the Chinese in San Francisco, Irwin supported the committee's work. He believed that the Chinese were responsible for the worker's plight, and he commented on the evils of Chinese immigration in his 1877 message, in which he called for Congress to restrict Chinese immigration.

FURTHER READING: H. H. Bancroft, *Chronicles of the Builders of the Commonwealth*, 7 vols., San Francisco, 1891; H. Brett Melendy and Benjamin F. Gilbert, *The Governors of California*, Georgetown, Calif.: Talisman Press, 1965; Alexander Saxton, *The Indispensable Enemy*, Berkeley: University of California Press, 1971.

ISSEI, a Japanese term that means the first generation of immigrants from Japan. The term is made up of two Japanese words: first or one and generation. When referring to the second generation, American-born children of Issei, the Japanese word Ni which means second, replaces the first word of the above term to become Nisei.* The third generation, children of Nisei, is called Sansei*; the first word of the term, san, means third or three.

Most of the Issei have now passed away, and those that are still alive today are over eighty years of age.

FURTHER READING: John W. Connor, *Tradition and Change in Three Generations of Japanese Americans*, Chicago: Nelson-Hall, 1977; Harry H. L. Kitano, *Japanese Americans: The Evolution of a Subculture*, Englewood Cliffs, N.J.: Prentice-Hall, 1969; Kataoka Susan McCoin, *Issei Women: A Study in Subordinate Status*, Ann Arbor, Mich.: University Microfilms International, 1980; Gordon G. Nakayama, *Issei*, Toronto, Canada: Britannia Printers Limited, 1983.

ITLIONG, LARRY DULAY (1914–1977), labor organizer. Itliong was born in 1914, long after the immigration of Asians to America for the purposes of cheap labor started. As a Filipino, he was concerned with the labor conditions of his co-workers in the fields. As late as the 1950s, Filipinos and other Asian immigrants were paid low wages and were unable to enter trade unions, even though Filipinos were the backbone of California's agricultural work force and provided much needed labor.

Unionization of field laborers was restricted until the 1960s, but a beginning was made when the AFL-CIO formed the Agricultural Workers Organizing Committee (AWOC) in 1959 and chose Larry Itliong to lead the committee to organize field workers. Larry worked diligently to organize union members, and in 1965 the AWOC led a strike against thirty-one grape growers in Delano, California. During the strike Cesar Chavez joined Itliong and his union, and Chavez's organization merged with the AWOC to become the United Farm Workers Organizing Committee* in 1966.

The committee was successful in its negotiations with the major wine-producing industries. Between 1969 and 1970 Itliong was able to produce three-year contracts with some major grape growers in Delano and San Joaquin Valley that established a $2 minimum wage for field workers.

Larry Itliong spent twelve years working to improve the rights of his fellow Filipinos and other minority groups. He resigned from the leadership of the United Farm Workers Organizing Committee in 1971 to embark on other causes. He died in 1977. (*See also* Grape Strike, Delano.)

FURTHER READING: Lorraine J. Crouchett, *Filipinos in California*, El Cerrito, Calif.: Downey Place Publishing House, 1982; Gary M. Fink, *Biographical Dictionary of American Labor Leaders*, Westport, Conn.: Greenwood Press, 1974.

IWAKURA MISSION, dispatched by the emperor of Japan to the United States and the major countries in Europe to negotiate the revision of treaties that would be more favorable to Japan. The mission was led by Prince Iwakura, and it arrived in San Francisco on January 15, 1872, aboard the steamer *America*. The total number of passengers was 107, of whom 49 belonged to the mission. The remainder were 5 women and 53 students and servants. They were accompanied by Charles E. DeLong, American Minister to Japan.

It was said that the prince wanted to meet all Japanese residents in San Francisco upon his arrival, and every effort was made to round up all Japanese to greet him. A total of thirty-seven Japanese residents were gathered for the occasion.

The mission was one of the most important diplomatic efforts launched by Meiji Japan to understand the West. Later, some of the members of the mission such as Ito Hirobumi, served in important government offices. Students who stayed behind to study in the United States also played prominent roles in Japanese society upon their return to Japan.

Prince Iwakura left two sons behind in the United States to study while he continued on a tour in Europe. During his European tour, Niijima Jo,* a Japanese student who had been studying at Andover Theological Seminary, served as interpreter for the mission. After the mission, Niijima returned to the United States, finished his study at the seminary, and then returned to his country to establish Doshisha University in Kyoto.

FURTHER READING: James F. Abbott, *Japanese Expansion and American Policies*, New York: Macmillan Co., 1916; Foster Rhea Dulles, *Yankees and Samurai: America's Role in the Emergence of Modern Japan, 1791–1900*, New York: Harper and Row, 1965; Yamato Ichihashi, *Japanese in the United States*, Stanford, Calif.: Stanford University Press, 1932; Charles Lanman, ed., *The Japanese in America*, New York: University Publishing Co., 1872.

J

JAMIESON, F. W. *See* Fukunaga Case.

JAPANESE AMERICAN BUSINESS PROMOTION COMPANY (Nichibei Kangyosha). *See* Abiko Kyutaro.

JAPANESE AMERICAN CITIZENS LEAGUE, a non-profit civic organization founded in 1939, with more than 30,000 members today. The national office is located in San Francisco. The Japanese American Citizens League (JACL) operates its official publication, *The Pacific Citizen,** which has been in existence since 1932. Although the JACL started as an organization whose membership was exclusively Nisei* when it began some fifty-five years ago, today its membership includes not only persons of other Asian ancestry, but also people whose ancestry is not Asian.

The effort to establish, maintain, and strengthen the JACL during the last half century has been hard and tortuous. It has suffered many defeats in its struggle to achieve justice for persons of Japanese ancestry, but it also has won some major victories.

The seeds of the organization were sown in San Francisco by a small group of Nisei college graduates who began to meet for lunch on a regular basis in 1918. Included in this lunch group were Thomas Okawara, Hayashi Tokutaro, Hayashi Hidebi, and Kay Tsukamoto, all of whom were concerned about the future of Nisei in America. Their lunch discussions finally led them to establish the American Loyalty Club,* but later the name was changed to American Loyalty League. The organization became virtually inactive by 1922.

Another group of Nisei in Seattle organized the Seattle Progressive Citizens League* with no knowledge of the existence of a league in San Francisco; their main concern was with legalized discrimination against aliens and ineligibility to citizenship. Another group of Nisei established the American Loyalty League of Fresno* under the leadership of Thomas Yatabe in 1923, and it was this organization to which the JACL today attributes its organizational foundation. In 1928 the Fresno League sent an invitation to the Seattle League asking it to send delegates to a conference of Nisei leaders that August. With delegates en route the meeting was canceled, but they continued to San Francisco and Los Angeles with the idea of establishing a coast-wide Nisei citizens' movement. Upon arriving in San Francisco they met with Kido Saburo,* Henry Takahashi, and Togasaki Susumu, and they all agreed to meet the following April with some concrete proposals for founding a national organization.

During the April meeting Clarence Arai made three proposals: to establish a national Nisei organization, to name it the Japanese American Citizens League, and to hold a founding convention in Seattle in the summer of 1930. As president pro tem of the league, Arai began to make preparations for a national convention in Seattle, and the convention was held on August 29, 1930, with 102 representatives from five states and the Territory of Hawaii. The delegates adopted the organization's constitution and passed a resolution, calling on Congress to grant veterans of Japanese ancestry American citizenship which they deserved after their loyal service to the country. The organization decided to send its lobbyist, Suma Sugi (later Mrs. Harry Yokotake), to have the Cable Act of 1922* repealed. She went to Washington, D.C., in February 1931 and was instrumental in getting the Cable Act repealed on March 3, 1931. The JACL lobbying efforts also led to legislation which allowed some 700 Nisei men who had served in the U.S. armed forces to be granted citizenship.

The JACL came under criticism during the internment years and immediately afterward because of its conservative policies and its cooperation with government authorities who decided to relocate all persons of Japanese ancestry during the Pacific War. Nonetheless, it has served the Japanese community well, seeking justice for persons of Japanese ancestry.

FURTHER READING: Bill Hosokawa, *Nisei*, New York: William Morrow and Co., 1969; *JACL in Quest of Justice: The History of the Japanese American Citizens League*, New York: William Morrow and Co., 1982.

JAPANESE AMERICAN COURIER, an all-English weekly started by James Yoshinori Sakamoto.* In 1927 he was the first Nisei* boxer to box professionally at Madison Square Garden in New York. Soon after he returned to Seattle, where he was born, and began to publish the *Japanese American Courier* in January 1928. The newspaper lasted fourteen years; it was closed when all persons of Japanese ancestry were ordered evacuated during the Pacific War. (*See also* Sakamoto, James Yoshinori.)

JAPANESE AMERICAN CREED, written by Mike Masaru Masaoka* in 1940 and included in the *Congressional Record* on May 9, 1941. It reflected not only Masaoka's loyalty to and belief in America and its Constitution, but also it represented most of the Nisei* who shared the same loyalty and belief expressed in the creed. It reads:

> I am proud that I am an American citizen of Japanese ancestry, for my very background makes me appreciate more fully the wonderful advantages of this nation. I believe in her institutions, ideals, and traditions; I glory in her heritage; I boast of her history; I trust in her future. She has granted me liberties and opportunities such as no individual enjoys in this world today. She has given me an education befitting kings. She has entrusted me with the responsibilities of the franchise. She has permitted me to build a home, to earn a livelihood, to worship, think, speak, and act as I please—as a free man equal to every other man.
>
> Although some individuals may discriminate against me, I shall never become bitter or lose faith, for I know that such persons are not representative of the majority of the American people. True, I shall do all in my power to discourage such practices, but I shall do it in the American way: above-board, in the open, through courts of law, by education, by proving myself to be worthy of equal treatment and consideration. I am firm in my belief that American sportsmanship and attitudes of fair play will judge citizenship and patriotism on the basis of action and achievement, and not on the basis of physical characteristics.
>
> Because I believe in America, and I trust she believes in me, and because I have received innumerable benefits from her, I pledge myself to do honor to her at all times and in all places; to support her Constitution, to obey her laws, to respect her flag; to defend her against all enemies, foreign or domestic; to assume actively my duties and obligations as a citizen, cheerfully and without any reservations whatsoever, in the hope that I may become a better American in a greater America.

(*See also* Masaoka, Mike Masaru.)

JAPANESE AMERICAN EVACUATION CLAIMS ACT, a law signed by President Harry S Truman on July 2, 1948, enabling Japanese Americans, who had lost their property because of their internment during World War II, to receive compensation for their losses. After the bombing of Pearl Harbor by the Japanese in December 1941, Japanese Americans on the Pacific West Coast were removed and relocated by the government according to Executive Order 9066* issued by President Franklin D. Roosevelt. Because of the evacuation order, Japanese Americans were forced to hastily liquidate their assets, pack what few belongings they could carry in their hands, and move to internment camps designated by the War Relocation Authority.* After the end of the war, Japanese Americans were allowed to return, but they had no homes, no property, and no jobs or income. Left with nothing, they turned to the government for assistance. With the help of the Japanese American Citizens League* (JACL), the Issei* and Nisei* began to make claims against the American government.

Eugene Rostow, a professor of law at Yale, made the connection between the moral obligation of making amends to the evacuees and another Supreme Court decision (Duncan v. Kahanomuku). Although unrelated to the Japanese American cases, it restored the principle of the primacy of civilian rights in wartime. Rostow asked the Supreme Court for material compensation for the Japanese

Americans, insisting that a democratic society should meet its responsibility by admitting that a wrong was committed and that it should right the wrong.

At its 1946 convention, the JACL passed a resolution calling on Congress to pass legislation to compensate evacuees for losses which the Federal Reserve Bank of San Francisco estimated at $400 million. Harold Ickes, U.S. Secretary of the Interior, had asked for compensation for damage inflicted on property during owners' absence from the West Coast, and his successor, J. A. Krug, urged Congress to pass an evacuation claims bill, a proposal endorsed by President Truman in the same month that he awarded the Seventh Presidential Distinguished Unit Citation to members of the 442nd Regimental Combat Unit.*

The law provided that Japanese Americans could make claims for damage to or loss of real and personal property, to be filed within an eighteen-month period. No claims were to be filed by those who had gone to Japan or for property confiscated under the Trading with the Enemy Act.

Offices on the Pacific Coast were set up to process claims. Congress appropriated $38 million and authorized payments of up to $2,500 for each claimant. By the January 2, 1950, deadline 23,924 claims for a total of approximately $132 million had been filed; half of the claims were reported to be under $2,500 and 95 percent were under $25,000. The smallest claim was for a child's tricycle, and the largest for a little over $1 million.

By 1950 only 210 claims were cleared, and only 73 people had actually received their money. Claims were being settled at the rate of four per month. The process not only was slow, but also proved to be very expensive because it cost the government over $1,000 to handle a $450 claim. The process was expedited somewhat by an amendment signed on August 17, 1951. This new law gave the Attorney General the authority to automatically settle all claims up to $2,500, or three-quarters of the amount of the compensable items, whichever was less. This made it no longer necessary to check each item individually, and by June 30, 1954, approximately $23 million for 19,750 claims had been given out. Because compensation was calculated on the basis of pre-war prices, it was estimated that the evacuees received on the average no more than ten cents on the dollar.

On July 9, 1956, President Dwight D. Eisenhower signed an amendment to further expedite the settlement of the relatively few outstanding but very large claims, and to correct some of the inequities of the 1948 law. This included allowing corporations with a majority of stockholders of Japanese ancestry to file claims. People interned by the Justice Department were allowed to file, and petitioners could ask compensation for property confiscated by the federal government under the Trading with the Enemy Act. Settling some of the remaining claims covered by this amendment took almost ten years.

In many cases, compensation to the Issei came too late. Many who were businessmen before the war became laborers because they were too old at the end of their internment to rebuild their practices. One man who claimed $75,000 accepted $2,500 because he knew that he would not live long enough to pursue further adjudication. Others died before they saw even that amount.

Today Nisei are still paying the price for whatever crimes they had committed during World War II. Internment of the Japanese Americans, although it was deemed necessary to many overzealous Americans after the bombing of Pearl Harbor, was a costly giant step backwards for both the Nisei and American democracy. (*See also* Commission on Wartime Relocation and Internment of Civilians.)

FURTHER READING: Frank F. Chuman, *The Bamboo People: The Law and Japanese-Americans*, Del Mar, Calif.: Publisher's Inc., 1976; Audrie Girdner and Anne Loftis, *The Great Betrayal: Evacuation of the Japanese-Americans During World War II*, New York: Macmillan Co., 1969; Bill Hosokawa, *JACL in Quest of Justice: The History of the Japanese American Citizens League*, New York: William Morrow and Co., 1982; Michi Weglyn, *Years of Infamy: The Untold Story of America's Concentration Camps*, New York: William Morrow and Co., 1976.

JAPANESE AMERICAN NEWS. *See* Sakamoto, James Yoshinori.

JAPANESE AMERICAN RESEARCH PROJECT (originally called the Issei History Project), a project initiated by Wakamatsu Shigeo, president of the Japanese American Citizens League* (JACL) in 1960 during its convention in Sacramento. Frank Chuman, who replaced Wakamatsu, appointed him to head the effort to direct the project as chairman of the committee charged with the responsibility of carrying out the work. Under Wakamatsu's leadership the committee, which included Mike Masaru Masaoka,* Satoda Yone, Satow Masao, William K. Hosokawa,* Mukaeda Katsuma, Nakamura Gongoro, and others, met during the 1962 JACL convention in Seattle and outlined the three major objectives of the project: to conduct a sociological survey based on a national sampling of Issei* and their Nisei* descendants; to publish a definitive history of the Japanese Americans; and to collect documents, including oral history and memorabilia. The JACL members donated $200,000 toward the goal, and the JACL gave a grant of $100,000 to the University of California at Los Angeles, which agreed to co-sponsor the project. Later the project would become known as the Japanese American Research Project. T. Scott Miyakawa became the first director of the project, and Robert A. Wilson was appointed to administer the fund. To this original grant was added $140,000 which the Carnegie Corporation generously contributed. In addition, the National Institute of Mental Health gave $400,000 to the project so that the project could include the Sansei* generation in the survey.

The project has produced the following authoritative and scholarly works: *The Japanese American Community* by Gene N. Levine and Robert C. Rhodes, published in 1981 by Praeger Press; *The Economic Basis of Ethnic Solidarity: Small Business in the Japanese American Community* by Edna Bonacich and John Modell, published in 1980 by the University of California Press; *The*

Bamboo People by Frank Chuman, published in 1976 by Publisher's Inc.; and *East to America* by Robert A. Wilson and Bill Hosokawa, published in 1980 by William Morrow and Company.

JAPANESE AND KOREAN EXCLUSION LEAGUE. *See* Asiatic Exclusion League.

JAPANESE ASSOCIATION OF AMERICA (also known as Beikoku Nihonjinkai), established by persons of Japanese ancestry in 1900, with its headquarters in San Francisco. Five years after its founding, it brought together a group of some thirty Japanese organizations scattered throughout the state for a conference that resulted in a federation of the local organizations, called the Japanese Association of America.
FURTHER READING: Bill Hosokawa, *Nisei*, New York: William Morrow and Co., 1969; Yamato Ichihashi, *Japanese in the U.S.*, Stanford, Calif.: Stanford University Press, 1932.

JAPANESE COMMERCIAL BANK, established in Seattle in 1907 by Furuya Masajiro, who took control of the Oriental American Bank in 1913. Furuya combined the two banks, a move that proved to be his downfall during the Great Depression when many other banks also failed. Other businesses of his also failed, and he later died in obscurity.

JAPANESE EXCLUSION ACT OF 1924. *See* Immigration Act of 1924.

JAPANESE EXCLUSION LEAGUE OF CALIFORNIA, organized as a pressure group on September 2, 1920, in San Francisco. Although State Senator J. M. Inman was elected president of the exclusionist organization, the real power of the organization was in the hands of Valentine Stuart McClatchy,* who had served as publisher of an influential newspaper, *The Sacramento Bee*, until 1920. The organization was established mainly to agitate for exclusion of Japanese immigration and to render support to individuals and groups working toward strengthening the Alien Land Act of California, 1913.* The organization was active for two years and then became dormant before it was dissolved in 1924 after the Japanese Exclusion Act passed through Congress.
FURTHER READING: Roger Daniels, *The Politics of Prejudice*, Berkeley: University of California Press, 1962; Valentine S. McClatchy, ed., *Four Anti-Japanese Pamphlets*, New York: Arno Press, 1978.

JAPANESE FEDERATION OF LABOR, organized in early December 1919 when representatives from various labor organizations met in Honolulu to establish an inter-island organization. Before the establishment of this organization, there were several labor federations on the major islands: the Maui Federation of Labor, the Oahu Federation of Labor, the Kauai Federation of Labor, and the

Labor Federation of Hawaii on the Big Island. The need for an organization to coordinate various labor demands necessitated an inter-island organizational structure.

After its organizational meeting the federation sent its demands for higher wages to the Hawaiian Sugar Planters' Association* (HSPA), but its demands were rejected. The leaders of the federation decided to strike only as a last resort and asked the HSPA to reconsider its demands. In the meantime the Filipino Federation of Labor,* under the leadership of Pablo Manlapit,* struck and urged the Japanese Federation of Labor to join it. On January 26, 1920, the Japanese Federation of Labor issued a general layoff order and scheduled its strike to begin on February 1. (*See also* 1920 Strike.)

JAPANESE GOSPEL SOCIETY, organized in 1877 by a group of Japanese students in San Francisco. Japanese students had met together to spend evenings in conversation, but they decided to establish a Bible study group under the leadership of Miyama Kanichi.

JAPANESE INTERDENOMINATION BOARD OF MISSION (DENDO-DAN), established in 1911 with its joint headquarters offices in San Francisco and Los Angeles. It published its own monthly paper and distributed it among Japanese Americans. Although it was related to American Mission Boards, which contributed $491.65 to its annual budget of $4,075.56 in 1913, it was largely a self-supporting organization drawing its strength from the Japanese community on the West Coast.

JODO SHINSHU, founded by Shinran (1173–1262) and one of the four denominations of Japanese Amida Buddhism in America. It is practiced by most Japanese Buddhists in Japan and in the United States. There are ten schools of Shinshu Buddhism in Japan, but only two of them are found among Japanese Americans: Nishi Hongwanji (West School of Original Vow of Amida Buddha) and Higashi Hongwanji (East School). Nishi Hongwanji was incorporated as the Buddhist Churches of America* and includes 75 to 90 percent of all Japanese Buddhists in America. (*See also* Buddhist Churches of America.)
FURTHER READING: *Buddhism in America, Tetsuden Kashima: The Social Organization of an Ethnic Religious Institution*, Westport, Conn.: Greenwood Press, 1977; Dennis M. Ogawa, *Kodomo no tame ni (For the Sake of the Children)*, Honolulu: University Press of Hawaii, 1978.

JOHN CHINAMAN, a perjorative term used against Chinese in the United States. A Chinese was seldom called by his or her own name when a wave of anti-Chinese feelings spread in America.

JOHNSON, ALBERT (1869–1957), congressman. Johnson was born in Springfield, Illinois, on March 5, 1869, and attended public schools at Atchison and Hiawatha, Kansas. He embarked on a very successful journalism career, starting with a job as a reporter on the *St. Joseph Herald* and then on the *St. Louis Globe-Democrat*. He later became news editor of the *Washington D.C. Post* in 1898. Journalism eventually brought him to the State of Washington where in 1898 he became editor and publisher of the *Grays Harbor Washingtonian*. Johnson remained in the newspaper business until 1907 when he ran for and was elected as a Republican to the 63d Congress of the United States from Washington. He served nine succeeding terms from March 4, 1913, to March 3, 1933.

During the 1924 session of Congress, Johnson introduced a bill in the House based on his views of the immigrating Asians he saw while living in Washington. The bill was passed by Congress and signed into law, becoming the Immigration Act of 1924.* By proposing this bill, Johnson made it all but impossible for Asians to immigrate to the United States. Johnson died on January 17, 1957, at American Lake, Washington. He was a victim of his own culture in which many believed that immigrants should be regulated unjustly or justly by the strong. (*See also* Immigration Act of 1924).

JOHNSON, HIRAM W. (1866–1945), California governor, U.S. senator. Johnson was born on September 2, 1866, in Sacramento, California, to a corporate lawyer, Grove L. Johnson, and his wife, Annie. He attended schools in his hometown, graduating from high school at the age of sixteen. He attended the University of California in 1884 but left in his junior year in order to marry. He worked as a shorthand reporter while studying at his father's office. He was admitted to the California bar in 1888 and joined his father's law firm.

Throughout his life Johnson was either well liked or extremely disliked, and he was a man of power. In 1910 he ran for governor with a clean, reform government platform, and a pledge to drive the Southern Pacific Railroad, of which his father was an attorney, out of politics. Admired for his simple, direct manner and his courage, he won the office and he also kept his pledges. He was a politician of the people. While in office, he gave counsel to supporters of the movement to deny aliens ineligible for U.S. citizenship the right to own land or to lease land for agricultural purposes in the State of California. When the Wilson administration asked him to use his veto power against the Alien Land Act of California, 1913* which the California Legislature passed, he refused to do so, saying that he could not go against the wishes of the elected representatives.

Johnson was elected to the U.S. Senate in 1916 and was reelected four times to serve as senator until his death in 1945 at Bethesda Naval Hospital in Maryland. As a senator he was no less anti-Asiatic than he had been as governor. He tried to pass an exclusion law through Congress that would exclude Asians from coming to the United States as immigrants. This effort was made in cooperation with Valentine Stuart McClatchy* in 1921.

FURTHER READING: Roger Daniels, *The Politics of Prejudice*, Berkeley: University of California Press, 1962; Franklin Hichborn, "The Party, the Machine, and the Votes," *California Historical Society Quarterly* 38 (1959) pp. 349–57; Irving McKee, "The

Background and Early Career of Hiram Johnson, 1866–1919,'' *Pacific Historical Review* 19 (1950) pp. 17–30; Brett Melendy and Benjamin Gilbert, *The Governors of California: From Peter H. Burnett to Edmund G. Brown*, Georgetown, Calif.: Talisman Press, 1965.

JOINT SPECIAL COMMITTEE OF CONGRESS ON CHINESE IMMIGRATION, created in 1876 when Congress decided to investigate Chinese immigration. The investigation came in response to pressure put on Congress by the Pacific Coast congressmen who believed that federal legislation on Chinese immigration was the only avenue left for them to seek, as various state laws passed on the Pacific Coast had been ruled unconstitutional by the courts. The committee was headed by Senator Oliver P. Morton of Indiana, and it included Edwin R. Meade, Wilson Cooper, Senator A. A. Sargent and W. F. Piper. The committee came to San Francisco and held public hearings, during which more than 129 witnesses were heard, and published a five-page report. The committee, through its report, recommended to the President and State Department that the Burlingame Treaty of 1868* with China be renegotiated, and it acknowledged the undesirability of Chinese immigration to the United States. However, contrary to the committee's majority report, a minority report written by Senator Morton before his death stated that Chinese labor in the Western states was a positive economic force bringing benefits to those states.

FURTHER READING: Mary Roberts Coolidge, *Chinese Immigration*, New York: Henry Holt and Co., 1909; Alexander Saxton, *The Indispensable Enemy: Labor and the Anti-Chinese Movement in California*, Berkeley: University of California Press, 1971.

JONES, HERBERT C. (1880-?), state senator. Jones was born on September 20, 1880, and received his A.B. at Stanford University in 1902. He served as California State senator from Santa Clara County from 1913 to 1934. His anti-Asiatic activities were confined to California, although he did affect the nation with his legislation on the issue of the racial classification of Malayans.

On January 18, 1933, Jones introduced Bills Nos. 175 and 176. These two bills would have amended Sections 60 and 69 of the Civil Code by adding the Malay race to non-white groups, which were prohibited from marrying whites. Sections 60 and 69 were intended to restrict the issuance of marriage licenses to whites and ''Negroes and Mongoloids.'' These bills came about after years of misconceptions about the racial classification of Filipinos, particularly with regard to racial intermarriage with whites. Not before 1933 did a high court rule on the issue of Filipino classification. On January 27, 1933, the Court of Appeals affirmed that Filipinos were not prohibited from marrying whites in California. This decision, handed down by the California Court of Appeals, was a result of the case of Salvador Roldan v. Los Angeles County* in which the county clerk had denied a marriage license to Salvador Roldan, who petitioned for a writ of mandate requiring the clerk to issue a marriage license. After the decision was handed down, Jones introduced his bills in an attempt to have Filipinos classified as part of non-white groups who were then to be prohibited from marrying whites. (*See also* California Senate Bills Nos. 175 and No. 176.)

JONES ACT OF 1916, passed by the U.S. Congress on August 29, 1916, in order to transform the Philippines into an autonomous and independent nation. By this act legislative power was turned over to the Filipinos, whereas the executive power was vested in the governor general appointed by the President and confirmed by the U.S. Senate. The act provided much of the power which Francis B. Harrison* needed as governor general appointed by President Woodrow Wilson to Filipinize much of the colonial bureaucracy established in the Philippines by Americans.

FURTHER READING: Theodore Friend, *Between Two Empires: The Ordeal of the Philippines, 1929–1946*, New Haven, Conn.: Yale University Press, 1965; H. Brett Melendy, *Asians in America: Filipinos, Koreans, and East Indians*, Boston: Twayne Publishers, 1977; Carlos P. Romulo, *Mother America: A Living Story of Democracy*, New York: Doubleday, Doran and Co., 1943.

JORDAN, SECRETARY OF STATE OF CALIFORNIA v. T. TASHIRO, a case argued in the U.S. Supreme Court in 1928 involving the question of whether persons ineligible for U.S. citizenship could purchase agricultural land. The Alien Land Act of California, 1913,* as amended by the California State Legislature on June 20, 1923, was ruled constitutional by the U.S. Supreme Court in the case of Porterfield v. Webb* in 1923. This meant that no person ineligible for U.S. citizenship was able to purchase land for agricultural purposes. Other states soon followed suit, legislating laws to prohibit aliens from purchasing land. Between November 12, 1923, when the Supreme Court ruled on the case of Terrace et al. v. Thompson, Attorney General of Washington,* and before May 20, 1927, when the Supreme Court of the State of California granted mandamus petition to T. Tashiro, Dr. Tashiro, a resident of California and citizen of Japan and ineligible for U.S. citizenship, presented to Frank M. Jordan, Secretary of State of California, articles proposing the incorporation of a "Japanese Hospital of Los Angeles." The articles proposed the creation of a business corporation with a share of $100,000. The corporation would construct and operate a general hospital in Los Angeles with a home for nurses and resident physicians, and it would lease land for that purpose. These articles complied with all statutes in California governing the formation of such a corporation.

The state, however, refused to file the articles on the grounds that because Dr. Tashiro was a citizen of Japan, ineligible for U.S. citizenship, the California Land Law would not permit an incorporation for such purposes. In response to the refusal, Tashiro filed for mandamus petition in which it was argued that the treaty between the United States and Japan, proclaimed on April 5, 1911, allowed citizens of Japan to incorporate in the United States for the purposes mentioned in the articles. The State Supreme Court granted mandamus, and the State of

California, through its secretary, petitioned for certiorari, which the Supreme Court of the United States granted.

The argument on this case was heard on October 9, and the case was decided on November 19, 1928, with Justice Harlan Stone delivering the opinion of the Court. The decision in favor of Tashiro was based on a more liberal interpretation of the treaty of April 5, 1911 between the two nations. The terms of the treaty authorized the citizens of Japan to lease land for residential and "commercial purposes," and, although a narrow interpretation of the word "commercial" is possible, according to the Justices of the Supreme Court a broader interpretation of the word should be given in order to "secure equality and reciprocity between the two nations."

FURTHER READING: Roger Daniels, ed., *Three Short Works on Japanese Americans*, New York: Arno Press, 1978 (originally published in 1929).

JOSS HOUSE, a term that supposedly originated from the Spanish Dios ("god"). It is a pejorative term used to ridicule the beliefs and religious rituals of Chinese worshipping in their temples.

JUDD, ALBERT FRANCIS (1838–1900), Attorney General during the reign of King Luanlilo and later a Justice on the Supreme Court of Hawaii. Judd was the son of Gerrit Parmele Judd.* Under the Dole Administration in Hawaii, he served as Chief Justice of the Supreme Court. He also worked for the Big Five* as its attorney and went to the Philippines to recruit for the Big Five Filipino laborers. He was able to recruit only fifteen laborers, who came to Hawaii aboard the *S.S. Doric* on December 20, 1906.

JUDD, GERRIT PARMELE (1803–1873), missionary and advisor to king of Hawaii. Judd was born at Paris, Oneida County, New York, and began to study medicine in his father's office at an early age. He graduated from medical school in 1825; the following year he was converted and became a missionary. In 1827 the American Board of Commissioners for Foreign Missions* sent him to the Sandwich Islands as a missionary. Through his medical profession he came into contact with the king and chiefs of Hawaii and developed a wealth of knowledge about Hawaii and its people. He learned the Hawaiian language until he was proficient and translated state papers for the king and chiefs.

Judd held a number of official positions under King Kauikeaouli; he was president of the Treasury Board in 1842 and managed the finances of the kingdom; he became Minister of Foreign Affairs unofficially in 1843 and officially in 1845. As a well-trusted advisor to the king, he developed a policy that was to unite the natives of Hawaii with foreigners in an independent, sovereign Hawaiian monarchy. His policy angered a number of foreigners, who brought impeachments against him. He was finally driven out of government and power in 1853.

JUS SANGUINIS, a principle by which a country may claim people as its citizens. According to this principle, a child born of parents of a given country takes the citizenship of his parents, regardless of where he or she was born. Japan, China, and Korea, among other nations, have maintained this principle by which they claim jurisdiction over children of their citizens born abroad. Therefore, children born in the United States of parents who are citizens of Korea, Japan, or China may have dual citizenship, because the United States practices the principle of *jus solis*,* which holds that a child takes the citizenship of the country of his birth regardless of his parents' citizenship.

JUS SOLIS, a legal principle which holds that a child born on its territory, regardless of the citizenship of his or her parents, takes the citizenship of the country of his or her birth.

K

KAHAHAWAI, JOSEPH. *See* Ala Moana Case.

KALAKAUA, DAVID (1836–1891), successor to King Lunalilo as King of Hawaii on February 3, 1874, when Lunalilo died without leaving an heir. Kalakaua was elected on February 12, 1874, by the Legislative Assembly that chose him over Queen Emma, widow of Kamehameha IV. As soon as he came to the throne, he adopted a friendlier attitude toward foreigners, repudiated his anti-foreign views, and expressed interest in reopening reciprocity negotiations with the United States. One year after he became king, the Kingdom of Hawaii and the United States reached a reciprocity agreement which brought about a revolutionary change in the Hawaiian economy and culture. King Kalakaua was also concerned with the immigration of foreigners to Hawaii. Interested in increasing Hawaii's dwindling population by allowing foreigners to immigrate to Hawaii, he directed the Legislative Assembly on April 30, 1874, to pay attention to this problem. In January 1881 his interest in promoting the immigration of Asians to Hawaii took him to Japan where he met with Japanese government officials to discuss the question of Japanese laborers immigrating to Hawaii. He even suggested that Princess Kaiulani, who was then only five years old and his heir apparent, be married to Prince Komatsu of Japan, with whom Kalakaua was very impressed during his trip to Japan. Upon his return to Hawaii, he encouraged Japanese immigration to Hawaii and concluded the Convention of 1886* with the Japanese government, an agreement through which Japanese immigration would be handled. On February 8, 1885, when the first group of Japanese immigrants arrived in Honolulu aboard the Pacific Mail steamer, *City of Tokyo*, the king was at dockside to welcome this group of 943 immigrants. His success in arranging Japanese immigration to Hawaii was hailed as a tremendous achievement, second only to the Reciprocity Agreement with the United States in its importance to Hawaii.

King Kalakaua died on January 20, 1891, while on a vacation trip to San Francisco.

FURTHER READING: Gavan Daws, *Shoal of Time*, Honolulu: University Press of Hawaii, 1968; Ralph S. Kuykendall, *The Hawaii Kingdom, Vol. III, 1874–1893: The Kalakaua Dynasty*, Honolulu: University of Hawaii Press, 1967; Dennis M. Ogawa, *Jan Ken Po: The World of Hawaii's Japanese Americans*, Honolulu: University Press of Hawaii, 1973; Sylvester K. Stevens, *American Expansion in Hawaii*, New York: Russell and Russell, 1945.

KALLOCH, ISAAC S. (1832–1890), mayor of San Francisco. Kalloch came to San Francisco from the East and established a Christian church located on Seventh Street, where he preached. As an abolitionist he defended the Chinese, but he learned quickly that defending the Chinese in San Francisco was neither popular nor politically expedient. He suddenly changed his views on the question of Chinese immigration and sided with the Workingmen's Party of California,* calling for the removal and expulsion of Chinese from California. He was elected mayor of San Francisco, but during the campaign he was opposed by the DeYoung brothers, one of whom, Charles DeYoung, shot and wounded him seriously. Kalloch recovered and was elected mayor in 1879. While campaigning for the mayor's office, he promised members of the Workingmen's Party that he would solve the Chinese problem by using the power already vested in the mayor and the city government.

FURTHER READING: L. F. Byington and Oscar Lewis, *The History of San Francisco*, Vol. 1, San Francisco: S. J. Clarke Publishing Co., 1931; M. M. Marberry, *The Gold Voice: A Biography of Isaac Kalloch*, New York: 1947; Alexander Saxton, *The Indispensable Enemy*, Berkeley: University of California Press, 1971.

KAMEHAMEHA DYNASTY of Hawaii, a dynasty that lasted from 1810, when the last unconquered island, Kauai, became the domain of King Kamehameha I, to 1872, when King Kamehameha V died without an heir. Kamehameha I (c. 1753–1819) was a powerfully built man, over six feet tall and excellent in every native sport. He was also a brawny, proud, fierce warrior who became a high-ranking chief at the age of nineteen. He was named Kamehameha, which means ''hard-shelled crab,'' because of his bravery in battle. The other Kamehamehas who succeeded him to the throne were probably less kingly and certainly less manly.

In 1782 the western half of Hawaii came under Kamehameha's control, and in 1791 he consolidated power over the entire island. In 1795 he started his push for control of the other major islands; he conquered all but Kauai, which finally came under his control in 1810. Although a number of major world powers attempted to take control of Hawaiian trade, Kamehameha I and American merchants on the Islands thwarted their attempts. Kamehameha I died on May 8, 1819, and was succeeded by his son, Liholiho, who assumed the throne at the age of twenty-three as Kamehameha II (1797–1824).

Although Kamehameha is considered a weak ruler by historians, he was loved by his people, and he laid the groundwork for Hawaii's future development. He abolished the old tabu system and worship of idols and later allowed missionaries to practice their religion and proselytize among his people, and to educate the royal youth. In addition, he approved a plan that permitted tenant lands to be passed on to the tenant's successors to work, a foundation for the future Great Mahele,* which put lands in the control of Caucasians and Asians. There were few Asians in Hawaii at this time, although a few Chinese entrepreneurs had come to the islands to explore the possibilities of sugar production. Kamehameha II died in England on July 14, 1824, leaving the throne to his brother, who had been designated the heir apparent before his departure for England. The following year, the twelve-year old Kauikeaouli (1813–1854) assumed the throne as Kamehameha III. His reign lasted thirty years, during which fundamental changes took place in Hawaiian society. During his reign, education became general for all people; the Alien Law of 1838 was passed to encourage foreigners to come and marry Hawaiians and become naturalized citizens; the king yielded some of his traditional authority and power voluntarily and created the Hawaiian "Magna Carta," which led to the establishment of the Constitution in 1840, bringing into existence a constitutional form of government with its three branches of separate power; and the first monetary system was created in 1846. Then came the Great Mahele, the breaking of the traditional land holding system. The Masters and Servants Act of 1850* was passed, which enabled Hawaii to obtain plantation workers abroad, and two years later, the first contracted Chinese laborers arrived, with more to follow. Kamehameha III died on December 15, 1854, without a son to succeed him to the throne. He named his nephew as his heir, and Alexander Liholiho assumed the throne as Kamehameha IV (1834–1863).

As young princes Alexander and his brother, Lot, were educated by the missionaries and were taken on a tour of Europe and America. They were less impressed with Americans than they were with British institutions, and Kamehameha IV welcomed the Anglican Church in his kingdom. His concern with the dwindling Hawaiian native population led him to appoint Charles St. Julian to study various peoples of Polynesia for their suitability as immigrants. Although he did not favor slavery or coolie trade,* he encouraged the immigration of Chinese laborers to his kingdom, recognizing the importance of their labor to the plantation system. Kamehameha IV's rule was brief, lasting only nine years. The death of his son on August 3, 1863 devastated him, and he died not long after, on November 30, 1863. The throne passed to Lot (1830–1872), who reigned as Kamehameha V. Upon assuming the throne, Kamehameha V was faced with two major problems: a dwindling population and a desperate need for laborers on the plantations. Although 300 Chinese coolies had been brought in 1852 by the Royal Hawaiian Agricultural Society, after having served their contract term many of them either went back to China or moved into towns in Hawaii to start small businesses of their own.

In order to decide what to do about these two problems, the king's Cabinet met shortly after his coronation and discussed the dilemma at some length. After the meeting, the king accepted a committee's recommendations to study the problem and suggested that 300 to 500 Chinese or Indian laborers be imported under government supervision. According to his instruction, a law was passed on December 30, 1864, creating a Bureau of Immigration which provided for strict governmental control of all contract laborers entering Hawaii. The bureau then sent its head administrator to China to recruit Chinese laborers. He was able to obtain 522 Chinese, including 95 women and 3 children, in 1865. In 1868 the first Japanese contract laborers were brought to Hawaii, although the success of this group as plantation workers was questioned. During the reign of King Kamehameha V, approximately 1,700 Chinese laborers were brought to the islands to work for very little recompense. The last king of the Kamehameha Dynasty died on December 11, 1872, without leaving an heir. The throne then went to William C. Lunalilo (1835–1874), who was elected by the Legislative Assembly on January 8, 1873. Lunalilo died on February 3, 1874, one year after he became king, and the throne went to David Kalakaua* (1836–1891). (*See* Kalakaua, David.)

FURTHER READING: Helena G. Allen, *The Betrayal of Liliuokalani: Last Queen of Hawaii, 1838–1917*, Glendale, Calif.: Arthur H. Clark Co., 1982; A. Grove Day, *Hawaii and Its People*, New York: Duell, Sloan and Pearce, 1955; Ralph S. Kuykendall, *The Hawaiian Kingdom*, Vols. 1, 2, and 3, Honolulu: University of Hawaii Press, 1947 (Vol. 1), 1953 (Vol. 2), 1957 (Vol. 3).

KAMEHAMEHA SCHOOLS, founded as a result of the will left by Princess Bernice Pauahi, (d. 1884), leaving almost one-ninth of all the land in the Hawaiian Islands for the purpose of educating the Hawaiian people. The income from the estate was to support one school for boys and one school for girls. The school for boys was founded in 1887, with William Brewster Oleson as its first principal. The school for girls did not begin operations until seven years later.

KANAGAWA, TREATY OF (1854), (TREATY OF PEACE, AMITY AND COMMERCE), signed on March 31, 1854, as a result of Commodore Perry's effort to establish diplomatic relations with Japan, the secluded nation that had pursued the policy of exclusion since 1638. Between 1638 and 1854, Japan excluded all foreigners, except for a number of small Dutch and Chinese traders. It also continued to ban the immigration of Japanese to other parts of the world until 1854. The treaty opened the port of Shimoda to American ships for securing wood, water, coal, and other provisions, and obligated Japan to open the port of Hakodata to American ships a year later. The treaty also provided that American silver and gold coins could be exchanged for Japanese coins and their goods. In accordance with the treaty provisions, the American government appointed as consul general Townsend Harris who concluded a commercial treaty with

Japan in 1858 known as the Treaty of Yedo, or the Commercial and Consular Treaty of 1858.
FURTHER READING: E. Manchester Boddy, *Japanese in America*, San Francisco: R. and E. Research Associates, 1970; Foster Rhea Dulles, *Yankees and Samurai: America's Role in the Emergence of Modern Japan: 1791–1900*, New York: Harper and Row, 1965; Yamato Ichihashi, *Japanese in the United States*, Stanford, Calif.: Stanford University Press, 1932.

KANAKA, a Hawaiian native term referring to people indigenous to Hawaii. This term is used in contrast with *haole*,* which means foreigners.
FURTHER READING: Andrew W. Lind, *Hawaii's People*, Honolulu: University Press of Hawaii, 1980.

KANG, YOUNGHILL (1903–1972), writer. Kang was born in a northern province of Korea in 1903 and moved to the United States just before the exclusionary Immigration Act of 1924 was passed by the Congress. He reportedly had only $4 in his possession when he arrived in America at the age of eighteen, but he managed to go to Harvard, where he excelled in his studies in literature. He taught at New York University and worked for the Encyclopaedia Britannica and the Metropolitan Museum of Art in New York. He also served as a language consultant for the U.S. government during World War II.

Kang is best known for his books. His first book, *The Grass Roof* (1931), was autobiographical and brought him fame as a Korean American writer. Other books followed, including *The Happy Grove* in 1933 and *East Goes West* in 1937, his last major novel. *The Grass Roof* describes Kang's life in Korea; *East Goes West* chronicles his search for identity and a place in an exclusionist America.
FURTHER READING: Elaine Kim, "Searching for a Door to America: Younghill Kang, Korean American Writer," *Korea Journal* 17, No. 4 (April 1977): 38–47; Elaine Kim, *Asian American Literature*, Philadelphia: Temple University Press, 1982.

K'ANG YU-WEI (1858–1927), Confucian scholar in its finest tradition, educator, philosopher, reformer, and founder of the Pao-huang Hui (Society to Protect the Emperor).* K'ang was born on March 19, 1858, the son of a district magistrate in a village in Nanhai (Namhoi) located southwest of Canton. He was educated in the Chinese classics, receiving many of his lessons from his grandfather and uncles. He studied—without success—for the examination for the Chu-jen degree in 1876 and for a time was very despondent, particularly after his grandfather's death. But his studies in government, history, geography, and Buddhism buoyed his spirits, giving him hope that he could free the world from its sufferings.

K'ang became interested in Western civilization, and by 1879 he visited Hong Kong. In 1882 he went to Shanghai where he toured the foreign concessions. As China's weakness in dealing with major crises became more pronounced, K'ang sent memorials to the emperor in which he pointed out the dangers of foreign invasions. Again in 1895, after he passed the examinations for the Chin-shih degree, he sent a memorial to the emperor urging him to reject the treaty between China and Japan by which Taiwan was to be ceded to Japan. During the same year he and Liang Ch'i-ch'ao* founded a reform newspaper, the *Chung-wai chi-wen*, and established a reform society, the Ch'iang-hsueh hui (Society for the Study of National Strengthening), with several friends. This association was popular among many Chinese officials, although it also aroused the hostility of powerful conservatives. During the next two years many reform organizations sprang up in China, while a number of national crises convinced many Chinese that the partition of China was imminent.

K'ang had his opportunity to reform the Chinese government when he was summoned to the emperor on June 16, 1898, five days after the Hundred Days Reform was proclaimed. He became an advisor to the emperor and wrote detailed recommendations for government reform. Because of a counterrevolution which placed the emperor in confinement, however, a number of reform officials were executed, including K'ang's younger brother, K'ang Kuang-jen (1867–1898). Upon leaving Peking, K'ang Yu-wei went to Japan, Great Britain, and Canada, where he began to organize overseas Chinese in a movement to save the Kuang-hsu emperor. While in Victoria, British Columbia, he founded the Pao-huang Hui in July 1899. During the next year, many branches of this organization were established among overseas Chinese in the United States, Hawaii, Japan, Southeast Asia, and Latin America. This organization presented strong competition to Dr. Sun Yat-sen* in the struggle for financial and other material support for the regeneration of China.

K'ang Yu-wei was a strong supporter of a constitutional monarchy in China and strove to regenerate Confucianism as a bulwark against moral and ethical degeneration in Chinese society. He died on March 31, 1927, at Tsingtao.

FURTHER READING: Harry Con, et al., eds., *From China to Canada: A History of Chinese Communities in Canada*, Toronto: McClelland and Stewart, Ltd., 1982; Philip Huang, *Liang Ch'i-ch'ao and Modern Chinese Liberalism*, Seattle: University of Washington Press, 1972; Jung-pang Lo, ed., *K'ang Yu-wei: A Biography and a Symposium* Tucson: University of Arizona Press, 1967.

KANRIN MARU, an escort corvette to the *U.S.S. Powhatan*. The *Kanrin Maru* entered the Golden Gate and anchored in San Francisco Bay on March 17, 1860. Among those aboard was Nakahama Manjiro,* the ship's official interpreter and navigation officer.

FURTHER READING: Bill Hosokawa, *Nisei*, New York: William Morrow and Co., 1969; Yamato Ichihashi, *Japanese in the United States*, Stanford, Calif.: Stanford University Press, 1932.

KAUIKEAOULI. *See* Kamehameha Dynasty.

KAWAKITA TOMOYA V. UNITED STATES, a case involving an American citizen of Japanese ancestry, Kawakita Tomoya, who in 1939 at the age of eighteen went to Japan with his father to visit his grandfather. He went on a

U.S. passport, and in 1940 he registered with an American consul in Japan as an American citizen. His father decided to return to the United States, but Kawakita remained to attend Meiji University, where he took a commercial course and military training. In 1941 he renewed his American passport when he was asked to give the oath of allegiance to the United States. He stayed in school, completing his studies in 1943, at which time it was impossible for him to return to the United States. In 1943 he entered his name in the Koseki, a family registry. Later during his trial he claimed that his registration in the family Koseki amounted to expatriation, or renouncement of his American citizenship.

During the war Kawakita worked for the Oeyama Nickel Company, Ltd., which used American prisoners of war in its mines and factories. Kawakita worked as an interpreter for the American prisoners and the company until the end of the war in August 1945. In that December he decided to return to the United States. He went to the U.S. consul at Yokohama and registered as an American citizen, stating that he had not committed any acts amounting to expatriation. He received a passport and came to the United States in 1946. In September 1947 a former prisoner of war, St. William L. Bruce, recognized Kawakita as he was coming out of a department store in Los Angeles and reported him to the Federal Bureau of Investigation, which then conducted a careful investigation into the accusations against Kawakita. A federal grand jury indicted Kawakita, charging him with fifteen counts in relation to his mistreatment of prisoners of war. The period covered in the indictment was August 8, 1944, to August 15, 1945. Kawakita went on trial in a Los Angeles courtroom before Federal District Judge William C. Mathes. During the trial Kawakita claimed he had expatriated himself by registering his name in the family registry, and therefore he could not be forced to stand trial as an American citizen. However, the jury found him guilty of treason, and Judge Mathes imposed the death sentence on Kawakita. His case was appealed to the Court of Appeals for the Ninth Circuit, but Judge Albert Lee Stephens upheld the lower court's decision. The case was then brought to the Supreme Court of the United States on certiorari for the defendant. The case was argued before the Court on April 3, 1952, and was decided on June 2, when Justice William O. Douglas delivered the opinion of the Court, which, by a four to three decision, rejected the defendant's claim that he was not an American citizen when the alleged acts were committed. The Court upheld the lower court's decision on both the conviction and death sentence. Kawakita was sent to the federal prison on an island in San Francisco Bay known as Alcatraz, where he spent almost sixteen years. On November 2, 1953, his death sentence was commuted to life imprisonment. President John F. Kennedy granted him a presidential pardon on condition that he return to Japan, never to reenter the United States.

FURTHER READING: Frank F. Chuman, *The Bamboo People: The Law and Japanese-Americans*, Del Mar, Calif.: Publisher's Inc., 1976; *Supreme Court Reporter* 72, 343 U.S. 717.

KAWANO, JACK. *See* Reluctant Thirty-Nine.

KEARNEY, DENIS (1847–1907), anti-Chinese agitator and political leader in California. Kearney was born in County Cork, Ireland, on February 1, 1847. His childhood was cut short when he went to sea at the age of eleven, and he sailed for some years under the U.S. flag. Finally, he became first officer on a coastal steamer, but his career ended after he was accused of deserting the ship in danger.

In 1868 Kearney came to San Francisco where he married in 1870. Two years later he bought a prosperous hauling business. Becoming a naturalized citizen in 1876, he represented the Draymen and Teamsters Union in the following year in presenting the complaints of organized labor to the government. In October 1877 he helped to organize the Workingmen's Party of California* and became its fiery leader, famed for his slogan, "Chinese Must Go!" The movement he launched against the Chinese, the Kearney movement or Kearneyism, protested against widespread unemployment, railroad domination, Chinese labor competition, and the two-party political system. Kearney constantly stressed the stoppage and exclusion of Chinese immigration, claiming that the Chinese deprived Americans of decent jobs.

Under Kearney's leadership, the Workingmen's Party showed surprising strength, capturing one-third of the seats in the California Legislature in 1878. With 51 delegates out of 152, the party introduced a series of anti-Chinese bills and was successful in changing California's Constitution. (*See also* California Constitutional Convention of 1879.)

FURTHER READING: S. L. Baldwin, *Must Chinese Go?: An Examination of the Chinese Question*, New York: Press of H. B. Elkins, 1890; Henry George, "The Kearney Agitation in California," *The Popular Science Monthly*, August 1890, pp. 433–439; Elmer C. Sandmeyer, *The Anti-Chinese Movement in California*, Urbana: University of Illinois Press, 1973; Alexander Saxton, *The Indispensable Enemy*, Berkeley: University of California Press, 1971.

KEARNEYISM. *See* Kearney, Denis.

KEIYAKU-NIN, a Japanese term meaning Japanese labor contractors. They entered into contract with employers willing to hire Japanese laborers, who were then recruited by *Keiyaku-nin*. The Issei* called them *bosu*, or boss, whose assistance the laborers needed in order to find work. Some of the labor contractors took advantage of their fellow countrymen by squeezing a profit out of the laborers' wages. Because immigrant laborers were not familiar with local conditions and could not communicate with potential employers, labor contractors were necessary, albeit often economically exploitative.

KENGAKU-DAN, student tour groups sent to Japan before World War II. This practice was popular among the Japanese, for it afforded them an opportunity to see Japan.

KENJIN-KAI, a Japanese term meaning prefectural organization. The term is made up of three words: *ken* or prefecture, *jin* or person, and *kai* or association. *Ken* or prefecture as an administrative system has little meaning in Japan, but it has significant meaning among Japanese immigrants abroad, particularly among Japanese immigrants and their descendants in America.

Japanese immigrants came to the United States primarily from nine or ten different prefectures. Upon their arrival in the United States, they created social organizations on the basis of their geographic origin. Apparently, they felt more comfortable and secure with fellow prefecture men than with their fellow countrymen. It was also believed that immigrants from the same prefecture were drawn to each other because of their common personality traits as well as behavior; people from Hiroshima Prefecture were known for their industriousness, whereas people from Wakayama were known to be hot-tempered and aggressive.

Kenjin-kai continues to sponsor many social functions in Japanese communities, including annual picnics, and also serves Japanese communities as welfare organizations.

FURTHER READING: Harry H.L. Kitano, *Japanese Americans: The Evolution of a Subculture*, Englewood Cliffs, N.J.: Prentice-Hall, 1969; William Petersen, *Japanese Americans: Oppression and Success*, New York: Random House, 1971; Frank Miyamoto, *Social Solidarity Among the Japanese in Seattle*, Seattle: Washington Asian American Studies Program, Occasional Monograph Series 2, 1981.

KHALSA, a Sikh congregation or community found among the Sikhs in the United States.

KHORANA, HAR GOBIND (1922–), geneticist, Nobel laureat. Khorana was born on January 9, 1922, in Pakistan and went to the University of Punjab, where he received his B.Sc. and M.Sc. in 1943 and 1945, respectively. He continued his studies at Liverpool University. In 1948 he received his Ph.D., and later he took up a Nuffield Fellowship at Cambridge University, where he became interested in nucleic acid research.

In 1960 Khorana began research projects at the University of Wisconsin where he became interested in decoding the genetic code. His hard work finally paid off when he succeeded in synthesizing each of the sixty-four nucleotide triplets that make up the code. For this monumental accomplishment he was awarded the Nobel Prize in physiology in 1968. In 1970 he was successful in developing the synthesis of the first artificial gene. He moved to the Massachusetts Institute of Technology that year, and by 1976 he was able to create a second gene.

KIBEI, Nisei,* or children born in the United States of Japanese immigrant parents, who were sent to Japan for their education. It was claimed that the Kibei retained their traditional Japanese ways and values because of their education in Japan. During and after the evacuation of all persons of Japanese ancestry during World War II, many Kibei were suspected of disloyalty to the United States, although they were citizens of the United States.

FURTHER READING: Christie W. Kiefer, *Changing Cultures, Changing Lives: An Ethnographical Study of Three Generations of Japanese Americans*, San Francisco: Jossey-Bass Publishers, 1974; Harry H.L. Kitano, *Japanese Americans*, Englewood Cliffs, N.J.: Prentice-Hall, 1969; Forrest E. LaViolette, *Americans of Japanese Ancestry*, Toronto: Canadian Institute of International Affairs, 1945; Andrew W. Lind, *Hawaii's Japanese: An Experiment in Democracy*, Princeton, N.J.: Princeton University Press, 1946.

KIDO, SABURO (1902–1977), leader of Japanese American Citizens League.* Kido was born in Hilo, Hawaii, in 1902 and moved to the mainland at the age of nineteen to study law at Hastings Law College in San Francisco, where he received his degree in 1926. He went into law practice on the fringes of Japantown. While practicing law in San Francisco, he became increasingly concerned with the future of the Nisei* and began to express his desire to establish an organization among Japanese Americans. He became a founding member of the Japanese American Citizens League* in the summer of 1930. His many years of service to the league were recognized when the league elected him president during its 1940 convention at Portland, Oregon. His ability as president proved critical during the Japanese evacuation during World War II. First, when he was offered a free trip to Japan before the war broke out, he refused to go because he felt strongly that it would be improper to accept an official Japanese invitation. Second, when the Japanese Association of North America,* an Issei* organization, asked Kido to raise funds jointly with the Japanese American Citizens League, he declined, because he believed there should be some distance between the two organizations. Third, he hired Mike Masaru Masaoka* to work as a full-time staff employee for the league. After the government decided to remove, evacuate, and relocate all persons of Japanese ancestry, Kido felt that the league should cooperate with the government, and he urged his members and people of Japanese communities to cooperate with the government to carry out its decision.

Immediately after the war, Kido developed a far-reaching program that would revitalize the league. During a convention held in December 1946, he presented his proposal which the delegates approved. Kido also worked to improve the league's official newspaper, *The Pacific Citizen.** He died on April 4, 1977.

FURTHER READING: Bill Hosokawa, *JACL in Quest of Justice*, New York: William Morrow and Co., 1982.

KIM, CHARLES (1884–1968), co-founder of the Kim Brothers Company.* Kim was born in Korea on May 25, 1884, and came to the United States in 1914. With his friend, Harry Kim (whose Korean name was Kim Hyung-soon), he founded the Kim Brothers Company in Reedley, California. Charles Kim, whose Korean name was Kim Ho, was very active in Korean community affairs, and he served as chairman of the United Korean Committee* in America in

1943. In May 1957, with the support of Harry Kim and Warren Kim,* he founded the Korean Foundation, to which the three Kims donated $500,000 worth of real estate. He died on January 5, 1968.

KIM HYUNG-SOON. *See* Kim, Charles.

KIM, WARREN (1896–), Korean American leader. Kim was born in Seoul on December 25, 1896, and came to the United States in 1917 to study law and government. He was active in Korean affairs throughout his lifetime. He served as general secretary of the Korean National Association* of Hawaii in 1933 and became editor of the *Korean National Herald* in 1936. He was elected chairman of the Board of Directors of the United Korean Committee* in America in April 1945, and in 1951, he was elected to the Central Committee of the Korean National Association of North America.

In 1957 Kim helped Charles Kim* establish the Korean Foundation and was in charge of the foundation, which awarded scholarships to students of Korean ancestry. He wrote a book, *Chaemi Hanin Osimnyon-sa*, or *A Fifty Year History of the Koreans in America* (1959).

KIM BROTHERS COMPANY, founded in 1921 by Charles Kim* and Harry Kim in Reedley, California. Their venture started as a small wholesale business dealing with fruit and nursery products, and expanded into orchards, fruit packing houses, and nurseries. In addition, the company began to develop new varieties of fruit trees, working mainly with nectarines and peaches. They succeeded in developing "fuzzless peaches" which today are known as "Le Grand" and "Sun Grand." Their business showed a net profit of $250,000 to $1 million annually until it was sold for $1.4 million in 1962 when Charles and Harry Kim retired. They remained active in Korean community affairs, donating $10,000 to help establish the Korean Community Center in Los Angeles and founding the Korean Foundation which awards scholarships to deserving students of Korean ancestry. (*See also* Kim, Charles.)
FURTHER READING: Bong-youn Choy, *Koreans in America*, Chicago: Nelson-Hall, 1979.

KIM-SHAN JIT SAN-LUK (GOLDEN HILLS' NEWS), the first Chinese newspaper published in San Francisco. At the end of April 1854, when the first issue came out, the newspaper promised to publish twice a week (on Wednesdays and Saturdays), but it quickly became a weekly by July 8, 1854. By December 1858 the *Golden Hills' News* was no longer in operation.

KIMM, DIAMOND v. GEORGE K. ROSENBERG, DISTRICT DIRECTOR, IMMIGRATION AND NATURALIZATION SERVICE, a case argued in the U.S. Supreme Court in 1960 involving the deportation of a Korean alien. Since 1789 a number of laws have been passed in the United States giving the government the power to expel aliens considered dangerous and undesirable because of their questionable moral character or their affiliation with a subversive organization. Starting with the 1798 act, which the Federalist Party pushed through, the government began to gain increasing power to expel aliens. But no aliens were expelled under the law until after the passage of the Chinese Exclusion Act of 1882* which contained provisions for deporting persons of Chinese ancestry who landed in the United States illegally.

In the Fong Yue Ting v. United States* case, brought before the Supreme Court in 1893, the Court supported the government position that it had inherent power to deport aliens. Subsequently, Congress strengthened the government's inherent power by passing laws in 1917, 1918, 1920, and 1940. In 1950 Congress passed the Internal Security Act amending the act of October 1918 which gave the government the power to exclude any alien from admission into the United States because of his or her affiliation with the Communist Party of the United States or any other totalitarian party.

Diamond Kimm came to the United States as a student in 1928 and continued his studies until 1938. His plans to return to his native country were disrupted when war broke out between China and Japan in 1937. After 1938 he worked at various jobs. This was the sole basis of his deportability, as noted in Justice William O. Douglas' dissenting opinion filed along with those of his colleagues, Chief Justice Earl Warren and Justice Hugo Black. When Kimm was ordered deported, he petitioned for suspension of the deportation order or his voluntary departure. The petition could be granted to an alien ordered deported under statutes giving the Attorney General discretion to suspend the deportation of deportable aliens who had proved their good moral character and who were not members of enumerated groups, including the Communist Party of the United States. When Kimm was asked before the hearing officer if he was a member of the Communist Party, he refused to answer the question, invoking the Fifth Amendment privilege. Consequently, he was refused the suspension because the officer felt that Kimm did not prove that he was a person of good moral character.

The case was heard on May 16 and 17, 1960, and was decided on June 13. The decision was made on a five to four vote, and the Court filed a per curiam opinion, with four of the Justices dissenting. In the per curiam opinion, it was argued that the burden of proof that the petitioner was a person of good moral character and that he was not a member of the Communist Party was on the petitioner, not on the government. Justice Douglas, in his dissenting opinion, eloquently argued that an alien invoking the Fifth Amendment should not be considered guilty until proven so. The fact that Kimm invoked the Fifth Amendment privilege did not mean that he was not a person of good moral character, and the Court could not "rest its decision on the ground that by invoking the Fifth Amendment the petitioner gave evidence of bad moral character." (*See also* Korean National Revolutionary Party.)

FURTHER READING: *Supreme Court Reporter* 80A, 363 U.S. 405, 1959.

KIMM, KIUSIC (1881–1950), Korean nationalist. Kimm was born on January 27, 1881, in Korea, and was orphaned in 1886 at the age of five. He was adopted by the Underwoods, an American missionary family, and was sent to America to study at Roanoke College, Roanoke, Virginia, in 1897. Although his Korean name was Kim Kyu-sik, he anglicized it to Kiusik Kimm. He also had a pen name, Usa, which he continued to use after 1919. Upon graduating from Roanoke College in 1903, he explored the possibility of staying in America for further study but returned to Korea, where he worked for the Underwoods in their missionary work.

As a result of Japanese oppression in Korea, he decided to go into exile in 1913, thus beginning his thirty-two years of life outside his homeland. During his years of exile in the United States, Europe, and China, he served as Foreign Minister of the Korean provisional government-in-exile in Shanghai, education minister of the same government, and head of delegates dispatched by the provisional government to many international conferences.

Kimm returned to the United States in 1919 to serve as chairman of the Korean Commission* to Europe and America but was unable to work with Syngman Rhee,* who was not very cooperative with Kimm. He left the United States on October 3, 1920, to go to Shanghai. Although he visited America once more in 1933, he spent most of his long years of exile in China, awaiting an opportunity to return to Korea to put his political skills into practice.

Kimm was elected president of the Korean National Revolutionary Party,* which was organized on July 4, 1935, in Nanking, China. This political organization established its branch party office in Los Angeles in 1943. (*See also* Korean National Revolutionary Party.)
FURTHER READING: Chong-sik Lee, *The Politics of Korean Nationalism*, Berkeley: University of California Press, 1965; Key S. Ryang, "Kim Kyu-sik as a Common Man and a Political Leader," *Korean Observer*, 13, No. 1 (Spring 1982): 36–54.

KING, WILLIAM LYON MACKENZIE (1874–1950), Prime Minister of Canada. King was born on December 17, 1874, in Berlin (now Kitchener), Ontario, and went to the University of Toronto, receiving a B.A. degree in 1895. In 1897 he received an M.A. degree in sociology from the same institution, and in 1909 he received his Ph.D. from Harvard University.

King's political career began when he was appointed Canada's first Deputy Minister of Labor in 1900. He was elected to represent Waterloo in the House of Commons where he served until 1911. He worked for the Rockefeller Foundation during World War I. He was elected again to serve in the House of Commons in 1921 and became Prime Minister, a position he held until 1930 when he was defeated by R. B. Bennett. But he made a political comeback in 1935 to become Prime Minister again, remaining in that position until his retirement in 1948.

Canada's restriction and exclusion of Asians go back to 1885 when the Dominion Parliament, under pressure from the British Columbia Parliament members, passed the 1885 Chinese Restriction Act, three years after the Congress of the

United States passed its Chinese Exclusion Act of 1882.* The 1885 law was revised somewhat, but it did not alter Canada's major policies toward Asian immigrants until the Dominion Parliament passed the 1923 Chinese Exclusion Act.

As a member of the Parliament as well as a member of the Canadian federal government, King presided over the passage and administration of these restrictive and exclusionist laws. When the Canadian government appointed a Royal Commission in 1907 to look into the methods by which Asian Indians immigrated to Canada, King was made head of the commission, and the commission submitted a report recommending more control over the entry of Asian Indians into Canada. But the government was faced with the problem of making its policies toward Asian Indian immigration appear fair and equal, while at the same time actually enforcing control over Asian Indians coming to Canada.

King did not use the traditional argument used by exclusionists, who claimed that people from Asia were inferior and that they should be excluded. He argued against Asian immigration to Canada, particularly Asian Indian immigration, on the grounds that Asian Indians were hurting their own self-interest by coming to Canada. He suggested that Asian Indians who had been accustomed to the conditions of a tropical climate were entirely unsuited to live in Canada. Under recommendations made by the commission, in 1910 the Parliament amended provisions included in the 1906 Immigration Act, particularly the "continuous journey" clause which stated that persons coming to Canada otherwise than by continuous journey from their native country would be prohibited from entering Canada. This particular clause was still in force when the *Komagata Maru* Affair* took place in 1914.

FURTHER READING: Stanislaw Andracki, "Immigration of Orientals into Canada with Special Reference to Chinese," Ph.D. diss., McGill University, 1958; Freda Hawkins, *Canada and Immigration*, Montreal: McGill-Queen's University Press, 1972.

KINGSTON, MAXINE HONG (1940–), writer. Kingston was born in Stockton, California, on October 27, 1940, the daughter of Tom and Ying Lan. Her parents bought a laundry business in Stockton after they immigrated to the United States in the 1930s. She went to the University of California at Berkeley where she received a degree in English. Kingston later took an advanced degree in education and began to teach in Hawaii in 1967, although her first teaching job was with a school in Hayward, California, where she taught English and mathematics between 1965 and 1967. She married Earll Kingston on November 23, 1962, thus acquiring the surname Kingston.

Kingston's best known works are: *The Woman Warrior* (1976) and *China Men* (1980). The first has variously been considered a novel, a memoir, and an autobiographical work, whereas the 1980 work attempts to describe the difference between the way a racist America perceived Chinese immigrant men and the way these men thought of themselves. (*See* Asian American Writers.)

FURTHER READING: Elaine Kim, *Asian American Literature*, Philadelphia: Temple University Press, 1982; Lina Mainiero, ed., *American Women Writers*, New York: Frederick Ungar Publishing Co., 1980.

KINSHIP ASSOCIATIONS (also known as clan associations), established among the Chinese in the United States. These associations exercised both supervision and oppression of their members, who were constantly reminded of their loyalty to the clan and to their family back in China. Clan associations were usually organized around a local merchant who assumed the leadership of his clan and provided shelter to his clan members. In return, he solicited his business and often monopolized the market among his clan members.

Even today, certain clans tend to concentrate in America's urban centers: the Lees in Philadelphia; the Toms in New York; the Loys in Cleveland; the Ongs in Phoenix; the Fongs and Yees in Sacramento; and the Moys and Chins in Chicago.

FURTHER READING: Gunther Barth, *Bitter Strength*, Cambridge, Mass.: Harvard University Press, 1964; Rose Hum Lee, *The Chinese in the United States of America*, Hong Kong: Hong Kong University Press, 1960; Stanford M. Lyman, *Chinese Americans*, New York: Random House, 1974.

KITANO, HARRY H. L. (1926–), sociologist. Kitano was born on February 14, 1926, in San Francisco, and went to the University of California at Berkeley, graduating from the university in 1948 with a B.A. degree. He received his Ph.D. in 1958.

Kitano began to teach in 1958 at the University of California at Los Angeles, where he is still professor of social welfare and sociology. He has written a number of books, including *Japanese Americans: The Evolution of a Subculture* (1969), *American Racism*, with Roger Daniels* (1970), and *Race Relations* (1974).

Kitano and Daniels together developed the theory of the two-category system which describes and explains race relations between whites and non-whites in American society. Kitano is also responsible for the concept of subculture,* which is often used in describing the Japanese American culture. According to this concept, the Japanese American culture constitutes a subculture in American society, and some of its subcultural values are shared by the members of the majority society.

FURTHER READING: Harry H. L. Kitano, *Japanese Americans: The Evolution of a Subculture*, Englewood Cliffs, N.J.: Prentice-Hall, 1969.

KITCHEN WORKERS UNION, organized by Harry Ueno in 1942 at the Manzanar Relocation Center. It was made up mainly of people who opposed the government's policy of evacuation and relocation of persons of Japanese ancestry during World War II. The union was directly involved in the Manzanar Incident.* (*See* Manzanar Incident.)

KNIGHTS OF LABOR, an outgrowth of the Garment Cutters Union (1862–1869), established in Philadelphia in 1869. The Knights of Labor began with only nine members, led by Uriah Stephens. It was organized as a secret society for the protection of its members from exploitation by employers. In order to enlist new members, the organization allowed all tradesmen to enter with an equal footing with the original members of the Garment Cutters Union, and they were exempt from paying dues.

During the first decade of its existence, the Knights grew very slowly, but by the end of 1873 there were approximately eighty local assemblies, the majority of which were located in Philadelphia and its vicinity. By 1879 the organization claimed a membership of nearly 10,000. In 1878 Stephens resigned, and Terence Vincent Powderly* took over as master workman. Powderly furthered the cause of the organization by adopting a new program of unionism, which was added to its previous craft-union emphasis. As the Knights took on a more national image, the organization separated itself from a religious connection, altered its rituals, and eliminated its oath of secrecy. The Knights continued to exclude lawyers, bankers, stockbrokers, and doctors, although it claimed that its membership did not exclude people on the grounds of racial origin, religion, or sex. The Knights became the first general labor organization to encourage the organization of women. However, the Knights drew the line when the question of including Chinese came up. The organization had no relations with California workers until 1878, the same year Denis Kearney* began to form his Workingmen's Party of California.* The Knights' first California branch was established in Sacramento in 1877 as Local Assembly 855.

Within ten years after its founding, the Knights became a powerful labor organization, using its power against the Chinese in California. They agitated for Chinese exclusion, claiming that the Chinese came to the United States as slaves sponsored by the Chinese Six Companies* and that they could not return to their home country until they had paid off their debt. Even after the Chinese Exclusion Act of 1882,* the Knights continued to agitate for the complete exclusion of Chinese, and incited its members to participate in anti-Chinese activities. These activities finally culminated during the summer of 1885 in an anti-Chinese riot at Rock Springs, Wyoming, where the local Chinese lost their lives and property. This incident is known as the Rock Springs Massacre of 1885.*

The Knights of Labor peaked in mid–1886 but began to lose strength quickly as a result of a series of strike failures and the Haymarket Square Riot. It continued to exist as an organization well into the 1900s, but its importance waned as its membership dwindled to 74,635 in 1893, when Powderly retired from the organization. Many of the Knights later joined the American Federation of Labor and other craft unions, and the fate of the Knights was sealed in 1917. (*See also* Powderly, Terence Vincent.)

FURTHER READING: Isaac H. Bromley, *The Chinese Massacre at Rock Springs, Wyoming Territory*, Boston: Franklin Press: Rand, Avery and Co., 1886; Henry J. Browne,

The Catholic Church and the Knights of Labor, Washington, D.C.: Catholic University of America Press, 1949; Ira B. Cross, *A History of the Labor Movement in California*, Berkeley: University of California Press, 1935; Alexander Saxton, *The Indispensable Enemy*, Berkeley: University of California Press, 1971; Nicholas A. Somma, "The Knights of Labor and Chinese Immigration," M. A. thesis, Catholic University of America, 1952; W. W. Stone, "The Knights of Labor on the Chinese Labor Situation," *Overland Monthly* 7 (January 1886).

KNIGHTS OF SAINT CRISPIN, organized on March 1, 1867, under the leadership of Newell Daniels in response to the rapidly expanding factory system introduced to the shoe-making industry during the Civil War. Before the 1860s, shoes were made by hand and sold to a unique market. Unlike the situation in other trades, prices varied for each customer or exchange, as a result of which custom shoemakers received the highest prices and pay for the highest wages. The craft was usually passed on from father to son. Between 1860 and 1870 the number of inventions of new machines increased at an alarming rate, making skilled artisans unnecessary for the construction of shoes. Some skilled workers, perceiving the threat to their livelihood, reacted violently to this transformation.

Newell Daniels, the shrewd founder of the Knights, felt that many of the shoemakers' problems could be traced to the employment of what he called "green hands"—people who were unskilled. He realized that whereas the organization could not prevent the machine transformation of the industry, a union could be organized to discriminate between the skilled workers and the unskilled, who could not become union members.

The so-called green hands were not the only threat to their way of life. Chinese immigrants were also feared as potential workers taking away their jobs. In 1869 the 600 union members in San Francisco successfully resisted Chinese entrance into the labor force, but by 1871, 1,000 Chinese were employed in San Francisco alone. By 1872 the Chinese had taken over slipper manufacturing and had driven the San Francisco chapter of the Knights out of existence. In 1879 a total of 5,000 Chinese were working and 800 whites were unemployed, thus converting the Knights' original fear into a nightmarish reality. Under these circumstances the Knights of Saint Crispin became hostile toward Chinese and Chinese immigration.

FURTHER READING: John Roger Commons, *History of Labor in the United States*, Vols. 2 and 3, New York: Macmillan Co., 1918–1935; Blanche Evans Hazard, *The Organization of the Boot and Shoe Industry in Massachusetts Before 1875*, (1921, rpt. 1968, Johnson Reprint Corp.); Don Divance Leschier, *The Knights of St. Crispin*, Madison: University of Wisconsin Press, 1910.

KNOX, FRANK (1874–1944), journalist. Knox was born on New Year's Day 1874 in Boston, the son of an oyster market man, William Edwin Knox. He grew up in Nova Scotia and Grand Rapids, Michigan. In 1893 he entered Michigan's Alma College but did not complete his education as he joined the army to become one of Teddy Roosevelt's Rough Riders. However, in 1912 Alma offered him a B.A. degree.

Knox embarked on a career in journalism when he accepted a job as a reporter for the *Grand Rapids Herald*. In 1902, he purchased the *Evening Journal* in Sault Ste. Marie, Michigan, and nine years later he became half-owner of the *Manchester Union & Leader*, one of the leading newspapers in Manchester, New Hampshire. Knox's journalism career was interrupted when he went abroad with the 78th Division during World War I. He came home and ran for governor of New Hampshire in 1924 but was defeated. He resumed his journalism career when William Randolph Hearst placed him in charge of the *Boston American and Advertiser* in 1927. The following year he became general manager of all Hearst papers. In 1931 Knox bought Chicago's *Daily News*, and he condemned the New Deal through his editorials. In 1936 he ran against Franklin Roosevelt on the Landon-Knox Republican ticket as vice-presidential candidate but was again defeated. Soon after his defeat he began to embrace some of Roosevelt's policies, particularly in the area of foreign affairs. In 1940 Roosevelt appointed him Secretary of the Navy.

After the Japanese bombed Pearl Harbor on December 7, 1941, Knox made a trip to Hawaii to inspect the damage done to the Pacific Fleet. Upon returning to Washington, he released his official report on December 16, 1941, in which he made no mention of any sabotage or any Japanese Fifth Column activities. But on the day preceding the release of his official report, during a meeting with newsmen, he stated that the most effective Fifth Column work was carried out in Hawaii, implying that Japanese in Hawaii spied on American military facilities. This irresponsible statement left the American public with the strong impression that Japanese Americans in Hawaii were spying for Japan.

FURTHER READING: Frank F. Chuman, *The Bamboo People*, Del Mar, Calif.: Publisher's Inc., 1976; Andrew W. Lind, *Hawaii's Japanese*, Princeton, N.J.: Princeton University Press, 1946; George H. Lobdell, "A Biography of Frank Knox," Ph.D. diss., University of Illinois, 1954.

KO. See *Tanomoshi*.

KOJONG (1852–1919), the penultimate king of Korea's Yi Dynasty (1392–1910). Kojong came to the throne in 1864 at the age of eleven, and ruled the dynasty until Japanese officials forced him to abdicate in 1907 in favor of his son.

When the American Minister, Horace N. Allen,* approached Kojong on the question of Korean immigration to Hawaii, he approved Allen's plan and established an office to handle Korean immigration to Hawaii. He was proud that his countrymen were able to go to the place where Chinese had been excluded. To him it was a matter of national pride that his subjects were accepted. At times he showed friendship toward Americans, particularly to those who were close to him, and adopted a pro-American attitude in his foreign policy. Tragically, he presided over many events of national infamy during his reign, including his own abdication imposed on him by the Japanese.

FURTHER READING: James B. Palais, *Politics and Policy in Traditional Korea*, Cambridge, Mass.: Harvard University Press, 1975; Wayne Patterson, *The Korean Frontier in America: Immigration to Hawaii, 1896–1910*, Ann Arbor, Mich.: University Microfilms International, 1977.

KOMAGATA MARU **AFFAIR,** incident that formed a small part of the Ghadar revolt in India. It was actually a test of an embargo on Asian Indian workers immigrating to Canada. In 1914 the Canadian government placed an embargo on Indian immigration, and there was also talk of ending Asian Indian immigration to the United States. At this time a wealthy Sikh by the name of Gurdit Singh established the Guru Nanak Navigation Company in Hong Kong and chartered a Japanese ship, the *Komagata Maru*. His plan was to confront the embargo law by sailing to Vancouver, British Columbia, and unloading Asian Indian workers. The Hong Kong authorities tried to stop the *Komagata Maru* but were unsuccessful. The ship then picked up Asian Indian workers in Shanghai, Kobe, and Yokohama on its way to Vancouver.

On the way to Vancouver anti-British and pro-Ghadar Party material was handed out on the *Komagata Maru*. This stirred up anti-British feelings and rowdiness among the workers. The ship arrived in Vancouver on May 23, 1914, with 376 passengers aboard, but Canadian officials refused to let the *Komagata Maru* dock. The ship then sat out in the harbor for two months, unable to get the workers ashore. Har Dayal* then suggested that if the Indian workers could enter Canada there would be no trouble in India.

On Saturday, July 18, the Japanese captain attempted to prepare for the voyage back, at which time a mutiny broke out among Asian Indians, who had no desire to return. Harbor officials responded by sending 120 police and 40 special immigration officials, with commanders, to retake the ship. The Indian passengers responded by throwing coal, bricks, steel, and homemade spears. The police were beaten back with a great deal of humiliation. The Canadians then surrounded the *Komagata Maru* with harbor boats and navy ships. One of them, a cruiser with two 6-inch guns, stood by ready for action. After four days the ship sailed out of Vancouver; while the ship was on its return trip, World War I broke out in Europe. Refused entry into Hong Kong and Singapore, the ship chose Calcutta as its final destination. When the ship docked at Budge Budge, a special train was ready to take the passengers to the Punjab at government expense. Only sixty workers took the train, and a riot broke out shortly thereafter in which eighteen Sikhs were killed. All but Singh and twenty-eight others were arrested, but they were released after five months, when the British felt that the revolt was over. (*See also* King, William Lyon MacKenzie.)

FURTHER READING: Emily Brown, *Har Dayal*, Tucson: University of Arizona Press, 1975; Robie L. Reid, "The Inside Story of the Komagata Maru," *British Columbia Historical Quarterly* 5 (January 1941), pp. 1–23.

KONG CHOW WUI KUN or KONG CHOW HUI KUAN. *See* Sze Yap (Sze-I); District Companies.

KONO, TOMMY (1921–), a health food salesman in Hawaii who won Olympic titles for the United States in 1952 and 1956 in weight lifting. He had previously won eight world and eight national titles. He broke no less than twenty-six world records.

KOOPMANSCHAP, CORNELIUS (1828–1882), labor contractor. Koopmanschap was born on February 13, 1928, in Weesperkarspel, near Amsterdam and came to California between 1850 and 1851, settling in San Francisco as an importer of Chinese goods. As his business grew, he made frequent trips to Hong Kong, where he established residence in the 1860s. His business connections with Chinese firms enabled him to take on a major role as contractor and importer of Chinese laborers to the United States and other parts of the world.

During the Chinese Labor Convention held on July 13, 1869, in Memphis, Tennessee, he reported to the delegates that the House of Koopmanschap had imported nearly 30,000 Chinese laborers and that he could secure Chinese laborers for the South who would come to work at Southern plantations at $20 per month.

When John C. Stanton, superintendent of the Alabama and Chattanooga Railroad,* asked Koopmanschap to ship Chinese laborers to work for his company, he promised to send Stanton 1,000 or 2,000 Chinese, but he was able to ship only 960 Chinese, who arrived in Alabama in early August 1870. He also sent 52 Chinese workers to work on Louisiana sugar plantations in October 1870.

Although Koopmanschap's reputation as a contractor and importer of Chinese workers was widespread in the South, he actually was credited with bringing only 1,200 Chinese laborers. Had his company not gone bankrupt in May 1872, he might have brought more Chinese to the South.

Koopmanschap died in 1882 in Rio de Janeiro, where he was negotiating to bring Chinese laborers to Brazil.
FURTHER READING: Gunther Barth, *Bitter Strength*, Cambridge, Mass.: Harvard University Press, 1964; Lucy M. Cohen, *Chinese in the Post-Civil War South*, Baton Rouge: Louisiana State University Press, 1984; Robert Seto Quan, *Lotus Among the Magnolias*, Jackson: University Press of Mississippi, 1982.

KOREAN AMERICAN EDUCATION CENTER, established in 1973 in San Francisco by concerned Koreans in the Bay Area who wanted their children to learn not only the Korean language, but also Korean history and culture. The center rented local school classrooms and began to hold classes ranging from kindergarten to sixth grade. Students attending school at the center were taught Korean and English on Sunday afternoons. Because the center emphasized instruction in the Korean and English languages, its programs were similar to those that had been offered at language schools operated by the Japanese, Korean, and Chinese in Hawaii.

KOREAN AGRICULTURAL AND COMMERCIAL CORPORATION, established by the Korean National Association* of Hawaii on March 4, 1911, in order to promote agriculture and commerce among Koreans in Hawaii. The total capital for the corporation was set at $100,000, with each share costing $10.

KOREAN CHRISTIAN CHURCH, established in 1917 after a group of seventy Korean Christians walked out of the Korean Methodist Church in Honolulu under the leadership of Syngman Rhee,* who believed that Koreans should have their own church. (*See also* Korean Churches.)

KOREAN CHURCHES, established in America beginning in 1903. The sociocultural characteristics of Korean immigrants to the United States were different from those found among Japanese and Chinese immigrants. The Korean laborers recruited for the Hawaiian Sugar Planters' Association* by David W. Deshler* were from various parts of the Korean peninsula, whereas Japanese and Chinese immigrants were recruited from within limited areas of their respective countries. In addition, Korean immigrants were different from their Japanese and Chinese counterparts in that they came to Hawaii not as sojourners* ready to return with their accumulated wealth, but as people willing to stay in their host country. Still more dissimilar from their Japanese and Chinese counterparts was their religious affiliation. Whereas Japanese and Chinese were not Christians, many Korean immigrants had already embraced Christianity when they were recruited.

Upon their arrival in Honolulu, the Koreans sought to establish a place of worship according to their own faith. These Christians avoided clan associations and organized themselves on the basis of their Christian faith. The first to establish a church were the Korean Methodists, and they called it the Korean Evangelical Society* in 1903. Two years later, the Korean Episcopal Church was established under the leadership of Chong Hyon-ku and Kim Ik-song. After Syngman Rhee* came to Honolulu, to carry out his work for Korea's independence, disputes developed within the church, and in 1916 Rhee led a group of seventy people to establish a separatist movement within Korean Christian Churches. This movement led to the establishment of the Korean Christian Church in 1917.

In mainland United States, the Korean Methodist Church of San Francisco, formerly the Korean Evangelical Society, started on October 8, 1905, whereas a group of Korean Christians in Los Angeles began to worship at a mission school in March 1904.

Even today, Christian churches in Korean communities in the United States continue to play a vital role by providing a variety of services that would not otherwise be available to many new immigrants coming from Korea.

FURTHER READING: Bong-youn Choy, *Koreans in America*, Chicago: Nelson-Hall, 1979; Hyung-chan Kim, *The Korean Diaspora*, Santa Barbara, Calif.: ABC-Clio Press, 1977; Eui-Young Yu et al., *Koreans in Los Angeles*, Center for Korean-American and Korean Studies, California State University, 1982.

KOREAN COMMISSION, established by Syngman Rhee* who became president of the Korean provisional government-in-exile in Shanghai in September 1919. Previously, propaganda activities to promote the cause of Korea's independence from Japan had been conducted by the Bureau of Korean Information,* which had been created as a result of the first Korean Liberty Congress.* But this bureau ceased to function when the Korean Commission was created by Syngman Rhee, acting as president of the government-in-exile, under criticism by officials of the government he was supposed to represent. At any rate, Rhee appointed Kiusic Kimm* to serve as chairman. Kimm arrived in 1919, but left following a disagreement with Rhee.

The commission carried out propaganda activities, including the publication of books such as *Korea's Fight for Freedom* and *The Case of Korea*. It also raised money to be used in its political propaganda work against Japan. Korean community people in the United States donated money to this organization, and Syngman Rhee issued government bonds amounting to $250,000. Although the commission was maintained until 1928, its active propaganda work ceased by 1922. (*See also* Kimm, Kiusic.)
FURTHER READING: Bong-youn Choy, *Koreans in America*, Chicago: Nelson-Hall, 1979; Chong-sik Lee, *The Politics of Korean Nationalism*, Berkeley: University of California Press, 1965.

KOREAN EPISCOPAL CHURCH OF HONOLULU, established among Korean immigrants to Hawaii on February 10, 1905, under the leadership of Kim Ik-song and Chong Hyong-ku. (*See also* Korean Churches.)

KOREAN EVANGELICAL SOCIETY, organized between November 3 and 10, 1903, under the leadership of Ahn Ch'ung-su and U Pyong-gil, who negotiated to secure a place of worship. It later became the Korean Methodist Church of Honolulu. (*See also* Korean Churches.)

KOREAN INDEPENDENCE. *See* Korean National Revolutionary Party.

KOREAN LIBERTY CONGRESS, held in 1919 to rally support for Korean independence. After more than ten years of oppression suffered under Japanese domination, Koreans arose on March 1, 1919, to protest against Japanese colonial administration. To this uprising Japan responded ruthlessly with guns and bayonets, killing and maiming thousands of innocent people. This tragic news reached Korean residents in the United States who held a mass rally on March 15, 1919, to protest Japan's occupation of Korea and to work toward Korea's independence.

A thirteen-point resolution was passed during the mass meeting which directed the Korean National Association* to execute activities related to the Korean independence movement and to ask Dr. So Jae-p'il (Philip Jaisohn)* to establish the Korean Information Office in Philadelphia for diplomatic and propaganda activities, to which the Korean National Association was to donate $800 per month.

After this mass rally, twenty-seven Korean community organizations sent their representatives to the first Korean Liberty Congress, held on April 14, 1919, in Philadelphia. The congress lasted three days, after which it passed a ten-point resolution calling on the League of Nations to recognize Korea. The name of the congress was later changed to the Bureau of Korean Information.* (*See also* Bureau of Korean Information.)

FURTHER READING: Bong-youn Choy, *Koreans in America*, Chicago: Nelson-Hall, 1979; C. W. Kendall, *The Truth About Korea*, San Francisco: Korean National Association, 1919; Chong-sik Lee, *The Politics of Korean Nationalism*, Berkeley: University of California Press, 1965; F. A. McKenzie, *Korea's Fight for Freedom*, London: F. H. Revell Co., 1920.

KOREAN METHODIST CHURCH OF LOS ANGELES, originally established by a retired missionary, Mrs. Sherman, on March 11, 1904, and financed by the Board of Education of Southern Methodist Churches. (*See also* Korean Churches.)

KOREAN METHODIST CHURCH OF SAN FRANCISCO, founded as the Korean Evangelical Society* on October 8, 1905, under the leadership of Mun Kyong-ho, who conducted church services at a private home located on Ellis Street. The church officially became the Korean Methodist Church on August 11, 1911. (*See also* Korean Churches.)

KOREAN NATIONAL ASSOCIATION, established on February 1, 1909, when two organizations, the Kongnip Hyophoe (Mutual Assistance Society*) in California and the Hanin Hapsong Hyophoe (United Korean Society*) in Hawaii, merged into the Tae-Hanin Kungmin-hoe or Korean National Association. The purpose of the association was to represent Korean interests in the United States. Its headquarters was established in San Francisco, and branch offices were opened in Hawaii, Siberia, and Manchuria. It required all Korean residents in the United States to become members and to pay dues to support the organization. From the start the association was actively involved in working toward Korea's independence from Japan, although factionalism within the association made its activities weak and ineffective.

After Korea's liberation from Japan in 1945, the association became dormant. Although it opposed the Syngman Rhee* regime in Seoul, its opposition did not affect his one-man dictatorship. Even today the association maintains an office

in Los Angeles, but it has no significant organizational basis among Koreans in
America.
FURTHER READING: Bong-youn Choy, *Koreans in America*, Chicago: Nelson-Hall,
1979; Hyung-chan Kim, *The Korean Diaspora*, Santa Barbara, Calif.: ABC-Clio Press,
1977.

KOREAN NATIONAL BRIGADE. *See* Pak Yong-man.

KOREAN NATIONAL REVOLUTIONARY PARTY, founded in 1935. After
Japan occupied Manchuria and made an advance toward Shanghai, Korean
independence fighters in China gathered in Nanking and established a united
front against Japan on October 23, 1932. Three years later, on June 20, 1935,
thirty-six representatives from nine different political organizations fighting for
Korean independence gathered in Nanking, and they agreed to establish a united
organization to work toward Korean independence. Five of the nine political
organizations decided to dissolve their party in order to create the Korean National
Revolutionary Party, which came into existence on July 5, 1935. In spite of
factionalism which continued to plague the party, its leadership maintained control
of the party until Kiusic Kimm,* Kim Won-bong, and Kim Sang-dok came to
Korea after Korea's liberation in 1945. In South Korea, the party continued to
carry out its work to establish a democratic Korea, in accordance with its party
platform proclaimed in February 1944 during its seventh party convention. The
party established ten different branch offices in and around Seoul.

The Korean National Revolutionary Party of Los Angeles began as an
organization to assist Chinese refugees who became victims of the Japanese
invasion of China in 1937. The organization, called the China-Aid Society, was
created among Koreans in America in October 1939, and it later changed its
name to the Korean Volunteers Corps Aid Society in China. The Korean Volunteer
Corps was originally established in China by Kim Won-bong, a leftist military
officer who once served as Minister of Defense in the Korean provisional
government-in-exile in Shanghai. In January 1945 the Korean Volunteers Corps
Aid Society in China changed its name to the Korean National Revolutionary
Party and became the American chapter of the party. The American chapter
began with only forty members. They appointed Kim Song-kwon, Hwang Sa-
yong, and Kwak Im-dae as members of the Executive Committee.

The party began to publish its own newspaper, *The Korean Independence*, on
September 5, 1943, under the leadership of Pyon Chun-ho, Diamond Kimm,
Choy Bong-youn, and Pak Sang-hyop, who served as editor of the newspaper.
After Korea's liberation in August 1945, the newspaper criticized American
policies toward Korea through its editorials. Because of their vitriolic criticism,
some members of the party were harassed by officials of the Justice Department,
which initiated deportation proceedings against such persons as Alice Whang
and Diamond Kimm. The case of Kimm, v. George K. Rosenberg*, District
Director, Immigration and Naturalization Service, went to the U.S. Supreme

Court which on June 3, 1960, ruled in favor of the government, thus upholding the lower court's decision to deport Diamond Kimm. The decision was moot, however, as Diamond Kimm had already left the United States for North Korea, where it was alleged he was purged.

FURTHER READING: Democratic National Front, ed., *The First-year History of Korean Liberation*, Seoul, Korea; Munwu Inswoi-kwan, 1946; Bong-youn Choy, *Koreans in America*, Chicago: Nelson-Hall, 1979; Warren Kim, *Fifty-year History of Koreans in America*, Los Angeles: Charles Ho Kim, 1959; Chong-sik Lee, *The Politics of Korean Nationalism*, Berkeley: University of California Press, 1965.

KOREAN PRESBYTERIAN CHURCH OF LOS ANGELES, organized in Los Angeles on May 10, 1906, by a group of Korean residents who negotiated for a place of worship with the Board of the Presbyterian Extension. It was not until April 9, 1921, that the church became an independent, self-governing body. (*See also* Korean Churches.)

KOREAN RESIDENTS ASSOCIATION (KYOMIN-DAN), established on March 21, 1921, when a group of Korean residents in Hawaii following the leadership of Syngman Rhee* split off from the Korean National Association* of Hawaii to establish the Korean Residents Association. It was established in order to assist Syngman Rhee in his efforts to achieve Korean independence through diplomatic activitics.

KOREAN RESIDENTS' ASSOCIATION (HAN-NIN-HOE), an organization found in many parts of the United States—particularly since the passage of the Immigration Act of October 3, 1965,* which enabled large numbers of Koreans to immigrate to America. The association may take on a different name in order to characterize its local peculiarity. For instance, the Korean Residents' Association in Southern California is called the Korean Association of Southern California, whereas Korean residents who established their organization in the Bay Area called it the Korean American Association of San Francisco and the Bay Area.

Most of the local resident associations established by Koreans claim to be non-profit and social in purpose, but they suffer from lack of participation by local Korean residents, many of whom do not feel they need such an organization.

The government in South Korea has frequently curried favor with leaders of associations by inviting them to Korea, where they are entertained at government expense. In return, the government asks their support for its policies, both domestic and international.

FURTHER READING: Bong-youn Choy, *Koreans in America*, Chicago: Nelson-Hall, 1979; Hyung-chan Kim, *The Korean Diaspora*, Santa Barbara, Calif.: ABC-Clio Press, 1977.

KOREAN SCHOOL OF AVIATION, established on February 20, 1920, under the leadership of Kim Chong-nim and Noh Baek-nin in Willows, California. Kim was a rice farmer who had more than 2,000 acres of rice fields, and he donated three airplanes to start the school. Noh was chief of the Bureau of Military Affairs of the Korean provisional government-in-exile in Shanghai. It was said that Kim gave $3,000 per month to maintain the school in operation. The school was founded to train pilots to fight against the Japanese in order to achieve Korea's independence.

KOREAN SPECIAL DIPLOMATIC MISSION TO AMERICA, 1883, a follow up to the treaty between Korea and the United States in 1882. The United States dispatched its ambassador, Lucius Foote, to Korea in 1883. King Kojong* of Korea wanted to reciprocate by sending a special diplomatic mission headed by Prince Min Yong-ik, who was assisted by Hong Yong-sik and three other secretaries and an American advisor. Foote made arrangements for the mission to be guests of the *U.S.S. Monocacy*, which carried them to Nagasaki, Japan. The mission went to Yokohama to board the *Arabic*, which left for San Francisco on August 18, 1883, arriving at its destination on September 2, 1883. Min Yong-ik was met by President Chester A. Arthur, and the mission made a nationwide tour before it returned to Korea. One of the members of the mission, Yu Kil-chun, was granted permission by Min to study at Dummer Academy of Salem, Massachusetts, under Samuel Morse. Yu became the first Korean student to study in America under Korean government sponsorship. (*See also* Chemulp'o, Treaty of [1882].)
FURTHER READING: Sung-joo Han, ed., *After One Hundred Years: Continuity and Change in Korean-American Relations*, Seoul, Korea: Asiatic Research Center, 1982; Tae-hwan Kwak et al., ed., *U.S.-Korean Relations, 1882–1982*, Seoul, Korea: Kyungnam University Press, 1982; Gary D. Walter, "The Korean Special Mission to the United States of America in 1883," *Journal of Korean Studies* 1 (1969):84–142.

KOREAN VOLUNTEERS CORPS AID SOCIETY. *See* Korean National Revolutionary Party.

KOREAN WOMEN'S PATRIOTIC LEAGUE, established on August 5, 1919, when all existing Korean women's organizations decided to merge into one organization. Delegates from various women's organizations gathered together in Dinuba, California, on August 2, 1919, and passed the league's constitution with three articles. Its main purpose was to support the Korean independence movement in cooperation with the Korean National Association.*

KOREAN YOUTH MILITARY ACADEMY. *See* Pak Yong-man.

KOREMATSU v. THE UNITED STATES, a case argued on October 11 and 12, 1944, and decided on December 18, 1944, involving an American citizen of Japanese ancestry, Fred Toyosaburo Korematsu, who was convicted of remaining in a military area contrary to Civilian Exclusion Order No. 34 issued by the commanding general of the Western Command. Korematsu remained in the city of San Leandro, California, a part of Military Area No. 1, and failed to report to authorities at the designated time and place, as he had been required.

In the brief *amicus curiae* filed by the American Civil Liberties Union on behalf of the petitioner, Korematsu's lawyers argued that the case did not involve only the question of the validity of exclusion, but more importantly the very question of whether or not exclusion as a means of internment was constitutional. Implicit in their argument was that Korematsu violated the order because he deemed it unconstitutional.

Justice Hugo Black, in his opinion for the court, stated that exclusion and internment or detention were two separate problems and therefore "may be governed by different principles." The lawfulness of one did not necessarily determine the lawfulness of the other. Insisting that the Justices "uphold the exclusion order as of the time it was made and when the petitioner violated it," Justice Black deemed the exclusion order justified because of military necessity.* He ruled out any possibility that Korematsu might have been excluded from the military area because of his race. Three of his associates, however, did not agree with him. Justices Owen Roberts, Frank Murphy, and Robert Jackson dissented and filed their separate opinions. In his dissenting opinion Justice Roberts delineated various events leading to the exclusion chronologically, presented to his colleagues "facts of which we take judicial notice," and concluded that the assembly center to which Korematsu was required to report was a "euphemism for a prison." In his opinion Korematsu had been deprived of his constitutional rights. Justice Murphy went further than Justice Roberts in characterizing the exclusion, when he said that "such exclusion goes over the very brink of constitutional power and falls into the ugly abyss of racism." Justice Jackson chastised his colleagues when he declared:

> A military order, however unconstitutional, is not apt to last longer than the military emergency. Even during that period a succeeding commander may revoke it all. But once a judicial opinion rationalizes such an order to show that it conforms to the Constitution, or rather rationalizes the Constitution to show that the Constitution sanctions such an order, the Court for all time has validated the principle of racial discrimination in criminal procedure and of transplanting American citizens.

(*See also* Hirabayashi v. United States.)
FURTHER READING: Milton R. Konvitz, *The Alien and the Asiatic in American Law*, Ithaca, N.Y.: Cornell University Press, 1946; *Supreme Court Reporter* 65, 323 U.S. 214, 1944; Robert A. Wilson, *East to America*, New York: William Morrow and Co., 1980.

KUHIO, JONAH KALANIANAOLE. *See* Hawaii Rehabilitation Act.

K'U-LI. *See* Coolie.

KUMI, a term that means a team or company in Japanese. Japanese immigrants in Hawaii developed the *kumi* system whereby a neighborhood consisting of between fifteen and twenty households engaged in cooperative activities, including weddings, funerals, and other community festivities. The *kumi* system was said to be the most important social organization in the Kona District.

FURTHER READING: John F. Embree, *Acculturation Among the Japanese of Kona, Hawaii*, American Anthropological Association, 1944; Dennis M. Ogawa, *Kodomo no tame ni* (For the Sake of the Children), Honolulu: University Press of Hawaii, 1978; William Petersen, *Japanese Americans: Oppression and Success*, New York: Random House, 1971.

KUMIAI, a Japanese term for partnership or association. It was established among Japanese farmers in the Kona District who grew coffee for their livelihood. The practice of engaging in cooperative activities through the *kumiai* system continued until the 1930s when it was discontinued because the Nisei* did not make use of it.

Dennis Ogawa, in his book *Kotomo no tame ni* (For the Sake of the Children), states that *kumi*, rather than *kumiai*, were Japanese farmer cooperatives. It is quite possible, however, that Japanese farmers used *kumiai* as cooperatives in the Kona District. In fact, Lawrence Fuchs in his book *Hawaii Pono* refers to *kumiai* as Japanese farmer cooperatives.

FURTHER READING: Lawrence Fuchs, *Hawaii Pono: A Social History*, New York: Harcourt, Brace and World, 1961; Dennis M. Ogawa, *Kotomo no tame ni* (For the Sake of the Children), Honolulu: University Press of Hawaii, 1978.

KUOMINTANG, an organization founded in 1905 to overthrow the Manchu government and to establish a democratic China in conformity with six principles adopted by the Revolutionary Alliance. When Dr. Sun Yat-sen* was in Honolulu, he established the Hing Chung Wui or Hsing Chung Hui* (Society for the Regeneration of China) in 1894 through which he raised funds for his revolutionary activities. A new phase in the development of this revolutionary organization occurred when a large group of delegates, mostly students studying in Japan, gathered to hold a conference in Tokyo in the autumn of 1905. Out of this conference emerged the T'ung Meng Hui or Revolutionary Alliance, which became the organizational basis for the Kuomintang. In 1911 the Alliance changed its name to the Kuomintang. During the same year Dr. Sun was made president of the Republic of China.

The Kuomintang became the Revolutionary Party of China in 1914 and the Kuomintang of China in 1924, a name which the Nationalist Chinese in Taiwan have retained. The government in Taiwan showed keen interest in the affairs of Chinese communities in the United States. It established Chinese community schools staffed by teachers regularly examined for their loyalty to the Kuomintang government. Instructional materials for Chinese community schools were examined to see if they were suitable for use in the schools supported by the Taiwan government.

The Kuomintang government frequently curried favor with Chinese community leaders, but it was also willing to use rather questionable methods to make disloyal Chinese conform to its expectations. Overseas Chinese today, wherever they are found, are faced with the problem of dealing with two governments in China claiming to represent the interests of overseas Chinese. (*See also* Henry Liu Murder Case.)

FURTHER READING: Stanford M. Lyman, *Chinese Americans*, New York: Random House, 1974; Harold Z. Schiffrin, *Sun Yat-sen and the Origins of the Chinese Revolution*, Berkeley: University of California Press, 1968; T. C. Woo, *The Kuomintang and the Future of the Chinese Revolution*, Westport, Conn.: Hyperion Press, 1975.

KURIHARA, JOSEPH YOSHISUKE (1895-?) World War II evacuee. Kurihara was born on Kauai Island, Hawaii, and came to Honolulu at the age of two with his family. He attended elementary school and a Catholic high school before he enrolled in St. Ignatius College in San Francisco. In 1917 he moved to Michigan where he enlisted in the U.S. Army. He served abroad and was honorably discharged.

During World War II Kurihara was interned, and he felt that he was betrayed by his own country. He was so embittered that he renounced his citizenship when given the opportunity and returned to Japan in February 1946 to become "a Jap a hundred percent and never to do another day's work to help this country fight this war."

KUROKAWA, COLBERT NAOYA (1890–1978) Japanese researcher. Kurokawa was born in a small village in Chiba Prefecture, Japan. His parents raised him to be a Buddhist priest, but he ran away at the age of fourteen and joined his uncle in Hawaii. Although he possessed only 50 cents upon his arrival in Hawaii, he built a successful career in America during the following twenty-five years. He attended Mid-Pacific Institute in Honolulu on a scholarship and went to Dickinson College from which he graduated in 1922. After his conversion to Christianity, he held a number of positions in the church related to community service. While in Hawaii, he also worked as an interpreter for the local Japanese consul general and came into contact with important government officials from Japan.

In 1935, after thirty years in Hawaii, Kurokawa decided to return to Japan with his family and taught English at Doshisha University in Kyoto. During the Pacific War he worked for a policy study organization called the South Seas Economic Research Center, which was established in 1937 to make policy recommendations to the Japanese government's Southern Affairs Department headed by Admiral Oka Takazumi. As a researcher he submitted an in-house report entitled "What Should Be Done with Hawaii?", which was dated April 1943. In the report Kurokawa made a number of policy recommendations to be used by the Japanese government in case of Japanese military conquest of the Hawaiian Islands.

FURTHER READING: John J. Stephen, *Hawaii Under the Rising Sun: Japan's Plans for Conquest After Pearl Harbor*, Honolulu: University of Hawaii Press, 1984.

KWANG TEK TONG. *See Tongs.*

KWOCK JAN FAT v. WHITE, COMMISSIONER OF IMMIGRATION,
a case argued in 1920 involving an American citizen of Chinese ancestry who
was denied entry into the United States on the basis of false evidence. In January
1915 Kwock Jan Fat, intending to visit China for a year, filed with the commissioner
of immigration for the port of San Francisco an application for a preinvestigation
of his claimed status as an American citizen by birth. This was required by law
of all persons of Chinese ancestry who wanted to gain reentry into the United
States.

Kwock was eighteen years of age, born in Monterey, California, and the son
of Kwock Tuck Lee, who also was born in America of Chinese parents and had
resided in Monterey for many years. The Department of Immigration made an
elaborate investigation of the facts pertaining to Kwock Jan Fat and accepted
testimony from three credible white men, verifying them. As a result of the
inquiry, the applicant was allowed to leave for China with a reentry permit.

During Kwock's absence, anonymous information reached the San Francisco
Immigration Office, in which there had been a change of officials, alleging that
the petitioner's name was not Kwock Jan Fat, but Lew Suey Chong and that he
had entered the United States in 1909 as a minor son of a merchant, Lew Wing
Tong, of Oakland, California.

Upon Kwock's return to the United States from China, he was denied entry
on the basis that his American citizenship had not been established to the
commissioner's satisfaction. Kwock's American citizenship was suspected on
the basis of testimony made by witnesses under the promise that their names
would not be disclosed. In addition, records on the testimony given against
Kwock were improperly kept.

The case came to the Supreme Court on writ of certiorari to the U.S. Circuit
Court of Appeals for the Ninth Circuit, was argued on April 30, 1920, and
decided on June 7, 1920. Justice John H. Clarke, delivering the Court's opinion,
affirmed the right of an alien to have a fair opportunity to be heard, when he
stated that a hearing based on an unfair report was not a fair hearing. He cautioned
against the use of excessive power when he argued that the power given to the
Secretary of Labor over Chinese immigrants by the acts of Congress was "to
be administered, not arbitrarily and secretly, but fairly and openly, under the
restraints of the tradition and principles of free government applicable where the
fundamental rights of men are involved, regardless of their origin and race."

The judgment of the Circuit Court of Appeals was reversed and the case was
remanded to the District Court for trial of the merits.

FURTHER READING: Milton R. Konvitz, *The Alien and the Asiatic in American Law*,
Ithaca, N.Y.: Cornell University Press, 1946; *Supreme Court Reporter* 40, 253 U.S. 454,
1920.

KYE, a Korean term referring to a form of rotating credit association similar to
the Chinese *hui* or the Japanese *tanomoshi.** (*See also Hui.*)

KYOP'O, a Korean term referring to all ethnic Koreans living abroad, regardless of their citizenship. The word *kyop'o* is usually placed after the name of the country or place where they are found. Therefore, the Koreans who live in the United States are called *Miguk* (America) *kyop'o*.

L

LADD, WILLIAM. *See* Ladd and Company.

LADD AND COMPANY, a company established by William Hooper, William Ladd, and Peter Brinsmade* in 1833. Two years later they received permission from chiefs to lease a tract of land at Koloa, Kauai, for fifty years at $300 per year. A year later, Hooper was proud to say that on his land there were 25 acres of cane under cultivation, twenty houses for the native workers, a house for the superintendent, a carpenter's shop, a blacksmith's shop, a sugar house, a boiling house, and a sugar mill. As his operation grew, he became dissatisfied with the native workers and began to think about employing Chinese workers. By 1838 Chinese were working for Hooper, who assigned them to the mill, while native Hawaiians were placed on the field.

In 1839, after a number of years of hard work, Hooper tired of his constant struggle with his workers and finally decided to bid farewell to Koloa Plantation. In 1845 the company ran into financial trouble and went out of business.
FURTHER READING: Gavan Daws, *Shoal of Time*, Honolulu: University Press of Hawaii, 1968; Ronald Takaki, *Pau Hana: Plantation Life and Labor in Hawaii*, Honolulu: University of Hawaii Press, 1983.

LADDARAN, ESTANISLAO P. v. LADDARAN, EMMA P., a litigation case involving Estanislao P. Laddaran, a Filipino, who requested annulment of his marriage to Emma, his white wife. The Superior Court, in handing down its decision in 1931, gave its opinion that the marriage was legal in California because Filipinos were not classified as Mongolians, and therefore his marriage could not be annulled. Two years later on January 18, 1933, Herbert C. Jones* of the California State Legislature introduced bills to reclassify the Filipinos so that they could not marry whites. (*See* Jones, Herbert C.)

LANGUAGE SCHOOLS, established by Chinese, Japanese, and Korean immigrants who wanted to preserve their culture. In view of the fact that they expected to return to their mother country someday, they established schools where their children were taught the culture and language of their homeland. In Hawaii, plantation owners were quite willing to provide their employees with financial support toward constructing language schools as they hoped that they would provide the infrastructure needed for meaningful community life.

The first Chinese language school on the mainland was established in San Francisco's Chinatown* in 1884. It was called the Ch'ing School, named after the dynasty, and some sixty students attended two classes. Even as late as the 1960s the Chinese community in San Francisco maintained language schools where approximately 650 children attended classes two hours a day, five days a week.

In Hawaii, the practice of teaching children the language of their parents' mother country was not uniform. Chinese immigrants sent their sons to China for their early education because there were no schools for Chinese language instruction during the early years of their settlement. As the number of children of school age grew and Chinese immigrants changed from sojourners* to more permanent residents, Chinese language schools were established. In Hawaii this occurred around 1910. On the other hand, Japanese immigrants established their language schools as early as 1896 and continued to operate them until toward the end of the 1930s. Enrollment reached its peak in 1934 when 41,192 children of Japanese ancestry received some instruction every day in a language school. By 1941 the number of children receiving language instruction began to decline. Language schools among Japanese, Korean, and Chinese immigrants in Hawaii did not operate without the government's attempt to restrict, control, and eventually eliminate them, as they were viewed by some as foreign and un-American. Particularly after World War I a flurry of bills was rushed through the Territorial Legislature, and in 1923 the Clark Bill was passed to give the Department of Education power to abolish the language schools. In 1925 the legislature amended the Clark Bill and passed An Act Relating to Foreign Language Schools and Teachers Thereof, whereby the Department of Education issued regulations requiring written permission for operation of language schools and a $1 fee per pupil. This law was challenged in the case of Farrington v. T. Tokushige et al.* on the grounds that it violated the Fourteenth and Fifth Amendments of the Constitution. Justice James McReynolds ruled on February 21, 1927, in favor of T. Tokushige. In his opinion for the Court, Justice McReynolds declared that the law and regulations went far beyond mere regulation of private schools: they deprived parents of the opportunity of instruction for their children in what they thought was important.

Language schools for Japanese immigrants lost their popularity when no large numbers of Japanese immigrants continued to come to the United States. Nonetheless, these schools are still important for recent immigrants from Korea and China.

FURTHER READING: Milton R. Konvitz, *The Alien and the Asiatic in American Law*, Ithaca, N.Y.: Cornell University Press, 1946; Gavan Daws, *Shoal of Time*, Honolulu: University Press of Hawaii, 1968; Clarence E. Glick, *Sojourners and Settlers*, Honolulu: University Press of Hawaii, 1980; Kum Pui Lai, "The Natural History of the Chinese Language School in Hawaii," M.A. Thesis, University of Hawaii, 1935; Andrew Lind, *Hawaii's Japanese: An Experiment in Democracy*, Princeton, N.J.: Princeton University Press, 1946; Gail Y. Miyasaki, *The Schooling of the Nisei in Hawaii*, Occasional Papers in Social Foundations of Education, No. 2, University of Hawaii, 1977; Dennis M. Ogawa, *Kodomo no tame ni* (For the Sake of the Children), Honolulu: University Press of Hawaii, 1978; John N. Hawkins, "Politics, Education and Language Policy: The Case of Japanese Language Schools in Hawaii," *Amerasia Journal* 5, No. 1 (1978), pp. 39–56.

LASKER, BRUNO (1880–1965), writer and social researcher. Lasker was born on July 26, 1880, in Hamburg, Germany, came to the United States in 1914, and became naturalized in 1921. He worked as a social research scientist as well as a writer, and in 1923, he joined the Institute of Pacific Relations as research associate, serving until 1928. In early 1931 the American Council of the Institute of Pacific Relations commissioned him to study Filipino immigration to the United States and to report on it within three months. He completed his study and issued a report which in 1931 was published under the title *Filipino Immigration: To Continental United States and to Hawaii*.

In 1928 Lasker moved to the Southeast Asia Institute, where he served until 1946, at which time he became a member of the United Nations Ad Hoc Committee on Slavery. He worked for the United Nations until his retirement in 1952. He was the author of many books, including *Racial Attitudes in Children* (1929), *People of Southeast Asia* (1944), *Asia on the Move* (1945), *Human Bondage in Southeast Asia* (1950), and *Standards of Living in Southern and Eastern Asia* (1954). He died on September 9, 1965.

LAU et al. v. NICHOLS et al., a case involving thirteen non-English speaking students of Chinese ancestry who filed suit in federal court against the San Francisco Board of Education. The case was heard on December 10, 1973, and was decided unanimously on January 21, 1974. This class suit asked for relief against the unequal educational opportunities which the petitioners claimed violated the Fourteenth Amendment. Specifically, the petitioners claimed that the inability or unwillingness of the San Francisco School Board to provide 1,800 students of Chinese ancestry with adequate instructional procedures violated Section 601 of the Civil Rights Act of 1964. This section excludes from participation in federal financial assistance recipients of aid who discriminate against racial groups. The San Francisco school system was a recipient of such aid.

This case had first been heard before the District Court, which had denied relief from the situation. It was then appealed, and the Court of Appeals upheld the decision of the District Court. Finally, the Supreme Court granted the petition for certiorari because of the "public importance of the question presented," as Justice William O. Douglas characterized the case in his opinion for the Court.

The Court relied on Section 601 of the Civil Rights Act of 1964 for its argument. Justice Douglas also cited a specific guideline to Section 601 that had been provided by the Department of Health, Education and Welfare (HEW) in 1970. The guideline stated that

> where inability to speak and understand the English language excludes national origin minority group children from effective participation in the educational program offered by a school district, the district must take affirmative steps to rectify the language deficiency in order to open its instructional program to these students. Any ability grouping or tracking system employed by the school system to deal with the special language skill needs of national origin minority group children must be designed to meet such language skill needs as soon as possible and must not operate as an educational dead-end or permanent track.

Because the San Francisco school system had contractually agreed to comply with the Civil Rights Act of 1964 and all requirements imposed by HEW, it clearly was in violation of the agreement it made by denying adequate English instruction to these 1,800 children of Chinese ancestry.

The Chief Justice and three other Justices concurred with Justice Douglas in the decision to reverse the judgment of the Court of Appeals, and the case was remanded for the "fashioning of appropriate relief."

FURTHER READING: Equal Educational Opportunity: Hearing before the Select Committee on Equal Educational Opportunity of the U.S. Senate, 92nd Congress, 1st Session, Part 9B, pp. 4715–4754; *U.S. Reports* 414, October Term 1973, Washington D.C.: U.S. Government Printing Office, 1975, pp. 563–72; Ling-chi Wang, "Lau v. Nichols: The Right of Limited-English-speaking Students," *Amerasia Journal* 2, No. 2 (Fall 1974), pp. 16–45.

LAURETA, ALFRED (1924–), first Filipino director of the Department of Labor and Industrial Relations. Laureta was born on May 21, 1924, in Hawaii to Laureano and Victoriana Laureta. He went to the University of Hawaii from which he graduated with a B.Ed. degree in 1947, and to Fordham University for his law study. In 1954 he was admitted to the Hawaii bar and began his practice in Honolulu as a partner with George Ariyoshi.* Governor John Anthony Burns* appointed him director of the Department of Labor and Industrial Relations in 1963. He held this position until 1967 when he was appointed to serve on Hawaii's Circuit Court One.

LEA, HOMER (1876–1912), writer, advisor to Sun Yat-sen.* Lea was born in Denver, Colorado, on November 17, 1876, the son of Alfred and Hersha Erkine. He attended the University of the Pacific, Occidental College, and Leland Stanford Junior University. Although he studied law, his real interest was in military history and tactics, and in major wars, particularly those involving Napoleon. He claimed that he was destined to be a great military leader, but people around him did not take him too seriously as he was physically fragile and a deformed hunchback who had been rejected by the U.S. Army.

In 1899 Lea left for China, where he assisted in the relief of Peking during the Boxer Rebellion. Lea impressed the Chinese with his military knowledge and courage. Soon he became associated with K'ang Yu-wei,* but his acquaintance with K'ang ended when he was forced to flee to Hong Kong. There he met Dr. Sun Yat-sen, who made Lea his chief advisor during the revolution of 1911 and 1912.

Lea became well known for his literary works, namely, *The Vermillion Pencil* (1909), *The Valor of Ignorance* (1912), and *The Day of the Saxon* (1912). In *The Valor of Ignorance*, he predicted the rise of militarism in the twentieth century, with a particular regard to war between Japan and the United States, while in *The Day of the Saxon*, he predicted a Japanese attack on the British Empire in the Far East. In his first book, he made some unfair characterizations about Asians. He died on November 1, 1912, in Ocean Park, California. (*See also* K'ang Yu-wei and Sun Yat-sen.)

FURTHER READING: Roger Daniels, *The Politics of Prejudice*, Berkeley: University of California Press, 1962.

LEAGUE OF DELIVERANCE, an organization that emerged out of a convention of labor and anti-Chinese organizations of the State of California, held on April 24, 1882, in San Francisco. It was headed by Frank Roney* and W. F. Eastman. Many branches of the league were established, especially in San Francisco where there was a membership of over 4,000 workers.

Frank Roney, who once worked with Denis Kearney* in the Workingmen's Party of California* serving as the temporary chairman of the party's first state convention and writer of the party's platform, broke with Kearney and organized the Seamen's Protective Union in 1880. He was the Protective Union's delegate to the San Francisco Representative Assembly of Trades and Labor Union in 1881, and within a month he was elected its president to serve during 1881 and 1882. As president of the Union, he undertook extensive organization and launched an anti-Chinese movement. After founding the league, he became the leading force behind the league's tactics used against Chinese. The main strategy was a boycott of Chinese-made goods. Advertisements separating Chinese-made goods from white-made goods were distributed and placed in store-front windows. As one example of the league's tactics, the business of a San Francisco shoe salesman who sold Chinese-made products was undermined when a boy was paid to stand in front of the store and pass out handbills requesting that the public not buy from the salesman. The boycott had a very real impact on the sale of Chinese-made goods and Chinese employment. One factory replaced its 600 Chinese workers with whites, and on July 31, 1882, the local newspaper noted with obvious enjoyment that many factories were discharging their Chinese employees and were hiring whites.

In addition to the boycott, the league adopted more extreme measures in order to expel Chinese by "whatever means available," but it never had to do anything in practice once Congress passed the Chinese Exclusion Act of May 6, 1882.* FURTHER READING: John Commons, *History of Labour in the United States*, Vol. 2, New York: Macmillan Co., 1918; Ira Cross, *A History of the Labor Movement in California*, Berkeley: University of California Press, 1935; Alexander Saxton, *The Indispensable Enemy*, Berkeley: University of California Press, 1971.

LEAGUE OF THE FRIENDS OF KOREA, organized by Floyd W. Tomkins on May 16, 1919, primarily to inform the American public about conditions in Korea. Among the league's other objectives was to secure religious liberty for the Korean Christians. An organization with the same name was established in England in 1920 after Frederick A. MacKenzie's book, *Korea's Fight for Freedom* (1920) was published. MacKenzie's book had great influence on public opinion in England.

LEAGUE OF KOREAN INDEPENDENCE (TONGNIP-DAN), established by Pak Yong-man* in Hawaii on March 3, 1919, only two days after his countrymen rose against Japanese oppression in Korea. The league had approximately 350 members who were united in their resolve to support the national independence movement of Korea financially and morally. The league was dissolved soon after its leader was assassinated by a Korean in 1928. (*See also* Pak Yong-man.)

LEAVE CLEARANCE, a bureaucratic procedure adopted by the War Relocation Authority* (WRA) to grant Japanese internees permission to leave relocation centers to work outside on a temporary or permanent basis. It was also used to separate potentially disloyal persons of Japanese ancestry in the relocation centers from those who showed willingness to comply with WRA policies. Under the direction of the War Department, WRA staff members were instructed to distribute DSS Form 304a and WRA Form 126 to all internees aged seventeen and over. All internees were required to execute WRA Form 126 which included two loyalty questions, Numbers 27 and 28. Question Number 27 read: "Are you willing to serve in the armed forces of the United States on combat duty, wherever ordered?" Question Number 28 read: "Will you swear unqualified allegiance to the United States of America and faithfully defend the United States from any or all attacks by foreign or domestic forces, and foreswear any form of allegiance or obedience to the Japanese Emperor or any other foreign government, power or organization?"

Question Number 28 created a great deal of conflict and controversy at the relocation centers for it had two important implications. First, the Issei* were citizens of Japan on the principle of *jus sanguinis** and were excluded from becoming American citizens because they were considered unassimilable. Had they answered "yes" to Question Number 28, they would have given up their only citizenship, which was Japanese, thereby becoming stateless persons. They could not become American citizens, even if they had given their allegiance to the United States. It is no wonder then that many of the Issei internees flatly refused to answer the question, but some of them gave a very qualified "yes." On the basis of their answer to the question, internees were judged loyal or disloyal to America, and those considered disloyal were sent to Tule Lake Segregation Center* for the purpose of segregation.

By July 31, 1944, 8,300 internees filed application for leave clearance, and 6,800 of them were granted indefinite leave or were considered eligible for leave. A total of 12,680 "disloyal" evacuees were sent to Tule Lake to be segregated, and others were either refused leave or were in the process of hearings and review.

FURTHER READING: Dillon S. Myer, *Uprooted Americans*, Tucson: University of Arizona Press, 1971; Jacobus ten Broek et al., *Prejudice, War and the Constitution*, Berkeley: University of California Press, 1970; Michi Weglyn, *Years of Infamy*, New York: William Morrow and Co., 1976.

LEE, DAVID (YI TAE-WI) (?–1928), Korean American community leader. Lee was born in Korea and came to the United States in 1905 as a political refugee. He attended the Pacific School of Religion in Berkeley, while actively engaged in Korean community affairs in San Francisco. He was one of the original members of the Korean National Association* and served as its president between 1913 and 1915, and again in 1918. He also served the first Korean community weekly newspaper, *The New Korea*, as editor. He invented a typesetting machine for the Korean writing system in 1915, which enabled all Korean publications in the United States to use *Han'gul*, to the exclusion of Chinese characters.

LEE, ROSE HUM (1904–1964) teacher and writer. Lee was born in Butte, Montana, on August 20, 1904, graduated from Carnegie Institute of Technology with a B.S. degree in 1942, and the following year received an M.A. degree from the University of Chicago. In 1945 Lee received her Ph.D. from the University of Chicago. She taught at a number of American institutions of higher learning, starting first with Roosevelt University in 1945 and then Phoenix College. Her teaching career and busy schedule notwithstanding, she actively involved herself in various service organizations which provided relief and social service to people in China during the Sino-Japanese War and World War II.

Lee wrote a number of books, including a pioneer work on Chinese in America entitled *The Chinese in the United States of America*, published in 1960 by Hong Kong University. In one of her many studies on Chinese communities in America, she predicted the decline and possible elimination of Chinatowns* in America. She died on March 25, 1964.

FURTHER READING: Rose Hum Lee, "The Growth and Decline of Chinese Communities in the Rocky Mountain Region," Ph.D. diss., University of Chicago, 1947.

LEE, SAMMY (1920–), Olympic gold medal winner for swimming. Lee was born in Fresno, California, on August 1, 1920, the son of Lee Soonkee and Eunkee, immigrants from Korea. He graduated from Occidental College in 1943 and the University of Southern California in 1947. He came to world attention in 1948 when he was awarded the high diving gold medal in the Olympic Games. Four years later, he won the medal again, thus becoming the first male diver in history to win it in two consecutive Olympics. In 1958 he became the first non-white to receive the James E. Sullivan Award for his outstanding achievements in sports.

LEE, TSUNG-DAO (1926–), physicist and Nobel laureate. Born on November 24, 1926 in Shanghai, China, Lee was educated primarily in his native country. He attended the National Chekiang University and the Southwest Associated University in K'un-ming before he came to the University of Chicago in 1946 on a fellowship to study physics. He received his Ph.D. in 1950. He spent a year at the University of California at Berkeley and then moved to the Institute for Advanced Study at Princeton where he joined Yang Chen-ning* to continue some speculations begun in 1945. Their joint project involved the principle of conservation of parity, which was later successfully proven by experiments undertaken by Wu Chien-shiung* and others. For this work Lee won the Albert Einstein Commemorative Award in Science and the Nobel Prize in Physics in 1957. He then became the second youngest Nobel laureate in history. Lee left Princeton for Columbia University in 1953, and in 1956 he became the youngest full professor on its faculty. (*See also* Wu, Chien-shiung, Yang Chen-ning.)

LEE KUM HOY, LEE KUM CHERK, AND LEE MOON WAH v. JOHN L. MURFF, a case argued before the U.S. Supreme Court on November 21, 1957, and decided by the Court on December 9, 1957. The case involved whether or not blood testing as a means of adjudicating derivative citizenship was a valid method, particularly when used exclusively for a group of people chosen on the basis of their race.

When some Chinese began presenting to the American consulate in Hong Kong questionable documents showing their derivative citizenship, the Immigration Service began blood testing to see if a person claiming to be the son or daughter of an American citizen was indeed the right person. A writ of habeas corpus was followed by a judicial hearing to decide if an exclusion order on the basis of blood group tests was valid. The U.S. District Court for the Southern District of New York sustained the writ and ordered Lee Kum Hoy and others admitted to the United States. The Immigration Service appealed, the Court of Appeals reversed the District Court order, and Lee and others brought certiorari. The Supreme Court ruled that blood group tests had been inaccurate and that their reports had been partly erroneous and conflicting. The case was then remanded with directions for further hearings before the Special Inquiry Officer.

FURTHER READING: S. W. Kung, *Chinese in American Life: Some Aspects of Their History, Status, Problems, and Contributions*, Seattle: University of Washington Press, 1962; *Supreme Court Reporter*, 355 U.S. 169.

LEGIONARIOS DEL TRABAJO, known as one of the "Big Three" Filipino fraternal organizations (along with Caballeros de Dimas-Alang* and Gran Oriente Filipino*), established on February 2, 1924, in San Francisco. At its peak the Legionnaires of Labor had 3,000 members with eighty-six different lodges in all the states, including Hawaii and Alaska. (*See also* Caballeros de Dimas-Alang; Gran Oriente Filipino.)
FURTHER READING: Fred Cordova, *Filipinos: Forgotten Asian Americans*, Dubuque, Iowa; Kendall and Hunt Publishing Co., 1983; Hyung-chan Kim and Cynthia C. Mejia, *The Filipinos in America, 1898–1974*, Dobbs Ferry, N.Y.: Oceana Publications, 1976.

LEM MOON SING v. UNITED STATES, a case heard in 1895 involving a Chinese merchant's attempt to reenter the United States after a trip to China. In the case of the United States v. Ju Toy,* the U.S. Supreme Court ruled that a decision by the Secretary of Commerce and Labor refusing to admit a Chinese who claimed to be an American citizen was final and was not subject to a judicial hearing, even if the person had exhausted all administrative remedies required. The Supreme Court came under criticism for this decision and thereafter modified its stance on the admissibility of Chinese who claimed to be American citizens. The Court later ruled that the executive hearings of Chinese who claimed to be American citizens must be fair and that the administrative hearing could not be conclusive if an alleged American citizen had been denied an opportunity to establish his citizenship at such a hearing.

The Lem Moon Sing v. United States case involved a Chinese merchant, Lem Moon Sing, who left the United States on January 20, 1894, for his native country for a temporary visit. He had lived in the United States for more than two years and had every intention of returning to his life in the State of California. While he was in China, Congress passed the Exclusion of Chinese Merchant Act which stated that "in every case where an alien is excluded from admission into the United States under any law or treaty now existing or hereafter made, the decision of the appropriate immigration or customs officers, if adverse to the admission of such alien, shall be final, unless reversed on appeal to the secretary of the treasury."

Lem Moon Sing returned to San Francisco on November 3, 1894, to reenter the state of his former residency but was denied permission to land. He was detained on board the steamship which brought him. Even though he had the credible testimony of two white persons who testified that he had previously resided in the United States and was not employed as a laborer, he was still refused his right to land. Lem Moon Sing then petitioned the District Court for the Northern District of California for a writ of habeas corpus, on the grounds that because he was a former resident of California, the Exclusion of Chinese

Merchant Act of August 9, 1894, was not applicable. The District Court ruled against him because it considered that customs officers had acted within their jurisdiction. His habeas corpus was denied. Lem Moon Sing appealed to the Supreme Court of the United States, which handed down its decision on May 27, 1895. The Court, upholding the lower court's decision, based its opinion on the precedent set in the case of Nishimura Ekiu v. United States.* According to the Court, an alien was entitled to the same rights as any person in the United States, as long as he or she remained in the country; but if the alien left of his or her own free will, upon returning he or she should be treated as any other alien seeking permission to enter the country. By this decision the U.S. Supreme Court strengthened the authority of the executive branch of the government in handling aliens seeking to enter the United States. (See also United States v. Ju Toy.)

FURTHER READING: Thomas A. Bailey, *A Diplomatic History of American People*, Englewood Cliffs, N.J.: Prentice-Hall, 1980; Milton R. Konvitz, *The Alien and the Asiatic in American Law*, Ithaca, N.Y.: Cornell University Press, 1946; *Supreme Court Reporter* 15, 158 U.S. 538.

LEUPP ISOLATION CENTER, an isolation camp in Arizona for evacuees during World War II. After the Manzanar incident* of December 6, 1942, leaders who were suspected of inciting anti-War Relocation Authority* sentiment among the evacuees at Manzanar Relocation Center were put under arrest. Included among them were Joe Kurihara, a veteran of World War I, and Harry Ueno, who had organized the Kitchen Workers Union* at Manzanar. Fifteen leaders were then sent to a heavily guarded isolation camp near Moab, Utah, on January 11, 1943, later to be transferred again to another isolation camp near Leupp, Arizona, on April 27, 1943. The center was closed down on December 2, 1943, as an economic measure, and a total of fifty-two inmates were then transferred to the Tule Lake Segregation Center.* Many of these people later renounced their American citizenship and were deported to Japan after the end of World War II. (*See also* Manzanar Incident.)

FURTHER READING: Audrie Girdner and Anne Loftis, *The Great Betrayal*, New York: Macmillan Co., 1969; Edward H. Spicer et al., *Impounded People: Japanese-Americans in the Relocation Centers*, Tucson: University of Arizona Press, 1969; Michi Weglyn, *Years of Infamy: The Untold Story of America's Concentration Camps*, New York: William Morrow and Co., 1976.

LI K. C. See Wah Chang Trading Company.

LI SUNG v. UNITED STATES, a case heard in the U.S. Supreme Court in 1900 involving the deportation of a Chinese alien. The Supreme Court allowed a writ of certiorari on February 1, 1899 in order to review a decision of the U.S. Circuit Court of Appeals for the Second Circuit dismissing a writ of habeas corpus and ordering deportation of a Chinese person. In June 1893 Li Sung, a resident of Newark, New Jersey, returned to China for a visit and then came back to the United States by way of Canada. He carried a certificate issued by the Chinese government through its consulate in New York, which was visaed at the U.S. consulate in Hong Kong. Li Sung presented the certificate to the U.S. collector of customs in Malone, New York, who canceled it on August 28, 1896, and permitted him to enter the United States. In January of the following year a U.S. inspector for the port of New York ordered Li Sung deported, claiming that he had entered the United States illegally as a Chinese laborer. Li Sung and his counsel, however, claimed that the action of the U.S. customs collector in allowing him to enter the United States was *res judicata* and that he was a merchant, not a laborer.

The Court heard the argument on April 18 and 19, 1900, and decided on the case on March 18, 1901. In delivering the opinion of the Court, Justice George Shiras stated that Congress could require aliens to prove their right to be in the United States. In addition, in the case of a Chinese laborer lacking the certificate of residence, he would have the burden of proving that the assumption made by the government that he was in the United States illegally was false. Furthermore, Justice Shiras strongly pointed out that an alien, in deportation proceedings, could not receive constitutional guarantee against unreasonable search and seizure, and cruel and unusual punishment. During the deportation proceedings the alien did not have the constitutional protection of trial by jury, according to Justice Shiras. This ruling strengthened the power of the executive branch in dealing with aliens. The Court had already ruled in its favor in the case of Fong Yue Ting v. United States,* affirming the deportation order on the grounds that Fong Yue Ting was not able to produce credible white witnesses supporting his status in the United States.

FURTHER READING: Milton R. Konvitz, *The Alien and the Asiatic in American Law*, Ithaca, N.Y.: Cornell University Press, 1946; *Supreme Court Reporter* 21, 180 U.S. 486, 1901.

LIANG CH'I-CH'AO (1873–1929), Chinese reform movement leader. Liang was a native of Xinhui (Sunwui), Kwangtung Province, from which many Chinese immigrants in America originated. He was born on February 23, 1873, the eldest son in a family of long farming tradition. At the early age of eleven, he showed his precocity when he passed the prefectural examinations to become a "sheng-yuan." Five years later, in 1889, he passed the provincial examinations in Canton and earned the title of "chu-jen." Later he traveled to Peking and took the metropolitan examinations, but he did not pass. Upon returning to Canton, he visited K'ang Yu-wei* at the Hsueh-hai-t'ang and was impressed with K'ang's knowledge. He immediately enrolled in K'ang's school where he studied Buddhism, the Philosophy of Institutional Reform, and Western Learning. In 1893 he began to teach at the school where he had studied.

Although he was in full sympathy with the revolutionaries who advocated the overthrow of the Ch'ing Dynasty in China, Liang decided to support the Pao-huang Hui (Society to Protect the Emperor),* and in the summer of 1899, he traveled to raise funds for this society established by K'ang Yu-wei. Thus, Liang came to the United States and gave lectures to people in Chinese communities concerning his fund-raising campaign. Before his return to Japan in November 1903, he visited President Theodore Roosevelt and Secretary of State John Hay in Washington.

Liang continued to work toward the goal of reforming Chinese society; sometimes he carried out his mission while serving in government, and at other times, he undertook his mission by voicing his reform ideas in writing. Liang was one of the most influential persons in the Chinese reform movement during the first two decades of this century.

FURTHER READING: Hao Chang, *Liang Ch'i-ch'ao and Intellectual Transition in China, 1890–1907*, Cambridge, Mass.: Harvard University Press, 1971; Philip C. Huang, *Liang Ch'i-ch'ao and Modern Chinese Liberalism*, Seattle: University of Washington Press, 1972; Jung-pang Lo, *K'ang Yu-wei: a Biography and a Symposium*, Tucson: University of Arizona Press, 1967; Shih-sahn Henry Tsai, *China and the Overseas Chinese in the United States, 1868–1911*, Fayetteville: University of Arkansas Press, 1983.

LIBERAL PATRIOTIC ASSOCIATION, organized in June 1889 in Honolulu, Hawaii, by Robert W. Wilcox, who was born on Maui in 1855 of a Hawaiian mother and an American father. Wilcox had been recruiting people who would conspire to overthrow the government led by King Kalakaua.* These people called themselves the Liberal Patriotic Association and held secret meetings to plan their conspiracy. Among his sympathizers were some local Chinese who had given Wilcox money to be used in executing his plan.

Wilcox's attempt to force Kalakaua to sign a new constitution failed. Wilcox was charged with treason but was later found not guilty. One of his Chinese sympathizers, Ho Fon, a journalist, was convicted of conspiracy and was fined $250.00.

FURTHER READING: Helena G. Allen, *The Betrayal of Liliuokalani: Last Queen of Hawaii, 1838–1917*, Glendale, Calif.: Arthur H. Clark Co., 1982; Gavan Daws, *Shoals of Time*, Honolulu: University Press of Hawaii, 1968; Ralph S. Kuykendall, *The Hawaiian Kingdom, Vol. III, 1874–1893*, Honolulu: University of Hawaii Press, 1967.

LIBERTY BANK, established in Hawaii by Chinese who felt that the banks run by whites were discriminatory. This bank, along with the Chinese American Bank,* has served the Chinese community in Hawaii very well.

LIGOT, CAYETANO, resident Philippine labor commissioner, appointed by Leonard Wood, governor-general of the Philippines (1921–1927), and sent to Hawaii to report on general conditions among Filipino plantation workers. The investigation was made by Hermenegildo Crus, director of the Philippine Bureau of Labor, who reported to Wood. The report was endorsed by Ligot, who had toured the plantations and had urged Filipinos to work enthusiastically. The report blamed labor unrest on Filipinos and was very sympathetic with the Hawaiian Sugar Planters' Association* (HSPA). Because of Ligot's sympathy toward the HSPA, Filipino workers felt that Ligot had fallen under that agency's control.

LIHOLIHO. *See* Kamehameha Dynasty.

LIHOLIHO, ALEXANDER. *See* Kamehameha Dynasty.

LILIUOKALANI (1838–1917), queen of Hawaii. Liliuokalani was born on September 2, 1838, ascended as queen to the Hawaiian throne on January 29, 1891, and was deposed on January 17, 1893, when her regime was overthrown by a group of revolutionaries who wanted to establish a republic along American lines. After she was deposed, Sanford Ballard Dole* was sworn in as president of the Republic of Hawaii on July 4, 1894. (See Committee of Safety; Dole, Sanford Ballard.)

LIN SING v. WASHBURN, a case involving the California police tax, a form of capitation tax, which was used to discriminate against Chinese in California. In 1862 the California State Legislature passed a police tax which required all Mongolians over eighteen years of age who were not engaged in the production of rice, sugar, tea, or coffee or who had not paid the California Foreign Miners' Tax* already, to pay $2.50 per month. This law was challenged in 1863 in the case of Lin Sing v. Washburn on the grounds that such a law was in violation of the constitution of the State of California. The California State Supreme Court ruled that the law was unconstitutional.
FURTHER READING: 20 California 535 (July 1862, pp. 534–586).

LIN YUTANG (1895–1976), professor of philology, writer. Lin was born on October 10, 1895, at Chang-chow, in the Fukien Province of China. He attended missionary schools and St. John's College in Shanghai before he came to Harvard University, from which he received his M.A. in 1921 in absentia. Upon graduation he traveled to such places as France and Germany, where he studied at Jena in the spring of 1921. Lin did much research in Indo-Germanic philology at Leipzig, where he eventually received a doctorate.

In 1923 Lin returned to China and became a professor of English philology at Peking National University. He also lectured on philology at Peking National Normal University, and served as dean and head of the English Department at Peking National Women's University. Lin entered politics briefly, serving as secretary of Foreign Affairs in the Wuhan government under Eugene Chen in 1927.

Lin came to America in 1930 to live for the next three decades. During this period he wrote many books for the American audience on Chinese culture and people, including *My Country and My People* (1935); *The Importance of Living* (1937); *Moment in Peking* (1939); *The Vigil of a Nation* (1944); and *Chinatown Family: On the Wisdom of America* (1950).

Lin's *Chinatown Family* reflects his views of what America was to him—a nation where people have opportunities to become whatever they want to become without government interference.

Lin died on March 26, 1976, in Hong Kong after a fruitful life that spanned more than eighty years.

LIPPMANN, WALTER (1889–1974), journalist. Lippmann was born on September 23, 1889, in New York, into a wealthy Jewish family. In 1910 he graduated from Harvard and took up his journalism career. During World War I, he served as Assistant Secretary of War and aided in the formulation of Woodrow Wilson's Fourteen Points. Between World War I and World War II, he wrote for many prestigious newspapers. He became a popular political critic and was known for his analyses of current issues in light of America's historical roots.

As a respected journalist, many Americans listened to what they considered to be Lippmann's wisdom concerning the Japanese Americans on the West Coast. After the Japanese attack on Pearl Harbor, public opinion began to weigh heavily on the Japanese, who were held under suspicion as a potential threat to America's security. Among the many influential people who advocated the removal and internment of persons of Japanese ancestry was Lippmann, who wrote ''The Fifth Column on the Coast,'' an essay circulated widely among the public as well as the Justice Department and the White House. On February 19, 1942, just seven days after Lippmann's article was printed, President Franklin D. Roosevelt signed Executive Order 9066.*

Lippmann enjoyed fame and prestige throughout his life, despite the questionable role he played in the fate of fellow Americans in the 1940s. Many have forgotten his abuse of the power of the pen against innocent citizens in American society. FURTHER READING: Masie Conrat and Richard Conrat, *Executive Order 9066*, Los Angeles: California Historical Society, 1972; Roger Daniels, *Concentration Camp U.S.A.*, San Francisco: Holt, Rinehart and Winston, 1972; Ronald Steel, *Walter Lippmann and the American Century*, Boston: Little, Brown, 1980; Jacobus ten Broek et al., *Prejudice, War and the Constitution*, Berkeley: University of California Press, 1954.

LITERACY BILL. *See* Immigration Act of February 5, 1917.

LODGE, HENRY CABOT (1850–1924), U.S. senator. Lodge was born on May 12, 1850, and graduated from Harvard University in 1871. He studied law at Harvard Law School, from which he graduated in 1874, and the following year he was admitted to the Boston bar. Lodge received his Ph.D. in 1876 and wrote a number of books, including *Life and Letters of George Cabot* (1878) and *Historical and Political Essays* (1892).

In 1886 Lodge was elected to Congress where he served until 1893. In that year he was elected to the Senate, where he served until his death on November 9, 1924.

Senator Lodge was responsible for the passage of the Immigration Act of 1924,* which excluded Japanese from immigrating to the United States. He capitalized on Japanese Ambassador Hanihara Masanao's* comment on the pending immigration bill, which, according to Hanihara, would bring "grave consequences" between the two nations, and persuaded his colleagues to vote for Japanese exclusion. (See Hanihara Masanao.)

FURTHER READING: Henry Cabot Lodge, *Speeches by Henry Cabot Lodge*, Boston: Houghton Mifflin Co., 1892; *Retention of the Philippine Islands, Speech of Honorable Henry Cabot Lodge of Massachusetts*, Washington, D.C.: U.S. Government Printing Office, 1900; John Arthur Garraty, *Henry Cabot Lodge: A Biography*, New York: Alfred A. Knopf, 1953; William Johnson Miller, *Henry Cabot Lodge: A Biography*, New York: Heineman, 1967; William C. Widenor, *Henry Cabot Lodge and the Search for an American Foreign Policy*, Berkeley: University of California Press, 1980.

LONDON, JACK (1875–1916), writer. London was born on January 12, 1875. William Chaney, his natural father, deserted his mother when she refused to abort their child. A few months after Jack's birth, his mother married John London. The younger London finished his public education at the age of thirteen in Oakland, California, and then went to work in a factory. He spent the next four years as a lobster thief, a hobo traveling across America, and a fish patroller in San Francisco. He came in contact with Chinese who caught shrimp illegally, while working as a fish patroller. At sixteen years of age, he signed on board a sealing ship headed for Alaska, which eventually took him to Japan, where he was exposed to an Asian culture.

Upon returning from his sea-faring adventure, London returned to school in Oakland, but he dropped out after less than a year. During the next three years his attempts at writing proved unsuccessful. He returned to school, this time to get an education at the University of California at Berkeley, but he dropped out again. During the gold strike of 1897 in the Alaskan Yukon, he went north in search of his fortune; not unlike many who looked for gold, he found nothing. His Yukon experience, however, provided him with raw material for a successful novel, *A Daughter of the Snows* (1902). London's reputation, based on his success as a writer, allowed him to visit the Far East to report on the Russo-Japanese War. Through his reporting London's intense dislike for the non-white race became apparent. He was a self-proclaimed Socialist. His racism and belief in white supremacy led him to recommend that the "lesser races" be eliminated by chloroform or electrocution. His racist attitude led one of his colleagues, Frederick Palmer, who served as a war correspondent with London in the Far East, to comment on London: "Jack London was the most inherently individualistic and un-Socialist of all Socialists I ever met and (was) really a philosophical anarchist."(O'Connor, p. 217.)

Upon his return to the United States, London wrote *The Yellow Peril* (1904) in which he concluded that there was an inherent weakness in the "yellow man." In another book, *The Star Rover* (1915), he describes Koreans as people who "delight in seeing stranded English sailors flogged in the streets." To London, these beatings represented nothing but the sadistic Korean mind. In *The Whale Tooth* (1910), London gives the impression that the Asians are cannibals, gluttons, and "frizzle-headed man-eaters." In much of London's writing, he leaves a strong misrepresentation of Asians in the minds of many unsuspecting Americans. He died on November 21, 1916, under suspicious circumstances.

FURTHER READING: Richard W. Etulain, *Jack London on the Road*, Logan: Utah State University Press, 1979; Joan D. Hedrick, *Solitary Comrade*, Chapel Hill: University of North Carolina Press, 1982; Earle Labor, *Jack London*, New York: Twayne Publishers, 1974; Jack London, *The Star Rover*, New York: Macmillan Co., 1963; Richard O'Connor, *Jack London, a Biography*, Boston; Little, Brown, 1964; Andrew Sinclair, *Jack: A Biography of Jack London*, New York: Harper and Row, 1977; Irving Stone, *Jack London: Sailor on Horseback*, Boston: Houghton Mifflin Co., 1938.

LOOMIS, AUGUSTUS WARD (1818–1891), missionary. Loomis was born in Andover, Connecticut. He graduated from Hamilton College, New York in 1841 and completed his study at Princeton Theological Seminary in 1844. Upon graduation he entered the mission field and went to China, where he served from 1844 until 1850. After returning to America, he served among the Creek Indians between 1852 and 1853. In 1859 he became a missionary to the Chinese in San Francisco, replacing William Speer* who had become ill in 1857.

As a result of his mission work among the Chinese in California, Loomis gained enough knowledge of the people to write a book, *English and Chinese Lessons*, which was published by the American Tract Society in 1872. (*See also* Speer, William.)

FURTHER READING: Gunther Barth, *Bitter Strength*, Cambridge, Mass.: Harvard University Press, 1964.

LOS ANGELES COUNTY ANTI-ASIATIC SOCIETY, an organization established in 1919 with the Japanese as special targets. Although the Alien Land Act of California, 1913* was passed in order to deprive Japanese of their livelihood, it proved less than effective in the eyes of the exclusionists. This issue lay dormant for seven years until 1920, when James D. Phelan* was up for reelection as Senator. In his various campaign speeches he delivered around the state, Phelan pointed to the necessity of closing loopholes in the 1913 law by approving the 1920 alien land initiative. His slogan, "Keep California White," rang loudly.

Phelan was supported by a number of organizations in California, especially the Native Sons of the Golden West. In October 1919 a joint Anti-Asiatic Committee convened in Los Angeles, and on November 15, 1919, the name of the committee was changed to the Los Angeles County Anti-Asiatic Society, which included the American Legion and organized labor. Serving as its chairman was Sheriff William I. Traeger.

The society proclaimed as its purpose the protection of racial purity, support for the alien land initiative, protection against the Japanese menace, abrogation of the Gentlemen's Agreement,* and constitutional amendment to repeal *jus soli** for children born of alien parents ineligible for U.S. citizenship, namely, Japanese immigrants.

FURTHER READING: John Modell, *The Economics and Politics of Racial Accommodation: The Japanese of Los Angeles, 1900–1942*, Urbana: University of Illinois Press, 1977.

LOS ANGELES JAPANESE ASSOCIATION (RAFU NIHONJIN KAI), established in 1906 as a defense organization to protect the general interests of the Japanese in the United States. The association merged with the Japanese Chamber of Commerce of Los Angeles in 1929, and the united organization adopted the English name Chamber of Commerce, while it decided to retain its Japanese name Rafu Nihonjin Kai, or Los Angeles Japanese Association.

The nature of the association became apparent when its secretary admonished the people in the community not to make too many demands on whites, who did not understand their feelings. He felt that white Americans would be more inclined to give to the Japanese if they came begging rather than demanding. The best strategy to use against whites, he said, was to make no move and to be quiet so that the Japanese would be forgotten.

FURTHER READING: John Modell, *The Economics and Politics of Racial Accommodation: The Japanese of Los Angeles, 1900–1942*, Urbana: University of Illinois Press, 1977.

LOS ANGELES RIOT OF 1871, mob action against Chinese residents in which nineteen Chinese were killed. Business recessions in 1854 and 1862 in California caused a great deal of bitterness between the working classes. Much of the blame for bad times was placed on the Chinese. The natives of California felt that they should be getting the jobs the Chinese had, only with a higher salary and improved working conditions. Resentment against the Chinese ran high, especially in the mining camps and railroad construction sites. Chinese were often killed, usually at the hands of tax collectors, who were seldom tried and almost never punished for their crimes. Conflicts became more widespread as a result of the increased demands of laborers and political campaigns to stop Chinese immigration. Accompanying the political campaigns were physical attacks on Chinese, whose homes and businesses were destroyed. The state courts did little to rectify this repression and lawlessness. One of the largest riots before the passage of the Chinese Exclusion Act of 1882* occurred on October 23, 1871, in Los Angeles.

The Los Angeles riot started with an argument between two *tongs*. Nin Yung Tong members accused the Hong Chow Tong Fraternal Organization of kidnapping a woman who belonged to their association. Officer Bilderrain tried to stop a shooting that broke out between the two *tongs* in Calle de los Negros. Bilderrain, Robert Thompson, who came to help subdue the mob, and two bystanders were wounded by bullet shots. Chinese and townsmen gathered at the Plaza of the

Calle de los Negros while at the same time another mob of "roughnecks" formed along Los Angeles Street.

Sheriff James Burns arrived to break up the rioters; he told the mob that the Chinese in the building would be arrested in the morning and that they might as well break up and go home. When it became obvious that the crowd was not going to leave but only grow more destructive with the passage of time, Burns went for help. When he returned, most of the besieged Chinese had fled. One unfortunate victim failed to escape and was hung by the lawless crowd.

All the while, the Chinese were being forced out of their buildings by another group of rioters. Holes were punched and hacked in the ceilings, so that the mobs could shoot at the helpless victims hiding inside. Those who escaped from the buildings were shot down in the streets. Other unfortunate Chinese were hung from bar awnings and prairie wagons. When the four hours of madness were over, nineteen Chinese were counted dead.

The riot attracted worldwide reaction. Christians in the East wanted to rush in their missionaries to help. In China people and their government protested, and in the Congress of the United States a bill was introduced to pay a large indemnity. Ten riot instigators were brought before Judge Ygnacio Sepulveda, who presided over the grand jury. During the trial the list of names of the people called to testify was lost, and there were people who came forward to testify in defense of the accused. After the trial, nine men were found guilty, but they were set free within one year. Congress failed to pass the bill to indemnify the Chinese for the loss of lives and property.

FURTHER READING: Lynn Bowman, *Los Angeles: Epic of a City*, Berkeley, Calif.: Howell North Books, 1974; S. W. Kung, *Chinese in American Life*, Seattle: University of Washington Press, 1962; Workers of the Writers' Program of the Work Projects Administration in Southern California, comp., *Los Angeles: A Guide to the City and Its Environs*, New York: Hastings House, 1941.

LOT. *See* Kamehameha Dynasty.

LOW, FREDERICK (1828–1894), governor of California, diplomat. Low was born near Frankfort, Maine, on June 30, 1828, and attended common schools there. Apprenticed to the East Indian firm of Russell, Sturgis and Company, Boston, at the age of fifteen, he learned much about California and the Far East. Stricken with the gold fever in 1849, he left for California in February of that year and panned some gold, earning over $1,500 during that summer. The following year he established a partnership in Marysville with his brother and successfully ran it for some time. In 1861 he was nominated to represent California in Congress, but he was not sworn into office until June 3, 1862 when Congress passed a special act to accept him. When his term expired, he chose not to run again, and in 1863 President Abraham Lincoln appointed him collector of the port of San Francisco. Low did not serve long in that federal post, for he was elected governor of California in 1863.

While in office as governor Low voiced his strong opposition to the mistreatment of Native Indians and Chinese. He believed, for example, that it was a disgrace to deny Chinese the right to testify against a white person in the courts of California.

In 1869, after a brief retirement, Low was appointed by President Ulysses S. Grant to serve as America's Minister to China, where he arrived prior to the outbreak of the Tientsin massacre. Commenting on the event that involved the killing of nineteen foreigners and the French consul, Low felt that the illegal actions taken by the French Catholic missionaries were mainly responsible for the outbreak. While serving in China as American Minister, he encouraged the exchange of students between the United States and China.

Although Low took a courageous stand against racial bigotry, he was also a victim of his times in certain of his notions. He believed, for instance, that the Chinese were incapable of assimilation with the American people and could not either intelligently or honestly vote or participate in the American body politic. He thought that they would only contribute to further corruption.

FURTHER READING: Frederick F. Low, *Some Reflections of an Early California Governor*, Sacramento: California Book Collection Club, 1959; H. Brett Melendy, *The Governors of California*, Georgetown, Calif.: Talisman Press, 1965.

LUCE-CELLER BILL (INDIAN IMMIGRATION BILL), a bill passed in 1946 placing a quota for Asian Indian immigration. The immigration of Asian Indians began in the late 1880s. From 1898 to 1903 approximately thirty Asian Indians per year moved to the United States and from 1904 to 1906 this number increased to 250 per year. By 1908 approximately 1,700 Asian Indians had come to the United States. This influx of Asian Indians aroused a strong anti-Hindu sentiment among white Americans, particularly among those on the West Coast. These people, alarmed by their own imagined danger of a Hindu invasion of America, agitated for the exclusion of Asian Indians from the privilege of coming to America as immigrants. In response to the exclusionists' demand, Congress passed the Immigration Act of February 5, 1917* with its Asiatic Barred Zone provision that excluded Asian Indians as a class of people from coming to the United States. The U.S. Supreme Court strengthened the power of the government to exclude Asian Indians when it interpreted the wording "white person" in the 1917 Immigration Act to mean only persons of European descent and not Hindus in connection with the decision on the case of United States v. Bhagat Singh Thind* in 1923.

The Immigration Act of 1924* prohibited the immigration of any person who was not eligible for citizenship in the United States. This act also revoked the citizenship of any woman who married an alien not eligible for citizenship as well as the citizenship of those immigrants who had been granted it prior to the enactment of this law.

In Tarak Nath Das,* an Indian, and his American wife initiated legal proceedings to have Das's citizenship reinstated. He was associated with Sailendra Nath

Ghose through the organization called the Nationalist Friends of Free India. Ghose won the support of Emanuel Celler,* a member of the House of Representatives from New York. In 1927 and 1928 Representatives Oren Sturman Copeland and Emanuel Celler introduced bills to recognize Asian Indians as Caucasians. These proposals were met with stiff resistance and were tabled in committee. Another bill similar to the bills of 1927 and 1928 was proposed by Representative John Lesinski, but it was tabled again in committee. During World War II India came to the attention of many Americans; as India became sympathetic to the American cause against Japan, Americans became concerned with India's struggle for self-rule.

In 1943 the Chinese Exclusion Act was repealed. The passage of this act, along with the placement of a quota for Chinese immigration and the eligibility for citizenship, represented steps toward establishing better relations with the Chinese, America's ally during World War II. In 1944, with the precedent set by the repeal of the Chinese Exclusion Act, Representatives Clare Boothe Luce and Emanuel Celler proposed the same treatment for the Asian Indians. This bill was endorsed and supported by many organizations, the media, and prominent citizens. Nevertheless, the bill was kept in committee too long and was allowed to die on the floor of the House. The bill was brought back again in 1945 by Luce, Celler, Everett Dirksen, Joseph H. Ball, and Arthur Capper. This time the Luce-Celler Bill was supported by the President and the State Department. However, a senator from Georgia rallied the opposition, and the bill again died in committee. The Luce-Celler Bill was revived for the last time in 1945 by President Harry Truman, who urged Celler to resubmit it, and the bill was introduced on June 20, 1945. It made it through the House and the Senate and was signed on July 2, 1946.

FURTHER READING: Ray E. Chase and S. G. Pandit, *An Examination of the Opinion of the Supreme Court of the United States*, Los Angeles, California, 1926; S. Chandrasekhar, *From India to America*, La Jolla, Calif.: A Population Review Book, 1982; E. P. Hutchinson, *Legislative History of American Immigration Policy, 1798–1965*, Philadelphia: University of Pennsylvania Press, 1981; Harold Isaacs, *Scratches on Our Minds, American Views of China and India*, New York: M. N. Sharpe, 1980.

LUNA, a term used on Hawaii's sugar plantations meaning an overseer responsible for supervising field workers. Of the total number of *lunas* and clerks in 1882, it was estimated that 88 percent were white. No *luna* was Chinese.

LUNG KEE SUN BO, originally called the *Tan Shan Sun Bo*, or *Hawaiian Chinese News*, and established by a group of young Chinese immigrants who thought of it as a commercial and literary venture. It began to publish a handwritten four-page newspaper in 1881. Two years later the paper acquired Ho Fon, who had once been involved in a conspiracy with Robert W. Wilcox to force King Kalakaua* to sign a new constitution. Along with a new manager, it acquired a new name, *Lung Kee Sun Bo*, or *The New Prosperous Business*

News, to which Dr. Sun Yat-sen* gave strong support. The publishers of the newspaper supported Dr. Sun's program of bringing revolutionary changes to China. Radical political views expressed in the news were opposed by people who belonged to the Pao-huang Hui,* which published the *Sun Chung Kwock Bo*, or *New China News*, in order to counter the propagation of Dr. Sun's revolutionary views.

As a result of declining subscriptions, *Lung Kee Sun Bo* was discontinued during the 1930s.

FURTHER READING: Clarence E. Glick, *Sojourners and Settlers*, Honolulu: University Press of Hawaii, 1980.

Mc

McCARRAN-WALTER IMMIGRATION AND NATURALIZATION ACT OF 1952. See Immigration and Nationality Act of 1952.

McCLATCHY, VALENTINE STUART (1857–1938), journalist. McClatchy was born in Sacramento, California, the son of James and Charlotte McClatchy. He attended public schools in his hometown before he went to Santa Clara College, from which he received his B.S. degree.

McClatchy took up journalism as his main career and wrote on immigration and trans-Pacific communication. He served as publisher of the very influential *Sacramento Bee* for forty years and helped establish the *Fresno Bee*. He also served as executive secretary of the California Joint Immigration Committee.

As an influential journalist in his home state, McClatchy aligned with Hiram W. Johnson* to champion the cause of California exclusionists who wanted to exclude Japanese immigration to the United States. In many of his writings about the Japanese, he pointed out that Japanese immigration posed a major threat to the United States, particularly to white Americans. He stated that the Japanese were not only unassimilable, but their birthrate was also high, implying that high birthrate among Japanese was a menace. The Japanese also presented unfair competition to American workers.

In March 1924, when Congress was considering the National Origins Act of 1924,* McClatchy came to Washington as a member of a three-man exclusionist delegation to testify before the Senate. Representing California exclusionists, McClatchy claimed that the Japanese were less assimilable and more dangerous than any other people living in the United States who were ineligible for citizenship. He advocated exclusion of the Japanese from the United States on the grounds that they would drive "the white race to the wall" given sufficient time.
FURTHER READING: Roger Daniels, *The Politics of Prejudice*, Berkeley: University of California Press, 1962; Carl Kelsey, ed., *Present-Day Immigration with Special Ref-*

erence to the Japanese, Philadelphia: American Academy of Political and Social Science, 1921; Valentine Stuart McClatchy, ed., *Four Anti-Japanese Pamphlets*, New York: Arno Press, 1978 (reprints).

McCREARY AMENDMENT TO THE GEARY ACT OF 1892, an amendment extending the deadline for Chinese residents to obtain certificates of residence. The Geary Act of 1892* prohibited Chinese persons from coming into the United States. It extended all existing laws restricting Chinese immigration for ten more years and required that all Chinese laborers carry a certificate of residence. The Chinese who were entitled to remain in the United States were required to apply to their district collector of Internal Revenue within one year after the passage of the act. If any Chinese laborer was found without a certificate of residence, he would be arrested and deported. In 1893 a large deportation seemed imminent, for few Chinese in America had registered. Congress hastily passed the McCreary Amendment on November 3, 1893, which extended the registration deadline another six months. If after the six-month period a Chinese laborer was found within U.S. boundaries without a legal certificate of residence, he was to be judged illicit within the United States and arrested and deported unless he could prove to the satisfaction of the judge that some unavoidable cause had prohibited him from attaining a certificate of residence.

The McCreary Amendment also imposed a more rigid definition of a merchant and a laborer. According to the bill, the word "laborer" inferred both skilled and unskilled manual laborers, including Chinese employed in mining, huckstering, fishing, and laundry work. This piece of legislation seemed designed to degrade the Chinese as much as possible. It stipulated that a merchant, as a person employed in the buying and selling of merchandise at a fixed place of business, must not during the time he was a merchant perform any manual labor except what was required to run his business. Thus, by implying that Chinese merchants should not engage in any kind of manual labor, the act made clear that labor was intended only for those of inferior standing.

FURTHER READING: Mary R. Coolidge, *Chinese Immigration*, New York: Henry Holt and Co., 1909.

McDOUGAL, JOHN (1818–1866), governor of California. McDougal was born into a poor family in Rose County, Ohio, and moved to a place near Indianapolis, Indiana, during his childhood. In 1846 he became superintendent of the Indiana State Prison, and in 1848 he left for California, arriving in San Francisco on February 28, 1849.

McDougal's political career started when he was elected as a delegate from the Sacramento District to the constitutional convention meeting at Monterey in the summer of 1849. As a delegate to the convention meeting, he made his name known when he made a proposal concerning California's eastern boundary as well as a separate proposal concerning the issue of admitting blacks into California.

He was elected first lieutenant governor in that year, and in January 1851 when Governor Peter Burnett resigned, he succeeded to the office.

As governor, McDougal took a firm stand against the First Vigilance Committee of 1851, organized in San Francisco. He denounced the works of various vigilance committees and called upon them to cooperate with elected officials in solving the state's crime problems. His stance against vigilance committees soon made him unpopular among Californians. Although he believed that Native Indians should be removed from the state, as President Andrew Jackson had done, he did not harbor any anti-Chinese sentiments. In fact, he praised Chinese as "one of the most worthy classes of our newly adopted citizens—to whom the climate and the character of these lands are peculiarly suited" and called on Chinese to settle the swamp and flooded lands. Few politicians of his time shared his friendly views toward Chinese immigration.

FURTHER READING: H. Brett Melendy, "Who Was John McDougal?" *Pacific Historical Review* 29 (1960) pp. 231–243; H. Brett Melendy and Benjamin F. Gilbert, *The Governors of California*, Georgetown, Calif.: Talisman Press, 1965.

McKINLEY ACT, legislation passed by the U.S. Congress and signed into law on October 1, 1890, by President Benjamin Harrison. The bill was to go into effect on April 1 of the following year. Under provisions of the law, foreign sugar was allowed to come into the United States free of duty, and a bonus of two cents a pound was paid on sugar produced in the United States. This would mean economic disaster for Hawaii, for Hawaiian sugar would lose the differential advantage it had enjoyed since the Reciprocity Treaty of 1875.* This loss of advantage became an additional incentive for some key professionals and businessmen to press for the annexation of Hawaii by the United States. There was widespread opposition to annexation, however. Planters feared that annexation would eliminate the contract labor system* which enabled them to bring in large numbers of Asian laborers, whereas merchants and professionals were afraid that "their" Hawaii would be overrun by masses of Asian laborers. Eventually, the revolution that ended the Hawaiian Kingdom was supported by the vast majority of white citizens.

FURTHER READING: Gavan Daws, *Shoal of Time*, Honolulu: University Press of Hawaii, 1968; Lawrence H. Fuchs, *Hawaii Pono: A Social History*, New York: Harcourt, Brace and World, 1961; Ralph S. Kuykendall, *The Hawaiian Kingdom, Vol. III, 1874–1893*, Honolulu: University of Hawaii Press, 1967.

McWILLIAMS, CAREY (1905–1980), writer. McWilliams was born in Steamboat Springs, Colorado, on December 13, 1905, and died in New York City on June 27, 1980. During his lifetime, he championed the powerless and the persecuted, and defended their rights to fair and equal treatment. He graduated from the University of Southern California in 1927 with a degree in law and immediately began his practice in a partnership with Black and Hammock. He stayed in the partnership until 1938 at which time he was appointed chief of the

Division of Immigration and Housing by Governor Culbert L. Olson* of California. This position had been created to help the migrating farm workers. During his work as a lawyer, McWilliams had become familiar with the social problems farm workers faced. When he was given a chance to apply his knowledge, he worked hard to help the farm workers. Eventually, he had to give up his law practice.

In 1939 McWilliams published a book, *Factories in the Field*, in which he focused attention on the poor conditions the migrant farm worker had to face. He became a national figure, championing better living and labor conditions for the migrant farm worker. In 1942 he wrote another book, *Ill Fares the Land*, in which he described the harsh conditions of the migrant farm worker who was being taken advantage of by large-scale industrial farming.

McWilliams' concerns with the powerless and the persecuted extended beyond the poor living and working conditions of the migrant farm worker; they also encompassed the agony and frustrations of people who were discriminated against and despised because of their color. *Brothers Under the Skin*, (1942) was a prophetic book about the treatment of minorities during World War II. In this book he urged the federal government to enforce the Bill of Rights and to enact a new federal civil rights act. He also advocated the formation of an Institute of Ethnic Affairs within the Interior Department for public educational purposes. He felt that all nationalities should be treated with equality in immigration, and he noted that the color of the world had changed as well as the color of America.

This work was followed by *Prejudice* (1944), in which McWilliams explained the plight of American citizens of Japanese ancestry who were removed from their homes and relocated against their will during World War II. He claimed that racial prejudice, not military necessity,* had compelled the federal government to remove Japanese Americans.

In January 1945 McWilliams joined the staff at the *Nation* and became editor of the journal, for which he continued to write, voicing firm opposition to all forms of militarism and exposing the private interests of American corporations that undermined the public good. He resigned from his position in 1975 and spent the remaining years of his life writing, as always, on behalf of the equality and freedom of all people of this country.

FURTHER READING: Carey McWilliams, *The Education of Carey McWilliams*, New York: Simon and Schuster, 1979; Alexander Saxton, "Goodbye to a Colleague: Carey McWilliams, 1905–1980," *Amerasia Journal* 7, No. 2 (1980), pp. v-vii.

M

MAGNUSON ACT OF 1943. *See* Act to Repeal the Chinese Exclusions Acts, to Establish Quotas, and for Other Purposes, December 17, 1943.

MANILA GALLEON TRADE, vigorous trade between Manila and Acapulco, Mexico, which brought goods to Manila from China, Japan, Malaysia, and other parts of the world, stimulated by the permanent occupation of the Philippines by the Spaniards in 1565. This trade, carried on by galleons that were built in shipyards near the city of Manila, resulted in a number of unexpected developments. First, because the galleon trade was heavily involved in bringing Mexican silver from Mexico in exchange for Chinese silk, many Chinese merchants came to Manila to settle. Their number increased so greatly that an exclusive Chinese colony known as the *parian*, meaning "the marketplace," was built near Manila. Second, the galleons that plied between Acapulco and Manila had Manilamen, or Indians as the Spaniards called them, as crew members, deckhands, and common seamen. Some of these Manilamen deserted their galleons and intermingled with the native Indians. Some married native women and settled in various parts of Mexico.

Other Filipinos, called Luzon Indians by Pedro de Unamuno, a Spanish explorer, were brought to California by the Spanish explorers as early as 1587 when they landed on Morro Bay. When Sebastian Rodriguez Cermeno, captain of the Manila galleon *San Agustin*, landed at San Luis Obispo on December 17, 1595, to further explore California, Filipinos came with him.

Manilamen were found along the bayous and marshes of Louisiana as early as 1763. They jumped ship because of the harsh treatment they received from their Spanish masters. Their descendants established what was probably the first social club of Filipinos in the United States, the Sociedad de Beneficencia de los Hispano Filipinas de Nueva Orleans.

FURTHER READING: Charles E. Chapman, *The Founding of Spanish California*, New York: Macmillan Co., 1916; Fred Cordova, *Filipinos: Forgotten Asian American*, Dubuque, Iowa: Kendall/Hunt Publishing Co., 1983; Marcie G. Holmes, *From New Spain by Sea to the Californias, 1519–1668*, Glendale, Calif.: A. H. Clark Co., 1916; John L. Phelan, *The Hispanization of the Philippines: Spanish Aims and Filipino Responses, 1565–1700*, Madison: University of Wisconsin Press, 1959; William L. Schurtz, *The Manila Galleon*, New York: E. P. Dutton, 1939.

MANILAMEN. *See* Manila Galleon Trade.

MANLAPIT, PABLO (1891–1969) labor leader. Manlapit was born on January 17, 1891, in Lipa, Batangas, in the Philippines and completed intermediate grades in his home country. He came to Hawaii in 1910 in order to work for the Hawaiian Sugar Planters' Association* (HSPA), which promoted him to foreman. Later he became a timekeeper but was dismissed from his job following his involvement with a labor union strike. After his dismissal, he came to Hilo where he started two newspapers and operated a pool hall. He studied law while working as a janitor in a law office. His study finally paid off when he was licensed to practice law, thereby becoming the first Filipino in Hawaii to pass the bar examination.

In November 1918, while studying law, Manlapit began to organize Filipino labor, and by August 1919 he had established the Filipino Federation of Labor* which launched vigorous recruitment drives on Oahu, Maui, and Kauai. The following year Manlapit initiated the Filipino Higher Wage Movement in order to improve living conditions among Filipino plantation workers in Hawaii. This became necessary because the pre-war wages remained unchanged, while inflation after World War I had driven the cost of living up 40 to 50 percent. The movement asked for an increase in wages from $0.72 to $1.25 per day, for an eight-hour day, a substantial change in the bonus system, overtime pay for work on Sundays and legal holidays, and leave with pay for women laborers for two weeks before and six weeks after giving birth. The HSPA turned down these demands. Manlapit then called for a strike by Filipino workers, who responded by staging a strike on January 19, 1920. This is known as the 1920 Strike.* On that day 3,000 workers struck four major sugar plantations on Oahu, and by February 1, Filipino and Japanese workers joined forces to make their demands.

In response to this united effort to improve their living conditions, the HSPA began to evict workers from plantation houses. It is estimated that at the height of the strike 12,100 workers, most of whom were Japanese, were evicted from their homes. In addition, the HSPA brought in large numbers of strike-breakers to break the will of striking workers, and it made arrangements with the territorial schools' central administration not to enroll children of striking workers. Under these circumstances, the striking workers were hard pressed to give up their demands and return to work. Although some 500 workers were still out on strike, most of the striking workers returned to work by the end of July 1920. The strike lasted 165 days, and there was still no solution to the labor unrest in Hawaii.

Manlapit continued to organize Filipino labor between 1920 and 1924 by recruiting freshly imported Filipino workers. By April 1, 1924, he was able to call a strike in Oahu, which later resulted in the bloodiest event in the history of labor movements in Hawaii. On September 9, sixteen strikers and four policemen were killed at Hanapepe, Kauai. This has become known as the Hanapepe Massacre.*

Because of his involvement in this bloody strike, Manlapit was convicted of conspiracy and was sentenced to two years in prison. He chose to go into exile but returned to Hawaii in 1932 to resume his labor union activities. Together with Antonio Fagel* and Epifanio Taok, he established a new Filipino labor union which later became known as Vibora Luviminda. Manlapit had to leave Hawaii in 1935 when the HSPA managed to put Taok in jail and had Manlapit banished to the Philippines permanently. (*See also* Filipino Federation of Labor; Hanapepe Massacre; and 1920 Strike.)

FURTHER READING: Robert N. Anderson et al., *Filipinos in Rural Hawaii*, Honolulu: University of Hawaii Press, 1984; Lawrence H. Fuchs, *Hawaii Pono: A Social History*, New York: Harcourt, Brace and World, 1961; H. Brett Melendy, *Asians in America: Filipinos, Koreans, and East Indians*, Boston: Twayne Publishers, 1977; Michi Kodama-Nishimoto et al., *Hanahana: An Oral History Anthology of Hawaii's Working People*, Honolulu: Ethnic Studies Oral History Project, University of Hawaii, 1984; John E. Resnecke, *Feigned Necessity: Hawaii's Attempt to Obtain Chinese Contract Labor, 1921–1923*, San Francisco: Chinese Materials Center, 1979; Luis V. Teodoro, Jr., *Out of This Struggle: The Filipinos in Hawaii*, Honolulu: University Press of Hawaii, 1981.

MANOA LIN YEE WUI (HUI), the oldest Chinese association in Hawaii to date, organized by a group of Chinese merchants in 1854. The association took care of burials in the plot in Manoa Valley, bought land to create a Chinese cemetery, and also handled arrangements for people who wanted to send the bones of their dead relatives back to China by exhuming graves and cleaning the remains at a building established on the cemetery. The association received its charter from the Hawaiian government in 1889 under the name of the Chinese Cemetery Association of Manoa, or Manoa Lin Yee Wui. The cemetery grounds became its possession in 1892.

MANZANAR CITIZENS FEDERATION, established in July 1942 by young Nisei* leaders from Los Angeles who felt that evacuees at the Manzanar Relocation Center should cooperate with the war effort and should try to establish a community. Most of these young Nisei were from Los Angeles County as well as Los Angeles, and they had been associated with the Japanese American Citizens League* before their evacuation. The league had come under severe criticism as a result of its mishandling of issues relating to the evacuation of all persons of Japanese ancestry. The young Nisei did not want to identify themselves with the league, but other evacuees identified them as league sympathizers and considered the Manzanar Citizens Federation an arm of the Japanese American Citizens League.

Opposed to the Manzanar Citizens Federation were many Kibei* and Issei* evacuees who denounced not only government policies for evacuation, but also those among the Nisei who had been accused of collaborating with the government. In addition, the Kitchen Workers Union* led by Harry Ueno opposed the federation. (*See also* Manzanar Incident.)

FURTHER READING: Edward H. Spicer et al., *Impounded People*, Tucson: University of Arizona Press, 1969; Michi Weglyn, *Years of Infamy: The Untold Story of America's Concentration Camps*, New York: William Morrow and Co., 1976; Toshio Yatsushiro, *Politics and Cultural Values: The World War II Japanese Relocation Centers and the United States Government*, New York: Arno Press, 1978.

MANZANAR INCIDENT, an incident that occurred on December 6, 1942, when approximately 1,000 angry evacuees gathered together to take further action on a Nisei* who had been suspected of collaborating with the War Relocation Authority* and had been hospitalized after he had been beaten by Harry Ueno. The crowd was also intent on rescuing Ueno from jail. Alarmed by the angry mob gathered in front of the Manzanar Camp jail, troops with submachine guns and rifles were deployed to surround the jail. Although tear gas was thrown to disperse the crowd, they kept on coming toward the jail. Shots were fired, and two evacuees were killed.

After order was reestablished at the Manzanar Camp, those suspected of having agitated evacuees were rounded up and sent to the Leupp Isolation Center* and later transferred to the Tule Lake Segregation Center.* Among them was Joseph Yoshisuke Kurihara.*

FURTHER READING: Audrie Girdner and Anne Loftis, *The Great Betrayal*, New York: Macmillan Co., 1969; Michi Weglyn, *Years of Infamy*, New York: William Morrow and Co., 1976; Toshio Yatsushiro, *Politics and Cultural Values*, New York: Arno Press, 1978; Arthur A. Hansen and David A. Hacker, "The Manzanar Riot: An Ethnic Perspective," *Amerasia Journal* 2, No. 1 (Fall 1974), pp. 112–157.

MARCUELO, D. L. See Salinas Lettuce Strike of 1934.

MARGINAL GENERATION, the sociological notion that people of one generation stand on the margins of two societies and cultures but are not accepted into either. It may be argued that the children of immigrant parents, regardless of where they came from, are more likely to manifest marginality as a result of cultural conflict between their parental culture and the culture of their host society than the children of succeeding generations.

FURTHER READING: Rose Hum Lee, *The Chinese in the United States of America*, Hong Kong: Hong Kong University Press, 1960; Gene N. Levine and Colbert Rhodes, *The Japanese American Community*, New York: Praeger Publishers, 1981; Minako K. Maykovich, *Japanese American Identity Dilemma*, Tokyo, Japan: Waseda University Press, 1972.

MARGINAL MAN, a sociological concept coined by Robert E. Park, who characterized the marginal man as one "whom fate has condemned to live in two societies and in two not merely different but antagonistic cultures." Park believed that the marginal man was a more civilized human being than those who are tied to their social conventions and prejudices. In contrast, Everett V. Stonequist described the marginal man as someone who was uncertain about his own identity and was confused over his loyalty. Stonequist's marginal man also suffered from self-hatred and an inferiority complex.

A true marginal man, if such a person exists, may not be found either in Park's prototype or in Stonequist's image of a man suffering from a lack of self-fulfillment. In rapidly changing societies, including the American society, role conflict and identity crises may create a sense of marginality in the minds of people.

FURTHER READING: Aaron Antonovsky, "Toward a Refinement of the Marginal Man Concept," *Social Forces* 35 (October 1956), pp. 57–62; David I. Golovensky, "The Marginal Man Concept: An Analysis and Critique," *Social Forces* 30 (October 1951–May 1952), pp. 333–339; Arnold W. Green, "A Re-examination of the Marginal Man Concept," *Social Forces* 26 (1957), pp. 167–168; Robert E. Park, "Human Migration and the Marginal Man," *American Journal of Sociology* 33 (May 1928), pp. 881–893; David Riesman, "Some Observations Concerning Marginality," *Phylon* (1951), pp. 113–127; J. S. Slotkin, "The Status of the Marginal Man," *Sociology and Social Research* 28 (September 1943), pp. 47–54; Everett V. Stonequist, "The Problems of the Marginal Man," *American Journal of Sociology*, 41 (1935), pp. 1–12.

MASAOKA, MIKE MASARU (1915–), Japanese American Citizens League* leader. Masaoka was born on October 15, 1915, in Fresno, California, the son of Masaoka Eijiro and Haruye (Goto). His family moved to Salt Lake City, Utah, when he was three years of age. His father operated a small fish market until he was killed in an automobile accident in 1924. Masaoka attended public schools there and went on to the University of Utah from which he graduated in 1937 with a B.A. degree.

Masaoka's involvement with the Japanese American Citizens League (JACL) started in 1938 when Walter Tsukamoto, executive secretary of the JACL, asked him to attend the national convention to be held in Los Angeles. Masaoka went to the convention and suggested a number of organizational changes, including qualifications for membership. He was seen as a trouble-maker and was told to leave the meeting. After this incident he came back to Utah and began to organize the Intermountain District Council,* becoming president of the council in 1939. This council was then accepted as a chapter of the JACL.

Masaoka was hired in 1941 under the recommendation of Kido Saburo,* then president-elect of the JACL, to work as its national secretary, in which office he served well until 1943. Between 1945 and 1952, Masaoka worked for the JACL as its Washington lobbyist. He worked diligently with congressmen to get the Japanese American Evacuation Claims Act* through Congress, which was eventually signed into law by President Harry S Truman on July 2, 1948.

Because of his cooperative attitude toward government authorities prior to and during the evacuation of persons of Japanese ancestry during World War II, Masaoka came under severe criticism by radical Japanese Americans. As national secretary of the JACL and as a lobbyist for this organization, however, he served Japanese communities well.

Masaoka's attitude toward America was well articulated in his Japanese American Creed,* which he wrote in 1940 and which was recorded in the *Congressional Record* on May 9, 1941. For his contributions to JACL and to Japanese communities in America, he was chosen Japanese American of 1950. (*See also* Japanese American Creed.)

FURTHER READING: Bill Hosokawa, *JACL in Quest of Justice*, New York: William Morrow and Co., 1982.

MASAOKA HARUYE, et al., v. THE PEOPLE, a case involving Mrs. Masaoka Haruye, a widow, and her five sons, including Mike Masaru Masaoka,* who brought legal action against the State of California in order to determine whether the Alien Land Act of California, 1913,* as amended in 1920, was constitutional. The Masaoka children, four of whom had served in the U.S. military (a fifth son was killed in action in France) wanted to build a home for their aged mother so that she could live out the rest of her life without major economic hardship. They bought a piece of property in Pasadena and deeded it to their mother, who was a Japanese alien and therefore ineligible for U.S. citizenship. According to the Alien Land Act of 1913, the property deeded to an alien ineligible for U.S. citizenship was subject to escheat action by the State of California.

In their legal action they specifically asked the following question:

> Can the State of California by statute relegate citizens of the United States to a position inferior to that of other citizens and, in some cases, inferior to aliens, merely because of their racial origin, in the matter of the right to make and enforce contracts; in the matter of providing for the security of persons and property; in the matter of the right to purchase land, sell, hold and convey real or personal property . . . ?

Judge Thurmond Clark of the Superior Court of Los Angeles, where the case was tried, initially ruled on March 16, 1950, in favor of the respondents when he found the California Alien Land Act in violation of the Fourteenth Amendment of the Constitution. The State of California then appealed to the state's highest court. The Supreme Court of California cited its decision on Fujii Sei v. State of California,* and stated that that case was controlling and "for the reasons there stated the judgment must be affirmed." However, the court was not unanimous; three judges filed a dissenting opinion on July 9, 1952, the day when the majority handed down its opinion. Judge Schauer, with whose opinion Judges Shenk and Spence concurred, felt that it was not the place of the state's Supreme

Court to intervene and determine that the Alien Land Act was unconstitutional; it was up to the Supreme Court of the United States and Congress to make that determination.
FURTHER READING: Frank Chuman, *The Bamboo People: The Law and Japanese-Americans*, Del Mar, Calif.: Publisher's Inc., 1976; Bill Hosokawa, *JACL in Quest of Justice*, New York: William Morrow and Co., 1982; 39 C. 2d 883; 245 P. 2d 1062.

MASSIE RAPE CASE. See Ala Moana Case.

MASTERS AND SERVANTS ACT OF 1850, also known as Act for the Government of Masters and Servants, passed by the National Legislature during the reign of King Kamehameha III in preparation for the plantation era that was expected to come to Hawaii. Even before the law was passed, the Royal Hawaiian Agricultural Society had taken up the question of importing laborers from abroad.

Under provisions of this law, anyone over twenty years of age could legally bind himself by contract to another in employment for no more than five years. In addition, labor contracts made in other countries for work to be performed in Hawaii could not exceed ten years. This was to be legally enforced, and anyone violating the terms of the contract could be arrested and forced to serve twice the time agreed, unless the master agreed to a compensation for his loss. Anyone not willing to comply with these demands would be sentenced to prison and hard labor until an agreement could be reached.

Two years after this law was passed, a shipload of Chinese was brought to Hawaii under the terms provided in the law, and they were immediately sent to work on plantations. Even before this "first" group of Chinese workers arrived, Hawaii already had seventy-one Chinese who were engaged in a variety of trades.
FURTHER READING: Katharine Coman, *The History of Contract Labor in the Hawaiian Islands*, New York: Macmillan Co., 1903; Ralph S. Kuykendall, *The Hawaiian Kingdom, 1854–1874*, Honolulu: University of Hawaii Press, 1953.

MASUMIZU KUNINOSUKE (?–1915), an original member of the Wakamatsu tea and silk farm colony.* Masumizu was reported to have married a black woman and operated a fish store in Sacramento, California. He had three daughters and a son, who worked as a barber in the city. He died in 1915 and is buried at Colusa, California.
FURTHER READING: Bill Hosokawa, *Nisei*, New York: William Morrow and Co., 1969; Harry H.L. Kitano, *Japanese Americans: The Evolution of a Subculture*, Englewood Cliffs, N.J.: Prentice-Hall, 1969.

MATSUDAIRA TADAATSU (1855–1888), engineer. Matsudaira was only seventeen years of age when he came from Japan to America in 1872. He attended Rutgers University and earned a degree in civil engineering. He worked as an engineer for the Union Pacific for a while and then decided to attend the Colorado School of Mining. Upon graduation he was appointed assistant inspector of mines. He married the daughter of a retired U.S. Army officer, General Archibald

Sampson, and enjoyed some measure of success, but he died young, at the age of thirty-three.

MATSUI, ROBERT TAKEO (1941–), U.S. congressman. Matsui was born on September 17, 1941, in Sacramento, California. He received a B.A. degree in political science from the University of California at Berkeley in 1963 and his J.D. degree from Hastings College in 1966. The following year he was admitted to the California bar and began his law practice in Sacramento. He served as a member of the Sacramento City Council beginning in 1971 and became very active in community affairs, particularly as a member and president of the Japanese American Citizens League.*

Matsui was elected to represent California's Third Congressional District in the House of Representatives in 1978, comfortably winning the election against Republican candidate Sandy Smoley. In Congress he has served on a number of committees, including the Commerce Committee.

MATSUNAGA, SPARK MASAYUKE (1916–), U.S. senator. Matsunaga was born in Kauai, Hawaii, on October 8, 1916, and graduated from the University of Hawaii with an Ed.B. degree in 1941. He went on to Harvard University where he studied law and received his J.D. degree in 1951.

Before he was elected to Congress, where he served seven terms beginning in 1963, Matsunaga served in Hawaii's Territorial House between 1954 and 1959. Preceding his service in the Territorial House, he served in various public offices, including the Civil Defense Agency and the Committee on Housing between 1947 and 1954. During World War II he worked for the U.S. government in military service, serving in the 108th and 442nd Regimental Combat Units.* He retired as a lieutenant colonel and was in the Judge Advisory General Corps. For his bravery and dedication he won many awards, including the Purple Heart with Oak Leaf Clusters.

In 1977 Matsunaga won a Senate seat in Hawaii, defeating his colleague, Representative Patsy Takemoto Mink.* He has been active in the Senate, strongly advocating nuclear arms control and proposing a bill to create a National Academy of Peace. The bill passed both the House and the Senate, and was signed into law by President Ronald Reagan on October 19, 1984.

FURTHER READING: Frank Chuman, *The Bamboo People: The Law and Japanese-Americans*, Del Mar, Calif.: Publisher's Inc., 1976; Spark M. Matsunaga, "An Academy of Peace: Training for a Peaceful Future," *The Futurist*, February 1985.

MEARES, JOHN (1756–?) British fur trader. Meares entered the British Royal Navy at a young age and reached the rank of lieutenant before he finally resigned to enter the lucrative fur trading business. In 1786 he sailed to the coast of Northwest America under the British flag, as the captain of the *Nookta*. Two years later, he made the voyage again, this time commanding the *Felice* and the

Iphigenia, in order to trade for furs from the Nootka Indians and to build a ship at Nootka Sound.

These two ships carried a number of volunteer Chinese laborers. Meares had these laborers build a ship, which was named the *Northwest America*. It set sail under the command of Robert Funter. Half of its crew were supposedly Chinese; they were the first known Chinese laborers in the Northwest.

FURTHER READING: James Colnett, ed., *The Journal of Captain James Colnett Aboard the Argonaut*, Toronto: Champlain Society, 1940; Frederic W. Howay, *The Dixon-Meares Controversy*, New York: Plenum Publishing Corp., 1969; John Meares, *The Memorial of John Meares*, ed. Nellie B. Pipes, Portland: Metropolitan Press, 1933.

MEHTA, ZUBIN (1936–), conductor of the New York Philharmonic Orchestra. Mehta was born in Bombay, India, on April 29, 1936, the son of Mehli Nowrowji and Tehmina (Daruvala) Mehta. His father was an accomplished musician, having taught himself to play the violin. He organized the Bombay String Quartet and the Bombay Symphony and served the Bombay Symphony as its first conductor. Under his father's tutelage, Zubin was introduced early in his life to music and conducting. He was allowed to work with the Bombay Symphony and had the experience of conducting a full orchestra rehearsal at the tender age of sixteen. Although his father encouraged him to prepare himself for a more stable profession, he finally decided against medicine in favor of music.

At the age of eighteen Mehta went to Vienna to study music at the Akademie für Musik and Darstellende Kunst where he learned conducting under Hans Swarowsky. Upon completing his study there in 1957, he entered the Liverpool International Conductor's Competition in 1958 and won first prize, which enabled him to lead the Royal Liverpool Philharmonic as its associate conductor. He remained in Europe in order to work with other orchestra groups until he was given an opportunity to come to Los Angeles in 1961, at which time he was offered the post of musical director of the Los Angeles Philharmonic. He became its conductor in 1962 and served there until 1978 when he was asked to lead the New York Philharmonic, succeeding its internationally renowned conductor, Leonard Bernstein.

MENOR, BENJAMIN (1922–), member of the Hawaii Supreme Court. Menor was born in the Philippines on September 27, 1922, the son of Angelo and Paulina Menor, and came to Hawaii in 1930 where he attended the University of Hawaii. He graduated from that institution in 1950 with a B.A. degree and studied law at Boston University. In 1953 he was admitted to practice in Hawaii and served as Hawaii county attorney until 1959. In 1974 he became the first Filipino to be appointed to the Hawaii State Supreme Court.

MERCHANT MARINE ACT OF 1936, legislation passed to help Americans find jobs during the Great Depression. Congress passed so many laws from 1933 to 1937 that they became known as Franklin Roosevelt's Alphabet Laws, or

Alphabet Reform. One of these laws, the Merchant Marine Act of June 29, 1936, required that 90 percent of the crews on American flag ships be American citizens. Under this law any officer, agent, or owner of any merchant ship who employed an alien without the proper identification was subject to a $50 fine for each alien so employed. The law was to be enforced by the Secretary of the Treasury.

The number of Filipinos hired to work on merchant ships increased from 5,500 in 1925 to 5,800 in 1932. This number reached its peak in 1930 when 7,869 were working on American merchant ships. Hence, many Filipino workers were subject to dismissal and unemployment after passage of the Merchant Marine Act of 1936.

Because of the economic hardship the law placed on Filipinos, particularly among the Filipinos in Louisiana, U.S. Senator Allen Ellender a Louisiana senator, introduced an amendment to the act on April 19, 1937. Filipinos in New Orleans and its vicinity sent their letters to members of Congress urging them to support Ellender's bill to amend the Merchant Marine Act of 1936.

FURTHER READING: Hyung-chan Kim and Cynthia C. Mejia, *The Filipinos in America, 1898–1974*, Dobbs Ferry, N.Y.: Oceana Publications, 1976; H. Brett Melendy, *Asians in America: Filipinos, Koreans, and East Indians*, Boston: Twayne Publishers, 1977; Merchant Marine Act, 1936, The Shipping Act, 1916 and Related Acts, Washington, D.C.: U.S. Government Printing Office, 1938.

METCALF, VICTOR HOWARD (1884–1936) U.S. congressman, Secretary of Commerce and Labor, Secretary of the Navy. Metcalf was born in Utica, New York, on October 10, 1884. He was educated at the Utica Free Academy and then attended Yale Law School. He practiced law in New York and Connecticut before he moved to Oakland, California. From 1900 to 1904 he served in Congress as a Republican from the Third District. Under President Teddy Roosevelt, Metcalf served as Secretary of Commerce and Labor from 1904 until 1906 when he was asked to serve as Secretary of the Navy, an office he served until 1908.

Metcalf played a prominent role in the San Francisco school segregation crisis of 1906, precipitated by the San Francisco School Board's resolution on October 11, 1906, ordering principals to send all Chinese, Japanese, or Korean children to the Oriental Public School. This order, which established a policy of educational segregation, touched off a major international crisis between the United States and Japan. Major newspapers in Tokyo printed the segregation order, and the Japanese government filed a strong protest with Washington against the segregation order. The official protest from Tokyo carried diplomatic weight, for Japan had just defeated Russia militarily. Fearful of any major military confrontation between the United States and Japan, Roosevelt sent his Secretary of Commerce and Labor to California to investigate the school crisis. Because Metcalf was the only Californian in the cabinet, Roosevelt naturally relied on him. Metcalf arrived in the San Francisco area on October 31 and stayed for two weeks. He did not produce his report until December 18, 1906. Meanwhile, Roosevelt and the

Justice Department planned a course of action that would include litigation to test the segregation order on constitutional grounds and restrictions on Japanese immigration later after the school crisis was over. Californians did not support Metcalf's report and dubbed him a traitor for it. Metcalf was guided by his strong conviction that Japanese residents in California deserved full protection from the state, and that if California could not provide them with that protection, then the federal government should step in.

FURTHER READING: Thomas A. Bailey, *Theodore Roosevelt and the Japanese-American Crisis*, Gloucester, Mass.: Peter Smith, 1964; Roger Daniels, *The Politics of Prejudice*, Berkeley: University of California Press, 1962, William Petersen, *Japanese Americans*, New York: Random House, 1971.

MIDDLEMAN MINORITY, a sociological concept used to compare the socioeconomic status of a minority with that of other minorities in a society where both are dominated by the majority. This concept is often used to single out Asian Americans in general and Japanese Americans in particular as either model minority* or middleman minority in the United States. It is argued that the middleman minority occupies the intermediate position in a society where they face hostility and discrimination because ethnic solidarity within the community of the middleman minority enables its members to start and develop their own economic niche.

The phenomenon of the middleman minority has been explained by a number of theorists, who can be divided into four groups: (1) pure-prejudice theorists, (2) contextual theorists, (3) cultural theorists, and (4) situational theorists. Pure-prejudice theorists attempt to find the roots of hatred against the middleman minority in the religion, culture, and psychology of its persecutors, whereas contextual theorists look for causes responsible for the existence of the middleman minority in the market situations. The cultural theorists focus on the cultural characteristics of the middleman minority in their attempts to find causes for the middleman minority phenomenon. Finally, the situational theorists believe that the history of immigration of a particular minority and of its interaction with the majority society can explain the middleman minority phenomenon.

FURTHER READING: Hubert M. Blalock, Jr., *Toward a Theory of Minority-Group Relations*, New York: John Wiley and Sons, 1967; Edna Bonacich and John Modell, *The Economic Basis of Ethnic Solidarity: Small Business in the Japanese American Community*, Berkeley: University of California Press, 1980.

MIEN, a small tribal group that moved to Laos from China some 200 years ago. Although there were 3 million Mien in China, there were only 50,000 Mien in Laos. Once in Laos they moved into the mountains between 3,000 and 4,000 feet high and refused to intermarry.

After the American debacle in Vietnam in 1975, many Mien moved to America to settle in such cities as Portland, Oregon, and Richmond, Oakland, San Jose, and Long Beach, California. It is estimated that there are approximately 4,000 Mien in the United States, 1,500 of whom live in Portland.

MILITARY INTELLIGENCE SERVICE LANGUAGE SCHOOL, originally established on November 1, 1941, as the Fourth Army Intelligence School at the Presidio in San Francisco. The idea of establishing a school where intelligence people would be taught the Japanese language was suggested by John Weckerling and Kai E. Rasmussen. They were given permission to start the school but received little encouragement when they got only $2,000 in funding.

With the outbreak of the Pacific War, the school became more important to the U.S. armed forces. It was reorganized as the Military Intelligence Service Language School and placed under direct War Department supervision. After the end of the war, the school changed its curriculum from military Japanese to general Japanese and civil affairs in order to train people to reconstruct the defeated Japan.

MILITARY NECESSITY, a concept used widely to justify the decision to impose a curfew law selectively on persons of Japanese ancestry on the West Coast and to remove and evacuate them during the Pacific War. The U.S. Supreme Court resorted to this concept in making decisions on two major cases, namely, the case of Hirabayashi v. United States* and the case of Korematsu v. United States.* The Court did not concern itself with a precedent established in 1866 in the Milligan case. The majority opinion in this case ruled that even military necessity could not be the only justification for suspending the Constitution; military authorities, even with the President's approval, could not hold the Constitution in suspension when dealing with citizens entitled to judicial protection guaranteed by the Constitution. There was only one exception, according to the majority opinion on the Milligan case, when military authorities could suspend the Constitution in this country: when the President declared martial law as there prevailed a clear impending danger in combat situations.

Because there was no clear and impending danger on the U.S. mainland, the military necessity concept was used as an expediency in order to impose the government's decision on a people who looked the same as America's enemies. FURTHER READING: Roger Daniels, *Concentration Camps U.S.A.: Japanese Americans and World War II*, New York: Holt, Rinehart and Winston, 1971; Jacobus ten Broek, Edward N. Barnhart, and Floyd W. Matson, *Prejudice, War and the Constitution: Causes and Consequences of the Evacuation of the Japanese Americans in World War II*, Berkeley: University of California Press, 1970.

MILLER BILL, a bill introduced by Senator John Franklin Miller of California on December 5, 1881, and reported out of committee unanimously on January 26, 1882. According to this bill, which was called A Bill to Enforce Treaty Stipulations Relating to Chinese, Chinese laborers were to be refused admission to the United States sixty days after passage of the bill and thereafter for twenty years. The bill passed through the House and the Senate and was sent to the President for his signature. President Chester A. Arthur used his veto power and returned the bill to Congress on April 4. In his veto message he pointed out that "good faith requires us to suspend the immigration of Chinese laborers for a period less than twenty years." (*See also* Chinese Exclusion Act of 1882.)

FURTHER READING: Mary Roberts Coolidge, *Chinese Immigration*, New York: Henry Holt and Co., 1909; Tien-Lu Li, *Congressional Policy of Chinese Immigration or Legislation Relating to Chinese Immigration to the United States*, Nashville, Tenn.: Publishing House of the Methodist Episcopal, South, 1916.

MINETA, NORMAN Y. (1931–), U.S. congressman. Mineta was born on November 12, 1931, in San Jose, California, where he spent his entire childhood and attended the public schools. He graduated from the University of California at Berkeley in 1953, having majored in business and political science.

Between 1953 and 1956 Mineta served in the U.S. Army and returned to his hometown to start an insurance business with his father. He became active in the city's Japanese American Citizens League,* an involvement that led him to become interested in other community organizations such as the San Jose Human Relations Commission, Chamber of Commerce, and the North San Jose Optimists Club. From 1967 to 1971 he was on the City Council of San Jose and worked for the San Jose Housing Authority. He became vice-mayor for three years and eventually became mayor of that city in 1971. He served in that office until 1974 when he ran for the 94th Congress as a Democrat. He was successful in his first bid to become a member of the House of Representatives. In Congress he was instrumental in establishing a Presidential Commission that was charged with investigating the issues involved in the wartime relocation and internment of Japanese American citizens. In his testimony on behalf of the bill (S. 1647), he stated that "such a comprehensive study was long overdue. Instead of focusing on second hand accounts, inaccuracies, and accepted myths, the Commission will force us as a society to concentrate on the facts: What really happened and what were the consequences?" This fact-finding bill was approved by Congress, and the commission eventually submitted its recommendation to Congress in 1983.

FURTHER READING: U.S. Government Printing Office, *Commission on Wartime Relocation and Internment of Civilians Act*, 96th Congress, Washington, D.C.: 1980.

MING QUONG HOME FOR YOUNG CHINESE GIRLS, opened on December 12, 1925, when a new building erected on McClellan Street in Oakland was dedicated and named Ming Quong, meaning "radiant light." This building was used to accommodate young Chinese girls who came from broken homes. They not only were given shelter, but also received training in useful skills. This was all made possible through the personal efforts of Donaldina Cameron.* (*See also* Cameron, Donaldina.)

MINING AND EMIGRATION REGULATIONS OF 1905 IN KOREA, enacted to protect Koreans and their interests, although Japan intended to use the law to restrict Korean immigration to Hawaii, where Korean laborers were often used as strike-breakers against Japanese workers on strike. After Japan took over the Korean peninsula as its protectorate in 1905, it began to tighten its control over general administrative affairs in Korea, including Korean immigration to Hawaii.

FURTHER READING: Wayne Patterson, *The Korean Frontier in America: Immigration to Hawaii, 1896–1910*, Ann Arbor, Mich.: University Microfilms International, 1977.

MINK, PATSY TAKEMOTO (1927–) U.S. representative. Mink was born on December 6, 1927, at Paia, Hawaii, where she grew up. She attended the University of Hawaii, graduating in 1948. Three years later she received a law degree from the University of Chicago. Since 1955 she has held a number of public and government positions: she served in the Hawaiian House of Representatives as House Attorney in 1955; she became president of the Hawaiian Young Democrats in 1956; she was elected to the Hawaiian Senate in 1958; and she became a member of Hawaii's state delegates to the Democratic National Convention in 1960.

In 1962 Mink was elected to the House of Representatives and served until 1977, when she ran for a seat in the U.S. Senate, only to be defeated by her colleague, Spark Masayuke Matsunaga.*

While in Congress, her attention focused on women's rights and education, with a particular emphasis on the disabled and minorities. She was actively involved in the hearings on the National Women's Conference and Sex Discrimination Regulations as well as the hearings on the Hawaiian Native Claims Settlement Act.*

MISCEGENATION, a word used in an anonymous pamphlet published in 1864, "Miscegenation: The Theory and the Blending of the Races." The pamphlet was written by Democrats David Croly and George Wakeman who were trying to place favorable views of racial mixing with the Republicans in order to give their Democratic candidate for President an edge. The candidates in the election were Republican Abraham Lincoln who was running for reelection and General George B. McLellan on the Democratic ticket.

As early as 1661, the State of Maryland outlawed marriage between whites and blacks, and as many as thirty-one states had anti-miscegenation laws* in 1945. These laws were also applied to marriages between whites and Asians. In 1967 the U.S. Supreme Court ruled in the case of Loving v. Virginia that states could not outlaw marriage between whites and non-whites. (*See also* Anti-miscegenation Laws.)

MISSISSIPPI VALLEY IMMIGRATION LABOR COMPANY, proposed by General Gideon S. Pillow during the Chinese labor convention held on July 13, 1869, in Memphis, Tennessee. According to the proposal, the company would be established when enough stocks, each of which was to be sold at $100, had been sold to create $100,000. The purpose of capitalizing such a company was to bring "as many Chinese immigrant laborers as possible, in the shortest time," but Pillow did not receive much support for his proposal, although he was able to raise $100,000 in stocks. Finally, in December 1869, the Tennessee Legislature passed a law forbidding the company from importing any Chinese labor. (*See also* Chinese Labor Convention in Memphis.)

FURTHER READING: Gunther Barth, *Bitter Strength*, Cambridge, Mass.: Harvard University Press, 1964; Lucy M. Cohen, *Chinese in the Post/Civil War South: A People Without a History*, Baton Rouge: Louisiana State University Press, 1984; Robert Seto Quan, *Lotus Among the Magnolias: The Mississippi Chinese*, Jackson: University Press of Mississippi, 1982.

MODEL MINORITY, a sociological concept used to compare Asian Americans with other minorities in the United States. This concept implies that other minorities should emulate Asian Americans in their thought and behavior, for members of the majority society view Asian Americans as docile, well-disciplined, hard-working, humble, and above all less demanding. Asian Americans are considered more successful because their values are similar to those of whites, whereas the values of less successful minorities are remote from those of whites. Small wonder, then that Asian Americans are presented as a model to other minorities.

FURTHER READING: Elaine H. Kim, *Asian American Literature*, Philadelphia: Temple University Press, 1982; Bob H. Suzuki, "Education and Socialization of Asian Americans: A Revisionist Analysis of the 'Model Minority' Thesis," in Russell Endo, Stanley Sue, and Nathaniel N. Wagner, eds., *Asian Americans: Social and Psychological Perspectives*, Vol. 2, Ben Lomond, Calif.: Science and Behavior Books, 1980; Don T. Nakanishi and Marsha Hirano-Nakanish, eds., *The Education of Asian and Pacific Americans: Historical Perspectives and Prescriptions for the Future*, Phoenix, Ariz.: Oryx Press, 1983.

MONCADO, HILARIO C. *See* Filipino Federation of America.

MOON, HENRY DUKSO (1914–1974) medical researcher. Moon was born in San Francisco on September 28, 1914, the first son of Mr. and Mrs. Moon Yang-mok, both of whom came to America as immigrants from Korea. He received the B.A. degree from the University of California at Berkeley in 1935, and two years later he received his M.A. in anatomy at the same institution. In 1940 he received his M.D. degree.

During his lifetime Moon was known for his research on hormones. He was part of the team that first isolated the ACTH hormone. He wrote some ninety-five articles on hormones which were published in well-established medical journals. He also served on the Scientific Advisory Board and on the National Board of Medical Examiners.

MOON SUN-MYUNG, REVEREND. See Unification Church.

MORGENTHAU, HENRY, JR. (1891–1967), Secretary of the Treasury. Morgenthau was born to a wealthy family in New York. His father, Henry Morgenthau, Sr., served as ambassador to Turkey. Through his father's connection with Franklin D. Roosevelt—they happened to live in the same neighborhood—Morgenthau became the business manager of Roosevelt's campaign when Roosevelt ran for the 1928 New York governorship. For his service, Morgenthau was rewarded with the chairmanship of the New York Agricultural Advisory Commission. Morgenthau was the campaign manager for Roosevelt's presidential race in 1932 and again was rewarded with a chairmanship, this time on the Federal Farm Board.

Morgenthau served as Secretary of the Treasury from January 1934 until July 17, 1945. On July 26, 1941, one day after Japan seized South French Indochina, Morgenthau called for a trade embargo on Japan and a freezing of Japanese assets in America. After Pearl Harbor, he took his first official action to increase security around the White House, for the Secret Service was under the authority of the Treasury Department. The second order from Morgenthau was to close the borders to all Japanese within the United States and revoke all licenses under which Japanese and their business firms were operating. This included not only Japanese residents, but also American citizens of Japanese ancestry. Although his staff members urged him to take over thousands of small businesses owned by Japanese on the West Coast, he thought their proposal "hysterical and impractical." Morgenthau was against a mass evacuation of all persons of Japanese ancestry; instead, he believed that only those who could hurt the country should be evacuated. His position did not carry much weight inasmuch as in the end the government did indeed remove all persons of Japanese ancestry from the West Coast.

FURTHER READING: John Morton Blum, *Roosevelt and Morgenthau*, Boston: Houghton Mifflin Co., 1970; John Morton Blum, *Years of War: From the Morgenthau Diaries*, Boston: Houghton Mifflin Co., 1967; Morton Grodzins, *American Betrayed*, Chicago: University of Chicago Press, 1949; Bill Hosokawa, *Nisei*, New York: William Morrow and Co., 1969.

MORIKAMI MUSEUM, a Japanese culture museum built on 140 acres of land donated by George Sukeji Morikami to Palm Beach County, Florida, for a park. Morikami came to Palm Beach County in 1906 when he joined the Yamato Colony, established in 1904.

MORRISON et al. v. PEOPLE OF THE STATE OF CALIFORNIA, a case that went to the U.S. Supreme Court as an appeal from the Supreme Court of the State of California. The case was argued on December 12 and 13, 1933, and was decided on January 8 of the following year. Justice Benjamin Cardozo delivered the opinion of the unanimous court in which he stated that a person of Japanese ancestry born in the United States was a citizen of the United States, but a person of Japanese ancestry born outside the United States, unless his father was a U.S. citizen, was not eligible for U.S. citizenship. The Court stated that the privilege of naturalization was confined to free white persons, members of the Caucasian race. Hence, no Japanese, Hindus, American Indians, or Filipinos were eligible for U.S. citizenship.

The case involved an indictment and conviction of a conspiracy charge against George Morrison and H. Doi, the latter being a Japanese alien ineligible for U.S. citizenship. The State of California claimed that the two conspired to violate the Alien Land Act of California, 1913.* The State of California particularly claimed that Doi, although he was ineligible for U.S. citizenship, did not inform Morrison of his alien status when he sought to lease land from Morrison.

The two were convicted of conspiracy as charged and were sentenced to serve two years in prison, but their sentence was suspended and they were put on probation. The defendants appealed to the District Court of Appeals for the Fourth District, which upheld the lower court's decision and ruled that the Fourteenth Amendment was not violated. The case went to the Supreme Court of California, where the defendants' contention that the Fourteenth Amendment right was violated was overruled, with three Justices dissenting.

The Supreme Court, by its unanimous decision, upheld Section 9(a) of California's Alien Land Act of 1913 as amended in 1927 as constitutional.
FURTHER READING: Frank Chuman, *The Bamboo People*, Del Mar, Calif.: Publisher's Inc., 1976; Milton R. Konvitz, *The Alien and the Asiatic in American Law*, Ithaca, N.Y.: Cornell University Press, 1946; *Supreme Court Reporter* 54, 291, U.S. 82, 1934.

MORTON, OLIVER. See Joint Special Committee of Congress on Chinese Immigration.

MUN LUN SCHOOL, established in Hawaii on February 4, 1911, under the auspices of the Pao-huang Hui (Society to Protect the Emperor)* just four days before the establishment of the Wah Mun School* by the T'ung Meng hui, which was established by Dr. Sun Yat-sen.* The Mun Lun School was staffed with two teachers from Yokohama, Japan, and it was the largest and best equipped Chinese language school in Hawaii. Its educational curriculum, unlike that of Wah Mun School, was centered around traditional Chinese cultural and classical education. This must have reflected the educational philosophy of K'ang Yu-wei,* who wanted to restore Chinese cultural splendor by means of Confucianism. The school received some financial support from China.
FURTHER READING: Clarence E. Glick, *Sojourners and Settlers*, Honolulu: University Press of Hawaii, 1980.

MUNG, JOHN. *See* Nakahama Manjiro.

MUNSON REPORT, a report prepared by Curtis B. Munson, who had been asigned to investigate the degree of loyalty to the United States among persons of Japanese ancestry both in Hawaii and on the West Coast of the United States.

He undertook this assignment during the month of October and the first weeks of November 1941, as policymakers on both sides of the Pacific began to prepare for war before the Japanese attack on Pearl Harbor. After his investigation as a special agent of the State Department, he filed a twenty-five page report in which he described each generation of persons of Japanese ancestry and pointed out their amazing degree of loyalty to America. A similar report in favor of Japanese Americans was submitted to Kenneth D. Ringle, who had been assigned to gather intelligence on Japanese Americans in Los Angeles. In spite of these reports, people in high places in Washington and on the West Coast removed and evacuated all persons of Japanese ancestry on the West Coast during the Pacific War.

FURTHER READING: Bill Hosokawa, *Nisei*, New York: William Morrow and Co., 1969; Michi Weglyn, *Years of Infamy*, New York: William Morrow and Co., 1976; Bob Kumamoto, "The Search for Spies: American Counterintelligence and the Japanese American Community, 1931–1942," *Amerasia Journal* 6, No. 2 (1979), pp. 45–75.

MURAYAMA MAKIO (1912–) medical researcher. Murayama was born on August 10, 1912, in San Francisco to Hakuyo and Namiye Maruyama. His father died when Makio was only four years of age, and the child was sent to Japan to live with a great-aunt. He stayed in Japan for the next ten years. He came back to San Francisco where he attended Lowell High School. After his graduation from high school in 1933, he entered the University of California at Berkeley where he majored in biochemistry and minored in bacteriology. He put himself through college by cleaning hotel bathrooms and finally graduated in 1938. He did graduate work at Berkeley where he majored in biochemistry and minored in nuclear physics; his interest in nuclear physics had more to do with the study of cyclotrons than with the atom's nucleus.

After the Japanese attack on Pearl Harbor, Murayama's family was sent to a concentration camp, but he was separated from his family when he was ordered to report to the Manhattan Project in Chicago as a physicist. With his Japanese ancestry, however, he was rejected. During the war he was followed by an FBI agent.

Murayama obtained his Ph.D. in 1953 and did his postgraduate work at the California Institute of Technology, where he worked under Linus Pauling on blood cell sickling. Murayama is a world renowned researcher on sickle cell diseases, and for his accomplishments in this area he was awarded the 1969 Association for Sickle Cell Anemia Award and the Martin Luther King, Jr., Medical Achievement Award in 1972.

MURIETA, JOAQUIN (19th century), a folk hero said to have been born in Quillota, Chile and to have come to California in search of gold. Some have suggested he was a character in fiction. Murieta was a bandit who defied law officers and state authorities after the Spanish-speaking miners had been driven out of the mines as a result of the California Foreign Miners' Tax* in 1850.

Some of these displaced miners joined gangs of bandits out of frustration and necessity and raided gold mines, stole horses, and robbed travelers. Murieta preyed on Chinese miners in particular because they were considered more defenseless. Murieta allegedly raided a Chinese camp near Rich Bar and robbed it of an estimated $10,000. According to another estimate, some 200 Chinese were robbed of their gold dust estimated at $30,000 by Joaquin and his bandits.

Because of widespread banditry, the California State Legislature created a temporary state ranger department to capture the bandits, known as the five Joaquins. They were identified by the legislature as Joaquin Valenzuela, Joaquin Ocomorenia, Joaquin Carillo, Joaquin Botellier, and Joaquin Murieta. It was said that an ex-Texas Ranger, Harry Love, was hired to help California capture the Joaquins, and his rangers shot and killed Joaquin Murieta on July 25, 1853. Love and his rangers collected their reward money as promised by the legislature.

FURTHER READING: Jay Monaghan, *Chile, Peru and the California Gold Rush of 1849*, Berkeley: University of California Press, 1973; Remi Nadeau, *The Real Joaquin Murieta: Robin Hood Hero or Gold Rush Gangster?*, Corona del Mar, Calif.; Trans-Anglo Books, 1974; Ralph J. Roske, *Everyman's Eden: A History of California*, New York: Macmillan Co., 1968.

MURRAY, HUGH CAMPBELL (1825–1857), Chief Justice, California Supreme Court. Murray was born on April 22, 1825, in St. Louis, Missouri, of Scottish ancestry. His family moved to Alton, Illinois, when he was very young. He lived there until he was twenty-one years of age, at which time he joined the army and served during the Mexican War. After the war, he returned to Illinois, where he was admitted to the bar. He practiced law for a short time until he was stricken with gold fever, which brought him to California in September 1849. In San Francisco he set up a law office, and several months later he was elected an associate justice of the First Superior Court of San Francisco.

In 1851 California Governor John McDougal* appointed Murray to the Supreme Court of the State of California, and the following year he became Chief Justice. He was elected again in 1853 and in 1855.

In 1854, in the case of the People v. George W. Hall,* Chief Justice Murray made a historic ruling. George Hall had been convicted of murder upon the testimony of Chinese witnesses. He later appealed to the Supreme Court of the State of California claiming that such evidence was inadmissible. His appeal was considered in light of a law passed by the California State Legislature on April 16, 1850, which stated that "no black, mulatto, or Indian shall be allowed to give evidence in favor of or against a white man." Chief Justice Murray used this law to consider the appeal, arguing that the term "Indian" was a generic one—applying to all persons who were not white, black, or mulatto. He ruled that a person of Chinese ancestry could not testify against a white man, and he reversed the judgment against George W. Hall, setting him free.

FURTHER READING: Cheng-Tsu Wu, ed., *"Chink!": A Documentary History of Anti-Chinese Prejudice in America*, New York: World Publishing, 1972.

MUTUAL ASSISTANCE ASSOCIATIONS, social and community organizations established among Southeast Asian refugees in America as cultural, educational, social, and recreational, as well as economic, institutions. In this respect, they are similar to the clan or district associations among early Chinese immigrants; *kenjin-kai,** or prefectural associations among early Japanese immigrants; and churches among early Korean immigrants.

MUTUAL ASSISTANCE SOCIETY, established in 1905 as the first political organization among Koreans in the United States. The organization had approximately 130 members by 1908. The following year it merged with the United Korean Society* in Hawaii to become the Korean National Association.* (*See also* Korean National Association.)
FURTHER READING: Bong-youn Choy, *Koreans in America*, Chicago: Nelson-Hall, 1979; Hyung-chan Kim, ed., *The Korean Diaspora*, Santa Barbara, Calif.: ABC-Clio Press, 1977.

MUTUAL SUPPLY COMPANY, a business firm established by Togasaki Kikumatsu who came to America in 1887. Togasaki was a graduate of a Japanese government school of law. He visited America with the intention of returning to Japan, but after his visit he decided to remain in America. He owned and operated a small roominghouse and later sold this business and operated a gift shop. When anti-Japanese pressure was applied on wholesale firms to cut off supplies for Japanese laundries, Togasaki organized a cooperative. This effort resulted in establishing the company. He married a Japanese woman, Shige Kushida, and had a son, George Kiyoshi Togasaki* born in 1895.

MUZUMDAR, HARIDAS THAKORDAS (1900–), worker for India's independence. Muzumdar was born on December 18, 1900, in Gujarat, India, and came to America to study at Northwestern University, where he received his B.A. degree in 1925. He received his Ph.D. degree in sociology at the University of Wisconsin in 1930.

Upon graduation from the University of Wisconsin, Muzumdar worked for India's freedom from Britain both in India and the United States. In 1939 he returned to India to participate in a round of talks with political leaders, including Nehru and Gandhi. He came back to the United States in 1940 as an unofficial ambassador, as he called himself, and promoted the cause of India's independence by publishing books and giving public lectures on the topic of India's independence. After India became independent, he became a naturalized citizen of the United States out of gratitude to his adopted country. His book, *America's Contributions to India's Freedom* (1962), is a contribution to our understanding of Asian Indian history in the United States.
FURTHER READING: Haridas T. Muzumdar, *America's Contributions to India's Freedom*, Allahabad, India: Central Book Depot, 1962.

MYER, DILLON S. (1891–1982), director, War Relocation Authority.* Myer was born on September 4, 1891, in Hebron, Ohio. He attended Ohio State University where he majored in agronomy. After he received his B.S. degree, he entered government service in 1916. Had he not been appointed director of the War Relocation Authority (WRA) created during World War II, he probably would have spent the rest of his life in anonymity. He was fifty years old at the time of his WRA appointment, and his political and social philosophy seems to have been born of a typically Midwestern mold—kindly but lacking in individual insight and conviction.

Little has been written about Dillon S. Myer, but some sketches of his character may be gleaned from his book, *Uprooted Americans*, written twenty years after his experience with the WRA. In his book he presents a fairly objective view of the WRA's activities, albeit a somewhat subjective and biased account of his own involvement.

On May 22, 1946, as an expression of gratitude, the Japanese American Citizens League* presented Myer with a citation, commending him for his humanity in dealing with the Japanese evacuees. Indeed, history shows that he made an effort to ease the pain of people who were so haplessly placed under his jurisdiction. Believing from the outset that the evacuation was not justified, he found himself in a hornet's nest of public prejudice and official resistance against his effort to help the evacuees. He went so far as to issue a statement in which he said: "It is not the American way to have children growing up behind the barbed wire and under the scrutiny of armed guards." He even submitted a plan in which the entire program could be eliminated. The response he received from the Secretary of War, Henry Lewis Stimson,* is indicative of the prevailing attitudes of the time. According to Stimson, any problems in the relocation centers* were the result of "failure to take aggressive action against those individuals who are actively working against the interests of the government."

Faced with such opposition, Myer's efforts can only be seen as commendable, although one may question his conclusions about the WRA twenty years later. Myer considered it a success. Inevitably, a more basic question arises: Is it moral to participate in an activity that is clearly both immoral and illegal? Does not obedience to an unjust law give it a tacit legitimacy? Myer meant well, but his actions left much to be desired. (*See also* War Relocation Authority.)

FURTHER READING: Allen R. Bosworth, *America's Concentration Camps*, New York: W. W. Norton and Co., 1967; Dillon S. Myer, *Uprooted Americans*, Tucson: University of Arizona Press, 1971; Michi Weglyn, *Years of Infamy*, New York: William Morrow and Co., 1976.

N

NAIM, HAM SAY v. NAIM, RUBY ELAINE, a case involving Naim Ham Say, a Chinese seaman, and Ruby Elaine Naim, a Caucasian, who traveled to North Carolina to marry on June 26, 1952, and then returned to Virginia to live as man and wife. The following year, September 30, 1953, Ruby Naim filed for annulment of her marriage to Naim Ham Say in Virginia on the grounds that the marriage had been illegal under Virginia law. She was granted the annulment, and Naim Ham Say appealed to the Supreme Court of Appeals of the State of Virginia, which upheld the annulment on June 13, 1955. The case was then appealed to the Supreme Court, which refused to make a decision on the case, stating that the decision handed down by the Supreme Court of Virginia made the case "devoid of a properly presented Federal question." (*See also* Anti–miscegenation Laws.)
FURTHER READING: S. W. Kung, *Chinese in American Life*, Seattle: University of Washington Press, 1962; *Supreme Court Reporter*, 350 U.S. 891 and 350 U.S. 985.

NAKADATE, PAUL T. *See* Fair Play Committee of One.

NAKAHAMA MANJIRO (1827–1898), (also known as John Mung), professor of English in Japan. Nakahama was born the son of a fisherman in Naka-no-hama, Ashizuri-misaki, in the Province of Tosa in Shikoku, Japan. Being a fisherman himself, he was out fishing in 1841 when his ship met a typhoon and was wrecked. He and four other fisherman reached a deserted island where they spent approximately six months before they were rescued by an American whaling ship, which brought them to the United States. Manjiro was then taken to Fairhaven, Massachusetts, where he was given a new name, John Mung, and was sent to school. It is said that, in addition to English, he learned mathematics, navigation, and surveying. In 1850 he went aboard an American ship and left the United States for Japan, arriving in Kagoshima in 1851. Although he was well treated upon his return, he was assigned to the lowest samurai rank. Two years later he became an official as a result of efforts made by Abe Masahiro on his behalf.

With his knowledge of English and navigation acquired while abroad Manjiro was put to work translating foreign documents pertaining to foreign missions and navigation. In 1860 he accompanied the official party which came to America on the *Kanin Maru* to ratify a commercial treaty between the United States and Japan.

In 1869, one year after the Meiji Restoration, Manjiro became a professor of English in the Kaisei Gakko, the forerunner of Tokyo University. The following year he accompanied another Japanese mission led by the military leader Oyama Iwao to Europe but returned to Japan the following year because of failing health. FURTHER READING: Hisakazu Kaneko, *Manjiro: The Man Who Discovered America*, Boston: Houghton Mifflin Co., 1956; Bill Hosokawa, *Nisei*, New York: William Morrow and Co., 1969.

NAKANO YOSUKE W. (1887–1961), architect. Nakano was born in Yamaguchi, Japan, and came to the United States when he was nineteen years of age. He attended high school in California before he enrolled in the school of architecture at the University of Pennsylvania. He joined Wark and Company, an architectural firm in Philadelphia, where he eventually became chief engineer. Nakano made his name as an expert in the use of reinforced concrete for the construction of large buildings and had a part in constructing more than 200 builidings on the East Coast. Among these buildings were the Bell Telephone Building, Gulf Oil and Sun Oil buildings, and the Presbyterian Hospital in Philadelphia.

NANHAI. *See* Sam Yap (Sze–I).

NATIONAL COMMITTEE FOR REDRESS, THE JAPANESE AMERICAN CITIZENS LEAGUE, established in 1976 to obtain compensation from the federal government for the illegal detention of Japanese Americans. The issue of making the federal government compensate Japanese Americans for their financial losses because of internment during World War II was discussed among Japanese Americans as early as 1946. Because of more urgent personal concerns— families to rear, careers to build, children to educate, and communities to rebuild— nearly thirty years passed before they resorted to legal avenues.

During the 1976 national convention of the Japanese American Citizens League held at Sacramento, California, when the issue of compensation once again surfaced, Edison Uno led the campaign to persuade the Japanese American Citizens League to file grievances. Uno traveled widely, visiting various Japanese communities and presenting his plan to make the federal government pay for its illegal detention of Japanese Americans, denial of constitutional protection, and their financial losses. After Uno's death in 1977, Clifford Uyeda assumed leadership of the campaign as chairman of the National Committee for Redress, the Japanese American Citizens League. The committe's plan was to ask the federal government for $25,000 tax-free compensation for every Japanese American evacuee who suffered illegal imprisonment during World War II. The plan submitted to the Japanese American Citizens League during its national convention in 1978 in Salt Lake City was amended to include among beneficiaries the heirs of deceased evacuees and persons of Japanese ancestry. The plan was unanimously approved by the convention delegates.

This decision was directly responsible for the introduction of a bill to Congress by Senators Daniel Ken Inouye,* Spark Masayuke Matsunaga,* Samuel Ichiye Hayakawa,* Alan Cranston, Frank Church, and James A. McClure to establish a national commission to investigate the evacuation of American citizens during World War II. (*See* Commission on Wartime Relocation and Internment of Civilians.)

FURTHER READING: Bill Hosokawa, *JACL in Quest of Justice*, New York: William Morrow and Co., 1982; Robert A. Wilson and Bill Hosokawa, *East to America: A History of the Japanese in the United States*, New York: William Morrow and Co., 1980.

NATIONAL DOLLAR STORES, LTD., a chain of fifty–four retail stores established by Joe Shoong* in California; Seattle, Washington; Salt Lake City, Utah; Arizona; and Hawaii. They carried men's and women's wear. The chain was originally established as the China-Toggery-Shoong Company in 1921, and the name was changed in 1928 to the National Dollar Stores, Inc. The stores reached an annual sales volume of $10 million based on a capital stock of $1 million, which was owned by the Shoong family. They employed approximately 600 persons, and the company net worth increased from $1.6 million in 1941 to $7 million in 1959. The company's headquarters are located in San Francisco. (*See also* Shoong, Joe.)

NATIONAL ORIGINS ACT OF 1924. *See* Immigration Act of 1924.

NATIONAL REFORM PARTY, organized in 1890 when two political groups, Hui Kalaiaina (the Hawaiian Political Association) and the Mechanics' and Workingmen's Political Protective Association, came together with the special purpose of defeating the Reform Party during the 1890 election in Hawaii. These two groups agreed that the Hawaiian Kingdom should remain free and independent and that Asians should not be allowed to ruin Hawaii. But they were not able to agree on the most important question—the right to rule. Native Hawaiians in the National Reform Party did not want to see white men gain power over them, whereas members of the Mechanics' and Workingmen's Political Association, most of whom were white, disliked the idea of natives wielding power over them.

The election results made this contention moot because the legislature was equally divided between Reform and National Reform members.

NATIONAL STUDENT RELOCATION COUNCIL, organized in May 1942 under the recommendations made to President Franklin Roosevelt by the governor of California, Culbert L. Olson,* who expressed his concern in a letter to the President. Olson stated that approximately 1,000 Nisei students were affected by the government's decision to relocate and detain them in the relocation centers and that their educational interruption might have a lasting impact on the Japanese American community in the future. Responding to Olson's letter, President Roosevelt directed one of his aides, possibly Milton Stover Eisenhower,* to ask Clarence Pickett to head a committee to help Nisei students.

The work of helping Nisei college students went to John W. Nason, president of Swarthmore College, who served as chairman of the National Student Relocation Council, with headquarters located in Philadelphia. By fall 1942 many Nisei students were enrolled in institutions of higher learning in the Eastern states.
FURTHER READING: Frank F. Chuman, *The Bamboo People*, Del Mar, Calif.; Publisher's Inc., 1976; Bill Hosokawa, *Nisei*, New York: William Morrow and Co., 1969.

NATIVE SONS OF THE GOLDEN STATE, organized in 1895 when Walter U. Lum, Joseph K. Lum, and Ng Gunn decided to establish an organization made up of native-born Chinese and persons born of Chinese ancestry in the United States. They strongly felt the need for an organization to fight for the protection and improvement of the civil rights of native-born Chinese.

The establishment of this organization in San Francisco (which changed its name to the Chinese Americans Citizens Alliance in 1915) marked a turning point in the history of Chinese social organizations: it broke off from the tradition of establishing social organizations on the basis of clan membership, district affiliation, sworn brotherhood, or language affiliation.

By the time the organization changed its name, it had established local chapters in Chicago, Detroit, Pittsburgh, Boston, Houston, San Antonio, Albuquerque, Los Angeles, Fresno, San Diego, Salinas, Portland, and Oakland. Its official newspaper, *The Chinese Times*, had the largest circulation of any Chinese language newspaper in the United States.

The organization had long been dominated by businessmen and professionals who leaned toward the Republican Party. As a result of this factor, coupled with the establishment of the Chinese-American Democratic Club, the organization's influence on Chinese communities began to decline.
FURTHER READING: Jack Chen, *The Chinese of America*, New York: Harper and Row, 1980; Rose Hum Lee, *The Chinese in the United States of America*, Hong Kong: Hong Kong University Press, 1960; H. Brett Melendy, *The Oriental Americans*, New York: Hippocrene Books, 1972.

NATURALIZATION ACT OF MARCH 26, 1790, a bill that required a two–year residence for citizenship and restricted citizenship to free whites. The second session of the 1st Congress saw the creation in the House of Representatives of a three–member committee to consider a uniform rule of naturalization as suggested by President George Washington. The committee presented the first clause of such a bill to the House:

> that all free white persons, who have, or shall migrate into the United States, and shall give satisfactory proof, before a magistrate, by oath, that they intend to reside therein, and shall take an oath of allegiance, and shall have resided in the United States for one whole year shall be entitled to all right of citizenship.

The debate on the proposed bill included no arguments on the racial restriction; the only disagreement was on the length of residence required for citizenship. Congress finally chose to include a two-year residence requirement for citizenship with no change in the racial restriction. The bill passed Congress and became the Act of March 26, 1790, entitled An Act to Establish a Uniform Rule of Naturalization. In 1795 Congress extended the residence requirement from two to five years.

Almost from the beginning, the United States established a system of discrimination by which only "free whites" were allowed to become citizens. This "free whites only" stipulation was revised to admit blacks into membership of the Union after the Civil War, when Congress granted naturalization privilege to "persons of African nativity or descent." Because Asians were neither "white" nor "persons of African nativity," they were ruled ineligible for U.S. citizenship from 1790 until 1952.

FURTHER READING: Frank Chuman, *The Bamboo People*, Del Mar, Calif.: Publisher's Inc., 1976; E. P. Hutchinson, *Legislative History of American Immigration Policy, 1798–1965*, Philadelphia: University of Pennsylvania Press, 1981; Benjamin B. Ringer, *We the People and Other*, New York: Tavistock Publications, 1983.

NEW CHURCH (SILLIP KYOHOE). *See* Korean Churches; Korean Christian Church.

NEW KOREA, THE (SINHAN MINBO), published on February 1, 1909, as a weekly in Korean under the editorship of Ch'oe Chong-ik. The publication had been in operation under another name, the *Mutual Cooperative News*, which saw its first publication on April 26, 1907. The office was moved from Oakland to San Francisco, and finally, when the Korean National Association* built its headquarters in Los Angeles, the *New Korea* also moved down to Los Angeles. There had been many newspapers among Korean communities in America, but this was the only newspaper that survived difficult times and is still in operation.

NEW PEOPLE'S SOCIETY (SINMIN-HOE), organized on August 7, 1903, in Hawaii under the leadership of Ahn Jong-su and Yun Byong-gu. This was the first political organization established among Koreans in Hawaii. Its purpose was to resist Japanese aggression in Korea and to rebuild Korea with people at home and abroad born of the new spirit of cooperation.

FURTHER READING: Hyung-chan Kim, ed., *The Korean Diaspora*, Santa Barbara, Calif.: ABC–Clio Press, 1977.

NEWSPAPERS, ASIAN AMERICAN, began as early as 1854. No major study has been done on the role of ethnic newspapers published by persons of Asian ancestry. Consequently no major generalization is possible. A number of studies have been done on the European ethnic press, but whether or not the findings of these studies are applicable to the Asian American experience is highly debatable, and should not be used without critical examination.

Asian Americans began to publish their newspapers as early as April 1854, when Chinese in San Francisco began to publish the *Kim-Shan Jit San-Luk*, or *Golden Hills' News*, first as a newspaper published twice a week, then as a weekly. Many others followed, and too many newspapers are published today by Chinese to mention. Among the early newspapers were the *Oriental*, published in San Francisco in 1855; the *Chinese Daily News* in Sacramento in 1856; the *Chinese World* in San Francisco in 1891, which was published as the first bilingual newspaper among Chinese in America; and the *New China Daily News*, published in Hawaii in 1900.

Japanese Americans, seeing the acute need for a medium to disseminate information and exchange ideas in their communities established a number of newspapers. Among the earliest ones were *The Nichi Bei Times*,* published in 1898; *North American Times*; the *Japanese American Courier*; *Nippu Jiji**; and the *Hawaii Hochi*. As of 1974, there were thirteen newspapers published by Japanese Americans, eleven of which were published either bilingually or had a Japanese vernacular section. Among these were *Gidra*, *Rafu Shimpo*, *Hokubei Mainichi*, Nichibei *Times*, *Chicago Simpo*, *Utah Nippo*, *New York Nichibei*, *Hawaii Times*, and *Pacific Citizen*.

Korean immigrants in the United States started their newspaper publication as early as 1905, when the *Korean News* was published between June 10, 1905, and September 1906 in Honolulu. It did not last long, but others followed. In mainland United States the *Mutual Cooperation News* was published on April 16, 1907, in San Francisco, followed by the *New Korean World*, published on October 3, 1907. Other newspapers published during the earlier years of Korean immigration were the *United Korean News*, the *United Korean Weekly*, the *Great Unity Information*, and the *New Korea*. None of them lasted too long except for the *New Korea* which is still published under the same title in Los Angeles.

Among Filipino newspapers in America there existed as many as twenty or more over the last seventy years. Among the earlier newspapers were *Kauai Filipino News*, which changed its name to *Filipino News* in 1931; *Commonwealth Courier* in 1931; *Philippine Advocate* in 1934; *Philippine Herald in 1920; and Philippines Mail** in 1930. The last is still published in Salinas, California.

These newspapers reported on the labor union movement, job opportunities, news from home countries, information about American culture, new immigration legislation, as well as new developments in their communities. A close examination of the content of these newspapers indicates that the Asian American ethnic press underwent three stages of development: the first stage was dominated by news from and about their home countries, and they were reported in their vernacular; the second was characterized by news reported in both English and their vernacular on political economic conditions of their home countries and the United States; and the third began to see the emergence of newspapers which were printed exclusively in English and dominated by social, political, and economic news on America, with minor attention given to news from and about their home countries.

Although this three–stage analysis may be applicable to newspapers published by earlier Asian immigrants, it may not be true that a similar condition prevails among recent immigrants from Asia. For these newly arrived people, it is quite possible that the first stage has begun all over again.

FURTHER READING: Irving Howe, *World of Our Fathers*, New York: Simon and Schuster, 1976; Charles Jaret, "The Greek, Italian, and Jewish American Ethnic Press: A Comparative Analysis," *Journal of Ethnic Studies* 7, No. 2 (1979), pp. 47–49; H. S. Nelli, "The Role of the Colonial Press in the Italian American Community of Chicago, 1886–1921," Ph.D. diss., University of Chicago, 1965; E. Olszyk, *The Polish Press in America*, Milwaukee, Wisc.: Marquette University Press, 1940; R. Sanders, *The Promised City*, Cambridge, Mass.: Harvard University Press, 1962.

NG FUNG HO et al. v. WHITE, COMMISSIONER OF IMMIGRATION, a case that went to the U.S. Supreme Court as petitioners brought certiorari, asking the Court to rule mainly on two questions. The first question dealt with whether or not a Chinese laborer who was found to be in the United States illegally before passage of the General Immigration Act of February 5, 1917,* could be deported on the basis of that act. The second question had to do with whether or not a Chinese laborer who claimed to be a citizen of the United States had, in deportation proceedings, the right to a judicial hearing as guaranteed by the federal Constitution. The case, argued on March 17, and 20, 1922, and decided on May 29, 1922, involved four Chinese: Ng Fung Ho and his son, Ng Yuen Shew, Gin Sang Get, and Gin Sang Mo. The first question was applicable to Ng Fung Ho and his son, whereas the second was related to Gin Sang Get and Gin Sang Mo, both of whom claimed they were foreign-born sons of a native-born citizen.

Justice Louis Brandeis delivered the opinion of the Court. He stated that Congress had the right to order the deportation of aliens considered dangerous to the country, and it could order this by means of executive proceedings, even if the alien was not deportable by executive proceedings at the time of his entry. Prohibition of *ex post facto* laws did not apply to the deportation of undesirable aliens. However, when the claim of citizenship by aliens was involved, they were protected by the federal Constitution to have a judicial hearing on their claim of citizenship, although the burden of proof, as far as Chinese were concerned, was on them, not on the government. Furthermore, according to the opinion of the Court, the alien claiming to be a citizen was not entitled to his discharge from custody but was to be held for trial on the question of his citizenship.

Ng Fung Ho and his son were ordered deported, and Gin Sang Get and Gin Sang Mo were detained for trial to determine their claim of citizenship.

FURTHER READING: Milton Konvitz, *The Alien and the Asiatic in American Law*, Ithaca, N.Y.: Cornell University Press, 1946; *Supreme Court Reporter* 42, October Term 1921, 259 U.S. 276, 1921.

NICHI BEI TIMES, THE, established in 1898 when Abiko Kyutaro* and four friends merged two Japanese language newspapers they had purchased. They named the newspaper *Nichi Bei*, or *Japanese American*, to highlight the presence of persons of Japanese ancestry in America. The newspaper is published in San Francisco in Japanese with a section devoted to news written in English and has been very influential in Japanese American communities.

NIHONJIN-KAI, a generic term used to refer to Japanese associations established among persons of Japanese ancestry in the United States. It was frequently used synonymously with kenjin kai,* or prefectural associations, although its meaning does not point to any association with organizations established on the basis of common prefectural membership. These associations were established in Japanese American communities in order to offer protection to their members against anti-Japanese violence and discrimination.

FURTHER READING: John W. Conner, *Tradition and Change in Three Generations of Japanese Americans*, Chicago: Nelson-Hall, 1977; Toshio Yatsushiro, *Politics and Cultural Values: The World War II Japanese Relocation Centers and the United States Government*, New York: Arno Press, 1978.

NIHON-MACHI, a generic term referring to towns established by Japanese from Japan and their descendants in the United States. *Nihon-machi* is often identified with Japantown or Little Tokyo and is considered as a central place of small businesses where the Japanese get their supplies for their ethnic foods and other comforts. It is also a center for cultural and social activities used by members of Japanese American communities. (*See also* Chinatown.)

NIIJIMA JO (1843–1890), interpreter for Iwakura Mission.* Niijima was born in Kanda in Edo, Japan, the son of a lower ranking samurai. At the age of thirteen the lord of his domain ordered him to study Western science and technology. In accordance with this order he attended the Kaigun Denshujo, where he studied mathematics and navigation. During this time he read a book written by an American missionary and developed an intense desire to go to America. Because no Japanese were allowed to leave Japan, he went to Hakodate, Hokkaido, where he was able to board an American ship bound for Shanghai in 1864. In Shanghai he became a stowaway on an American ship, the *Wild Rover*, and came to Boston. With the assistance of A. Hardy, the owner of the ship, he attended school and graduated from Amherst College in 1870. He served the Japanese Mission to America, led by Prince Iwakura, as an interpreter and accompanied the Mission to Europe where he also worked as an interpreter. Returning to the United States, he completed his study at Andover Theological Seminary in 1874 and went back to Japan with a donation of $5,000 to found a Christian college in Japan. He established a school in Kyoto called Doshisha. (*See also* Iwakura Mission.)

1920 STRIKE, a strike that started on January 19, 1920, under the leadership of Pablo Manlapit,* president of the Filipino Federation of Labor.* Preparation for the strike began as early as 1917 when a group of plantation workers organized the Association of Higher Wage Question. The association then began to investigate actual wages paid to workers by sending a letter to each plantation, but the Hawaiian Sugar Planters' Association* (HSPA) directed all managers to ignore the letter. When their letter of inquiry went unanswered, the Association of Higher Wage Question called for the establishment of a labor union. Two years later, on October 19, 1919, seventy-five delegates from the Japanese Young Men's Association met in Hilo and called for an eight-hour day, an increase in wages, and abolition of the bonus system. This particular association changed its name to the Hawaii Federation of Labor, thus becoming a catalyst to the development of the Japanese Federation of Labor* in Hawaii.

The Japanese Federation of Labor, made up of four island-wide labor federations, supported Manlapit's efforts to negotiate for an increase in wages for Filipino plantation workers when the Filipino Federation of Labor was refused a pay raise by the HSPA. Manlapit issued an order for Filipino plantation workers to strike on January 19, 1920. He also called on Japanese workers to strike with his union members. Japanese workers did not join him immediately, but by the middle of February, 5,871 Japanese on Oahu and 2,625 Filipino workers were on strike. The HSPA swiftly retaliated against the strikers by evicting them from their houses that had been furnished by the HSPA.

The strike started with a demand for an increase in wages from $0.77 to $1.25 per day. It failed because the HSPA resisted and fought against the strikers by importing Portuguese, Puerto Ricans, Chinese, and Koreans as strike–breakers. (*See also* Filipino Federation of Labor; Japanese Federation of Labor.)

FURTHER READING: Lawrence H. Fuchs, *Hawaii Pono: A Social History*, New York: Harcourt, Brace and World, 1961; John E. Reinecke, *Feigned Necessity; Hawaii's Attempt to Obtain Chinese Contract Labor, 1921–1923*, San Francisco: Chinese Materials Center, 1979; Ronald Takaki, *Pau Hana: Plantation Life and Labor in Hawaii, 1835–1920*, Honolulu: University of Hawaii Press, 1983.

NING YUNG WUI KUN. *See* District Companies.

NIPPU JIJI, THE, Japanese–English newspaper that began as the *Yamato* in 1895 in Hawaii but changed its name to *Nippu Jiji* in 1906. It continued publication until the Japanese attack on Pearl Harbor. After a month's interruption, the newspaper appeared again, and in November 1942 the name was changed to *Hawaii Times*. It is still published in both Japanese and English.

NISEI, a Japanese term meaning the second generation of children born in the United States of their immigrant parents from Japan. Many sociological and anthropological studies have been conducted on this particular generation of people by American scholars, who considered them quiet, docile, meek, and compliant. William K. Hosokawa* has called the Nisei the "quiet Americans."
FURTHER READING: John W. Connor, *Tradition and Change in Three Generations of Japanese Americans*, Chicago: Nelson-Hall, 1977; Bill Hosokawa, *Nisei: The Quiet Americans*, New York: William Morrow and Co., 1969; Christie W. Kiefer, *Changing Cultures, Changing Lives*, San Francisco: Jossey-Bass Publishers, 1974; Minako K. Maykovich, *Japanese American Identity Dilemma*, Tokyo, Japan: Waseda University Press, 1972; Daniel I. Okimoto, *American in Disguise*, New York: Walter/Weatherhill, 1971.

NISHIKAWA, MITSUGI v. JOHN FOSTER DULLES, SECRETARY OF STATE, a case argued on October 28, 1957, before the U.S. Supreme Court and decided on March 31, 1958, involving the constitutional issue surrounding the question of whether or not an American citizen of Japanese ancestry who had served in the Japanese Army involuntarily lost his U.S. citizenship because of that fact and that fact alone. The petitioner, Nishikawa Mitsugi, was born in Artesia, California, in 1916 and was educated in schools there until 1939. In August of that year, after graduating from the University of California in engineering, he traveled to Japan where he intended to stay two to five years. Nishikawa's father had registered him in the family register in Japan. But in November 1939, the petitioner's father passed away, leaving the petitioner without any financial means to return to the United States.

In June 1940 the petitioner was required to take a physical, and in March of the following year he was drafted into the Japanese Army where he served as a maintenance man/mechanic in the Air Force regiment in China. The petitioner alleged that because of his statements that Japan could not win the war against the United States, he was beaten repeatedly for a month and afterwards was beaten "a couple days a month."

After the war, Nishikawa applied to the U.S. consulate in Japan for an American passport. But instead of a passport, he received, more than a year later, a Certificate of Loss of Nationality of the United States. The petitioner brought judicial action against the Secretary of State and asked that his citizenship be restored. The U.S. District Court for the Southern District of California, Central Division, ruled against the plaintiff, declaring that he lost his U.S. citizenship. He appealed to the U.S. Court of Appeals for the Ninth Circuit, which also ruled against him. Then he brought certiorari to the U.S. Supreme Court.

Chief Justice Earl Warren delivered the opinion of the Court, with Justices John Harlan and Tom Clark dissenting. In his opinion for the Court, the Chief Justice declared that expatriation cases require a strict standard of proof, and the government in the case of Nishikawa failed to prove that his service in the Japanese Army was done voluntarily. Because "no conduct results in expatriation, unless that conduct is engaged in voluntarily," Nishikawa did not lose his American citizenship, Justices Hugo Black and William O. Douglas, in their concurring opinion, went further, emphasizing that the American citizenship of any person is his or her constitutional birthright and Congress cannot expatriate any citizen against his or her own will.

FURTHER READING: Frank F Chuman, *The Bamboo People: The Law and Japanese Americans*, Del Mar, Calif.: Publisher's Inc., 1976; *Supreme Court Reporter* 78, 356, U.S. 129.

NISHIMURA v. UNITED STATES, a case brought to the U.S. Supreme Court as a result of a Japanese woman, Nishimura Eki, who was refused the right to land in the United States. Commissioner William H. Thornley did not permit her to land because he believed that the provisions of the act of Congress of August 3, 1882, applied to Mrs. Nishimura, who arrived at San Francisco from Yokohama on May 7, 1891 on the *S. S. Belgic*. The act imposed a head tax of 50 cents on each alien coming by vessel at the port of entry, and it excluded from entry people who were deemed to be lunatics, idiots, or convicts, or any person unable to take care of himself or herself without becoming a public charge.

Nishimura presented her passport which stated that she came in the company of her husband who had been in America for two years. She did not know where he was, but she said that she was to go to a hotel in San Francisco and wait for him. She had $21 in U.S. currency to prove that she had as much money as any average immigrant brought to America.

On May 13, 1891, Nishimura petitioned for a writ of habeas corpus against the commissioner of immigration, alleging that she was illegally detained and was refused permission to land without due process of law. The commissioner excluded the evidence offered as the petitioner's right to land and reported that the question of the right had been tried and determined by a duly constituted and competent tribunal having jurisdiction; that the decision of J. L. Hatch, who was appointed inspector of immigration, was conclusive on the right of the petitioner to land and could not be reversed by the court but only by the commissioner of immigration and the Secretary of Treasury; and that the petitioner was not unlawfully restrained of her liberty.

On July 24, 1891, the Circuit Court confirmed its commissioner's report and ordered Nishimura remanded to the custody of J. L. Hatch to be dealt with "as he finds the law required." Nishimura and her lawyer appealed to the U.S. Supreme Court on the grounds that Hatch's appointment was illegal because it was made by the Secretary of Treasury and should have been made by the Superintendent of Immigration. The Constitution does not allow Congress to vest the appointment of inferior officers elsewhere than "in the President alone, in the court of law, or in the heads of departments." The act of 1891 contemplated and intended that the inspectors of immigration be appointed by the Secretary of Treasury; appointment of such officers by the Superintendent of Immigration could be upheld only by presuming them to be made with the concurrence or approval of the Secretary of Treasury.

It was also argued that Hatch's proceedings did not conform with Section 8 of the act of 1891 because it did not appear that he took testimony on oath and because there was no record of any testimony or of his decisions.

Justice Horace Gray delivered the Court's opinion, stating that the statute did not require the inspector to take any testimony at all and allowed him to decide on his own inspection and examination of the question of the right of any alien immigrant to land. The provision merely empowered inspectors to take oaths and testimony, and required only testimony so taken to be entered on record. Because the decision was in conformity with the act of 1891, there could be no doubt that it was final and conclusive against the petitioner's right to land in the United States.

This was the first Supreme Court case involving a person of Japanese ancestry. The ruling on the case also led the two governments to work on a new treaty that would allow citizens of one country to enter, travel, or reside in any part of the territories of the other contracting party.

FURTHER READING: Frank F. Chuman, *The Bamboo People*, Del Mar, Calif.: Publisher's Inc., 1976; Milton Konvitz, *The Alien and the Asiatic in American Law*, Ithaca, N.Y.: Cornell University Press, 1946; Nishimura v. United States, 142 U.S. 651, 1892.

NITOBE INAZO (1862–1933), writer and lecturer. Nitobe was born in Morioka, Japan, on September 1, 1862, into a high–ranking samurai family. His father died when he was five, but his mother, grandfather, and uncle never let him forget his samurai heritage. At an early age he sensed the importance of change in Japanese society caused by the Meiji Restoration, and he became interested in Western culture.

In 1877 Nitobe entered Sapporo Agricultural College. After being influenced by American missionaries he became a Christian. He graduated from Sapporo in 1881 and entered Tokyo Imperial University to study English and economics. In 1884 Nitobe went to Johns Hopkins University to study economics, history, and literature. Three years later he went to Germany to study statistics and agricultural economics at Halle, from which he received his Ph.D. degree in 1890. In 1891 he returned to the United States and married Mary Patterson Elkinton, a Philadelphia Quaker, with whom he returned to Japan that same year.

Because his wife was an American and because of his continuing interest in Western culture, Nitobe wanted to improve United States-Japan relations. He wrote books on Japanese culture and society for Western readers and books on American culture and society for Japanese readers. Among these are *Bushido: The Soul of Japan*, and *The Japanese Nation: Its Culture and Its Life*, both of which were written in English.

Nitobe retired from his position as Under-Secretary General of the League of Nations at the outbreak of the Manchurian incident. Although he was retired, he had not forgotten his youthful dream of "building a bridge across the Pacific." He continued to write and lecture to further East-West understanding.

When the United States passed the National Origins Act of 1924,* which excluded Japanese from the classes of people eligible to come to the United States as immigrants, Nitobe's hopes for Japanese-American understanding were jolted. He felt that this law was the reason for the increasingly aggressive posture of Japanese foreign policy. He decided not to step on American soil until it was repealed, but fear of American misunderstanding of the Japanese problem prompted him to reverse his decision, and he and his wife came to America in 1932 to lecture and explain Japanese actions to suspicious Americans. The following year he came to the Banff Conference of the Institute of Pacific Relations as head of the Japanese delegation. His death came on October 15, 1933, in Victoria, British Columbia, Canada.

FURTHER READING: Hilary Conroy and T. Scott Miyakawa, *East Across the Pacific*, Santa Barbara, Calif.: ABC-CLIO Press, 1972; George Oshiro, "He Dreamed of a Bridge Joining People of Pacific," *Asia Pacific Report*, Institute of Asian Research, University of British Columbia, Vol. 8, No. 3, 1984.

NOGUCHI ISAMU (1904-), sculptor. Noguchi was born in Los Angeles on November 17, 1904. His father was Noguchi Yone, a poet and artist, and his mother, Leonie Gilmour, was an American writer. In 1906 Noguchi moved with his parents to Tokyo where he remained for the next eleven years. There he attended Japanese and Jesuit schools. At the age of thirteen his parents sent him to a school in northern Indiana. Upon graduation he served as an apprentice to sculptor Gutzon Borglum at Stamford, Connecticut. When Borglum told him that he would never be a sculptor, he enrolled in Columbia University as a pre-med student. In 1924, however, he enrolled in Leonardo da Vinci School in New York, and after only three months, he was featured in a one-man exhibition.

In 1926, at the age of twenty-two, Noguchi won the Guggenheim Award, which enabled him to travel to Paris where he worked with Constantin Brancusi. At night he studied drawing at the Academie Grande Chaumiere. He returned to New York in 1929 and became a highly successful sculptor of bronze heads. Among his subjects were Martha Graham, Buckminster Fuller, and George Gershwin. By 1938 the young artist had been featured in several important exhibitions.

In 1942 Noguchi left New York to voluntarily intern himself at a Japanese relocation center* at Poston, Arizona. According to one of his biographers, his objective "was to help relocation by contributing his services as an artist in developing the area." When he returned to New York after six months in the camp, he wrote an article for *The New Republic* entitled "Trouble Among Japanese Americans." The article highlighted the demoralized state of Japanese

Americans interned in relocation camps, and it stressed the need for fairness in dealing with the reassimilation of these people into American society.

Noguchi has an international reputation as a sculptor. His outdoor sculptures can be found at the Associated Press Building in Rockerfeller Center, in Seattle, and on the campus of Western Washington University at Bellingham, Washington. His best known landscape is the UNESCO Gardens in Paris. He has also designed gardens for the Israeli Museums, Chase Manhattan Bank, and IBM in New York. FURTHER READING: Allen H. Eaton, *Beauty Behind Barbed Wire*, New York: Harper and Brothers, Publishers, 1952; Paul Bailey, *City in the Sun*, Los Angeles: Westernlore Press, 1971; Nancy Grove and Diane Botnick, *The Sculpture of Isamu Noguchi*, New York: Garland Publishing Co., 1980; Isamu Noguchi, "Trouble Among Japanese Americans," *New Republic* 108 (1943).

NYE-LEA BILL, signed into law by President Franklin Roosevelt on June 24, 1935, granting U.S. citizenship to 500 persons of Asian ancestry, most of whom were Japanese, who had served with the U.S. armed forces during World War I. The bill was sponsored by Congressman Clarence F. Lea of California in the House, and Senator Gerald Nye of North Dakota introduced a similar bill in the Senate. Tokutaro Slocum, who had served with the 82nd Division during World War I, went to Washington to lobby for this bill.

NYIN FO FUI KON (also called the Yin Fo Society), established in San Francisco at the turn of the century by the Hakkas,* who felt they needed an organization to protect themselves against the Puntis,* as well as against others. An organization for the Hakkas in Hawaii was organized in 1921 when a group of Hakkas decided to form their own society. The Puntis, who were more numerous than the Hakkas in Hawaii, looked down on the Hakkas. Although the society was organized in 1921, it did not have a headquarters building until 1937.
FURTHER READING: Tin-Yuke Char, ed., *The Sandalwood Mountains: Readings and Stories of the Early Chinese in Hawaii*, Honolulu: University Press of Hawaii, 1975; Clarence E. Glick, *Sojourners and Settlers: Chinese Migrants in Hawaii*, Honolulu: University Press of Hawaii, 1980.

O

OCEANIC GROUP, a group of six Japanese businessmen who arrived in San Francisco on the *Oceanic* in early 1876. Their destination was New York, where they arrived by train in March of that year. The six were Arai Ryoichiro; Morimura Toyo; Sato Momotaro; Date Chushichi, who came to America to promote trade in ceramics and art goods for the Mitsuis; Masuda Rinzo, who came to establish markets for Sayama tea, silks, and other Japanese merchandise; and Suzuki Toichi, who came to represent the Maruzen organization. (*See also* Hinode Company.)

OKADA, JOHN (1923–1971), novelist. Okada was born in Seattle in 1923 and attended public schools there before he completed his college education at the University of Washington. During World War II he was interned by the government but volunteered to serve in the U.S. armed forces. He came back to go to Columbia University, graduating in 1949 with his M. A. degree in sociology.

Okada is known for his novel, *No-No Boy*, (1957) the only book he wrote before he died of a heart attack in February 1971. The book is set in Seattle where a no-no boy, Ichiro, returned after four years of imprisonment because of his refusal to serve in the U.S. armed forces. To the Japanese community of Seattle also returned Kenji, a "yes-yes boy," who lost his leg and eventually would lose his life but was admired by people in the community for his "patriotic contributions" to the war. Ironically, a no-no boy, who refused to serve in the U.S. armed forces because the government refused to accept him and his people as its citizens, was condemned as a traitor, whereas a yes-yes boy, who volunteered to serve to prove his loyalty to a nation that had refused to accept him as equal to other citizens was regarded as a hero to be envied and admired. Acceptance by and identity with white America, no matter what price the community and its individual members had to pay, became an obsession for the Nisei.*

FURTHER READING: Elaine Kim, *Asian American Literature: An Introduction to the Writings and Their Social Context*, Philadelphia: Temple University Press, 1982; John Okada, *No-No Boy*, Rutland, Vt.: Charles E. Tuttle Co., 1957.

OKAMOTO KIYOSHI v. UNITED STATES, a case involving the conviction of seven members of the Fair Play Committee of One,* which had been organized by Okamoto Kiyoshi at Heart Mountain Relocation Camp. These seven draft resisters, who were on the Fair Play Committee's executive council, were Okamoto Kiyoshi, Horino Isamu Sam, Paul T. Nakadate, Wakaye Tsutomu, Frank Seishi Emi, Kubota Gentaro, and Tamesa Minoru, all of whom were charged with "unlawful conspiracy" to help violators of the draft. James Matsumoto Omura, English editor of the *Rocky Shimpo* was charged with the same offense.

With the exception of James Omura, who was acquitted, the seven draft violators were found guilty. Okamoto and his co-defendants then appealed to the Federal Circuit Court of Appeals, insisting that their rights specified in the First Amendment of the Constitution had been infringed on by the government. The Appeals Court reversed the Federal District Court's decision on December 16, 1945, on technical grounds of an improper jury instruction. (*See also* Fair Play Committee of One.)
FURTHER READING: Frank F. Chuman, *The Bamboo People: The Law and Japanese-Americans*, Del Mar, Calif.: Publisher's Inc., 1976; 152 F. 2nd 905, December 26, 1945.

OKEI (1852–1871), an original member of the Wakamatsu Tea and Silk Farm Colony,* who died of fever at the age of nineteen. The stone over her grave reads: "In Memory of Okei, died in 1871, age 19 years, a Japanese girl." (*See also* Wakamatsu Tea and Silk Farm Colony.)

OKIMURA KIYOKURA v. ACHESON, SECRETARY OF STATE, a 1952 case involving the revocation of citizenship of an American-born Japanese who served in the Japanese Army and voted in a Japanese election. Until World War II, it was customary for Japanese immigrant parents to send their American-born children to Japan for their education. These children were called Kibei.* During the Pacific War many of these children of Japanese immigrant parents were stranded in Japan. Some of them were inducted into the Japanese Army, and others were forced into activities against their will. The U.S. government revoked the citizenship of those Americans of Japanese ancestry who had served in the Japanese Army or had voted in the Japanese elections.

One of these individuals was Okimura Kiyokura, born in 1921 of Japanese parents in Kauai, Hawaii. He was sent to Japan by his parents for his education at the age of four and stayed in Japan until 1932 when he returned to Hawaii. After two years in Hawaii, he went back to Japan in order to study Japanese so that he could teach in a Japanese language school in Hawaii. He only had a Hawaiian certificate of citizenship issued by the U.S. Immigration and Naturalization Service in accordance with regulations. He did not register in

Japan as an American citizen with any U.S. consul. In 1939 Okimura's classmates, who were also U.S. citizens, returned to the United States to avoid the Japanese military conscription law, and Okimura had planned to return with them. His parents, however, wanted him to stay so that he could complete his education. In order to satisfy his parents' wishes, he attended Japanese middle school and normal school. Upon graduation he was ordered to take a teaching job in Miwa because his education at the normal school was subsidized by the Japanese government which had the right to assign him to a teaching position.

In June 1942 Okimura was asked to report for a Japanese Army physical examination. He took the physical fearing imprisonment by the military police if he did not. He tried to excuse himself by claiming his U.S. citizenship but was called an "ideological criminal." In 1942 Okimura was inducted into the Japanese Army and served in China until he was captured in August 1945. In 1946 he returned to Japan, which was then under American military rule. His hopes of becoming a Japanese language teacher were frustrated by the war, and so he decided to become a Buddhist monk, receiving training for a year in Japan. In Japan there was an intensive program by occupation authorities to encourage Japanese to participate in elections, and Okimura voted in the 1947 election. In 1949 Okimura was ready to return to Hawaii as a Buddhist monk and applied for a U.S. passport. He was denied on the grounds that he had lost his citizenship by having served in the Japanese Army and having voted in Japanese elections. This decision was in accordance with Section 801 (c) and (e) of Title 8, United States Code, which states:

> A person who is a national of the United States, whether by birth or naturalization, shall lose his nationality by: (c) Entering, or serving in, the armed forces of a foreign state unless expressly authorized by the laws of the United States, if he has or acquires the nationality of such foreign state; or
> (d)Voting in a political election in a foreign state or participating in an election or plebiscite to determine the sovereignty over foreign territory.

Through his lawyers, Okimura argued that Congress did not have power to revoke the citizenship of an American born in America because of service in the Japanese Army and voting in an election in Japan. The District Court stated that Congress had plenary power over citizenship by naturalization but no power to interfere with U.S. citizenship by birth. The only way a citizen could destroy his or her citizenship by birth was to undergo a foreign procedure equivalent to the U.S. system of naturalization. The District Court also stated that Congress could not devise ways of losing citizenship that had no relationship to how it was acquired. It concluded that the government's justification for denying Okimura his citizenship was unconstitutional, and the petition was granted. On October 6, 1952, and April 14, 1953, the defendant, Secretary of State Dean Acheson, took a direct appeal to the Supreme Court. The Supreme Court remanded the case and asked for additional information, which was filed on October 6, 1952, and amended April 14, 1953. The additional information did not affect the prior decision. Judge Gerald McLaughlin, representing the District Court, ruled in favor of Okimura and stated that the specific findings of fact in regard to Okimura were made available as directed by the Supreme Court.

FURTHER READING: Frank F. Chuman, *The Bamboo People*, Del Mar, Calif.: Publisher's Inc., 1976.

OLSON, CULBERT L. (1876–1962), Governor of California. Olson was born in Fillmore, Utah, on November 7, 1876, to Daniel and Delilah (King) Olson. He grew up in Utah and attended Brigham Young University between 1890 and 1891 and again between 1893 and 1895. He studied law at Columbian Law School, Washington, D.C., between 1897 and 1899 and received an LL.B. degree from the school in 1901. He was admitted to the Utah bar in 1901 and began his practice in Salt Lake City, Utah. He continued his private law practice in Salt Lake City until 1920, when he decided to move to California where he served as California State senator from 1934 to 1938. He ran for the office of governor of California and was elected on November 8, 1938, when he defeated incumbent Republican Governor Frank F. Merriam. He was sworn into office on January 2, 1939, and served until 1942 when he was defeated by Republican Earl Warren.*

Immediately after the bombing of Pearl Harbor, Olson summoned leaders of the Japanese American community on the West Coast to Sacramento and suggested that they accept his evacuation plan. The plan involved sending all Japanese males to inland concentration camps where they would stay at night but would go out by day to work on farms in order to continue California's food production.

Although a few of the leaders thought that Olson's plan was worthy of their serious consideration, most of them were outraged by his suggestion and asked him to provide Japanese Americans with police protection. The meeting broke up with no progress. When all persons of Japanese ancestry were ordered evacuated from the West Coast, he did not oppose the evacuation order.

In May 1942 Olson wrote a letter to President Franklin Roosevelt expressing concern about the disruption in education of the college-age Nisei.* This letter was answered by President Roosevelt, who directed his assistants to develop a plan to accommodate the educational needs of the college-bound Nisei. (*See also* National Student Relocation Council.)

FURTHER READING: Bill Hosokawa, *JACL in Quest of Justice*, New York: William Morrow and Co., 1982; Bill Hosokawa, *Nisei*, New York: William Morrow and Co., 1969; H. Brett Melendy and Benjamin F. Gilbert, *The Governors of California*, Georgetown, Calif.: Talisman Press, 1965.

ON, one of the Japanese cultural norms which means "ascribed obligation or duties one has because of what he is, not because of what he has accomplished." One has obligations as son, father, teacher, or pupil. It is believed that the deity has dispensed blessings (*on*), and it is up to each individual to pay back the blessings he or she has received. It is suggested that children in Japanese culture are strongly admonished to develop this sense of obligation to family and community by means of *on*.

FURTHER READING: Harry H. L. Kitano, *Japanese Americans*, Englewood Cliffs, N.J.: Prentice-Hall, 1969; Minako K. Maykovich, *Japanese American Identity Dilemma*, Tokyo, Japan: Waseda University Press, 1972; Dennis M. Ogawa, *Kodomo no tame ni* (For the Sake of the Children), Honolulu: University Press of Hawaii, 1978; Toshio Yatsushiro, *Politics and Cultural Values: The World War II Japanese Relocation Centers and the United States Government*, New York: Arno Press, 1978.

ON LEE v. UNITED STATES, a case argued before the U.S. Supreme Court on April 24, 1952, and decided on June 2, 1952. The case of On Lee v. the United States involved not only the illegal sale of opium, but also the question of the legality of the search and seizure techniques used in obtaining evidence against the defendant, On Lee.

The defendant, On Lee, was convicted in the U.S. District Court for the Southern District of New York of making an illegal opium sale. The case was appealed and brought before the Supreme Court because of the question of unlawful search and seizure.

The defendant owned a laundry business in Hoboken. An old acquaintance and former employee of On Lee, Chin Poy, was an undercover agent for the Bureau of Narcotics. Upon On Lee's request, Chin Poy entered Lee's establishment and engaged Lee in conversation. At that time, Lee made incriminating statements dealing with the sale of opium, but, unknown to Lee, Chin Poy had a small microphone in his coat pocket and was transmitting their conversation to an agent of the Bureau of Narcotics, Lawrence Lee. A few days later, Lee and Poy met on the street, and again On Lee made incriminating statements. During the trial the defendant maintained that the search and seizure process was unlawful, according to the Fourth Amendment of the Constitution. He claimed that the use of listening devices was illegal, and therefore the evidence received from the transmission was inadmissible.

Justice Robert Jackson, in delivering the majority opinion of the divided Court, stated that justice was better served if the methods used in obtaining evidence were questioned not on the basis of law, but on issues of credibility. But Justice William O. Douglas, in his dissenting opinion, cautioned his colleagues against men willing to encroach on basic freedoms guaranteed by the Constitution out of "zeal and well-meaning, but without understanding." Justice Felix Frankfurter, with whom Justice Harold Burton concurred, stated in his dissenting opinion that such questionable methods of collecting evidence were nothing but "encouragement to lazy, immoral conduct by the police," and it did not "bode well for effective law enforcement."

Later, Chin Poy recanted his testimony in a signed affidavit in which he admitted that no such incriminating conversation took place, but On Lee was denied a new trial.

FURTHER READING: Stanford Lyman, *Chinese Americans*, New York: Random House, 1974; *Supreme Court Reporter* 72, 343, U.S. 747.

ONUKI HACHIRO (1849–1921), businessman. Onaki was born in Japan and came to America with a group of American naval cadets, who probably had smuggled him into their ship. He arrived in Boston in 1876 and later moved to Phoenix, Arizona, where, in 1886, he received a franchise from the city of Phoenix to supply the city with "Illuminating gas or electric light or both." Between 1876 and 1886 he changed his Japanese name to Hutchlon Ohnick and married Catherine Shannon in 1888.

His enterprise became a huge success, and in 1901 he moved to Seattle where he started the Oriental American Bank with two other Issei.* The bank was later purchased by Furuya Masajiro.* (*See also* Furuya Masajiro.)

OPERATION BABY LIFT, originally suggested by American ambassador to Saigon Graham Martin to President Thieu of South Vietnam in 1975 as a means of gaining American support. Thieu agreed to airlift 2,000 Vietnamese orphans, and they began to be airlifted on April 4, 1975. During the operation a World Airways C–5A crashed, killing 150 orphans and 50 adults. Operation Babylift was a purely political decision made by high government officials from the two governments in order to gain American public support for the continuing war effort by easing America's guilt about the war. It was characterized as a humanitarian act that would "offer new hope for the living," as President Gerald Ford put it, but little advanced planning was done to bring the operation to its successful conclusion. In fact, it could be said that more planning was done for Operation Gold Lift, through which the $70 million private fortune of President Thieu and Lon Nol was secretly transported from Vietnam to Switzerland.
FURTHER READING: Shana Alexander, "A Sentimental Binge," *Newsweek*, April 18, 1975; "BabyLift," *Commonweal*, May 9, 1975; Gloria Emerson, "Operation Babylift," *New Republic*, April 26, 1975; "Ford Saddened by Crash," *Department of State Bulletin*, April 28, 1975; "Let the Children Come," *Saturday Review*, May 17, 1975.

OPIUM WAR, 1840–1842, the war fought between the Ch'ing Dynasty of China and Britain over the conflict on opium trade, or the "Poison Trade" as it was commonly called in those days (in contrast to the "Pig Trade," which was selling Chinese coolies to plantation owners in the Western Hemisphere who were in need of cheap labor to replace black slaves).

The Chinese defeat in this war resulted in a number of drastic changes that finally brought about the end of the dynasty. Internally, the Ch'ing court showed its deep suspicion of its own people, who learned of the rampant corruption of government officials in high places. Internationally, China was forced to open its ports to Western nations through unequal treaties, of which terms were dictated to her, thus becoming vulnerable to the colonial and imperialistic trade policies of capitalist nations. China exposed to the outside world its military weakness and social degeneration, and Western nations descended to prey on the country. When China was found to be incapable of defending its own people, Chinese were kidnapped off the streets of their own towns and hamlets to be shipped to California gold mines or sugar plantations in the Caribbean.

The opium-producing poppy was first introduced to China by the Turks and Arabs in the late seventh century, and by the eighteenth century, the Chinese habit of burning opium extract over a lamp and inhaling its fumes through a pipe had spread throughout China. Alarmed by this development, an imperial edict was issued in 1729 to prohibit the domestic sales and consumption of opium, and 1796 importation and domestic cultivation of opium were also banned. In spite of these measures taken by the Ch'ing court, the opium trade grew as Portugal, East India, and Britain continued to export opium to China. In 1821 the Ch'ing government took strict prohibition measures, but the opium smuggling continued on an ever increasing scale.

In 1834 the British government appointed Charles Elliot as chief superintendent. Elliot was instructed to establish diplomatic relations with the Ch'ing government and to demonstrate aggressive policies to have more Chinese ports open to the opium trade. When none of the demands he placed before China was satisfied, Elliot reported that a war between Britain and China was imminent and that China would have to bear the entire responsibility for it.

In March 1839 High Commissioner Lin Tsu-hsu, who had been appointed by the government in Peking to "investigate port affairs" (a Chinese euphemism for stamping out opium trade) confiscated opium. He ordered 20,000 chests of opium destroyed in June of that year, thus showing his determination to eradicate the Poison Trade. In response to Lin's drastic measures, Elliot pushed ahead with plans for an aggressive war, and he repeatedly urged his government to start a war. An incident that occurred at a little village of Chien-sha-tsui on July 1939 became a catalyst for a number of naval skirmishes between the British Navy and Chinese Navy. These little wars fought during the latter part of 1839 were a prelude to the war between the two nations.

In January 1840 High Commissioner Lin ordered the port of Canton closed, and in June 1840 British naval forces began to arrive off the Kwangtung coast ready for an invasion attempt. Because the Kwangtung coast was well defended, the British sailed north to attack Amoy, although it was also well defended. On July 2, the British reached Tinghai and captured it on July 5. Other forts fell to the British invading forces during that year, and by the end of May of the following year, the British forces had surrounded Canton. The Chinese were forced to sign the Peace Convention of Canton, as dictated by the British.

The war was resumed in 1841 when Chinese peasants attacked the British forces in the small village of San-yuan-li. The British forces swiftly retaliated and attacked China and won the battle on October 10, 1841. Three days later Ningpo fell to the British. The decisive battle that sealed China's fate occurred in March 1842 when Chinese forces were soundly defeated at Chinkiang. The fall of Chinkiang on July 21, 1842, forced the Ch'ing court to negotiate for peace for two reasons. First, it did not want Britain to continue further into the Yangtze Valley for fear of dividing the country in two. Second, the government was afraid of a revolt from the Chinese people against the government.

At the end of the hostilities, on August 29, 1842, the signing of the Sino-British Treaty of Nanking marked the beginning of the end of the mighty Manchu Empire. This treaty was followed by other unequal treaties which China was forced to conclude with the United States and France. Riding on the coattails of the British success, the United States decided to take advantage of the defeated and decrepit China and to force an unequal treaty on the country. Caleb Cushing was sent to China to represent American interests, but China did not desire another unequal treaty. Cushing then threatened China with war, which China did not want. China was forced to conclude a treaty with the United States at the small village of Wanghia, outside Macao. The Americans condemned the opium trade as contraband in the treaty and promised not to give any protection to opium traffickers, but in 1858 one-fifth of all the opium entering China was carried by American ships.

The Opium War also served as a catalyst for creating anti-Chinese feelings in the United States. The unfavorable image of China created in the minds of the American people, who were also influenced by other negative stereotypes of Chinese, led finally to the congressional action taken against Chinese in the form of the Chinese Exclusion Act of 1882.*

FURTHER READING: Jack Beeching, *The Chinese Opium War*, New York: Harcourt Brace Jovanovich, 1975; J. Chesneax, M. Bastid, and M. Bergere, *China, From the Opium War to the 1911 Revolution*, New York: Pantheon Press, 1976; Peter Ward Fay, *The Opium War, 1840–1842*, Chapel Hill: University of North Carolina Press, 1975; Rodney Gilbert, *The Unequal Treaties: China and the Foreigner*, London: John Murray, Albermarle Street W., 1929; P. C. Kuo, *A Critical Study of the First Anglo-Chinese War*, Westport, Conn.: Hyperion Press, 1973; C. Miller, *The Unwelcome Immigrant*, Berkeley: University of California Press, 1969; Ssu-yu Teng, *Chang Hsi and the Treaty of Nanking, 1842*, Chicago: University of Chicago Press, 1944.

OPUKAHAIA. *See* Hopu, Thomas.

ORGANIC ACT OF GUAM, a bill passed by the U.S. Congress on August 1, 1950, conferring U.S. citizenship on the inhabitants of the Territory of Guam. This meant that Guamanians would be able to move to the United States without restrictions. As of 1978 there were approximately 20,000 Guamanians in Los Angeles alone. No accurate census data on Guamanian immigrants to the United States are available today as they have not been identified as a separate ethnic or racial group in the U.S. method of collecting census data.

FURTHER READING: F. P. King, ed., *Oceania and Beyond: Essays on the Pacific Since 1945*, Westport, Conn.: Greenwood Press, 1976; Faye Untalan Munoz, *An Exploratory Study of Island Migration: Chamorrow of Guam*, Ann Arbor, Mich.: University Microfilms International, 1979.

ORGANIC ACT OF 1900, a bill signed by President William McKinley on April 30, 1900, thus incorporating Hawaii as a Territory of the United States and creating the territorial government. Under the constitution spelled out by Congress of the United States, Hawaii was to govern itself for the next sixty years. The Organic Act brought mixed blessings to Hawaii. On one hand, it brought education, sanitation, welfare, safety, highways, and public works which were under the governor's control. On the other hand, it created some new political and labor problems. First, the Organic Act gave native Hawaiians the right to vote as citizens of the United States, although persons of Asian ancestry were deprived of this privilege. This played havoc on the political system of Hawaii which had been under the control of the white oligarchy. Second, the Organic Act made contract labor illegal. As a result, while the Organic Act was being debated in Congress, between 1898 and 1900 the Hawaiian Sugar Planters' Association* brought some 40,000 Japanese laborers, 26,000 of whom came in 1899. This was done to forestall any possible labor shortage.

FURTHER READING: A. Grove Day, *Hawaii and Its People*, New York: Duell, Sloan and Pearce, 1955; Lawrence H. Fuchs, *Hawaii Pono: A Social History*, New York: Harcourt, Brace, and World, 1961; Wayne Patterson, *The Korean Frontier in America: Immigration to Hawaii, 1896–1910*, Ann Arbor, Mich.: University Microfilms International, 1977; Theon Wright, *The Disenchanted Isles: The Story of the Second Revolution in Hawaii*, New York: Dial Press, 1972.

ORIENTAL AMERICAN BANK. *See* Furuya Masajiro; Onuki Hachiro.

ORIENTAL FOOD PRODUCTS OF CALIFORNIA, a company established by Peter Hyon in 1926 in Los Angeles that produced twenty–seven different canned Oriental foods by 1939. Its assets in 1958 were estimated at $2 million. It now operates under a different name, the Jan-U Wine Food Corporation.

ORIENTAL TRADING COMPANY (TOYO BOEKI KAISHA), established by Yamaoka Ototake in Seattle, Washington, in 1898, importing Japanese laborers to the Puget Sound area on the West Coast of the United States. Yamaoka was said to make frequent trips to his native Shizuoka Prefecture where he recruited Japanese laborers and issued fradulent passports to them.

OVERSEAS CHINESE MERCHANTS' ASSOCIATION (also known as the Wah Kiu Seong Wui in Chinese), established in 1911 by those Chinese in Hawaii who followed the leadership of Dr. Sun Yat-sen.* This association was created in response to the establishment of the Chinese Merchants' Association, or Chung Wah Chung Seong Wui, which was later renamed the Chinese Chamber of Commerce.* When Yuan Shih-k'ai took over the reins of power in China, his government recognized the Chung Wah Chung Seong Wui and ignored the Wah Kiu Seong Wui. Therefore, the Overseas Chinese Merchants' Association was dissolved.

OYAMA v. CALIFORNIA, a case involving an escheat action taken by the State of California against the property owned by Fred Y. Oyama, the son of Oyama Kajiro, who had purchased real property and had it registered under his son's name. He became a guardian of his son, who was a miner at the time the property was purchased in 1934. The case was argued before the U.S. Supreme Court on October 22, 1947, and was decided on January 19, 1948.

The case reached the nation's highest Court on writ of certiorari to the Supreme Court of California, which had upheld the Alien Land Act of California, 1913,* as constitutional in 1946. Petitioners Fred Y. Oyama and Oyama Kajiro challenged the constitutionality of California's Alien Land Law on the grounds that it deprived Fred Y. Oyama, a U.S. citizen, of the equal protection of the laws and of his citizen's privileges; it deprived Oyama Kajiro of equal protection of the laws; and it violated the due process clause.

Chief Justice Frederick Vinson delivered the opinion of the Court, with Justices Robert Jackson, Stanley Reed, and Harold Burton dissenting. Justice Vinson in his opinion stated that when there is a conflict between the rights of the state to formulate a policy of land holding in its bounds and an American citizen's right to hold land anywhere in the United States, the rights of the citizen may not be infringed on because of his or her ancestry. Justice Hugo Black, with whom Justice William O. Douglas concurred, stated that because America was committed to observance of the United Nations' Charter to promote "fundamental freedoms for all without distinction as to race, sex, language, or religion," it was incumbent on the United States to faithfully carry out its pledge before the international community. The Supreme Court reversed the decision of the Supreme Court of California and held California's Alien Land Act to be unconstitutional.

FURTHER READING: Frank F. Chuman, *The Bamboo People*, Del Mar, Calif.; Publisher's Inc., 1976; Robert A. Wilson and Bill Hosokawa, *East to America*, New York: William Morrow and Co., 1980; *Supreme Court Reporter* 68, 332 U.S. 633.

OZAWA SEIJI (1935–), conductor and musical director. Ozawa was born in Hoten, Manchuria, on September 1, 1935, to Japanese parents, Kaisaku and Sakura Ozawa. He was their third son. His family moved to Tokyo in 1944, where he began to receive private piano lessons. In 1953 he was accepted as a student at Toho School of Music, which offered training in the European and American musical traditions. Graduating from the school in 1959, he demonstrated his future potential when he conducted the Japan Radio Orchestra and the Japan Philharmonic Orchestra. He was named the outstanding talent for the year by a music magazine, *Friends of Music*.

In 1960 he left Japan for study in Europe. He studied with Eugene Bigot in France and with Herbert von Karajan in Berlin. While in Europe he entered the International Competition for Young Orchestra Conductors at Besançon, France, and won first prize. In the United States during the same year, he won the Koussevitsky Memorial Scholarship for Conducting at the Berkshire Music Center in Lenox, Massachusetts.

He was offered one of the three assistant conductor positions for the 1961–62 season and made his debut with the New York Philharmonic Orchestra on April 14, 1961. He was named the sole assistant conductor for the 1964–65 season and the following year was appointed permanent conductor for the Toronto Symphony Orchestra. He served in that capacity until the end of the 1969 season and moved to Boston to become music director of the Boston Symphony Orchestra. He has been serving in that position since 1970.

OZAWA TAKAO v. UNITED STATES, was a case involving a Japanese citizen, Ozawa Takao, a graduate of a high school in Berkeley California, who later became a student of the University of California. He applied for U.S. citizenship on October 16, 1914, but was denied. Subsequently, the case reached the nation's highest Court on writ of certiorari to the Circuit Court of Appeals for the Ninth Circuit. The case was argued on October 3 and 4, and it was decided on November 13, 1922. Justice George Sutherland, in an opinion for the unanimous court, held that Ozawa was ineligible to become a U.S. citizen because of his race. According to his reason, the naturalization act adopted in 1790 granted U.S. citizenship to any alien "being a free white person." After the Civil War, this provision was changed to include aliens of African nativity and of African descent. Furthermore, Congress passed a bill entitled An Act to Establish a Bureau of Immigration and Naturalization, and to Provide for a Uniform Rule for the Naturalization of Aliens Throughout the United States, Section 2169 of Title XXX, which specified that provisions for citizenship apply to aliens, being "free white persons, and to aliens of African nativity and to persons of African descent." Because Ozawa was neither white nor African, he was ruled ineligible for U.S. citizenship.
FURTHER READING: Frank F. Chuman, *The Bamboo People*, Del Mar, Calif.: Publisher's Inc., 1976; Milton R. Konvitz, *The Alien and the Asiatic in American Law*, Ithaca, N.Y.: Cornell University Press, 1946; *Supreme Court Reporter* 43, 260 U.S. 178.

P

PACIFIC CITIZEN, THE, a monthly newspaper published in San Francisco and adopted by the Japanese American Citizens League* in 1932 as its official national publication. Since then, *The Pacific Citizen* has undergone some major changes both in terms of its format as well as editorship. Larry Tajiri and Harry Honda have served *The Pacific Citizen* as editors. Today, *The Pacific Citizen* is published as a weekly, and its headquarters is located at 125 Weller Street, Los Angeles.

PACIFIC MAIL STEAMSHIP COMPANY, a company that provided steamship service on the Pacific Coast. A bill to incorporate the Pacific Mail Steamship Company was introduced to the New York State Senate on April 1, 1848, and three days later it was approved. On April 12, the New York Assembly approved the bill, thus enabling William Aspinwall to create steamship service on the Pacific Coast. The company was incorporated with the capital stock of $500,000 divided into 500 shares, and its president, William Aspinwall, was to receive 2.5 percent of all receipts from all sources at home and abroad. The company was successful in obtaining an annual government subsidy of $348,250 in exchange for mail service on the Pacific Coast. It prospered during the next two years as the company's capital stock increased from $500,000 to $2 million.

Fifteen years later, a mail contract was obtained to open a steamship service to Japan and China from the United States by way of Panama, and service began on January 1, 1867. This expansion came as a result of the preparations for the completion of the transcontinental railway which would curtail its business conducted by way of Panama.

As early as February 1852, the company expressed its interest in establishing steamship service between San Francisco and Honolulu. Its agent inquired about the possibility of acquiring two lots on the Honolulu waterfront for a line of steamers that would run between California and China, and between San Francisco and Honolulu.

The Pacific Mail Steamship Company ran its first service on January 1, 1867, when its steamer, the *Colorado*, sailed from San Francisco for China. This was made possible by a bill passed by Congress in 1865 under the title An Act to Authorize the Establishment of Ocean Mail-Steamship Service between the United States and China, and the government awarded the contract to the Pacific Mail Steamship Company with an annual subsidy of not over $500,000. Later, in March 1867, Congress enriched the annual subsidy by adding $75,000 in order to attract a steamship service between San Francisco and Honolulu. The Pacific Mail Steamship Company provided the service beginning on April 27, 1873, when its steamer, the *Costa Rica*, arrived in Honolulu from San Francisco on that day.

Ten years later, in 1883, the Pacific Mail Steamship Company was one of two lines allowed to bring Chinese laborers to Hawaii by the government of Hawaii, and the number of Chinese allowed to come was not to exceed 600 in any three-month period. After that time, the Pacific Mail Steamship Company became the largest company carrying Chinese immigrants to the United States and Hawaii. It was said that as many as 1,400 Chinese would be carried by a company's ship in its steerage, along with other passengers.

FURTHER READING: Jack Chen, *The Chinese of America*, New York: Harper and Row, 1980; John H . Kemble, *The Panama Route, 1848–1969*, New York: Da Capo Press, 1972; John H. Kemble, "The Genesis of the Pacific Mail Steamship Company," *California Historical Society Quarterly*, Vol. 13, no. 3, (1934) pp. 240–254, No 4, (1934), pp. 386–406, Ralph S.Kuykendall, *The Hawaiian Kingdom, 1854–1874: Twenty Critical Years*, Honolulu: University of Hawaii Press, 1953; Ralph S. Kuykendall, *The Hawaiian Kingdom, 1874–1893: The Kalakaua Dynasty*, Honolulu: University of Hawaii Press, 1967.

PAK YONG-MAN (1881–1928), advocate of military means to free Korea from Japan. Pak was born in Kangwon Province, Korea, and came to the United States for his studies in October 1904. He went to Lincoln, Nebraska, for his English education in preparation for his study at an institution of higher learning. Later, he majored in political science at the University of Nebraska, graduating in 1910. While he was a student at the university, he established the Korean Youth Military Academy at Hastings, Nebraska, and upon graduation, he moved to Hawaii in December 1912 when he was invited to become editor of the *National Herald*. The following year he consolidated all the existing military training programs in Hawaii into the Korean National Brigade, which was officially created on August 29, 1914. This military unit had about 311 cadets under training to engage in the military struggle against Japan for the liberation of Korea.

Pak was a strong advocate of Korea's liberation from Japan by military means. Opposed to him was Syngman Rhee,* who believed that such a strategy for gaining Korea's independence from powerful Japan was unrealistic. This disagreement between Pak and Rhee was the beginning of factionalism among Koreans in the United States.

Pak was assassinated in Peking on October 17, 1928, by an agent allegedly hired by Kim Won-bong, who had established the Korean Volunteer Corps in China. (*See also* Korean National Revolutionary Party.)

PANYU (PUNYU). *See* Sam Yap (Sze–I); Pearl River Delta.

PAO-HUANG HUI (Society to Protect the Emperor), established in Japan among the overseas Chinese by K'ang Yu-wei* after he and Liang Ch'i-ch'ao* escaped from China to Japan in 1898. When K'ang Yu-wei came to Canada to raise money for his reformist activities, he organized the Chinese in Victoria, British Columbia, where the society was established in July 1899. The Society was organized mainly to overthrow the conservative government, led by the Empress Dowager, by assassinating her and restoring Emperor Kuang-hsu to found a constitutional government. For this cause K'ang traveled to many nations where overseas Chinese were found to raise money for his political programs. Liang Ch'i-ch'ao, a student of K'ang and his co-worker for the society, came to Hawaii in 1899 and campaigned for the society in order to raise money and support. The society was supposedly established in Maui, and it was led by Dr. Sun Yat-sen's* brother, Sun Mei, who was introduced by Sun Yat–Sen. Liang was able to raise $90,000 from the local Chinese communities.

Members of the society in Hawaii applied for a charter of incorporation to the territorial government, but they were refused. When the Society decided to assist in founding a newspaper, the *Sun Chung Kwock Bo* (New China News), an office became available for the society's activities. The Society's name was later changed to Dai Kwock Hin Jing Wui, or Constitutional Monarchy Society, which was incorporated as a charitable society under the laws of the Territory of Hawaii in 1908. (*See also* K'ang Yu-wei; Liang Ch'i-ch'ao; and Sun Yat-sen.)

FURTHER READING: Hao Chang, *Liang Ch'i-ch'ao and Intellectual Tradition in China, 1890–1907*, Cambridge, Mass.: Harvard University Press, 1971; Clarence E. Glick, *Sojourners and Settlers: Chinese Migrants in Hawaii*, Honolulu: University Press of Hawaii, 1980; Philip C. Huang, *Liang Ch'i-ch'ao and Modern Chinese Liberalism*, Seattle: University of Washington Press, 1972; Jung-Pang Lo, *K'ang Yu-wei; A Biography and a Symposium*, Tucson: University of Arizona Press, 1967.

PAPALAGI, (prounced pahLONG–ee), a Samoan term for Caucasians meaning "sky burster."

PAPER SONS (or slot cases). Paper sons were fabricated by those who wanted to sell fraudulent certificates to Chinese willing to pay for their entry into the United States. Paper sons were Chinese who would come to the United States as sons born abroad of Chinese fathers, who were citizens of the United States and therefore were allowed to bring their sons under the legal provisions made on February 1, 1855. This law existed until 1934, when it was changed to require that the citizen-father be a resident of the United States for at least ten years before the birth of the children, who then could claim derivative citizenship. This privilege of Chinese who were citizens of the United States was abused in fabricating sons who were legal only on paper. The U.S. government responded to this scheme by creating blood tests of "paper sons" to determine whether they were real children of their fathers as they claimed. (*See also* Lee Kum Hoy, Lee kum Cherk, and Lee Moon Wah v. John L. Murff.)

PARIS, TREATY OF (1898), signed on December 10, 1898, between the United States and Spain, thus terminating the war fought between the two nations. The treaty made the Philippine Islands part of the United States and declared their inhabitants U.S. nationals, who owed allegiance to the United States without having privileges of U.S. citizenship. The treaty was ratified by the U.S. Senate on February 6, 1899.

PARIS-PARIS (also known as "pareja-pareja"), a term meaning paring off. It was used by Filipino workers in Hawaii who, lacking steerage fare to get their wives to join them, had them pose as wives of new recruiters, who were allowed to bring a wife and two children at the expense of the Hawaiian Sugar Planters' Association.* In the 1930's the steerage fare between Manila and Honolulu was $84.50, plus $5 tax for an adult.

PARROTT'S CHINESE CASE. *See In re* Tibercio Parrott.

PASS BOOK SYSTEM, a system used by Hawaiian plantation managers to prevent sugar plantation laborers from uniting to make demands for wage increases. This system was used in order to curtail the number of laborers leaving plantations as the Organic Act* abolishing contract labor went into effect on June 14, 1900. (*See also* Organic Act of 1900).

PAYNE-ALDRICH TARIFF ACT, a bill signed into law on August 5, 1909, allowing free trade between the Philippine Islands and the United States. Prior to passage of this law, the existing tariff laws of the United States were applied to articles brought to the continental ports of the United States from the Philippine Islands. On the same day, the Philippine Tariff Act went into effect, and these two acts were used to regulate trade between the United States and the Philippine Islands. Later, on October 3, 1913, the Underwood-Simmons Act was passed to supersede the Payne-Aldrich Tariff Act, thus establishing complete free trade by eliminating the quota limitations on sugar and tobacco.

PEARL RIVER DELTA, an area about 2,900 square miles in size formed by the joining of the three major rivers in the Province of Kwangtung, China, namely, the West River, the East River, and the North River. The West and North rivers come together about fifty miles west of Canton, whereas the East River meets them at Whampoa, a traditional Chinese trade port, where the French signed a treaty with China in 1844 at the end of the First Opium War. The Pearl River, which originates from the district of Sanshwui, meets the three rivers at Whampoa and forms a large estuary about fifty miles in length before it empties into the South China Sea.

In this delta were located twelve districts grouped into two administrative prefectures of the Kwangtung Province, one of the most populous provinces of China. The province's population in 1787 was estimated at 16,014,000, a number that grew to 28,182,000 by 1850, a net gain of 75.6 percent. This exponential population growth put a great deal of pressure on the available agricultural land. The Sze Yap (Sze-I)* region, in particular, where four districts—Enping (Yangping), Kaiping (Hoiping), Xinhui (Sunwai), and Taishan or Hsinning (Sinning)—are located, had only limited land for agricultural use. The region surrounded by mountains on three sides was hilly, rocky, and unproductive, with only 10 percent of land arable. Living in these districts were three groups of people: the Punti,* or natives of the region; the Hakka,* or guests who migrated to the region from northern China; and the Tanka,* or the "boat people." These people spoke the same dialect which was intelligible only to them. Because of their rural backgrounds and dialect, they were considered inferior by the residents of Sam Yap* or Three Districts, which included Nanhai (Namhoi), Panyu (Punyu), and Shunde (Shuntak), which surrounded the city of Canton, the provincial center.

A number of sociocultural and economic factors drove these people out of their land to countries in Southeast Asia and ultimately to the United States. It is claimed that villagers from Sze Yap, especially from the Hsinning District, outnumbered Chinese immigrants from all other districts in China. (*See also* District Companies.)

FURTHER READING: Gunther Barth, *Bitter Strength*, Cambridge, Mass.: Harvard University Press, 1964; H. Brett Melendy, *The Oriental Americans*, Boston: Twayne Publishers, 1972; George B. Cressey, *China's Geographical Foundations*, New York: McGraw–Hill, 1934; Ping-ti Ho, *Studies on the Population of China, 1368–1953*, Cambridge, Mass.: Harvard University Press, 1959; Kil Young Zo, *Chinese Emigration into the United States, 1850–1880*, New York: Arno Press, 1978.

PEI, IEOH MING (1917–), architect. Pei, was born in Canton, China, on April 26, 1917, the son of a banker, and grew up in Shanghai where he attended St. John's Middle School. He came to the United States in 1935 to study architecture at the Massachusetts Institute of Technology, from which he received his Bachelor's in Architecture in 1940. In 1946 he received his Master's in Architecture from Harvard Graduate School of Design. He stayed at Harvard as instructor but left to join Webb and Knapp, Inc., where he served as director of architecture. In 1954 he became a naturalized citizen of the United States, and the following year he established his own architectural firm, I. M. Pei and Partners in New York.

Pei has established an astonishing list of accomplishments in the field of architecture. The Mile High Center in Denver, Colorado, was designed by Pei and was built in 1956, and in 1964 he was given the assignment of designing the John F. Kennedy Library built in Cambridge, Massachusetts. All in all, his firm has designed over fifty major buildings, including several of the largest civic and corporate constructions of the 1970's.

Pei was awarded the Gold Medal from the American Institute of Architects in 1979.

PENSIONADO ACT OF 1903, approved by the Philippine Commission on August 26, 1903, under the Taft Administration. The act, which went into operation in November of that year, enabled young Filipinos to come to America for their training and education at various institutions of higher learning at government expense. The first 100 students were selected from 20,000 applicants, and they were placed in American homes to learn about life in the United States. Their fields of study were education, engineering, agriculture, and medicine. By 1907 there were 183 Filipinos enrolled in 47 schools and colleges. At the end of their education in 1910, all *pensionados* returned to assume important positions in the Philippine Islands under American control.

PEOPLE v. DOWNER, a case that went to the Supreme Court of California as an appeal from the District Court of the Twelfth Judicial District on behalf of the people, who had been denied the right to collect $12,750 as passenger tax from the owner of the ship, Stephen Baldwin, which brought 250 Chinese from Hong Kong. According to the Passenger Tax, or the Act of 1855, as it was officially called, a tax of $50 was to be imposed on every person arriving in the State of California by sea who was not able to become a U.S. citizen.

Justice Solomon Heydenfeldt, in delivering his opinion for the court, with which Justice Hugh Murray* concurred, declared the Act of 1855 approved by the State of California unconstitutional on the grounds that Congress had exclusive power to regulate commerce with foreign nations. This ruling by the Supreme Court of California dealt a severe blow to Chinese exclusionists, who were then compelled to seek other means of excluding Chinese from the United States.
FURTHER READING: Mary R. Coolidge, *Chinese Immigration*, New York: Henry Holt and Co., 1909; 7 Cal. 169, January 1857.

PEOPLE v. GEORGE W. HALL, a case that involved George W. Hall, who had been convicted of murder, on the basis of testimony given by Chinese witnesses. He appealed on the grounds that such evidence given by Chinese was inadmissible under the laws of the State of California. The specific law in question was Section 394 of the Civil Practice Act which stated that "no Indian or Negro shall be allowed to testify as a witness in any action in which a white person is a party."

Chief Justice Hugh C. Murray,* in his opinion for the court, with which Justice Solomon Heydenfeldt concurred, argued that the terms used in legislating Section 394 of the Civil Practice Act, namely, Indian, Negro, and white, were generic in nature and white in this case meant the exclusion of Negroes, Indians, and yellow and all other colors. Therefore, the lower court's conviction of George Hall was reversed, and the case was remanded. Justice Alexander Wells dissented from his colleagues' opinion. (*See also* Murray, Hugh Campbell.)
FURTHER READING: Jack Chen, *The Chinese of America*, New York: Harper and Row, 1980; 4 Cal. 399, October 1854.

PEOPLE v. MCGUIRE, a case that went to the Supreme Court of California as an appeal from the County Court of the city and county of San Francisco where the defendant, McGuire, had been convicted of assault against a Chinese, Sam Wah, who was a native and subject of China. During the trial Sam Wah was called as a witness against the objections of the defendant, who claimed that a Chinese witness was not admissible. However, the County Court permitted Sam Wah to testify against McGuire, who appealed to the Supreme Court of the State of California.

The highest court of the State of California had ruled twice that Mongolians or Chinese could not testify for or against any white person. In the case of the People v. George W. Hall,* the court ruled that terms such as "Negroes" and "Indians" were used in a generic sense, and therefore Asians were also considered to be Indians. Therefore, Chinese could not give witness in favor of or against any white man. In the case of the People v. Brady which was decided by the court in 1854, the same year when the previous case was ruled, it was the opinion of the court that forbidding a Chinese witness in favor of or against a white person was not in violation of the Fourteenth Amendment of the U. S. Constitution. After these decisions were rendered, the California State Legislature passed a law that repealed all laws forbidding Chinese from testifying against white men. This law was to go into effect after January 1, 1873. The lower court convicted McGuire in anticipation of the new law that went into effect in January 1873. The Supreme Court reversed the lower court's decision and remanded for a new trial on the grounds that courts in the State of California were not free to disregard the decisions handed down by the Supreme Court of the State of California because they considered the decisions unsound.
FURTHER READING: 45 Cal. 56, October 1872.

PETERSEN, WILLIAM. *See* Subnation.

PHELAN, JAMES D. (1861–1930), mayor of San Francisco, U. S. senator. Phelan was born in San Francisco on April 20, 1861. He attended St. Ignatius University in San Francisco and graduated in 1881. He then studied law at the

University of California at Berkeley. Upon graduation he joined the family banking business, which he eventually inherited. In 1897 he ran for the office of mayor of San Francisco and was elected with the help of a prominent newspaper, *The Bulletin*. He served three terms as mayor and did much to clean up the graft and corruption that plagued the city during that era. He went on to serve the State of California as a U. S. senator from 1915 to 1921. He also served as president of the University of California for sixteen years.

During his three terms in office as mayor of San Francisco, Phelan did much to reform the city administration and to beautify the city by cleaning the streets and establishing parks and art works. During his administration he gave comfort and support to those who agitated for Asian exclusion. He even engaged in a public debate with the Chinese consul general to discuss the merits and disadvantages of Chinese immigration. When San Francisco hosted the California Chinese Exclusion Convention in November 1901, he gave the main address to delegates, who believed that Chinese exclusion was the only way to preserve Western civilization. As mayor he took actions that demonstrated his policies toward the Chinese. In 1900 he allowed a regular blockade of Chinatown* because he thought it was a firetrap. Again, when the Board of Health allegedly found a Chinese person who had died of bubonic plague, he allowed Chinatown to be put under quarantine.

Phelan also championed Japanese exclusion and used the issue politically during his campaign for reelection in 1920, when he supported the Alien Land Act of California, 1913.*

FURTHER READING: Roger Daniels, *The Politics of Prejudice*, Berkeley: University of California Press, 1962; John Modell, *The Economics and Politics of Racial Accommodation: The Japanese of Los Angeles, 1900–1942*, Urbana: University of Illinois Press, 1977; Robert A. Wilson and Bill Hosokawa, *East to America*, New York: William Morrow and Co., 1980.

PHILIPPINE MAIL, THE, successor to the first newspaper for Filipinos in the continental United States, the *Philippine Independent News* (published in Salinas, California, 1921). The *Philippine Mail*, begun on November 3, 1931, was also published in Salinas California, under the editorship of Delfin Cruz. The newspaper reported news from the Philippine Islands as well as from the United States, including Hawaii, and it was published in English. This is the longest surviving newspaper among the Filipinos in America.

PHILIPPINE TARIFF ACT. *See* Payne-Aldrich Tariff Act.

PICTURE–BRIDE, a term that originated from the manner in which marriages between Japanese residents already in the United States and their future spouses were arranged and consummated. The husband usually sent his picture to his home country and had a close relative or friend arrange his marriage to a woman, who was, in turn, asked to send her picture to her future husband. Their marriage was, therefore, strictly speaking, completed by proxy. After the marriage was thus consummated, picture–brides were allowed to join their husbands in the United States under the agreement made between the United States of America and Japan in 1908, which was called the Gentlemen's Agreement.* (See also Gentlemen's Agreement.)

PIG TRADERS, those engaged in selling and buying Chinese coolie laborers immediately after the end of the Opium War* of 1842. Coolie trade,* or pig trade, by American ships was banned in February 1862. (See also Coolie Trade.)

PINEAPPLE GROWERS ASSOCIATION OF HAWAII, organized in 1907 to coordinate advertising, research, and marketing. The production of pineapple, the second most important agricultural product in Hawaii, started in 1900 when James Dole started growing the fruit. The following year he established the Hawaiian Pineapple Company for which he served as general manager until October 1932, when the company reorganized to avoid a financial disaster. In 1903 he was able to can 1,800 cases of pineapple, thus introducing pineapple as a viable cash crop next to sugar. He encouraged others in Hawaii to grow pineapple and by 1907 there were enough people to organize the Pineapple Growers Association of Hawaii.

In order to obtain cheap labor for their cash crop, the Pineapple Growers Association worked closely with the Hawaiian Sugar Planters' Association.* During the first few years of operation, pineapple canneries and plantations used surplus labor available from sugar fields. Later, the Pineapple Growers Association paid an annual stipend to the Hawaiian Sugar Planters' Association to recruit Filipino laborers to work on pineapple plantations.

FURTHER READING: Lawrence H. Fuchs, *Hawaii Pono: A Social History*, New York: Harcourt, Brace and World, 1961; Brett Melendy, *Asians in America: Filipinos, Koreans, and East Indians*, Boston: Twayne Publishers, 1977.

PINKHAM, LUCIUS EUGENE (1850–1922), business leader in Hawaii. Pinkham was born on September 19, 1850, at Chicopee Falls, Massachusetts, the son of Lucius Moulton Pinkham, a cotton mill owner who also did some manufacturing. Pinkham did well in his studies in the public schools of Hartford, Connecticut, and planned to attend Yale University until a serious accident prevented him from pursuing his goal.

Pinkham's business career, started in 1873, was extended to many parts of the world; consequently, Pinkham traveled widely to Europe, Siberia, the Orient, the Philippines, and the Hawaiian Islands, where he lived between 1891 and 1894 and again from 1898. When Pinkham lived on Oahu, he worked for Benjamin Dillingham as a bookkeeper at the Oahu Railroad and Land Company, while he was also working as manager of the Pacific Hardware Company. In 1904 Governor George Robert Carter appointed him president of the Territorial Board of Health. Pinkham held this position for four years. While serving as president of the Board of Health, he gained a reputation for handling the bubonic plague and cholera effectively and economically. During this time he also worked with the lepers of Molokai, whose surroundings were greatly improved through his hard work. Upon leaving his position as president of the Board of Health, he became affiliated with the Hawaiian Sugar Planters' Association* (HSPA). This affiliation furthered the work of the former Royal Hawaiian Agricultural Society and the Planters' Labor and Supply Company.

In the 1890's the HSPA could only recruit unskilled labor from four sources: the Chinese, who were soon to be excluded; the Japanese, who were considered undesirable; the Portuguese, who turned out to be too expensive; and the Filipinos. For these reasons the HSPA encouraged the immigration of agricultural workers from the Philippines.

Recruiting in the Philippines began in 1906 with a plan to get 300 families, but the initial recruiting effort failed—only 15 laborers were recruited. In 1907, however, 150 laborers were recruited. Two years later Oswald A. Steven, a Honolulu auctioneer, and Lucius E. Pinkham began full-scale recruiting. While Steven sent out his hired agents to recruit Filipinos in and around Cebu, Pinkham was in Hong Kong to set up and arrange transportation for the people recruited.

Lucius Eugene Pinkham was appointed governor of Hawaii by President Woodrow Wilson for the 1913–1917 term. He retired in June 1918. He moved to San Francisco where he died on November 2, 1922.

PINOY, Filipino agricultural workers who came from the Philippines to California to do stoop labor. These Filipinos called themselves pinoys.

PORTERFIELD v. WEBB, a case argued before the U.S. Supreme Court on April 23 and 24, 1923, and decided on November 12, 1923, when Justice Pierce Butler delivered the opinion of the Court on the question of the constitutionality of the Alien Land Act of California of 1913,* as amended in 1920.

The appellants, W. L. Porterfield and Y. Mizuno, appealed through the U.S. District Court for the Southern District of California to the Supreme Court to enjoin Attorney General of the State of California U.S. Webb from enforcing the Alien Land Law of California. Porterfield had 80 acres of land in Los Angeles County which he wanted to lease to Mizuno, a Japanese citizen and alien who was not eligible for U.S. citizenship. In accordance with the Alien Land Act of California, 1913, such a lease transaction would be in violation of the law because of Mizuno's legal status.

Justice Pierce Butler, in his opinion for the Court, affirmed the lower court's decision and held the Alien Land Act of California to be constitutional. He brushed aside the appellants' arguments that the treaty between Japan and the United States allowed citizens of Japan to ''own and lease and occupy homes, manufactories, warehouses and shops,'' or ''to lease land for residential and commercial purposes'' because he believed that the treaty was not applicable to leasing agricultural land. He also ruled that the Fourteenth Amendment of the

Constitution was not violated on the grounds that aliens who were eligible for U.S. citizenship, but who had not declared their intention to become U.S. citizens were also included in this class of people who could not own land in California. FURTHER READING: Consulate-General of Japan, San Francisco, *Documental History of Law Cases Affecting Japanese in the United States, 1916–1924*, Vol. 2, San Francisco: 1925; Frank F. Chuman, *The Bamboo People: The Law and Japanese-Americans*, Del Mar, Calif.: Publisher's Inc., 1976; Milton R. Konvitz, *The Alien and the Asiatic in American Law*, Ithaca, N.Y.: Cornell University Press, 1946.

POSTON STRIKE, an incident that occurred on November 18, 1942, at the Poston War Relocation Camp where approximately 9,000 persons of Japanese ancestry had been interned since their removal from their homes on the West Coast. This particular incident, known as the Poston Strike, originated from a beating incident on November 14, when a Kibei* who served as a councilman was beaten up by a number of assailants, who left him almost dead. After this incident, about fifty evacuees were investigated, two of whom were detained by the FBI agents for further investigation.

Sympathy from evacuees centered around the two persons detained, and a large crowd formed around the center jail where the two were held. At nightfall, an Emergency Committee was created, made up of representatives from all the blocks under which residents of the camp were organized. The committee was immediately controlled by leaders of the Issei Advisory Board, which called for a general strike against the administration. While the strike was on, there were some tense moments. But negotiations took place on November 23 and 24, and law and order were restored in the camp. One of the detainees was released, and the other was released for trial by the camp Judicial Commission. FURTHER READING: Audrie Girdner and Anne Loftis, *The Great Betrayal*, New York: Macmillan Co, 1969; Alexander H. Leighton, *The Governing of Men*, Princeton, N. J.: Princeton University Press, 1945; Dillon S. Myer, *Uprooted Americans*, Tucson: University of Arizona Press, 1971; Edward H. Spicer et al., *Impounded People*, Tucson: University of Arizona Press, 1969.

POWDERLY, TERENCE VINCENT (1849–1924), labor leader, immigration offical. Powderly was born on January 22, 1849, in Carbondale, Pennsylvania. He was one of twelve children born to Terence Powderly and Margery Walsh who had come from County Meath, Ireland, to the United States in 1827 in search of a better life. Powderly attended school until the age of thirteen but later went on to become a self-educated lawyer. Powderly was a firm believer in the value of an education, not only for the individual but also for society.

In 1871, at the age of twenty–two, Powderly began his labor activities in the Machinists' and Blacksmiths' Union of Carbondale. Three years later, he became an organizer and was initiated into the order of the Knights of Labor.* In 1878 he was elected mayor of Scranton, Pennsylvania, and the following year he became General Master Workman of the Knights of Labor, thus becoming head of the then most powerful labor organization in the history of America.

With the eventual decline of the Knights of Labor, Powderly took an intense interest in his own political ambitions, and in 1894 he campaigned for William McKinley until his election as President in 1897. As a reward for his assistance, McKinley appointed Powderly to the position of U.S. Commissioner General of Immigration in charge of the Bureau of Immigration created by Congress in 1891. He held this position until he was removed from office in 1902 by President Theodore Roosevelt, who then appointed Frank Pearce Sargent* to succeed Powderly. In 1906 Roosevelt appointed Powderly to study the causes of emigration from Europe, and in 1907 Powderly became Chief of the Division of Information of the Bureau of Immigration, a position he held until 1921. Powderly's last appointment was as a member of the Board of Review of the Department of Immigration, which he held until an illness which preceded his death in 1924.

Powderly was strongly opposed to the immigration of foreign laborers to the United States, particularly to the immigration of Chinese laborers. He strongly supported the Chinese Exclusion Act of 1882* and played an instrumental role in persuading President Grover Cleveland to push for the passage of the Alien Contract Labor Law of 1885 through Congress. Throughout his long career associated with immigration, he made it more difficult for Chinese to enter the United States as he had power to establish new rules and regulations controlling Chinese entry into this country. On December 8, 1900, Powderly issued new regulations requiring Chinese to possess a through ticket, furnish a bond of $500, and assure immigration officials that they were truly passing through the United States for their stated prupose, and not to stay in the United States.

FURTHER READING: Jack Chen, *The Chinese of America*, New York: Harper and Row, 1980; Delber L. McKee, *Chinese Exclusion Versus the Open Door Policy, 1900–1906*, Detroit: Wayne State University Press, 1977; George E. McNeill, ed., *The Labor Movement*, New York: M. W. Hazen Co., 1888; Terence V. Powderly, *Thirty Years of Labor*, Columbus, Ohio: Excelsior P. House, 1890; Terence V. Powderly, *The Path I Trod: The Autobiography of Terence V. Powderly*, New York: Columbia University Press, 1940.

PREFECTURE. *See Kenjinkai.*

PRESIDENTIAL PROCLAMATION 2762. *See* Executive Order 9814.

PRESIDENT'S ADVISORY COMMITTEE ON REFUGEES, created by President Gerald Ford on May 12, 1975, when he appointed seventeen persons on the committee in order to advise the President and the heads of government agencies on the matter of settling Indochinese refugees.

PROPOSITION 13 OF CALIFORNIA, 1956, initiated by the Japanese Americans Citizens League* (JACL) which asked the California State Legislature to repeal the Alien Land Act of California, 1913,* by putting it to vote. The repeal measure was placed on the November 4, 1956 general election ballot, and it was called Proposition 13. The JACL campaigned vigorously for repeal of the Alien Land Act, and Joe Masaoka, a brother of Mike Masaru Masaoka,* rallied throughout the state to gather support for this important issue. The repeal measure was approved as 2.5 million people voted by a two to one majority in favor of doing away with the Alien Land Act.

PROPOSITION 15. *See* Validation of Legislative Amendments to Alien Land Law.

PUBLIC LAW 95–145, a law passed by the U.S. Congress on October 28,1977, authorizing Indochinese refugees to become permanent residents upon request. Refugees could, therefore, apply for U.S. citizenship after five years of residence from the date of their arrival in the United States.

PUBLIC LAW 405, a law that went into effect on July 1, 1944, when President Franklin Roosevelt signed the legislation that amended the Nationality Act of 1940, authorizing Japanese evacuees in relocation centers* to renounce their U.S. citizenship by filing a written declaration. After the passage of this law, approximately 5,700 evacuees applied for renunciation of their citizenship and expatriation to Japan.

PUBLIC LAW 503, signed by President Franklin Roosevelt on March 21, 1942, making it a federal offense to violate any order issued by the military commander, as specified in Executive Order 9066.* This was done in order to execute the provisions specified in Executive Order 9066 signed by President Roosevelt on February 19, 1942.

PUBLIC PROCLAMATIONS, a series of orders issued by General John Lesesne DeWitt* after President Franklin Roosevelt signed Executive Order 9066* authorizing military commanders to designate military zones from which all civilians could be excluded. Public Proclamation No. 1, issued on March 2, 1942, established Military Area No. 1, which included the western halves of California, Oregon, and Washington and the southern half of Arizona. Public Proclamation No. 2 was issued on March 16, which came five days after the Wartime Civil Control Administration was established. Through this proclamation, the execution of change of residence notices required by Public Proclamation No. 1 was extended to enemy aliens and persons of Japanese ancestry residing within the geographical limits of the Western Defense Command. Eight days later, on March 24, 1942, Proclamation No. 3 was issued, establishing military curfew and travel regulations on enemy aliens and persons of Japanese ancestry. The curfew was to be enforced between 8:00 P.M. and 6:00 A.M. to begin on March 27 in Military Area No. 1. On the same day when the curfew was to go into effect, General DeWitt issued Public Proclamation No. 4, forbidding further voluntary migration of persons of Japanese ancestry from the West Coast military area. This was to go into effect on March 29,1942. This action meant that persons of Japanese ancestry were not able to move out of the areas designated as military zones, and soon they were to be told they could not stay in those areas either. The process was initiated by a series of Civilian Exclusion Orders* issued by the same general. Public Proclamation No. 5 was issued on March 30 to provide a basis for exempting certain classes of people from curfew and travel regulations imposed by Proclamation No. 3. Proclamation No. 6, issued on June 2, 1942, forbade the voluntary migration of persons of Japanese ancestry from the eastern half of California, and they were to be sent to the war relocation centers directly from this area, according to the same proclamation. After persons of Japanese ancestry were interned, General DeWitt issued Proclamation No. 15, rescinding the curfew and travel regulations contained in Proclamation No. 3 on December 24, 1942

Public Proclamation No. 17, issued by General DeWitt on April 19, 1943, authorized Nisei* soldiers to return to the West Coast while on leave from active combat duty. After America's victory over Japan, the Western Defense Command issued Public Proclamation No. 24, revoking civilian exclusion orders and restrictions against persons of Japanese ancestry. This proclamation came on September 4, 1945.

FURTHER READING: Roger Daniels, *The Decision to Relocate the Japanese Americans*, Philadelphia: J. B. Lippincott Co., 1975; Masako Herman, *The Japanese in America, 1843–1973*, Dobbs Ferry, N.Y.: Oceana Publications, 1974; Dillon S. Myer, *Uprooted Americans*, Tucson: University of Arizona Press, 1971; U.S. Department of War, *Final Report: Japanese Evacuation from the West Coast, 1942*, Washington D.C.: U.S. Government Printing Office, 1943.

PUNTI, a Chinese term referring to the natives of Kwangtung Province located in the southeastern region of China and particularly the natives of the Pearl River Delta* from which many Chinese came to the United States as immigrants and sojourners* during the second half of the nineteenth century. (*See also* Hakka.)

PUUNENE STRIKE OF 1936, a labor strike by members of a Filipino labor union known as Vibora Luviminda which was organized by Pablo Malapit,* Antonio Fagel* and Epifanio Taok, after Manlapit had returned to Hawaii from California. The union, organized in 1932, went underground after Taok was jailed and Manlapit was exiled to the Philippine Islands in 1935. In June 1936 Fagel led members of his underground union to strike, demanding a wage increase. The Hawaiian Sugar Planters' Association* brought in strike–breakers in response to this strike organized exclusively by Filipino plantation workers, who were urged by the Philippine resident commissioner in Washington, D.C., and Manuel Quezon* to go back to their jobs. After a long strike that lasted eighty–five days, the Hawaiian Sugar Planters' Association agreed to give a 15 percent pay increase, and the strike ended successfully. This was the first successful strike led by

Filipino workers, and it was also the last strike led by a single ethnic group in Hawaii.

FURTHER READING: Luis V. Teodoro, Jr., ed., *Out of This Struggle: The Filipinos in Hawaii*, Honolulu: University Press of Hawaii, 1981.

Q

QUEZON, MANUEL (1878–1944), Filipino patriot who paved the way for Philippine independence. Quezon was born on Luzon on August 19, 1878, and died in Saranac Lake, New York, on August 1, 1944. During the six decades of his life, he worked for the modernization and improvement of the lives of his people.

Quezon fought in the 1901 insurrection against the United States with Emilio Aguinaldo,* but after its failure he cooperated with the territorial administration and resumed his study of law. He was admitted to the bar in 1903. He later became majority leader of the first Philippine Assembly under U.S. rule in 1907 and served as Filipino resident commissioner in Washington, D.C. from 1909 to 1916. Quezon was instrumental in the passage of the Jones Act of 1916* which granted autonomy to the Filipinos and provided for a bicameral Philippine legislature. Upon his return to the Philippines in 1916, he was elected president of the Philippine Senate, an office he held until 1935. Quezon led the successful protest against the Hare-Hawes–Cutting Act* and negotiated for better legislation. In 1934 the Congress of the United States approved the Tydings-McDuffie Act* promising Philippine independence. Independence finally came on July 4, 1946.

QUON QUON POY v. JOHNSON, a case argued on December 9 and 10, 1926, and decided on February 21, 1927, involving the foreign-born son of a native-born Chinese father living in the United States. The appellant, Quon Quon Poy, was a boy of fifteen when he arrived at the port of Boston in June 1924 and applied for admission to the United States, claiming that he was the foreign-born son of Quon Mee Sing, a native-born citizen of the United States. In June 1924, he was detained by the inspector of the port of Boston, and in September he was questioned under oath and at length by the inspector who also separately examined Quon Mee Sing and an alleged brother.

The Board of Special Inquiry was held as required under the Immigration Act of February 5, 1917* and told Quon Quon Poy that he could have a relative or friend with him, but he stated that he did not wish to have anyone. After the hearing, he was refused admission to the United States. He then applied for a writ of habeas corpus against John P. Johnson, U.S. Commissioner of Immigration at the port of Boston.

The case went to the U.S. Supreme Court as an appeal from the District Court of the United States for the District of Massachusetts, which was allowed under Section 238 of the Judicial Code.

Justice Edward Sanford, in his opinion for the unanimous Court, stated that the appellant was not entitled to a judicial hearing and that the immigration officers made proper administrative decisions. Because there was no evidence of any abuse of discretion, the District Court's decision was affirmed by the Supreme Court *nunc pro tunc*.

FURTHER READING: *Supreme Court Reporter* 47, 273, U.S. 352, 1926.

QUOTA IMMIGRATION ACT OF 1921, the first quota act passed by Congress in American history, signed into law by President Warren Harding on May 19,1921. It limited the number of aliens coming to the United States as permanent residents to 3 percent of the number of foreign-born persons of that national origin who were enumerated in the 1910 Census. The 1910 Census was used mainly because during that year and the year preceding the United States saw the greatest number of immigrants from England, Ireland, Scotland, and the Scandinavian countries. In this way, it was thought that America could be kept "white."

FURTHER READING: Marion T. Bennett, *American Immigration Policies: A History*, Washington, D.C.: Public Affairs Press, 1963; E. P. Hutchinson, *Legislative History of American Immigration Policy, 1798–1965*, Philadelphia: University of Pennsylvania Press, 1981; George M. Stephenson, *A History of American Immigration, 1820–1924*, New York: Russell and Russell, 1964.

QUOTA IMMIGRATION ACT OF 1924. *See* Immigration Act of 1924.

R

RAFU SHIMPO, one of the most influential newspapers published by Japanese Americans. It is still published daily, except Sunday, in Los Angeles. (*See also* Newspapers, Asian American.)

RAGHEAD, a pejorative term used by Californians against the Sikhs, who wear *pagri* or turbans.

RAI, LAL LAIJAT. *See* India Home Rule League of America.

RECIPROCITY TREATY OF 1875, concluded between the Hawaiian Kingdom and the U.S. government, allowing both sides to establish free trade on major goods across the Pacific. Negotiations for this treaty were facilitated when King Kalakaua* visited Washington in November and December of 1874. According to the agreement reached between Henry Alpheus Peirce Carter, the commissioner appointed by the Hawaiian Kingdom to negotiate a treaty with the United States, and Hamilton Fish, Secretary of State, Hawaii was allowed to export unrefined sugar, rice, castor oil, bananas, fruits, nuts, vegetables, and other goods to the United States duty free, and American goods such as wool, iron, steel, and textiles were allowed duty-free entry into Hawaii. The treaty was to be in effect for seven years, and either party was allowed to terminate it after twelve months' notice.

King Kalakaua ratified the treaty on April 18, 1875, and President Ulysses S. Grant gave his approval on May 31, 1875. But Congress did not pass the enabling legislation until May 8, 1876, and the Senate approved it on August 14, thus putting the treaty into operation on September 9, 1876.

Business in Hawaii in 1875 was rather sluggish; good arable land went to waste for lack of investment. With the Reciprocity Treaty of 1875, however, the Hawaiian economy was suddenly revived with a drastic increase in sugar and rice output. Sugar imports from Hawaii to the United States increased from an estimated 17,063,133 pounds in 1875 to 115,325,077 in 1883. The sudden boom in sugar export business from Hawaii to the United States created demands for plantation labor, particularly cheap labor, and the mad race to supply sugar plantations with Asian labor and labor from other parts of the world changed the size and character of the population in the Hawaiian Islands. At the beginning of the reciprocity period (1876–1900) Hawaii had a population of 55,500; of these, 46,500 were native Hawaiians, 3,000 part-Hawaiians, 3,500 Caucasians, and 2,500 Chinese. By 1900, the last year of the reciprocity period, the population increased to 154,000; of these 30,000 were native Hawaiians, 27,000 Caucasians, and 87,000 Asians. Of these 87,000 Asians, 26,000 were Chinese and the rest Japanese.

FURTHER READING: Gavan Daws, *Shoal of Time*, Honolulu: University Press of Hawaii, 1968; Ralph S. Kuykendall, *The Hawaiian Kingdom*, Vol. 3, Honolulu: University of Hawaii Press, 1967; Merze Tate, *The United States and the Hawaiian Kingdom: A Political History*, New Haven, Conn.: Yale University Press, 1965; Merze Tate, *Hawaii: Reciprocity or Annexation*, East Lansing: Michigan State University Press, 1968.

REFORM SOCIETY, an organization originally established in 1903 in Hawaii under the name the Central Japanese League, whose members felt they were exploited by immigration companies run by Japanese. The organization was created for the purpose of redressing Japanese workers' problems of collecting 100 yen which each of them had deposited in the steamship company providing passage. It was not able to help them, however. It was succeeded by the Reform Association in 1905.

The requirement that all Japanese workers have at least $50 in their possession or a written employment contract developed as a result of a law passed in 1894. Accordingly, a Japanese worker had to give $50 to the steamship company providing his passage in return for a certificate of deposit. The emigre then brought the certificate to Hawaii and surrendered it to agents of the immigration company who, in turn, deposited it in the Keihin Bank. The workers, however, found that they were unable to collect their certificates unless they applied for reimbursement in Tokyo. The Reform Association requested that the Japanese government abandon this practice, and after it accomplished its purpose, it disbanded itself in 1916.

REFUGEE ACT OF 1980, a bill signed into law on March 17, 1980, by President Jimmy Carter after it was approved by both the House and the Senate on March 4, 1980. The Refugee Act of 1980, or Public Law 96–212, was enacted in response to increasing numbers of people seeking asylum from Vietnam, Kampuchea, and Cuba, and as a means of amending the Migration and Refugee Assistance Act of 1962. The act increased the number of refugees allowed to enter the United States from 17,400 to 50,000 annually, and the President was empowered to admit additional refugees in consultation with Congress. Among the law's other provisions were the creation of the Office of the United States Coordinator for Refugee Affairs and the Office of Refugee Resettlement, a new definition of refugee, and a wide-ranging federal program to assist refugees in their resettlement process. For this purpose the act authorized the government to spend $200 million annually on special projects, programs, and services for refugees.

FURTHER READING: Edward M. Kennedy, "Refugee Act of 1980," *International Migration Review* 15, (1981) pp. 141–156; Tricia Knoll, *Becoming Americans*, Portland, Oreg.: Coast-to-Coast Book, 1982; Barry Wain, *The Refused: The Agony of the Indochina Refugees*, New York: Simon and Schuster, 1981.

REGAN v. KING, a case tried before the U.S. District Court for the Southern District of California on July 2, 1942. Jon T. Regan, with the help of his lawyers, one of whom was U.S. Webb, an anti-Asian exclusionist, brought suit against Cameron King, registrar of voters in the city and county of San Francisco, State of California, in order to force King to eliminate from the list of voters the names of more than "2,600 Japanese of full blood born in the United States and the State of California, of alien parents born in the Empire of Japan." He claimed that these people were erroneously registered as eligible voters and that his rights as a voter were infringed upon by allowing ineligible persons to vote. Defending the registrar of the city and county of San Francisco were City Attorney John J. O'Toole, with Wayne M. Collins* filing *amicus curiae* for the American Civil Liberties Union.

District Judge Adolphus Frederic St. Sure, in his opinion for the court, ruled that persons born of Japanese ancestry in the United States were U.S. citizens on the basis of the Supreme Court ruling in the case of United States v. Wong Kim Ark,* and therefore they were entitled to be registered to vote. Regan then petitioned for a writ of certiorari, but the Supreme Court denied his petition on May 17,1943.

FURTHER READING: Frank F. Chuman, *The Bamboo People*, Del Mar, Calif.: Publisher's Inc., 1976; 49 F. Supp. 222, July 2, 1942; *Supreme Court Reporter* 63, 310 U.S. 753.

RELOCATION CENTERS, concentration camps set up for persons of Japanese ancestry in the United States during World War II. After the Japanese attack on Pearl Harbor on December 7, 1941, President Franklin Roosevelt signed Executive Order 9066* on February 19, 1942, that set in motion a series of bureaucratic decisions creating mechanisms for establishing concentration camps for persons of Japanese ancestry in the United States. On the following day, Secretary of War Henry Lewis Stimson* delegated responsibility for carrying out the Executive Order to General John Lesesne DeWitt,* who issued Public Proclamation No. 1 on March 2, 1942, setting up Military Areas 1 and 2 on the West Coast. This was followed by some different orders issued by General DeWitt and other government officials.

In March 1942 President Roosevelt issued Executive Order 9102* creating the War Relocation Authority* to supervise and control people evacuated from the West Coast. These evacuees were then transferred to concentration camps, or relocation camps as they were called euphemistically. Ten concentration camps were established in different states, and approximately 112,000 persons of Japanese ancestry, including American citizens, were interned and detained in these camps. California had two centers, one at Manzanar with 10,000 evacuees and another at Tule Lake with 16,000 capacity. Colorado had a concentration camp established at Granada in Prowers County, with a capacity of 8,000 people. Arkansas had two centers, one at Rohwer and the other at Jerome. Each camp was able to detain 10,000 internees. Arizona also had two camps, one at Poston and the other at Gila River. Poston was built with a capacity of 20,000 detainees, and the Gila River camp was smaller with a capacity of 15,000 persons. Other camps were established at Heart Mountain, Wyoming, at Minidoka, Idaho, and at Topaz, Utah. Each of them was able to receive approximately 10,000 internees. FURTHER READING: Lillian Baker, *The Concentration Camp Conspiracy: A Second Pearl Harbor*, Lawndale, Calif: AFHA Publications, 1981; Richard Conrat et al., *Executive Order 9066: The internment of 110,000 Japanese-Americans*, San Francisco: California Historical Society, 1972; Roger Daniels, *Concentration Camps: North American—Japanese in the United States and Canada During World War II*, Malaba, Fla.: Robert E. Krieger Publishing Co., 1981; Roger Daniels, *Concentration Camps, U.S.A.: Japanese Americans and World War II*, New York: Holt, Rinehart, and Winston, 1971; Edward T. Spicer et al., *Impounded People*, Tucson: University of Arizona Press, 1968; Jacobus ten Broek et al., *Prejudice, War and the Constitution*, Berkeley: University of California Press, 1954; Dorothy Swaine Thomas and Richard S. Nishimoto, *The Spoilage*, Berkeley: University of California Press, 1946.

RELUCTANT THIRTY-NINE, a group of people who were called to testify before the House Un-American Activities Committee in April 1950 when the Congressional Committee came to Hawaii to investigate the allegation that the top leadership of the International Longshoremen's and Warehousemen's Union* had been infiltrated by Communists. This allegation was made by Izuka Ichiro in a pamphlet, *The Truth About Communism in Hawaii*, in which he named members of the labor union who were party members. Among those whom Izuka named were Jack Hall and Jack Kawano, former president of the labor union. Charges against Hall, Kawano, and other union members were made in the wake of a dock strike that had almost crippled Hawaii's economy.

The Territorial Legislature of Hawaii asked the House Un-American Activities Committee to investigate the allegation, and the committee called a total of sixty–six people. Of these, thirty–nine witnesses refused to answer questions put to them by the committee, which found them in contempt of Congress. However, the following year Federal Judge Delbert E. Metzger ruled that even self-admitted Communists, as well as others who were described as Communist, were entitled to take refuge in the Fifth Amendment of the Constitution.

As a result of this ruling, all thirty-nine witnesses were acquitted. Five of them were later tried for violation of the Smith Act. (*See also* Hawaii Seven.)
FURTHER READING: Gavan Daws, *Shoal of Time*, Honolulu: University Press of Hawaii, 1968; Lawrence H. Fuchs, *Hawaii Pono*, New York: Harcourt, Brace and World, 1961; Paul C. Phillips, *Hawaii's Democrats: Chasing the American Dream*, Washington, D.C.: University Press of America, 1982.

REPATRIATION, JAPANESE, action taken by persons of Japanese ancestry in the United States to go to Japan either voluntarily or under duress, while they were in internment camps. Some internees, finding their lives unbearable in the concentration camps, decided to go back to Japan. Others lost their faith in America and decided to give up their citizenship. A total of 4,724 persons of Japanese ancestry went to Japan on five different dates: 4 on June 11, 1942; 314 on September 2, 1943, 423 on November 25, 1945; 3,551 on December 29, 1945; and 432 on February 23, 1946. This amounted to less than 4 percent of the total evacuees during World War II. While in the internment camps, 5,766 U.S. citizens of Japanese ancestry renounced their citizenship, and of these 1,116 decided to go to Japan. Afterwards 5,409 asked that their citizenship be restored, and 4,978 recovered their citizenship. Only 357 people failed to apply for restoration of their U.S. citizenship. (*See also* Inouye, Yuichi et al. v. Clark; Public Law 405.)
FURTHER READING: Frank F. Chuman, *The Bamboo People*, Del Mar, Calif.: Publisher's Inc., 1976; Dillon S. Myer, *Uprooted Americans*, Tucson: University of Arizona Press, 1971.

REPATRIATION ACT OF 1935. *See* Filipino Repatriation Act of 1935.

REPORT TO THE CALIFORNIA STATE SENATE OF ITS SPECIAL COMMITTEE ON CHINESE IMMIGRATION. *See* California Senate Address and Memorial of 1876.

REPRESENTATIVE COUNCIL OF THE FEDERATED TRADES AND LABOR ORGANIZATIONS OF THE PACIFIC COAST. *See* Roney, Frank.

REPRESENTATIVE COUNCIL OF TRADES AND LABOR UNIONS, organized in 1878 in California by a group of dissatisfied union members who had opposed Denis Kearney's* domination within the Workingmen's Party of California.* Also known as the Trades Assembly, the council was led by Frank Roney* who steered his organization toward agitation for anti-Chinese movement in 1882. (*See also* Roney, Frank.)

RESTRICTIVE COVENANTS (also known as protective covenants as well as race restrictive covenants), widely used method before 1948 of creating and maintaining residential segregation between whites and non-whites in the United

States. This method was also used on the West Coast to segregate whites and Asians. Property owners usually agreed on restrictive covenants at the time land was platted for building houses. Included in their joint agreements was a provision pertaining to the exclusion of non-white people. Any owner violating this provision could be taken to court and forced to comply with the agreement. The courts were not sympathetic to non-whites who wanted to purchase these properties.

In 1948, however, the U.S. Supreme Court ruled in the case of Shelley v. Kraemer that it was unconstitutional for state courts to enforce racially restrictive covenants.

RHEE, SYNGMAN (1875–1965), first president of the Republic of Korea. Rhee was born on Arpil 26, 1875, in the village of Pyong-san, Hwanghae Province, Korea, the only son of Yi Kyong-son. Rhee was educated in the Chinese classics before he entered a modern school run by a group of Methodist missionaries. There he learned English and came into contact with Western civilization. Upon graduation from the school, he remained to teach English before he involved himself in political activities of the Independence Club, whose purpose was to demand political and social reforms within the government. Because of his agitation for mass demonstration, Rhee was imprisoned in 1897; he was not released until 1904. During these years he was converted to Christianity and developed his faith in God and in democratic values. While in prison he wrote a book, *Tongnip Chongsin* (1900), or *The Spirit of Independence*.

In the winter of 1904 Rhee traveled to the United States to appeal the case of the ever-fragile independence of Korea to President Theodore Roosevelt, who turned a deaf ear to Rhee's plea for the United States to use its good offices as it had promised in the Treaty of Chemulp'o, 1882.*

While in Washington, D.C., Rhee enrolled in George Washington University in 1905 and graduated in 1907. He went to Harvard to do his postgraduate work in international relations. In 1908 he received his Master's degree from Harvard and continued his studies in international relations at Princeton where he received his Ph. D. degree in 1910. He returned to his native country upon graduation and stayed there briefly as a YMCA organizer, but he came back to the United States in 1912 and did not go back to Korea until it was liberated from Japanese rule by the Allied forces in August 1945.

In 1913 when Pak Yong-man* asked him to become principal of the Korean Compound School in Honolulu, Hawaii, Rhee accepted the position and worked diligently to teach children of Korean immigrants their native language and culture. He was chosen the first president of the Korean provisional government in April 1919, which was established after the March 1 Independence Movement in Korea. From 1919 on, Rhee strove to work toward Korea's independence through diplomatic means, for he believed that Korea's independence would come only if the Great Powers of the world worked together to force Japan to relinquish its colonial rule on Korea. In his efforts to regain Korean independence, Rhee gathered Korean residents in Hawaii who shared a similar political philosophy and organized Tongji-hoe, or the Comrade Society,* in November 1920. The society was to assist the Korean provisional government-in-exile in Shanghai financially and to follow the policies established by the president of the government-in-exile who was none other than Syngman Rhee.

After Korea's liberation in 1945, Rhee returned to Korea with his Austrian wife and became the first president of the Republic of Korea in 1948. His government was overthrown by student revolutionaries in April 1960 in the midst of charges of corruption against government officials. He was secretly taken out of Korea and was flown to Hawaii where he lived out his life in exile. He died on July 19, 1965.

FURTHER READING: Richard C. Allen, *Korea's Syngman Rhee, an Unauthorized Portrait*, Rutland, Vt.: Charles E. Tuttle, 1960; Bong-youn Choy, *Koreans in America* Chicago: Nelson-Hall, 1979; Chong-sik Lee, *The Politics of Korean Nationalism*, Berkeley: University of California Press, 1963; Robert Oliver, *Syngman Rhee: The Man Behind the Myth*, New York: Dodd, Mead, 1954.

RINGLE, KENNETH D. *See* Munson Report.

RIZAL, JOSE (1861–1896), Filipino national hero. Rizal was born on June 19,1861 at Calamba in the Philippine Province of Laguna, the son of Francisco Mercado who later chose Rizal, orginally Racial, as the family's surname. He requested that his name be changed to Rizal, but Spanish authorities refused. The family continued to use Rizal, however. At the age of nine, Jose was taken to Binan to attend a Latin school and at eleven was sent to Manila to begin his studies at the famous school, the Ateneo Municipal. He received a bachelor of arts degree in 1877 and studied at the University of Santo Tomas before he left for Spain in 1882 to study at the Central University of Madrid, where he completed medical and humanistic studies.

While in Spain, Rizal wrote a number of books, including *Noli Me Tangere* (1887), which was banned by Spanish authorities. However, he continued to express his anti-colonial points of view. His revolutionary stance took a decisive turn when his family was driven out of their land by the colonial government which decided to side with the Dominican friars who owned the land legally.

Rizal came home on August 5, 1887, but left again six months later for Europe when he realized that his presence in the Philippines contributed to the persecution of his family by Spanish authorities. While in Europe he completed another book, *El Filibusterismo* (1891), which was dedicated to the memory of three Filipino priests executed in 1872.

The same anguish over his family's plight that had sent him into exile in Europe brought Rizal to Manila on June 26, 1892. Before his arrival in Manila he spent some time in Hong Kong where he contemplated establishing a Filipino community in Borneo and drafted the constitution of the Liga Filipina, which was founded on July 3, 1892. Although it did not last too long, its presence inspired Andres Bonifacio to organize the first Filipino revolutionary party known as Katipunan. This organization spearheaded the revolution against Spain in 1896.

Rizal was placed under arrest by Governor-General Despujol on July 6,1892, for having brought anti-friar handbills to the Philippines. On July 14, Rizal was deported to Dapitan, Mindanao, where he remained for four years. During these years of banishment he worked to improve the lives of inhabitants by practicing opthalmology, building a school, waterworks, and other community improvement projects.

In February 1895 revolution broke out in Cuba, where an epidemic of yellow fever began to spread concurrently. As a result, the Spanish government appealed to doctors under forty–five years of age to volunteer to serve in the army. Rizal successfully appealed to the Spanish government to join the Spanish Army and was on his way to Spain to enlist when the Philippine revolution broke out. The news was received at Port Said. Rizal was told by the ship's captain that he was under arrest and was to be deported to the Philippines, where Rizal arrived on November 3, 1896. He was then tried and convicted of treason and complicity with the revolution, and was executed on December 30, 1896.

The Filipinos consider Rizal a national hero, and the Filipinos in America commemorate his execution on Rizal Day. (*See also* Filipino League (La Liga Filipina.)

FURTHER READING: Austin Coates, *Rizal, Philippine Nationalist and Martyr*, Hong Kong: Oxford University Press, 1968; Austin Craig, *Lineage, Life and Labors of Jose Rizal*, Manila: Philippine Education Co., 1913; James A. LeRoy, *The Americans in the Philippines*, Boston: Houghton Mifflin Co., 1914; Rafael Palma, *Biografia de Rizal*, Manila: Manila Bureau of Printing, 1949; Charles Edward Russell, *The Hero of the Filipinos*, New York: Century Co., 1923.

ROBERTS COMMISSION REPORT, a report released in 1942 by a special commission appointed to investigate the Japanese attack on Pearl Harbor. The commission was chaired by Associate Justice Owen J. Roberts, and it released its findings on January 25, 1942, only one day after General John Lesesne DeWitt* expressed his opinion that a widespread sabotage against military installations on the West Coast by Japanese Americans was yet to come.

The release date of the report was as important as what was said about Japanese Americans in Hawaii. The commission concluded that Japanese residents in Hawaii had engaged in widespread espionage activities. This conclusion was influential in protraying Japanese Americans on the U.S. mainland as dangerous to the national security.

FURTHER READING: Roger Daniels, *Concentration Camps, U.S.A.: Japanese Americans and World War II*, New York: Holt, Rinehart and Winston, 1971; Charles A. Leonard, *Philosophy of Justice: Owen J. Roberts*, New York; Kennikat Press, 1971; Robert A. Wilson and Bill Hosokawa, *East to America*, New York: William Morrow and Co., 1980.

ROBINSON v. L. E. LAMPTON, COUNTY CLERK OF LOS ANGELES,
a litigation case involving Mrs. Stella Robinson who petitioned to the Superior
Court of the County of Los Angeles for a writ of prohibition so that her daughter,
Ruby, could not marry a Filipino, Tony V. Moreno. Judge J. A. Smith ruled
in 1930 that Filipinos were Mongolians and therefore could not marry whites,
thus upholding, in essence, the decision handed down in the case of the State
of California v. Timothy S. Yatko.*
FURTHER READING: Jesse Quinsaat, ed., *Letters in Exile*, Los Angeles: Regents of
the University of California, 1976.

ROCK SPRINGS MASSACRE OF 1885, an attack on the Chinese quarter of
a small coal mining town, Rock Springs, Wyoming Territory, on September 2,
1885 by an armed mob of white men. The mob killed twenty–eight Chinese,
wounded another fifteen, and drove the rest of the Chinese population into the
surrounding hills. It is estimated that in the following weeks another fifty Chinese
died of exposure and starvation. The senseless massacre was apparently touched
off by a fist fight between white and Chinese coal miners, but the real reason
was that white miners as well as white businessmen wanted to get rid of the
Chinese because they posed an economic threat to whites. As Alexander Saxton
points out in his book, *The Indispensable Enemy* (1971), members of the local
Knights of Labor* were concerned about the less favored position of the whites
caused by diminishing high–yield seams of coal; by white labor becoming more
plentiful and cheaper because of a depression in the East; and by Chinese labor
becoming more expensive because of the Chinese Exclusion Act of 1882.*

On September 11, 1885, Cheng Tsan Ju, the Chinese Minister in Washington,
D.C., wrote Secretary of State Thomas F. Bayard to complain of the attack on
the Chinese residents at Rock Springs. Bayard expressed his regrets and informed
the Minister that two army officers had been detailed to assist the Chinese
counsels who were on their way to Rock Springs to investigate the mob attack.
While this investigation was going on, another massacre of Chinese residents
occurred in Seattle, Washington Territory.

As the investigation proceeded, it became clear to the Chinese that the men
who committed the crimes would never be brought to justice unless martial law
was invoked. But both the civil and federal governments were reluctant to do
that. Politically, the Grover Cleveland administration, which was the first
Democratic shift in twenty–four years, was reluctant to alienate its support from
the West, even though it recognized the inhumanity of the massacre. In view
of this situation, the Chinese officials' only option was to push for indemnity
from the federal government and to negotiate for protective measures for the
future.

On November 30, 1885, Chinese Minister Cheng delivered to Secretary Bayard
a lengthy letter, supported by reports from his investigating counsels and a
detailed list of damage claims. The letter made it evident that the Chinese Minister
had done his homework. The previous administration had denied having authority

to act on a riot that had occurred against Chinese at Denver, Colorado, on the grounds that the federal government could not interfere in the administration of state law. Cheng inferred that because Wyoming was instead a territory and not a state the federal government would have jurisdiction to bring the criminals to justice. In addition, because China had historically been quick to indemnify the losses of American citizens caused by riots in China, he argued that the U.S. government should respond in kind with payment. (In 1858 China had paid the U.S. government $735,258.97 in full liquidation of American losses resulting from riots in China.)

In his message to Congress on March 1, 1886, President Cleveland emphatically denied that the U.S. government was under any obligation to pay, but he admitted that an indemnity payment should be made for "benevolent consideration for the innocent and peaceful strangers' maltreatment." But it took another full year before Congress passed the final bill, granting the sum of $147,748.74 to the Chinese government. (*See also* Seattle Anti–Chinese Riots.)

FURTHER READING: Jerry M. Cooper, *The Army and Civil Disorder*, Westport, Conn.: Greenwood Press, 1980; Paul Crane and Alfred Larson, "The Chinese Massacre," *The Annals of Wyoming* 12, No.1 (January 1940); Richard E. Lingenfelter, *The Hardrock Miners*, Berkeley: University of California Press, 1974; Alexander Saxton, *The Indispensable Enemy*, Berkeley: University of California Press, 1971; Charles Collan Tansill, *The Foreign Policy of Thomas F. Bayard*, New York: Fordham University Press, 1940; Shi-Shan Henry Tsai, *China and the Overseas Chinese in the United States, 1868–1911*, Fayetteville, University of Arkansas Press, 1983; 49th Congress, Session II, Statutes at Large, Volume 24, Chapter 253, February 24, 1887.

ROHMER, SAX (1883–1959), adventure story writer. Rohmer was born Arthur Henry Zarfield Wade of Irish parents in Birmingham, England, on February 15, 1883. As a student Rohmer developed a fond curiosity for ancient Egypt, studied hieroglyphics, and pursued a lifetime interest in the occult. After his schooling was finished, he tried a number of unsuccessful careers before he wrote his first stories, "The Leopard Couch" and "The Mysterious Mummy." These stories helped to establish him as an adventure story writer. But his best known adventure series is the "Dr. Fu Manchu" stories. In this series Asian males, through the character of Dr. Fu Manchu, were always portrayed as "evil geniuses" or "amazingly horrible," and their physical characteristics as "green eyes like a leopard" or "cat-like poise." Rohmer created many negative stereotypes for the Chinese: notably, their yellow skin color; long, bony fingers; long, narrow eyes; lean, yellow necks; either short in stature or tall and gaunt. Chinatown* itself was characterized as a mysterious place with many strange smells; full of gangs and gangsters; a center of crime, especially murders. Influenced by what they read, Americans saw the caricature of Chinese as realistic, and they based their prejudice on what they wanted to see—probably because the villainous prototype was more exciting. Rohmer captured the excitement and exaggeration in one character, Fu Manchu. Fu Manchu's popularity brought Rohmer a fortune in 1955 when he sold the television, radio, and film rights for Fu Manchu to Republic Pictures for $4 million.

FURTHER READING: Isaac Anderson, "New Mystery Stories," *New York Times Book Review*, New York: New York Times Company, April 5, 1931; Will Cuppy, "Mystery and Adventure," *New York Herald Tribune Books*, New York: New York Tribune, November 13, 1932; Stanley J. Kunitz, *Twentieth Century Authors: First Supplement*, New York: H. W. Wilson Co., 1955; Ralph Hobart Phillips, "Sax Rohmer's 'The Insidious Dr. Fu Manchu,'" *Bookman*, New York: Dodd, Mead, and Co., September 1913–1914; John M. Reilly, *Twentieth Century Crime and Mystery Writers*, New York: St. Martin's Press, 1980.

ROLDAN, SALVADOR v. LOS ANGELES COUNTY, a case involving Salvador Roldan who had been denied a marriage license to marry Marjorie Rogers in 1931 by the county clerk. The couple then decided to petition for a writ of mandate to the California Court of Appeals, requesting that it direct the county clerk to issue them a marriage license.

On January 27, 1933, the Appeals Court ruled that Filipinos were not prohibited from marrying whites, thus upholding the lower court's opinion that Filipinos were not to be included in the classification of "Mongolian." But it was a hollow victory: on April 20, 1933, the California State Legislature approved Bill No. 175, which was to go into effect on August 21, 1933, thus making all marriages of white persons with non-whites illegal in the State of California. (*See also* Jones, Herbert C.*)

ROMULO, CARLOS P. (1899–), Filipino patriot, president of the U.N. General Assembly, journalist. Romulo was born on January 14, 1899, in Manila, the son of a Filipino guerrilla fighter who was an active member of the revolutionary government of Emilio Aguinaldo* during the American Filipino War. Ironically, Carlos Romulo would gain prominence as America's most trusted Asian spokesperson in his later life. By his own admission he was filled with hatred toward Americans and all things American when he was growing up in the Philippines. On the other hand, probably because of his American education, he would gain some respect for American ways and ideals.

Romulo received his B. A. degree from the University of the Philippines and a Master of Arts degree in English from Columbia University in 1921. Upon completion of his graduate studies in the United States, he returned to the University of the Philippines to work as an English professor, as well as chairperson of the same department, a position he held from 1923 to 1928. In 1929 he was appointed a regent of the University of the Philippines. Among the many honors he received during his long life, perhaps two accomplishments stand out: first, he was chosen as the first Asian to become president of the United Nations General Assembly in 1949; and second, he was the only Filipino journalist who was awarded the highly prestigious Pulitzer Prize for a series of outstanding articles on the Southeast Asian political situation in the late 1930s and early

1940s. During World War II Romulo joined the staff of General Douglas MacArthur as press relations secretary and was commissioned a major in the U.S. Army. By 1945 he was promoted to the rank of brigadier general and accompanied MacArthur in the recapture of Manila.

Romulo served his home country as a seasoned diplomat in various negotiations with the United States, including various amendments attached to the Philippine Rehabilitation Act of 1946. This particular negotiation was carried out while Romulo was serving as the Philippine resident commissioner in Washington, D.C., in 1945.

Romulo authored a number of books, including *I Saw the Fall of the Philippines* (1942), *Mother America* (1943), *My Brother Americans* (1945), *Crusade in Asia* (1955), and *I Walked with Heroes* (1961).

FURTHER READING: Milton Walter Myer, *A Diplomatic History of the Philippine Republic*, Honolulu: University of Hawaii Press, 1965; Carlos P. Romulo, *Mother America*, New York: Doubleday, Doran and Co., 1943; Carlos P. Romulo, *I Walked with Heroes*, New York: Holt, Rinehart and Winston, 1961; George E. Taylor, *The Philippines and the United States: Problems of Partnership*, New York: Frederick A. Praeger, 1964.

RONEY, FRANK (1841–1925), labor leader and anti-Chinese agitator. Roney was born in Belfast, Ireland, on August 13, 1841. A Roman Catholic and a son of a wealthy contractor, he was married three times, fathering three children. As a young man, he was associated with the Fenians, a revolutionary movement dedicated to the overthrow of British rule in Ireland. Because of his leadership position in the organization, he was arrested and charged with treason, but he was able to avoid a prison sentence by promising never to return to his homeland. He immigrated to the United States and lived in New York and Chicago before he settled in Omaha, Nebraska, where he secured a job with Omaha Smelting as an iron molder. He joined the Iron Molders Union, Local 190, and served as secretary and president. Roney became active in the National Labor Reform Party, which was the political arm of the National Labor Union (NLR). He was elected president of the Nebraska arm of the NLR party.

Roney moved to California in search of work in 1875, and found employment at Pacific Iron Works in San Francisco. That same year he also became a naturalized citizen of the United States. Two years later Roney joined the Workingmen's Party of California* and championed the anti-Chinese movement of the party. Roney was elected temporary chairman of the Workingmen's Party during its first state convention on January 21, 1878. While acting as temporary chairman, he wrote the party platform and constitution. Its platform contained ten major points, some of which were anti-Chinese.

When Denis Kearney* was released from prison on May 4, 1878, Roney was deposed from the leadership role. However, he led the anti-Kearney faction in an attempt to represent a more radical and socialist platform. After this unsuccessful attempt, he severed connections with both factions within the Workingmen's

Party and became a socialist and an active trade unionist. He joined the International Workingmen's Association, a forerunner of the Socialist Labor Party.

Roney became temporary chairman of the Seaman's Protective Association when sailors and firemen formed the organization on September 5, 1880. The following year Roney went to the Representative Assembly of Trades and Labor Unions as a delegate from the Seaman's Protective Union. Roney drafted a bill requiring that two-thirds of the crew on every U.S. ship be American citizens after it was rumored that Chinese seamen were untrustworthy. With the intent to organize opposition against Chinese, the Trade Assembly called for a state convention of labor and anti-Chinese organizations to be held in San Francisco on April 24, 1882. At this convention the League of Deliverance* was formed with Roney as chairman. The league boycotted products from businesses that employed any Chinese or Mongolian directly or indirectly, in any capacity. The goal of the league was to exclude the Chinese from the United States. With the passage of the Chinese Exclusion Act of 1882,* the league was disbanded.

Roney was also involved in founding the Representative Council of the Federated Trades and Labor Organization of the Pacific Coast, an anti-Knights of Labor federation dominated by the International Workingmen's Association. He served as its president from 1885 through 1887. He continued to work as labor organizer and leader until 1915, when he served as secretary treasurer for the Iron Council of Los Angeles. He lived a lonely, poverty-stricken life until his death on January 24, 1925, in Long Beach, California.

FURTHER READING: John R. Commons et al., *History of Labor in the United States*, Vol, 2, New York: Macmillan Co., 1918; Alexander Saxton, *The Indispensable Enemy*, Berkeley: University of California Press, 1971; Philip Taft, *Labor Politics American Style: The California State Federation of Labor*, Cambridge, Mass.: President and Fellows of Harvard College, 1968; Paul S. Taylor, *The Sailors Union of the Pacific*, New York: Ronald Press Co., 1923.

ROQUE ESPIRITU DE LA YSLA v. UNITED STATES, a case involving the right of a person born in the Philippines, but owning allegiance to the United States, to become a naturalized citizen of the United States. The petitioner, Roque Espiritu de la Ysla, had applied for U.S. citizenship but was denied by the Los Angeles Superior Court. He appealed to the U.S. Circuit Court of the Ninth Circuit, which upheld the lower court's decision on April 23, 1935.

In his brief, prepared for presentation before the Supreme Court, it was argued that the petitioner was not an alien and was entitled to constitutional protection as a citizen of the Philippines who owed allegiance to the United States. On October 15, 1935, the Supreme Court ruled not to grant the petitioner writ of certiorari, thereby upholding the lower court's decision.

FURTHER READING: Hyung-chan Kim and Cynthia Mejia, *The Filipinos in America, 1898–1974*, Dobbs Ferry, N.Y.: Oceana Publications, 1976; *Supreme Court Reporter* 56, 296, U.S. 575, 1935.

ROYAL HAWAIIAN AGRICULTURAL SOCIETY. *See* Hawaiian Sugar Planters' Association.

S

SAKADAS, a group of Filipino laborers recruited from the Philippines to work on Hawaii's sugar plantations. The word "Sakada" means a laborer-recruit as well as the process used in recruiting temporary workers. Among Hawaiian Filipinos, however, the term is used to separate Filipino laborers who came to Hawaii between 1906 and 1946 from other Filipinos.
FURTHER READING: Ruben R. Alcantara, *Sakada: Filipino Adaptation in Hawaii*, Washington, D.C.: University Press of America, 1981.

SAKAMOTO, JAMES YOSHINORI (1903–1955), prize–fighter, journalist. Sakamoto was born in Seattle, the son of Sakamoto Osamu and Tsuchi, and attended public schools in Seattle before he decided to go to New York to begin his career in prize-fighting. In 1927 he became the first Nisei* to fight at Madison Square Garden. He came back almost blind from the blows he had received as a fighter, and started a newspaper, *The Japanese American Courier*,* which was published in English on January 1, 1928. Sakamoto later served as president of the Japanese American Citizens League* in 1938. He died in Seattle in 1955.

SAKE BILL, a law entitled An Act to Increase the Duty on Liquors, Still Wines and Other Beverages Made from Materials Other Than Grape Juice. It was approved by the legislature of the Republic of Hawaii over President Sanford Ballard Dole's* veto in June 1896. The law went into effect on July 1, 1897.

With the increasing number of Japanese immigrants entering Hawaii to replace Chinese laborers, white citizens began to react against them. One of the measures taken to discourage Japanese immigration to Hawaii was to restrict the amount of sake available for consumption by Japanese in Hawaii. Sake had been consumed by Japanese in Hawaii, and it was singled out as the target of anger and frustration over Japanese immigration to Hawaii.

The law imposed an almost prohibitive tax on the importation of this favorite drink of the Japanese, thereby discouraging further Japanese economic expansion and immigration to Hawaii.

FURTHER READING: Francis Hilary Conroy, "The Japanese Expansion into Hawaii, 1868–1898," Ph.D diss., University of California, 1949.

SALII, LAZARUS EITARO (1936–), political leader of Micronesia. Salii was born in Anaguar, Palau, Micronesia, on November 17, 1936, the son of Edward and Concepcion Salii. He attended the University of Hawaii where he majored in government. Upon graduation from the university in 1961, he entered public administration by becoming an employee of the Office for Political and Social and Economic Affairs, Palau District, Micronesia, and worked there until 1964. He became secretary for the Palau Legislature in 1964, and in 1968 he became a member of the Micronesia Senate from Palau District. He served as chairman of the House Ways and Means Committee and as Special Advisor to the United States Delegation to the United Nations Trusteeship Council.

In 1967 Salii became chairman of the Congressional Committee on the Future Status of Micronesia, and at the same time he began to negotiate with the government of the United States on the political future of Micronesia. Since 1969 he has served as chairman of the Future Political Status Commission established by the Congress of Micronesia.

Under Salii's able political leadership, Micronesia began to lean toward the United States under a formula called free association. This policy was to give Micronesians autonomy in local affairs in exchange for financial assistance from the United States, which was also given the right to use the islands for military purposes. Micronesia's foreign affairs were to be controlled by Washington.

FURTHER READING: F. P. King, ed., *Oceania and Beyond: Essays on the Pacific Since 1945*, Westport, Conn.: Greenwood Press, 1976; Robert Trumbull, *Tin Roofs and Palm Trees: A Report on the New South Seas,* Seattle: University of Washington Press, 1977.

SALINAS LETTUCE STRIKE OF 1934, a strike called against the Central California Vegetable Growers and Shippers' Association by the newly established Filipino Labor Union* on August 27, 1934. The Filipino Labor Union, established on November 30, 1933, had completed its organization and had established various local chapters by the end of 1933. Under the leadership of D. L. Marcuelo, who published the *Three Stars*, a major Filipino newspaper that had urged Filipinos to organize, and Rufo Canete, a Filipino labor contractor, the Filipino Labor Union demanded that the hourly wage of 30 cents be raise to 40 cents, but its demand had been refused by the Central California Vegetable Growers and Shippers' Association. Three days later, on August 27, 1934, approximately 7,000 workers, both men and women, walked off their jobs, thus paralyzing the $50,000 daily lettuce industry in Central California.

During the course of the strike attempts by local mobs, local government authorities in collusion with the Growers and Shippers' Association were made to harass and discourage striking workers and their leaders from continuing their strike. Rufo Canete found his labor camp set on fire on September 21,1934, and he himself was placed under arrest on a misdemeanor charge but was later released. In addition, D. L. Marcuelo, president of the Filipino Labor Union, was pressured to resign from his office, although he gave his failing health as his reason for his resignation.

As a result of mounting pressure on striking members, the union's Strike Committee decided to call off the strike on September 23, 1934. This was followed by two days of intensive and hard negotiations. The workers returned to the fields, and the Filipino Labor Union was recognized as a legitimate farm union. Filipino farm workers were given a wage increase of 10 cents, lifting their hourly wage to 40 cents. This was a minor victory for the members of the Filipino Labor Union. More important to Filipinos in America in general, however, was that the Salinas Lettuce Strike changed the image of Filipinos from happy-go-lucky people willing to work for low wages to people willing to stand up for their rights.

FURTHER READING: Howard A. DeWitt, "The Filipino Labor Union: The Salinas Lettuce Strike of 1934," *Amerasia Journal* 5, No.2 (1978) pp. 1–21; Stuart Jamieson, *Labor Unionism in American Agriculture*, Washington, D.C.: U.S. Government Printing Office, 1946; Hyung-chan Kim and Cynthia Mejia, *The Filipinos in America, 1898–1974*, Dobbs Ferry, N.Y.: Oceana Publications, 1976; U.S. Government Printing Office, *Hearings Before a Subcommittee of the Committee of Education and Labor*, U.S. Senate, Part 54, Agricultural Labor in California, Washington, D.C.: U.S. Government Printing Office, 1940.

SAM YAP (SAN-I), the three districts surrounding the city of Canton, Kwangtung Province, located in the southeastern part of China. These districts —Nanhai (Namhoi), Panyu (Punyu), and Shunde (Shuntak)— sent many of their inhabitants to the United States, where they later established their own social organization known as Sam Yap Wui Kun (Hui Kuan) in 1851. (*See also* District Companies; Pearl River Delta.)

FURTHER READING: Gunther Barth, *Bitter Strength*, Cambridge, Mass.: Harvard University Press, 1964; Corinne K. Hoexter, *From Canton to California: The Epic of Chinese Immigration*, New York: Four Winds Press, 1976; Kil Young Zo, *Chinese Emigration into the United States, 1850–1880*, New York: Arno Press, 1978.

SAM YAP WUI KUN. *See* District Companies.

SAMOAN CIVIC ASSOCIATION, a secondary social organization established among Samoans on the United States' West Coast, to which they immigrated from Samoa. As of 1970 approximately 15,000 to 20,000 Samoans were living in San Diego, Oceanside, the greater Los Angeles area, and the San Francisco Bay area. Traditionally, after the introduction of Christianity to Samoa, churches became a most popular secondary social organization among Samoans. But in 1960 some 200 Samoans decided to organize the Samoan Civic Association in order to sponsor a number of community projects.

FURTHER READING: Joan Ablon, "The Social Organization of an Urban Samoan Community," in Emma Gee, ed., *Counterpoints*, Regents of the University of California, 1976; Cluny MacPherson, Bradd Shore, and Robert Franco, eds., *New Neighbors . . . Islanders in Adaptation*, Santa Cruz, Calif.; Center for the South Pacific Studies, University of California at Santa Cruz, 1978.

SAN FRANCISCO BOARD OF SUPERVISORS, REPORT OF SPECIAL COMMITTEE ON CHINATOWN (1884), special committee appointed by the San Francisco City Board of Supervisors on February 2, 1884, to report on general conditions in Chinatown.* A three-man committee set out to investigate the social, economic, and cultural life of Chinese residents in an area occupying twelve blocks within the boundaries of California Street on the south, Kearney Street on the east, Broadway on the north, and Stockton Street on the west. Within this limited area to which the Chinese were confined to establish their community, the committee found living conditions to their disliking. The report condemned prostitution in Chinatown, the abuse of Chinese women and children, unhealthy conditions prevailing in the community, and general lawlessness and violations of laws by Chinese residents. It accused the Chinese of deliberately violating municipal laws in defiance of city authorities.

The report made a number of recommendations to force the Chinese to comply with health standards. Among the recommended measures were strengthening and enforcing municipal laws. The report submitted by W. B. Farwell and John E. Kunkler concluded by calling on Congress to prohibit Chinese immigration.

FURTHER READING: Willard B. Farwell, *The Chinese at Home and Abroad*, San Francisco: A. L. Bancroft and Co., 1885.

SAN FRANCISCO SCHOOL BOARD SEGREGATION ORDER OF 1906, an order requiring that all Japanese children be sent to the Oriental Public School. With the large influx of Japanese immigrants into the United States, anti-Japanese sentiment gradually developed among whites on the West Coast where many Japanese residents concentrated. The first anti-Japanese protest meeting was held in 1900, and the San Francisco Labor Council decided to push for the exclusion of all Japanese from American soil the following year. Three years later the American Federation of Labor endorsed the exclusion stance of the San Francisco Labor Council. Adding fuel to the already burning issue was the printing of derogatory articles and statements on Asians in California in major San Francisco newspapers, especially *The San Francisco Chronicle*.

The first resolution of the San Francisco School Board regarding segregation came in May 1905 and declared its intention to establish separate schools for Chinese and Japanese. Although it was not enforced, it opened the door for the segregation order that came one year later. On October 11, 1906, the San

Francisco School Board ordered school principals to send all Japanese children to the Oriental Public School, later to be called Commodore Stockton. Shocked and insulted by this racist order, parents of the children refused to comply with the order and kept their children at home.

The official Japanese response to the outrageous treatment of Japanese residents was swift and strong. A major newspaper in Tokyo urged the government to send warships, and the Japanese consul in San Francisco filed a protest with the board. Viscount Aoki Keikichi, the Japanese ambassador to the United States, claimed, during a meeting with Secretary of State Elihu Root, that the segregation order of the San Francisco School Board was in violation of the Treaty of 1894.

On October 26, 1906, worried about a potential boycott of Japanese trade on top of the already present Chinese boycott, President Theodore Roosevelt sent his Secretary of Commerce and Labor, Victor Howard Metcalf,* to study the situation and report on the exclusion of the Japanese children from public schools. Upon arrival in San Francisco, Metcalf, who was from Oakland, attempted to persuade the board to rescind its segregation order but without success. His efforts were denounced by people who attended a mass labor meeting on December 23 in San Francisco.

While the Roosevelt administration searched for ways to resolve the conflict between the San Francisco School Board and the federal government's interest in protecting Japanese children's rights, it also prepared for a lawsuit against the school board. On January 17, 1907, U.S. Attorney Robert Devlin filed his brief on behalf of Aoki Keikichi against M. A. Deane, the principal of Redding School, claiming that Section 1662 of the law in question excluded only Chinese and Mongolians, and because Japanese were neither Chinese nor Mongolian, they should not be excluded.

The case of Aoki v. Deane was dismissed, however, because the San Francisco School Board agreed to rescind its segregation order in exchange for the promise by the Roosevelt administration that Japanese immigration to the United States would be restricted and that Japanese laborers would not be allowed to come to the U.S. mainland from Hawaii, Mexico, or Canada. The Roosevelt administration then negotiated with the Japanese government for conclusion of the Gentlemen's Agreement,* which went into effect in 1908.

FURTHER READING: Thomas A. Bailey, *Theodore Roosevelt and the Japanese-American Crises*, Gloucester, Mass.: Peter Smith, 1964; Roger Daniels, *The Politics of Prejudice*, Berkeley: University of California Press, 1962; Philip A. Lum, "The Creation and Demise of San Francisco Chinatown Freedom Schools: One Response to Desegregation," *Amerasia*, 5, No.1 (1978) pp. 57–73; David Brudnoy, "Race and the San Francisco School Board Incident: Contemporary Evaluations," in Roger Olmsted and Charles Wollenberg, eds., *Neither Separate Nor Equal: Race and Racism in California*, California Historical Society, 1971; Charles Wollenberg, *All Deliberate Speed: Segregation and Exclusion in California Schools, 1855–1975*, Berkeley: University of California Press, 1976.

SANDALWOOD MOUNTAINS, another name for the Hawaiian Islands, where sandalwood was found in abundance in the past. The Chinese developed trade with Hawaiian natives, who suffered greatly from forced labor in gathering sandalwood. The Chinese used sandalwood in making incense, fans, and other objets d'art.

SANSEI, a Japanese term meaning the third generation of persons of Japanese ancestry born in the United States. Most persons of Japanese ancestry belonging to this generation are between twenty-five and fifty years of age. Many studies have been conducted on the personality and behavior of the third–generation Japanese Americans. It is commonly believed that Sansei are different from their parental generation, which is generally characterized as unwilling or unable to speak out against the injustices they suffered during World War II. (*See also* Issei; Nisei.)

FURTHER READING: John W. Connor, *Tradition and Change in Three Generations of Japanese Americans*, Chicago: Nelson-Hall, 1977; Christie W. Kiefer, *Changing Cultures, Changing Lives: An Ethnographic Study of Three Generations of Japanese Americans*, San Francisco: Jossey-Bass Publishers, 1974; Minako K. Maykovich, *Japanese American Identity Dilemma*, Tokyo, Japan: Waseda University Press, 1972.

SARGENT, FRANK PEARCE (1854–1908), labor leader, commissioner general of the Bureau of Immigration. Sargent was born in East Orange, Vermont, on November 18, 1854, to a family whose forebears had lived in Massachusetts as early as 1633. He attended local schools during childhood and worked on farms in the surrounding area. He spent one year at Northfield Academy, Northfield, Massachusetts, before he was force to come to Arizona because of health problems. In 1878 he enlisted in the U.S. Calvary there, and was active in a military campaign against the Apache Indians. He was discharged two years later and went to work for the Southern Pacific railroad as an engine wiper. In 1881 Sargent was initiated into the Brotherhood of Locomotive Firemen, thus beginning his long involvement with the American labor movement. He rose through the ranks to lead a number of major labor strikes, including the Chicago, Burlington and Quincy strike in 1888 and the American Railway strike against the Great Northern Railroad in 1894.

On May 7, 1902, President Theodore Roosevelt nominated Sargent to become commissioner general of the Bureau of Immigration to succeed Terence Vincent Powderly,* and his nomination was approved the following day. With his appointment the close ties between the American Federation of Labor and the Bureau of Immigration during the Powderly years of office became even closer, and they had devastating effects on Chinese in America as well as Chinese desiring to enter the United States.

Sargent was committed to the restriction and exclusion of immigrants to the United States from South and Southeastern Europe and Asia. At the same time he wanted to encourage Northern European immigrants who belonged to the

Germanic race. This prejudice was reflected in his writings. In one of his articles published in 1904, "The Need of Close Inspection and Greater Restriction of Immigrants," Sargent stated that America was becoming a "dumping ground" for the diseased, poor, and unwanted immigrants, and he advocated the exclusion of these people. In another article published in the same year, "Problems of Immigration," he tried to soften his prejudice by claiming that U.S. immigration laws were made not to exclude people but to select them. He believed that America needed certain desirable immigrants, especially the Irish and German.

During his tenure in office between 1902 and 1908, Sargent made numerous recommendations that were basically anti-Chinese in nature, and he encouraged immigration officials to intimidate and harass Chinese residents in America. He defended the mass arrests of Chinese in Boston on October 11, 1903, on the grounds that too many Chinese had been smuggled into the United States. He was also instrumental in introducing the Bertillon system* of identification that was used against Chinese. (*See also* Powderly, Terence Vincent; Bertillon System.)

FURTHER READING: Delber L. McKee, *Chinese Exclusion Versus the Open Door Policy, 1900–1906: Clashes over China Policy in the Roosevelt Era*, Detroit, Mich.: Wayne State University Press, 1977; Frank Sargent, "The Need of Close Inspection and Greater Restriction of Immigrants," *Century Magazine* 67, (November 1903-April 1904), pp. 470–473; Frank Sargent, "Problems of Immigration," *Annals of the American Academy of Political and Social Science* 24, (July-November 1904), pp. 153–158.

SATOW MASAO (1908–1977), leader of the Japanese American Citizens League.* Satow was born on February 14, 1908, in San Mateo, California, to Satow Shuzo and Kiyose. Like many of his colleagues who worked for the Japanese American Citizens League, "Mas" came from very modest origins. When he was still a toddler, his family moved to Los Angeles where his father supported the family by doing menial day work. After his high school years, Satow scraped together enough money to attend the University of California at Los Angeles and graduated in 1929. He continued his education at Princeton Theological Seminary where he received a Bachelor of Theology degree in 1932.

In 1932 Satow joined the Japanese American Citizens League, which had just begun to emerge as a national organization for persons of Japanese ancestry born in the United States. As the years passed, Satow became more involved in this organization. He was elected to the position of assistant executive secretary in 1936 and was allowed a nominal travel expense of $150 for the two-year term. In the same year he was appointed to chair the Second Generation Development Program. This program helped Nisei* to become more closely integrated into the nation's economic, political, and social life.

During World War II Satow was interned but was released in December of 1944 from Granada. He took the position of a national board field representative for the Young Men's Christian Association (YMCA) in Milwaukee. He continued to work for the Japanese American Citizens League as the Eastern-Midwest district representative before he was asked to serve as the organization's national secretary when that position was vacated by Mike Masaru Masaoka,* who had left for Washington, D.C., to lobby for legislation to equalize Japanese American rights. Satow accepted his new position and began his twenty–five years of service as national secretary of the Japanese American Citizens League during which he worked hard to develop the organization. When he became the national secretary in 1947, there were only 3,100 members in twenty–five chapters with only two chapters on the West Coast; in 1972 when Satow retired, there were ninety–four chapters from coast to coast constituting 27,000 members. His contributions to the organization were recognized when the Japanese American Citizens League headquarters in San Francisco was renamed the Satow Building. A Library in Gardena, California, was also named after Satow. He died on March 3, 1977.

SAUND, DALIP SINGH (1899–1973), U.S. Congressman. Saund was born on September 20, 1899, in a village in northern India called Chhajalwadi. Although his parents were illiterate, they valued education and sent their son to schools in the Punjab town of Amritsar. Saund graduated from the Sikh College and went to the University of Punjab with a degree in 1919. Although he could have worked in India's British-controlled civil service, he rejected this opportunity and came to America in 1920, as a result of his interest in the ideologies of Woodrow Wilson and Abraham Lincoln.

Saund came to California to study the cannery industry with the intention of setting up his own cannery in India. He enrolled in the University of California at Berkeley, and during the summers he worked in cannery factories. He graduated with an M. A. in mathematics in 1922 and earned his Ph. D. two years later.

Saund's ability to speak publicly on subject matters pertaining to India made him a popular speaker in the Imperial Valley of California. He decided to run for public office but was unable to qualify because of the citizenship restrictions against Asian Indians. He then worked to organize the India Association of America and served as its president in 1942. With the support of this organization he pushed for Asian Indian rights to become U.S. citizens.

In 1949 Saund became a naturalized citizen of the United States, and in 1956 he ran for a seat in Congress against a popular Republican, Jacqueline Odlum. He defeated his opponent by 3,200 votes, thus becoming the first Asian to be elected to Congress. In Congress he served on the House Foreign Affairs Committee, which assigned him to survey the U.S. foreign aid program in Asia. In an address to the Parliament of India in 1957 he vigorously denied discrimination against non-whites in the United States. He served in Congress from 1957 to 1962. He was defeated in his bid for the 88th Congress.

SCHNELL, JOHN HENRY. *See* Wakamatsu Tea and Silk Farm Colony.

SCOTT ACT OF 1888, approved by the U.S. Congress against a background of controversy as to whether or not China had rejected a treaty with the United States. The treaty in question was negotiated between the two governments and was approved on March 12, 1888, prohibiting Chinese laborers from returning to the United States if they were not already in the country. While China was considering the treaty, a London dispatch of September 2, 1888, reported that China had rejected the treaty. The following day Rep. William L. Scott of Pennsylvania introduced a bill that would deny the Chinese laborers' reentry into the United States after their visit to their native country. It was estimated that as many as 20,000 Chinese laborers were in transit at the time of the passage of the bill, which was signed into law on October 1, 1888, by President Grover Cleveland. The certificate of identity issued to them was ruled null and void, and no more certificates were issued.

FURTHER READING: Jack Chen *The Chinese of America*, New York: Harper and Row, 1980; Tien-Lu Li, *Congressional Policy of Chinese Immigration*, Nashville, Tenn.: Publishing House of the Methodist Episcopal Church, South, 1916; Stanford M. Lyman, *Chinese Americans*, New York: Random House, 1974.

SEATTLE ANTI-CHINESE RIOT, a riot that took place on February 8, 1886, when Chinese residents in Seattle, Washington Territory, were driven out of town by an angry mob of Sinophobes who felt strongly that "law and order" had to be restored by expelling Chinese from their city. A number of factors were directly responsible for Chinese expulsion from Seattle. First, there was a widespread belief that the Chinese were willing to work more hours for less pay and that their labor was too cheap for whites to compete with. This somewhat distorted perception was particularly strong during the hard times of 1885–1886 in influencing unemployed people to take "law and order" into their own hands. Second, Chinese were perceived as sojourners* who were concerned not with local economic conditions, but only with how much money they could send to their homeland. Third, racial prejudice played a major role in anti-Chinese agitation. Given these conditions in a depressed economy, Seattle inevitably followed the examples of Eureka, California, Rock Springs, Wyoming Territory, and Tacoma, Washington Territory.

The agitators bent on expelling Chinese residents from Seattle tried to have them removed by peaceful means. For their part local authorities tried to prevent rioting against Chinese. After the Chinese were expelled from Tacoma, Sheriff John H. McGraw asked Governor Watson Carvosso Squire* to send for military aid. The U.S. military arrived in Seattle, and all was quiet as long as the soldiers were there. But the agitators continued to hold meetings where they planned to expel the Chinese, and after the soldiers left, they put their plan into action. About 1,500 men were estimated to have participated in the Chinese evacuation. They went into the Chinese quarter of town and collected all Chinese belongings and had them loaded onto wagons. Then the Chinese were escorted to the docks to be shipped to San Francisco aboard the *Queen of the Pacific*. Not surprisingly, the Chinese offered no resistance.

At the docks, the Chinese were given tickets and put aboard the ship; those Chinese who could not board the ship waited on the docks with all of their belongings. The *Queen of the Pacific* left with a large cargo of Chinese, but those who were left behind were escorted back to the courthouse, where a fight broke out between deputies and the angry mob. During the fight shots were fired, killing one man and injuring four others. After this incident Governor Squire declared martial law, establishing a regular military system of government. President Grover Cleveland approved this measure and dispatched a regiment of U.S. infantry to the scene.

The ringleaders of the riot were brought to court for their violent attack on the Chinese, but none of them was ever prosecuted or convicted. (*See also* Squire, Watson Carvosso; Rock Springs Massacre of 1885.)

FURTHER READING: C. B. Bagley, *History of Seattle, Washington*, Vol. 3, Chicago: S. J. Clarke Publishing Co., 1916; Lorraine B. Hildebrand, *Straw Hats, Sandals and Steel*, Tacoma: Washington State American Revolution Bicentennial Committee, 1977; Jules Alexander Karlin, "The Anti-Chinese Outbreaks in Seattle, 1885–1886," *Pacific Northwest Quarterly* 39 (1948), pp.103–130; Shih-shan Henry Tsai, *China and the Overseas Chinese in the United States, 1868–1911*, Fayetteville: University of Arkansas Press, 1983.

SEATTLE PROGRESSIVE CITIZENS LEAGUE, a civic organization established in 1921 in Seattle, Washington, by Nisei* Americans to combat legalized discrimination against Americans of Japanese ancestry. The organization was established under the instigation of two Issei* Japanese, Henry H. Okuda and Ito Chusaburo. Ozawa Shigeru served as president when the league was organized, but it was not very active, holding only three meetings between 1921 and 1928. The organization was revived after an editorial calling for reorganization of the league appeared in the first issue of the *Japanese American Courier* on January 1, 1928. This time Clarence Arai was elected president. In that year he went to Portland, Oregon, to help organize the Portland Progressive Citizens League. In the middle of 1928 he made a trip to San Francisco and Los Angeles and met a number of Nisei leaders in both cities. In April of the following year, Arai met with Kido Saburo* and Thomas T. Yatabe, and presented them with three proposals: that a Nisei organization be established nationwide; that it be named the Japanese American Citizens League*; and that a convention to found such an organization be held in Seattle in the summer of 1930. The founding convention of the Japanese American Citizens League was held in Seattle on August 29, 1930.

FURTHER READING: Bill Hosokawa, *Nisei*, New York: William Morrow and Co., 1969; Bill Hosokawa, *JACL in Quest of Justice*, New York: William Morrow and Co., 1982.

SECOND FILIPINO INFANTRY BATTALION, originally activated on October 14, 1942, as the First Battalion, Second Filipino Regiment, with authorization from Headquarters of the Army Ground Forces. It was later reorganized as the Second Filipino Infantry Battalion on March 27, 1944, and was stationed at Camp Cooke. In 1943 the battalion was sent to Brisbane,

Australia, and participated in a battle in New Guinea before it landed in the southern Philippines.

SECRET SOCIETIES. *See Tongs.*

SELECT COMMITTEE INVESTIGATING NATIONAL DEFENSE MIGRATION. *See* Tolan Committee.

SELF-DEFENSE SOCIETY. *See* Bow On Guk.

SEWARD, GEORGE FREDERICK (1840–1910), Minister to China. Seward was born on November 8, 1840, the son of George W. and Tempe Leddell Seward of Florida, New York. His education included Seward Academy in Florida and a brief stint at Union College which he entered in 1857 but from which he never graduated. Through his kinship to William Seward, then Secretary of State, George Seward was appointed U.S. consul to China at Shanghai on October 24, 1861, and by September 2, 1863 he was promoted to consul general. He married Kate Sherman on August 4, 1870.

Seward served as consul for many years before he was appointed Minister to China. As Minister, he served with considerable distinction and success; he apparently had a genuine interest in helping to modernize China and was instrumental in developing the steam railroad line at Woosung.

Seward was outspoken in his opposition to strict and unfair immigration quotas levied against the Chinese people in the latter half of the nineteenth century. He argued at length on behalf of the Chinese, attacked negative stereotypes, and challenged erroneous assumptions prevalent in America in his time. But because his opinions clashed with those of his superiors, his diplomatic career was cut short. His resignation as Minister to China was requested before he could complete an immigration treaty with China. He returned to this country in 1880 and wrote a significant book, *Chinese Immigration: Its Social and Economical Aspects* (1881). He died in New York on November 28, 1910.

FURTHER READING: George F. Seward, *Chinese Immigration: Its Social and Economical Aspects*, New York: Charles Scribner's Sons, 1881.

SHANGHAIED, a term referring to the kidnapping of men for compulsory service aboard a ship bound for the city of Shanghai, China. Kidnapping occurred on the streets of San Francisco in the 1860s and 1870s. It was said that a man with the nickname "Shanghai Brown" kidnapped numerous men in the city. In 1896 he was kidnapped himself and was placed aboard a ship going around Cape Horn. The word "Shanghai" also means the kidnapping of Chinese peasants in China, who were then sold into slavery as coolies to work on sugar plantations in the Caribbean Islands.

SHANGHAI RIOTS OF 1859, provoked by kidnapping of Chinese coolies. Shanghai, the largest port in China, was open to foreign trade in 1842 and had four foreign settlements established by Japanese, French, British, and Americans. The British and American settlements merged to become the International Settlement in 1863, whereas the Japanese and French kept their settlements until they were returned to China at the end of World War II.

Although the coolie trade* and Chinese emigration through the port of Shanghai were small, the presence of foreigners who were suspected of kidnapping Chinese to be sold into slavery aroused intense feelings of hostility. After the French coolie ship *Gertrude* sailed with Chinese coolies aboard who had been kidnapped, the anger of the local people ran high, and when they saw two British sailors who were mistaken as kidnappers they attacked them, leaving one dead and the other seriously wounded. This incident occurred on July 29, 1859, and the following day six Siamese were attacked by a group of angry Chinese. One of them drowned, and the rest had to be sent home under military escort. Under pressure from the Chinese government as well as from local people, the ship returned August 1, and 157 Chinese were released to their families.

When a Chinese ship intercepted a fishing boat that carried thirty–four kidnapped Chinese to be sold into slavery, local people became angry and killed two foreign sailors. These provocative events alarmed Chinese officials who attempted to persuade foreign governments to discourage citizens from engaging in the coolie traffic. The cooperation the Chinese government sought from foreign governments did not come; instead, the Chinese government was forced to allow its citizens to emigrate abroad under the joint supervision of British and Chinese officials. FURTHER READING: Robert L. Irick, *Ch'ing Policy Toward the Coolie Trade, 1847–1878*, San Francisco: Chinese Materials Center, 1982; Sing-wu Wang, *The Organization of Chinese Emigration, 1848–1888*, San Francisco: Chinese Materials Center, 1978.

SHOONG, JOE (1879–1961), businessman, philanthropist. Shoong was born in San Francisco on December 29, 1879, the son of Joe Gon and Wong Shee Shoong. His father immigrated from China to the United States in the middle of the nineteenth century. Joe Shoong grew up in San Francisco, attending its public schools. He was employed in a dry goods store in Vallejo, California, until 1903 when he decided to establish a small shop where he made and sold women's apparel. In 1905 he moved this store to the Fillmore district in San Francisco and began operating the business under the name of China Toggery. In 1928 the name was changed to the National Dollar Stores, Ltd.,* woth forty–three branch stores in California, two in Utah, two in Nevada, one in Washington, and four in Hawaii. The company had $20,000 capital when it started, but an estimated $1 million by 1928.

Shoong was active in the San Francisco Chinese community affairs. He contributed liberally to community causes, including $24,000 for the construction costs of the Chinese Hospital in San Francisco. He established the Joe Shoong Foundation through which a number of scholarships have been generated to benefit Chinese Americans. He died on April 13, 1961. (*See also* National Dollar Stores, Ltd.)

SHUNTE. *See* Sam Yap.

SINGH, RAM. *See* Chandra, Ram.

SINGH, SIDAR JAGJIT. *See* India League of America.

SINHWUI. *See* Sze Yap.

SINNING. *See* Sze Yap (Sze-I).

SINO-KOREAN PEOPLE'S LEAGUE, established in Hawaii in December 1938 under the leadership of Haan Kilsoo, who warned Americans against a possible Japanese attack. He claimed that Japanese Americans would support Japan in its war with the United States. The organization was established to assist the Chinese in their war against Japan and to promote anti-Japanese activities. The organization was dissolved in 1945.

SISSON, WALLACE AND COMPANY, established in San Francisco as a mercantile firm and active in recruiting Chinese laborers for the construction of the transcontinental railroad in the 1860s. It was said that Charles Crocker's* brother, Clark W. Crocker, had a leadership position with the firm. The company initially recruited Chinese laborers from various mines as placer mining began to decline, but the number of Chinese recruited was not sufficient. Later the company sent its recruiting agents to China to bring more Chinese, who upon their arrival in the United States were organized into work gangs of twenty–five to thirty. Each Chinese work gang had its own leader, who worked under a white boss responsible for supervising several gangs.
FURTHER READING: Gunther Barth, *Bitter Strength*, Cambridge, Mass.: Harvard University Press, 1964; Jack Chen, *The Chinese of America*, New York: Harper and Row, 1980; Brett Melendy, *The Oriental Americans*, Boston: Twayne Publishers, 1972; Alexander Saxton, *The Indispensable Enemy*, Berkeley: University of California Press, 1971.

SIX COMPANIES. *See* Chinese Six Companies; District Companies.

SLOCUM, TOKUTARO. *See* Nye-Lea Bill.

SLOT CASES. *See* Paper Sons.

SLOT RACKET. *See* Paper Sons.

SMALLPOX EPIDEMIC OF 1853, disease brought to Hawaii by sailors and settlers who gave it to natives with little immunity. In 1848 and 1849 an epidemic of measles was introduced from Mexico, and it spread throughout Hawaii. This was followed by whooping cough and influenza which killed about 10,000 people. Then on February 10, 1853, the *Charles Mallory*, an American merchant ship from San Francisco, appeared off Honolulu sending a distress signal with a yellow flag indicating that a serious disease was aboard. The passenger suffering from smallpox was immediately segregated on a reef at Kalihi, and others came ashore to be vaccinated and quarantined. The smallpox seemed to have been subdued, but it broke out again in May with more ferocity to kill natives. It was under control by the end of January 1854 after painstaking work by many concerned people who did everything they could to care for those stricken by the disease. Before it was brought under control, however, it had killed 2,485 people according to an official account, but it was estimated that about 6,000 people actually died of the disease. This number represented more than one-fifth of the total native population in Hawaii at that time. (*See also* Committee of Thirteen.)

FURTHER READING: A. Grove Day, *Hawaii and Its People*, New York: Duell, Sloan and Pearce, 1955; Gavan Daws, *Shoal of Time: A History of the Hawaiian Islands*, Honolulu: University Press of Hawaii, 1968; Gerrit P. Judd, IV, *Hawaii: An Informal History*, New York: Collier Books, 1961; Ralph S. Kuykendall, *The Hawaiian Kingdom*, Vol. 3: 1874–1893, Honolulu: University of Hawaii Press, 1967.

SO JAE-P'IL (PHILIP JAISOHN) (1866–1951), medical doctor and Korean patriot. So was born in South Cholla Province, Korea, on October 28, 1866, but was brought to his uncle's home in the capital city of Korea for his education. At the age of thirteen, he passed the state examination and was later sent to Japan by Kim Ok-kyun for his military training. He returned to Korea in 1884 and participated in the 1884 coup d'etat in order to reform Korean society. After three days of power, the coup leaders were driven out of Korea. So fled to Japan and subsequently came to America.

So attended the Harry Hillman Academy and Lafayette College at Easton, Pennsylvania, before he studied medicine at George Washington University. Because of financial difficulties, he was not able to complete his education at Lafayette. He moved to Washington where he was given the job of translating Japanese medical books into English, while studying medicine at George Washington University. In 1895 he received his M. D. degree and married a Miss Armstrong. The following year he returned to Korea and started a newspaper printed both in the vernacular and English. It was called *The Independence*. He changed his name to Philip Jaisohn when he was naturalized, and he continued to work for Korea's independence when he was asked to leave his own country. In 1898 he came back to the United States where he practiced medicine. In 1919 Koreans, in protest against Japanese colonial policy in Korea, held mass demonstrations. The March 1 mass protest movement spread quickly among overseas Koreans, including Koreans in America. So Jae-p'il was instrumental in organizing the First Korean Liberty Congress* in Philadelphia, which was held between April 16 and 19, 1919. He continued to work for Korean independence by speaking out against Japanese colonial policy. When Korea was liberated from Japanese colonialism in 1945, he visited his home country briefly. He died on January 5, 1951, after many decades of devotion and service to his native country.

FURTHER READING: Channing Liem, *America's Finest Gift to Korea: The Life of Philip Jaisohn*, New York: William-Frederick Press, 1952.

SOJOURNER MENTALITY, the condition or state of mind of sojourners* whose lives in a strange land are held in suspension, while they are working to save enough money to go back to their native country where they are expected to live a real life. Under this psychological condition, everything in the life of the sojourner becomes temporary and takes on little meaning unless it enhances his or her chance of returning home to live in comfort. The majority of Chinese immigrants during the middle of the nineteenth century in America were sojourners bent on returning, but many of them became settlers, developing roots in America.

FURTHER READING: Jack Chen, *The Chinese of America*, New York: Harper and Row, 1980; Clarence E. Glick, *Sojourners and Settlers*, Honolulu: University Press of Hawaii, 1980; Rose Hum Lee, *The Chinese in the United States of America*, Hong Kong: Hong Kong University Press, 1960.

SOJOURNERS, persons temporarily out of their own native country in search of work or a new opportunity for financial or economic success. Sojourners tend to think of their host society as a temporary place of work and are always inclined to return to their home country as soon as they are financially able to do so. Because of this orientation toward their home country, sojourners do not actively participate in the social and cultural life of their host society where they feel themselves to be strangers. They tend to avoid any effort for social or cultural assimilation and insulate themselves against the host society. Chinese immigrants during the middle of the nineteenth century in America were by and large sojourners.

FURTHER READING: Clarence E. Glick, *Sojourners and Settlers: Chinese Migrants in Hawaii*, Honolulu: University Press of Hawaii, 1980; Rose Hum Lee, *The Chinese in the United States of America*, Hong Kong: Hong Kong University Press, 1960.

SOKOKU SEINEN-DAN. *See* Hokoku Seinen-dan.

SOKUJI KIKOKU HOSHI-DAN (ORGANIZATION TO RETURN IMMEDIATELY TO THE HOMELAND TO SERVE), a dues-charging organization established on November 1, 1944, by a group of residents of the Tule Lake Segregation Center* who had petitioned for resegregation. Membership was limited to those who not only petitioned for resegregation but also wished to return to Japan and pledged absolute loyalty to Japan. They were required to sacrifice life and property in order to serve Japan. Officers of the organization were elected, and they were to work with and supervise leaders of the Sokoku

Kenkyu Seinen-dan, which later changed its name to Hokoku Seinen-dan.*. The organization's name was usually abbreviated to Hoshi-dan, and it published a monthly magazine called the *Hokoku* (Service to Mother Country).

The Hoshi-dan worked through the Hokoku to agitate Tule Lake residents to renounce their American citizenship if they were citizens and to go to Japan immediately. Their goal was partially achieved when the Department of Justice decided to accept applications for renunciation. During the month of January 1945 alone, 3,400 Nisei* and Kibei* in Tule Lake applied for renunciation of their American citizenship. (*See also* Hokoku Seinen-dan.)

FURTHER READING: Gary Y. Okihiro, "Tule Lake Under Martial Law: A Study in Japanese Resistance," *Journal of Ethnic Studies* 5, No. 3, (Fall 1977) pp. 71–85; Dorothy S. Thomas and Richard Nishimoto, *The Spoilage: Japanese-American Evacuation and Resettlement During World War II*, Berkeley: University of California Press, 1969.

SONE, MONICA (1919–), writer, clinical psychologist. Sone was born in Seattle, Washington, in 1919, shortly after the Armistice of World War I was signed. She grew up in Seattle and attended Bailey Gatzet School. She lived with her parents in the old Carrollton, which was a hotel her parents took care of. Sone's father came to America in 1904 in order to study law at Ann Arbor, Michigan, but was unable to save enough money to finance his education.

Sone wrote of her experiences as a Nisei* at the age of thirty–four in her autobiographical book, *Nisei Daughter* (1953). In her book, she tells of the disillusioned and astonished Japanese Americans shocked at the news of the Japanese attack on Pearl Harbor. She also tells of her experience of living at a relocation center* called Camp Minidoka. She moved to Chicago and later enrolled in Wendell College in southern Indiana, where her interests were in music, history and current events, religion, philosophy, and sociology. She later majored in clinical psychology at Western Reserve University. At the time the 1979 edition of *Nisei Daughter* was published, Sono was living in Canton, Ohio, where she practiced clinical psychology.

FURTHER READING: Elaine Kim, *Asian American Literature*, Philadelphia: Temple University Press, 1982; Monica Sone, *Nisei Daughter*, Boston: Little, Brown and Co., 1953.

SOUTHERN CALIFORNIA RETAIL PRODUCE WORKERS UNION, a union of exclusively Japanese workers established in 1937. Japanese immigrants who came to the West Coast of the United States, particularly California, went into truck farming and supplied fresh vegetables for their Caucasian customers. The Japanese retail produce industry was an important economic force in the Japanese community in southern California where many Japanese were concentrated. The industry grew rapidly, and with the expansion of fruit stands, more Nisei* workers were hired. By 1941 half of the people engaged in the Japanese retail produce industry as managers and proprietors were Nisei. These entrepreneurs of small businesses did not like unionization of workers, particularly

Nisei workers who were expected not to develop any labor interest which was distinctly different from that of their employers. They were supposed to work for ethnic solidarity among the Japanese.

When the workers in the wholesale produce industry were organized in 1936 to create the Market Workers Union, which later recruited Japanese workers in that industry, the Japanese community, probably under the instigation of Japanese businessmen, reacted to this new development with an organization of workers in the retail produce industry. Some 450 Nisei workers were organized into the Southern California Retail Produce Workers in 1937. Membership was restricted to Japanese workers in retail produce, and it was to include all workers in that industry. The purpose of the organization was not to represent workers' grievances, but rather to suppress them in order to present Japanese ethnic solidarity in that industry. Because of this organizational defect as a labor union, it came under attack by Local 770, Retail Food Clerks.

The union was later reorganized under another name, the Fruit and Vegetable Store Employees' (Japanese) Union, Local 1510, which was dissolved after persons of Japanese ancestry were interned during World War II. When the internment was over, Japanese workers in the retail produce industry joined Local 770. They found that they were limited to certain categories of jobs and positions, although Local 770 was a common union where segregation and discrimination were not to be practiced.

FURTHER READING: John Modell, *The Economics and Politics Of Racial Accommodation The Japanese of Los Angeles, 1900–1942*, Urbana: University of Illinois Press, 1977.

SPECIAL COMMITTEE ON CHINESE IMMIGRATION OF THE CALIFORNIA STATE SENATE. See California Senate Address and Memorial of 1876.

SPECIAL JAPANESE SOCIETY (RINJI NIHONJIN-KAI), organized after the outbreak of bubonic plague in Honolulu in December 1899. During the plague, buildings affected were ordered burned, and they were set on fire on January 20, 1900. But the fire went out of control quickly, and twelve blocks of the Asian quarters were destroyed. The Chinese community filed claims for losses estimated at $1,761,112 and the Japanese quickly organized Rinji Nihonjin-kai, or the Special Japanese Society, which filed claims totaling $639,742. Congress appropriated $1 million, and claims were finally settled in 1903. It was estimated that people who lost their property recovered about 50 cents on the dollar. A total of $333,730 was paid to the Japanese, and the Chinese received $845,480.

FURTHER READING: Robert A. Wilson and Bill Hosokawa, *East to America: A History of the Japanese in the United States*, New York: William Morrow and Co., 1980.

SPEER, WILLIAM (1822–1904), missionary to China. Speer was born on April 24, 1822, in New Alexandria, Pennsylvania, the son of Dr. James Ramsey Speer, a physician in Pittsburgh. He spent one year at Jefferson College and transferred to Kenyon College, Gambier, Ohio, graduating in 1840. Speer began his study in medicine but changed to the study of theology in preparation for missionary work. He entered Allegheny Seminary, now Western Theological Seminary, in Pittsburgh and graduated in 1846. Upon graduation he was ordained a Presbyterian minister in June and immediately sailed to China for missionary work there.

Speer organized the first Presbyterian mission work in China in Canton, but because of the death of his wife and child, he returned to America in 1850. As Chinese immigrants began to come to the West Coast of the United States in large numbers, Speer felt called to their service, and he came to San Francisco in 1852 to establish the first Chinese church. The first Chinese Presbyterian Church outside China was established in June 1854. Speer also established a weekly newspaper, *The Oriental*, printed in both Chinese and English. Speer's service to the Chinese community in San Francisco was cut short because of his ill health. He was replaced by Augustus Ward Loomis,* who began his mission work in 1859.

Speer defended Chinese rights to come and live in America and shielded them against the racial antipathy which was rampant among white citizens on the West Coast. He wrote a number of books on the basis of his experiences with the Chinese in both China and America. (*See also* Loomis, Augustus Ward.)
FURTHER READING: William Speer, *The Great Revival of 1800*, Philadelphia: Presbyterian Board of Publications, c. 1862; William Speer, *The Oldest and Newest Empire: China and the United States*, Hartford, Conn.: S. Scranton and Co., 1870.

SPONTANEOUS INTERNATIONAL MIGRATION, a sociological concept used by Darrel Montero and others to describe the unique phenomenon of Vietnamese exodus from their homeland and their subsequent settlement in the United States. This model differs from the immigration pattern of earlier Chinese and Japanese immigrants who came to America after the middle of the nineteenth century. Whereas Japanese and Chinese immigrants entered the stage of ethnic enclaves upon their arrival in the United States and subsequently underwent the stage of assimilation, the Vietnamese refugees, most of whom were compelled to leave their homeland, were temporarily accommodated in various refugee camps where they were refugees for a time. Their camp life stage was followed by a period of sponsorship by private citizens of the United States. The sponsorship program helped to disperse Vietnamese refugees throughout the United States. This stage of dispersion was still temporary as many Vietnamese began to move into ethnic enclaves which they are now forming in many parts of America. Many Vietnamese may have to undergo this stage before they are assimilated into American society.

FURTHER READING: Jacqueline Desbarats and Linda Holland, "Indochinese Settlement Patterns in Orange County," *Amerasia Journal* 10, No. 1 (Spring/Summer 1983), pp. 23–46; William T. Liu, *Transition to Nowhere: Vietnamese Refugees in America*, Nashville, Tenn.: Charter House Publishers, 1979; Darrel Montero, *Vietnamese Americans: Patterns of Resettlement and Socioeconomic Adaptation in the United States*, Boulder, Colo.: Westview Press, 1979.

SQUIRE, WATSON CARVOSSO (1838–1926), governor of Washington Territory, U.S. Senator. Squire was born on May 18, 1838, at Cape Vincent, New York, the only son of a Methodist Episcopal minister, Orra Squire, and his wife Erreta (Wheeler) Squire. He graduated from Wesleyan University, Middletown, Connecticut, in 1859 and worked as principal of Moravia Institute at Moravia, New York, the following year. He began his law study, which was interrupted briefly by the Civil War in 1861 when he enlisted as a private. He resumed his law study the same year and was admitted to the bar. He organized the 7th Independent Company of Ohio Sharpshooters; he became captain and was later promoted to colonel.

Following the war, Squire rose through the ranks of management with E. Remington and Sons, an ammunition and firearms manufacturing company in New York. As a result of his hiring, the company obtained huge contracts for sales of rifles, carbines, and pistols to foreign countries, as well as the first contract in the world for the manufacture of typewriters. Squire's affiliation with the Territory of Washington was instigated by his vast land investments in the Seattle area in 1876. For the next three years he traveled to European capitals, Mexico, and other foreign lands until his need to withdraw from the commercial field led him to permanently settle in Seattle. His land investments and spirit of motivation, coupled with the ties he maintained with friends in the East and the Republican Party, spawned the extensive interest and development of the Territory that resulted in his appointment as governor by President Chester A. Arthur in 1884. Durning this term he was noted for his action in suppressing anti-Chinese riots in the Seattle area which followed the riots in Thurston and Pierce counties.

By the time the Central Pacific Line had been completed in 1869, many unemployed Chinese had drifted north, which agitated Washington residents already suffering from an economic depression. Anti-Chinese sentiment became acute, and local public meetings brought destructive results. The media heightened the situation with articles similar to the *Seattle Post-Intelligencer*'s editorials calling for scalps of "the treacherous almond-eyed sons of Confucius." Subsequently, on September 5, 1885, three Chinese were killed and many were wounded at the hop ranches in Squaw Valley; Chinese were forced to evacuate the mines at Coal Creek, and their quarters were burned; and on November 3, 1884, in Tacoma, a mob of 300 men gave the Chinese the ultimatum, allowing them thirty days to get out of town, and then proceeded to run them out as they torched the Chinese homes. Prior to these incidents, and to no avail, Governor Squire had deputized numerous men to maintain peace and had summoned

General John Gibbon from Washington, D.C., to quiet the agitators through deliberation.

When the mayor of Seattle notified Squire on February 7, 1886, that Seattle residents were attempting a similar evacuation of Chinese as that in Tacoma, Squire immediately called out the National Guard and demanded order through proclamation. In spite of his firm measures, the rioters were turbulent and determined to accomplish their goal of Chinese expulsion.

The day following Squire's proclamation, 600 to 800 Chinese were taken before Seattle's Chief Justice Roger S. Greene and were interrogated as to whether or not they would evacuate by vessel to San Francisco. After the ship's capacity was reached, those remaining were escorted to safe quarters by the National Guard when they became targets of violence as the mob attempted to disarm the peace-keeping troops. At this point, five mob ringleaders were shot down. Governor Squire responded by declaring martial law and inaugurating a regular military system of government. Squire received full support from President Grover Cleveland, who enforced the decision by sending a regiment of U.S. infantry to the scene. This occupation lasted until the end of February 1886.

In 1889, two years after Squire's tenure as governor had ended, he was called on to preside over a committee that was to draft an act for Congress requesting statehood. That same year, statehood was granted to Washington, and Squire was elected to the first of this two terms as senator. During this time (1889–1897), Senator Squire made a number of contributions to the State of Washington and the nation: the gaining of railroad land grants; appropriations to improve rivers and harbors and create national parks and forest reserves; the securing of Bremerton naval station and the military posts of Fort Lawton and Spokane; and the most noted success—his question and proposal of national coastal defense.

During his last senatorial term, Squire recommended to Congress that strong enforcement of the Chinese restriction act be carried out. (*See also* Seattle Anti–Chinese Riot.)

FURTHER READING: C. B. Bagley, *History of Seattle, Washington*, Vol 3, Chicago: S. J. Clarke Publishing Co., 1916; Lorraine B. Hildebrand, *Straw Hats, Sandals and Steel*, Tacoma: Washington State American Revolution Bicentennial Committee, 1977; Edmond S. Meany, *History of the State of Washington*, New York: Macmillan Co., 1924; William Farrand Prosser, *History of the Puget Sound Country*, Vol. 2, New York: Lewis Publishing Co., 1903.

STANFORD, LELAND (1824–1893), railroad builder, member of Big Four, U.S. senator. Stanford was born on March 9, 1824, in Watervliet, New York, the fourth of Josiah Stanford's seven sons. He grew up on his father's farm, attending public schools during the winter and working on the farm during the summer. In 1842, at the age of twenty–four, Leland left Albany where he had studied law and headed for Port Washington, Wisconsin, where he established his practice. When his law firm was destroyed by fire, Stanford, with suggestions from his brothers, departed Wisconsin and headed west to California, where he arrived on July 12, 1852. Before he left for California, Leland went back to Albany to marry June Lathrop.

When he arrived in California, Stanford joined his two brothers selling equipment to miners and within a four-year period was able to save enough money to move to Sacramento in 1856. In Sacramento, his attention, along with that of three other prominent men of his period, focused on the railroad business. These four were later known as the "Big Four." Together they joined the Pacific Ocean with the Atlantic by connecting the rails of the Southern Pacific with those of the transcontinental railroad. Stanford had the privilege of spiking in the golden spike on May 28, 1869, marking the completion of the transcontinental railway.

Stanford's political career in California began when he ran for governor on the Republican ticket in 1859. Although he lost the election, other Republicans saw his value and invited him to the Republican convention in 1860, where he became a staunch supporter of Abraham Lincoln. While Stanford worked alongside Lincoln during Lincoln's transition into the White House, Republicans back in California nominated Stanford for the governorship, which he won convincingly in 1861. In his inaugural message to the California Legislature, he characterized Asians as dregs who were inferior to white people and suggested that all available legislative means be used to discourage the immigration of Asians to the United States. His racist attitude toward Chinese did not hamper his success in American politics and economy. He and his associates used Chinese labor to complete the transcontinental railroad. Stanford later served as U.S. senator from 1885 until his death on June 21, 1891.

At the time of his death Stanford's wealth was estimated at $50 million, wealth that would not have been possible had the thousands of Chinese not labored in the heat of the California deserts. (*See also*, Crocker, Charles; Central Pacific Railroad Company.)

FURTHER READING: Thomas J. Curran, *Xenophobia and Immigration, 1820–1830*, Boston: Twayne Publishers, 1975; Richard Dillion, *Humbugs and Heroes*, Garden City, N.Y.: Doubleday and Co., 1970; H. Brett Melendy and Benjamin F. Gilbert, *The Governors of California*, Georgetown, Calif.: Talisman Press, 1965; Norman Tutorow, *Leland Stanford: Man of Many Careers*, Menlo Park, Calif: Pacific Coast Publishers, 1971.

STATE OF CALIFORNIA v. HAYAO YANO AND TETSUBUMI YANO,

a case involving Yano Hayao who had purchased 14 acres of farmland valued at $3,000 and had title to the land transferred to his daughter, Yano Testubumi, age two, who was a native-born citizen of the United States. Yano admitted that he had transferred the title to his daughter because he knew he could not hold title to the land as an alien ineligible for U.S. citizenship, according to the Alien Land Act of 1920. He filed a petition with the Superior Court of Sutter County in order to become the guardian of his daughter and the estate. He was denied by the Superior Court to be the guardian, and he appealed to the Supreme Court of the State of California.

In 1922 the state's highest court reversed the Superior Court's decision, declaring Section 4 of the Alien Land Act of 1920 unconstitutional as it denied the minor child equal protection of the laws guaranteed by the Constitution. The state's Supreme Court also ruled that the right of a father to become a legal guardian did not have anything to do with his nationality.

This crucial decision went in favor of Japanese alien residents in America who were then given legal right to purchase land and transfer it to their minor children born in the United States.

FURTHER READING: Consulate-General of Japan, *Documentary History of Law Cases Affecting Japanese in the United States, 1916–1924*, San Francisco, 1925; Frank F. Chuman, *The Bamboo People: The Law and Japanese-Americans*, Del Mar, Calif.: Publisher's Inc., 1976.

STATE OF CALIFORNIA v. TIMOTHY S. YATKO, a case tried in 1925 involving Timothy S. Yatko, a Filipino who had been accused of stabbing to death a white man who was found in bed with Yatko's Caucasian wife, Lola Butler. The counselor for the state wanted Yatko's wife to testify against her husband, and he claimed that the marriage between Lola Butler and Yatko was null and void because Yatko was a Filipino and therefore was prohibited from marrying a white woman. Lola Butler testified against Yatko, who was found guilty of killing Harry L. Kidder on May 11, 1925. He was sentenced to life imprisonment in San Quentin.

STATE OF CALIFORNIA v. *S.S. CONSTITUTION*, a case involving the question of the constitutionality of a law passed by the California State Legislature on May 3, 1852, requiring the masters of vessels to post a per capita bond of $500, or no less that $5 but no more than $10 per passenger, to be used in medical care and other relief work for alien passengers. The income from this tax was to be distributed among the major hospitals of the state. The State Treasury collected a total of $433,654.94, and the Chinese paid no less than 45 percent of that amount. Just one year before the law was ruled unconstitutional, the Chinese paid 85 percent of the amount of tax money collected.

William H. Hudson, master of the *S.S. Constitution*, had brought four persons as passengers from New Granada but had failed to pay the required amount of money. Because of this failure, a lien was imposed on the vessel to force the owner to pay. A lower court decided in favor of the state, the plaintiff; the defendant appealed.

The only question before the Supreme Court of the State of California was whether or not the law in question, An Act Concerning Passengers Arriving in the Ports of the State of California, was constitutional.

Judge Joseph B. Crockett, in his opinion for the court, stated that a state "has the power to exclude from its limits paupers, vagabonds, and criminals, or sick, diseased, infirm, and disabled persons, who were liable to become a public charge," but it did not have the power to exclude people who were neither paupers, vagabonds, nor criminals, or affected with any mental or bodily deformity. According to Crockett, the power to regulate commerce belonged to Congress exclusively. Therefore, he ruled that the law under question was unconstitutional. FURTHER READING: Mary Roberts Coolidge, *Chinese Immigration*, New York: Henry Holt and Co., 1909; 42 California 578, 1872.

STEVEN, OSWALD A. *See* Pinkham, Lucius Eugene.

STEVENS INCIDENT. *See* Chang In-hwan.

STIMSON, HENRY LEWIS (1867–1950), Secretary of State. Stimson was born on September 21, 1867, in New York City, the only son of Lewis Atterbury Stimson and Candace (Wheeler) Stimson. His family line in America could be traced to the Massachusetts Bay Colony in the early seventeenth century. He graduated from Andover in 1884, Yale in 1888, and Harvard Law School in 1890. The following year he was admitted to the New York bar and joined the law firm of Root and Clark. He ran for the governorship of New York in 1910 but was defeated. The following year he was appointed Secretary of War by President William Howard Taft. He served in World War I as an artillery officer. From 1927 to 1929 he was the governor-general of the Philippines. In 1931 Stimson authored the Stimson Doctrine, primarily to counter Japanese aggression in Manchuria. In 1932 he supported the Kellogg Pact.

President Franklin Roosevelt, who called Stimson ''a leading Republican internationalist'' appointed him Secretary of War in June 1940, and he served in that office until September 1945 when he decided to retire. During these five years, his decisions affected the lives of millions of people around the world including persons of Japanese ancestry, and people who lived in Hiroshima and Nagasaki.

Immediately after the Japanese bombing of Pearl Harbor, rumors circulated that Japanese residents in America were spying on American military installations for Japan. There were also false rumors of sabotage committed by Japanese Americans. Secretary Stimson admitted before the Tolan Committee* that the War Department had received no information of sabotage committed by Japanese during the attack on Pearl Harbor. Nevertheless, he did nothing to silence the rumors. When pressured by his subordinates, including General John Lesesne DeWitt* of the Western Command, he argued for the evacuation of all persons of Japanese ancestry from the West Coast, even though he knew that such action was in violation of the Constitution. When he received a report from General DeWitt who claimed that a ''Jap'' was a ''Jap'' regardless of his citizenship, Stimson did not question this racist premise. In one entry in his diary, Stimson himself wrote that the racial characteristics of Japanese Americans made it impossible to understand or trust them.

As the major architect of the decision to evacuate and intern the Japanese Americans during World War II, Stimson insisted that his decision was a matter of "military necessity."* He drafted the proclamation and sent it to the President for him to issue. Later, he covered up the unconstitutionality of his decision by submitting a bill to Congress to legalize his unlawful decision.

FURTHER READING: Richard N. Current, *Secretary Stimson: A Study in Statecraft*, New York: Archon, 1970 (rev.); Peter Irons, *Justice at War*, New York: Oxford University Press, 1983; Elting E. Morison, *Turmoil and Tradition: A Study of the Life and Times of Henry L. Stimson*, Boston: Houghton Mifflin Co., 1960; Henry L. Stimson, *On Active Service in Peace and War*, New York: Harper, 1948.

STRASSER, ADOLPH. *See* Cigar Makers' International Union.

STROBRIDGE, JAMES. *See* Crocker, Charles.

SUBCULTURE, a sociological concept developed by Harry H. L. Kitano* who described the cultural value orientation of the Japanese Americans as being quite distinct from those held by other Americans. Because of the distinct quality of their values, Japanese Americans are believed to have established a subculture. On the other hand, some Japanese American values are considered to be very similar to those of other Americans, particularly white Anglo-Saxon Protestants. (*See also* Subnation.)

FURTHER READING: Harry H. L. Kitano, *Japanese Americans: The Evolution of a Subculture*, Englewood Cliffs , N.J.: Prentice-Hall, 1969; Robert A. Wilson and Bill Hosokawa, *East to America*, New York: William Morrow and Co., 1980.

SUBNATION, a term used by William Petersen to describe and explain ethnic solidarity among Japanese Americans. Because of the Japanese Americans' concern about their community welfare and reputation, individual members have been careful about their conduct both in and out of their immediate environs. Petersen argues that there has been a mutually supporting system between the Japanese American community and its individual members. Individual members were given support by their community in times of need, but they were also expected to conform with the community's values which were quite distinct from those of other American communities. The Japanese Americans have been living in their subnation, which is now being dissolved as a result of the socioeconomic success Japanese Americans have achieved. Petersen hopes that the subnation of Japanese Americans will never be totally dissolved into the "national pot," as he puts it.

FURTHER READING: Robert E. Park, *Race and Culture*, New York: Free Press, 1950; William Petersen, *Japanese Americans: Oppression and Success*, New York: Random House, 1971.

SUDDEN DEATH SYNDROME, a medical condition among Hmong* refugees in America and other places abroad which claimed fifty–nine lives of Hmongs between 1978 and 1983. The death may result from a combination of psychological, cultural, and physical factors which the Hmong refugees have undergone in their war-torn country as well as in the United States. It usually occurs at night, but the cause is still unknown.

FURTHER READING: Bruce T. Downing and Douglas P. Olney, *The Hmong in the West*, Minneapolis, Minn.: Center for Urban and Regional Affairs, 1982; Jacques Lemoine and Christine Mougne, "Why Has Death Stalked the Refugees?" *Natural History* 92, No. 11 (November 1983), pp. 6–19.

SUGAR BEET AND FARM LABORER'S UNION OF OXNARD, formed on February 11, 1903, when a group of labor contractors in cooperation with their Japanese workers decided to establish their own union. This move came about after a successful strike against the sugar beet owners who had wanted to employ the Japanese workers directly without the mediation of Japanese labor contractors. In retaliation, the contractors called off their workers and asked for more pay for them.

The union asked the American Federation of Labor to give it recognition as a charter. Samuel Gompers,* president of the American Federation of Labor, demanded that the union accept no Chinese or Japanese members.

SUGI SUMA. *See* Cable Act of 1922.

SUMIN-WON, established on November 16, 1902, by Korea's penultimate king, Kojong,* who issued an imperial edict creating a Department of Emigration, or Sumin-won. This office was charged with responsibility for processing Korean immigrants to Hawaii. King Kojong may have been initially reluctant to let his people immigrate to Hawaii, but Horace N. Allen* persuaded him to allow his people to go.

SUN CHUNG KWOCK BO (THE NEW CHINA NEWS). See Lung Kee Sun Bo.

SUN YAT-SEN (1866–1925), first president of Republic of China. Sun Yat-sen was born on November 12, 1866, in the Hsiang-shan village of Ts'ui-heng on the Pearl River Delta,* Kwangtung Province, China. The Hsiang-shan District was famous for many Chinese who introduced Western culture to China. The name of the district was later changed to Chung-shan after its favorite son, Sun Yat–sen. He had acquired the name while exiled in Japan.

Sun lived in his hometown until he was thirteen years of age when his mother took him to Hawaii where he stayed with his older brother Sun Mei. In Hawaii he enrolled in Iolani School, an Anglican institution in Honolulu under the directorship of Bishop Willis. At this school Sun learned not only English but also the constitutional form of government and Christianity. By the time he graduated from the school he won second prize in English grammar which was a great accomplishment considering that when Sun entered the school he did not know a word of English.

Upon graduation from Iolani, Sun entered Oahu College, where he developed an interest in government and medicine. But his brother, opposed to Sun's desire to convert to Christianity, sent Sun back to China in 1883. Sun did not stay long in his village. He went to Hong Kong, where he enrolled in another Church of England school, and in 1884 he finally embraced Christianity as his religion. He returned to China in April 1886. He graduated from the college of medicine attached to the newly established Alice Memorial Hospital in Hong Kong in June 1892, with a certificate of proficiency in medicine and surgery. In the spring of 1893 he began to practice medicine in Hong Kong.

Because of his involvement in the Canton revolt of 1895, Sun became a political fugitive with a price on his head. For the next sixteen years he lived in exile working for his revolutionary cause outside China. He escaped to Japan in November 1895 and established a branch of the Hing Chung Wui* (Hsing Chung Hui or the Society for the Preservation of China). This was originally established in Hawaii by Sun Yat-sen, when he was able to persuade a group of twenty young Chinese to form an anti-dynastic organization on November 24, 1894. The organization concentrated its effort on raising funds for Sun's political activities. In 1903 he returned to Hawaii where he called on the Hawaiian Hua-ch'iao* (the Hawaiian Chinese) to support his organization, Hsing Chung Hui. After five months in Hawaii he traveled to the U.S. mainland between April and December 1904. During these months he gained much support from the Chinese in the United States, although he was also denounced by supporters of K'ang Yu-wei.* He left for England in December 1904 and spent many of his years of exile in Europe and Japan before he went to Canada and the United States in 1909, meeting Homer Lea* on the West Coast whom he appointed "Commanding General." In February 1911 Sun came to Vancouver, Canada, where he sold $70,000 worth of bonds in Hong Kong currency.

Sun left for Europe in October 1911 where he entered into a series of negotiations with the French government to obtain French recognition of the revolutionary government in China. He then sailed for China, where he arrived on December 25, 1911. He was welcomed as a national hero by members of the T'ung Meng Hui, which Sun Yat-sen had established in Japan in 1905. Four days later he was elected president of a provisional republican government, and on January 1, 1912, he took office and formally proclaimed the establishment of the Republic of China. (*See also* Hing Chung Wui; Chung Wah Tung Ming Wui.)

FURTHER READING: Clarence Glick, *Sojourners and Settlers*, Honolulu: University Press of Hawaii, 1980; Bernard Martin, *Strange Vigour: A Biography of Sun Yat-sen*, New York: Augustus M. Kelley Publishers, 1970 (Reprints, 1944); Harold Z. Schiffrin, *Sun Yat-sen and the Origins of the Chinese Revolution*, Berkeley: University of California Press, 1968; Sun Yat-sen, *Memoirs of a Chinese Revolutionary*, New York: AMS Press, 1970 (Reprints, 1927); T. C. Woo, *The Kuomingtang and the Future of the Chinese Revolution*, Westport, Conn.: Hyperion Press, 1975 (Reprints, 1928).

SUNWUI (XINHUI). *See* Sze Yap (Sze–I).

SUTTER, JOHN AUGUSTUS (1803–1880), soldier, builder, fortune seeker, and rancher. Sutter was born in Switzerland in 1803; he studied at a military college and became a captain in the French Army. At the age of thirty, he came to the United States in search of better opportunities for vine growing. The group of friends and relatives that accompanied him asked him to find a suitable place for the project. Sutter came as far as Missouri, made necessary preparations for the project, but suffered a great loss when the steamboat carrying his supplies sank. He went to California and built a stockade, known as Sutter's Fort, which is now within the city limits of Sacramento. He received a land grant from Mexico and called the colony New Helvetia to honor his native land. Sutter decided to build a sawmill on his property, a decision that would affect the lives of millions of people throughout the world, including those of Chinese who were attracted to California in search of wealth. Sutter hired James Wilson Marshall to find an appropriate place for the sawmill. Marshall found it at Coloma on the American River, located about 35 miles east of the fort. Marshall and his men built a tailrace in order to get rid of the debris resulting from rock blasting, by turning the water of a nearby stream over the tailrace overnight. He would go out in the morning to see what had to be done for the day's work. On January 24, 1848, as he had done so many times before, he went out to work and to his surprise he found yellow particles in the dirt covering part of the tailrace. This was how gold was discovered in California.

After the discovery of gold on Sutter's property, which included 48,400 acres in the Sacramento Valley, many miners came to squat on his land. This led to Sutter's economic downfall. He was unable to recover his land and when he died in Washington, D.C., in 1880 he was virtually penniless.

FURTHER READING: Johann A. Sutter, *New Helvetia Diary: A Record of Events Kept by John A. Sutter and His Clerks at New Helvetia, from September 9, 1845 to May 25, 1848*, San Francisco: Grabhorn Press, 1939; James P. Zollinger, *Sutter, the Man and His Empire*, New York: Oxford University Press, 1939; Gordon V. Axon, *The California Gold Rush*, New York: Mason/Charter, 1976.

SUTTER CREEK STRIKE, one of many strikes that took place during June 1869 and August 1871 in California's mines. Labor demanded that the mine owners discontinue using "giant powder" as a blasting agent, that equal pay for above-ground and underground workers be guaranteed, that pre–1869 wages be kept, that the length of working shifts be reduced, and that Chinese workers not be hired. The mine owners honored only the demand about Chinese employment.

The conflict between white skilled miners and the Chinese grew as many Chinese released by the Central Pacific Railroad Company* after completion of the transcontinental railway drifted into mines in search of work. Because many

Chinese who had worked for the Central Pacific were skilled in using "giant powder," white miners opposed their employment.

FURTHER READING: Ping Chiu, *Chinese Labor in California, 1850–1880: An Economic Study*, Madison: State Historical Society of Wisconsin, 1963.

SZE YAP (SZE-I), the four districts located on the Pearl River Delta,* in Kwangtung Province, China, from which many Chinese immigrated to the United States. These districts are Enping (Yangping), Kaiping (Hoiping), Xinhui (Sunwui), and Taishan or Hsinning (Sinning). The Chinese emigrants from these four districts organized Sze Yap Wui Kun, or the four–district association, toward the end of 1851. The association included the Ning Yung, Hop Wo, Kong Chow, and Sue Hing companies.

T

TA TING LEU LEE (OR FUNDAMENTAL LAW OF THE CH'ING DYNASTY), a law proclaimed in 1712 by the Ch'ing Dynasty to discourage Chinese from going abroad. The penalty imposed on those who were caught in the act of leaving the country or in the act of conniving or cooperating with those who left the country was death. Government officials found negligent in their duty to enforce this law were to be demoted or dismissed from their office. This policy of banning foreign emigration was changed in 1868 when the Ch'ing Dynasty signed a treaty with the United States allowing Chinese to go abroad. FURTHER READING: Tin-Yuke Char, *The Sandalwood Mountains*, Honolulu: University Press of Hawaii, 1975; H. F. MacNair, *The Chinese Abroad*, Shanghai, China: Commercial Press, 1924.

TACOMA EXPULSION OF CHINESE. On November 3, 1885, a group of white citizens of Tacoma, Washington, encouraged by Mayor J. Robert Weisbach, drove the Chinese residents from the city. There had been anti-Chinese sentiment in Tacoma, but no major incidents occurred until 1884. In March 1884, a Workingmen's Union was organized; it was powerful enough to elect J. Robert Weisbach, a merchant who set his heart against the Chinese. Upon his election he and other law officers and community leaders encouraged agitation against the Chinese in the city.

On February 21, 1885, a mass meeting was held at the instigation of Mayor Weisbach and an anti-Chinese committee was established. The committee adopted various measures, one of which was to discourage merchants from having any business dealings with the Chinese. Another meeting was held on October 8, where emphasis was placed on discharging all Chinese employees before November 1. On the following day, October 9, committee men visited Chinese homes in Tacoma and told the Chinese to leave the city before November 1. When it was found that 200 of the 700 Chinese residents had not left, white citizens loaded all of the Chinese belongings on wagons and escorted the Chinese to the railroad station to ship them out of town. As the train pulled out of town with the defenseless Chinese aboard, their homes were set on fire by white citizens.

Although the ten men responsible for this incident were indicted, the jury refused to convict and Judge John P. Hoyt discharged the accused.

FURTHER READING: Roger Daniels, ed., *Anti-Chinese Violence in North America*, New York: Arno Press, 1978; Tricia Knoll, *Becoming Americans*, Portland, Oregon: Coast to Coast Books, 1892.

TAFT COMMISSION, estabished in 1900 by President William McKinley to study the social and political conditions prevailing in the Philippines after the United States acquired the islands from Spain through the Treaty of Paris on December 10, 1898, the treaty that ended the Spanish-American War. On February 6, 1900, President McKinley appointed William Howard Taft, U.S. Judge of the Sixth Judicial Circuit, to be the president of the new Philippine Commission. Taft served from March 13, 1900, to February 1, 1904. The commission was composed of Henry Ide, a former lawyer from Vermont who had served as U.S. commissioner to Samoa in 1891; General Luke Wright, a lawyer from Memphis and a veteran of the Civil War; and Bernard Moses, a professor of political economy at the University of California at Berkeley. Each member of the commission was assigned to his special area of interest and expertise: Taft handled situations involving crown lands, land titles, the church, and civil service; General Wright was responsible for looking into internal improvements, constabulary, commerce, corporation franchises, and the criminal code; Ide's responsibilities included banking, currency, and the organization of civil courts; and Bernard Moses was to look into revenue, taxation, and schools.

After many months of investigation, the commission recommended that the people of the Philippines should be given more local autonomy to deal with local affairs. Then the commission passed a law that appropriated $1 million for the repair and construction of highways and bridges. It also made a provision for the reorganization of the Bureaus of Forestry, Mining, and the Court of Justice. For the improvement of Manila harbor, $1 million were appropriated to complete the work that had been started under Spanish colonial rule. One of the commission's major legislative actions was the Pensionado Act of 1903* which established a government-sponsored program through which many young Filipinos were sent to the United States for their education and training. *See also* Pensionado Act of 1903.)

FURTHER READING: W. Cameron Forbes, *The Philippine Isands*, Vols. 1 and 2, Boston: Houghton Mifflin Co., 1928; George E. Taylor, *The Philippines and the United States: Problems of Partnership*, New York: Frederick A. Praeger, 1964; Leon Wolff, *Little Brown Brothers*, New York: Doubleday and Co., 1961.

TAGORE, RABINDRANATH (1861-1941), novelist and playwright, Nobel laureate in literature. Tagore was born on May 7, 1861, in Calcutta, India, the fourteenth of fifteen children born to the Maharishi Debendranath Tagore and

Sarada Devi. He grew up in a large home on the outskirts of Calcutta surrounded by older brothers and sisters, but he was deprived of maternal affection because of his mother's ill health and her preoccupation with running the large household in the absence of her husband.

Tagore began writing poetry at the age of eight, and his first poem was published when he was fourteen. He wrote thousands of poems and more than 1,200 songs, most of which he also set to music. He wrote thirty–eight plays and directed or acted in many of them. He is credited with twelve novels and nearly 200 short stories. He won a Nobel Prize for Literature in 1913. When he was awarded the Nobel Prize, an American newspaper published an article regretting that such an honor was bestowed on a non–white person. Tagore assoiciated this kind of blatant racism with North America. When he visited San Francisco in 1916, he was humiliated when police had to protect him from a rumored assassination plot by his own countrymen. American newspapers used this incident to implicate him as a German spy in the Hindu Conspiracy Trials* of 1918. When Tagore cabled President Woodrow Wilson to ask that his name be cleared, his request was ignored. Again in 1929, after lecturing in Canada, Tagore reacted to the humiliation of being fingerprinted by U.S. immigration authorities after he had lost his passport by declining invitations to appear in the United States. Despite inconveniences he encountered in America, he travelled widely and enjoyed his fellowship with friends and followers. During his trip to the United States in 1929, he was received by President Herbert Hoover.

FURTHER READING: Krishna Kripalani, *Rabindranath Tagore: A Biography*, London: Oxford University Press, 1962; Mary M. Lago, *Rabindranath Tagore*, Boston: Twayne Publishers, 1976; Vishwanath S. Naravane, *An Introduction to Rabindranath Tagore*, Columbia, Mo.: Macmillan Co. of India, Limited, 1978.

TAJIRI, LARRY. *See Pacific Citizen, The*.

TAKAHASHI TORAO v. FISH AND GAME COMMISSION, a case that reached the U.S. Supreme Court on writ of certiorari to the Supreme Court of the State of California, and was argued on April 21 and 22, 1948, and finally decided on June 8, 1948. The case involved the right of an alien who was ineligible for U.S. citizenship to fish off the coast of California for a living. Takahashi Torao was born in Japan and came to the United States in 1907. He worked as a fisherman off the coast of California from 1915 to 1942 with a commercial fishing license. In 1942 he was sent to an evacuation camp along with other persons of Japanese ancestry. In 1943 the Fish and Game Commission adopted a law prohibiting "alien Japanese" from getting a commercial fishing license. To make the law constitutional, in 1948 the commission altered the existing law to include persons "ineligible to citizenship" because alien Japanese residents were included in this category under federal law.

Takahashi took the commission to the Superior Court of Los Angeles County to compel it to issue him a license. Judge Henry M. Willis ordered the commission to issue Takahashi a license, holding that the state code was in violation of the Fourteenth Amendment of the Constitution. But on appeal to the State Supreme Court, the lower court's decision was reversed. Justice Douglas M. Edmonds ruled that the state had a proprietary interest in the fish which could be caught off the coast and sold in California for commercial purposes. According to this opinion, this interest justified the state in barring all aliens in general and "aliens ineligible to citizenship" in particular from fishing either within or outside the three–mile coastal belt.

Takahashi then appealed to the U.S. Supreme Court. The Court decided in favor of Takahashi by seven to two votes. Justice Hugo Black delivered the opinion of the majority of the Court, reversing the decision of the Supreme Court of California and dismissing the arguments presented by the State of California that the code under question was passed to conserve fish. First, he supported the petitioner's contention that the code was directed against Japanese. Second, he dismissed the state's contention that the state could adopt laws similar to those passed by Congress in order to keep out non-white people from the state. The fact that the United States regulates immigration and naturalization on the basis of color and race does not mean that a state can do the same. Third, he brushed aside the argument presented by the State of California to the effect that fish off the coast of California belonged to the special public interest to be protected by the state. Black argued that, even if ownership of California were granted, it could not prohibit aliens from fishing. Justice Stanley Reed filed his dissenting opinion, with which Justice Robert Jackson concurred.

This was one of many anti-Asian laws that began to lose force after the end of World War II.

FURTHER READING: Frank F. Chuman, *The Bamboo People*, Del Mar, Calif.: Publisher's Inc., 1976; Bill Hosokawa, *Nisei*, New York: William Morrow and Co., 1969; William Petersen, *Japanese Americans: Oppression and Success*, New York: Random House, 1971; *Supreme Court Reporter* 68, 334 U.S. 410.

TAMESA MINORU v. UNITED STATES, a case taken to the U.S. Supreme Court by Tamesa Minoru who was one of sixty–three defendants found guilty of violating a draft law. After sixty–three Japanese Americans who had been interned at Heart Mountain Relocation Camp refused to report for pre-induction physical examinations, a federal grand jury in Cheyenne, Wyoming, indicted them on May 10, 1944, and Judge T. Blake Kennedy found them guilty of having violated the draft. The case was known as Fujii Shigeru v. United States. As one of the defendants, Fujii Shigeru appealed to the Federal Circuit Court of Appeals, which upheld Judge Kennedy's decision on March 1945.

One of the three appeals justices, Walter A. Huxman, stated that the defendants had been reclassified from 4-C to I-A, showing that they were above reproach and should therefore serve in the U.S. armed services as any other eligible U.S. citizen. He also opined that the defendants should have exhausted all "administrative remedies" while complying with the orders given them.

On appeal to the Supreme Court of the United States, the Court decided on June 18, 1945, to uphold the decisions reached by the lower courts.
FURTHER READING: Frank F. Chuman, *The Bamboo People*, Del Mar, Calif.: Publisher's Inc., 1976; United States v. Shigeru Fujii, 55 Federal Supplement 928; United States v. Shigeru Fujii, 148 Federal 2nd 298. 325 U.S. 868, 1945.

TAN SHAN SUN BO (HAWAIIAN CHINESE NEWS). See Lung Kee Sun Bo.

TAN SHAN TONG. *See Tongs.*

TANG TUN v. HARRY EDSELL, a case that reached the Supreme Court of the United States on writ of certiorari to the U.S. Circuit Court of Appeals for the Ninth Circuit, which had reversed the decision of the District Court of Washington, Northern Division. The District Court had ruled in favor of Tang Tun and had allowed his admission to the United States.

Tang Tun was born in the United States in 1879 but left for China in 1884 and stayed there for thirteen years. He returned to the United States, being admitted by the customs officer in 1897, and worked for Wa Chong and Co. until 1905 when he made yet another trip to China, this time to marry Leung Kum Wui. In 1906 he tried to return to the United States with his wife, but they were refused admission by Harry Edsell, Chinese inspector in charge of Port Sumas, Washington.

In support of his application for admission, Tang Tun had affidavits supporting his claim that he was born in the United States and the endorsement of the inspection officer on October 1, 1905, the date he left the United States for China. The white witnesses who signed the affidavits testified on his behalf, but the Chinese witness informed the inspector that he did not wish to testify. Tang Tun then produced a copy of the identification papers he used when he returned to the United States in 1897 to work. The papers had the endorsement of the collector as to the fact of admission but Inspector Edsell found that in the official records of the customs office in Port Townsend, the town where Tang Tun had arrived in 1897, it was stated that he had been rejected.

The inspector questioned Tang Tun about the discrepancy and told him that the testimony of the witnesses on his behalf was not satisfactory. Tang Tun was then asked to present further evidence but was unable to do so. Edsell then refused Tang Tun and his wife admission on July 5, 1906. Tang Tun appealed to the Secretary of Commerce and Labor, who upheld Edsell's decision on September 5, 1906.

The case was then brought to the District Court which ruled that the petitioners, Tang Tun and his wife, had been denied the hearing required by the Chinese Exclusion Act, that Tang Tun had established his citizenship and therefore could stay in the United States. The decision was reversed on appeal by the Circuit Court of Appeals, which stated that the requirements of the law had been complied with and that there were no grounds for judicial intervention. The Circuit Court thus supported the legal principle that the decision of the immigration officer was final unless reversed by the Secretary of Commerce and Labor or unless the officers had acted improperly.

Tang Tun then appealed to the Supreme Court on the grounds that the immigration officers had acted improperly and abused their discretion. But on March 11, 1912, Justice Charles E. Hughes in his opinion for the unanimous Court stated that the decision of the Circuit Court was correct. Tang Tun was refused permission to return to his own country after a trip to China. (*See also* United States v. Ju Toy.)

FURTHER READING: Milton R. Konvitz, *The Alien and the Asiatic in American Law*, Ithaca, N.Y.: Cornell University Press, 1946; *Supreme Court Reporter* 32, 223 U.S. 673.

TANKA (also known as tan-chia or boat people), people who lived on the rivers that formed the Pearl River Delta,* Kwangtung Province, China. The Cantonese treated them as social outcasts and forbade them to intermarry with the Cantonese, who held them in contempt. In addition to the Punti* and Hakka people, the Tanka people also immigrated to the United States.

TANOMOSHI, the Japanese form of rotating credit association very similar to Chinese *hui.* Ivan Light speculates that this form of economic cooperative system was brought to Japan from China in the thirteenth century. The term *tanomoshi* was used among Japanese in northern California, Hawaii, and the Pacific Northwest, whereas the term *mujin* was more popular among Japanese in southern California. The term *ko* was preferred by Japanese in their home country.

Regardless of what term the Japanese in America used to signify their mutual cooperative economic institution, *tanomoshii* played an important role both as an economic force and as a cultural bond that tied Japanese together. Members of a *tanomoshi* were mutually bound by the principle of collective obligation, and in return, each member was assured of his group's assistance in time of need.

Members of a *tanomoshi* met once a month, according to John Embree, and they pooled their funds. Through this method Japanese were able to capitalize their businesses in spite of discrimination against them by white-owned banks.

FURTHER READING: John Embree, *Acculturation Among the Japanese of Kona, Hawaii*, American Anthropological Association, Memoirs, No.59, 1941; Ivan Light, *Ethnic Enterprise in America: Business and Welfare Among Chinese, Japanese and Blacks*, Berkeley: University of California Press, 1972; John Modell, *The Economics and Politics of Racial Accommodation: The Japanese of Los Angeles, 1900–1942*, Urbana: University of Illinois Press, 1977; Toshio Yatsushiro, *Politics and Cultural Values; The World War II Japanese Relocation Centers and the United States Government*, New York: Arno Press, 1978.

TAOK, EPIFANIO. *See* Manlapit, Pablo.

TAPE v. HURLEY, a case involving litigation between Joseph Tape representing his daughter, Mamie Tape, and Mamie's school principal, Jennie M. A. Hurley of Spring Valley School, who was instructed by San Francisco School Superintendent A. J. Moulder not to admit Chinese students to Spring Valley. Moulder's decision was ratified on October 21, 1884, by the Board of Education. The case was originally tried by Judge Macguire in Municipal Court of San Francisco who required Miss Hurley to enroll Mamie Tape, declaring that public schools were open to all children and denying that a child born of Chinese parents was in violation of the laws of the State of California.

A writ of mandate was issued to Miss Hurley and A. J. Moulder, and they appealed to the Supreme Court of California. Judge J. R. Sharpstein in his opinion for the unanimous court upheld Judge Macguire's decision and stated that teachers could not justify a violation of law, claiming that they were ordered to do so by the Board of Education. The victory was short–lived, however, as the Board of Education decided to create a separate school for children of Asian ancestry. Mamie Tape was then sent to that school.

FURTHER READING: H. Brett Melendy, *The Oriental Americans*, Boston: Twayne Publishers, 1972; Charles Wollenberg, *All Deliberate Speed: Segregation and Exclusion of California Schools, 1855–1975*, Berkeley: University of California Press, 1976; Tape v. Hurley, 66 California Supreme Court Reports, March 3, 1885.

TAXI-DANCE HALLS, entertainment establishments popular among Filipino men during the 1920s and 1930s. Girls were hired in these halls to dance with their male customers, who were charged ten cents per dance lasting one minute. Because of the unbalanced sex ratio between males and females within the Filipino population in the United States and the Filipino men's love of dancing, Filipino men frequented these places where they were often cheated out of their hard-earned money.

These taxi-dance halls were found in Honolulu, Chicago, Los Angeles, Stockton, California, and other major urban centers where a concentration of Filipinos were found. "Floating taxi-dance halls" also followed the Filipino migratory workers.

The association between Filipino men and white women of questionable moral character outraged many white citizens who felt that crimes committed by Filipinos were directly related to their affiliation with white girls.

FURTHER READING: Paul G. Cressey, *The Taxi-Dance Hall: A Sociological Study in Commercialized Recreation and City Life*, Chicago: University of Chicago Press, 1932; H. Brett Melendy, *Asians in America*, Boston: Twayne Publishers, 1977; Sonia Emily Wallovits, *The Filipinos in California*, San Francisco: R. and E. Research Associates, 1972.

TENNEY, JACK B. (1898-?), California state senator. Tenney was born in Los Angeles County, California, which he represented as a Democrat in the California State Legislature. During his political career he compiled a long list of anti-Japanese and anti-Communist legislation to his credit. After Japan officially joined the Axis Powers, Tenney felt that persons of Japanese ancestry would try to spy for Japan, and pushed through anti-spy, anti-sabotage, and anti-subversive legislation with the help of Senators Nelson S. Dilworth and Herbert W. Slater.

In December 1942 the California Department of the American Legion appointed Senator Tenney to investigate the relocation of Japanese. Soon afterward the American Legion went on record against ever letting the Japanese return to their homes. It also decided to delete Nisei* war veterans' names from the Legion roll call lists.

After the Lowrey bill, which proposed to tighten the existing Alien Land Laws* of the State of California, died, Senator Jack Tenney incorporated the Lowrey bill into his own Tenney bill. It was passed and signed into law by the governor. Tenney was empowered by the California State Legislature when he was named head of the Joint Fact-Finding Committee on Un-American Activities, or the "little Dies Committee" as it was often called after the Texas Republican who headed the House Committee on Un-American Activities in Congress. The Tenney committee investigated Japanese sympathizers as well. One sympathizer, George Roth, received a misdemeanor charge for refusing to answer the committee's questions concerning American-born Japanese sponsors of his radio show. The Tenney committee was busy with investigations into war relocation centers, * Communist subversion, and the Mexican "zoot suiters," among others. It charged that the Japanese evacuees had been pampered by the War Relocation Authority* and recommended turning the camps over to the army completely. His committee also labeled organizations which defended the rights of Japanese Americans as Communist–controlled.

In 1945 Senator Jack Tenney and Senator Hugh M. Burns of Fresno County introduced Proposition 15, a measure entitled Validation of Legislative Amendments to Alien Land Law,* but the California voters defeated the measure. It would have closed all loopholes in the California Alien Land Laws for the purpose of prohibiting persons ineligible for citizenship from purchasing or leasing farmland in California.

FURTHER READING: Frank F. Chuman, *The Bamboo People*, Del Mar, Calif., Publisher's Inc., 1976; Audrie Girdner and Anne Loftis, *The Great Betrayal*, New York: Macmillan Co., 1969; Jack B. Tenney, *Red Facism*, Los Angeles: Federal Printing Co., 1947.

TERRACE et al. v. THOMPSON, ATTORNEY GENERAL OF WASHINGTON, one of six major cases that reached the U.S. Supreme Court challenging the constitutionality of the Alien Land Laws* of Western states, particularly those to the states of Washington and California. The Court ruled all six cases (Cockrill et al. v. People of the State of California, * Frick v.

Webb,* Morrison v. People of the State of California,* Porterfield v. Webb,* Terrace et al. v. Thompson,* Attorney General of Washington,* and Webb v. O'Brien*) constitutional, although their decisions were based on different grounds.

The Terrace et al. v. Thompson case reached the Court as an appeal from the U.S.District Court for the Western District of Washington. It was argued on April 23 and 24 before the Court, and it was decided on November 12, 1923, as was the case of Porterfield v. Webb. James B. Howe argued on behalf of his clients, Mr. and Mrs. Frank Terrace and Elizabeth Terrace, as well as N. Nakatsuka, that the Washington Alien Land Law of 1921 was in violation of due process of law, the equal protection clause of the Fourteenth Amendment of the Constitution, and Article 1 of the existing treaty between the United States and Japan. Justice Pierce Butler, who delivered the opinion of the Court, ruled that the Alien Land Act of 1921 of the State of Washington was not in violation of the Fourteenth Amendment of the Constitution. Neither was it in violation of the 1911 Treaty between the United States and Japan, according to his opinion. FURTHER READING: Frank F. Chuman, *The Bamboo People*, Del Mar, Calif.: Publisher's Inc., 1976; Consulate-General of Japan, *Documentary History of Law Cases Affecting Japanese in the United States, 1916–1924*, Vol. 2, San Francisco, 1925; Milton R. Konvitz, *The Alien and the Asiatic in American Law*, Ithaca, N.Y.: Cornell University Press, 1946; *Supreme Court Reporter* 44, 263 U.S. 197, 1924.

THEO. DAVIES AND COMPANY. *See* Big Five.

THREE-POWER CONVENTION OF 1899, the agreement reached between three nations, namely, Germany, Great Britain, and the United States, to carve out their own spheres of interest concerning Samoa. Ten years earlier, in 1889, the same three nations had reached an agreement by which they had established a joint commission to rule over Samoa. In 1899 Samoa was divided in two by the three nations, just as other small and powerless nations were later divided against their own will after the end of World War II. The United States took over control of six smaller eastern islands, later to be called American Samoa, whereas Germany was given Upolu, Savai'i, and their satellite islands. Great Britain made no territorial claims on Samoa but was assured of Germany's withdrawal from Tonga, Niue, and the Solomons for the concessions it made to Germany.

Although the United States was awarded Eastern Samoa, the accession was not formally approved by Congress until 1926, when the President placed the administration of Samoa in the care of the Navy Department. FURTHER READING: Paul M. Kennedy, *The Samoan Tangle: A Study in Anglo-German- American Relations, 1878–1900*. New York: Barnes and Noble, 1974; Douglas Oliver, *The Pacific Islands*, Cambridge, Mass.: Harvard University Press, 1951; Robert Trumbull, *Tin Roofs and Palm Trees*, Seattle: University of Washington Press, 1977.

THURSTON, ASA. *See* American Board of Commissioners for Foreign Missions.

THURSTON, LORRIN A. *See* Committee of Safety; Hawaiian League.

TIAO YU TAI MOVEMENT, a movement that arose from a dispute between Japan and China in 1968 over the question of which nation controlled eight small uninhabited islands known as the Tiao Yu Tai. These islands, located 120 miles from Taipei and 240 miles from Okinawa, had been neglected and ignored until 1968 when geological studies sponsored by the United Nations Economic Commission for Asia and the Far East reported that this area could be developed as one of the largest oil–producing areas in the world. After this report was released, Japan suddenly made its claim to the islands and decided to explore the area for possible oil production. This aggressive Japanese territorial claim did not bring any strong protest from the Nationalist Chinese government in Taiwan. Chinese students and intellectuals in America, however, protested against the Nationalist government for abandoning its territorial rights.

A group of Chinese students initiated the movement in December 1970 at Princeton University, and it quickly spread to the major university campuses in New York. As a result, a committee called the New York Action Committee was organized on December 22, 1970, and a decision was made to hold a demonstration in New York on January 30, 1971.

After the demonstration, in which more than 1,000 people from thirty different colleges participated, the Tiao Yu Tai Committees established across the country wrote an open letter on March 12, 1971, to President Chiang Kai-shek of the Nationalist government in Taiwan. The letter listed ten demands. When the government did not respond to their demands, the movement took a decisive turn by linking itself with the People's Republic of China. The People's Republic made its claims to the islands on December 4, 1970, through its official news agency, Hsinhua, which was later repeated in *Peking Review* on December 11 and in *Jenmin Jih Pao* on December 29 of the same year.

The movement's linkage with the People's Republic of China brought it into conflict with the government in Taiwan as well as those who had been working for the independence to Taiwan in America. Nevertheless the Tiao Yu Tai activists continued to hold meetings, staged demonstrations, and lobbied in Washington. The activists also wrote an open letter to President Richard M. Nixon which was published on May 23, 1971, in the *New York Times*.

This sudden outpouring of protest from Chinese who had traditionally been silent helped awaken the political consciousness of young Chinese in America. In addition, what had been launched as a protest to the Nationalist government in Taiwan became a social and cultural movement providing a variety of social services in Chinatowns* across the country.

FURTHER READING: James Lee, ''The Story of the Tiao Yu Tai Movement,'' *Bridge* 1, No.3 (November-December 1971), pp. 4–16; Stanford M. Lyman, *Chinese Americans*, New York: Random House, 1974.

TIDE LAND RECLAMATION COMPANY, established in California by George D. Roberts and Solomon Heydenfeldt, former Associate Justice of the Supreme Court of California, who ruled in January 1857 on the case of the People v. Downer.* The company engaged large numbers of Chinese workers, who were hired to reclaim Tule land between the delta of the Sacramento and San Joaquin rivers. In his testimony before a congressional commission, Heydenfeldt reported that the wealth created by Chinese workers who had reclaimed Tule land was equal to $90 million a year.

FURTHER READING: Jack Chen, *The Chinese of America*, New York: Harper and Row, 1980; George F. Seward, *Chinese Immigration: Its Social and Economical Aspects*, New York: Charles Scribner's Sons, 1881.

TIGER BRIGADE (MAENGHO-KUN), established by Korean residents in the United States immediately after the Japanese attack on Pearl Harbor. The brigade was incorporated into the California National Guard under the command of Colonel Hughes and went into training on December 29, 1941. Initially, only fifty Koreans enlisted, but the number grew to 100. The brigade was not sent into actual combat.

TING, SAMUEL CHAO CHUNG (1936–), Nobel Prize winner in physics. Ting was born in Ann Arbor, Michigan, on January 26, 1936, to Ting Kuan Hai and Wang Tsun-Ying, both professors. He spent his childhood in mainland China and his teens in Taiwan. His father taught at the National Taiwan University. Ting came to the United States in 1956 to study at the University of Michigan from which he received his B.A. in engineering. He received his Master's and Ph.D. degrees in physics in 1960 and 1962, respectively.

Ting went to work for the European Nuclear Research Center upon graduation and came back to teach at Columbia University before he joined the Massachusetts Institute of Technology (MIT) in 1967. While at MIT he joined a team of research scientists at the Brookhaven National Laboratory at Upton, Long Island, where they discovered a new atomic particle known as the "psi" particle. For this discovery Ting was awarded the Nobel Prize in physics in 1976 which he shared with Professor Burton Richter of the Stanford Linear Accelerator. On December 10, 1976, when he was presented with the award, he delivered half of his speech in Chinese. He became the first American-born Asian scientist to receive a Nobel Prize.

TINGLEY, GEORGE B. *See* Coolie Bill.

TOGASAKI, GEORGE KIYOSHI (1895–), Japanese business leader. Togasaki was born in San Francisco to Togasaki Kikumatsu and was one of twenty–five Nisei* children subjected to the school segregation policy decided on by the San Francisco School Board on October 15, 1906. The board had decided to send all Chinese, Japanese, and Korean children to the Oriental School. George later served in the army during World War I, and upon returning home he joined a discussion group of Nisei Japanese who were determined to claim their rightful place in American society. The discussion group later developed into the American Loyalty League. This league finally paved the way for the establishment of the Japanese American Citizens League.* Togasaki finally moved back to Japan, making his home in Tokyo, and became president of the *Japan Times*. He also served as the first chairman of the Board of Japan Christian University as well as president of Rotary International, with its 600,000 members, in 1968–1969. (*See also* San Francisco School Board Segregation Order of 1906.)

TOISHAN (also known as Hsinning), a district located on the Pearl River Delta.* It is one of the four districts that were called Sze Yap (Sze–I). Many early Chinese immigrants in the United States came from this district. (*See also* Pearl River Delta; and District Companies.)

TOKYO CLUB, a gambling house established in 1919 in Los Angeles. A gambling house with the identical name was also established among the Japanese in Seattle in 1919. These two clubs did not have any business connections with each other. The rationale for establishing gambling houses among Japanese was to keep the money within the Japanese community, for the Japanese had previously gambled in gambling houses run by Chinese owners. Itami Chojiro, the boss of the Tokyo Club in Seattle between 1919 and 1927, was said to have had a surplus of $250,000. He was later succeeded by Yasuda Yasutaro who headed the club until his death in 1931. Although Yasuda was known for his ruthlessness, he was also benevolent; during his domination, the Tokyo Club contributed to various community projects.
FURTHER READING: Bill Hosokawa, *Nisei*, New York: William Morrow and Co., 1969.

TOKYO ROSE. *See* D'Aquino, Iva Ikuko Toguri.

TOLAN COMMITTEE, appointed by the House of Representatives to investigate various aspects of the defense migration. The committee was headed by John H. Tolan, a Democrat elected to represent California's Seventh District in 1935. He had graduated from the University of Kansas Law School and practiced law in Oakland, California, before he was elected. He died on June 30, 1947.

The House Select Committee, investigating National Defense Migration, was composed of five other members of the House: John Sparkman of Alabama, Frank Osmers of New Jersey, Carl T. Curtis of Nebraska, Laurence Arnold of Illinois, and George H. Bender of Ohio. The committee came to the West Coast and held its first public hearings on February 21, 1942, in the post office building in San Francisco. The first witness to testify was Angelo J. Rossi, mayor of San Francisco, who agreed with the President's Executive Order 9066,* for he firmly believed that all enemy aliens should be removed from the Western Defense zones. He did not advocate the same treatment for the Italian and German aliens, however. Following him, Earl Warren,* attorney general of the State of California, testified and presented maps of Japanese populations and land owned and occupied by Japanese aliens. Warren's main argument was that the Japanese lived and worked in the coastal defense areas and were very close to war industries. But he did not point out that the Japanese population had been located in those same areas long before World War II began. During his testimony, he suggested that the Japanese could be incarcerated by declaring them enemy aliens and then suspending the writ of habeas corpus. His second suggestion was more drastic: he recommended that martial law be declared.

The Tolan Committee then moved to Portland, Oregon, Seattle, and Los Angeles to hold public hearings. During these hearings members of the community as well as city, county, state, and federal officials were interviewed to get their opinions on the relocation of aliens as well as Japanese Americans. The opinions were as varied as the people who testified. Japanese American citizens' groups recommended against internment but also gave their solemn pledge to cooperate with the government. Friends of the Japanese testified, stating that they were trustworthy, self-sufficient, intelligent, and hard-working people. The testimony of some elected officials reflected their racism and prejudice. Prejudice against Japanese Americans abounded on the West Coast both before and during the Pacific War. The mayor of Portland, Earl Riley, spoke for many when he said, "Every Axis alien is under suspicion, and I don't want them in my locality." A large segment of the population felt the same way as Riley, and although there was no justification for their prejudice, they were easily swept up into the flood of racism against the Japanese population.

The findings of the Tolan Committee, which included a recommendation that the Japanese population be evacuated, were moot. On March 2, 1942, the day when the Tolan Committee was to conclude its hearings in Seattle, General John Lesesne DeWitt* issued Public Proclamation No. 1, establishing Military Area No. 1, which included the western halves of California, Oregon, and Washington, and the southern half of Arizona.

FURTHER READING: Frank F. Chuman, *The Bamboo People*, Del Mar, Calif.; Publisher's Inc., 1976; Audrie Girdner and Anne Loftis, *The Great Betrayal*, New York: Macmillan Co. 1969; Bill Hosokawa, *JACL in Quest of Justice*, New York: William Morrow and Co., 1982; Michi Weglyn, *Years of Infamy*, New York: William Morrow and Co., 1976; Tolan Committee, *Hearings Before the Select Committee Investigating National Defense Migration*, San Francisco, February 21 and 23, 1942, Washington, D.C.: U.S. Government Printing Office, 1942.

TOM HONG v. UNITED STATES, a case dealing not only with Tom Hong, but also with two of his former business partners, Tom Dock and Lee Kit. These three men owned and operated the Kwong Yen Ti Company from 1891 to 1895 in New York. They classified themselves as merchants. They bought and sold goods at their store, performed the necessary bookkeeping functions of their trade, and had the required articles of partnership. The law at that time could be interpreted so that it would require their names to be listed in the name of the company. Their company, which was operated as a partnership, listed none of their names in its title.

The provisions of the Chinese Exclusion Act of 1892, renewing the Chinese Exclusion Act of 1882,* and amended by the 1893 act, required that certain Chinese laborers obtain a certificate of residence and that those found without the certificate were to be deported. In addition, the law described Chinese laborers as both skilled and unskilled manual laborers in mining, fishing, huckstering, peddling, laundry, and those engaged in selling shell or other fish for home use.

The Kwong Yen Ti Company ceased to operate in 1895 after years of operation. During that period the Chinese Exclusion Act of 1892 did not require them to obtain a certificate of residence because they were merchants. Shortly after the turn of the century, the three were found to be in violation of the act because they did not have the certificate required of certain laborers. They were brought before the commissioner of the Eastern District of the State of New York, B. Lincoln Benedict, who ruled that they were not merchants as defined in the act during 1894. Rather, they were now laborers without certificates and should be deported. The commissioner did not contest the fact that the men operated the Kwong Yen Ti Company; he based his deportation order on the grounds that they failed to show that they were bona fide merchants. The Chinese Exclusion Act of May 5, 1892, as amended by the Act of November 3, 1893, defined a merchant as "a person engaged in buying and selling merchandise at a fixed place of business, which business is conducted in his name, and who, during the time he claims to be engaged as a merchant, does not engage in the performance of any manual labor except such as is necessary in the conduct of his business as such merchant."

The case went to the Supreme Court as an appeal from the District Court to review an order affirming an order of deportation of the three Chinese merchants. The case was heard on January 12, 1904, and was decided on March 21, 1904. Justice William Rufus Day delivered the opinion of the Court to the effect that the three men did not have to list their names. The purpose of the requirement was to make sure that they were, in fact, merchants. The judgment was reversed because the three men were not required to register for a certificate at the time. FURTHER READING: *Supreme Court Reporter* 24, 193 U.S. 517, 1903.

TONGHOE, the village council established on each plantation in Hawaii with more than ten Korean families. Tongjang, or the village chief, was elected once a year to head the village. The village council was an important social and political organization for Koreans in Hawaii because it was empowered to arrest, prosecute, and punish any Korean found guilty of violating the community's code of ethics. In 1907 the *tonghoe* of various plantations came together to form a single organization called the Hanin Hapsong Hyop-hoe, or the United Korean Society.*

TONGJANG. *See Tonghoe.*

TONGS (TANGS), Chinese organizations. The Chinese word *tong*, or *tang* as pronounced in Mandarin, refers to a variety of Chinese organizations. This has created a great deal of misunderstanding about Chinese organizations in the United States. *Tong* could mean a hall, a mansion, a club, or a large residence. Used in combination with other words, it could also mean church as in *gau tong* or school as in *hawk tong*. *Tong* as it is understood by people in North America is commonly associated with the notion of Chinese secret societies.

Tong as a social organization among Chinese at home and abroad is a mutual aid society organized to render assistance to its members in time of need. In practice, however, a *tong* became an extralegal organization among overseas Chinese whose members were engaged in illegal activities.

The *tongs* sometimes referred to as Hoong Moon Societies* or Triad or Three Dots Societies were developed in China during the seventeenth century when China came under the control of the Manchus who were resented by the followers of the Ming Dynasty. It was said that the Ch'ing Dynasty outlawed these organizations because of their identity as rebels against the dynasty.

When the Chinese came to America, they came with their social organizations. A Hoong Moon Society was found in existence in San Francisco in 1854, when the city police raided its headquarters during an initiation ceremony. Obviously, the organization had been in existence much earlier. As Gunther Barth observes in his well–known study of early Chinese immigrants in the United States, there were such *tongs* as the Hung Shun Tong, the Kwang Tek Tong, the Hsieh I Tong, and Tan Shan Tong. All these *tongs* were collectively known as the Chee Kung Tong.*

Tongs were largely responsible for organized crime or illegal activities such as running the gambling houses and the houses of prostitution, selling narcotics and opium, and even murdering those who refused to cooperate with their demands. Killing occurred between members of rival *tongs* over their property rights. *Tong* wars were frequently reported, particularly during the last two decades of the nineteenth century. (*See also* Hoong Moon Societies; Chee Kung Tong.)

FURTHER READING: Gunther Barth, *Bitter Strength*, Cambridge, Mass.: Harvard University Press, 1964; Steward Culin, *The I Hing or Patriotic Rising*, San Francisco: R. and E. Research Associates, 1970 (originally published in 1887); Richard Dillon, *The Hatchet Men, 1880–1906*, New York: Coward-McCann, 1962; Rose Hum Lee, *The Chinese in the United States of America*, Hong Kong: Hong Kong University Press, 1960; Charles R. Shepherd, *The Ways of Ah Sin*, New York: Fleming H. Revell, 1923.

TONG WARS. *See Tongs.*

TOYOTA HIDEMITSU v. UNITED STATES, a case argued on March 18, 1925, and decided on May 25, 1925, when Associate Justice Pierce Butler upheld the decision of the Circuit Court to cancel Toyota's certificate of citizenship granted to him by the District Court. Toyota came to the United States from Japan in 1913 and subsequently served in the U.S. Coast Guard until 1923. On May 14, 1921, he filed a petition for naturalization in the District Court for the State of Massachusetts. The District Court granted him the petition on the basis of the Act of 1918, and a certificate of citizenship was issued. According to the Act of 1918, all aliens who had served in the armed forces of the United States and had been honorably discharged were granted naturalization privileges.

The government was not satisfied, however, and appealed to the Federal Circuit Court of Appeals for the First Circuit, which subsequently decided to revoke Toyota's citizenship on the grounds that it had been illegally obtained. On appeal the case went to the U.S. Supreme Court with two certified questions: (1) May a person born in Japan of Japanese race be legally naturalized under the seventh subdivision of section 4 of the Act of June 29, 1906, as amended by the Act of May 9, 1918; and (2) may such a person be legally naturalized under the Act of July 19, 1919?

Associate Justice Butler, who delivered the opinion of the Court with which the Chief Justice dissented, reasoned that the words "all alien" used by Congress when it passed the Act of 1918 did not mean to enlarge the classes of aliens eligible for citizenship. Because it had been the policy of the U.S. government to maintain the distinction of race and color in naturalization laws, a person born of the Japanese race could not be naturalized.

FURTHER READING: Frank F. Chuman, *The Bamboo People*, Del Mar, Calif.; Publisher's Inc., 1976; Milton R. Konvitz, *The Aliens and the Asiatic in American Law*, Ithaca, N.Y.: Cornell University Press, 1946; Robert A. Wilson and Bill Hosokawa, *East to America*, New York: William Morrow and Co., 1980; *Supreme Court Reporter* 45, 1924, 268 U.S. 402.

TREATY OF AMITY AND COMMERCE OF 1882 BETWEEN KOREA AND THE UNITED STATES. *See* Chemulp'o, Treaty of (1882).

TREATY OF COMMERCE AND NAVIGATION OF 1858 BETWEEN JAPAN AND THE UNITED STATES. *See* Yedo, Treaty of (1858).

TREATY OF COMMERCE AND NAVIGATION OF 1894 BETWEEN JAPAN AND THE UNITED STATES, a pact concluded on November 22 and proclaimed on March 21, 1895. This treaty was one of the most comprehensive agreements ever concluded between Japan and the United States, for it included twenty–nine articles covering such subjects as mutual freedom of trade and travel, import and export duties, and equality of shipping as well as port regulations. Particularly relevant to Japanese arriving in the United States as immigrants after 1895 was Article I of the treaty which stated: "The citizens or subjects of each of the two High Contracting Parties shall have full liberty to enter, travel, or reside in any part of the territories of the other Contracting Parties, and shall enjoy full and perfect protection for their persons and property."

Because of this particular article, the treaty came under review by the Supreme Court of the United States when it rendered a decision in the case of Yamataya Kaoru v. Thomas M. Fisher* on April 6, 1903. (*See also* Yamataya Karou v. Thomas M. Fisher.)

FURTHER READING: Roger Daniels, ed., *Three Short Works on Japanese Americans*, New York: Arno Press, 1978.

TREATY OF COMMERCE AND NAVIGATION OF 1911 BETWEEN JAPAN AND UNITED STATES. *See* Washington, Treaty of (1911).

TREATY OF 1880 BETWEEN CHINA AND THE UNITED STATES, an agreement concluded on November 8, 1880, but not signed until November 17, 1880. The Treaty of 1880 is also called the Angell Treaty after James B. Angell, the head of the commission appointed to review the Burlingame Treaty of 1868,* who at that time was president of the University of Michigan.

The necessity of revising the Burlingame Treaty of 1868 or abrogating it altogether arose as a result of pressure by West Coast residents on the Congress and the President to exclude Chinese laborers. The whites were blaming the 1868 treaty for the depressed economy. President Rutherford B. Hayes, who with the upcoming election in 1880 had a political decision to make, decided to send a team of commissioners to renegotiate a new treaty with the Chinese government. Angell was initially reluctant to accept the appointment as he was not convinced that absolute prohibition of Chinese immigration was the answer. When he was assured that the government was seeking limited restraints on Chinese immigration, he accepted the appointment and left for China with other commissioners, namely, John F. Swift of California and William H. Trescot of South Carolina. They left for China on June 19, 1880, on the ship *Oceanic* and arrived in Shanghai on July 27, at which time they proceeded to Chefoo where they arrived on August 1, 1880.

Facing the possibility of absolute prohibition of Chinese immigration to the United States, the government in Peking sought some concessions from the American government, particularly protection of Chinese who were already in the United States. The Ch'ing government agreed to the regulation, limitation, and suspension, but not absolute prohibition, of immigration of Chinese laborers as long as other classes of Chinese were not affected by the agreement. In return, the American government promised to give protection to Chinese residents in America. (*See also* Burlingame Treaty of 1868.)

FURTHER READING: Jack Chen *The Chinese of America*, New York: Harper and Row, 1980; Mary R. Coolidge, New York: Henry Holt and Co., 1909; Tien-Lu Li, *Congressional Policy of Chinese Immigration or Legislation Relating to Chinese Immigration into the United States*, Nashville, Tenn.: Publishing House of the Methodist Episcopal Church, 1916; Shi-shan Henry Tsai, *China and the Overseas Chinese in the United States, 1868–1911*, Fayetteville: University of Arkansas Press, 1983.

TREATY OF 1894 BETWEEN CHINA AND THE UNITED STATES (also known as the Gresham-Yang Treaty), an agreement concluded on March 17, 1894. The Senate debated the treaty in May and again in August, and the treaty was ratified and proclaimed in December. Two factors apparently helped relax the hitherto strained relations between China and the United States. First, trade between China and the United States decreased markedly, a change that led the American government to think about renegotiating a new treaty. Second, the Chinese government threatened to retaliate against Americans in China in reaction to the passage of the Geary Act of 1892.*

According to the new treaty, China accepted the absolute prohibition of immigration of Chinese laborers and registration requirement as stipulated in the Geary Act of 1892. In return, the United States allowed Chinese with valid certificates to return to America, thus replacing the punitive Scott Act of 1888.* The treaty also gave Chinese the right of transit and required American laborers in China to register with the Chinese government—an empty gesture in light of the small number of American laborers in China.

FURTHER READING: Jack Chen *The Chinese of America*, New York: Harper and Row, 1980; Mary R. Coolidge, *Chinese Immigration*, New York: Henry Holt and Co., 1909; Delber L. McKee, *Chinese Exclusion Versus the Open Door Policy, 1900–1906*, Detroit, Mich.: Wayne State University Press, 1977.

TREATY OF PARIS 1899 BETWEEN SPAIN AND THE UNITED STATES. *See* Paris, Treaty of (1899).

TREATY OF PEACE, AMITY AND COMMERCE OF 1854 BETWEEN JAPAN AND THE UNITED STATES. *See* Kanagawa, Treaty of (1854).

TRIAD SOCIETY. *See Tongs;* Hoong Moon Societies.

TSUKIYAMA, WILFRED C. (1897–1966), Chief Justice of Hawaii Supreme Court. Tsukiyama was born in Hawaii and was educated at the University of Chicago Law School. He joined the Republican Party in 1924, stating that he idealized Abraham Lincoln.

Upon his return to his home state, Tsukiyama was appointed deputy attorney for the city and county of Honolulu in 1929, an important political office for a Japanese born in Hawaii to hold at that time. He continued to serve until he became chief attorney four years later. During his tenure as deputy attorney the famous Ala Moana Case* was heard.

In 1940 when relations between Japan and America deteriorated, Tsukiyama went into private law practice; his withdrawal from public life was later criticized by a new generation of politicians of Japanese ancestry. In 1958 he was asked to run against John Anthony Burns* for the governorship but refused. Instead, he ran for a seat in Hawaii's Senate from the Fifth District of Oahu and won it.

Soon after the election he resigned to become the first Chief Justice of the Supreme Court of Hawaii, following Hawaii's admission to statehood in 1959.

In 1963, Tsukiyama was awarded the Order of the Sacred Treasure Second Class by Japan for his contributions to the promotion of good relations between Japan and the United States.

FURTHER READING: Gavan Daws, *Shoal of Time*, Honolulu: University of Hawaii Press, 1968; Lawrence H. Fuchs, Hawaii Pono: A Social History, New York: Harcourt, Brace and World, 1961; Theon Wright, *The Disenchanted Isles*, New York: Dial Press, 1972.

TULE LAKE SEGREGATION CENTER, one of ten relocation centers* in which Japanese Americans were interned during World War II. Tule Lake, opened in 1942, was one of the first four centers. Located in the foothills of the Sierra Nevada Mountain Range, it was within the evacuation zone of the West Coast. Its peak population of 18,734 was recorded on January 1, 1945.

On July 6, 1943, the U.S. Senate passed a resolution asking the War Relocation Authority* (WRA) to segregate Japanese evacuees whose loyalty did not rest with the United States. Accordingly, on July 15, 1943, the WRA announced a policy of segregating the loyal Japanese Americans from disloyal persons of Japanese ancestry. The Tule Lake Center was chosen because it already had the highest percentage of residents who were probably destined to be segregated.

Because of its segregation, life at Tule Lake was tense from the moment it opened. It had more military police guards than any other center. Moreover, it was the only center to have more than two or three non-evacuee policemen. Although most of the evacuees at Tule Lake were law-abiding citizens, they were questioned and harassed so much that many evacuees developed a dislike for the investigation of authorities.

A minor incident in the fall of 1943 was mishandled by authorities and became a major crisis. A truck carrying farm workers was overturned, and one of the workers was killed in the accident. When the evacuees learned that an inexperienced minor had been the driver of the truck, they blamed the WRA for the accident. They then enacted a work stoppage. The project director caused further unrest by refusing use of the public address system for a massive public funeral for the killed worker. His funeral took place without the system. The explosive situation was worsened when it was learned that the monthly compensation to the widow was very low.

While continuing their work stoppage, the Negotiating Committee formed by the Japanese residents at Tule Lake met with the project director and complained of overcrowding, unacceptable sanitary conditions, and deficiencies in their diet. The committee demanded that farm production be confined to the needs of Tule Lake and that no produce be shipped elsewhere. While these demands were being heard, plans were being made to break the work stoppage by bringing in ''loyal'' workers from other centers to harvest the crops.

When Dillon S. Myer,* national director of the WRA, visited Tule Lake on November 1, over 5,000 men, women, and children formed a human barricade around the administration building for three hours. During this time, Myer and administration heads listened to the residents' grievances. After the meeting ended, Myer addressed the demonstrators outside, after which the residents dispersed. No violence occurred.

Three days later, however, a minor scuffle prompted the army to invade Tule Lake. The army established a stockade, officially called Area B, behind a barbed wire fence that separated the white administration area from the evacuees' area. Japanese residents who were considered leaders of the massive non-cooperation were arrested and held in the stockade.

Eventually, martial law was declared, and the army ran the center until January 15, 1944, when it returned control of the center to the WRA. The army continued to run the stockade, however, until May. The stockade was finally closed on August 24, 1944. While it was in operation, there were series of hunger strikes, reports of beatings of stockade inmates, raids into evacuee housing, and disruption of food and other supplies throughout the center. In fact, tensions and unrest continued until the center was closed on May 4, 1946, and turned over to the Bureau of Reclamation.

FURTHER READING: Dillon S. Myer, *Uprooted Americans*, Tucson: University of Arizona Press, 1971; Gary Y. Okihiro, "Tule Lake Under Martial Law: A Study in Japanese Resistance," *The Journal of Ethnic Studies* 5, No. 3 (Fall 1977) pp. 71–85; Jacobus ten Broek et al., *Prejudice, War and the Constitution*, Berkeley: University of California Press, 1975; Michi Weglyn, *Years of Infamy*, New York: William Morrow and Co., 1976.

TUNG HING KUNG SI. *See* Hoong Moon Societies.

TWAIN, MARK (1835–1910), writer. Twain was born Samuel Langhorne Clemens on November 30, 1835, in Florida, Missouri, but moved to Hannibal, Missouri, on the Mississippi River, the setting for *Tom Sawyer* and *The Adventures of Huckleberry Finn*. *Huckleberry Finn* is still the focus of scholarly debates and attention. As recently as March 1985 the *Christian Science Monitor* published an article examining whether Twain was a racist.

He himself claimed that he was not racially prejudiced; all he cared to know, he said, was "that a man is a human being—that is enough for me: He can't be worse." In spite of this disclaimer, it is quite possible that he was influenced by racial prejudices of people around him. The townspeople of Hannibal had strong anti-Catholic and anti-foreign feelings which are reflected in Twain's writings. In his correspondence with the *Muscatine Journal*, for example, he expressed indignation over the number of foreigners in Eastern cities. In August 1853 he wrote home expressing how appalled he was by the "mass of Human vermin" he encountered in the immigrant district of New York. He also wrote of his shock upon encountering the immigrants in Philadelphia.

Mark Twain travelled to the West Coast, where he came into contact with Chinese. His description of the Chinese quarters of New York and Virginia City, California, reflected the stereotypes so predominant in the anti-Chinese literature of the time. But when Twain finally came to know the hard–working Chinese he found that the stereotypes he had followed were not based on the truth. In *Roughing It* (1871), he describes the Chinese as "a harmless race when white men leave them alone or treat them no worse than dogs. They are almost entirely harmless anyhow for they seldom think of resenting the vilest insults or the cruelest injuries."

Twain also characterized the Chinese as people who loved to herd themselves and to imitate, although he claimed that they were quick to learn and were very industrious. Most damaging to his reputation was his characterization of the Chinese as good house servants.

But to call Mark Twain a racist would be too simplistic. On the positive side he defended the Chinese for their diligence, their love of peace, and their intelligence. He praised the Burlingame Treaty of 1868* for finally giving the Chinese some rights.

Furthermore, Twain devoted himself to exposing "the brutally outrageous treatment" of the Chinese in the land of the free, a subject which engaged the attention of few American writers of the time.

FURTHER READING: Louis J. Budd, *Mark Twain: Social Philosopher*, Bloomington: Indiana University Press, 1962; Philip S. Foner, *Mark Twain: Social Critic*, New York: International Publishers, 1958; Maxwell Geismar, *Mark Twain and the Three R's*, New York: Bobbs-Merrill Co., 1973; A. L. Scott, *Mark Twain at Large*, Chicago: Henry Regnery Co., 1969; W. S. Shepperson, *Restless Strangers: Nevada's Immigrants and Their Interpreters*, Reno: University of Nevada Press, 1970; Janet Smith, *Mark Twain on the Damned Human Race*, New York: Hill and Wang, 1962; Mark Twain, *Roughing It*, New York: Harper and Brothers Publishers, 1871; Mark Twain, *Sketches New and Old*, New York: Harper and Brothers Publishers, 1899; Dixon Wecter, *The Love Letters of Mark Twain*, New York: Harper and Brothers Publishers, 1949.

TWO–CATEGORY SYSTEM, THEORY OF. *See* Daniels, Roger; Kitano, Harry H. L.

TYDINGS-McDUFFIE ACT OF 1934 (known as the Second Filipino Independence Act), negotiated between Manuel Quezon* and leaders of Congress, including Senator Millard Tydings, chairman of the Senate Committee on Territories and Insular Affairs. Quezon had led the opposition against the Hare-Hawes-Cutting Act* of 1933, because he felt that he could get a better bargain from Congress. He came to America in December 1933 and held a round of talks with President Franklin Roosevelt, Secretary of War George Dern, and Senator Tydings. After much maneuvering, Quezon was able to settle on the bill introduced by Senator Tydings which promised the Philippine Islands political independence ten years after the passage of the bill. It also provided a progressive 5 percent export tax on Philippine products beginning in 1941. All Philippine products were to have 100 percent tariff on them after independence, which came in 1946.

Although Quezon sought more advantageous political and economic legislation, he received terms that were no better than what the Hare-Hawes-Cutting Bill had promised. The issue revolving around Filipino immigration to the United States did not change substantially, and Filipino residents in the United States were reclassified from nationals to aliens after the Tydings-McDuffie Act passed on March 23, 1934. The President signed the bill the following day. The Philippine legislature approved the bill on May 1, 1934, thus setting in motion the process of establishing the Commonwealth of the Philippines.

FURTHER READING: Theodore Friend, *Between Two Empires; The Ordeal of the Philippines, 1929–1946*, New Haven, Conn.: Yale University Press, 1965; H. Brett Melendy, *Asians in America; Filipinos, Koreans and East Indians*, Boston: Twayne Publishers, 1977; George E. Taylor, *The Philippines and the United States: Problems of Partnership*, New York: Frederick A. Praeger, 1964.

U

UKUPAU SYSTEM, a Hawaiian term meaning "job done." Under the *ukupau* system of work, Chinese workers on Hawaii's sugar plantations gained some independence and discretion when they were allowed to work as rapidly or as slowly as they wanted as long as a certain amount of work was done daily. The plantation owners who hired Chinese laborers also used the contract system. Under this system a Chinese contractor hired Chinese laborers to work for a stipulated sum of money to be paid for a certain amount of work completed.

UNIFICATION CHURCH, officially founded in 1954 in Seoul, Korea, by the Reverend Moon Sun-myong, who is known as "the Master" by his followers. Moon was born in North P'yongan Province, North Korea, in 1920 and later came to Seoul where he studied electrical engineering. He states that he received a vision from Jesus, who told Moon that he was destined to restore the Kingdom of God on earth. This divine vision occurred on Easter Sunday morning of 1936, when Moon was only sixteen years old.

Upon graduation from high school, Moon went to Tokyo, where he attended Japan's most prestigious institution of higher learning, Waseda University. At the end of the Pacific War in 1945 he came back to North Korea, where he began his ministry in P'yongyang. Because of his Christian ministry in North Korea he was imprisoned on February 22, 1948, and was not freed until 1950 after the United Nations Forces moved north. He came to Pusan after he was freed and began to gather a small group of converts to his religious views.

Moon studied, meditated, and prayed from 1946 until 1955 when he put together *The Divine Principle*, which his church uses as its spiritual guide. His church is founded on four major principles: (1) perfection of the individual, (2) perfection of the family, (3) restoration of the nation, and (4) restoration of the world.

The church remained small in Korea during the 1960s. It was unable to recruit many new members because many Koreans considered it to be an unorthodox, if not sectarian, group. When the church was transplanted to America in an era of social turmoil and conflict when the young were questioning their parents' values as well as their own, the church finally began to gain converts. Three individuals were largely responsible for the development of the church in America: Kim Oong Young, who translated *The Divine Principle* from Korean into English and went to California to work for the church; David S. C. Kim, who moved to Oregon; and Pak Bo Hi, who came to Washington, D.C. The church was officially incorporated as the Holy Spirit Association for the Unification of World Christianity under California law on September 2, 1961, and its office was located in San Francisco.

As membership began to grow in America and rumors of mind control and indoctrination began to spread across the country, the public began to question the legitimacy of the church and its way of converting young people to be followers of the Reverend Moon. Some former converts of the church, also known as "Moonies," went through the process of deprogramming in order to free themselves from the influence of the church.

In 1982 the Reverend Moon was prosecuted for violation of tax laws and was sent to prison in 1984. On July 4, 1985, he was released to a half-way house. FURTHER READING: Robert Boettcher, *Gifts of Deceit: Sun Myung Moon, Tong Sung Park, and the Korean Scandal*. New York: Holt, Rinehart and Winston, 1980; David G. Bromley, *Moonies in America*, Beverly Hills, Calif.; Sage, 1979; Christopher Edwards, *Crazy for God*, Englewood Cliffs, N.J.: Prentice-Hall, 1979; Irving L. Horowitz, *Science, Sin and Scholarship: The Politics of Rev. Moon and the Unification Church*, Cambridge, Mass.: MIT Press, 1978; Report of the Subcommittee on International Organizations of the Committee on International Relations, U.S. House of Representatives, *Investigation of Korea-American Relations*, Vol. 2, Washington, D.C.: U.S. Government Printing Office, 1978; Barbara Underwood, *Hostage to Heaven*, New York: C. N. Potter, 1979.

UNITED CANNERY, AGRICULTURAL, PACKING AND ALLIED WORKERS OF AMERICA, chartered by the Congress of Industrial Organizations in 1937, although efforts to organize workers in agricultural and cannery industries had been made as early as 1934. Carlos Bulosan,* author of *America Is in the Heart* (1946), helped to found the union. Once chartered, leaders of the union launched a strong and aggressive membership drive, particularly among Filipino and Mexican seasonal workers, in competition with the American Federation of Labor. The Union changed its name to the Food, Tobacco and Agricultural Workers International before it was ousted from the Congress of Industrial Organizations because of heavy infiltration of the Union by Communists.

UNITED CHINESE SOCIETY, established in late 1882 when a group of twenty-five Chinese merchants in Hawaii gathered at the Chinese fire station in Honolulu to organize the Chung Wah Wui Goon, or the Chinese Union as it was called in English. For a long time the Chinese in Hawaii were in need of a centralized organization to deal effectively with outside pressure. As the number of Chinese immigrants coming to Hawaii increased, the Hawaiian government attempted to restrict Chinese immigration, and white citizens in Hawaii began to discriminate against the Chinese.

The initiative to establish a centralized Chinese organization did not originate from within the Chinese community in Hawaii. It came from the Chinese government which began to show increasing interest in the welfare of its subjects abroad, particularly after the Burlingame Treaty of 1868.* When Chen Lan-pin, Chinese Minister to Washington, D.C., passed through Honolulu, he donated $1,000 toward construction of a community headquarters, and upon his return to China he dispatched two commissioners, who were highly knowledgeable about the workings of the Chinese Six Companies* in San Francisco, to help local Chinese in their efforts to establish an organization.

The organization elected C. Alee (or Ching King Chun) as president and Goo Kim (or Goo Kim Fui) as vice-president. A secretary and an assistant secretary, a treasurer and an assistant treasurer, and twenty-four directors were also elected to complete the organization's personnel needs. It was the first time in the history of the Chinese in Hawaii that the Puntis* and Hakkas* came together to work in a single organization, for C. Alee was a Punti, and Goo Kim was a Hakka. Previously, the Chinese in Hawaii had established organizations on the basis of clan, language, or birthplace. This marked the beginning of the collective consciousness among the Chinese in Hawaii who felt they had to unite in order to combat the prejudice against them.

The organization served the Chinese community in Hawaii for more than fifty years both as a social and a political organization. It made efforts to stave off government attempts to restrict Chinese immigration unsuccessfully; it sent protests against anti-Chinese laws; and it intervened when the Chinese were mistreated or were unjustly dealt with by their employers.

FURTHER READING: Clarence E. Glick, *Sojourners and Settlers*, Honolulu: University Press of Hawaii, 1980; Ralph S. Kuykendall, *The Hawaiian Kingdom*, Vol. 3: 1874–1893, Honolulu: University of Hawaii Press, 1967.

UNITED FARM WORKERS ORGANIZING COMMITTEE, an organization of Filipino and Chicano farm workers established in August 1966, when the Agricultural Workers Organizing Committee, an organization whose membership was predominately Filipino, merged with the National Farm Workers Association which was originally established by Cesar Chavez. Filipino immigration to the U.S. mainland was modest until the passage of the Immigration Act of 1924,* which prohibited Japanese immigration. After that date, large numbers of Filipino farm workers known as *pinoy** were brought to work in California and other agricultural states. They were brought under contract to pick tomatoes, pack peas, harvest grapes, peaches, and berries, cut asparagus, and plant celery and lettuce. By the early 1930s there were as many as 45,000 *pinoys* in the United

States, most of whom were found in California. Numerous attempts were made to organize them into labor unions, but most of these attempts failed as a result of strong opposition from the Associated Farmers of California, although the Filipino Agricultural Workers Association* had some success in the 1940s.

After World War II, Filipino agricultural workers began to demand higher wages and better working conditions, but they were not very successful because they lacked organization. In the early 1960s they began to organize under the leadership of Larry Dulay Itliong,* who led the Agricultural Workers Organizing Committee local dominated by the Filipino farm workers. The Agricultural Workers Organizing Committee that was formed by the AFL-CIO in 1959 struck against thirty-three grape growers in Delano, California, under Itliong's leadership, and Cesar Chavez joined the strike eight days later. The seven-month strike created much public sympathy, and the striking union members won a victory when Schenley Industries, owner of the largest vineyards of the thirty-three decided to recognize Chavez's National Farm Workers Association as the sole bargaining agent. The two organizations merged to form the United Farm Workers Organizing Committee of the AFL-CIO. (*See also* Grape Strike, Delano.)
FURTHER READING: Paul Fusco and George D. Horowitz, *La Causa, the California Grape Strike*, New York: Collier Books, 1970; Dick Meister and Anne Loftis, *A Long Time Coming*, New York: Macmillan Co., 1977; Brett Melendy, *Asians in America*, Boston: Twayne Publishers, 1977.

UNITED JAPANESE SOCIETY OF HAWAII, organized in June 1958 when representatives from fifty Japanese organizations met to establish an island-wide organization that would cut across the interests of small groups represented by businessmen, church people, veterans, and politicans. The society had 30,000 members who were expected to participate in promoting friendship between Japanese and white citizens, helping the elderly, and protecting their rights.

UNITED KOREAN COMMITTEE, created on April 20, 1941, when a group of representatives of nine Korean social and political organizations met in Honolulu, Hawaii, to find ways of supporting the Korean provisional government in Shanghai. The representatives decided to form the United Korean Committee to carry out a nine-point program to assist the Korean provisional government in its struggle against Japan. It proclaimed a Declaration of All-Korean Convention.* Haan Kil-soo was appointed as the liaison between the U.S. government and the committee, which was to carry out all diplomatic activities in relation to Korea's independence. (*See* Declaration of All-Korean Convention; Rhee, Syngman.)

UNITED KOREAN SOCIETY, self-governing body representing Korean interests in Hawaii, established in 1907. Upon arrival in Hawaii in 1903, Korean immigrants organized *tonghoe** and established some semblance of community life. A *tonghoe* was established in each plantation with more than ten Korean families. These *tonghoes* came together to establish the United Korean Society (or Hanin Hapsong Hyophoe). In 1909, it merged with the Mutual Assistance Society* on the U.S. mainland to become the Korean National Association.* (*See also* Mutual Assistance Society; *Tonghoe*.)

UNITED STATES v. BHAGAT SINGH THIND, a case argued before the U.S. Supreme Court on January 11 and 12, 1923, and decided on February 19, 1923. The case reached the Court on Certificate from the U.S. Circuit Court of Appeals for the Ninth Circuit, as the federal government brought suit against Bhagat Singh Thind requesting that his certificate of citizenship be canceled. The District Court that had tried the case dismissed the government's arguments, and the government appealed to the Circuit Court of Appeals, which certified to the Supreme Court the question of whether or not a high-caste Hindu was a white person, and whether or not the Immigration Act of February 5, 1917* did not qualify him for naturalization.

Justice George Sutherland, who delivered the opinion of the Court, pointed out that the Naturalization Act of March 26, 1790* that conferred the right of naturalization to "only free white persons" meant to include almost exclusively immigrants from the British Isles and Northwestern Europe. According to his reasoning, the definition of "a free white person" as it was used by Congress at the time the law was passed did not mean a scientific definition; it only meant the understanding of the term by the common man.

In his opinion on the case of Ozawa Takao v. United States* which was decided on November 13, 1922, Justice Sutherland said that Ozawa was not eligible for U.S. citizenship because he was not a Caucasian. But, in the present case, the same Justice changed his point of view, if not denying his previous opinion. He now said that although Thind was a member of the Caucasian race, he was not eligible for U.S. citizenship because he did not fit into the common man's understanding of "a white person."

Thind's appeal for certificate was denied by the Supreme Court. This decision had a far-reaching impact on those Asian Indians who had acquired U.S. citizenship prior to this decision and those who desired to acquire it after the decision. (*See also* Ozawa Takao v. United States.)
FURTHER READING: S. Chandrashekhar, ed., *From India to America*, La Jolla, Calif.: Population Review, 1982; Ray E. Chase and S. G. Pandit, *An Examination of the Opinion of the Supreme Court of the United States*, Los Angeles: n.p., 1926; Milton R. Konvitz, *Civil Rights in Immigration*, Ithaca, N.Y.: Cornell University Press, 1953; Milton R. Konvitz, *The Alien and the Asiatic in American Law*, Ithaca, N.Y.: Cornell University Press, 1946; *Supreme Court Reporter* 43, 261, U.S. 204, 1922.

UNITED STATES v. JU TOY, a case involving a U.S. citizen who was denied entry into his own country because he was of Chinese descent. Ju Toy left the United States for a visit to China. On returning to the United States he applied for reentry on the grounds that he was a citizen. After examining Ju Toy's case, the immigration officers denied him admission. He appealed to the Secretary of

Commerce and Labor, who upheld the immigration officer's decision. He then appealed his case to the District Court and asked for a writ of habeas corpus. The District Court decided in Ju Toy's favor on the grounds that he was a native-born citizen of the United States. The case went to the Supreme Court on a certificate from the Circuit Court of Appeals presenting certain questions of law to which the Supreme Court was asked to respond. The first question raised was whether habeas corpus should be granted on behalf of a person of Chinese descent whose right to enter the United States had been denied by the immigration officers and affirmed on appeal by the Secretary of Commerce and Labor, and citizenship was the only grounds alleged in making the detention unlawful. The second question before the Court was whether or not the writ should be dismissed under such circumstances or whether a further hearing should be granted. The Court was also asked to answer the question of whether or not the decision of the Secretary of Commerce and Labor was conclusive in the absence of abuse of authority.

The case was argued on April 3, 1905, and was decided on May 8, 1905. Justice Oliver Wendell Holmes, in delivering the opinion of the Court, responded to these questions by saying that the answer to the first question should be no, because the Court decided previously on the case of the United States v. Sing Tuck* (194 U.S. 161) that a person covered under the Chinese Exclusion Law did not have the right to a habeas corpus proceeding, even when habeas corpus was requested on the grounds of citizenship. The answer to the third question was affirmative, because the Court also ruled previously on the case of Nishimura v. United States* that the decision made by an executive officer was due process. As to the second question, the writ was to be dismissed.

The Court did not feel that by denying Ju Toy a habeas corpus hearing it violated the Fifth Amendment which guarantees U.S. citizens due process of law. Ju Toy was not allowed to enter the United States by this decision.

FURTHER READING: Milton R. Konvitz, *The Alien and the Asiatic in American Law*, Ithaca, N.Y.: Cornell University Press, 1946; *Supreme Court Reporter* 25, October Term, 1904, 198 U.S. 253, 1904.

UNITED STATES v. JUNG AH LUNG, a case tried before the United States Supreme Court in 1888 involving the reentry of a Chinese into the U.S. from China. In the case of Chew Heong v. United States* the right of a Chinese laborer who had left the United States before passage of the Chinese Exclusion Act of 1882,* as amended on July 5, 1884, was upheld by the U.S. Supreme Court. According to the opinion of the Court, Chew Heong could not have gotten the certificate of identity as specified in Section 4 of the Chinese Exclusion Act of May 6, 1882, as amended on July 5, 1884, because he had left the United States before the law went into effect. Soon after this decision, another case came before the Court asking for its opinion. Jung Ah Lung, a Chinese laborer, was a lawful resident in San Francisco between November 17, 1880, and October 24, 1883, when he left the United States for China. When he left he obtained a certificate of identity that entitled him to reentry into the United States, as specified in Section 4 of the Chinese Exclusion Act of May 6, 1882. Any Chinese laborer leaving the United States was required to register with the collector of the customs of the district from which he was to depart and was required to carry the certificate of identity. But he was not required to present it as "the only evidence permissible to establish his right of re-entry" to the United States as specified in Section 4 of the Chinese Exclusion Law, which amended the Chinese Exclusion Law of May 6, 1882.

Jung Ah Lung was absent from the United States between October 24, 1883, and August 25, 1885, at which time he tried to reenter the United States. He was detained by the local customs authority, because he was unable to produce the certificate of identity he was required to carry. Jung Ah Lung claimed that his certificate was stolen by pirates who attacked the boat he was aboard. He filed for a habeas corpus securing release from detention. Subsequently, in the judicial review by the Circuit Court, his right to land and remain in the United States was upheld. The government appealed the case to the Supreme Court and the Court ruled on the case on February 13, 1888. Justice Samuel Blatchford delivered the opinion of the Court, supported by five of his colleagues; three Justices, Stephen Field, John Harlan, and Lucius Lamar, dissented.

According to the Court, Jung Ah Lung had satisfactorily met the requirements for identification and reentry under the Chinese Exclusion Act of May 6, 1882. Because he left the United States prior to the 1884 amendment and the 1884 amendment was not retroactive, he was allowed to reenter the country. It was the opinion of the Court that the wording of Section 4 of the original Chinese Exclusion Act was vague and that it did not explicitly state that a Chinese laborer must present the certificate of identity for his reentry. This lacuna in the original Chinese Exclusion Act was closed tightly by Congress when it passed an amendatory act to the original Chinese Exclusion Act of May 6, 1882, under the title An Act to Amend an Act Entitled, "An Act to Execute Certain Treaty Stipulations Relating to Chinese Approved May sixth eighteen hundred and eighty-two."

FURTHER READING: Jack Chen, *The Chinese of America*, New York: Harper and Row, 1980; Milton R. Konvitz, *The Alien and the Asiatic in American Law*, Ithaca, N.Y.: Cornell University Press, 1946; Tien-Lu Li, *Congressional Policy of Chinese Immigration*, Nashville, Tenn.: Publishing House of the Methodist Episcopal Church, South, 1916; *Supreme Court Reporter* 8, October Term, 1887, 124 U.S. 621, 1887.

UNITED STATES v. SAKHARAM GANESH PANDIT, a case heard before a Court of Appeals in 1926 involving the government's attempt to cancel the citizenship of an Indian American. Sakharam Ganesh Pandit, a high-caste Hindu, was issued his citizenship on May 7, 1914. This was before February 19, 1923, when the U.S. Supreme Court ruled on the case of United States v. Bhagat Singh Thind,* taking Thind's citizenship away because he was not a white person eligible for U.S. citizenship. After the Supreme Court ruling, the government tried to cancel the citizenship of a number of Asian Indians who had been naturalized before 1923. Pandit was one of those Asian Indians whose citizenship was to be canceled because it was illegally procured, according to the government's claim.

Pandit was educated at Orthodox Sanskrit University and received a Ph.D at Dgarwar. He studied law and was admitted to the bar to practice in California in 1917. He was a member in good standing in all courts. He was also appointed by the governor of California to the office of notary public. In his defense he claimed that he would lose his property as well as his notarial commission if his citizenship were canceled. He also used the plea of *res judicata*, claiming that the original court granted him his citizenship in 1914 after it had heard the government's protest and that his citizenship had not been challenged since then.

The District Court and Circuit Court of Appeals supported Pandit's claim, and the Supreme Court also agreed with Pandit.

FURTHER READING: S. Chandrashekhar, *From India to America*, La Jolla, Calif.: Population Review, 1982; H. Brett Melendy, *Asians in America*, Boston: Twayne Publishers, 1977.

UNITED STATES v. SING TUCK, a case that reached the Supreme Court of the United States on a writ of certiorari to the U.S. Circuit Court of Appeals to the Second Circuit. The Supreme Court was asked to review the judgment made by the Circuit Court of Appeals which had reviewed the judgment made by the Circuit Court of the Northern District of New York and reversed it. The case was argued on April 7, 1904, and decided on April 25, 1904.

Five Chinese, including Sing Tuck, tried to enter the country through Canada and were prevented from entering by a Chinese inspector who questioned their rights. They all claimed that they were U.S. citizens. After they gave their names upon questioning, they refused to answer any further questions. They were then detained at a detention house for deportation purposes. The detainees challenged the government's right to detain them through their lawyer who filed for a petition. The Circuit Court ruled that the detention was proper and lawful. The case was then appealed to the Circuit Court of Appeals which reversed the lower court's decision on the grounds that the detainees were entitled to a judicial investigation. The government then appealed to the Supreme Court.

The Supreme Court had established the legality of the Chinese Exclusion Act of 1882* in its decisions on Fong Yue Ting v. United States* in 1893 and Chin Bak Kan v. United States* in 1902. In the Chin Bak Kan case, the Supreme Court ruled that a person seeking entry into the country claiming to be a citizen had the burden of proof. In the present case, a more restrictive interpretation was given by the Supreme Court in the Court's opinion delivered by Justice Oliver Wendell Holmes, who ruled that the detainees should have exhausted all the administrative remedies before they sought judicial relief.

Two Justices, David Brewer and Rufus Peckham, dissented and filed their own opinion. Justice Brewer insisted that Chinese entering the country should not be asked to comply with the rules established by the government, if the same rules were not applied to members of other races seeking reentry and claiming that they were citizens.

FURTHER READING: Milton R. Konvitz, *The Alien and the Asiatic in American Law*, Ithaca, N.Y.: Cornell University Press, 1946; *Supreme Court Reporter* 24, 194 U.S. 161.

UNITED STATES v. WONG KIM ARK, a case decided by the U.S. Supreme Court on March 28, 1898, in which the Court handed down a major constitutional decision affirming that a person of Chinese descent born in the United States had a right to citizenship. Wong Kim Ark, born in 1873 of Chinese immigrant parents, was denied his right to enter the United States as a citizen upon his return from China. When he was born, Wong Kim Ark's parents had permanent domicile in San Francisco. When he was seventeen years of age, he went to China on a short visit. The same year he returned to San Francisco without any problems. But when he returned from another visit to China when he was twenty-one years of age, he was denied permission to land in San Francisco by the collector of customs.

The question before the Court was the following: If a child was born in the United States of parents of Chinese descent who, at the time of his or her birth, although subjects of the emperor of China, had a permanent residence in the United States, and were carrying on business and not employed in any diplomatic capacity under the emperor of China, did that child become a citizen of the United States at the time of his or her birth? Justice Horace Gray, in his opinion for the majority, argued in favor of Wong Kim Ark on the basis of the Fourteenth Amendment. Although Congress had adopted the policy to exclude Chinese immigrants from American territory and to deny them U.S. citizenship by naturalization, there were no compelling reasons for the Court to fail to give full effect to the clear language of the amendment. Chief Justice Melville Weston Fuller and Justice John Harlan dissented.

This case strengthened and reaffirmed the meaning of the Fourteenth Amendment of the Constitution as it applies to the citizenship of persons born in America of Asian parentage. However, it also reaffirmed the Chinese Exclusion Act of 1882,* when Justice Gray stated that the rights of the United States, as exercised by and under this act, to exclude or expel from the country persons of the Chinese race, born in China and continuing commercial domicile in the United States, had been upheld by this Court.

FURTHER READING: Milton R. Konvitz, *The Alien and the Asiatic in American Law*, Ithaca, N.Y.: Cornell University Press, 1946; *Supreme Court Reporter*, 169 U.S. 649 (1898), pp. 456–88.

USHIJIMA, GEORGE (1863–1926), potato farmer. Ushijima was born in Fukuoka Prefecture, Japan, and came to California in 1889 where he worked as a laborer. He was largely responsible for converting much of the swamp land along the San Joaquin River into potato fields. He was later known as the "Potato King."

UYEDA, CLIFFORD. *See* National Committee for Redress, Japanese American Citizens League.

V

VALIDATION OF LEGISLATIVE AMENDMENTS TO ALIEN LAND
LAW (known as Proposition 15), introduced on May 18, 1945, to change
Section 17 of Article I of the Constitution of the State of California. The California
State Legislature had passed a number of amendments to the Alien Land Law
of 1920, and it became necessary for the legal residents of California to approve
the amended law, because a law approved by the people of the State of California
through initiative had to be voted again by the people if the law was to be
amended. This amended law was to close all loopholes left in the Alien Land
Act of 1920.

The Japanese American Citizens League* under the leadership of Mike Masaru
Masaoka* campaigned rigorously against the measure, and Proposition 15 was
voted down by the voters of California.

VAN REED, EUGENE. *See Ganen-Mono*.

VARONA, FRANCISCO (?–1941), inspector sent to Hawaii by Governor-
General Francis B. Harrison in 1920 to investigate conditions among Filipino
laborers working on Hawaii's sugar plantations. After his tour of various labor
camps, Varona filed a report indicating that much of the labor problems originated
from racial prejudice against the Filipinos by Japanese and whites. He
recommended a number of measures to the plantation owners, and he negotiated
transportation for the Filipinos who did not have any means to get home.

Varona was appointed assistant to Philippine Resident Commissioner Joaquin
M. Elizalde* in 1939 and was actively involved in a number of labor disputes
between Filipino workers and their employers as a mediator. He served as Chief
of the National Division of the Philippine Resident Commissioner's Office until
his death in June 1941. (*See also* Honolulu Contract.)

VEDANTA SOCIETY OF AMERICA. *See* Vivekananda, Swami.

VIBORA LUVIMINDA. *See* Filipino Federation of Labor.

VISCO v. LOS ANGELES COUNTY, a litigation case involving Gavino C. Visco, a Filipino who petitioned for order of alternative mandamus to get a license to marry a Mexican-Indian, Ruth M. Salas. Judge Walter Guerin, Superior Court of Los Angeles County, ruled in 1931 that California law did not prevent marriages between Indians and Filipinos. Furthermore, he stated that he would have approved Visco's petition, had Ruth M. Salas been a white woman.

VIVEKANANDA, SWAMI (1863–1902), Hindu guru. Vivekananda was born Narendra-nath Datta in Calcutta, India, on January 12, 1863, of high-caste parents. He adopted the name Vivekananda after his religious conversion. He received an English education, studying the philosophy of Mill, Hume, and Spencer, which he soon rejected. Toward the end of 1881 Vivekananda met the great Hindu guru Ramakrishna Paramashamsa, who persuaded the young man to join his community of disciples. After Ramakrishna's death in 1885, Vivekananda assumed leadership of the organization.

In 1893 Vivekananda was invited to attend the Chicago meeting of the Parliament of Religions as a representative of Hinduism. He spoke before the Parliament no less than five times and was very successful in influencing the members. This success led to many invitations to lecture on the Vedanta (Monism) philosophy. In 1896, Vivekananda established the Vedanta Society of New York, a branch organization of the Vedanta Society of America located in Calcutta. He returned to India in 1897 but came back to America in 1899 and visited California where he helped establish Vedanta centers in Los Angeles and San Francisco.

FURTHER READING: Bhupendranath Datta, *Swami Vivekananda, Patriot-Prophet: A Study,* Calcutta, India: Nababharat Publishers, 1954; R. C. Majumdar, ed., *The History and Culture of the Indian People: British Paramountcy and Indian Renaissance, Part II,* Bombay, India: Bharatiya Vidya Bhavan, 1965; Swami Nikhilananda, *Vivekananda: A Biography,* 3d ed., Calcutta, India: Advaita Ashrama, 1975.

VOLAG, an acronym referring to voluntary agencies established in America in the 1940s, under contract with the U.S. government, to help resettle refugees from around the world in cooperation with sponsors. Examples of these religious voluntary agencies are the U.S. Catholic Conference, Lutheran Immigration and Refugee Service, World Relief Service, and Church World Services. Other voluntary agencies are non-sectarian, including the International Rescue Committee, the American Council for Nationalities Service, the Tolstoi Foundation, the American Fund for Czechoslovakian Refugees, and Travelers' Aid-International Social Services.

After Saigon fell to the North Vietnamese Communists in 1975, Vietnamese refugees began to pour into the United States. Voluntary agencies under contract with the Interagency Task Force* found sponsors to help refugees resettle in America. The government gave these agencies $500 per refugee as a resettlement grant. (*See also* Interagency Task Force.)

FURTHER READING: Gail Paradise Kelly, *From Vietnam to America*, Boulder, Colo.: Westview Press, 1977; Tricia Knoll, *Becoming Americans*, Portland, Oreg.: Coast to Coast Books, 1982; William T. Liu, *Transition to Nowhere*, Nashville, Tenn.: Charter House, 1979; Darrel Montero, *Vietnamese Americans: Patterns of Resettlement and Socioeconomic Adaptation in the United States*, Boulder, Colo.: Westview Press, 1979.

W

WAH CHANG TRADING COMPANY, incorporated under New York law in 1916 by Li K. C., a metallurgical engineer trained at the Royal School of Mines in England. The company operated the world's largest tungsten refinery in 1953. It took over a number of other companies engaged in mining and refining other metals, and by the end of 1958 the company's assets totaled $4.5 million. Li died in 1961 and was succeeded by his son, Li K. C., Jr., who still serves as chairman of the board.

Li K. C. created a foundation called the Li Foundation to provide scholarships to students desiring to study and work in the United States. Created in 1944, the scholarship provides each student with $5,000, in addition to round-trip transportation.

WAH KIU, a different way of pronouncing Hua-ch'iao* referring to the overseas Chinese, regardless of their nationality. (*See also* Hua-ch'iao.)

WAH KIU SEONG WUI (OVERSEAS CHINESE MERCHANTS' ASSOCIATION). *See* Chinese Chamber of Commerce.

WAH MUN SCHOOL, founded on February 8, 1911, under the auspices of the Tung Ming Wui of Dr. Sun Yat-sen,* who during his trip to Hawaii in 1910 had suggested that a Chinese school be established for the children of Chinese immigrants where they could be taught their native language. Besides teaching Chinese, the school put heavy emphasis on Dr. Sun's political principle, the San Min Chu I, or the Three Principles of Government.

In 1927 the name of the school was changed to Sun Yat-sen School in honor of Dr. Sun Yat-sen.

WAI WAH YEE YUEN (Chinese Hospital), a hospital built with donations toward the construction of a hospital to care for the sick Chinese in Hawaii. The United Chinese Society* launched a vigorous campaign to raise the necessary funds, and the China Fire Engine Company donated $1,950. The hospital was officially opened by Goo Kim, president of the United Chinese Society, in March 1897, at a public ceremony attended by leading Chinese merchants and prominent white citizens of Hawaii.

According to hospital regulations, Chinese patients in need of hospital care could not be admitted without permission from the president, vice-president of the United Chinese Society, and the director of the hospital. Any Chinese too poor to pay was to be cared for free of charge. In the case of death, known relatives were required to pay $14 for burial expenses. The hospital was closed in 1906.

WAKAMATSU TEA AND SILK FARM COLONY, an agricultural community established by a group of Japanese immigrants who were led by John Henry Schnell. These early Japanese pioneers arrived in San Francisco on May 27, 1869, and may have been political refugees who had supported *shoguns* on the losing side. They were known to have come from the vicinity of Aizu Wakamatsu, about 200 miles northeast of Tokyo. The group reached Gold Hill, where their leader, Schnell, had arranged to purchase 600 acres of land to grow tea and silkworms. The colony lasted less than two years. (*See also* Okei.)
FURTHER READING: Bill Hosokawa, *Nisei*, New York: William Morrow and Co., 1969; Robert A. Wilson and Bill Hosokawa, *East to America*, New York: William Morrow and Co., 1980.

WAR AGENCY LIQUIDATION DIVISION, established in 1946 to facilitate the Japanese evacuees' readjustment to a new environment outside the camps where they had been detained. After the U.S. Supreme Court rendered its decision on Endo, ex parte* on December 18, 1944, it was evident that the government could no longer detain persons of Japanese ancestry against their will in concentration camps. Therefore the War Relocation Authority* (WRA) announced on the same day that it was to terminate all camps within six months. In anticipation of liquidating all the programs administered by the WRA by June 30, 1946, a War Agency Liquidation Division was established to operate under the Office of the Secretary of Interior with a staff of eighty people. Congress recommended a supplemental budget of $173,000 for the agency. It functioned about a year after June 30, 1946, before it was closed.

WAR BRIDES ACT OF 1945, a bill passed during the first session of the 79th Congress, introduced by Representative Samuel Dickstein of New York, allowing alien wives, children, and husbands of the members of the U.S. armed forces to come as non-quota immigrants, and eliminating provisions concerning mental and physical defectives. The bill was signed into law on December 28, 1945.

Under the provisions of the War Brides Act of 1945, a total of 722 Chinese and 2,042 Japanese were admitted into the country between 1946 and 1953.
FURTHER READING: Marion T. Bennett, *American Immigration Policies: A History*, Washington, D.C.: Public Affairs Press, 1963; E. P. Hutchinson, *Legislative History of American Immigration Policy, 1798–1965*, Philadelphia: University of Pennsylvania Press, 1981; S. E. Kung, *Chinese in American Life*, Seattle: University of Washington Press, 1962.

WAR RELOCATION AUTHORITY (WRA), established by Executive Order 9102* on March 18, 1942, by President Franklin D. Roosevelt, who on February 19, 1942 had announced Executive Order 9066,* making it possible to exclude civilians from the militarily strategic areas. Milton Stover Eisenhower* was named director of the WRA and was later replaced by Dillon S. Myer* who was appointed to direct the agency on June 17, 1942. The WRA was created to provide for the relocation, maintenance, supervision, and placement in public and private employment of persons whose removal from areas designated by military commands was deemed necessary in the interest of national security.

Over 110,000 persons of Japanese ancestry were taken from their homes and removed, under guard, to assembly centers* and relocation centers* at an average rate of 3,750 per day because high government officials thought they should be removed for military necessity.* The evacuees were allowed only a few specified personal belongings, and they had five days after official notice of their removal in which to sell, rent, loan, store, or give away their real estate and possessions. The Japanese suffered heavy financial losses during this time. The evacuation and internment in assembly centers were completed by August 7, 1942.

Twelve assembly centers were set up in California and one each in Oregon, Washington, and Arizona. The people were kept there until more "permanent" relocation centers could be built and prepared for "human occupancy." The assembly centers were under the control of the Wartime Civil Control Administration (WCCA), which laid down the policies to be followed in educational and religious institutions, and in press activities. Considerable latitude was given the evacuees in setting up educational and recreational facilities. The WCCA gave the evacuees permission to establish center newspapers, but writing in English (Japanese was not allowed) was carefully censored.

Ten relocation centers were built and were brought under WRA control. The transfer of evacuees from the assembly centers to these barracks—accomplished in a great hurry—took place during the summer and was completed by November 3, 1942, when the last group of evacuees arrived at the Jerome Center in Arkansas from Fresno, California.

The WRA continued to operate these concentration camps until the Supreme Court of the United States ruled on Endo, ex parte,* that a citizen claiming to be loyal to the United States could not be detained against his or her own will. On December 18, 1944, the same day the Supreme Court handed down its decision, the WRA announced the termination of relocation centers, and by June 30, 1946, the WRA was liquidated. (*See also* Assembly Centers.)

FURTHER READING: Roger Daniels, *Concentration Camps, U.S.: Japanese Americans and World War II*, New York: Holt, Rinehart and Winston, 1971; Dillon S. Myer, *Uprooted Americans*, Tucson: University of Arizona Press, 1971; War Relocation Authority, *The Administrative Highlights of the WRA Program*, Washington, D.C.: U.S. Government Printing Office; War Relocation Authority, *WRA, A Story of Human Conservation*, Washington, D.C.: U.S. Government Printing Office, 1946.

WARREN, EARL (1891–1974), Chief Justice of the U. S. Supreme Court. Warren was born on March 19, 1891, in Los Angeles but grew up in Bakersfield, California, where his family moved in 1894. He attended the University of California at Berkeley between 1908 and 1914 as an undergraduate and a law student. He graduated in 1914 and served as deputy district attorney of Alameda County, California, before he became district attorney for the same county. He served in that office from 1925 to 1939. Warren was Attorney General for the state from 1939 until 1943, when he ran successfully for the office of governor of California. He held that office until 1953, when President Dwight D. Eisenhower appointed him Chief Justice of the Supreme Court of the United States.

President Eisenhower reportedly wanted to appoint a Chief Justice who would take a stand on a difficult issue, yet not be radical in his thinking. Vice-President Richard M. Nixon and Senator William Knowland recommended Warren because his political philosophy seemed to coincide with that of Eisenhower's. Once appointed as the fourteenth Chief Justice of the Supreme Court, however, Warren proved everyone wrong: he was neither conservative nor a traditional politician. In his first term, he spoke out against school segregation in his famous handling of the Brown v. Board of Education of Topeka in 1954. In this case Warren eliminated the legal basis for discrimination in education, public facilities, and transportation. Some people have labeled the Warren years "The Warren Revolution," because he was willing to go against the white majority's views. With regard to the issue of school prayer, Warren felt that children should not be forced to pray because not every child shares the same religion and not every child or person prays the same way to his God. He vehemently defended the Bill of Rights. Because of his radical views on civil rights, Warren endured a prolonged crusade for his impeachment.

This strong defender of the civil rights of all Americans made one major mistake in his career, however. In 1942, when he was called to testify before the Tolan Committee* investigating national defense migration, he supported the evacuation of persons of Japanese ancestry from the West Coast and suggested that the writ of habeus corpus be suspended for Japanese Americans. In his autobiography (1977) he deeply regretted this testimony and also emphasized that he had no prejudices against the Japanese. (*See also* Tolan Committee.)

FURTHER READING: Frank F. Chuman, *The Bamboo People*, Del Mar, Calif.: Publisher's Inc., 1976; Bernard Schwartz, *Super Chief: Earl Warren and His Supreme Court—*

A Judicial Biography, New York: New York University Press, 1983; Earl Warren, *The Memoirs of Earl Warren*, New York: Doubleday and Co., 1977; G. Edward White, *Earl Warren: A Public Life*, New York: Oxford University Press, 1982.

WARTIME CIVIL CONTROL ADMINISTRATION. *See* Assembly Centers; War Relocation Authority.

WASHINGTON, TREATY OF (1911), known as the Treaty of Commerce and Navigation of 1911, a renegotiation of earlier unequal treaties between the United States and Japan. Ever since Japan was forced to conclude unequal treaties with the West, starting with the Kanagawa Treaty of 1854* with the United States, one of the major Japanese foreign policy goals was to remove all unequal treaties for the sake of its national interest as well as its honor. As early as 1872 the Japanese government dispatched a diplomatic mission known as the Iwakura Mission* to renegotiate with the United States for a treaty that would be more favorable than earlier ones. The Iwakura Mission was not successful, and diplomatic efforts following its failure were made with this particular goal in mind.

The Japanese government prepared to replace the 1894 treaty with a more favorable one by creating a section in the Foreign Ministry in 1906 that would be responsible for investigating issues related to treaty revision. In addition, in 1908 a Board of Commissioners for the Preparation of Treaty Revision was established by imperial decree, with Foreign Minister Komura as its chairman. According to Huntington Wilson, Third Assistant Secretary of State, the board had twenty-five of the ablest men in Japan working toward developing strategies for a treaty renegotiation with the United States.

Although the two nations initially disagreed on the date of expiration for the 1894 treaty, they came to a mutual understanding and began to revise the old treaty. Meanwhile, President William Howard Taft was concerned about the anti-Japanese feelings of people on the West Coast, which he felt might jeopardize the Panama Pacific International Exhibition to be held in 1915 in San Francisco. Therefore, he invited California Governor-elect Hiram Johnson* to the White House and warned him that if any anti-Japanese riots were to break out in California, endangering treaty negotiations, then San Francisco would not be the site of the exhibition. Johnson promised the President that he would keep California's anti-Japanese agitators under control.

The new treaty, known as the Treaty of Commerce and Navigation of 1911, was signed on February 21, 1911, by the representatives of both governments and was proclaimed on April 5, 1911. The treaty, also known as the Washington Treaty, placed more restrictions on the rights of Japanese citizens in the United States than the 1894 treaty, as it only guaranteed the U.S. government's "constant protection" of Japanese person and properties. The 1894 treaty had provided "full and perfect protection of the same."

Most crucial for the Japanese in California was the inability of the Japanese government to receive concessions from the U.S. government for its citizens to be able to purchase, rent, or lease land for agricultural purposes. This flaw in the treaty led directly to California's enactment of the Alien Land Act of California, 1913.* (*See also* Alien Land Act of California, 1913.)

FURTHER READING: Frank F. Chuman, *The Bamboo People*, Del Mar, Calif.: Publisher's Inc., 1976; Roger Daniels, ed., *Three Short Works on Japanese Americans*, New York: Arno Press, 1978; Yamato Ichihashi, *Japanese in the United States*, Stanford, Calif.: Stanford University Press, 1932; Akira Iriye, *Across the Pacific: An Inner History of American-East Asian Relations*, New York: Harcourt, Brace and World, 1967; T. Iyenaga and Kenoske Sato, *Japan and the California Problem*, New York: G.P. Putnam's Sons, 1921; Teruko Okada Kachi, *The Treaty of 1911 and the Immigration and Alien Land Law Issue Between the United States and Japan, 1911–1913*, New York: Arno Press, 1978.

WATSONVILLE ANTI-FILIPINO RIOT, race riot aimed against Filipinos, January 19–23, 1930. With the passage of the National Origins Act of 1924* or the Asiatic Exclusion Act, as it was called among Asians in America, the immigration of laborers from Asian countries was virtually cut off. Filipinos were recruited as agricultural laborers because they were not subjected to the 1924 National Origins Act and they were classified as U.S. nationals. But with a large influx of Filipino laborers on the West Coast, violent reactions set in against them on both economic and social grounds.

The first major incident occurred in Washington's Yakima Valley on September 19, 1928, when a group of white laborers, fearing competition from their Filipino counterparts, expelled Filipinos from the valley. A year later another major racial violence occurred on October 24, 1929, when a white man was stabbed at a carnival in Exeter in San Joaquin Valley. This incident touched off wide-spread retaliation against the Filipinos by whites, and the Filipinos had to flee from Exeter.

A more serious race riot occurred on January 19, 1930, in Watsonville, California, and it continued through January 23 before it ended. During the four-day rioting one Filipino was shot to death, 46 Filipinos were terrorized and beaten, Filipino property was destroyed, and many Filipino residents were intimidated into leaving town. As Emory Bogardus points out, the race riot was caused by the perceived threat of competition from Filipino workers, racial prejudice against them, their going out with white girls, and the general breakdown of law and order in Watsonville.

Eight leaders of the riot were brought to trial at the Supreme Court of Monterey County and were sentenced to serve two years in the county jail. Four of them were given probation immediately, and the other four were sent to the county jail for only thirty days, however. The murderer of Fermin Tober, a laborer who was shot to death on January 22, 1930, was never apprehended.

FURTHER READING: Emory S. Bogardus, *Anti-Filipino Race Riots: A Report Made to the Ingram Institute of Social Science of San Diego*, San Diego: Ingram Institute of

Social Science, 1930; Norris Hundley, ed., *The Asian American: The Historical Experience*, Santa Barbara, Calif.: ABC-Clio Press, 1976; Bruno Lasker, *Filipino Immigration*, Chicago: University of Chicago Press, 1931; Jesse Quinsaat, *Letters in Exile*, Los Angeles: Regents of the University of California, 1976; Sonia Emily Wallovits, *The Filipinos in California*, San Francisco: R. and E. Research Associates, 1972.

WATUMULL FOUNDATION, established by Gobindram Watumull in 1942 to provide students from India with scholarships in the United States with the purpose of returning to their country to work. The foundation also proposed to support an academic chair at the University of Hawaii which was to be devoted to teaching Indian culture. The foundation also gave travel funds to scholars and professionals in India to come to the United States. The foundation was still actively engaged in supporting academic programs as of 1976. (*See also* East India Store.)

WEBB-HENEY BILL OF 1913. *See* Alien Land Act of California, 1913.

WEBB v. O'BRIEN, a case that reached the U.S. Supreme Court in 1923 on appeal by the State of California on the grounds that the district court that had tried the case originally erred. J. J. O'Brien was a citizen of the United States and owned 10 acres of agricultural land in Santa Clara County, California. J. Inouye was a citizen of Japan, and was therefore ineligible for U.S. citizenship and subject to the Alien Land Act of California, 1913.* O'Brien and Inouye entered into a cropping contract covering the planting, cultivating, and harvesting of crops grown on the land. This arrangement was considered to be in violation of the Alien Land Act of California, however, and Attorney General of California Ulysse S. Webb as well as the district attorney threatened to criminally prosecute them and take O'Brien's land. O'Brien filed a suit to enjoin the State of California from enforcing the Alien Land Law and was granted the interlocutory injunction. The State of California, however, appealed the lower court decision.

The case was decided on November 19, 1923, the same day the case of Frick v. Webb* was ruled by the Court. Justice Pierce Butler delivered the opinion of the Court upholding the constitutionality of the Alien Land Act of California. He argued against O'Brien's claim that the cropping arrangement was a contract for the performance of labor and therefore constituted the relationship between employer and employee. According to Justice Butler, such a cropping arrangement was more than a contract of employment; cropping arrangements would give the alien the right to share in the benefits from the land for agricultural purposes. He concluded that Japanese residents in America were not given the right as provided in the 1911 treaty between the United States and Japan, and they should be forbidden from having that right.

FURTHER READING: Frank F. Chuman, *The Bamboo People*, Del Mar, Calif.: Publisher's Inc., 1976; Consulate-General of Japan, *Documental History of Law Cases Affecting Japanese in the United States 1916–1924, Vol. II*, San Francisco, 1925; Milton

R. Konvitz, *The Alien and the Asiatic in American Law*, Ithaca, N.Y.: Cornell University Press, 1946.

WELCH BILL, the Filipino Repatriation Act of 1935,* which enabled Filipinos to go back to the Philippines at U.S. government expense. The bill introduced by Congressman Richard J. Welch from California was designed to send back large numbers of Filipinos to their home country during the Great Depression, but it did not work as few Filipinos were willing to return. (*See* Filipino Repatriation Act of 1935.)

WESTERN DEFENSE COMMAND, established on December 11, 1941, and placed under the direction of Lieutenant General John L. DeWitt* who was known for his racist views on the Japanese in America. He said: "A Jap's a Jap. They are a dangerous element. . . . There is no way to determine their loyalty. . . . It makes no difference whether he is an American citizen; theoretically he is still a Japanese, and you can't change him. . . . You can't change him by giving him a piece of paper."

Although no general martial law was declared, the West Coast was considered a theatre of war. The Western Defense Command, therefore, decided to remove all persons of Japanese ancestry from the West Coast for military necessity.* (*See also* DeWitt, John Lesesne.)

WHITE v. CHIN FONG, a case heard before the U.S. Supreme Court in 1920 involving the attempt of a person of Chinese ancestry to reenter the United States. Chin Fong, a person of Chinese ancestry, resided in the United States for more than one year before leaving for China on a business trip, but when he returned, he was refused permission to land by Edward White, commissioner of immigration for the port of San Francisco, who held him for deportation. White argued that Chin had initially entered the country illegally, and he should therefore be deported to China. Chin contended that he had entered the country and established a fixed residence for more than one year, and his stay in China was meant only to be temporary. He further argued that the commissioner, as a representative of the executive branch of the government, did not have the authority to determine that his original entry was unlawful. The District Court ruled in favor of the commissioner, but the Circuit Court of Appeals ruled in favor of the defendant. The judgment of the Court of Appeals was made certiorari to review, and the Supreme Court heard the case on April 22, 1920. On May 17, 1920, Justice Joseph McKenna delivered the opinion of the Court, stating that there was a difference between "the situation of a Chinese person in the United States, and the one seeking to enter it." He ruled that the latter was subject to executive action and decision, whereas the Chinese in the United States was entitled to a judicial inquiry and determination of his rights. Because Chin had been a resident of the United States for more than a year and he had every intention of returning to his former residence, his right to enter the United

States, as provided under the act of November 3, 1893, should not have been determined by the executive branch of the government, but should have been investigated and determined judicially. Chin was given permission to enter on this technicality.

FURTHER READING: Milton R. Konvitz, *The Alien and the Asiatic in American Law*, Ithaca, N.Y.: Cornell University Press, 1946; *Supreme Court Reporter* 40, 253 U.S. 90, 1920, October Term 449–450.

WILCOX, ROBERT W. *See* Liberal Patriotic Association.

WONG, ANNA MAY (1907–1961), film actress. Wong was born in Los Angeles' Chinatown* and was named Liu Tsong at birth on January 3, 1907. She was the daughter of Chinese parents who operated a laundry in Chinatown. Against her parents' wishes, she began acting at the age of twelve. After a string of appearances in silent films, she got her first major role at the age of sixteen in Douglas Fairbanks' *The Thief of Bagdad*, in which she played a Mongol slave. She would be typecast in such roles throughout her career.

Wong was usually cast as a "villainous member of the Yellow Peril."* She became so well established in this role that film critic Pauline Kael, describing classic Hollywood stereotypes, referred to "the bitchy Oriental dragon lady out of an old Anna May Wong movie." In 1932 Wong appeared in *Shanghai Express* which was nominated for an Oscar, but her films of the late 1930s and 1940s were mostly cheap crime melodramas in which she was the mysterious Oriental villainness. Among her other roles were the Chinese mistress of a Chicago gangster and an Eskimo. Even in her last film in 1960, she was reviewed by the *New York Times* as being "merely inscrutable as the suspicious housekeeper."

Besides her American film appearances, Wong made several films in Europe and appeared on the stage. *Circle of Chalk* featured Laurence Olivier as a Chinese prince with her as his leading lady. John Cottrell, Olivier's biographer, claims, however, that Anna Wong, physically perfect for the role, shattered the Oriental illusion with her "broad American accent."

As Eugene Wong has documented in his work on racism in films, the majority of good character roles for Asians (and for non-whites, in general) have historically been given to whites who were then made up to look like the ethnics they portrayed. Sexual taboos also prohibited interracial relationships. Anna May Wong was occasionally allowed a love interest in her films, but she was never permitted to kiss an Occidental until later in her career. The films in which she appeared, though numerous, were not monumental. However, the roles she played live on, reinforcing the stereotype of the Oriental.

FURTHER READING: John Cottrell, *Laurence Olivier*, Englewood Cliffs, N.J.: Prentice-Hall, 1975; Emma Gee, *Counterpoint: Perspectives on Asian America*, Los Angeles: Regents of the University of California, 1976; Pauline Kael, *Going Steady*, Boston: Little, Brown and Co., 1970; Eugene F. Wong, *On Visual Media Racism*, New York: Arno Press, 1978.

WONG WING v. UNITED STATES, a case argued before the U.S. Supreme Court in 1896 as an appeal from the Circuit Court of the United States for the Eastern District of Michigan. Wong Wing and three others were found to be illegally within the United States on July 15, 1892. The commissioner of the Circuit Court in Michigan ruled that the four be sent to prison at hard labor for sixty days and then be removed from the United States in compliance with the Act of May 5, 1892, also known as the Geary Act.* The Chinese then applied for a writ of habeas corpus claiming that the prosecution was without any fair jurisdiction on the part of the commissioner, but the writ was discharged and the Chinese were sent back to prison to serve out their original sentence.

The Chinese then appealed to the Supreme Court, claiming that prosecution without due process of law and at hard labor was unconstitutional. Justice George Shiras, Jr., delivered the opinion of the Court on May 18, 1896, reversing the judgment of the Circuit Court, and declaring Section 4 of the Act of May 5, 1892 to be in violation of the Fifth and Sixth Amendments of the Constitution.

This was the only case in which the Supreme Court of the United States defended the rights of illegal Chinese immigrants even if they were subject to deportation because of their illegal entry into the country.

FURTHER READING: Milton R. Konvitz, *The Alien and the Asiatic in American Law*, Ithaca, N.Y.: Cornell University Press, 1946; *Supreme Court Reporter* 16, 163 U.S. 228, 1895.

WOO YEE-BEW (1864–1930), Christian missionary. Woo was born in Fat San, near Canton, China. He was converted to Christianity at an early age and sent to the Lutheran Mission School in Canton. There he studied the Chinese classics as well as German and religion. In 1880, when he was sixteen years of age, he went to Hong Kong and entered St. Stephen's College to study theology.

Three years later Woo left Hong Kong for San Francisco to do graduate work in theology under the auspices of a family friend. After his benefactor died, he went to Hawaii, arriving in Honolulu on December 8, 1883. There he lived with Goo Kim (or Goo Kim Fui) and later with Chang Young Siu, with whom he lived for a period of six years. He also opened a camp with his roommate for Chinese plantation workers in Kohala, Hawaii.

Woo began his Christian ministry in December 1887, when he was appointed evangelist to the Chinese community in Kohala, where the St. Paul Chinese Mission was later established through his efforts. The following year he was asked to come to Honolulu to work with Chinese Christians who had moved there from Kohala. On January 6, 1902, he was appointed missionary for the Church of St. Paul, Makapala, Kohala, Hawaii, and on November 23 of the same year, he was appointed priest. He stayed with the St. Paul Church until 1915 when he decided to move to Honolulu.

As the first Chinese clergyman of the Episcopal Church in Hawaii, the Reverend Woo contributed to the Chinese community through his Christian ministry of serving the Chinese in Hawaii.

WORKINGMEN'S PARTY OF CALIFORNIA, a political party that grew out of both national and local economic conditions in the 1870s. Nationally, economic recovery following the Civil War had been slow and labor was restless during these economically hard times. Labor unrest finally exploded during the railroad strikes, which spread quickly to major urban areas such as Chicago, Pittsburgh, and Baltimore where law and order had to be reestablished by the use of troops. Locally, a number of economic factors prevailed to agitate workers in California where land was concentrated in the hands of a few rich people and corporations. This arrangement prevented small business people from purchasing land, conditions that were resented by workers. Also contributing to the general unrest among working people in California was the declining value of mining stocks. Small investors felt threatened, and after the Bank of California failed in 1875 this feeling was intensified.

California workers could not count on the Central Pacific Railroad Company* for their labor policy, which advocated using Chinese labor which was readily available, easy to control, and rather inexpensive. White workers saw this particular policy as a direct threat to their lives. Resenting Chinese laborers whom they saw as competitors, they wanted to have them removed.

This labor unrest was exploited by people such as Denis Kearney* and John Day who worked to organize the Workingmen's Trade and Labor Union of San Francisco on August 22, 1877. A number of other meetings soon followed where the Chinese were blamed for national and, in particular, California's economic ills. On October 5, 1877, the Workingmen's Party was officially organized, with Denis Kearney as its president. The party then adopted its platform calling for the destruction of the land monopoly in California, the expulsion of Chinese from the state and the nation, the election of competent workers to office, and taking the government away from the rich.

Soon after its organization, the party began to exert its influence on local politics by electing its men to office in Oakland, Sacramento, Alameda, and Santa Clara counties. Particularly during the 1878 election, the Workingmen's Party was able to have fifty-one of their men elected as delegates to the California Constitutional Convention. Although they did not constitute a majority, they had an important influence on shaping a new constitution, when the California Constitutional Convention was called to order on September 28, 1878.

One of the major issues debated during the convention was what to do with the Chinese. A committee was established to consider the problem, and three of the Workingmen's Party delegates were placed on the committee. They introduced a number of proposals to exclude Chinese from the United States, to prohibit them from doing business, and to prevent them from public works. When California's new constitution was finally ironed out by the delegates of varying interests, the Chinese were the losers. They were prevented from being employed on public works, were discouraged from coming to America, were not to be employed by California's corporations, and were considered a threat to peace in the community. (*See* California Constitutional Convention of 1878.)

FURTHER READING: Ralph Kauer, "The Workingmen's Party of California," *Pacific Historical Review* 13 (1944), pp. 278–279; Carey McWilliams, *California: The Great Exception*, New York: A.A. Wyn, Publisher, 1949; Andrew F. Rolle, *California: A History*, 2d ed., New York: Thomas Y. Crowell Co., 1969; Alexander Saxton, *The Indispensable Enemy*, Berkeley: University of California Press, 1971; Earl G. Walters et al., *The Rumble of California Politics, 1848–1970*, New York: John Wiley and Sons, 1970.

WU CHIEN-SHIUNG (1912–   ), physicist. Wu was born on May 29, 1912, in Shanghai, China, and was educated at National Central University in China where she received her B.S. degree in 1934. She went to the University of California at Berkeley, where she studied with Nobel Prize winner Earnest Lawrence. She received her Ph.D. degree in physics in 1940. At the age of twenty-seven she was appointed to teach nuclear physics at Princeton University. Later she moved to Columbia University where she participated in the Manhattan Project during World War II.

Wu worked with physicists Lee Tsung-dao* and Yang Chen-ning* in their efforts to prove that the principle of the conservation of parity was incorrect. She performed the necessary experimental tests in collaboration with a team of scientists at the National Bureau of Standards and presented the data in support of the new anti-theory. The two physicists received their Nobel Prize for their contributions to our understanding of the changing world of physics.

Although she did not receive a Nobel Prize, Wu received many awards and honorary degrees during the lifetime. In 1958 she became the first female recipient of the Research Corporation Award. She also achieved first status at Princeton University when she was made the first woman to receive an honorary doctorate in physics. In 1975 she became the president of the American Physical Society.

WU TING-FANG (1842–1922), diplomat. Wu was born on July 9, 1842, in Singapore and moved to his father's native place when he was three years of age. He received a traditional Chinese education in Sunwui, Kwangtung, where his father had been a merchant for many years. He graduated from the British Central School in Hong Kong in 1860. Wu was called to the bar in 1877 and practiced law in Hong Kong until 1882 when he joined the secretariat of Li Hung-chang at Tientsin. He participated in the negotiations and signing of a treaty between China and France in 1885. Later, he was involved in building railroads in China. He also participated in treaty negotiations with Japan after China was defeated in the Sino-Japanese War of 1894.

Wu was Chinese Minister to the United States during 1897–1902 and again during 1907–1909. He was exceptionally well qualified to represent his nation's interests. As the first English-speaking Chinese diplomat in Washington, he made a deep impression on people around him. He traveled extensively and was a popular speaker. Through his speeches he appealed to the American people to oppose the discrimination against Chinese in America. Wu probably did more than any other individual to present China's case to the American public.

Wu believed that the American public went along with the anti-Chinese movement because the Chinese had a bad image. Many of his articles sought to create an understanding between the races. The *New York Times* (January 27, 1900) quoted him as saying that "persons are generally disliked on account of their indolence, immorality, and other bad qualities, but this is the first instance in history that a people are considered undesirable and excluded because of their industry, perseverence, honesty, and other good qualities."

Unlike some other Ch'ing officials, Wu was interested in all people and was not solely preoccupied with the rich and powerful. He was a spokesman for the powerless. He used his eloquence as a strong and cutting weapon to defend and advance the cause of his people.

FURTHER READING: Harley F. McNair, *The Chinese Abroad*, Shanghai, China: Commercial Press, 1933; Kenneth W. Rhea, *Early Sino-American Relations, 1841–1912*, Boulder, Colo.: Westview Press, 1977; Shih-shan H. Tsai, *China and the Overseas Chinese in the United States, 1868–1911*, Fayetteville: University of Arkansas Press, 1983; Wu Ting-fang, *America Through the Spectacles of an Oriental Diplomat*, New York: Frederick A. Stokes Co., 1914.

Y

YAMASAKI MINORU (1912–), architect. Yamasaki was born on December 1, 1912, in Seattle, Washington, and went to the University of Washington, graduating from that university in 1934. He continued his studies in architecture at New York University. He is known for his outstanding contribution to architectural designs. Among his works are the Reynolds Metal Company Building in Detroit, the Public Housing Development in St. Louis, the Oberlin College Music Conservatory Structure, the Woodrow Wilson School of Public and International Affairs at Princeton University, the Northwestern National Life Insurance building in Minneapolis, and the World Trade Center in Manhattan.

Yamasaki is probably best known for his design work at the World's Fair held in Seattle in 1962. The same year he was cited by the Japanese American Citizens League* as the Nisei of the Biennium. Part of the citation reads: "By artfully blending his understanding of Japanese art and culture with that of Western architecture, he has attained in his profession a philosophy of humanism which seeks to elevate the dignity of man in his environment, a philosophy dedicated to and consistent with the highest ideals of democracy."

FURTHER READING: Masako Herman, *The Japanese in America, 1843–1973*, Dobbs Ferry, N.Y.: Oceana Publications, 1974; Bill Hosokawa, *Nisei*, New York: William Morrow and Co., 1969; Noel L. Leathers, *The Japanese in America*, Minneapolis, Minn.: Lerner Publications, 1967.

YAMASHITA SOEN (1898–). Yamashita was born in Yasuura, Hiroshima Prefecture, Japan and came to Hawaii at the age of sixteen to learn English. He enrolled in Honolulu's Iolani School. Upon completion of his study he was hired by the *Nippu JiJi** and was sent to Japan in 1933 as its correspondent. He later assumed the directorship of an organization established in Tokyo: Dai Nisei Rengokai, or the League of Nisei* Organizations, financed and supervised by the Foreign Ministry of Japan.

He was one of the Hawaii *doho*,* who came back to Japan to live after they had spent a number of years in Hawaii. It was estimated that there were as many as 14,000 Hawaii-born Nisei living in Japan in 1938. In addition to the Hawaii Nisei, there were also people like Yamashita, George Kunimoto and Colbert Kurokawa* who were born in Japan but came to Hawaii to live a considerable number of years before they decided to go back to Japan for various reasons. Most of these Issei* and Nisei were loyal to America, although some of them advocated Japanese national interest in Hawaii as well as Japanese colonization of the islands. For instance, Yamashita claimed that Japanese first discovered the Hawaiian Islands and that Japanese conquest of the islands would have been natural. Furthermore, he believed that Hawaii was to be the first base of Japanese expansion in the Pacific.

FURTHER READING: Carey McWilliams, *Prejudice*, Boston: Little, Brown and Company, 1944; John J. Stephan, *Hawaii under the Rising Sun: Japan's Plans for Conquest After Pearl Harbor*. Honolulu: University of Hawaii Press, 1984.

YAMASHITA TAKUI et al. v. HINKLE, a case argued on October 3 and 4, 1922, and decided on November 13, 1922, dealing with the question of whether or not a Japanese born in Japan was entitled to become a naturalized citizen of the United States. Yamashita first brought his case to the Supreme Court of the State of Washington when J. Grant Hinkle, then Secretary of the State of Washington, refused to receive and file articles of incorporation for Yamashita's Japanese Real Estate Company. Hinkle refused to file these articles on the grounds that Yamashita was not eligible for citizenship and therefore was not qualified to file articles for or form a corporation under Washington State law. To complicate the matter somewhat, Yamashita had been granted U.S. citizenship by a Washington Superior Court prior to 1906. When the Washington State Supreme Court ruled in favor of Hinkle, the case was appealed to the Supreme Court on writ of certiorari, allowing the Court to call up the records of the lower court.

Before the Supreme Court Yamashita argued that since he had been granted citizenship, he was therefore qualified to file these articles and should be allowed to do so. As far as the Supreme Court was concerned, the only issue involved was whether or not Yamashita, being a Japanese born in Japan, was eligible for U.S. citizenship. On the same day, the Court ruled that a person born in Japan could not be naturalized, in the case of Ozawa Takao v. United States.*

Justice George Sutherland, in his opinion for the Court, ruled that Yamashita could not be naturalized under U.S. law and that the Superior Court in Washington that had granted Yamashita citizenship in 1906 had done so without jurisdiction. It was declared void by the Supreme Court of the United States.

FURTHER READING: *Supreme Court Reporter* 43, 260, U.S. 199, 1921.

YAMATAYA KAORU v. THOMAS M. FISHER, a case argued before the U.S. Supreme Court on February 23, 1903, and decided on April 6, 1903, dealing with the question of whether or not a Japanese person who was a pauper or person who was likely to become a public charge had the right to enter the United States.

On July 11, 1901, Yamataya Kaoru, a Japanese subject, landed at the port of Seattle, Washington, and four days later an immigration inspector, Thomas Fisher, decided that she had come to America in violation of the law because she was a pauper and likely to become a public charge. The inspector presented evidence to the Secretary of the Treasury, who was the only one authorized under the Act of Congress of October 1888 to issue warrants. The warrant was issued on July 23, 1901, stating that she came into the United States contrary to the provisions laid down in the Act of March 3, 1891, and that she was to be taken into custody to be returned to Japan.

Before the inspector could execute the warrant, an application was presented for a writ of habeas corpus, alleging that imprisonment of the appellant would be unlawful and that Yamataya did not come to America in violation of the Act of 1891.

The writ was dismissed, however, and Yamataya was ordered remanded to the custody of the Secretary of the Treasury for deportation. She then appealed to the U.S. Supreme Court. Justice John Harlan, in his opinion for the Court, upheld the lower court's decision. In his opinion he took note of the Treaty of Commerce and Navigation of 1894 between Japan and the United States,* but ruled that the Act of March 3, 1891, was not in violation of that treaty. The Act of March 3, 1891, was made to insure public security, which was provided in the treaty. Because judgment on whether or not a person was a pauper or was likely to be one was a matter of public security, the inspector was correct in taking her into custody for deportation. (*See also* Treaty of Commerce and Navigation of 1894 Between Japan and the United States.)
FURTHER READING: *Supreme Court Reporter* 23, 189 U.S. 86, 1902.

YAMATO, THE. See *Nippu Jiji*.

YAN WO WUI KUN. *See* District Companies.

YANG CHEN-NING (1922–   ), Nobel Prize winner in physics. Yang was born in Hofei, Anhwei, China, but grew up in Peking, where he attended the Chung Te middle school. With the Japanese invasion of China, his family moved to Kunming where he attended the National Southwest Associated University, where he met Lee Tsung-dao,* who later worked jointly with Yang on a project that would finally give them the Nobel Prize in physics. Upon graduation from the university in 1942, Yang entered Tsinghua University, where his father taught mathematics.

Upon completion of his Master's degree, Yang taught in a Chinese high school. In 1945 he came to the University of Chicago on a scholarship and began his study in physics. Yang received his Ph.D. in physics in 1948 and decided to stay with the University of Chicago as an instructor. In 1949 he was named member of the Institute for Advanced Study in Princeton, where he became a full professor in 1955 at the age of thirty-three.

In the summer of 1956 he and his friend, Lee Tsung-dao, suggested that the principle of conservation of parity, a theory that had been considered valid since 1925, was not a fundamental concept in nuclear physics, thereby challenging the conventional wisdom in physics. The two Chinese scientists published a series of scientific papers in which they suggested that parity was not conserved, and they suggested several ways of proving their contention. Dr. Wu Chien-Shiung* and a team of scientists at the National Bureau of Standards set up experiments to test their contention and prove that parity was not conserved. For their theory, Lee and Yang shared the Nobel Prize in physics for 1957.

In 1966 Yang became Albert Einstein Professor of Physics and director of the Institute of Theoretical Physics at the State University of New York at Stony Brook.

YASUI MINORU v. UNITED STATES, a case that came to the U.S. Supreme Court as a companion case to Hirabayashi v. United States* in 1943. Yasui was born, raised, and educated in Portland, Oregon. He served three years in Japanese language school and later attended the University of Oregon. He was a member of the bar of Oregon and a second lieutenant in the U.S. Army Infantry Reserve. Yasui also was an employee of the Japanese Consulate Office in Chicago but resigned after the bombing of Pearl Harbor.

After Public Proclamation No. 3 was issued on March 24, 1942, imposing a military curfew on all "enemy aliens," including the Japanese on the West Coast, Yasui wanted to test the constitutionality of the curfew regulation. He discussed his intentions with an FBI agent and then voluntarily violated the order and requested that he be arrested in an attempt to get a writ of habeas corpus for his release.

His case was brought to the Federal District Court of Oregon, where Judge Agler Fee ruled Public Law 503* unconstitutional as it applied to American citizens. However, Law 503 was held constitutional in the Yasui case, because he had renounced, or was thought to have renounced, his citizenship when he went to work for the Japanese Consulate Office in Chicago. Yasui testified that he had never renounced his citizenship, but the same judge who ruled Public Law 503 unconstitutional sentenced Yasui to one year imprisonment, despite his testimony.

In January 1983 Yasui, with the help of his lawyer, Peter Irons, filed a petition for a writ of error *coram nobis* in Portland in order to seek the reversal of his conviction in 1943. The case was dismissed after the government vacated the original ruling on the Yasui Case. (*See also* Hirabayashi v. United States.)

FURTHER READING: Frank F. Chuman, *The Bamboo People*, Del Mar, Calif.: Publisher's Inc., 1976; Peter Irons, *Justice at War: The Story of the Japanese American Internment Cases*, New York: Oxford University Press, 1983; Milton R. Konvitz, *The Alien and the Asiatic in American Law*, Ithaca, N.Y.: Cornell University Press, 1946.

YATABE, THOMAS T. *See* Seattle Progressive Citizens League.

YEDO, TREATY OF (1858), also known as the Treaty of Commerce and Navigation of 1858, negotiated by Townsend Harris representing the U.S. government. Harris had suggested to Japanese officials preceding the treaty negotiation that Britain, France, and Russia were scheming to invade Japan. Japanese officials were convinced that an open door trade policy with the United States would be beneficial to Japan. This was the first commercial treaty Japan signed with a Western nation. The official ceremony for the treaty took place on July 29, 1858, when representatives of the two governments signed the treaty aboard the American war vessel, *Powhatan*.

The first commercial treaty was an unfair treaty for Japan: Japan was required to open additional treaty ports, to grant extraterritoriality to foreign residents in Japan, to accept a fixed tariff on Japanese goods, and to grant religious freedom to Americans in Japan. The treaty was to be revised after July 4, 1872.

When the treaty was about to expire, Japan dispatched the Iwakura Mission* to renegotiate a treaty that would be more favorable to Japan's national interest, but the mission was unsuccessful. (*See also* Iwakura Mission.)

FURTHER READING: E. Manchester Boddy, *Japanese in America*, Los Angeles, 1921; Foster Rhea Dulles, *Yankees and Samurai: America's Role in the Emergence of Modern Japan, 1791–1900*, New York: Harper and Row, 1965; Yamato Ichihashi, *Japanese in the United States*, Stanford, Calif.: Stanford University Press, 1932; Akira Iriye, *Across the Pacific: An Inner History of American-East Asian Relations* (New York: Harcourt, Brace and World, 1967; Chitoshi Yanaga, *Japan Since Perry*, New York: McGraw-Hill Book Co., 1949.

YELLOW PERIL, catch-word used mainly for Japanese and Chinese in the United States to signify the Asians as a great menace to Western civilization. Immigrants from all over the world have come to America in search of work, freedom, and prosperity. Some were readily accepted, but others were treated unjustly. The Japanese and Chinese have received their share of discrimination from white Americans. Upon their arrival in America they were charged with having low standards of living, "vile habits," a high birthrate, and an inability to assimilate into the American way of life as if it were built into their biological makeup. Asians were viewed as a threat to the American society and the American way of life. Thus, the Japanese and Chinese were often referred to as the "yellow peril," a term used extensively by 1905 in the United States.

The first use of the term is generally ascribed to Kaiser Wilhelm II, who described an allegorical picture entitled "die gelbe Gefahr," drawn by a German artist, H. Knackfuss. The picture was sent to the Russian Tsar as a gift from the German ruler. It depicted the archangel Michael represented by Germany, protecting a group of fair maidens, representing Russia, France, Britain, Austria, Italy, Spain, and Portugal from the yellow peril.

The idea of yellow peril probably came to America from Europe, although it is difficult to say at exactly what date. Once the term was grafted onto the American mentality sometime in the 1880s, however, it gained the full force of mass media propaganda to be used by newspapers, politicians, and labor leaders against the defenseless Asians. Between 1880 and 1882 scare literature began circulating, warning of the invasion of the yellow peril. The Japanese immigration fueled newspapers in America about the likelihood of America being invaded by an Asian power. The yellow peril theory held that Japan was the Germany of Asia and had a long-range plan to infiltrate California. The Pacific Coast should therefore prepare for a major Japanese attack. Many Americans were convinced of this preposterous propaganda due to yellow journalism.

William Randolph Hearst and his paper, *The Examiner*, were instrumental in spreading the yellow peril scare. Hearst was believed to have been involved with the Germans and to have worked together with them to spread anti-Japanese propaganda. A Senate committee investigation showed that Hearst himself concocted some of the yellow peril propaganda.

Before World War II yellow peril was used effectively as a tool to get Americans to discriminate against the Asian immigrants. Through all the anti-Asian literature and mass media, Americans became convinced of the yellow peril. It was not too difficult to persuade Americans, especially Californians, that the Asians were a threat to their livelihood, inasmuch as they were going through economic problems at the time. Many Americans wanted to believe that more jobs would be available immediately if they could just get rid of "Asians willing to work for almost nothing."

The yellow peril myth still lingers in the minds of many Americans today. For example, in May of 1981, white fishermen attempted to gain legislative support to exclude Vietnamese Americans from the fishing industry. In the previous two years three Vietnamese boats had been burned, and several threats of injury to life and property were perpetrated by white fishermen who perceived the Vietnamese as a threat to their livelihood.

In recent years the American auto industry has attempted to brainwash Americans into believing that Japanese imports are responsible for America's faltering auto industry and its depressed economy in general. Unfortunately, these attitudes become manifest in tragic and violent cases like the beating death of Vincent Chin. This incident exposed the racist attitudes not only of white auto workers, but also of a racist judicial system.

FURTHER READING: A. C. Floyd, *White Man-Yellow Man*, New York: Abingdon-Cokesbury Press, 1947; C. R. Hensman, *China Yellow Peril? Red Hope?*, London: SCM Press Ltd., 1968; Homer Lea, *The Valor of Ignorance*, New York: Harper and Row, 1909; Marsden Manson, *The Yellow Peril in Action*, San Francisco: Britton and Rey, 1907; Robert McClellan, *The Heathen Chinee: A Study of American Attitudes toward China, 1890–1905*, Columbus: Ohio State University Press, 1971; Stuart C. Miller, *The Unwelcome Immigrant*, Berkeley: University of California Press, 1969; Richard Austin Thompson, *The Yellow Peril, 1890–1924*, New York: Arno Press, 1978; William F. Wu,

The Yellow Peril: Chinese Americans in American Fiction, 1850–1940, Hamden, Conn.: Archon Books, 1982.

YEONG WO WUI KUN. *See* District Companies.

YICK WO v. HOPKINS, a case that reached the Supreme Court of the United States on writ of error to the Supreme Court of the State of California and was decided on May 10, 1886. Yick Wo and some 150 Chinese engaged in laundry businesses in San Francisco were imprisoned by the city of San Francisco for allegedly violating City Ordinance 1569. This ordinance, passed on May 26, 1880, prescribed conditions under which laundry businesses could be operated within the limits of the city and county of San Francisco. All laundry businesses operated in wooden buildings were required to obtain permission from the Board of Supervisors of the city. At the time there were about 320 laundry businesses, 240 of which were owned and operated by Chinese. Out of 320 laundries, 310 were constructed of wood.

On August 24, 1885, Yick Wo petitioned to the Supreme Court of the State of California for the writ of habeas corpus, claiming that he had been illegally deprived of his personal liberty. In response to the claim, the sheriff of San Francisco defended his action on the grounds that Yick Wo violated certain city ordinances established by the Board of Supervisors.

The Supreme Court of the State of California ruled in favor of the city and county of San Francisco, stating that the Board of Supervisors had authority to prohibit and regulate all occupations that were against good morals, contrary to public order and decency, or dangerous to public safety. Furthermore, the court claimed that City Ordinance 1569 was not "unjust, unequal . . . or oppressive."

The U.S. Supreme Court did not agree with this judgment in its opinion delivered by Justice Stanley Matthews, who reversed the decision of the Supreme Court of California. He stated that the ordinance passed by San Francisco vested unusual discretion in the Board of Supervisors of the city. He stated that whatever the intent of the ordinance, its effect was to deny equal protection of the laws to a certain select group of individuals. It was, therefore, in violation of the Fourteenth Amendment of the Constitution. The Court also specified that the Fourteenth Amendment was not confined to the protection of citizens but that no state could deny any person life, liberty, or property without due process of law.

FURTHER READING: *Supreme Court Reporter* 6, 118 U.S. 356, 1885.

YOUNG INDIA. *See* India Home Rule League of America.

YU CONG ENG et al. v. TRINIDAD, a case argued on April 12 and 13, 1926, and decided on June 7, 1926. The case before the U.S. Supreme Court dealt with the validity of the Philippine Chinese Bookkeeping Act No. 2972, approved by the Philippine legislature on February 21, 1921, which declared it illegal for any person, partnership, company, or corporation making money in the Philippine Islands "to keep its account books in any language other than English, Spanish, or any local dialect." The act was designed to help collect sales and income taxes, and it prohibited a person from keeping a duplicate set of account books. When a person was found in violation of the act, his property could be taken without due process of law and equal protection of the laws. This denial of constitutional protection was in violation of the Philippine Autonomy Act which ensures all persons living on the Philippine Islands liberty and property, due process of law, and equal protection of the laws.

Yu Cong Eng, a Chinese merchant in a wholesale lumber business in Manila, could not read, write, or understand English, Spanish, or any other local dialect. He kept his accounting books in Chinese. Therefore, he was in violation of the Philippine Chinese Bookkeeping Act of 1921. Subsequently, he was arrested, his books were seized, and his trial was about to begin, when the petition was filed on his behalf. The Supreme Court of the Philippine Islands denied him the petition, and the petitioners brought suit to the U.S. Supreme Court on writ of error to the Supreme Court of the Philippine Islands.

Chief Justice William Howard Taft delivered the opinion of the Court ruling that the Philippine Chinese Bookkeeping Act was invalid on the grounds that it deprived Chinese of their liberty and property without due process of law, and denied them the equal protection of the laws.

FURTHER READING: *Supreme Court Reporter* 46, 271 U.S. 500, 1925.

YUN CH'I-HO (1864–1945), Korean scholar, politician. Yun was born on December 26, 1864, in Korea and received a traditional education in the Chinese classics. Although he aspired to become a government official, he did not participate in any state-qualifying examinations. Because of his father's connections with high government officials, he was sent to Japan in 1882 as a student attendant to the Gentlemen's Tour Group dispatched to the modernizing Japan by King Kojong.* He did not return to Korea immediately. Instead, he decided to study English at Doshisha Institute in Kyoto. In 1883 he was hired as an interpreter for Lucius Foote, American Minister to Korea, and returned to Seoul, Korea. Because of his association with a group of radical politicians, including So Jae-p'il (Philip Jaisohn)* who plotted to overthrow the government and take the reins of power in their hands, he had to leave Korea in 1885.

Yun went to Shanghai and attended the Anglo-Chinese Institute where he studied modern science, mathematics, English, and other subjects. Upon completion of his education he was sent to Vanderbilt University in Nashville, Tennessee, in 1883 by a group of American benefactors who arranged for Yun to study theology. Yun arrived in Nashville on November 4, 1888, and stayed there until 1891 when he transferred to Emory College, Oxford, Georgia. He graduated from the college in 1893 and returned to the Anglo-Chinese Institute to teach there until 1895 when he was able to go back to his native country.

Upon his return to Korea, Yun was immediately engulfed by local politics against his own will and became president of the Independence Club in 1898, when So Jae-p'il* was forced to return to America. Yun also took over the management and control of the *Independent*, the first modern newspaper in the history of Korea. In 1904 he was appointed vice-minister of the Foreign Affairs Ministry, and the following year he was sent to Hawaii by King Kojong to investigate the charges that Korean laborers working on Hawaii's sugar plantations were being mistreated. He made a tour around the islands, visiting almost every Korean labor camp and encouraging his countrymen to work hard.

Upon returning to Korea, Yun retired from politics as Korea became a protectorate of Japan in 1905. He spent the rest of his life educating Korea's youth.

FURTHER READING: Hyung-chan Kim, *Letters in Exile: The Life and Times of Yun Ch'i-ho*, Oxford, Georgia: Oxford Historical Shrine Society, 1980.

YUNG WING (1828–1912), one of the first Chinese graduates of America's colleges. Yung was born on November 17, 1828, in the village of Nam Ping in Southern China, a small town located about four miles southwest of Macao. He came to America under the auspices of the Reverend Samuel Robins Brown, a graduate of Yale, class of 1832. Yung and his Chinese friends, Wong Hsing (Shing) and Wong Foon, arrived in New York on April 12, 1847, thus becoming the first group of Chinese to arrive in America to study. They enrolled in the Monson Academy in Monson, Massachusetts. One of them, Wong Hsing, had to leave for China because of poor health, but Yung and Wong continued their studies at the academy until they graduated in 1850.

Wong Foon went to Scotland and entered the University of Edinburgh, while Yung enrolled in Yale, graduating in 1854. When Yung returned to China, he entered the tea business for a short period of time. In 1863 he worked for Tseng Kuo-fan, the most prominent Chinese of the day. His patron sent him to the United States to purchase machinery for making modern arms and had the machinery installed in Shanghai, thus beginning the Kiangnan Arsenal. He was successful in persuading his patron to establish a school of mechanical engineering. At his suggestion in 1870, the Chinese government created the Chinese Educational Mission,* and Yung served as its first commissioner. He was responsible for bringing many Chinese students to study at American institutions of higher learning. He was not only the first Chinese to graduate from a prestigious American college, but also the first to initiate a cultural exchange between China and the United States.

FURTHER READING: Thomas E. LaFargue, *China's First Hundred*, Pullman: Washington State College Press, 1942; Shih-shan Henry Tsai, *China and the Overseas Chinese in the United States, 1868–1911*, Fayetteville: University of Arkansas Press, 1983; Edmund H. Worthy, Jr., "Yung Wing in America," *Pacific Historical Review* 34 (1965), pp. 265–287; Yung Wing, *My Life in China and America*, New York: Henry Holt and Co., 1909.

APPENDIX A

Select Bibliography

Abbott, James Francis. *Japanese Expansion and American Policies*. New York: Macmillan Co., 1916.

Adams, Romanzo. *The Peoples of Hawaii*. New York: Institute of Pacific Relations, 1933.

Alcantara, Ruben R. *Sakada: Filipino Adaptation in Hawaii*. Washington, D.C.: University Press of America, 1981.

Anderson, Robert N., et al. *Filipinos in Rural Hawaii*. Honolulu: University of Hawaii Press, 1984.

Archer, Jules. *The Chinese and the Americans*. New York: Hawthorn Books, 1976.

Arino, Vincent A. *Contributions of Filipino Farm Labor to California Industrialized Agriculture Development Problems in Selected California Areas*. Berkeley: University of California Press, 1953.

Auerbach, Frank. *Immigration Laws of the United States*. Indianapolis: Bobbs-Merrill Co., 1955.

Ayscough, Florence. *Chinese Women, Yesterday and Today*. Boston: Houghton Mifflin Co., 1937.

Bailey, Thomas A. *Theodore Roosevelt and the Japanese-American Crisis*. Stanford, Calif.: Stanford University Press, 1934.

Baldwin, S. L. *Must the Chinese Go? An Examination of the Chinese Question*. Boston: Rand, Avery and Co., 1886.

Bancroft, Hubert Howe. *History of California*. 7 vols. San Francisco: A.L. Bancroft Co., 1890.

Banerjee, Kalyan Kumar. *Indian Freedom Movement: Revolutionaries in America*. Calcutta, India: Jijnasa, 1969.

Barth, Gunther. *Bitter Strength: A History of the Chinese in the United States, 1850–1870*. Cambridge, Mass: Harvard University Press, 1964.

Beach, Walter G. *Oriental Crime in California: A Study of Offences Committed by Orientals in the States, 1900–1927*. New York: AMS Press, 1971.

Beck, Louis J. *New York's Chinatown*. New York: Bohemia Publishing Co., 1898.

Bennett, Marion T. *American Immigration Policies*. Washington, D.C.: Public Affairs Press, 1963.

Bernard, William S. *American Immigration Policy: A Reappraisal*. New York: Harper and Brothers, 1950.

Boddy, E. Manchester. *Japanese in America*. Los Angeles: By the Author, 1921.

Bogardus, Emory S. *Immigration and Race Attitudes*. Boston: D.C. Heath, 1928.

Bonacich, Edna, and Modell, John. *The Economic Basis of Ethnic Solidarity: Small Business in the Japanese American Community*. Berkeley: University of California Press, 1980.

Bosworth, Allan R. *America's Concentration Camps*. New York: W.W. Norton and Co., 1967.

Bradley, Harold Whitman. *The American Frontier in Hawaii: The Pioneers, 1789–1843*. Stanford, Calif.: Stanford University Press, 1942.

Broom, Leonard, and Riemer, Ruth. *Removal and Return: The Socio-Economic Effects of the War on Japanese Americans*. Berkeley: University of California Press, 1949.

————. *Removal and Return: The Japanese American Family in World War II*. Berkeley: University of California Press, 1956.

Brown, Emily C. *Har Dayal: Hindu Revolutionary and Rationalist*. Tucson: University of Arizona Press, 1975.

Buaken, Manuel. *I Have Lived with the American People*. Caldwell, Idaho: Caxton Printers, 1948.

Bulosan, Carlos. *America Is in the Heart: A Personal History*. New York: Harcourt, Brace and Co., 1946.

California State Senate. *Chinese Immigration: Its Social, Moral, and Political Effect*. Sacramento, Calif.: State Office, 1878.

Campbell, Persia Crawford. *Chinese Coolie Emigration to Countries Within the British Empire*. London: P.S. King and Sons, Ltd., 1923.

Cariaga, Roman R. *The Filipinos in Hawaii: Economic and Social Conditions, 1906–1936*. Honolulu: Filipino Public Relations Bureau, 1937.

Cather, Helen V. *The History of San Francisco's Chinatown*. San Francisco: R. and E. Research Associates, 1974.

Chandrasekhar, S. *From India to America*. La Jolla, Calif.: A Population Review Book, 1982.

Chang, Hao. *Liang Ch'i-ch'ao and Intellectual Transition in China, 1890–1907*. Cambridge, Mass.: Harvard University Press, 1971.

Chang, Pao-min. *Continuity and Change: A Profile of Chinese Americans*. New York: Vantage Press, 1983.

Char, Tin-Yuke, ed. *The Sandalwood Mountains: Readings and Stories of the Early Chinese in Hawaii*. Honolulu: University Press of Hawaii, 1975.

Chen, Jack. *The Chinese of America*. New York: Harper and Row, 1980.

Cheng, Lucie, and Bonacich, Edna, eds. *Labor Immigration Under Capitalism: Asian Workers in the United States Before World War II*. Berkeley: University of California Press, 1984.

Chesneaux, Jean, et al. *China from the Opium Wars to the 1911 Revolution*. New York: Pantheon Books, 1976.

Chinn, Thomas W., ed. *A History of the Chinese in California*. San Francisco: Chinese Historical Society of America, 1969.

Choy, Bong-Youn. *Koreans in America*. Chicago: Nelson-Hall, 1979.

Chui, Ping. *Chinese Labor in California, 1850–1880*. Madison: State Historical Society of Wisconsin, 1963.

Chuman, Frank F. *The Bamboo People: The Law and Japanese-Americans*. Del Mar, Calif.: Publisher's Inc., 1976.

Cohen, Lucy M. *Chinese in the Post-Civil War South: A People Without a History*. Baton Rouge: Louisiana State University Press, 1984.

Coleman, Elizabeth. *Chinatown, U.S.A.* New York: John Day, 1946.

Coman, Katherine. *The History of Contract Labor in the Hawaiian Islands*. New York: Macmillan Co., 1903.

Condit, Ira M. *The Chinaman As We See Him*. New York: Fleming H. Revell, 1900.

Connor, John W. *A Study of the Marital Stability of Japanese War Brides*. San Francisco: R. and E. Research Associates, 1976.

————. *Tradition and Change in Three Generations of Japanese Americans*. Chicago: Nelson-Hall, 1977.

Conroy, Francis Hilary. *The Japanese Expansion into Hawaii, 1868–1898*. San Francisco: R. and E. Research Associates, 1973.

————, and Miyakawa, T. Scott. *East Across the Pacific*. Santa Barbara, Calif.: ABC-Clio Press, 1977.

Consulate-General of Japan. *Documental History of Law Cases Affecting Japanese in the United States, 1916–1924*. 2 vols. San Francisco, 1925.

Coolidge, Mary R. *Chinese Immigration*. New York: Henry Holt, 1909.

Cordova, Fred. *Filipinos: Forgotten Asian Americans*. Dubuque, Iowa: Kendal/Hunt Publishing Co., 1983.

Courtney, William J. *San Francisco Anti-Chinese Ordinances, 1850–1900*. San Francisco: R. and E. Research Associates, 1974.

Cressey, Paul G. *The Taxi-Dance Hall*. Chicago: University of Chicago Press, 1932.

Crouchett, Lorraine Jacobs. *Filipinos in California: From the Days of the Galleons to the Present*. El Cerrito, Calif.: Downey Place Publishing House, 1982.

Damon, Ethel M. *Sanford Ballard Dole and His Hawaii*. Palo Alto, Calif: Pacific Books, 1957.

Daniels, Roger. *Concentration Camps U.S.A.: Japanese Americans and World War II*. New York: Holt, Rinehart and Winston, 1971.

————. *The Decision to Relocate the Japanese Americans*. New York: J.B. Lippincott Co., 1975.

————. *The Politics of Prejudice: The Anti-Japanese Movement in California and the Struggle for Japanese Exclusion*. New York: Atheneum, 1972.

————, and Kitano, Harry H. L. *American Racism: Exploration of the Nature of Prejudice*. Englewood Cliffs, N.J.: Prentice-Hall, 1970.

Das, Rajani Kanta. *Hindustani Workers on the Pacific Coast*. Berlin: Walter DeGruyter, 1923.

Davis, Winfield. *History of Political Conventions in California, 1849–1892*. Sacramento: California State Library, 1892.

Daws, Gavan. *Shoal of Time: A History of the Hawaiian Islands*. Honolulu: University Press of Hawaii, 1968.

Day, A. Grove. *Hawaii and Its People*. New York: Duell, Sloan and Pearce, 1955.

Dillon, Richard. *The Hatchet Men: The Story of Tong Wars in San Francisco's Chinatown*. New York: Coward-McCann, 1962.

Divine, Robert A. *American Immigration Policy, 1924–1952*. New Haven, Conn.: Yale University Press, 1957.

Dobie, Charles C. *San Francisco's Chinatown*. New York: Appleton-Century, 1936.

Dulles, Foster Rhea. *Yankees and Samurai: America's Role in the Emergence of Modern Japan: 1791–1900*. New York: Harper and Row, 1965.

Duuas, Masayo. *Tokyo Rose: Orphan of the Pacific*. Tokyo, Japan: Kodansha International Ltd., 1979.

Eaves, Lucile. *A History of California Labor Legislation*. Berkeley: University of California Press, 1910.

Eberhard, Wolfram. *Chinese Festivals*. New York: Henry Schuman, 1952.

Elegant, Robert S. *The Dragon's Seed: Peking and the Overseas Chinese*. New York: St. Martin's Press, 1959.

Elstob, Winston. *Chinatown, a Legend of Old Cannery Row*. Orinda, Calif.: Gondor's Sky Press, 1965.

Esberg, A. I., ed. *Forty-Nine Opinions on Our Japanese Problem*. San Francisco: Grabhorn Press, 1944.

Esthus, Raymond A. *Theodore Roosevelt and Japan*. Seattle: University of Washington Press, 1966.

Fairbank, John King. *The United States and China*. Rev. ed., New York: Viking Press, 1955.

Farwell, Willard B. *The Chinese at Home and Abroad*. San Francisco: Bancroft 1885.

Fenn, William Purviance. *Ah Sin and His Brethren in American Literature*. Peking: College of Chinese Studies, 1933.

Fisher, Lloyd H. *The Harvest Labor Market in California*. Cambridge, Mass.: Harvard University Press, 1953.

Fisk University, Social Science Institute. *Orientals and Their Cultural Adjustment*. Nashville, Tenn.: Fisk University, 1946.

Fitzgerald, Stephen. *China and the Overseas Chinese: A Study of Peking's Changing Policy*. Cambridge, England: Cambridge University Press, 1972.

Flowers, Montaville. *The Japanese Conquest of American Opinion*. New York: George H. Doran, 1917.

Forbes, Cameron W. *The Philippine Islands*. 2 vols. Boston: Houghton Mifflin Co., 1928.

Friend, Theodore. *Between Two Empires: The Ordeal of the Philippines, 1929–1946*. New Haven, Conn.: Yale University Press, 1965.

Fuchs, Lawrence H. *Hawaii Pono: A Social History*. New York: Harcourt, Brace and World, 1961.

Fukei, Budd. *The Japanese American Story*. Minneapolis, Minn.: Dillon Press, 1976.

Galarza, Ernesto. *Farm Workers and Agri-business in California, 1947–1960*. Notre Dame, Ind.: Notre Dame University Press, 1950.

Galloway, J. D. *The First Transcontinental Railroad—Central Pacific and Union Pacific*. New York: Simmons Boardmen, 1950.

Gardner, Robert W., Robey, Bryant, and Smith, Peter G. *Asian Americans: Growth, Change, and Diversity*. Washington, D.C.: Population Reference Bureau, Inc., 1985.

Garis, Roy L. *Immigration Restruction*. New York: Macmillan Co., 1928.

Gee, Emma, ed. *Counterpoint: Perspectives on Asian America*. Los Angeles: UCLA Asian American Studies Center, 1976.

Gibson, Otis. *The Chinese in America*. Cincinnati: Hitchcock and Walden, 1877.

Gibson, William M. *Aliens and the Law*. Chapel Hill: University of North Carolina Press, 1940.

Girdner, Audrie, and Loftis, Anne. *The Great Betrayal: The Evacuation of the Japanese-Americans During World War II*. New York: Macmillan Co., 1969.

Given, Helen L. *The Korean Community in Los Angeles*. San Francisco: R. and E. Research Associates, 1974.

Glazer, Nathan. *Ethnic Dilemmas, 1964–1982*. Cambridge, Mass.: Harvard University Press, 1983.

Glick, Clarence E. *Sojourners and Settlers: Chinese Migrants in Hawaii*. Honolulu: University Press of Hawaii, 1980.

Gordon, Milton. *Assimilation in American Life*. New York: Oxford University Press, 1964.

Graff, Henry F. *American Imperialism and the Philippine Insurrection*. Boston: Little, Brown, 1969.

Grodzins, Morton. *Americans Betrayed: Politics and the Japanese Evacuation*. Chicago: University of Chicago Press, 1949.

Gulick, Sidney L. *American Democracy and Asiatic Citizenship*. New York: Charles Scribner and Sons, 1918.

———. *The American Japanese Problem: A Study of the Racial Relations of the East and the West*. New York: Charles Scribner's Sons, 1914.

Hansen, Gladys C., ed. *The Chinese in California*. Portland, Oreg.: R. Avel, 1970.

Harrison, Earl G. *Immigration and Nationality Laws as of March 1, 1944*. Washington, D.C.: U.S. Government Printing Office, 1944.

Hata, Donald Teruo, Jr. *"Undesirables": Early Immigrants and the Anti-Japanese Movement in San Francisco: 1892–1893*. New York: Arno Press, 1978.

Herman, Masako. *The Japanese in America, 1843–1973*. New York: Oceana Publications, 1974.

Hess, Gary R. *America Encounters India, 1941–1947*. Baltimore: Johns Hopkins University Press, 1971.

Higham, John. *Strangers in the Land: Patterns of American Nativism, 1860–1925*. New Brunswick, N.J.: Rutgers University Press, 1955.

Hosokawa, Bill. *Nisei: The Quiet Americans*. New York: William Morrow and Co., 1969.

———. *Thirty-Five Years in the Frying Pan*. New York: McGraw-Hill Book Co., 1978.

———. *JACL in Quest of Justice: The History of the Japanese American Citizens League*. New York: William Morrow and Co., 1982.

Howard, Alan. *Ain't No Big Thing: Coping Strategies in a Hawaiian-American Community*. Honolulu: University Press of Hawaii, 1974.

Hoy, William. *The Chinese Six Companies*. San Francisco: Chinese Consolidated Benevolent Association, 1942.

Hoyt, Edwin P. *Asians in the West*. New York: Thomas Nelson Publishers, 1974.

Hsu, Francis L.K. *Americans and Chinese: Two Ways of Life*. New York: Henry Schuman, 1953.

———. *The Challenge of the American Dream*. Belmont, Calif.: Wadsworth Publishing Co., 1971.

Hsu, Kai-yu, and Palubinski, Helen. *Asian American Authors*. Boston: Houghton Mifflin Co., 1972.

Huang, Tsen-ming. *The Legal Status of the Chinese Abroad*. Taipei, Taiwan: China Cultural Service, 1954.

Huie, Kin. *Reminiscence*. Peking: San Yu Press, 1932.

Hundley, Norris, ed. *The Asian American: The Historical Experience*. Santa Barbara, Calif.: ABC-Clio Press, 1976.

Hurh, Won Moo, and Kim, Kwang Chung. *Korean Immigrants in America: A Structural Analysis of Ethnic Confinement and Adhesive Adaptation*. Cranbury, N.J.: Fairleigh Dickinson University Press, 1984.

Hutchinson, E. P. *Legislative History of American Immigration Policy, 1798–1965*. Philadelphia: University of Pennsylvania Press, 1981.

Hwuy, Ung. *A Chinaman's Opinion of Us and of His Own People*. New York: Frederick A. Stokes and Co., 1927.

Ichihashi, Yamato. *Japanese Immigration: Its Status in California*. San Francisco: Marshall Press, 1915.

————. *Japanese in the United States: A Critical Study of the Problems of the Japanese Immigrants and Their Children*. Stanford, Calif.: Stanford University Press, 1932.

Ichioka, Yuji. *A Buried Past*. Berkeley: University of California Press, 1974.

Ignacio, Lemuel F. *Asian Americans and Pacific Islanders*. San Jose, Calif.: Filipino Development Associates, 1976.

Inouye, Daniel K. *Journey to Washington*. Englewood Cliffs, N.J.: Prentice-Hall, 1967.

Irick, Robert L. *Ch'ing Policy Toward the Coolie Trade, 1847–1878*. San Francisco: Chinese Materials Center, 1982.

Iriye, Akira. *Across the Pacific: An Inner History of American-East Asian Relations*. New York: Harcourt, Brace and World, 1967.

Irons, Peter. *Justice at War: The Story of Japanese American Internment Cases*. New York: Oxford University Press, 1983.

Irwin, William H. *Old Chinatown*. New York: M. Kennerly, 1913.

Ishigo, Istelle. *Lone Heart Mountain*. Los Angeles: Anderson, Ritchie and Simon, 1972.

Ito, Kazuo. *Issei: A History of Japanese Immigrants in North America*, trans. Shinichiro Nakamura and Jean S. Girard. Seattle: Executive Committee for Publication of Issei, 1973.

Iyenaga, T., and Sato, Kenoske. *Japan and the California Problem*. New York: G.P. Putnam's, 1921.

Jacobs, Paul, and Landau, Saul, with Pell, Eve. *To Serve the Devil, Vol. II: Colonials and Sojourners*. New York: Random House, 1971.

Jamieson, Stuart M. *Labor Unionism in American Agriculture*. U.S. Bureau of Labor Statistics Bulletin No. 836. Washington, D.C.: U.S. Government Printing Office, 1945.

Jo, Yung-hwan. *Political Participation of Asian Americans*. Pacific/Asian American Mental Health Research Center, 1980.

Joesting, Edward. *Hawaii: An Uncommon History*. New York: W.W. Norton, 1972.

Jones, Dorothy B. *The Portrayal of China and India on the American Screen*. Cambridge, Mass.: MIT, Center for International Studies, 1955.

Joseph, Philip. *Foreign Diplomacy in China, 1894–1900*. London: George Allen and Unwin Ltd., 1928.

Judd, Gerrit P. IV. *Hawaii: An Informal History*. New York: Collier Books, 1961.

Kachi, Teruko Okada. *The Treaty of 1911 and the Immigration and Alien Land Law*

Issue Between the United States and Japan, 1911–1913. New York: Arno Press, 1978.

Kang, Younghill. *East Goes West*. New York: Charles Scribner's, 1937.

Kanzaki, Kichi. *California and the Japanese*. San Francisco: n.p., 1921.

Kashima, Tetsuden. *Buddhism in America: The Social Organization of an Ethnic Religious Institution*. Westport, Conn.: Greenwood Press, 1977.

Kawakami, K. K. *The Real Japanese Question*. New York: Macmillan Co., 1921.

Kelly, Gail Paradise. *From Vietnam to America: A Chronicle of the Vietnamese Immigration to the United States*. Boulder, Colo.: Westview Press, 1977.

Kiefer, Christie W. *Changing Cultures, Changing Lives: An Ethnographic Study of Three Generations of Japanese Americans*. San Francisco: Jossey-Bass Publishers, 1974.

Kim, Bok-Lim C. *The Asian Americans: Changing Patterns, Changing Needs*. Montclair, N.J.: Association of Korean Christian Scholars in North America, 1978.

Kim, Byong-suh, ed. *The Korean Immigrant in America*. Montclair, N.J.: Association of Korean Christian Scholars in North America, 1980.

Kim, Elaine H. *Asian American Literature: An Introduction to the Writings and Their Social Context*. Philadelphia: Temple University Press, 1982.

Kim, Hyung-chan, ed. *The Korean Diaspora: Historical and Sociological Studies of Korean Immigration and Assimilation in North America*. Santa Barbara, Calif.: ABC-Clio Press, 1977.

————, and Patterson, Wayne, eds. *The Koreans in America, 1882–1974*. Dobbs Ferry, N.Y.: Oceana Publications, 1974.

————, and Mejia, Cynthia C., eds. *The Filipinos in America, 1898–1974*. Dobbs Ferry, N.Y.: Oceana Publications, 1976.

Kim, Illsoo. *New Urban Immigrants: The Korean Community in New York*. Princeton, N.J.: Princeton University Press, 1981.

Kim, Warren. *Koreans in America*. Seoul, Korea: Po Chin Printing Co., 1971.

King, F. P., ed. *Oceania and Beyond: Essays on the Pacific Since 1945*. Westport, Conn.: Greenwood Press, 1976.

Kitano, Harry H.L. *Japanese Americans: The Evolution of a Subculture*. Englewood Cliffs, N.J.: Prentice-Hall, 1969.

Knoll, Tricia. *Becoming Americans: Asian Sojourners, Immigrants, and Refugees in the Western United States*. Portland, Oreg.: Coast to Coast Books, 1982.

Kodama-Nishimoto, Michi; Nishimoto, Warren S.; and Oshiro, Cynthia A. *Hanahana: An Oral History Anthology of Hawaii's Working People*. Honolulu: Ethnic Studies Oral History Project, University of Hawaii at Manoa, 1984.

Kodapi, C. *Indians Overseas, 1838–1939*. New Delhi: Indian Council of World Affairs, 1951.

Konvitz, Milton R. *The Alien and the Asiatic in American Law*. Ithaca, N.Y.: Cornell University Press, 1946.

————. *Civil Rights in Immigration*. Ithaca, N.Y.: Cornell University Press, 1953.

Kung, S. W. *Chinese in American Life*. Seattle: University of Washington Press, 1962.

Kuo, Chia-ling. *Social and Political Change in New York's Chinatown: The Role of Voluntary Associations*. New York: Praeger Publishers, 1977.

Kuykendall, Ralph S. *The Hawaiian Kingdom*, 3 vols. Honolulu: University of Hawaii Press, Vol. 1, 1938; Vol. 2, 1953; Vol. 3, 1967.

La Fargue, Thomas E. *China's First Hundred*. Pullman: Washington State College, 1942.

Lai, Him Mark; Lim, Genny; and Yung, Judy. *Island: Poetry and History of Chinese Immigrants on Angel Island, 1910–1940*. San Francisco: Hoc Doi, 1980.

Lanman, Charles, ed. *The Japanese in America*. New York: University Publishing Co., 1872.

Lasker, Bruno. *Filipino Immigration*. Chicago: University of Chicago Press, 1931.

La Violette, Forrest E. *Americans of Japanese Ancestry*. Toronto: Canadian Institute of International Affairs, 1945.

Lee, Calvin. *Chinatown, U.S.A.*. Garden City, N.Y.: Doubleday and Co., 1965.

Lee, Chong-sik. *The Politics of Korean Nationalism*. Berkeley: University of California Press, 1965.

Lee, Rose Hum. *The Chinese in the United States of America*. Hong Kong: Hong Kong University Press, 1960.

———. *The Growth and Decline of Chinese Communities in the Rocky Moutain Region*. New York: Arno Press, 1978.

Leighton, Alexander H. *The Governing of Men*. Princeton, N.J.: Princeton University Press, 1945.

Le Roy, James A. *The Americans in the Philippines, 2 vols.*. Boston: Houghton Mifflin Co., 1914.

Li, Tien-Lu. *Congressional Policy of Chinese Immigration*. Nashville, Tenn.: Publishing House of the Methodist Episcopal Church, South, 1916.

Light, Ivan H. *Ethnic Enterprise in America: Business and Welfare Among Chinese, Japanese and Blacks*. Berkeley: University of California Press, 1972.

Lin, Yutang. *Chinatown Family*. New York: John Day, 1948.

Lind, Andrew W. *Hawaii's People*. 4th ed. Honolulu: University Press of Hawaii, 1980.

Levine, Gene N., and Rhodes, Colbert. *The Japanese American Community: A Three-Generation Study*. New York: Praeger Publishers, 1981.

Liu, William T. *Transition to Nowhere: Vietnamese Refugees in America*. Nashville, Tenn.: Charter House Publishers, 1979.

Loewen, James W. *The Mississippi Chinese: Between Black and White*. Cambridge, Mass.: Harvard University Press, 1971.

Lowenstein, Edith. *The Alien and the Immigration Law*. Dobbs Ferry, N.Y.: Oceana Publications, 1958.

Lyman, Stanford M. *The Asian in North America*. Santa Barbara, Calif.: ABC-Clio Press, 1970.

———. *Chinese Americans*. New York: Random House, 1974.

McClatchy, Valentine S., ed. *Japanese Immigration and Colonization: Brief Prepared for Consideration of the State Department*. San Francisco: R. and E. Research Associates, 1970 (Reprint).

———. *Four Anti-Japanese Pamphlets*. New York: Arno Press, 1978.

McClellan, Robert. *The Heathen Chinese: A Study of American Attitudes Toward China, 1890–1905*. Columbus: Ohio State University Press, 1971.

McHenry, Donald F. *Micronesia: Trust Betrayed*. New York: Carnegie Endowment for International Peace, 1975.

McKee, Delber L. *Chinese Exclusion Versus the Open Door Policy, 1900–1906*. Detroit: Wayne State University Press, 1977.

McKenzie, R. D. *Oriental Exclusion*. Chicago: University of Chicago Press, 1928.

McLeod, Alexander. *Pigtails and Gold Dust*. Caldwell, Idaho: Caxton Printers, 1947.

MacNair, Harley Farnsworth. *The Chinese Abroad: Their Position and Protection: A*

Study in International Law and Relations. Shanghai, China: Commercial Press, 1924.

Macpherson, Cluny, et al., eds. *New Neighbors . . . Islanders in Adaptation*. Santa Cruz, Calif.: Center for South Pacific Studies, 1978.

McWilliams, Carey. *Brothers Under the Skin*. Boston: Little, Brown and Co., 1942.

———. *Prejudice: Japanese-Americans, Symbol of Racial Intolerance*. Boston: Little, Brown and Co., 1944.

———. *California, the Great Exception*. New York: Current Books, 1949.

Majumdar, R. C., ed. *Struggle for Freedom*. Bombay, India; Bharatiya Vidya Bhavan, 1969.

Mariano, Honoranti. *The Filipino Immigration in the U.S.* San Francisco: R. and E. Research Associates, 1972.

Mark, Diane Mei Lin, and Chih, Ginger. *A Place Called Chinese America*. Dubuque, Iowa: Kendall/Hunt Publishing Co., 1982.

Martin, Mildred Crowl. *Chinatown's Angry Angel: The Story of Donaldina Cameron*. Palo Alto, Calif.: Pacific Books, 1977.

Maykovich, Minako K. *Japanese American Identity Dilemma*. Tokyo, Japan: Waseda University Press, 1972.

Mears, Eliot Grinnell. *Resident Orientals on the American Pacific Coast: Their Legal and Economic Status*. Chicago: University of Chicago Press, 1927.

Melendy, H. Brett. *The Oriental Americans*. Boston: Twayne Publishers, 1972.

———. *Asians in America. Filipinos, Koreans, and East Indians*. Boston: Twayne Publishers, 1977.

———, and Gilbert, Benjamin F. *The Governors of California: Peter H. Burnett to Edmund G. Brown*. Georgetown, Calif.: Talisman Press, 1965.

Miller, Stuart Creighton. *The Unwelcome Immigrant: The American Image of the Chinese, 1785–1882*. Berkeley: University of California Press, 1969.

Misrow, Jogesh C. *East Indian Immigration on the Pacific Coast*. San Francisco: R. and E. Research Associates, 1971.

Miyamoto, Frank. *Social Solidarity Among the Japanese in Seattle*. Seattle: University of Washington, 1939.

Modell, John, ed. *The Kikuchi Diary: Chronicle from an American Concentration Camp*. Urbana: University of Illinois Press, 1973.

———. *The Economics and Politics of Racial Accommodation: The Japanese of Los Angeles, 1900–1942*. Urbana: University of Illinois Press, 1977.

Munoz, Alfred. *The Filipinos in America*. Los Angeles: Mountainview Press, 1971.

Munoz, Faye Untalan. *An Exploratory Study of Island Migration: Chamorrow of Guam*. Ann Arbor, Mich.: University Microfilms International, 1984.

Montero, Darrel. *Vietnamese Americans: Patterns of Resettlement and Socioeconomic Adaptation in the United States*. Boulder, Colo.: Westview Press, 1979.

———. *Japanese Americans: Changing Patterns of Ethnic Affiliation Over Three Generations*. Boulder, Colo.: Westview Press, 1980.

Muzumdar, Haridas T. *America's Contributions to India's Freedom*. Allahabad, India: Central Book Depot, 1962.

Myer, Dillon S. *Uprooted Americans: The Japanese Americans and the War Relocation Authority During World War II*. Tucson: University of Arizona Press, 1971.

Nakanishi, Don T., and Nakanishi-Hirano, Marsha. *The Education of Asian and Pacific*

Americans: Historical Perspectives and Prescriptions for the Future. Phoenix, Arizona: Oryx Press, 1983.

Nakayama, Gordon G. *Issei: Stories of Japanese Canadian Pioneers*. Toronto, Canada: Britannia Printers, Ltd., 1983.

Nee, Victor, and deBary, Brett. *Longtime Californ'*. Boston: Houghton Mifflin Co., 1974.

Nelson, Douglas W. *Heart Mountain: The History of an American Concentration Camp*. Madison: Department of History, University of Wisconsin, 1976.

Nordyke, Eleanor C. *The Peopling of Hawaii*. Honolulu: The University of Hawaii Press, 1977.

Norr, William. *Stories of Chinatown: Sketches from Life in the Chinese Colony of Mott, Pell and Doyers Streets*. New York: W. Norr, 1892.

Ogawa, Dennis M. *Jan Ken Po: The World of Hawaii's Japanese Americans*. Honolulu: University Press of Hawaii, 1973.

————. *Kodomo no tame ni (For the Sake of the Children, the Japanese American Experience in Hawaii)*. Honolulu: University Press of Hawaii, 1978.

Okada, John. *No-No Boy*. Rutland, Vt.: Charles E. Tuttle Co., 1957.

Okimoto, Daniel. *American in Disguise*. New York: Walker-Weatherhill, 1971.

Okubo, Mine. *Citizen 13660*. New York: Columbia University Press, 1946.

Oliver, Douglas L. *The Pacific Islands*. Cambridge, Mass.: Harvard University Press, 1951.

Olmsted, Roger, and Wollenberg, Charles, eds. *Neither Separate Nor Equal*. San Francisco: California Historical Society, 1971.

Owan, Tom Choken, ed. *Southeast Asian Mental Health*. Rockville, Maryland: National Institute of Mental Health, 1985.

Pajus, Jean. *The Real Japanese California*. Berkeley, Calif.: James J. Gillick, 1937.

Palmer, Albert W. *Orientals in American Life*. New York: Friendship Press, 1934.

Palmer, Phil. *Chinatown, San Francisco*. Berkeley, Calif.: Howell-North, 1960.

Patterson, Wayne. *The Korean Frontier in America: Immigration to Hawaii, 1896–1910*. 2 vols. Ann Arbor, Mich.: University Microfilms International, 1979.

Paul, Rodman W. *The Abrogation of the Gentlemen's Agreement*. Cambridge, Mass.: Harvard University Press, 1936.

Penrose, Eldon R. *California Nativism: Organized Opposition to the Japanese, 1890–1913*. San Francisco: R. and E. Research Associates, 1973.

Petersen, William. *Japanese Americans: Oppression and Success*. New York: Random House, 1971.

Phelan, John Leddy. *The Hispanization of the Philippines*. Madison: University of Wisconsin Press, 1959.

Phillips, Paul C. *Hawaii's Democrats: Chasing the American Dream*. Washington, D.C.: University Press of America, 1982.

Prangle, Gordon W. *At Dawn We Slept: The Untold Story of Pearl Harbor*. New York: McGraw-Hill Book Co., 1981.

Quan, Robert Seto. *Lotus Among the Magnolias: The Mississippi Chinese*. Jackson: University Press of Mississippi, 1982.

Quinsaat, Jesse, ed. *Letters in Exile: An Introductory Reader on the History of Filipinos in America*. Los Angeles: UCLA Asian American Studies Center, 1976.

Reinecke, John E. *Feigned Necessity: Hawaii's Attempt to Obtain Chinese Contract Labor, 1921–23*. San Francisco: Chinese Materials Center, 1979.

Remer, C. F. *A Study of Chinese Boycott with Special Reference to Their Economic Effectiveness*. Baltimore: Johns Hopkins University Press, 1933.

Riddle, Ronald. *Flying Dragons, Flowing Streams: Music in the Life of San Francisco's Chinatown*. Westport, Conn.: Greenwood Press, 1983.

Riggs, Fred W. *Pressures on Congress: A Study of the Repeal of Chinese Exclusion*. New York: King's Crown Press, 1950.

Ritter, Edward; Ritter, Helen; and Spector, Stanley. *Americans All, Our Oriental Americans*. New York: McGraw-Hill Book Co., 1965.

Rohmer, Sax. *Tales of Chinatown*. New York: Doubleday, Page and Co., 1922.

Ross, Edward A. *The Changing Chinese, the Conflict of Oriental and Western Cultures in China*. New York: Century Co., 1911.

Sabin, Edwin L. *Building the Pacific Railway*. Philadelphia: J.B. Lippincott Co., 1919.

Sandmeyer, Elmer Clarence. *The Anti-Chinese Movement in California*. Urbana: University of Illinois Press, 1939.

Saran, Parmatma, and Eames, Edwin. *The New Ethnics: Asian Indians in the United States*. New York: Praeger Publishers, 1980.

———. *Asian Indian Experience in the United States*. Cambridge, Mass: Schenkman Publishing Corp., 1985.

Saxton, Alexander. *The Indispensable Enemy: Labor and the Anti-Chinese Movement in California*. Berkeley: University of California Press, 1971.

Seward, George F. *Chinese Immigration: Its Social and Economic Aspects*. New York: Charles Scribner's Sons, 1881.

Sidney, Kansas. *Immigration and the Nationality Act*. New York: Immigrations Publications, 1953.

Smith, William C. *The Second Generation Oriental in America*. Honolulu: Institute of Pacific Relations, 1927.

———. *Americans in Process*. Ann Arbor, Mich.: J.W. Edwards, 1937.

Sone, Monica. *Nisei Daughter*. Boston: Little, Brown and Co., 1953.

Spicer, Edward H.; Hansen, Asael T.; Luomala, Katherine; and Opler, Marvin K. *Impounded People: Japanese-Americans in the Relocation Centers*. Tucson: University of Arizona Press, 1969.

Starr, M. B. *The Coming Struggle: On What the People on the Pacific Coast Think of the Coolie Invasion*. San Francisco: Excelsior Office, Bacon and Co., Book and Job Printers, 1873.

Stephan, John J. *Hawaii Under the Rising Sun: Japan's Plans for Conquest After Pearl Harbor*. Honolulu: University of Hawaii Press, 1984.

Stephenson, George M. *A History of American Immigration, 1820–1924*. New York: Russell and Russell, 1964.

Strong, Edward K. *The Second Generation Japanese Problem*. Stanford, Calif.: Stanford University Press, 1934.

Strong, William Ellsworth. *The Story of the American Board: An Account of the First Hundred Years of the American Board of Commissioners for Foreign Missions*. Boston: Pilgrim Press, 1910.

Sue, Stanley and Morishima, James. *The Mental Health of Asian Americans*. San Francisco: Jossey-Bass Publishers, 1982.

Sue, Stanley, and Wagner, Nathaniel N. *Asian-Americans: Psychological Perspectives*. 2 vols. Ben Lomond, Calif.: Science and Behavior Books, 1973–1980.

Sung, Betty Lee. *Mountain of Gold: The Story of Chinese in America*. New York: Macmillan Co., 1967.

Ta, Chen. *Chinese Migrations, With Special Reference to Labor Conditions*. Taipei, Taiwan: Ch'eng-Wen Publishing Co., 1967.

Tachiki, Amy; Wong, Eddie; and Odo, Franklin, eds. *Roots: An Asian American Reader*. Los Angeles: UCLA Asian American Studies Center, 1971.

Takashima, Shizuye. *A Child in Prison Camp*. New York: William Morrow and Co., 1974.

Tate, Merze. *The United States and the Hawaiian Kingdom: A Political History*. New Haven, Conn.: Yale University Press, 1965.

————. *Hawaii: Reciprocity or Annexation*. East Lansing: Michigan State University Press, 1968.

Taylor, George E. *The Philippines and the United States: Problems of Partnership*. New York: Frederick A. Praeger, 1964.

Telamaque, Eleanor Wong. *It's Crazy to Stay Chinese in Minnesota*. New York: Thomas Nelson, 1978.

ten Broek, Jacobus; Barnhart, Edward N.; and Matson, Floyd W. *Prejudice, War and the Constitution: Causes and Consequences of the Evacuation of the Japanese Americans in World War II*. Berkeley: University of California Press, 1970.

Teng, Ssu-Yu. *Chang Hsi and the Treaty of Nanking, 1842*. Chicago: University of Chicago Press, 1944.

Teodoro, Luis V., Jr., ed. *Out of This Struggle: The Filipinos in Hawaii*. Honolulu: University Press of Hawaii, 1981.

Thomas, Dorothy S. *The Salvage*. Berkeley: University of California Press, 1952.

————, and Nishimoto, Richard. *The Spoilage: Japanese-American Evacuation and Resettlement During World War II*. Berkeley: University of California Press, 1946.

Thompson, Richard Austin. *The Yellow Peril, 1890–1924*. New York: Arno Press, 1978.

Tow, J. S. *The Real Chinese in America*. Orange, N.J.: Academy Press, 1923.

Townsend, L. T. *The Chinese Problem*. Boston: Lee and Shepard Publishers, 1876.

Trumbull, Robert. *Tin Roofs and Palm Trees: A Report on the New South Seas*. Seattle: University of Washington Press, 1977.

Tsai, Shih-shan Henry. *China and the Overseas Chinese in the United States, 1868–1911*. Fayetteville: University of Arkansas Press, 1983.

Tuiteleleapaga, Napoleone A., Chief. *Samoa: Yesterday, Today and Tomorrow*. Great Neck, N.Y.: Todd and Honeywell, 1980.

Tung, William L. *The Chinese in America, 1820–1973*. Dobbs Ferry, N.Y.: Oceana Publications, 1974.

Uyeda, Clifford L. *A Final Report and Review: The Japanese American Citizens League National Committee for Iva Toguri*. Occasional Monographs Series 1, Seattle: Asian American Studies Program, University of Washington, 1980.

Wallovits, Sonia. *The Filipinos in California*. San Francisco: R. and E. Research Associates, 1972.

Wang, Sing-su. *The Organization of Chinese Emigration, 1848–1888*. San Francisco: Chinese Materials Center, 1978.

Weglyn, Michi. *Years of Infamy: The Untold Story of America's Concentration Camps*. New York: William Morrow and Co., 1976.

Whitney, James A. *The Chinese and the Chinese Question*. New York: Tibbals Book Co., 1888.

Williams, Frederick Wells. *Anson Burlingame and the First Chinese Mission to Foreign Powers*. New York: Charles Scribner's Sons, 1912.

Wilson, Robert A., and Hosokawa, Bill. *East to America: A History of the Japanese in the United States*. New York: William Morrow and Co., 1980.

Wolff, Leon. *Little Brown Brother: How the United States Purchased and Pacified the Philippine Islands at the Century's Turn*. Garden City, N.Y.: Doubleday and Co., 1961.

Wollenberg, Charles. *All Deliberate Speed: Segregation and Exclusion in California Schools, 1855–1975*. Berkeley: University of California Press, 1976.

————, ed. *Ethnic Conflict in California History*. Los Angeles: Tinnon-Brown, 1970.

Wong, Bernard P. *Chinatown: Economic Adaptation and Ethnic Identity of the Chinese*. New York: Holt, Rinehart and Winston, 1982.

Wong, Eugene F. *On Visual Media Racism: Asians in the American Motion Pictures*. New York: Arno Press, 1978.

Wood, Ellen Rawson. *Californians and the Chinese: The First Decade*. San Francisco: R. and E. Research Associates, 1974.

Wright, Theon. *The Disenchanted Isles: The Story of the Second Revolution in Hawaii*. New York: Dial Press, 1972.

Wu, Cheng-Tsu. *"Chink!"* New York: World Publishing, 1972.

Wu, Ching Chao. *Chinese Immigration in the Pacific Area*. San Francisco: R. and E. Research Associates, 1974.

Wu, William F. *The Yellow Peril: Chinese Americans in American Fiction, 1850–1940*. Hamden, Conn.: Archon Books, 1982.

Yanagisako, Sylvia Junko. *Transforming the Past: Tradition and Kinship among Japanese Americans*. Stanford, Calif.: Stanford University Press, 1985.

Yatsushiro, Toshio. *Politics and Cultural Values: The World War II Japanese Relocation Centers and the United States Government*. New York: Arno Press, 1978.

Yee, Carl, ed. *Dwell Among Our People*. Berkeley: University of California-Berkeley, Asian American Studies Department, 1977.

Yen, Ching-hwang. *Coolies and Mandarins*. Singapore: Singapore University Press, 1985.

Yoneda, Karl G. *Gunbattle: Sixty-year Struggle of a Kibei Worker*. Los Angeles: Asian American Studies Center, UCLA, 1983.

Yoshida, Jim, and Hosokawa, Bill. *The Two Worlds of Jim Yoshida*. New York: William Morrow and Co., 1972.

Yu, Eui-Young; Phillips, Earl H.; and Yang Eun Sik, eds. *Koreans in Los Angeles: Prospects and Problems*. Los Angeles: Koryo Research Institute, 1982.

Yung, Wing. *My Life in China and America*. New York: Henry Holt and Co., 1909.

Zo, Kil Young. *Chinese Emigration into the United States, 1850–1880*. New York: Arno Press, 1978.

Chronology of Asian American History

1820	The arrival of the first Chinese in the United States is reported by the Immigration Commission.
1821–1840	Ten more Chinese are reported to have come to the United States during the two decades.
1843	May 7. Captain William Whitfield of the *John Howland* rescues Nakahama Manjiro (1827–1898), known to Americans later as John Mung, and brings him to New Bedford, Massachusetts.
1844	July 3. The Treaty of Peace, Amity and Commerce between the United States and China is concluded at Whanghia, giving American citizens in China extraterritorial rights, but the same rights are not offered to Chinese in the United States.
1847	April 12. The first group of three Chinese students, Yung Wing (1828–1912), Wong Hsing (Shing), and Wong Foon, arrives in New York for their study at the Monson Academy, Monson, Massachusetts. Yung Wing later plays a major role in promoting Sino-American relations.
1848	January 24. Gold is discovered at John Sutter's property in California. This becomes a catalyst for bringing large numbers of Chinese to the West Coast.
	The *Bald Eagle* brings two Chinese men and one Chinese woman, an employee at the home of Charles Gillespie who returns from Hong Kong with them.
1850	The total number of Chinese in California reaches 4,000 by the end of the year.
	A monthly tax, known as the Foreign Miners' License Tax, is enacted by the California Legislature to discourage Chinese miners. It is ruled unconstitutional in 1870, but during the two decades Chinese miners pay 98 percent of $1.5 million of this tax.

Hamada Hikozo (1837–1897) is rescued by the American sailing ship *Auckland* and is brought to San Francisco. He moves to Baltimore where he is educated. He becomes the first American citizen of Japanese ancestry.

1851
The Chinese population in California grows from 4,000 to 25,000 within one year.

1852
280 Chinese are recruited by the Royal Hawaii Agricultural Society to work on plantations.

More than 20,000 Chinese arrive in San Francisco.

1853
March 30. The California Legislature passes An Act to Provide for the Protection of Foreigners, and to Define Their Liabilities and Privileges, through which special taxes are imposed on foreign gold miners. This tax as well as the discovery of gold in Australia reduces the number of Chinese coming to the United States. Only 4,470 Chinese are reported to have come to the United States this year.

1854
October. Chief Justice Hugh Campbell Murray (1825–1857) of the Supreme Court of the State of California rules on the People, Respondent, v. George W. Hall, Appellant that Chinese cannot testify against a white person as a witness. This ruling is later affirmed in another case, The People of the State of California, Respondents, v. James Brady, Appellant, during the same year.

April. The San Francisco-based newspaper, *Kim-Shan Jit San-Luk* (Gold Hills News), is published, the first such paper in Chinese America. It becomes a weekly on July 8.

March 31. The Treaty of Kanagawa, also known as the Treaty of Peace, Amity and Commerce, is concluded between the United States and Japan. It opens the port of Shimoda to American ships for securing wood, water, coal, and other provisions, and promises to open the port of Hakodata to American ships a year later.

Chinese in California establish their district companies known as Six Companies.

1855
April 28. California Legislature passes An Act to Discourage the Immigration to This State of Persons Who Cannot Become Citizens Thereof as part of the attempt to restrict the socioeconomic activities of the Chinese in California. This law requires that the master, owner, or consignee of any ship carrying passengers ineligible for citizenship pay $50 per passenger. The law is ruled unconstitutional in 1857 by Justice Solomon Heydenfeldt of the Supreme Court of the State of California on the grounds that Congress has exclusive power to regulate commerce with foreign nations.

1856
The Chinese Daily News is published in Sacramento but lasts only two years.

1857   The Act of April 28, 1855 passed by the California Legislature is
                ruled unconstitutional.

                Mixed marriages between Chinese men and Irish and German
                women are reported in *Harper's Weekly*.

1858   April 26. The California Legislature passes An Act to Prevent the
                Further Immigration of Chinese or Mongolians to This State.

                July 29. The Yedo Treaty, also known as the Treaty of Commerce
                and Navigation, is concluded between Japan and the United States.
                This particular treaty had been under negotiation between the two
                nations during the preceding two years.

1859   The Ch'ing Dynasty changes its traditional policy of prohibition
                on the emigration of its subjects and allows Chinese to go abroad
                after it concludes the Treaty of Tientsin with foreign powers in
                1858.

1860   March 17. Nakahama Manjiro, who had been the first Japanese
                in the United States in 1843, arrives in San Francisco aboard the
                Kanin Maru. Nakahama returns as an interpreter for the Japanese
                Grand Embassy.

                March 29. The Japanese Grand Embassy arrives in San Francisco
                aboard the *U.S.S. Powhatan*, led by Masaaki Shimmi, Bunzen-
                no-kami.

                According to the 1860 Census, there are 34,933 Chinese in the
                United States.

1861   During the year 8,434 Chinese are reported to have come to the
                United States and 3,594 Chinese to have left the country.

1862   April 26. The California Legislature passes An Act to Protect Free
                White Labor Against Competition with Chinese Coolie Labor, and
                to Discourage the Immigration of the Chinese into the State of
                California.

                The same legislature passes a police tax requiring Chinese in Cal-
                ifornia over eighteen years of age to pay $2.50 per person if they
                have not paid the Foreign Miners' License Tax.

1863   California Police Tax is ruled unconstitutional by the Supreme
                Court of the State of California in the case of Lin Sing v. Washburn.

1864   Niijima Jo (1843–1890), also known as Joseph Hardy Neesima,
                comes to the United States as a stowaway aboard the *Wild Rover*
                which brought him from Shanghai, China. The ship owner sends
                him to Phillips Andover Academy and Amherst College. In 1874
                he completes his study at Andover Theological Seminary before
                he goes back to Japan to establish Doshisha University in Kyoto,
                Japan.

Chinese are hired to build the transcontinental railroad.

1865   More Chinese are recruited to work on the transcontinental railroad. At the peak of its construction more than 10,000 Chinese are hired by the Central Pacific Railroad Company.

1866   Chinese workers are found on the sugar cane fields of Louisiana. Some of them are brought to Louisiana from Cuba.

1867   Fukuzawa Yukichi (1835–1901), educator, lecturer, and author, visits the United States for the third time. He was mainly responsible for introducing Japan to the Western world.

1868   June 19. The first group of Japanese emigrants to Hawaii, known as *Ganen-Mono* arrive. They are contract laborers recruited by Eugene Van Reed. When information on mistreatment of these people by their employers reaches the Japanese government, it stops Japanese emigration for the next seventeen years.

July 28. The Burlingame Treaty is concluded between the United States and China, allowing free immigration of citizens to both countries. It does not grant Chinese the right of naturalization in the United States to become American citizens.

1869   May 27. The first group of Japanese immigrants comes to mainland United States and settles in Gold Hill, California. They establish the Wakamatsu Tea and Silk Farm Colony under the leadership of John Henry Schnell.

The transcontinental railroad is completed, and approximately 15,000 Chinese workers are no longer wanted in the West.

July 13. A group of plantation owners hold a Chinese labor convention in Memphis, Tennessee, in order to find the best and cheapest way to import Chinese workers.

1870   February 11. A joint resolution is passed by the Colorado Legislature to welcome Chinese immigrants, but this attitude does not last long. An anti-Chinese riot breaks out in Denver ten years later.

Approximately 600 Chinese workers are hired to build the Alabama and Chattanooga Railroad.

Congress grants permission to twelve Japanese students to attend Annapolis Naval Academy.

1871   October 23. An anti-Chinese riot breaks out in Los Angeles. A Chinese is hung by the lawless crowd and other Chinese are lynched by the unruly mob.

1872   January 15. The Iwakura Mission led by Prince Iwakura is dispatched to the United States by the emperor of Japan. It arrives in San Francisco and proceeds to Washington, D.C., where Prince

Iwakura makes efforts to renegotiate a more equitable treaty. Fifty-three Japanese students who came with the mission are left behind in the United States for study.

The Chinese Education Mission is organized through the efforts made by Yung Wing, one of the first Chinese students to graduate from an American university. A group of thirty Chinese students, aged between ten and fifteen years, are brought to the United States for education. During the subsequent years, until the mission is disbanded in 1875, more Chinese students are sent to America for study.

1873   The International Workingmen's Association adopts an official anti-coolie policy which is, in essence, an anti-Chinese policy.

1874   White union workers engaged in the cigar-making industry discourage business people from selling Chinese-made cigars. Labels and other devices are used to sell only cigars made by white workers in San Francisco.

1875   The U.S. Congress passes an immigration act prohibiting convicts and prostitutes from coming to the United States. This is considered the first exclusion law passed by Congress to affect certain classes of aliens, as other laws passed before have been ruled unconstitutional.

May 31. The Reciprocity Treaty between the Kingdom of Hawaii and the United States is signed by President Ulysses S. Grant. The House approves it on May 8 and the Senate acts on it on August 14, but it does not go into effect until September 9 of the following year. The treaty enables Hawaii to export unrefined sugar to mainland United States duty free. This revives the Hawaiian economy, particularly the sugar-based economy, thus contributing to the further immigration of Asians to Hawaii.

Ch'en Lan-pin and Yung Wing are appointed by the Ch'ing Dynasty of China as commissioners to the United States, Peru, and Spain.

1876   A typical Japanese house is built by Japan for the Centennial Exhibition held in Philadelphia.

1877   A group of Japanese students led by Miyama Kanichi organizes the Japanese Gospel Society in San Francisco.

August 22. The Workingmen's Party of California is organized under the leadership of Denis Kearney.

1878   The Board of Supervisors of the city and county of San Francisco is required to increase police protection, but the same service is not provided for the city's Chinese quarters.

Ch'en Lan-pin and Yung Wing present their credentials to the U.S. government.

1879

California adopts a new Constitution as a result of the Second Constitutional Convention held between September 28, 1878, and March 3, 1879. The constitution contains many discriminatory measures against Chinese. It deprives the Chinese of employment on any municipal, county or state public works.

January 18. The Fifteen Passenger Bill is passed by the House of Representatives and is later sent for the Senate's approval. According to this law, no ship is allowed to carry more than fifteen Chinese. President Rutherford B. Hayes vetoes it on the grounds that it contradicts the Burlingame Treaty of 1868.

Sun Yat-sen (1866–1925), founder and president of the Republic of China, arrives in Hawaii to be with his brother. He later attends Iolani School in Honolulu.

1880

The U.S. government takes the initiative in revising the Burlingame Treaty, and a new treaty is concluded between China and the United States on November 8, although it is not signed until November 17. The Chinese government agrees to the limitation and restriction of Chinese immigrants to the United States, and receives, in turn, from the U.S. government, assurance that the Chinese residents in America will receive government protection for their persons and property. But this is an empty promise.

An anti-Chinese riot breaks out in Denver, Colorado, and many Chinese homes and businesses are lost in the riot.

During the decade between 1871 and 1880, 149 Japanese immigrate to the United States, according to the U.S. Bureau of Census.

1881

Congress passes an act to suspend Chinese immigration to the United States for twenty years contrary to the provisions made in the 1880 treaty. Because of provisions included in the law which were considered unreasonable, President Chester A. Arthur vetoes the bill.

1882

April 24. The League of Deliverance is established in San Francisco under the leadership of Frank Roney (1841–1916), who is behind the anti-Chinese tactics used to boycott Chinese-made goods.

May 6. The first federal exclusion law aimed at excluding a specific nationality is passed by the U.S. Congress and is forwarded to President Chester A. Arthur for his signature. The law, known as the Chinese Exclusion Act of 1882, or An Act to Execute Certain Treaty Stipulations Relating to Chinese, is signed into law, suspending Chinese immigration for the next ten years. This is further extended by the Geary Act in 1892.

May 22. The Treaty of Amity and Commerce is concluded between Korea and the United States. Article VI of the treaty allows Koreans to immigrate to the United States, although less than three weeks before the conclusion of the treaty, Chinese are not allowed to immigrate to America.

August 3. Congress enacts the first general immigration law establishing federal policies for immigration.

1883

September 3. The Korean diplomatic mission led by Prince Min Yong-ik arrives in San Francisco. Yu Kil-jun (1856–1914), a member of the mission, decides to stay in America for his study at the Governor Dummer Academy.

1884

July 5. Congress passes An Act to Amend an Act Entitled an Act to Execute Certain Treaty Stipulations Relating to Chinese, Approved May Sixth, eighteen hundred and eighty-two. The law imposes more restrictions on both Chinese residents in America and Chinese immigrants.

So Jae-p'il (1866–1951) comes to America as a political refugee and studies at George Washington University. He becomes a physician after graduation from the university. He changes his name to Philip Jaisohn and is naturalized.

1885

February 8. The first shipload of Japanese laborers, recruited by Robert Irwin, arrives in Honolulu, Hawaii. This immigration is a result of the treaty concluded between the Kingdom of Hawaii and Japan. This is the beginning of large-scale immigration of Japanese to Hawaii.

An anti-Chinese riot breaks out in a mining town (Rock Springs, Wyoming), killing some thirty Chinese and destroying properties.

November 30. Congress passes an act to prohibit contract labor.

1886

Japan legalizes the emigration of its people abroad. Japanese emigration had been stopped by the government after news of mistreatment of Japanese laborers in Hawaii reached Tokyo.

February 8. An anti-Chinese riot breaks out in Seattle, killing one man and injuring four others. The Chinese residents in Seattle are driven out of the city and sent to San Francisco.

May 10. The Supreme Court of the United States rules on the case of Yick Wo v. Hopkins, establishing the principle that no state may deny any person his or her life, liberty, or property without due process of law. The Court rules unconstitutional city ordinances of the city of San Francisco that prohibit Chinese from conducting their laundry businesses.

1887   Togasaki Kikumatsu arrives in the United States and later estab-
                            lishes the Mutual Supply Company in San Francisco.

1888   September 13. Congress passes another act to impose further re-
                            strictions on Chinese immigration.

                            October 1. The Scott Act is passed by Congress. It prohibits reentry
                            of Chinese laborers who had gone to China for a temporary visit.
                            Because of this law, over 20,000 Chinese are trapped outside the
                            United States, although they are former residents of the United
                            States.

1889   The Supreme Court of the United States rules on the case of Chae
                            Chan Ping v. United States. The Court states that the U.S. gov-
                            ernment has the right to exclude any alien and that the reentry
                            permit issued to aliens can be revoked. In essence, this ruling
                            upholds the constitutionality of the Scott Act which revoked all
                            reentry permits.

1890   There are 107,488 Chinese in the United States according to the
                            1890 Census report.

1891   *The Chinese World*, the first bilingual daily published both in
                            Chinese and English, appears in San Francisco.

1892   Congress passes the Geary Act, thus extending the Chinese Ex-
                            clusion Act of 1882 for another decade. The law also requires
                            Chinese residents in the United States to carry the certificate of
                            residence.

1893   May 15. The Supreme Court rules on the case of Fong Yue Ting
                            v. United States. The Chinese community desires to test the con-
                            stitutionality of the Geary Act and raises money to challenge the
                            law in court. The Court rules that Congress has the right to legislate
                            expulsion of Chinese through the order of executive officers.

                            The San Francisco Board of Education decides to send all Japanese
                            children to a segregated Chinese school. Japanese Consul Chinda
                            Sutemi protests the board's decision, and the board decides to
                            rescind the resolution.

1894   March 17. China and the United States conclude a treaty known
                            as the Gresham-Yang Treaty. China accepts absolute prohibition
                            of Chinese immigration to the United States. In return, the United
                            States allows Chinese with valid certificates to return to their for-
                            mer place of residence, thereby doing away with the punitive Scott
                            Act of 1888.

                            Hing Chung Wui, or Hsing Chung Hui (Society for the Regen-
                            eration of China), is established in Honolulu, Hawaii, by Sun Yat-
                            sen.

| 1895 | China is defeated by Japan. This makes Chinese in the United States more receptive to Sun Yat-sen's Hsing Chung Hui. |

The Native Sons of the Golden State is organized under the leadership of Walter U. Lum, Joseph K. Lum, and Ng Gunn. The organization changes its name to the Chinese American Citizens Alliance in 1915.

1896   November 2. During the meeting of the Executive Council of the Board of Immigration of Hawaii, a proposal is submitted by a Mr. Grunwaldt who wants to import Korean laborers to replace Chinese and Japanese workers. The council adopts a resolution to accept Grunwaldt's proposal but does not take any other action on the proposal.

1897   August 27. The Executive Council of the Board of Immigration of Hawaii denies permission to H. Hackfeld Company to bring Korean laborers to Hawaii.

1898   July 6. A joint resolution for the annexation of Hawaii is made by the Senate, and Hawaii's sovereignty is handed over to the United States on August 12, 1898. Congress makes Hawaii a Territory of the United States in January of the following year.

July 7. Congress passes a joint resolution prohibiting Chinese immigration to Hawaii. It also prohibits Chinese already in Hawaii from coming to mainland United States.

Abiko Kyutaro (1865–1936) establishes the *Nichi Bei Times* in San Francisco.

March 28. The Supreme Court of the United States rules on the case of United States v. Wong Kim Ark, establishing the principle that a person born in the United States is a citizen of the United States regardless of his or her parentage. Wong Kim Ark was born of Chinese parentage.

December 10. The United States acquires the Philippine Islands from Spain through the Treaty of Paris which officially ends the Spanish-American War.

1899   February 4. The Filipino-American War starts.

September 2. The Buddhist Churches of America are established as a result of the arrival of two Buddhist priests from Japan.

1900   April 29. Congress passes An Act Making Appropriations for Sundry Civil Expenses of the Government for the Fiscal Year Ending June 13, 1901, and for Other Purposes. One of the results of this act is to empower the immigration commissioner to take charge of the administration of the Chinese Exclusion Law.

April 30. The Organic Act is signed into law by President William McKinley, thus establishing the territorial government in Hawaii. Under this act Chinese in Hawaii are required to apply for certificates of residence.

June 3. The members of the Taft Commission arrive in Manila.

June 14. Hawaii is incorporated as a territory of the United States.

The Japanese Association of America is established in San Francisco. The purpose of the organization is to fight against racial discrimination.

1901   January 9. The first Korean immigrant, Peter Ryu, arrives in Hawaii on a Japanese ship, *Hongkong Maru*.

March 3. Congress passes An Act Supplementary to an Act Entitled an Act to Prohibit the Coming of Chinese Persons into the United States, Approved May 5, 1892.

July 4. William Taft becomes the first civil governor of the Philippines.

1902   April 29. Congress passes An Act to Prohibit the Coming into and to Regulate the Residence Within the United States, Its Territories and All Territory under Its Jurisdiction, and the District of Columbia, of Chinese and Persons of Chinese Descent. By this act restrictions are imposed on the Chinese in the Philippines.

234 Chinese are illegally imprisoned in Boston.

July 1. The Philippine Organic Act passes the Senate. This law is the basis for the Philippine policy of the United States during the Taft era (1901–1913).

The Hawaiian Sugar Planters' Association employs David Deshler in Korea to recruit Korean laborers.

December 22. The first group of Korean emigrants aboard the *Gaelic* leaves Korea for Hawaii.

1903   January 13. 102 Koreans arrive in Hawaii on the *S.S. Gaelic* and are inspected aboard the ship. Later they are divided into small groups and are sent to plantations.

About 1,000 Japanese and Mexican sugarbeet workers go on strike at Oxnard, California.

August 26. The *pensionado* program is authorized.

November 3. A group of 100 young Filipinos arrive in California for their education. This is the beginning of the *pensionado* program through which a total of 209 Filipinos and Filipinas receive education in the United States by 1912. It costs the U.S. government $479,940.

1904

September 23. Executive Order 38 is issued by the government of the Philippine Islands, applying U.S. government regulations concerning Chinese to the Philippines.

November 29. Syngman Rhee (1875–1965) arrives in Hawaii aboard the *Siberia* and begins to organize Korean immigrants there for the Korean national liberation movement.

Asian Indians begin to emigrate to the United States, and by 1923 there are approximately 7,000 Asian Indians in the United States, most of them on the West Coast.

1905

February 10. The Korean Episcopal Church in Honolulu is founded.

May 14. The Asiatic Exclusion League is established in San Francisco.

A nationwide boycott against American goods is launched in China in order to protest American discrimination and prejudice against Chinese.

The Korean Evangelical Society is organized in San Francisco.

The Mutual Cooperation Federation is established among Koreans in San Francisco.

1906

March 16. A branch office of the Mutual Cooperation Federation is established in Los Angeles.

San Francisco has an earthquake which destroys the old Chinatown.

Anti-Japanese sentiment is intensified as a result of the earthquake.

July 18. Future Senator Samuel Hayakawa is born in Vancouver, British Columbia, Canada.

The San Francisco School Board creates an international incident by ordering children of Japanese and Korean residents to attend the segregated Oriental Public School.

October 26. Secretary Victor Metcalf (1884–1936) is sent to San Francisco by President Theodore Roosevelt to confer with city officials on the question of school segregation.

Lajpat Rai (1865–1928), founder of the India Home Rule League of America, comes to the United States.

December. Negotiations with Japan for an agreement to restrict Japanese immigration start. They are carried out successfully, and a Gentlemen's Agreement is reached between the United States and Japan in 1908.

December. A group of fifteen Filipino workers arrive in Hawaii to work for the Hawaiian Sugar Planters' Association.

1907   January 17. U.S. Attorney Devlin files a brief on behalf of Aoki Keikichi against Deane, principal of Redding School, in order to test the constitutionality of the school segregation order issued by the San Francisco School Board. But the case of Aoki v. Deane is dismissed after the school board rescinds its segregation order.

February 26. The Regulation Governing the Admission of Chinese is issued to provide procedures for interrogating Chinese entering the United States.

February 20. President Theodore Roosevelt signs into law a bill passed by Congress to impose further restrictions on Japanese immigration.

March 13. The San Francisco School Board rescinds its school segregation order.

March 14. On the basis of the February 20, 1907, Immigration Law, President Roosevelt issues an Executive Order prohibiting Japanese from coming to mainland United States via Hawaii, Mexico, or Canada.

September 2. Representatives from twenty-four Korean organizations meet in Honolulu and decide to create the United Federation.

October 22. The United Federation publishes its newspaper, *United Korean News*.

1908   March 9. The Gentlemen's Agreement between the United States and Japan is officially concluded.

March 23. Chang In-hwan (1875–1930), a Korean patriot, shoots to death an American, Durham Stevens, who supports Japanese takeover of Korea as a protectorate.

May 23. The Korean Women's Association is established in San Francisco.

1909   February 1. The Mutual Cooperation Federation and the United Federation are merged into one organization to work together for Korea's independence. The new organization is called the Korean National Association, and it publishes a newspaper, *The New Korea*, beginning on that day.

August 5. The Payne-Aldrich Tariff Act goes into effect. The Philippine Tariff Act also becomes effective on the same day. The Payne-Aldrich Act is replaced by the Underwood-Simmons Act of October 3, 1913, establishing free trade between the Philippines and the United States.

Yung Wing publishes his autobiography, *My Life in China and America*.

Japanese sugar plantation workers go on strike in Hawaii. This is the first major strike by Japanese workers in Hawaii.

1910

Twenty-seven anti-Japanese proposals are introduced by the California Legislature. Governor Hiram Johnson is persuaded by his friends in the White House to discourage the California Legislature from approving these proposals.

Picture-brides married to Japanese men arrive from Japan to the United States.

Japan makes Korea its colony.

October 10. Syngman Rhee returns to Korea after receiving a Ph.D. degree from Princeton University. He is the first Korean to receive such a degree from an American institution of higher learning.

November 28. Sara Choe, married to Yi Nae-su, arrives in Hawaii. She is the first of 951 picture-brides from Korea.

1911

February. Har Dayal (1884–1939), an Asian Indian political leader, arrives in the United States and later works toward India's independence.

Intervention from President William Howard Taft stops the California Legislature from passing anti-Japanese laws.

Yi Bom-jin, Korean Minister to Russia, commits suicide in protest against Japanese seizure of Korea. He wills $3,000 to the Korean National Association to be used for its political work.

Ahn Chang-ho (1878–1938) returns to the United States from Korea where he had gone in 1907.

1912

January 1. The Republic of China is founded by Dr. Sun Yat-sen (1866–1925), who becomes its first president.

January 29. The North American Business, Inc., is established by Ahn Chang-ho. The company makes investments in agriculture and business.

September 16. The Korean Youth Corps, established in Hastings, Nebraska, under the leadership of Pak Yong-man (1881–1928), graduates its first class of thirteen students.

1913
May 13. The Corps for the Advancement of Individuals is organized among Koreans in America. Ahn Chang-ho serves as chairman of the Board of Directors of the organization.

May 19. The California Legislature passes the Alien Land Act, and it is signed into law, affecting not only Japanese but also Koreans. According to the law, a person ineligible for U.S. citizenship is not allowed to purchase land for agricultural purposes.

The Korean Boarding School changes its name to the Central Institute, and Syngman Rhee becomes its principal.

November 1. The Hindu Association on the Pacific Coast is established under the leadership of Har Dayal.

1914
June 10. The Korean Military Corps is organized by Pak Yong-man who believes that Korea's independence will come only if Japan is defeated militarily.

1915
"Japan Plans to Invade and Conquer the U.S. . . . " is published by the Hearst newspapers, thereby launching an anti-Japanese campaign.

March 11. *The New Korea* is printed by an Intertype machine invented by Yi Dae-wi.

October 15. Mike Masaoka, future national secretary for the Japanese American Citizens League, is born.

1916
The Wah Chang Trading Company is established in New York by Li K. C.

October 8. Future Senator Spark M. Matsunaga is born in Kauai, Hawaii.

1917
February 5. President Woodrow Wilson vetoes a bill passed by Congress on December 14, 1916, but Congress overrides his veto and it becomes effective on this day. The law known as the Asiatic Barred Zone Act excludes immigration from South and Southeast Asia. Asian Indian immigration is prohibited by this law.

March 6. Chandra K. Chakravarty, founder of the Pan Asiatic League, is placed under arrest in connection with the Hindu Conspiracy case. Ram Chandra, who worked with Har Dayal for India's independence, is put on trial as a dependent in the Hindu Conspiracy case. During the trial he is shot to death in the courtroom by one of his countrymen on April 23, 1918.

1918	July 29. The New Church is established among Koreans in Hawaii, and it is led by Syngman Rhee.
1919	March 1. Koreans in Korea protest Japanese colonial rule by holding a non-violent nationwide demonstration. Many Koreans are killed by Japanese police. News of the March Independence Movement reaches Koreans in Hawaii and mainland United States on March 9. The Korean National Association launches a fund-raising campaign for independence funds. It collects $10,000.

April 14–16. 150 Koreans attend the First Korean Liberty Congress in Philadelphia in order to draw the world's attention to the plight of Koreans in Korea.

September. Valentine Stuart McClatchy (1857–1938) forms the California Joint Immigration Committee and uses it effectively to drum up support for his anti-Japanese activities.

The American Loyalty Club is organized in San Francisco by a small group of Nisei Americans.

1920	The Alien Land Act passed by the California Legislature in 1913 is amended in order to close the loopholes in the original law.

February 20. The School of Aviation is founded in Willows, California, when Kim Chong-nim donates three airplanes. Future pilots are to be trained to fight against the Japanese Empire.

January 19. Under the leadership of Pablo Manlapit (1891–1969), president of the Filipino Federation of Labor, more than 8,000 Japanese and Filipino sugar plantation workers go on strike demanding higher wages and better working conditions.

Charles Ho Kim and Kim Hyong-sun establish the Kim Brothers Company in Reedley, California.

1921	January 22. The Caballeros de Dimas-Alang is established in San Francisco as a fraternal organization.

The Philippine Independent News, the first Filipino newspaper in mainland United States, is published in Salinas, California.

March 21. The Korean Resident Association is created in Hawaii.

May 19. President Warren Harding signs into law the Quota Immigration Act of 1921. This is the first quota immigration act passed by the Congress of the United States and eventually leads to the 1924 National Origins Act.

The Seattle Progressive Citizens League is established by Nisei Americans to fight against racial discrimination.

July 7. The Comrade Society is organized, and it is led by Syngman Rhee.

1922 September 22. Congress passes the Cable Act which revokes the American citizenship of any citizen woman marrying an alien ineligible for U.S. citizenship.

November 13. The Supreme Court of the United States rules on the Ozawa Takao v. United States case, declaring that the Japanese immigrants cannot become naturalized.

1923 February 19. The Supreme Court of the United States rules on the case of United States v. Bhagat Singh Thind, declaring that Asian Indians are not eligible for U.S. citizenship.

March 5. The American Loyalty Club of Fresno is organized, and Yatabe is chosen president of the organization. This is the beginning of the Japanese American Citizens League.

1924 February 2. The Legionarios del Trabajo is organized in San Francisco.

May 26. President Calvin Coolidge signs into law the Immigration Act of 1924, also known as the Quota Immigration Act as well as the National Origins Act. It excludes the immigration of all Asian laborers. The law is known to many Asians as the Asian Exclusion Act.

September 7. Future Senator Daniel Inouye is born in Honolulu, Hawaii.

1925 May 25. The Supreme Court of the United States rules against Toyota Hidemitsu, declaring that although he has served in the military, he is not eligible to become a U.S. citizen, because he is neither white nor black. On the same day the Court also rules on the case of Chang Chan et al. v. John D. Nagle, declaring that Chinese wives of American citizens are not allowed to come to America in accordance with the 1924 Immigration Law.

1926 The China Institute in America, Inc., is founded to promote cultural understanding between China and the United States.

1927 The Supreme Court upholds the ruling of the Circuit Court of Appeals on the case of Weedin v. Chin Bow and declares that a person born abroad of an American parent or parents who has never lived in the United States cannot be a citizen of the United States.

James Sakamoto (1903–1955), who later becomes an important figure in the development of the Japanese American Citizens League, becomes the first Nisei to fight professionally at Madison Square Garden.

During the annual convention of the American Federation of Labor, a resolution is passed to encourage Congress to enact legislation to prohibit Filipinos from coming to the United States.

1928   January 1. *The Japanese American Courier* is published by James Sakamoto in Seattle, Washington.

May 18. House Bill 13,900 is introduced by Congressman Richard J. Welch and Senator Hiram Johnson of California. The bill is designed to exclude Filipinos from the United States.

June 29. *The Samil Sinbo*, or the Samil News, is published by a group of Korean students in New York. Among them are Chang Dok-su, Yun Ch'i-yong, and Ho Chung, all of whom have major roles in South Korean politics after the end of World War II.

1929   February 28. Philippine Labor Commissioner Cayetano Ligot recommends to the Hawaiian Legislature that Filipinos be prevented from coming to Hawaii unless they have guaranteed jobs or sufficient funds with which to return home.

April. Kido Saburo, Thomas Yatabe, and Clarence Arai propose the establishment of the Japanese American Citizens League.

1930   January 22. Fermin Tober is killed during the anti-Filipino riot in Watsonville, California.

Kang Younghill (1903–1972) publishes *The Grass Roof*, which is well received by the American public.

February 26. A Los Angeles Superior Court judge, J. K. Smith, hands down a ruling that classified the Filipinos as members of the Mongolian race. This opens the way for invalidating more than 100 marriages performed after 1921.

August 29. The Japanese American Citizens League holds its first national convention in Seattle, Washington.

1931   The Cable Act is amended to allow women who are American citizens to retain their citizenship after their marriages to aliens ineligible for U.S. citizenship.

The India Society of America is founded by Hari G. Govil in New York.

Bruno Lasker is commissioned to study Filipino immigration to Hawaii and the United States.

March 1. Koreans in Kauai establish the United Society.

September 18. Japan invades Manchuria.

1932   Because of U.S. concerns with the Japanese military occupation of Manchuria, Secretary of State Henry Stimson declares a doctrine of non-recognition of any situation created by means of force. Chinese in the United States support American policy and render financial support.

December 20. Congress passes the Hare-Hawes-Cutting Act and excludes Filipinos from immigrating to the United States as they are ruled ineligible for U.S. citizenship.

1933   Japan withdraws from the League of Nations.

November 30. The Filipino Labor Union is founded and establishes a number of branch offices in central California by the end of 1933.

1934   March 24. President Franklin D. Roosevelt signs the Tydings-McDuffie Act which prohibits the immigration of Filipinos to the United States. It also promises political independence to the Philippine Islands ten years after the passage of the bill. It allows 50 Filipinos to come to America as immigrants per year.

August 27. The Salinas Lettuce Strike is called against the Central California Vegetable Growers and Shippers' Association. The strike is led by the Filipino Labor Union.

October 8. Syngman Rhee marries an Austrian woman, Francesca Donner, and draws a great deal of criticism from the Korean community in Hawaii because of his marriage to a white woman.

1935   July 10. The Filipino Repatriation Act is signed into law, allowing Filipinos in America to go back to the Philippine Islands at government expense, but once home they are not allowed to return to the United States.

August 17. The Philippine Commonwealth is organized and elects M. D. Guervarra as president.

Lin Yutang (1895–1976) publishes *My Country and My People*.

1936   Abiko Kyutaro (1865–1936), founder of the *Nichi Bei Times*, dies.

After the Sian Incident, which involves the involuntary detention of Chiang Kai-shek by his generals, Chinese in America send cables to the rebels urging them to release Chiang. Chiang is released on December 25.

Ahn Ik-t'ae (1906–1965), a Korean composer in Philadelphia, completes his composition of the Korean national anthem.

1937   One of the first sociological studies on Koreans in Hawaii is completed by Bernice B.H. Kim at the University of Hawaii.

July 7. Full-scale war between Japan and China begins. Many concerned Chinese in America send their financial contributions to help China repel aggression.

October 21. Haan Kil-soo, a Korean resident in Hawaii, states during his testimony before the Congressional State Committee that the Japanese government is attempting to unite Orientals in Hawaii against the whites.

1938   March 24–26. The first Filipino National Conference is held in Sacramento, California.

Hiram Fong (1907–   ) is elected to the legislature of the Territory of Hawaii.

V. S. McClatchy (1857–1938), leader of the anti-Japanese movement, dies.

1939   Intermountain District Council of the Japanese American Citizens League is organized by Mike Masaoka.

June 30. The *Filipino Journal* is published by the Filipino Agricultural Workers Union.

1940   March 9. Leaders of the Japanese American Citizens League meet with the Los Angeles City Council and assure their loyalty.

March 21. Leaders of the Japanese American Citizens League meet with officials of the Army and Navy Intelligence Services and pledge their loyalty and cooperation.

September 7. Haan Kil-soo urges Koreans in Hawaii, registering as aliens under the Alien Registration Act of 1940, to register as Koreans and not as Japanese subjects.

1941   Haan Kil-soo charges that Japan has been making plans to attack the United States and that the Japanese in Hawaii are ready to assist Japan in case of war with the United States.

May 9. The Japanese American Creed by Mike Masaoka is published in the *Congressional Record*.

July 26. The United States abrogates the treaty of commerce and friendship with Japan and freezes the assets of Japanese nationals in the United States.

December 7. Japan makes a surprise attack on Pearl Harbor.

Kido Saburo (1902–1977), president of the Japanese American Citizens League, sends a telegram to President Franklin Roosevelt pledging the loyalty and cooperation of the Nisei.

1942
February 19. President Franklin Roosevelt signs Executive Order 9066 authorizing the Secretary of War or his designated military commander to establish military areas and to evacuate civilians from these areas. This action is responsible for removing and relocating more than 110,000 persons of Japanese ancestry from the West Coast.

February 21. The Tolan Committee holds its first meeting in San Francisco.

March 2. General John L. DeWitt, commander of the Western Defense Command, issues Proclamation No. 1.

March 11. General DeWitt establishes the Wartime Civil Control Administration.

March 18. President Roosevelt signs Executive Order 9102 establishing the War Relocation Authority.

March 23. General DeWitt issues Civilian Exclusion Order No. 1, ordering the removal of persons of Japanese ancestry from Bainbridge Island, Washington.

April 22. The War Department completes the formation of the First Filipino Infantry Battalion.

June 5. Japanese are removed from Military Area No. 1 which includes the western half of Washington, Oregon, and California and southern Arizona.

November 18. The Poston Strike occurs at the Poston War Relocation Center.

1943
January 28. Secretary of War Henry Stimson makes the decision to allow the formation of an all-Nisei combat unit.

April 9. The nationals of the United States and citizens of the Philippines are no longer prevented from holding real property in California, according to Robert W. Kenny, Attorney General of California.

June 21. The Supreme Court of the United States rules on Hirabayashi v. United States, declaring that the curfew law imposed on all persons of Japanese ancestry is constitutional.

December 4. Military Order No. 4, which exempts Koreans in America from enemy alien status, is issued.

December 9. The Senate passes Senate Joint Resolution 93 which grants Philippine independence by presidential proclamation soon after the Japanese have been defeated and normal conditions have been restored in the islands.

December 17. Congress passes An Act to Repeal the Chinese Exclusions Act, to Establish Quotas, and for Other Purposes. This law allows Chinese to become naturalized citizens and gives China a quota of 105 immigrants to come to the United States per year.

1944

July 1. President Franklin Roosevelt signs Public Law No. 405, allowing America citizens to renounce their citizenship in time of war.

August 1. Manuel Quezon (1878–1944) dies in New York.

December 18. The Supreme Court of the United States rules on the case of Korematsu v. United States and Endo, Ex parte. In the Korematsu case the Supreme Court rules the evacuation order constitutional, while in the Endo case, the same court decides that the government cannot hold a loyal citizen of the United States in detention against his or her own will.

On the same day the War Relocation Authority announces that all relocation centers will be closed by the end of 1945.

The Philippine Cultural Society is established in San Francisco.

The Indian Society of Yuba and Sutter Counties is organized by a group of Asian Indians who live along the Feather River and in Yuba City.

August 6. The United States drops the atomic bomb on Hiroshima, Japan.

August 9. The United States drops the atomic bomb on Nagasaki, Japan.

August 15. Japan surrenders unconditionally.

August 30. Koreans in mainland United States organize the Post-War Assistance Society and begin to send relief goods to Korea. A society with the identical name has been established in Hawaii on March 10, and it begins to collect relief goods to be sent to Korea after the war.

September 7. Public Proclamation No. 24 is issued by the Western Defense Command which revokes exclusion orders and military restrictions against persons of Japanese ancestry.

December 28. President Harry S. Truman signs into law the War Brides Act of 1945, allowing 722 Chinese and 2,042 Japanese to come to the United States between 1946 and 1953.

1946   February 23. A group of 432 persons of Japanese ancestry are repatriated to Japan. They are known as disloyal citizens.

June 14. President Harry S Truman signs into law the Filipino Naturalization Act.

June 30. The War Relocation Authority program is officially finished.

July 2. The Luce-Celler Bill is signed into law, thus allowing Asian Indians to become U.S. citizens and establishing a quota of 100 immigrants from India to the United States per year.

July 4. The Philippines gain independence from the United States which promised Philippine independence in 1934 when the Tydings-McDuffie Act was passed.

1947   Chinese in the United States send $70 million to their families, relatives, and organizations in China between 1938 and 1947.

1948   The Supreme Court of the United States rules on the case of Takahashi v. Fish and Game Commission, declaring Section 990 of the Fish and Game Code of California unconstitutional.

June 25. President Harry S Truman signs into law the Displaced Persons Act of 1948, allowing as many as 15,000 Chinese in the United States to adjust their legal status.

July 2. President Truman signs into law the Japanese American Evacuation Claims Act, enabling former evacuees to file claims against the government for their financial losses during evacuation.

October 6. The Supreme Court of the United States declares California's legal ban on interracial marriage unconstitutional.

1949   October 7. Iva Toguri D'Aquino (1916–   ), also known as Tokyo Rose, is sentenced to a ten-year prison term in San Francisco. She is released from prison on January 28, 1956.

1950   June 25. The Korean War begins.

1951   Chinese in America are prevented from sending money to their families and relatives in mainland China.

So Jae-p'ill (1866–1951), also known as Philip Jaisohn, dies. He was the first Korean to become a naturalized citizen.

1952	December 24. The McCarran-Walter Immigration and Naturalization Act goes into effect. It repeals the National Origins Act of 1924 and allows immigration quotas to Japan and other Asian countries.
1953	The Refugee Relief Act, which is to expire at the end of 1956, allows Chinese political refugees to come to the United States.
	May 2. The day is declared Korean Day in the United States, and Americans are encouraged to make donations in money and materials to assist Koreans.
	July 23. The armistice ending the Korean War is signed.
1954	Chinese in the United States having technical knowledge are allowed to leave for mainland China.
1955	James Wong Howe (1898–1975) wins an Oscar for cinematography.
1956	The Filipino United Community Organization is established in San Jose, California.
	Harry Holt, a resident of Creswell, Oregon, brings over from Korea eight Korean orphans whom he adopts. Later he establishes the Holt Adoption Agency which is responsible for bringing thousands of Korean orphans to the United States.
1957	Yang Chen-ning (1922–) and Lee Tsung-dao (1926–) share the Nobel Prize for Physics.
	Sessue Hayakawa (1889–1973) stars in *Bridge on the River Kwai*.
	May 1. The Korean Foundation is organized with Kim Ho as its president. The purpose of the foundation is to promote higher education among Koreans in America.
1959	Hawaii becomes the fiftieth state of the Union.
	Hiram Fong is elected U.S. senator.
	Daniel Inouye is elected U.S. representative.
1962	Daniel Inouye is elected U.S. senator.
1964	Patsy Takemoto Mink is elected U.S. representative.
1965	October 3. President Lyndon B. Johnson signs into law a new immigration law that not only repeals the National Origins Act of 1924, but also establishes a new immigration policy to enable large numbers of immigrants from many Asian countries to come to the United States.
	The Filipino American Political Association is established in San Francisco.

1968   Har Gobind Khorana (1922–   ) is awarded the Nobel Prize for Physiology.

1974   January 21. The U.S. Supreme Court rules on the case of Lau et al. v. Nichols et al., declaring that bilingual education has to be provided to non-English speaking students.

1975   April 15. The Interagency Task Force is created to coordinate all U.S. government activities in evacuating U.S. citizens and certain Vietnamese citizens from Vietnam.

May 24. The Indochina Migration and Refugee Assistance Act is passed to provide funds for resettlement programs.

1976   September 10. The Indochinese Refugee Children Assistance Act is passed in an attempt to provide funds for the education of refugee children from Vietnam, Kampuchea, and Laos.

Samuel Ting (1936–   ) shares the Nobel Prize for Physics with Burton Richter.

Executive Order 9066, responsible for the evacuation, removal, and detention of persons of Japanese ancestry during World War II, is officially rescinded.

1977   January 19. Iva Toguri D'Aquino is pardoned by President Gerald Ford.

1980   The Refugee Act of 1980 is signed into law by President Jimmy Carter, enabling more refugees to enter the United States.

July 31. The Commission on Wartime Relocation and Internment of Civilians is created to gather facts that will help in determining if any wrong was committed against American citizens affected by Executive Order 9066.

The 1980 U.S. Census reports that there are 3,726,440 Asians and Pacific Islanders in the United States.

1982   June 22. Vincent Chin, a Chinese American in Detroit, is beaten to death by two assailants who mistake Chin for a Japanese. The murderers blame Japanese for their unemployment.

1983   Subrahmanyan Chandrashekhar (1910–   ) is awarded the Nobel Prize for Physics.

1984   October 18. The assassination of Henry Liu by agents of the government of Taiwan touches off an international incident. As a result of this incident, the U.S. government changes its policy toward the Nationalist government.

1985   *The Asian Week* reports that there are 4.8 million Asians in the United States and that this population will reach 6.5 million by 1990.

1980 Census Data

Asian and Pacific Islander Population: 1980

Data based on sample.

United States Regions and Divisions States	All races	Asian and Pacific Islander						
		Total		Chinese	Filipino	Japanese	Asian Indian
		Number	Percent				
United States..........	226 545 805	3 726 440	1.6	812 178	781 894	716 331	387 223
REGIONS AND DIVISIONS							
Northeast..........	49 135 283	599 294	1.2	217 624	77 051	46 913	132 560
New England..........	12 348 493	88 425	0.7	33 113	8 311	7 474	17 010
Middle Atlantic..........	36 786 790	510 869	1.4	184 511	68 740	39 439	115 550
North Central..........	58 865 670	435 391	0.7	74 944	80 928	46 254	89 588
East North Central..........	41 682 217	334 418	0.8	59 581	69 958	35 789	75 051
West North Central..........	17 183 453	100 973	0.6	15 363	10 970	10 465	14 537
South..........	75 372 362	513 005	0.7	91 415	85 626	47 631	90 602
South Atlantic..........	36 959 123	280 973	0.8	50 730	58 943	25 998	50 061
East South Central..........	14 666 423	45 484	0.3	7 312	5 668	4 932	9 748
West South Central..........	23 746 816	186 548	0.8	33 373	21 015	16 701	30 793
West..........	43 172 490	2 178 750	5.0	428 195	538 289	575 533	74 473
Mountain..........	11 372 785	114 239	1.0	19 959	14 181	29 471	7 229
Pacific..........	31 799 705	2 064 511	6.5	408 236	524 108	546 062	67 244
STATES							
New England:							
Maine..........	1 124 660	3 073	0.3	433	680	302	475
New Hampshire..........	920 610	3 364	0.4	900	286	356	742
Vermont..........	511 456	1 640	0.3	206	115	221	520
Massachusetts..........	5 737 037	52 615	0.9	24 882	3 180	4 290	8 943
Rhode Island..........	947 154	6 617	0.7	1 744	1 001	464	904
Connecticut..........	3 107 576	21 116	0.7	4 948	3 049	1 841	5 426
Middle Atlantic:							
New York..........	17 558 072	330 972	1.9	147 250	35 630	24 754	67 636
New Jersey..........	7 364 823	109 383	1.5	23 492	24 470	10 263	30 684
Pennsylvania..........	11 863 895	70 514	0.6	13 769	8 640	4 422	17 230
East North Central:							
Ohio..........	10 797 630	53 166	0.5	10 584	7 966	6 271	13 602
Indiana..........	5 490 224	24 355	0.4	4 491	3 507	2 503	4 746
Illinois..........	11 426 518	172 213	1.5	28 847	44 317	18 432	37 438
Michigan..........	9 262 078	62 641	0.7	10 824	11 132	6 460	15 363
Wisconsin..........	4 705 767	22 043	0.5	4 835	3 036	2 123	3 902

West North Central:							
Minnesota	3 734	3 191	2 628	4 558	0.8	32 226	4 075 970
Iowa	2 424	1 024	1 058	1 973	0.5	13 847	2 913 808
Missouri	4 276	2 897	3 883	4 520	0.5	24 962	4 916 686
North Dakota	252	225	496	387	0.4	2 292	652 717
South Dakota	157	305	312	200	0.3	1 917	690 768
Nebraska	1 106	1 212	945	1 285	0.5	8 190	1 569 825
Kansas	2 588	1 611	1 648	2 440	0.7	17 539	2 363 679
South Atlantic:							
Delaware	1 227	412	789	1 174	0.8	4 627	594 338
Maryland	13 788	4 656	11 763	15 037	1.6	67 949	4 216 975
District of Columbia	873	808	1 255	2 308	1.1	6 883	638 333
Virginia	9 046	5 173	19 111	9 495	1.3	70 569	5 346 818
West Virginia	1 936	508	1 282	1 095	0.3	5 902	1 949 644
North Carolina	4 855	3 594	2 869	3 229	0.4	23 150	5 881 766
South Carolina	2 572	1 584	3 797	1 204	0.4	13 370	3 121 820
Georgia	4 725	3 596	2 825	4 258	0.5	26 009	5 463 105
Florida	11 039	5 667	15 252	12 930	0.6	62 514	9 746 324
East South Central:							
Kentucky	2 669	1 170	1 417	1 381	0.3	11 823	3 660 777
Tennessee	3 392	1 752	1 761	2 904	0.3	15 252	4 591 120
Alabama	2 374	1 427	1 089	1 416	0.3	10 660	3 893 888
Mississippi	1 313	583	1 401	1 611	0.3	7 749	2 520 638
West South Central:							
Arkansas	1 194	697	732	1 184	0.3	7 232	2 286 435
Louisiana	3 036	1 671	2 650	3 091	0.6	25 123	4 205 900
Oklahoma	3 168	2 249	1 681	2 384	0.7	19 765	3 025 290
Texas	23 395	12 084	15 952	26 714	0.9	134 428	14 229 191
Mountain:							
Montana	154	803	501	395	0.4	3 097	786 690
Idaho	247	3 102	759	701	0.7	6 721	943 935
Wyoming	104	757	194	441	0.4	2 044	469 557
Colorado	2 565	10 841	2 764	4 224	1.2	34 257	2 889 964
New Mexico	622	1 353	1 200	1 412	0.6	7 728	1 302 894
Arizona	2 078	4 629	3 799	6 681	0.9	24 562	2 718 215
Utah	932	508	1 138	2 913	1.4	20 224	1 461 037
Nevada	527	2 478	3 826	3 192	1.9	15 606	800 493
Pacific:							
Washington	4 267	27 389	25 662	17 984	2.7	111 607	4 132 156
Oregon	2 265	8 580	4 800	7 918	1.6	40 958	2 633 105
California	59 774	268 814	358 378	325 882	5.5	1 312 973	23 667 902
Alaska	230	1 545	3 193	536	2.1	8 314	401 851
Hawaii	708	239 734	132 075	55 916	61.2	590 659	964 691

Asian and Pacific Islander Population: 1980–Con.

United States Regions and Divisions States	Asian and Pacific Islander—Con.					Other Asian and Pacific Islander		
	Korean	Vietnamese	Hawaiian	Samoan	Guamanian	Total[1]	Asian	Pacific Islander
United States......	357 393	245 025	172 346	39 520	30 695	183 835	166 377	17 005
REGIONS AND DIVISIONS								
Northeast............	68 357	22 021	4 273	522	1 952	28 021	27 318	679
New England..........	9 327	5 199	835	172	572	6 412	6 283	129
Middle Atlantic......	59 030	16 822	3 438	350	1 380	21 609	21 035	550
North Central........	64 573	32 949	5 476	991	1 816	37 872	36 845	909
East North Central...	47 895	17 238	3 442	389	984	24 091	23 562	451
West North Central...	16 678	15 711	2 034	602	832	13 781	13 283	458
South................	70 999	76 916	11 427	1 784	4 757	31 848	30 555	1 218
South Atlantic.......	44 880	26 882	5 719	900	2 549	14 311	13 684	601
East South Central...	6 985	5 316	1 800	291	423	3 009	2 971	38
West South Central...	19 134	44 718	3 908	593	1 785	14 528	13 900	579
West.................	153 464	113 139	151 170	36 223	22 170	86 094	71 659	14 199
Mountain.............	13 374	9 516	3 860	1 751	1 297	13 601	10 689	2 912
Pacific..............	140 090	103 623	147 310	34 472	20 873	72 493	60 970	11 287
STATES								
New England:								
Maine................	480	260	84	28	79	252	233	19
New Hampshire........	519	136	76	12	5	332	308	24
Vermont..............	332	94	11	14	21	106	94	12
Massachusetts........	5 369	2 847	352	93	251	2 408	2 371	37
Rhode Island.........	612	287	63	-	116	1 426	1 389	37
Connecticut..........	2 015	1 575	249	25	100	1 888	1 888	-
Middle Atlantic:								
New York.............	33 260	5 849	1 950	151	1 017	13 475	13 120	341
New Jersey...........	13 173	2 846	579	112	199	3 565	3 489	76
Pennsylvania.........	12 597	8 127	909	87	164	4 569	4 426	133
East North Central:								
Ohio.................	7 756	2 751	823	64	137	3 212	3 140	72
Indiana..............	3 940	2 137	503	60	119	2 349	2 288	61
Illinois.............	24 351	6 287	964	88	367	11 122	10 942	127
Michigan.............	8 948	4 364	894	90	199	4 367	4 222	138
Wisconsin............	2 900	1 699	258	87	162	3 041	2 970	53

West North Central:								
Minnesota	6 676	5 316	315	51	102	5 655	5 544	111
Iowa	2 057	2 101	301	50	95	2 764	2 721	43
Missouri	3 356	3 134	780	357	203	1 556	1 450	100
North Dakota	360	288	69	-	18	197	188	9
South Dakota	325	265	41	39	46	227	227	-
Nebraska	1 203	1 276	177	48	109	829	717	90
Kansas	2 701	3 331	351	57	259	2 553	2 436	105
South Atlantic:								
Delaware	501	171	77	5	45	226	226	-
Maryland	14 783	4 162	630	86	323	2 721	2 660	58
District of Columbia	312	435	194	38	89	571	571	-
Virginia	12 797	9 451	1 033	194	548	3 721	3 546	164
West Virginia	489	168	85	32	29	278	278	-
North Carolina	3 694	1 966	954	132	388	1 469	1 323	146
South Carolina	1 766	1 113	467	57	182	628	605	23
Georgia	5 590	2 339	795	134	503	1 244	1 177	60
Florida	4 948	7 077	1 484	222	442	3 453	3 298	150
East South Central:								
Kentucky	2 170	1 461	378	122	208	847	822	25
Tennessee	2 405	1 158	438	111	66	1 265	1 252	13
Alabama	1 761	1 220	583	38	62	690	690	-
Mississippi	649	1 477	401	20	87	207	207	-
West South Central:								
Arkansas	596	1 900	212	6	65	646	632	7
Louisiana	2 009	10 853	626	69	230	888	864	24
Oklahoma	2 757	4 174	695	117	261	2 279	2 140	131
Texas	13 772	27 791	2 375	401	1 229	10 715	10 264	417
Mountain:								
Montana	325	82	122	16	11	688	646	42
Idaho	635	443	293	103	42	396	311	85
Wyoming	240	43	87	27	10	141	113	28
Colorado	5 143	3 247	825	135	506	4 007	3 949	58
New Mexico	759	936	214	66	43	1 123	1 108	15
Arizona	2 543	1 756	854	179	346	1 697	1 482	215
Utah	1 397	1 991	913	1 171	64	4 197	1 995	2 202
Nevada	2 332	1 018	552	54	275	1 352	1 085	267
Pacific:								
Washington	13 441	8 933	2 840	1 837	1 739	7 515	6 986	509
Oregon	4 998	5 743	1 555	97	366	4 636	4 126	454
California	102 582	85 238	24 245	18 087	17 009	52 964	45 986	6 830
Alaska	1 616	306	419	102	129	238	210	28
Hawaii	17 453	3 403	118 251	14 349	1 630	7 140	3 662	3 466

[1]Includes 453 persons who provided Asian and Pacific Islander write-in entries which could not be specifically classified as either "Asian" or "Pacific Islander."

Index

Page numbers in *italics* indicate main entries in the dictionary.

About the Editor

HYUNG-CHAN KIM is Professor, Department of Educational Administration and Foundations, Western Washington University in Bellingham, Washington. He is the author of *The Koreans in America*, *The Korean Diaspora*, *The Filipinos in America*, and *Letters in Exile: The Life and Times of Yun Ch'i-ho*.